THE HISTORY OF DUNSTER CHURCH AND PRIORY

THE MOHUNS, THE LUTTRELLS AND THEIR CASTLE

"Cry Dunster and St George"

VOLUME ONE

Joan Jordan

HALSGROVE

First published in Great Britain in 2007

British Library Cataloguing-in-Publication Data.
A CIP record for this title is available from the British Library.

ISBN 978 1 84114 569 3

HALSGROVE
Halsgrove House
Ryelands Industrial Estate,
Bagley Road, Wellington
Somerset TA21 9PZ
Tel: 01823 653777
Fax: 01823 216796
E-mail: sales@halsgrove.com
Website: www.halsgrove.com

Printed and bound in Great Britain by
The Cromwell Press Ltd, Wiltshire

The publication of this volume has been
made possible with the generous support of
the Luttrell Arms Hotel, Dunster.

ACKNOWLEDGEMENTS

I am most grateful to the initial band of volunteers who rescued my hand-written script from oblivion and put it on to computer. My first volunteer was David Harvey, followed by various students of the Advanced Learning Associates in Minehead, headed by Bridget O'Brien BSC Hons, PGCE. Two chapters were printed by Chris Brinkman and Laurence Hambrook BSc,MSc,C Chem, MRSC, who also assisted me.

The enormous task of typing from my manuscript all the chapters comprising my original volume II, with only one exception, was the devoted voluntary work of the late Mr Edward Beer. He displayed a dedicated appreciation and enthusiasm for the work.

Most importantly, the great interest and advice of Sir David Money-Coutts KCVO whose wife is a descendant of the 19th-century vicar of Dunster, the Rev. Richard Utten-Todd. Mr Julian Luttrell traced ownership of the Luttrell Table Carpet. My article on the heraldic carpet was published in the *Coat of Arms* magazine by John Brooke-Little CVO, Clarenceux King of Arms.

From the research angle, I acknowledge the unfailing help received from Mr David Bromwich MA, ALA, Librarian of the Somerset Local Studies Library in Taunton, and also the help of Minehead Library and the Heraldry Society. I am also most grateful to the Society of St George, to Manette and John Nelson, for the unfailing support of Maureen Tuttle over many years, and for grants received from the Marc Fitch fund.

If I have failed to acknowledge any literary sources, I trust the authors concerned will treat my omissions with generosity.

Finally, the interest and financial support of Mr Paul Toogood of the Luttrell Arms Hotel has made publication possible, and I thank him most warmly.

CONTENTS

DEDICATION

To my husband and all the friends and
organizations who have supported this
project over many years.

CHAPTER ONE

RESEARCHES

The Cross

The 23rd of April 1988 was a most appropriate date on which to start a history, in part based on the Church of St George the Martyr, from whose tower his flag, lively in the wind, was flying; it was that saint's feast day.

The earliest mention of the church at Dunster is found in an undated charter of William de Mohun I which was issued during the episcopacy of John de Villula, bishop of Bath from 1088 and the reign of William II 'Rufus' (1087-1100). The charter must therefore date between 1088 and 1100.

The rallying cry of "Cry Dunster and St George" was inspired by the war cry of St George, a popular saint to whom many churches were dedicated as early as 1061 (Doncaster). Although little can be authenticated of his life and martyrdom, his historical existence is now generally accepted. Possibly he suffered martyrdom at Lydda before the time of Constantine (d.337 AD). The legend of the slaying of the dragon first appeared in the 12th century and probably grew out of the myth of Perseus's slaying of the sea monster which was popularised in the 13th century in Voragine's *Golden Legend*, translated in 1483/5 by Caxton (*Dictionary of the Christian Church*, p.549).

The adoption of St George as the saint of the crusading armies goes back to the First Crusade (1096-1102) which was predominantly French in character. The French knights were not eager to adopt the banner of the warrior saint of Byzantium, Demetrius. It is said that they discovered the tomb of St George in their newly acquired territory of Lydda. Here were the bones of a Christian saint who had shown exemplary courage in adversity at or near Lydda; a martyr who could readily be transformed into a military saint. In 1099 at the first siege of Jerusalem, it was said that he was the first to scale the ladders. At Antioch thousands were reputed to have seen him mounted on his great white horse, dressed all in red-crossed white, leading the Christian knights in a last desperate and victorious charge.

Before the end of the 12th century, Richard Coeur de Lion placed his army under the martial protection of St George and returning troops added to his popularity and his cult in the West grew rapidly. In the 13th century the Teutonic knights placed themselves under his protection and three of the greatest crusading ports, Venice, Genoa and Barcelona adopted him as their patron saint. By the end of the century the war cry of St Edward the Confessor ceased to be heard and was replaced by that of St George in answer to the French shouts of St Denis and Montjoie their famous Knight of Arms.

In 1345 eighty pennons with the red cross fluttered from the flagship of Edward III and eight hundred more from the mast and spars of the ships taking the English army across the Channel for the campaign which ended on 16 August 1346 with the defeat of the French at Crécy. Edward III, fostering the knight's image enshrined in the cults of King Arthur and St George, replaced the mock battles of 13th-century England with formal tournaments and single combat in the lists. In 1348 he founded the Order of the Garter and placed it under the protection of St George. He established its headquarters in the "noble college" of Windsor Castle, which was later to hold the heart of St George, given by Sigismund, emperor of Alemagne, to Henry V (1413-22) as a precious relic. Before the end of the 14th century, Richard II in his Scottish wars required that every man should have "a sign of his arms both before and behind." In 1415 Montjoie surrendered victory at Agincourt to Henry V and in that year St George became a national hero.

In the 16th century the man-of-war in the allegorical painting of Sir John Luttrell flies the cross of St George and round his upper arm the red and white material wraps Sir John in this emblem and proclaims 'England and St George'.

On 23rd April 1988 I was feeling particularly excited because after months of research into its history, a fascinating part of the jigsaw fell into place. The Rev. Robert Doré had shown me a stone carving, in the form of a cross, standing on the 13th/14th-century altar slab in the small chapel then called the St Lawrence chapel, on the north-east side of the church. It was apparently the carving of a Madonna and Child; her head gently inclined toward the child and with a third figure at her feet.

Mr Peter Tudball, bell-ringer and a former choir-boy, who had taken the photograph, also said that he had a vague memory of a cross being taken down from the apex of the west gable of the church which was confirmed by the report of an inspection in February 1948 by Messrs. Gallennaught & Nicholls at the request of the church architect, Mr Baganel. The inspection had been confined to "obtaining sufficient information to advise on the removal, or otherwise, of the ancient cross on the apex of the gable." The detailed report and recommendations were to examine: "the ancient stone cross at present built into the apex of the west gable, with a view to ascertaining whether it could be removed (for better preservation) and replaced with stone coping in a manner not to impair the appearance. In view of the ancient character of this cross it is recommended that it be removed from its present position. The question as to its future position, where it can be seen and appreciated, to be considered later. Also, the space then left in the gable coping to be closed with stone in colour and design to match the existing." On 1 March 1948 the Rev. G.D. Dunlop wrote to Prebendary Arford, archdeacon of Taunton:

> ... The ancient cross on the West Gable is the head of the thirteenth century Churchyard cross which must have been erected about 70 years ago. It is gradually disintegrating and it is our wish to take it down and display it somewhere inside the church. The pinnacle is in a dangerous condition, and sways to and fro in a high wind; if it were to fall, it would crash on the north aisle or transept and do serious damage.

The Church of St George, Dunster (1953) records: "the Cross Head from the thirteenth century Churchyard Cross had been removed at some time in history, and placed on the Western Gable of the Church, where it was in danger of disintegration and collapse. It has now been brought down from that position, and treated with the utmost care, and under expert advice. It will eventually be exhibited in the Parish Church. The figures are indistinct after seven hundred years, but there is the faint outline of Our Saviour on one side of the Cross; and a clearer figure of the Blessed Virgin Mary on the other side." The parochial church minutes, dated 11 August 1954, note that "the head of the Churchyard Cross had been taken from the roof and had been renovated by Mr Sparks. It was decided to place the Cross in the South Transept at the side of the old Font and that a notice be exhibited giving details of the Cross," though by April 1955 they had moved it again.

I had visited a small workshop in Exeter where two young men were using tools, unchanged in design from those used in the Middle Ages, with undiminished skill, carving in wood and stone to freely drawn designs. The Managing Director, Hugh Harrison, told me that, if I sent him a photograph, he might be able to get it identified by a friend at the Council for the Care of Churches. On 28 May 1988, he received a reply:

> The cross is probably the one removed from the apex of the west gable. This you could check simply by seeing if there is a ghost of a crucifixion on the reverse side. If there is, then the cross is from the west gable and placed there by the Victorians, but originating from the Churchyard Cross. The date, according to our files, is thirteenth century even though, to my untutored eye, it is late and more likely fourteenth century. The figure is the B.V.M. and Christ Child. The right hand is raised, not in benediction, but as a gesture of acknowledgement of the Miracle of God made flesh in Christ The infant is carried on the Virgin's left arm. Only the lower legs are visible – or legible – even though there is something of the shoulder remaining. There is a kneeling "donor" figure at the Virgin's feet (right-hand side). Is the stone lias? Late medieval iconography is not my bag. There does seem to be a correlation between front and back (if the crucifixion is present), possibly summed up by the word "Grace."

(The theological meaning of "grace" is "favour of God, divine regeneration and inspiring influence." In another place, "the divine influence which operates in men to regenerate and sanctify and impart strength to endure trial and resist temptation.")

After matins that Sunday morning Rev. Doré and I looked at the cross. We turned it round and there it was "the ghost of the crucifixion." The "donor" figure at the Virgin's feet is, I believe, that of Sir John de Mohun III (b. *c.*1269 d.1330), the great benefactor of the priory of Dunster, and this ties in with the dating by the Council for the Care of Churches.

The origins of the cross are in fact closely connected with the ceremonies of Palm Sunday, which involve rituals of procession representing Our Lord's triumphal entry into Jerusalem, and the blessing of the palms first recorded at the abbey of Bobbio near Genoa.[1]

The earliest reference to the "palme crosse" is in 1443 when the contract for building the two upper storeys of the tower states that "the sayde paroch schall bryng all suffycyant material withyn the palme crosse of the sayde church." (The palm cross is the churchyard cross, here used for the churchyard itself.) It would therefore appear that it was complete with its circular stepped base or calvary, in 1443, but when it became detached is entirely unclear. It is possible that it was moved by the monks before they left Dunster in 1539; some alterations took place at the west end of the church in the 1530s and the elevation of the cross to the gable would have ensured it some protection. Alternatively it may have suffered at the hands of the Puritan iconoclasts in the 17th century, but it was certainly not in its original position on top of the shaft in the churchyard by 1808. In the *Gentleman's Magazine* of that year we read: "In the Churchyard opposite the West door is the pedestal and shaft of an old cross on three steps, and a venerable yew of large dimensions."[2] The cross is visible on the west gable in the 1845 west view from the Braikenridge Collection. The specification for the great Victorian restoration, begun in August 1874, reads: "Re-set the coping of the West Gable, and provide the same with all necessary copper cramps, make good wherever defective all gable copings with stone of the same description and restore gable copings to old line where defective. All of approved wrought stone and to detail to be provided by the Architect. Carefully preserve the Gable Cross when re-setting the West Gable."

In *Dunster and its Lords* (1882), Sir Henry Maxwell Lyte recorded the iconography incorrectly for he wrote: "an interesting little cross, bearing a figure of St Michael, which is still to be seen above the western gable of Dunster Church." He did not, however, connect this with the churchyard cross for he wrote of "the 'Early English' Cross which stood in the Churchyard, the steps and a short stump only remain in their old position."

So, our "palme crosse" now finds sanctuary on the stone altar slab that escaped the destruction which befell many churches in the reign of Edward VI (1547-53), when monuments were defaced, wall-paintings covered with whitewash, statues destroyed and roods removed together with stained glass windows which showed a medieval superstitious character and which may have included the destruction of the image of St Christopher which was in the church in 1419.

The Chantry Chapels

The layout of the church had long posed interesting questions about the relationship between the church and the priory, and the various chantry chapels, in particular the position of the St Lawrence and de Mohun chapels.

The chantry of the Holy Trinity may have received a second dedication after the laity was excluded from the chancel containing the original altar of St George (the high altar). There is mention of the chantry of the Trinity or St George in the reign of Edward VI,[3] and again in Elizabeth's reign when "the whole lands belonging to the Trinity Chantry are worth £4, which yet remain in the Crown's hands."

THE NORTH-EAST CHAPEL (DE MOHUN)

When the Victorian designation of the north-east chapel as "the Sacristy" was dropped, the chapel reverted to that of St Lawrence assigned to it by C.H. Samson, Lyte (1882) and Hancock, while the Rev. Richard Utten Todd's preference for the "Old Chantry" or "Mohun Chapel" had been quietly laid aside. In the course of my research, however, I discovered that Sir Henry Maxwell Lyte had come to a different conclusion in his later book, *A History of Dunster* (1909), from that which he had reached in 1882. (Sir Henry Maxwell Lyte KC.B. was the keeper of the archives at Dunster castle and deputy keeper of the archives at the Tower of London.) He was supported by Dr Francis Eeles O.B.E. DLitt. F.R.Hist.S, the first secretary to the Council for the Care of Churches which he ran from "Earlham," in St George's Street and who had written the excellent 1934 and 1940 guides to the church.

The Rev. Richard Utten Todd, rector of Dunster during the Victorian period, referred in the parish magazine (February 1877) to the north-eastern chapel as the "Old Chantry" or "Mohun Chapel." This was entirely feasible since Sir John de Mohun III is said to have been buried on the north side of the sanctuary of the priory church, the grave being marked only by an aperture in the wall on the west of the door to the chapel at ground level. However, the ground plan by C. H. Samson, F.R.I.B.A. of the church before restoration shows at (2) the chantry of St Lawrence sited at the north-east and at (6) the chantry of the Holy Trinity or St George sited in the south-east.

In John Buckler's drawing (in the Pigott Collection) showing the north-east view of the church in 1839, the roof of this chapel is sloping and continues the line of the gable roof of the east end of the church; the east window is blocked up and there are no apertures in the north face. During the 1874/6 restoration the chapel was taken down and re-built on new foundations and set back 1 foot 6 inches from the face of the east wall in order to show the old buttress in the angle of the latter. The specification states, "the old buttress of Sacristy to be re-built stone for stone," and further that, "the old stone altar in the Sacristy is to be most carefully preserved and protected and, if necessary, re-fixed in its old position." The western jamb of the doorway from the chancel to the Sacristy was also "to be re-built and well-bonded into the wall." The 19th-century re-building gave us the present flat-topped and battlemented chapel with windows to the east and to the north. At that time the red and cream and black encaustic tiles were gathered from various places in the church and the fragments were put together to form the 13th/14th-century tiled floor in the chapel.

The renaming of the chapel as the Sacristy illustrates its new role in accommodating the sacred vessels and vestments for use at the high altar, or altar of St George, in the priory church. The high altar was the original altar of the undivided church, and now in 1876 it was to be re-instated. One of the great discoveries made during the restoration was the altar slab which was found reversed in the north aisle. This was placed on alabaster columns in what was thought to have been its original position. For my part I think it is equally possible that it was the altar slab of the chapel of the Holy Trinity at the extreme west end of the north aisle which Dr Eeles deemed to be the aisle of the Holy Trinity.

THE SOUTH-EAST CHAPEL (ST LAWRENCE)

Of the south-east chapel Lyte wrote: "in January 1357, as it appears, a very interesting agreement (pees) was made, in the presence of Sir John de Mohun (the last de Mohun lord of Dunster), between Richard of Childeston, Prior of Dunster and the monks on the one side, and the parishioners on the other, with regard to the services of the church, the provision of lights, and the repair and maintenance of the aisles (les eles) and the central tower (le clocher).[4] The following is a summary of the terms which are recorded in clumsy French :- (I quote the relevant item): (3) The Prior shall repair and roof (covera) the tower suitably without defect, and shall receive from the parishioners 8 marks in three instalments. He shall roof and forever maintain (amendera) the chapel of Our Lady and the dorter aisle (la ele dortur). The parishioners shall forever maintain the chapel of St Leonard and the aisle between the chapel of St Lawrence and the tower ... Proceeding to important questions with regard to the fabric of the church, the agreement presupposes that the monks were responsible for the maintenance of the chancel, and the parishioners for that of the nave. Both parties were interested in the tower. In the division of liability for the rest of the church, the monks undertook the Lady Chapel and the adjoining northern transept, styled the 'dorter aisle', from which a flight of steps led up to their 'dorter', or dormitory. The parishioners undertook the southern transept giving access to the chapel of St Lawrence, which may be located to the east of it."[5]

Lyte further says of alterations to this chapel: "The chapel of St Lawrence on the east side of the southern transept seems to have been enlarged and rebuilt in the later part of the fifteenth century." It is strange that in spite of these comments, in his ground plan whilst showing the St Lawrence chapel as the south-east aisle he places a query at No. 7 in the key to this plan. Dr Eeles writing about the 1357 agreement remarks: "the chapel of St Leonard seems to have been in the south choir, that of St Lawrence was on the south side of the nave, the aisle between it and the tower being the south transept[6] ... the parish maintaining the chapel of St Leonard and the aisle between the chapel of St Lawrence and the tower."[7] In writing about the mid-15th century, he says: "while on the south side of the nave the chapel of St Lawrence opened into the nave by an arch, or arches, near the east end. West of it there may have been a south aisle."[8] In the 1498 Glastonbury award the chapel of St Lawrence was included as part of the south aisle.[9]

In Lyte's *Dunster and Its Lords* (1882) he wrote that the effigies of Sir Hugh Luttrell (d.1428) and Lady Catherine Beaumont, his wife, (d.1435) lay on a table-tomb: "on the north side of the High Altar, in the thickness of the wall that separates the chancel from a small outlying chapel"... the only evidence indeed of the existence of an earlier chapel on the site is a massive stone altar which can hardly be later than the first half of the 13th century. There are fair grounds for believing that it was, 'the lower Chapel of St Lawrence' mentioned in the 1254 agreement between Sir Reynold de Mohun and the Prior and Convent of Bath."

Preb Hancock also favoured the north-east chapel as being that of St Lawrence, for in

Dunster Church and Priory, published in 1905, he wrote: "the parishioners of Dunster have come to be thankful for their beautiful church and its numerous services, when they look back only some fifty or sixty years. We have seen the terrible condition of neglect into which the priory church had fallen as Collinson found it. In the middle of the last century it was only used as a depository for all kinds of rubbish. The windows were decayed; the pavement rough and broken up; the Chapel of St Lawrence a mere ruin barely protected by a slanting roof, while stone walls shut the church off the North and South transepts."

The first mention of the St Lawrence chapel was the elaborate agreement which Sir Reynold de Mohun II made in 1254 with the prior and convent of Bath. His eldest son John had died in Gascony between 1252 and 1254 and his body had been brought back to England. He was buried at Bruton priory in Somerset and his heart was interred at Newenham abbey (Devon) before the high altar.[10] The agreement was for masses to be said for the benefit of this beloved son John and also for Sir Reynold's own soul (he died in 1257/8) and for the souls of his wives Hawis and Isabel, his ancestors and his successors. (It is of interest that it was Isabel's younger sister Joan who married John. They were the daughters of William Ferrers, earl of Derby.) The monks "undertook that mass should be celebrated daily to the end of time by one of their own number attached to the Priory of Dunster, or by a respectable secular chaplain, in the 'upper chapel' of Dunster Castle dedicated to St Stephen, unless prevented by war, by ecclesiastical interdict, or by order of the castellan," in any of which events it was to be celebrated in the chapel of St Lawrence belonging to the Priory below ("inferius"). To ensure due performance of this, they gave Reynold de Mohun right of distraint upon their land at Alcombe. He on his side granted to them fifty marks for the purchase of rents and undertook that the necessary books, vestments, lights and ornaments should be provided by himself and his heirs, owners of the Castle. Although the prior's deed is dated at Ottery, in Devonshire, the witnesses came from the neighbourhood of Dunster.[11] The chantry chapel of St Lawrence was normally served by a secular chaplain more or less independent of the prior and the vicar. It is 1420 before we hear any more of it, when John Batelyn of Dunster bequeathed a pair of silver cruets to hold the Eucharistic wine or water, to the altar of St Lawrence. John Batelyn must have been a wealthy man for he also bequeathed a pair to the high altar and a pair to the parochial altar.[12] It is thought that he worshipped at these various altars on particular days or at particular hours. The parochial altar was that of the Holy Rood on top of the rood screen formerly creating a bridge between the two western piers of the crossing tower and was served by the vicar. The main altar of the undivided church, the high altar or altar of St George was served by a monk.

The "upper chapel" of Dunster castle received its dedication in 1254. It was on the keep on the summit of the Tor. This was the site of the original medieval castle and the majority of the present "mansion" was built in the early 17th century and much altered in the 19th century. There was a knight's hall and chapel in the 13th century and buildings in the lower ward. In 1650 the present castle remained, but the chapel on the Tor was demolished and in the early 18th century the keep was levelled and converted into a bowling green. Any relics of the chapel of St Stephen and other castle buildings which had survived the attentions of the three hundred men employed in 1650 to dismantle the castle's fortifications, were then swept away. All that remained of the medieval castle of the Mohuns was located around the 13th-century gateway of Sir Reynold de Mohun II and the rounded bastion in the curtain wall.

Until the 15th century, the chantry chapel of St Lawrence and the chapel of Our Lady in the north-east were either apsidal chapels or square ended chapels with access to the presbytery of the priory church, if any, by means of a low arch. It is interesting to speculate about the length of these chapels off the presbytery. On the south side the remains of an

Early English lancet window can still be seen to the east of the mid-16th-century arcading now existing between the chancel and the south-eastern aisle. There could have been more of these lancet windows in existence before the erection of the Perpendicular arcading which would indicate a small chapel off the south transept. It is apparent from the masonry that the arcading was cut out of an earlier and more massive outer wall.

The re-built chapels of St Lawrence and Our Lady of mid-15th-century date had been functioning for just under a hundred years when the Edward VI's edict suppressing the chantries and the ensuing demolition of side-altars came into effect in 1548 and it would have been unacceptable to raze them. They were, however, inappropriate for the services prescribed by the new book of Common Prayer and, in the middle part of the 16th century, they were turned into side chapels by piercing apertures, or enlarging such apertures as then existed. Four-centred arches of two bays were erected, their piers having in their diagonals two-wave mouldings. The details of these pillars and arches are of a very debased character denoting their Late Perpendicular date. This is very evident when contrasting them with the mid-15th-century arch which connects the former chapel of Our Lady with the north transept.

In 1546 the following return was made by Henry VIII's commissioners: "The chauntrie of Saincte Laurence with the paryshe churche ther…is yerely worthe in Landes, rente and hereditamente in the tenure of sondery psones as maye appere pticulery more at large by the –

> Rentall of the same   ix li viijs. iiijd
>   whereof in
> Rents resolute paide yerely   xxs
>   and so
> Remaynethe clere   viij li viijs iiijd
> Plate and ornament. A Chalice, a pax, ij cruetts and too candelsticks of silv̄ waying lxxij oz.
> Ornamentes praysed at   ixs iiijd
> Memord. John Bayly clerk of the age of lx yeres, a singing man, incumbent ther."

There follows a return of the possessions of this chantry in consequence of the statute for the suppression of chantries etc. passed by Edward VI (Hancock D.C.P. 25/26)

HOLY TRINITY ALTAR AND AISLE

The site of the altar and aisle of the Holy Trinity has now to be considered. This was a source of disagreement between Preb F. Hancock, Sir H. Maxwell Lyte and Dr F. Eeles.

The earliest reference to Holy Trinity occurs in 1348 when R. de Cogston, bequeathed 6s. 8d. towards the building of the new screen or parclose of the Holy Trinity. In 1348 it does not appear to have been a chantry chapel. In William Pynson's will of 1419, 71 years later, the screen was apparently not completed: "To the work of the new Solarium of the Holy Trinity in the said church, 6s. 8d."[13]

Sir H. Maxwell Lyte wrote of this: "Later in the fifteenth century (the last date mentioned being 1420) a chantry was founded at the altar of the Holy Trinity, which is described vaguely as situate "in the parochial church of Dunster'." Its exact position is not defined. The founders of it appear to have been Henry Frank and Christina, his wife, and William Cadman, alias Clerke, and Alice, his wife. Some of the original trustees had died before 1491, when the survivors assigned the endowments to a secular chaplain named Richard Baker for the term of his life. His primary duty was to celebrate mass daily for the founders and the trustees at the altar of the Holy Trinity, but he was also bound to assist "in the choir" of the "parochial church" on Sundays and holy days "with the priests," presumably the monks, and the chaplain of the chantry of St Lawrence.[14]

The version of this document, i.e. DCB 94, as given in *Dunster Church and Priory* by Preb F. Hancock is considered by Lyte to have been "unfortunate." Hancock wrote of the "Holy Trinity Chantry": "This chantry was founded by Henry and Christine Franke and Alice Cudman (v. presentation by Feoffors, AD.1491). R. de Cogston, who died in AD 1348, bequeathed towards the building of the new screen or parclose of the Holy Trinity 6s. 8d. – Dunster Church Book. The right of presentation to the chantry was in the hands of Feoffors, and the chantry priest appointed by them was quite independent of the incumbent of the parish church."

In the Dunster Castle book we find the two following presentations to this chantry by the Feoffors.

7 Henry VII, 1491 (94). Grant by Sir Giles Daubeny of Daubeny, Kt., Alexander Sydenham, Richard Sydenham, George Stukely, John Loty, John Chaundeler Clerk, Philip Lucas, John Loker, Richard Inner and Adam Wilkin – to Richard Baker, Chaplain of the messuages, lands, oblations, services, etc., in Dunsterre and hundred of Carhampton which they held together with Walter Essen, Richard Browning, and others now dead – of the gift of Henry Franke and Christine his wife and Alice the late wife of William Cudman alias Clarke of Dunsterre for his life – of capital lords of these fees on the condition that (and here we go to p.15 which Lyte says is an unfortunate account of this document) the said Richard Baker Chaplain every day on which he shall be disposed shall celebrate Mass at the Altar of the Holy Trinity in the Parish Church of Dunsterre aforesaid and other divine Services and devout prayers according to his good conscience and devotion daily for the souls of the aforesaid Henry Franke, Christine his wife, William Cudman alias Clarke, and others specified on a certain tablet [which apparently no longer exists] and of all their parents children and benefactors and of all faithful dead and for the health and wealth of the said Giles, Alexander and Richard Sydenham, George Stukely, John Loty, John Chaundeler, and the other aforesaid feoffors, and also if it befalls that the said Richard Baker Chaplain on any Sunday or festival shall be attending other priests and there administering at their bedside, of the aforesaid parish Church of Dunsterre unless some other reasonable cause seeks to excuse his absence. Dunster Church Book.[15]

The Dunster Church Book, written in 1716 by Thomas Watts contained copies of 100 deeds which were at that time stored in a chest in Dunster church. Later these were added to the DCM (Dunster Castle Muniments) which are now in the Somerset Archives and Records Office. The DCB has, I understand, been re-numbered. According to Lyte, "There was in the eighteenth century, a collection of nearly a hundred medieval documents in Dunster Church relating to the rights of the burgesses and the endowments of the local chantries. Many of the more important of them have disappeared, a former incumbent of the parish having apparently considered himself free to do what he would with such things. A century ago [Lyte was writing at the beginning of the 20th century] a well known antiquary unblushingly referred to some of the originals as being in his own possession; one of them has found its way to the Castle. The former contents of one of the three ancient chests in the Church are now represented by a volume of indifferent transcripts made in 1716, which is in the possession of Mr Luttrell."[16]

Preb Hancock continues his account as follows:

AD 1538. Indenture made 20th day of June, 29th HVIII, between William Marchant, John Atwoode and Andro Ellsworthy feoffees of the Trynyte Chantry in the parish Church of Dunsterre, etc., on the one part with the assent of the burgesses and dwellers in town and John Ryse, Clerk, on the other part with the assent and consent of the burgesses and dwellers of the town hath constituted and ordayned the said John Ryse and to him hath allowed gevyn and graunted ther full and hole power, as often as the rents and profits thereof do extend suffycyently to the maintenance and fynd of a priest and that the said John Ryse shall yerly acownte to all seyd feofors of all gyfts or legacys that he receve of any person or persons of there devoytion to the mentaynaunce of the said Chauntre or of the Chapelyn celebrayting therein, and that the said feofors their heyres etc., nor none of the Burgesses and dwellers of the towne shall not receve nor take any rents or profytts of the said Chauntre during the praefate terme but only the sayd John Ryse or hys assygnes. Provided that yf the sayd John Ryse do not observe and kepe well and faythfully all the premises and admonyshed by the said feoffors and do not amend withyn the space of vi monethes that then ytt shall be lawfull for the sayd feoffors to receve and take the rents and profytts of the sayd Chauntre and exclude the sayd John Ryse thys Indenture or anythyng theryn specifyed to the contrary in any wyse notwithstandyng. Except that yf the seid John Ryse Clerke chaunce or happe to be sicke or by any other impotency cannot serve hys cure of Dunster that then the sayd John Ryse to have all the rents and profytts of the seid Chauntre to his own fyndyng and mauntenayance and to the reparyng of the howses without any interruption of the feoffors, burgesses or dwellers of the towne duryng the praefate terme of xx yeres. (Dunster Church Book, No. 17.)

The Royal Commission appointed, in February 1548, to enquire into the revenues of such chantries and chapels as still existed, report with regard to the chantry of the Holy Trinity at Dunster:

Land and possessions assigned to the use and maintenance of a chaplain there, celebrating in the Chantry of the Trinity or St George:

Divers persons hold ten tenements and five acres and a half of land there and render per annum, total … iiij li

Deduct in Rent resolute to John Luttrell Kt. for free rent for the premises, per ann vij s.

And remains over, per annum…lxxiij s.

Land assigned to the use and maintenance of a Light perpetually burning in the parish church there.

– holds half an acre of land lying in Watchet and renders per ann xvij d.

Deduct in Rent resolute to Fulforde, Kt., for free rent for the same half acre of land per annum … vj d.

And remains over, per annum…xij d.   (Somerset Record Society, vol. 2)[17]

[The "j" was the final form of "i" and was prolonged below the line, the tail became a curve and the dot gave rise to the modern letter "j." In the 17th century the two forms of the letter came to be differentiated, "i" remaining for the vowel and "j" used for the consonant, with the capital "J" being introduced. li = libra, a pound, s = solidus, a shilling, d = denarius, a penny.]

Another entry states that Joan Gryme, widow, of Dunster, "by her will proved Jan. 26, 1517, leaves… My body to be buried in the Church of S. George of Dunster, Light of the high cross in the said Church, 3s.4d. Devotion light 20d. Light of the Blessed Mary 12d. Light of S. George 12d. Repair of the aisle of the Holy Trinity 20d. Prior of Dunster for tithes forgotten 20d. Vicar of Dunster 2s. 6d."[18] John Gryme, yeoman, had died in 1509. He was "of Freckeford in the parish of Dunster" and decreed that: "my body to be buried in the

Churchyard of St George of Dunster. To the fabric of the parish Church of Dunster £6. 13s. 4d., to the light of the high cross 20d., the light of the dead there 20d. To the prior of Dunster for tithes forgotten 6s. 8d. Sir John Assheley Monk 12d. Sir John Holcomb my confessor and curate there at that time, 6s. 8d." (Med Wills S.R. Society, 139).[19] Later, Hancock mentions "three monks of the foundation," Sir John Wykys, Sir Thomas Kagnesah and Sir John Assheley, to whom John Gryme leaves 12d.[20] However, John Gryme did not leave money, as did his widow, to the chantry of the Holy Trinity or its aisle. His will was proved on 21 February 1509. Although no habitation remains at Frackford today I believe that it stood where Peter Creech used to grow dahlias and keeps his bees.

There is an account of the Trinity chantry in the *Gentleman's Magazine* of 1808 by William Hamper: "Trinity Chantry 7 Hen. VII 1491. Giles Daubeney, knight, Alexander Sydenham, Richard Sydenham, George Stukeley, and others...conveyed unto Richard Baker, Chaplain, sundry houses and lands in Dunster and Carhampton, on condition that whenever Mass was celebrated at the Altar of the Holy Trinity, in the Parish Church of Dunster, he should pray for the souls of Henry Franke, Cristina his wife, and others; and for the faithful departed this life; and for the good estate of the said Giles, Alexander, etc." Then, in 1537 (29 Hen. VIII), "The feofers of the Trynytye Chauntre" granted to John Ryse, Clerk, "ther full and hole power to receve the p'fytts of the said Chauntre duryng the terme of xxij yeres"; therewith to repair the houses belonging to it, and to maintain "an honest Chapleyn to say masse and to praye for the sowles of the founders, feofers, and benefactors of the seid Chauntre." The Altar of St James the Apostle, the Chapel of St Mary, and the "wex silver light," are named in antient wills, etc.; but the present article has already so far exceeded the indulgence granted by Sylvanus Urban to his Correspondents, that it must be here concluded.[21]

"John Greyme, yoman" was one of those named in the Star Chamber Proceedings[22] (Henry VII (no. 122.)) who with the vicar, Sir William Harries, was accused by the prior and convent of Bath of "certain wrongs... done to their brethren at Dunster";[23] the outcome of this dispute was the Glastonbury Agreement of 1498.

According to Eeles, "The re-building of the north aisle with larger windows and a waggon roof must have followed very soon after [the Glastonbury Agreement], for in 1504 Thomas Upcot of Dunster left 10 tons of iron to the fabric, "that is to the new aisle there to be built or repaired on the north side" on condition that work be undertaken in three years."[24] There was almost certainly a north aisle beside the eastern part of the nave, probably with a lean-to roof. The south aisle was not built until 1500 or, at the earliest the mid-15th century, while the chapel of the Holy Trinity existed in 1348 and became a chantry chapel in 1491. It is known that there was an adjunct on the north side from the earliest times, probably from 1177. Elsewhere Eeles dates the north aisle and the north transept to the mid-15th century. We also know that William of Dunster, former abbot of Cleeve, a Cistercian foundation which owned much property in Dunster, and appointed in 1491, seems to have contributed considerably to the erection of the north aisle.

A document of 1537, written during the short period when there were two distinct churches under one roof describes the chantry of the Holy Trinity as being in the "parochial" church of Dunster, the non-monastic section. It may thus be located either on the northern or on the southern side of the nave: almost certainly the north aisle. The chapel of Our Lady was at the east end of this aisle, and therefore the chantry of the Holy Trinity must have been at the west end, under the window. In the reign of Edward VI there is mention of the Chantry of the Trinity or St George; the second dedication seems to have been made when the laity had been excluded from the chancel containing the original altar of St George.[25]

Lyte tells us that 'the parishioners shall forever maintain (*amendera*) the chapel of St Leonard'. In 1510 Robert Loty left money to the light of this chapel and to the lights of

Our Lady and St George in the parochial part of the building. "Robert Lotey. My body to holy grave in the church of St. John the Baptist of Carhampton. To the light of B.M. 20d. The light of St. John Baptist 20d. The lights of the Holy Cross, St Nicholas, St Radegund, the dead, and St Christopher, 3s. 4d. The lights of St Leonard in the priory church of Dunster and of B.M. and St George in the parish church of Dunster, 6s. 8d. To Sir John Fyhilly vicar of Carhampton for tithes forgotten and not fully paid, 6s. 8d."[26] (Radegunde (518-87) was the daughter of a prince of Thuringen and wife of Clothaire I (c.540) who founded a monastery of nuns outside Poitiers.)

ALTAR SLABS
Closely connected with the question of the location of the chantry chapels is the identity of the altar slab found in the north aisle in 1876.

Side altars were abolished in 1548, but Lyte says, "One very ancient altar-slab that was suffered to remain in its original position in the little sacristy on the northern side of the chancel, where it is still to be seen (now called the de Mohun chantry chapel)." After the expulsion of the monks in 1539, the Vicar is hardly likely to have used it for the celebration of mass. Hence perhaps its immunity from the fate of other altars in constant use, such as those of Our Lady, St Lawrence, the Holy Rood, and the Holy Trinity.[27] This is the first altar slab.

At the Reformation altar slabs bearing their distinctive identity of consecration crosses were reversed and used to receive the carved epitaphs of the departed. The second altar slab is that on which the epitaph of Edward Poyntz was carved. He died in 1583 and "was buried in the parish church of Dunster, apparently in the eastern part of the northern aisle of the nave."[28]

At the time of the restoration in 1874/6 it may have been the altar slab of the chantry chapel of the Holy Trinity and St George that was set on alabaster columns on the site of the original high altar and altar of St George in the Priory Church. If it was the altar slab which bore the epitaph of Edward Poyntz these details were removed and they were inscribed with details also of his 18th-century descendants on a Victorian brass.

DUNSTER PROPERTIES

Various burgages in Dunster were given or bequeathed to the popular chantry of St Lawrence before the Reformation.[29] One of these was the house which adjoined the Cage House[30] to the west, both of which were rebuilt in the 19th century and now appear as one. In the very early 15th century and perhaps earlier, the Cage House was known as the "Cornershoppe" but in 1410 William Snell rebuilt it and it acquired its curious name, presumably due to its shape and wooden construction.[31] The more sober appearance we see today results from the later rebuilding by Dr Abrahams, whose memorial brass is on the floor of Dunster church. Dr Abrahams purchased the property from John Fownes Luttrell (1752-1816). It is now a bookshop called Shakespeare and Hall. The house next door once belonged to the abbey of Cleeve and was known as "le Smyth."[32] This, if not rebuilt, also has a later facade.

The Nunnery
The Victorian rector of Dunster, the Rev. Richard Utten Todd, writing in the parish magazine for August 1882, quoted from *Dunster and its Lords* by Sir Henry Maxwell Lyte:

Part of the revenue of the Chantry of St Lawrence at Dunster, which in the reign of Edward VI amounted to £9 a year, was derived from a very picturesque weather-tiled house generally called the 'Nunnery', on the north side of Middle Street in Dunster. The name however is of modern origin and quite misleading, the house in question having been known as 'The High House', even in the present century. In former times it was described as 'The Tenement of St Lawrence'.

There was a connection between the Benedictine priory of Dunster and the Cistercian abbey of Cleeve. One of the abbots of Cleeve, William Seylake, is thought to have been a Dunster man, commemorated as "W donesterre Abbas de Cliva" (William of Dunster, Abbot of Cleeve) in the Victorian windows in the vestry (formerly the chapel of Our Lady), which were copied from medieval fragments.

We first hear about the so-called "Nunnery" in the reign of Edward III. "In 1346, Hugh Pyrou [or Pero] of Oaktrow in Cutcombe, obtained royal licence to grant to the abbot and Convent of Cleeve in mortmain three messuages and a yearly rent of 12d in Dunster." His benefaction probably included the site of the "Nunnery" which may have been erected by the monks soon afterwards. The finials of the two gables and a small original window in the eastern wall seem to date from the fourteenth century.[33] This would make it about 300 years older than the Yarn Market The reason that the revenue of the chantry of St. Lawrence was said to be derived from the "Nunnery" is unclear since it belonged to the abbots of Cleeve, but they may well have devoted money to this very popular guild chapel. The abbots of Cleeve owned several other properties in the town including "le Smythe" and a fulling mill at the western end of the town. In 1535 they drew rents amounting to £4 7s. of which they paid 4s. to Dunster castle, presumably the old rent of four burgages. They distributed, out of these rents, 17s. in alms for the soul of their benefactor Pyrou and others.[34] All the property belonging to the abbey of Cleeve passed to the Crown at the Dissolution of the Monasteries and they, in turn, were liable to the Luttrells for the rent of 4s.

In 1609 a Londoner came upon the Dunster scene. His name was George Salter described as "of the parish of St Dunstan in the West, London gentleman."[35] He bought up houses and land in many different parts of England, speculating either for his own profit or acting as agent on behalf of other people and bought from the Crown the houses in Dunster formerly held by Cleeve abbey. He did not retain his purchases, but split them up and disposed of them until eventually by 1620 Robert Quirke of Minehead, the mariner who built the almshouses in Minehead, acquired what were then two separate tenements, "commonly known by the name or names of 'the Highe Howse or Howses,' subject to a yearly rent of £1 to the Crown."[36] In 1683 the property again came on the market and "comprised four several dwellings" although by 1703 it was inhabited by only three tenants. By 1781 it had changed its role and although described as "that dwelling house called or known by the name of 'the High House' … lately converted into a malt-house, with a kiln thereon for drying malt." By 1834 the maltster had been replaced by a joiner. There seems to have been no consistency regarding the name for in 1804 it was correctly designated in a conveyance by its ancient and descriptively appropriate of the "High House," but in 1769 and perhaps earlier in that century, it was known as the "Old Nunnery." This name belies the fact that apparently there never were any nuns in Dunster. Lyte, writing at the beginning of this century, said, "the building now comprises two dwellings not used for trade."[37]

TWO OF THE DUNSTER STREETS, AND CASTLE BAILEY

Church Street

The "Nunnery" stands in the street now called Church Street which has also undergone a series of name changes. "In 1367, it is called simply 'the street which leadeth from Market Street [High Street] towards the churchyard'. In 1636 it is called 'the strete which leadeth from the Markett Crosse towards the church of Dunster'. It was generally known as 'New Street' in the 15th and 16th centuries. Conveyances of the years 1781, 1804 and 1834 described it as 'Middle Street' while the parochial authorities of 1760 and 1782 called it 'Church Street'." [38]

West Street

"In front of the churchyard, the main road through Dunster turns sharply to the south-west and assumes the name of West Street. It is mentioned by that name in the 13th century and it has borne it ever since. The point at which it is intersected by a road on either side was known in the 17th century as Spear's Cross. In 1486 there is mention of 'the cross opposite to the dwelling-house (*mansionem*) of William Sper', doubtless identical with 'la crosse in la Westestrete' mentioned in 1413. There is a Wesleyan chapel of 1878 (now Chapel Crafts) which does not harmonize with its picturesque surroundings." [39]

Castle Bailey

This road, leading through the gateway and up the hill to the stables "was formerly one of the principal streets of Dunster, containing houses belonging to different freeholders. From its position immediately under the stronghold of the Mohuns and the Luttrells it was called, in the 14th and 15th centuries, 'Castelbayly', 'le Castellebale', 'le Baley Strete', or simply 'le Baleye'."

Near the stables "one branch of it turned northward into Market Street [High Street], another southward up the hill to the gate of the castle [this is a reference to the 13th-century gateway of the Lower Ward]. Eastward it led to St Benet's Well, to the Hanger Park, and to the Barton, or home farm of the medieval lords of Dunster. In course of time the Luttrells bought out all the smaller properties in the street, and put their dependants in such houses as they did not demolish. This process was completed by 1791 when the road is described as 'Castle Street'. The older name of 'Castle Bailey' was in use as late as 1769. The road has no name at present and it has long ceased to be a public thoroughfare...Here are the dairy, the stables, the coachhouse and the farm-yard pertaining to the Castle alone." [40] (Lyte, writing at the beginning of the 20th century was wrong about its lack of name. The road is now the way visitors approach the castle.)

In 1381 a William Garland was admitted tenant for life of a burgage in "la Baleye" between the ditch and the king's highway. The "ditch" was mentioned as a moat in 1318 when John de Mohun III was lord of Dunster. In 1409 the accounts of Sir Hugh Luttrell include the item, "To Thomas Skynner for the rent of a house in the Bailly in which to put my lord's dogs, 3s.4d." [42] The dog kennels remained in the castle bailey until the present houses were built in the 20th century. On 29 April 1488, in the time of another Sir Hugh Luttrell (d.1521), the accounts show, "That nobody shall henceforth winnow (ventulat) his grain in 'le Castell Bayly' and at 'le Barrys' unless forthwith remove the chaff arising therefrom, under pain of every one delinquent therein 12d. every time." [43]

FAMILIES OF DUNSTER

When the sea-port of Dunster was an area of bustling activity, Lower Marsh was not the rather isolated dwelling on the marshes which it has become. Although it stands in the parish of Carhampton, its successive owners, with whom we are concerned, were closely connected with life in the town of Dunster.

Ryvers family

The present house known as Lower Marsh was built in the 15th century, but in the 13th century Agnes of Marsh held a ferling of land in exchange for 16 capons which were to be rendered at Christmas and Easter: "she does suit like the said Gilbert (atte Cross), and she shall have in every year six cows and six calves in La Waterlete quit of herbage."[44] Sixteen capons were rendered to the lady of the manor (Lady Joan de Mohun) in the late 14th century by John Ryvers for his tenement at Marsh.[45] In 1411 during the time of the first Luttrell lord of Dunster, Sir Hugh Luttrell (d. 1428), John and Robert Ryvers were fined 6d. in the court of the borough of Dunster for a breach of the peace against Thomas Yarte. The constables seized his stick and his dagger but the stick was of no value and the dagger was sold for 4d. and it is thought that the owner paid the 4d. to get his dagger back.[46] In 1421 John Ryvers paid 3s. 4d annually for his pasture at East Marsh and in addition 16 capons for his freehold at Marsh. As woodward to Sir Hugh Luttrell he had a rent-free house with twenty acres of land.[47]

Robert Ryvers, like John Ryvers also served Hugh Luttrell. In this case firstly as bailiff of Dunster and steward of the household. Later, in the time of Sir Hugh's son, John Luttrell (d. 1430) Robert was the receiver-general, a role he fulfilled for John Luttrell's widow Margaret, the daughter of Lord Audley or Touchet of Nether Stowey castle. Dame Margaret got into financial difficulties with Robert Ryvers. This lady overspent her income and Robert Ryvers must have been a man of wealth for he was in a position to advance sums of money to his employer and he acquired silver vases and cups as part payment.[48] His accounts for the six months ending March 1432 survive in the Dunster Castle Muniments (1.17; XXXVII. 12) and are quoted by Lyte: "The same Robert has received of the same Margaret, as in silver vases bought of her 20s. And the same has received of her, as in silver cups (ciphis) bought of the same Margaret, 7l. 5s. And the same Robert has received of the same Margaret, as in a silver pot (alia) bought of her, 58s. 9d. And the same Robert has received of the same Margaret, as in a white bed of 'worstede' with other clothes (vestibus) bought of her and received in part payment of his aforesaid excess, 33s. 4d."[49] Even after this, she still owed £90! Robert Ryvers died in April 1441 leaving as his co-heirs four young daughters. All his property in Dunster and Carhampton was conveyed to feoffees in 1440 and probably most of it had already been sold.[50]

Loty family

We first hear about the Loty family on 16 March 1411: "John Spere chaplain drew a knife against John Loty, contrary to the peace. Therefore he is in mercy, 6d. And John Loty drew a dagger forfeited to the lord, against John Spere, chaplain. Therefore he is in mercy, 6d."[51] It is not explained why, but the former Ryvers estate became vested in the Loty family and John Loty, "the younger" and his descendants were in possession for more than three hundred years.[52] John had become a burgess of Dunster in 1440 and, like his predecessors the Ryvers, he served the lords of Dunster, becoming constable of their castle in the later years of Henry VI.

The Luttrells had always supported the Lancastrian cause and at the battle of Wakefield in 1460, Sir James Luttrell and others murdered Edward, duke of York. He was attainted of high treason and all his castles and manors were forfeit but he died of wounds received at the second battle of St Albans in 1461. John Loty "the younger," as the trusted feofee of the late Sir James, acted in various legal transactions[53] in the first year of the reign of Edward IV, probably concerned with Sir James Luttrell's will. John Loty died in September 1462 and was succeeded by his son, the third John.[54] By 1481, at the latest, the rent at Lower Marsh of 16 capons was converted to a monetary one of 8s.[55]

John Loty III may perhaps be responsible for the earliest part of the existing house at Lower Marsh. This includes a chapel over the porch, three mullioned windows, two niches for statues and a carved wooden roof. He was the largest owner of burgages at Marsh and in the main thoroughfares of Dunster; in the later part of the 15th century he paid in excess of 14s. annually at Martinmas[56] (11 November) and in 1496 he owned various lands in

Carhampton.[57] Opportunities of acquiring small areas of land were readily available to both the Ryvers and the Lotys acting as they did as agents to the Luttrells. Sometimes they purchased these lands and sometimes they came their way by the foreclosure of mortgages.[58] It is probable that John Loty III built Lower Marsh for his bride and that it was at that time that the form of the rent changed. He married Joan, stated to have been the daughter of Richard Chichester of Arlington in Devonshire, when she was the widow of John Bratton of Bratton, near Minehead. Richard Chichester was a party to the settlement made upon her by her second husband,[59] though in the *Visitations of Devon* under Chichester or Raleigh, Richard is shown as a fourth son who died without an heir, and no daughters are given. John Loty III died in June 1499. His widow "continued to occupy his free tenement then called 'Mershe Place',"[60] which Lyte identified with Higher Marsh, a farmhouse, which "seems to occupy the site of Marsh Place the cradle of the Stewkleys."[61] Joan and John Loty III had four children. There appears to have been no love lost between Robert and his mother who for some unknown reason filed a bill in chancery against her "unnatural" son, perhaps something to do with her three daughters, Margaret, Elizabeth and Jane, whose interests she was intent upon protecting. Robert Loty predeceased his mother, who died in 1518.[62] His will was proved in 1510 and he directed that he should be buried in the church at Carhampton. In the early 14th century there is mention of a second church at Carhampton dedicated to St Carantoc,[63] although the existing church is dedicated to St John, the Baptist. He also remembered St George's church, Dunster and left money to "the light of St Leonard in the Priory Church of Dunster and to the light of Our Lady and St George" in the parochial part of that building.[64]

Robert Loty had married Joan Flamank. Joan was a colourful character who enjoyed a varied experience of matrimony. Her second husband was Silvester Sydenham of North Petherton who died in 1525.[65] She then married John Luttrell, the younger brother of Sir Andrew Luttrell (*c*.1498-1538), but the marriage was dissolved in the legatine court of Cardinal Wolsey. Although the grounds of the divorce are unknown it was granted "according to the lawys of the church," which Lyte interpreted as perhaps being due to "some question of a pre-contract."[66] She then married for a fourth time, to Peter Fauntleroy of Fauntleroy's Marsh in Dorset.[67]

Joan's father, Thomas Flamank, a lawyer, together with Michael Joseph, a smith, raised an army of 15,000 men to lead a rebellion which erupted in Cornwall in 1497. They sought to force the king, Henry VII, to dismiss Archbishop Morton and Sir Reginald Bray, his financial advisers, who had brought in a poll tax to "pill and poll" the people to pay for Henry's endeavour to humble the Scots and to force the impostor Perkin Warbeck to surrender. The Bodmin blacksmith and the lawyer argued that liability for the defence of England against the Scots properly rested upon the northern barons.[68] The insurgents marched to London and encamped on Blackheath. Their rebellion ended in defeat by the royalist army under Lord Daubeny on 7 June 1497 and Thomas Flamank, Michael Joseph and their leader Lord Audley were all executed.[69] Thomas's daughter, Joan, as the wife of Peter Fauntleroy, shared with him persistent persecution from John Luttrell during the greater part of 1528.[70] It is said that, "he and his men drove away three hundred of her sheep on one occasion and sixty on another. They killed her doves and pigeons."[71] At various times, "they carried off deeds, household goods and even wearing apparel." Most dastardly of all, "they also flooded the lower chambers by cutting the dykes in the neighbourhood."[72] In short the Fauntleroys were boycotted and the tenants on the Luttrell estate were incited, not only to ignore them, but to withhold supplies of meat and drink.[73] The persecution even extended to Dunster church where the pew which her second husband Silvester Sydenham had erected with the parishioners' consent, was broken up by William Horsman. Joan Fauntleroy had her own domestic chaplain but John Luttrell carried off the chalice and the celebration of mass was prevented. As lessee of the priory of Dunster and the rectories of Dunster and Kilton, John Luttrell was a spurned husband who seems to have behaved in a less than Christian fashion. He was buried in the chapel of Our Lady in 1558.[74]

Poyntz family

It is supposed that by virtue of John Luttrell's marriage to the widow of Silvester Sydenham he claimed the enjoyment of all the lands and rents that had come to his wife in April 1510 when Robert Loty, her first husband, had died. She was summoned to attend the court of the hundred of Carhampton in 1534 and the court of the borough of Dunster in 1536. She must have been successful for at her death the entire property covered by the entail of 1510 was inherited by her sister-in law, Elizabeth Poynes, or Poyntz, of Mettcombe in Devon. Elizabeth was one of those three sisters of Robert Loty and daughter of Joan Chichester and John Loty III. Lyte refers to Elizabeth "as the relict of Richard Poyntz, whose eldest son Edward ... etc." but in the Pedigree of Poyntz of Devon & Somerset from the *Memoirs of the family of Poyntz* by Sir John Maclean, Edward Poyntz, son and heir, of Dunster, is shown as the son of Richard Poynes of Mettcombe in the parish of Marwood and Johan. Johan, Jane and Joan were synonymous names but it would appear that Edward's mother was certainly one of the three sisters. Edward established himself at Dunster but migrated between Dunster and Devon. He married Margaret, the daughter of Amias Chichester. Amias was the son of John Chichester of Ralegh, and was the first of the renowned Roman Catholic family to be seated at Arlington (Devon). Sir John Maclean, somewhat archly, wrote, "This Amassia (Amias), by Joan, his wife, daughter of Sir Roger Giffard, knight had nineteen sons, every one of which (what you may think much stranger) had no less than four sisters; fourteen of the nineteen lived to be proper gentlemen, though not above three of them had issue. When they went all to church, the first would be in the church porch, before the last would be out of the house."[75]

In the Dunster Parish Registers we find "Edward Poynts alias Poynes was buried 1579."[76] This was probably the eldest son of Edward and Margaret. Edward the elder would appear to have had a residence at Arlington where he made his will on 29 July 1583, in which he directed that his body should be buried in the church of Dunster; his interment does not appear in the Dunster Register of Burials but one of the ancient altar slabs was appropriated as his gravestone. In the will he names his five younger children Ann, Gartred, Mary, Philip and Charles, his two eldest sons Robert Poyntz and John Poyntz, and desires the latter to be good to his mother. He leaves the residue of his goods to his wife Margaret Poyntz, and names his brother-in-law Henry Chichester, Gent., and his brother John Poyntz, with his friend John Over, as overseers of his will. At the Inquisition taken at Chard, on 8 August 1584, he is described as Edward Poyntes, alias Poynes, Burgess of Dunster,[77] who on the day on which he died he was seized of "twenty-two burgages and two messuages in Dunster in free socage (as of the castle of Dunster) at a yearly rent of £1.2s.2d. to George Luttrell," their actual value being twenty times as much. His messuage called "Foremarsh," with fifty acres adjoining was found to be held of the manor of Carhampton at a fixed yearly rent of 15s. 4d. also far below the value.[78] This rent of 15s. 4d. was composed of a "high rent" of 12s. and 3s. 4d for common at the Marsh.[79]

Sir Edward Poyntz, in his young days had been at the court of King Henry VIII and he is mentioned by Professor Scarisbrick: "Sir Edward Poyntz who, like Sir Richard Weston, Sir William Kingston, Sir John Peachy, Sir Edward Neville and Sir Henry Guildford replaced Henry VIII's more boisterous courtiers when a court purge took place in May 1519. Nicholas Carew and Francis Bryan with whom he had diced and tilted and generally made merry were expelled and Henry decided to reform his way, and to avoid doubtful companions and to devote himself to more godly endeavours."[80] (In the 13th century an earlier Nicholas Carew's son John married Eleanor de Mohun, daughter of Sir William de Mohun of Ottery Mohun, a son of Reynold de Mohun II and his wife Isabel de Ferrers.) Edward had a son Robert (d. 1611) who lived at Leigh in the parish of Old Cleeve where he was buried. Through his cousin, Ursula Sydenham, he had secured a grange and land there. When he died he left money to the chapel at Leigh, and his manor at Foremarsh and lands in Dunster and Carhampton to his eldest son Giles.[81]

Giles Poyntz became a student of the Inner Temple in 1619 and in 1631 "he paid £30 to the Crown for relief from the burden of the duties imposed by his knighthood."[82] He lost his lands at Leigh, Dunster and Carhampton when he was denounced by the authorities of the Commonwealth as a Papist Delinquent. His estates were forfeited for treason and sold to Thomas Wharton of Gray's Inn, although his then wife Agnes seems not to have been so harshly treated for she was allowed to retain a fifth part of the lands. Lower Marsh was, at this time, rented by Nicholas Blake of Dunster.[83] Giles had sought to compound his estates but the petition had been rejected. He married a second time and in his will made after the Restoration in 1660 he left 20s. to each of his Catholic servants and £200 to his wife Prudence, "to be paid in a manner known to his wife." It is presumed that it was for the maintenance of a priest at Leigh.[84] Prudence was the daughter of George Rowe of Staverton,[85] and when her son Clement Poyntz, having succeeded his father in 1660, died without issue in 1685, his mother inherited all his lands. Her legacy from her husband and her son caused enormous trouble in the family because the heir-at-law was Giles Poyntz of Arlington (d. 1714), a great grandson of Edward Poyntz (d. 1583), and he appears to have contested the inheritance. The widow, Prudence, took the will to London, but she became caught up in the turmoil surrounding the escape of James II. William of Orange had landed at Brixham on 5 November 1688; James had been apprehended but he had escaped again and on Christmas day 1688, all was in a state of turmoil when news broke that James had landed in France. Three days later, William III entered London and Prudence, fearful about the safety of her precious document in her lodgings in Drury Lane, took it to nearby Wild Street, where she thought it would be safe in the Spanish ambassador's house. However, "the wrabble being very tumultuous," broke into the Embassy and "ryffled it" scattering the contents of her trunk "up and down the streets."[86] She manage to recover some of her possessions, and above all the precious will, for it was eventually upheld.[87] By her will of 1691, Robert Rowe of Kingston in the parish of Staverton (Devonshire), her nephew, became her principal legatee but her will contained a provision that: "notwithstanding the unkindness shown to her by Giles Poyntz of Bachet in Arlington, and in consideration of his relationship to her late husband, he should be allowed to have her lands on payment of 600l to Robert Rowe, her principal legatee."[88] Giles Poyntz came to terms with Robert Rowe and obtained the property at Dunster and Carhampton, which was from that time quite separate from the property at Leighland and Leigh Barton. He died at Yarnscombe in Devon in 1714 and was buried there. His manor, "or reputed manor" of Foremarsh in the parishes of Dunster and Carhampton was composed of houses and fields under the shadow of Dunster castle and was put into the hands of trustees, but his widow Anne got the barton of Marsh, or Lower Marsh and some adjacent land for her lifetime instead of a dower and she also received £5 per annum out of the "conventionary and other rents of the said manor."[89] She was registered in the reign of George I as a Roman Catholic landowner in Somerset.[90]

We have no evidence that Anne Poyntz ever kept a resident priest to serve in the little chapel over the porch at Lower Marsh. It is known, however, that until the early part of the 19th century, there was usually a Benedictine or a Jesuit priest in residence at Leighland. [91] Here Prudence Poyntz had made specific arrangements for a Benedictine chaplain who was to have free food, a horse and a salary of £7. It may be that a priest from Leighland officiated occasionally in the small chapel at Lower Marsh. Lyte says: "a cursory glance at a Poyntz pedigree, showing three Prudences, three Temperances and a Christian, might suggest that the family had a leaning towards Puritanism, if intermarriages with Chichester and Rowe did not show it to have been Catholic. Several members of it are recorded to have been buried at Arlington without a priest, that is to say, 'unattended by a lawful presbyter of the Church of England'."[92]

The names of the members of the Poyntz family whose names are inscribed on the Victorian brass are the three daughters of Giles (d.1714) and Anne Poyntz: Prudence, Mary (Clark), and Elizabeth who died in 1716, 1726, and 1729 respectively. Giles, their brother is not recorded on the brass but he was buried at Dunster in May 1731. After Giles' death his brother John inherited the property under an entail. He was of Gray's Inn and one of his unmarried sisters lived at Weston in Buckinghamshire and another at Arlington (Devon).[93] All their houses and lands in Dunster and Carhampton were let for life and were sold to Henry Fownes Luttrell for £2,400 in 1760. If these sisters sold their properties in 1760, they must have been the two younger sisters, for Prudence, Mary and Elizabeth had already died. Thus from the mid-16th century until 1760 the Poyntz family possessed Lower Marsh and were a powerful land-owning Catholic family.

Among the properties Henry Fownes Luttrell acquired were: "18 messuages 25 cottages 40 gardens 20 orchards 150 acres of arable land 30 acres of meadow 80 acres of pasture 10 acres of woodland 100 acres of furze and heath 20 acres of moor together with common of pasture for all manner of cattle in Dunster Marsh, East Marsh, Lutts (Loty's) Marsh, Coleborrow, Croydon, Townswood, Holly Hill, etc. together with the manor of Foremarsh. The farm at Lower Marsh yielded £49 a year and the property comprised houses in High St, New St, St George's St, West St and Gallocks St and other isolated pieces of land adjacent to others belonging to the Luttrell estate,"[94] including a small piece of land near Hensty where he was making the deer park at this time. The Luttrells' only loss was the ancient "chief rent" of 12s. and the burgage rents of £1 2s. 2d. due from Poyntz and his predecessors.[95]

CHAPTER TWO

THE DE MOHUNS

William de Mohun I

The first de Mohun, lord of Dunster, was William de Mohun I and the last was John de Mohun V. Perhaps the two most influential members of the family were William de Mohun I who granted the charter to build the Church and John de Mohun III who was the great benefactor of Dunster Priory.

William de Mohun I was alive in 1066 and 1090. The 12th-century Anglo-Norman historical poet, Robert Wace, wrote two chronicles in verse, the *Roman de Brut,* a translation of Geoffrey de Monmouth's *Historia Britonum,* which was later put into English verse by Layamon (medieval English poet), and the *Roman de Rou,* an account in octo-syllabic verse of the Norman dukes who accompanied William I, the "Conqueror," to England. The reference Wace makes to William de Mohun I is : *"Le viel William de Moion, Out avec li maint compaignon."* This first William was not necessarily old when he came to England but the adjective served to differentiate him from his son, William de Mohun II. A list of fifty-seven knights is included and these names are the same, and in an identical order, as those given in a somewhat dubious 14th-century account, presumably for the gratification of Sir John de Mohun V, the last de Mohun lord of Dunster, provided by an abbot of Newenham abbey, near Axminster in Devon. (Newenham abbey was founded in the 13th century by Reynold de Mohun II). This account professes to enumerate William de Mohun I's retinue and begins: "Be it known that in the year of the grace of our Lord Jesus Christ one thousand and sixty-six, on Saturday the feast of St Calixtus, came William the Bastard, Duke of Normandy, cousin of the noble king St Edward, the son of Emma of England, and killed King Harold and took away the land from him by the aid of the Normans and other men of other lands; among whom came with him Sir William de Moion the old, the noblest of all the host. This William de Moion had in his retinue in the host all the great lords after named, as it is written in the Book of the Conquerors." The list of fifty seven (or forty seven) "stout knights of name and repute" which then follows includes the names Marmion, Paignel, Basqueville, Corcye, Lacy, Columbers, Bullebek, Tregoz, Montfichet, and Bigot.[i] This great retinue was described as "a following worthy of an Emperor."[ii] The number of knights accompanying William the Conqueror is uncertain. Lyte says "there is an oft-repeated statement that he then had in his retinue fifty seven (or forty-seven) 'stout knights'" etc.[iii] In Hutchins' *Histories and Antiquities of Dorset*[iv] it is recorded that William de Mohun came to England with a retinue of forty-seven knights of note.

Apart from Mohun, the names of Corcye/Courci/Courcy and Painel/Paganell/Paynel/Paynell are of particular interest in the history of Dunster. The family Corcye gave its name to Stoke Curci or Stogursey. The family of Paynel married into both the de Mohun and Luttrell families. The foundation of the subsequent prosperity of the Luttrells was laid when Sir Geoffrey Luttrell, the progenitor of the house of Luttrell married Frethesant Paynell. Frethesant was the co-heiress with her sister Isabel, of their father William Paynell, a younger scion of the famous house of Paynell from whom they inherited fifteen knights' fees. Frethesant bore Sir Geoffrey Luttrell a son, Sir Andrew Luttrell of East Quantoxhead, who was the third cousin of Maurice of Gaunt, the heir of the elder branch of the Paynell family. It is from the union of Sir Andrew Luttrell and Pernel, his wife, that the two branches of the Luttrell family came into being. Their eldest son, Geoffrey was the ancestor of the Luttrells of Irnham (Lincs) and their younger son, Sir Alexander retained the seat of their father at East Quantoxhead.

The de Mohuns came from Moyon (now shown on the maps as Moon), near St Lo in Normandy which, in 1027, was part of the dower of Adela, duchess of Normandy. It appears that William de Mohun was also lord of Lion-sur-Mer which he later exchanged for Bruton/Brewton Priory which had previously been a dependency of Troarn abbey. There is great variety in the spelling of this family's name which appears as Moion, Moiun, Moyon, Moyun, Moun, Mooun, Moyhun and Mohun. It is known that William de Mohun, the first lord of Dunster, was sheriff in 1084 and, at the time of the Domesday survey of 1086, he was a tenant-in-chief in Somerset where he held fifty-six separate manors. In Dorset he held eleven manors and in Devon and Wiltshire he held one apiece. That year he assigned many of the manors to other Normans who, in exchange, agreed to abide by the customary conditions of military service. Although subject to this new Norman overlord, an Englishman, Brictric, was permitted to retain the lands which he had held of William Sordemaneford. Brictric had held these lands in the days of King Edward the Confessor.[v] By assigning his lands to other Norman knights William de Mohun strengthened his military hand and if he, or the king, required assistance it was readily available. He retained in his own hands eighteen manors in Somerset and six in Dorset but gradually these too were reduced either by the enfeoffment of more knights or by grants he made to religious establishments. Before 1100 he had concentrated his lands by exchanging outlying manors with the king for that of Carhampton and the Hundred of Carhampton. Eventually the little Hundreds of Cutcombe and Minehead, mentioned in the Gheld Inquest of 1084, were absorbed into the Hundred of Carhampton.[6]

It is thought that the fortress of William de Mohun I was higher up than the present castle and "crowned the Tor, a conical hill, whose summit, artificially levelled, measures about thirty-five yards east and west by about seventy north and south."[7] This lonely Torra, mentioned in the Exeter Domesday Book: "William has a manor which is called Torra" had been held by Aluric and gave its name to the little town variously known as Dunestore, Dunsterre, or Dunesthor. Lyte surmised "that Dunster Castle never had one great tower, quadrangular, like that of Rochester, or circular like that of Arundel."[8] The site was naturally impregnable but the uppermost part was made more so by being scarped to a perpendicular slope of eighty feet. It was already a most precipitous place and, whilst we have no knowledge of the fabric, it is thought that its very position abnegated the need for a massive keep and that there were several buildings, connected by walls of medium height. This first structure may indeed have been constructed of wood.

The castle of the de Mohuns became the head of an important Honour or Barony. By the middle of the 12th century the manors retained and owned by the first of the de Mohuns were Dunster, Minehead, Kilton, Carhampton and Cutcombe (where William de Mohun I kept thirty-six brood mares) and also Ham in Dorset. His estate at Stockland came to be called "the sheriff's town" later corrupted to Shereveton and Shurston. Some of his land near Kilton was also known as Shervidge. He also owned Sheriff's Brompton known to us today as Brompton Ralph. This name was acquired when it was held under the lord of Dunster, by Ralph, the grandson of Durand de Mohun. It is not known if this Durand de Mohun, steward (dapifer) was related to the lords of Dunster or if he simply hailed from Moyon.[9]

The de Mohuns established many religious foundations but William de Mohun I is notable for his gift of the church of St George, Dunster to the monks of Bath abbey. Dunster priory never became a large foundation and the main reason for its existence was as a centre from which the large estates granted to the Benedictine abbey of Bath by William de Mohun I could be administered and the underlying power remained with the prior of Bath. In 1088 John de Villula, a Norman, was made bishop of Bath. He had obtained both the city and the Saxon abbey, dating from 781 AD, from William II, "William Rufus." Villula built an abbey so vast that the east end of the present 15th-century abbey extends only as far as its crossing. The western arch, of rounded Norman form, still remains and encloses the inner later Perpendicular window over the high altar. This was one of the four arches which supported the original crossing tower of the Benedictine abbey.

The bishops of Somerset had been seated at Wells for two hundred years but the ambitious Villula ruthlessly destroyed the canonical buildings there and turned the canons out to fare for themselves as best they could. In 1107 he started to build his great abbey and its ancillary buildings at Bath and thus seven years after the last possible date of St George's charter (1088-1100), he established, during his episcopate, the supremacy of Bath. However, when Bishop Robert of Lewes (1136-66) became bishop of Bath he sought to redress the deeds of Villula and to restore Wells to its rightful state. Whilst conceding the precedence which Bath had acquired, he resolved the problem by having a *cathedra*, or bishop's throne, placed in both places and he laid down that he should be elected by both the chapter of Wells and that of Bath conjointly. Human ambitions being rarely satisfied, Bishop Savaric (1192-1205), who was said to have been "even more ambitious and unscrupulous than John de Villula," obtained the bishopric of Bath without reference to the chapter of Wells and then cast acquisitive eyes on Glastonbury and, in the reign of King John, he obtained it by violence and became bishop of Bath and Glastonbury. Pope Innocent IV confirmed the accession of Bishop Roger as bishop of Bath in 1244, although the monks of Bath had not consulted with Wells, and decreed that the agreement of Robert of Lewes should henceforth be adhered to and that the bishop should use the title of Bath and Wells. However, following the Reformation and the dissolution of Bath abbey in 1539, the bishops, whilst still known as bishops of Bath and Wells, have been elected by the chapter of Wells only and have been enthroned there.

William de Mohun I expressly stated in his deed of gift that he conferred the church of St George on the monks of the cathedral church of Bath that they might build and edify it (*œdificent et exaltent*). They received from William de Mohun I extensive lands, the manor of Alcombe, the advowson *(or right to appoint)* of the church of Dunster and the tithes of Dunster, Minehead, Broadwood, Carhampton, Newton (now known as Bicknoller), Broomfield, Stockland (now known as Shurton) and Kilton, held by William de Mohun in desmesne. Two fisheries were also given to the monks which are thought to have been in the little river Avill or on the seashore.

William de Mohun I's charter was confirmed by William "Rufus" and by that pioneer of scholasticism, St Anselm, who was appointed archbishop of Canterbury in 1093. The charter of the king and of Anselm have both disappeared. William de Mohun I's charter is as follows:

> Be it known to all faithful members of the Catholic Church both present and future that I, William de Moione, pricked by the fear of God, give and grant in perpetuity for the weal of my soul and that of William, King of the English, and those of all my ancestors and successors to the church of St Peter of Bath and to John, Bishop of that monastery, and to the monks both present and future, the church of St George of Dunestore, and myself, and the tithe of the same town, both of vines and of ploughs and of the market as also of all sheep, and the whole town of Alcume and all things

belonging to it, free and quit of all service, that is to say a hide of land, and a moiety of the tithe of Maneheafe, (Minehead) and the whole tithe of Bradeuude, (Broadwood) and all the tithe of Carentun, (Carhampton) so far as it belongs to me and the whole tithe of Niwetun, (Newton) and a moiety of the tithe of Brunfield, (Broomfield) and the whole tithe of Stokelande, (Stockland) and the whole tithe of Kilvestune, (Kilton) and two fisheries, the one belonging to Dunesthor and the other to Carentun, and the whole tithe of my mares on the moors. And I grant all these things to the aforesaid church of Bath by consent of my wife Adelisa, in order that the Bishop and monks of the same may build and raise the church of St George. Of this benefaction there are these witnesses on my behalf - Henry de Port, and Durand the steward, and Ogis and Geroius, and Walter de Celsui, and Robert le Blond *(flavus)* and Geoffrey and Robert my sons, and Wilmund my brother, and Odo de Altaribus, and William de Hermodville, and Robert son of Richard, and Humphrey de Pierrepont *(Petreponte)*, and Ralph, son of Osbern, and Herbert of Kent, and Richard le Blond and Picot, and Engelram, son of Juelin, and Alexander de Percy. These are on behalf of the Bishop, that is to say, Gireward the monk, and Girebert the archdeacon, and Dunstan the priest, and Gilbert the priest, and William the clerk, and Adelard the steward, and Turald and Sabian."[10]

The unreserved gift of the whole of Alcombe to the Benedictine monks of Bath caused it to become part of the endowment of their cell at Dunster. Sometime after 1341, the monks of Bath interpolated a mention of the tithes of Shurton, Coombe, Codford and Exford into this first charter of William de Mohun I.[11] This actual charter has disappeared but an earlier copy at Cambridge and several confirmations show clearly that these tithes were not named as part of the original endowment. This falsification by the monks was apparently not necessary to support some of these claims.[12]

Reference is made in the charter to vines and to the fact that the monks of Bath were to receive the tithe of William de Mohun I's vines. The expense of cultivating the vineyard and the sale of the local wine are alike mentioned in 1177.[13] In 1266, in the time of John de Mohun II, thirty four of the villeins were required to dig half a perch (2¾ yards) apiece of the lord's vineyard every year for which they received ½d.[14] The vineyard comprised 7 acres[15] and the production in 1279 was valued at 18s.[16] In 1284 when John de Mohun III was lord of Dunster there was mention of a wine-press. In 1376 the year after the last de Mohun lord of Dunster, Sir John de Mohun V died, there was a "keeper of the vines" who was in receipt of a regular salary.[17] Doubtless he was possessed of special skills and an expert knowledge of the subject. The vineyard was on the sunny slope behind the Luttrell Arms. This exact position is specified in a deed of 1419.[18] The first Luttrell lord of Dunster, Sir Hugh Luttrell (d.1428) abolished the vineyard and turned it into ordinary pasture land within the Hanger Park. The vineyard was known as "le Wynard" and the name survived for some time in the yearly accounts of the reeve of Carhampton and Dunster.[19] There was a vineyard at Minehead and Lady Joan de Mohun, widow of John de Mohun V used to have wine sent to her from this source after she left Somerset.[20] Her successor, Sir Hugh Luttrell probably preferred Bordeaux wine which would have been well-known to him since he spent much time in France. Today, descendants of the medieval vines of Dunster grow wild in the hedgerows and indeed on 13 August 1988, I brought home a great armful for the decoration of the church during the Flower Festival. The vines still bear grapes; small and hard but nevertheless a link with our mediaeval past.

William de Mohun II

In William de Mohun I's charter to the church of St Peter at Bath made between 1088 and 1100, the names of his wife Adelisa and of his sons Geoffrey and Robert appear. The charter is by consent of Adelisa and the two sons are the witnesses. However, the name of William de Mohun II, who succeeded his father as lord of Dunster, is not mentioned and it would therefore appear that he was not the eldest son. We know that Geoffrey and Robert were both alive in 1090. We first hear about this second William in 1131 when, being present at the Council of Northampton, he witnessed Henry I's charter to Salisbury cathedral.[21] He, like his father, was a benefactor of Bath abbey and he gave the monks a moiety of the tithes of Exford and some land at Avelham, at the southern end of Dunster and three furlongs of land at Northcombe in the neighbouring parish of Cutcombe.[22] These gifts were for the benefit of the soul of his deceased eldest son Ralph.

In 1134 after the rout of Winchester, Matilda fled to Gloucester. William de Mohun II deserted her cause and went over to Stephen's side. King Henry I died on 1 December 1135 and Stephen was crowned. However in 1138 William again espoused the cause of Matilda and Dunster castle became one of her main strongholds and was by this time a stone fortress of military pretensions. The chronicler who wrote the *Gesta Stephani* (the Deeds of Stephen) suggested that there was a lower ward to the castle, and in view of its war-like role at this time there would have been a need for the accommodation of many soldiers and horses. There is no traceable evidence of Norman work but the earliest masonry exists at the north eastern angle and is of great size. It is thought that it was William de Mohun II who stipulated that his feudal tenants, apart from their military obligations, should lend assistance to the repair of the walls of the castle.

In 1905 Prebendary Hancock wrote: "When the late extensive and skilful restoration was carried out...a large portion of the Norman west wall was exposed to view and also the jambs of the Norman west door. The Norman doorway had been built up in Late Perpendicular times, and a smaller doorway of Perpendicular style inserted. The jambs of the earlier door were found to have been much injured by fire, as if in some early émeute - perhaps when King Stephen lay about the castle, endeavouring in vain to reduce it - the church had been held by one side or the other, and an attempt made by the besiegers to effect an entrance by fire."[23] This earlier door may be of the first half of the 16th century.

For his services to her cause, sometime between April and June 1141 Matilda, also known, through her first marriage to the Emperor Henry V as the Empress Maud, created William de Mohun II an earl[24] and as Earl William de Moion he attested a charter issued by her at Westminster in the midsummer of that year.[25] The earldom conferred was that of Dorset although William called himself earl of Somerset. Both counties had a common sheriff and were administered as one.

Stephen, the younger son of Adela, the daughter of William the Conqueror, was born c.1096 and Matilda, daughter of Henry I the youngest son of William the Conqueror was born in 1102, so Stephen and Matilda were first cousins. Stephen had an elder brother Theobald of Blois, who had the support of some Norman barons, and a younger brother Henry of Blois, who King Henry I made abbot of Glastonbury, bishop of Winchester and became the wealthiest cleric in England. However, after the death of his father, Stephen Henry, count of Blois in the Holy Land, Henry I was exceptionally generous to Stephen, bestowing on him so many estates in England and France that he became the most affluent man in his uncle's kingdom. When Henry I died in December 1135, Stephen was crowned and all proceeded calmly for two years. In 1138 Geoffrey of Anjou, Matilda's second husband, invaded Normandy and Matilda's uncle David I, king of Scots, moved into the north of England. Her half-brother, Robert of Gloucester, an illegitimate son of King Henry I, raised her standard in the west country and it was only in a few shires that she gained any support. She was never crowned but her victory lay in the succession of her son, King Henry II to the throne after the death of King Stephen's heir Eustace, in 1152. Thus was founded the Angevin line which reigned in England in the persons of Henry II and his two sons Richard I and John.

The events of 1138 and William de Mohun II's part in them is best recorded by the *Gesta Stephani* as follows: "At that time, William de Moiun, a man not only of the highest rank but also of illustrious lineage, raised a mighty revolt against the King, and, collecting some bands of horsemen and footmen at his fortress, which he had placed in a fair and impregnable position by the sea-shore, began to overrun all that part of England in warlike manner, sweeping it as with a whirlwind. At all places and at all times, laying aside his loyalty, he set himself to work his cruel will, to subdue by violence not only his neighbours but others living afar off, to oppress with robbery and pillage, with fire and sword, any who resisted, and mercilessly to subject all wealthy persons whom he met to chains and tortures. By so doing, he changed a realm of peace and quiet, of joy and merriment, into a scene of strife and rebellion, weeping and lamentation. When in course of time these things were made known to the king, he gathered his adherents together in a mighty host and marched with all speed to put an end to William's savagery. But when he came to a halt before the entrance to the castle and saw the impregnable defences of the place, inaccessible on the one side where it was washed by the tide and very strongly fortified on the other by towers and walls, by a rampart *(vallo)* and outworks, he gave up all hope of carrying it by siege, and, taking wiser counsels blockaded the castle in full view of the enemy, so that he might the better hold them in check and occupy the neighbouring country in security. He also gave orders to Henry de Tracy, a skilled soldier, oft approved in the hazards of war, that acting in his stead, because he was called away to other business, he should with all promptitude and diligence bestir himself against the enemy. Henry, therefore, in the King's absence, set forth from Barnstaple, a town belonging to him and enjoying privileges granted to him by the King, and made vigorous and determined attacks on his foes, so that he not only restrained their wonted sallies and their unbridled, marauding raids in the neighbourhood, but also captured a hundred and four horsemen in one cavalry encounter. At length, he so reduced and humbled William that he was able to abandon further hostilities against him and leave the country more peaceful and free from such disturbances."[26]

It may be surprising to find Dunster castle described as "by the sea-shore" and as "bounded by the sea on one side." It is quite possible, however, that the level ground, now known as "the Lawn" or "Dunster Lawns," on the eastern side of the Tor, was, in the middle of the 12th century, occasionally covered by water. However the situation of the mill and of the haven, precludes any idea of the sea having extended over the Lawn at low water within historical times.

William de Mohun II, this "cruel and violent man," like all his contemporaries, was forever in fear of eternal damnation and sought to expunge his evil deeds by buying his way into heaven. This dichotomy of medieval man is illustrated by his founding of the Augustine priory of Bruton in Somerset,[27] and to the regular canons of that order he granted the church at Bruton together with tithes, dues and rights, and common pasture in his manor of Brewham.[28] The charters by which he is said to have made these grants are undated but if Lyte's proposition of the year 1142 is correct,[29] it would apply to William de Mohun II who is known to have been alive in 1131 and to have died before 1155. Lyte also says that it was by this lord of Dunster's advice that Robert son of Geoffrey, one of his feudal tenants, bestowed upon the Augustinian canons of Bruton the church of Luxborough, near Dunster, and that William de Mohun II increased the endowment.[30] All this information would appear to be fully substantiated by the Bruton Cartularies. "Between the years 1138 and 1160, the monks of Bath obtained from Theobald, Archbishop of Canterbury, a solemn confirmation of the lands and tithes granted to them at Dunster, Carhampton, Stockland, Kilton, Avelham, Staunton, Minehead and Exford with the church of Dunster. They must have must have acquired the tithes of Staunton from the person who held that manor of the lord of Dunster by military service, as it is not mentioned in any of the early charters issued by the Mohuns. For some reason unknown, the archbishop ignores the tithes of Broadwood,

Newton and Broomfield, specified in successive charters. If correctly transcribed, his charter is remarkable as recognising the canonization of his eminent predecessor, Anslem of Aosta."[31] The Augustinian canons of Taunton were not forgotten and to them William de Mohun II, or his son, granted land at Lydeard.[32]

The manor of Whichford in south Warwickshire came to the Mohuns through the marriage of William de Mohun II to Agnes[33] a lady of the highest lineage. The village of Whichford lies between Long Compton and Brailes and, at the time of the Domesday Survey of 1086, it belonged to Gilbert de Gaunt whose son Walter founded a priory of Augustinian canons at Bridlington in Yorkshire. During the reign of King Henry I, William de Mohun II and Agnes gave the church at Whichford to these canons of Bridlington.[34] For a short time this grant ceased to be the gift of this family but Reynold de Mohun I, Williams de Mohun II's great grandson, obtained it again from King John.[35] According to Lyte whilst the grant was originally limited to the lives of William and Agnes it later reverted to that family and was enjoyed by them and their descendants, the Stranges and the Stanleys, until the reign of Elizabeth.[36] The name of Agnes' father is not stated but Lyte suggests that she was the daughter of Walter of Gaunt, son of Gilbert of Gaunt, grandson of Baldwin, count of Flanders, the first cousin of William "Rufus" and Henry I. It may be that the chronicler who referred to William de Mohun II as "a man not only of the highest rank but also of illustrious lineage"[37] might have been alluding to the very high social position that marriage to Agnes accorded him. If Agnes' grandfather was Gilbert of Gaunt who held Whichford this would account for this benefaction to a religious house situated in Warwickshire so far from Dunster.

William de Mohun III

William de Mohun III was the second son and the heir of William de Mohun II. The eldest son Ralph was remembered by his father who gave some land at Avelham, south of Dunster, to the monks of Bath for masses to be said "for the benefit of the soul of his son."[38] William also gave three furlongs of land at Northcombe, in the parish of Cutcombe to the mother church of Dunster. William de Mohun III's connection with Bruton dated from c.1142 when he attested his father's charter to the canons of that place, for the foundation of an Augustinian priory.[39] His link with Bruton was strong and he endowed the canons with sixty acres of land near the pond at Brewham, together with further property there and at Redlinch. It was at Brewham that his grandfather William de Mohun I had kept twenty-two brood mares. In Selwood forest William de Mohun III gave the canons pannage for a hundred hogs[40] and he further endowed them with the church at Cutcombe where his grandfather had also kept thirty six brood mares. He also confirmed the gifts of his grandfather and father to the Benedictine monks of Bath. Abroad in Normandy, he also endowed the canons of Bruton with the church of Lyons, or Lion-sur-Mer, near Caen, and with the tithe of the fisheries there.[41]

All these gifts both in England and France were for the benefit of the souls of his father, who had died in 1155, his mother Agnes and his brothers. Apart from his elder brother Ralph, William de Mohun III had four more brothers younger than himself. Henry, who seems to have inherited his mother Agnes' estate at Whichford, for which, in 1162, he paid scutage for a knight's fee in Warwickshire[42] and a person of that name had connections in Hampshire in 1167 and had brothers, Ivan, Richard and Peter.[43] Nothing appears to be known about Ivan, but Richard and Peter were both in Holy Orders and Richard, though generally resident in England, held the benefice on the paternal estate in Normandy. William de Mohun III's charter to the Benedictine monks of Bath confirmed the gifts of his grandfather and father, but there appear to have been some variations. For example: "among the tithes of Dunster it specifies those of the mills and copses, and it mentions the church of Kilton as well as the tithes of that parish. On the other hand it contains no reference whatever to the monks of Bath, all the endowments being described as belonging to the church of Dunster."[44] Lyte also adds a note: "It is worthy of remark that a bull of Pope Honorius the Third dated at the Lateran 13 Kal.Dec.a.p.7.(AD1224) confirms to the monks of Dunster only two churches, those of Dunster and Carhampton."[45]

William de Mohun III married Godehold, or Godeheut, and around 1160 she and their son, yet another William, were witnesses to the charter to Bruton in which William granted the tithe of his fisheries at Lyon, or Lion-sur-Mer, to the canons. The words "tithe of his cuttlefish *(sepiarium)* and waters *(ewiarum)* at Lyons" appears in the *Complete Peerage*. Godehold's marriage portion was the manor of Brinkley in Cambridgeshire.[46] Her husband did not style himself earl of Somerset, the title bestowed on his father by the Empress Maud. Presumably, King Stephen declined to recognise this title. Stephen died on 25 October 1154 and William de Mohun II died in 1155 and therefore William de Mohun III never inherited the earldom.

The Honour of Dunster was a large one of 46½ fees held by different military tenants. Of these 5½ were feoffments created during the reigns of King Stephen and King Henry II. These William de Mohun III refused to recognise and when, on the occasion of Henry II's eldest daughter Matilda's marriage in 1168,[47] a levy was raised, William de Mohun III refused to pay this aid money on more than forty-one fees. He persisted in this refusal until he died in 1176.[48] He was accountable to King Henry II for only five of the eleven knights who owed him allegiance in Normandy.[49] On his death, William de Mohun III left the widow Godehold and at least seven children. She presumably, as her share for life of her late husband's estate, had Minehead and Kilton. Additionally she had her own property at Brinkley. Apart from the heir, William de Mohun IV, when Godehold died in 1186 there were ramifications for his brothers and sisters.

William de Mohun IV

Of the six manors which William de Mohun I had retained in Dorset in 1086, one was Ham Mohun, later corrupted to Hammoon. This manor was granted by William de Mohun IV to his next brother Geoffrey under the usual feudal terms of military service, it was held under the Honour of Dunster in return for Geoffrey's military aid should this be required. Geoffrey forfeited his lands for joining in the rebellion which John, count of Mortain, later King John, raised when his brother King Richard I was a prisoner of the Emperor, Henry VI in Germany. The king forgave his brother but, for his treachery, he was left landless and, as one of his adherents, Geoffrey lost to the king's ministers the profits of Ham which according to the Pipe Rolls amounted to £7. It was not until 1198, that Geoffrey's brother John, apparently by inheritance, regained possession of Ham. We are told that he had to promise to pay £30 to the Crown, "a sum six times as large as that which was ordinarily exacted by way of relief on succession to one knight's fee."[50]

William de Mohun IV had inherited Brinkley from his mother Godehold but this too had been taken by the king. John de Mohun, who had earlier been given the manor by his brother William, had, in 1201 to pay 20 marks before he could regain possession of the manor. In 1201 John de Mohun held the two fees of Ham and Brinkley. This is known from the accounts for scutage. Scutage was originally paid by those knights unable to render military service. It later degenerated into yet another method of extortion demanded even from those from whom military service was still expected. It was also known as "shield money." Around 1208 John's rights to these manors of Ham and Brinkley were challenged by Reynold de Mohun, the son and successor of William de Mohun IV. The outcome of the two law suits was that John de Mohun held both Ham and Brinkley under the lord of Dunster. However, for siding with the barons against King John he was deprived of his lands in Dorset, that is to say Ham. In 1217, the year after King Henry III came to the throne, they were restored to him.[51]

John de Mohun was the ancestor of the Mohuns of Ham and he died in 1221.[52] His dying wish was to be buried at Salisbury in the cathedral church of the diocese in which he normally resided. This wish was not, at first, carried out. The corpse rested for the night in the church at Bruton and the prior and convent decided to inter it there with his ancestors and cousins. This caused the bishop and chapter of Salisbury to be extremely angry and the prior of Bruton had publicly to apologise and hand over the remains of Sir John de Mohun of Ham.[53] Agnes, a sister of William de Mohun IV had, as her portion on her marriage to William of Windsor, an estate at and near Bicknoller. Her descendants for several generations held this estate of the Honour of Dunster in exchange for military service.[54] Agnes' sister Yolenta married Ralph, son of William, son of Durand de Mohun, and he gave his name to Brompton Ralph, known in the time of William de Mohun I as Sheriff's Brompton.[55]

When William de Mohun III died in 1176, his heir, William de Mohun IV was a minor and he became a ward of King Henry II, who appointed Richard of Ilchester, bishop of Winchester as William's guardian to look after his person and administer his estates. By royal order £18 was provided for the maintenance of the young heir during his minority which lasted for 18 months.[56] In 1176, Richard became the Norman justiciar. Before he became bishop of Winchester he was the archdeacon of Poitiers. He, and John of Oxford, later to become the bishop of Norwich, were appointed royal judges. They were joined by John Cumin who ended a very demanding life in the king's service, by becoming the archbishop of Dublin. These three of the royal court party were the king's ambassadors and fulfilled missions to Rome and France and to the Imperial Court of the Emperor, Frederick I Barbarossa.[57] When the vacancy arose at Winchester, the king sent the following writ to the monks of that place: "Henry, king of the English & c. to his faithful monks of the church of Winchester, greeting. I order you to hold a free election, but, nevertheless, I forbid you to elect anyone except Richard my clerk, the archdeacon of Poitiers."[58] Richard had, with Geoffrey Ridel been openly hostile to Thomas à Becket during his long struggle with the king and with John of Oxford. John Cumin had taken part in the complicated manoeuvres which had resulted in Becket's exile. In 1177, the bishop of Winchester, as William de Mohun IV's guardian, paid 54s "to the monks of St George, Dunster" for tithes from his ward's estate for the previous eighteen months.[59]

This is therefore a very significant date in the history of the church for it is the first specific reference to a religious house at Dunster and the Benedictines were settled at Dunster on the northern side of the parochial church.[60] This was the year William de Mohun IV came into his inheritance. The Crown lost the rents and tolls and the revenues from the mills at Dunster and Carhampton; the normal rents of these manors was £44 3s 4d but part of Dunster was described as "waste." Perhaps, in order not to declare all the assets to the Crown, it was said that the tolls did not yield the amount expected, that the mills showed a decline in revenue. The mill had to be repaired and there were charges for the cultivation of the vineyard and the wages of the servants,[61] all minuses as far as the Crown was concerned. However, quite apart from the proceeds of the rentals, the king received £19 from the sale of corn and wine.[62] A charter which "if authentic, must be ascribed to the fourth of that name defines the boundaries of the hide of land at Alcombe belonging to the monks of Dunster."[63] It also refers to some of these endowments, for instance, that they were to benefit from the tithe of the demesne of Shurton and land at Kersham near Luxborough. Apparently this charter, which may have been forged, refers to Kynewordisham which, according to a document of 1291, was Kersham.[64]

Another brother of William de Mohun IV, Thomas, benefited from the family holdings in France and subject to the life interest of Thomas, William made over his ecclesiastical patronage of Moyon, Tessy-sur-Vire and Beaucoudrai and Deodville in Normandy and Brinkley, Minehead and Todbere (Devon) for the canons of Bruton who also received confirmation of all the gifts of his grandfather and father and various tenants in Normandy and he further added such advantages as the endowment of the church at Minehead and the tithes of his mills at Cutcombe.[65]

By a charter published at Montchaton in 1186 William granted the Premonstratensian, or Norbertine canons, of the abbey of the Holy Trinity at La Luzerne the tithe of his mills at Moyon, Tessy-sur-Vire and Beaucoudrai on condition that they observed his anniversary and that one of their number successively be found to offer prayers for the soul of his mother Godeheut (Godehold).[66] These canons took their name from the mother house at Premontré in the forest of Coucy,[67] or from St Norbert, the son of a baron in the duchy of Cleves who, in his teens, had been a canon of Xanten cathedral in Lorraine. William de Mohun IV permitted the Austin canons of Bruton Priory to choose their prior from among their number provided that the man chosen was presented to him or his heirs whether in Normandy or in England.[68] This practice continued until the last de Mohun of Dunster, Sir John de Mohun V, died on 15 September 1375 leaving only three daughters and no male heir, and the senior male line of the family became extinct. Then the canons of Bruton continued to present their newly-elected prior by custom to the Luttrells of Dunster. In the middle of the 14th century an ancient custom prevailed whereby whenever the lord or lady of Dunster went to stay at Bruton priory, the canons provided two wax candles to burn throughout the night in their bed-chamber.[69]

William de Mohun IV married a lady named Lucy about whom no more is known. He arranged that his anniversary should be observed every year at Bruton priory and reference was made in these arrangements to his intention of going on pilgrimage to Jerusalem. He died abroad in 1193, possibly on the Third Crusade, and at Michaelmas in 1194 the escheats in London and Middlesex refer to the "portsoken of William de Moun."[70] This soke or soken was a district held by socage (i.e. shield money, a type of land tenure) which fell to the Crown since the heir was a minor. The "soke of Mohun" was given by his grandson, Reynold de Mohun II, to his daughter Alice on her marriage to Robert de Beauchamp of Hache/Hatch.[71] William de Mohun IV's heir, Reynold de Mohun I, was about ten years of age when his father died. He had an elder brother William who was a witness when he was still a minor to three of his father's charters, he died in 1194. By 1197 Dunster was described as a borough which yielded £20 a year to its lord.[72] Between 1042 and 1660 the boroughs in Somerset were: Axbridge, Bath, Bridgwater, Chard, Dunster, Ilchester, Langport, Estover, Milborne Port, Nether Weare, Taunton, Wells, and Yeovil.[73]

Reynold de Mohun I

Since the heir was a minor the Honour of Dunster was administered by the king, Richard I, whose agents were William de Ste Mère Eglise, William of Wrotham, Nicholas Puinz, Reginald of Clifton, Hugh de Gurnai and the famous Hubert de Burgh who was his guardian. The outgoings were said to be very small and the accounts made no reference to the expenses of the heir. Lyte tells us that at the "a doorkeeper and watchman were maintained by royal order" and that "a clerk named Richard who had a pension of the gift of William de Mohun, may have been the last surviving son of the earl of Somerset,"[74] William de Mohun II, who had died before 1155. This Richard would therefore have been one of Reynold de Mohun I's grandfather's brothers. Lyte further tells us that there was some trouble at Dunster, perhaps of a political nature, between the death of Richard I and the coronation of his brother.[75] Richard I died on 6 April 1199, and King John was crowned on 27 May 1199 in Westminster Abbey. When Reynold de Mohun, who was still legally under age, was in 1203 given the choice of surrendering his lands in France to King John or undertaking the journey to France with the doubtful chance of obtaining acceptable terms from the king who was at Le Mans, King John gave instructions to the seneschal of Normandy to make over to Hubert de Burgh all the land of Reynold de

Mohun in the duchy of Normandy "except some that had been committed to another person."[76] This may have been Reynold's mother, Lucy, who had obtained from the crown a lease of her late husband's estate at Moyon for an annual rent of £50 and a fine of £20.

By May 1203, a warning was sent from Falaise: "Hubert de Burgh, the Chamberlain, was commanded by letters patent to warn and induce Reynold de Moyhun to accept from the King an exchange in England for his land at Lyons near Caen, and for this cause to send him to the King or else his letters patent."[77] Lyte's explanation is: "In other words, a young man, legally under age, was to be compelled by his guardian to execute a deed surrendering part of his patrimony, unless he preferred to undertake a journey across the sea on the chance of obtaining tolerable terms from the King. The rolls of the period do not contain any further reference to the subject."[78] Maylis Baylé suggests that in the 13th century Reynold de Mohun was given Brewton/Bruton, previously a dependency of Troarn Abbey in exchange for Lyon, (i.e. Lion-sur-Mer) near Caen,[79] but according to Lyte, Bruton was established by William de Mohun II in the twelfth century and Sir William de Mohun III gave the church at Lyons to Bruton. Reynold de Mohun had had to choose between allegiance to King John or to the French King Philip. He chose King John and thus after Philip conquered Normandy, Maine, Anjou and Touraine in 1204, Reynold's French estates were administered by Richard de Humez.[80] Hubert de Burgh was the warder at Falaise of Arthur of Brittany who, as the son of the late Geoffrey, elder brother of King John, was a serious rival for the throne. It was Hubert who saved Arthur from being blinded and castrated, the terrible fate advised to King John as a way of eliminating his rival. The murder of Arthur of Brittany took place on 3 April 1203, and it is due to William de Briouze, lord of Bramber in Sussex, Radnor, Brecon and Abergavenny in Wales and Barnstaple and Totnes in Devon, that we know what happened, for it was he who supplied the information that King John slew Arthur when he was in a drunken rage in his castle at Rouen, and that he disposed of the body by tying a heavy stone to it and casting it into the Seine where it was recovered by a fisherman and finally buried at the priory of Bec in Normandy. This information appears in the annals of Margam abbey, the Cistercian abbey in Glamorgan of which the Briouzes were patrons.

In 1204 Reynold de Mohun came of age and into possession of Dunster Castle and must have been the occasion for rejoicing in Dunster. But it was also the year in which his French estates were lost to the French Crown. Some of these French possessions were eventually recovered by a younger branch of the de Mohun family. At home, Reynold confirmed all the gifts of his ancestors to the canons of Bruton. From his great grandmother Agnes, the wife of William de Mohun II, he inherited in September 1204, the manor of Whichford and, as the heir of his grandmother Godehold, he had the rights of the manor of Brinkley.

In 1206 Reynold set off to France in the service of King John[81] who was bound for Poitou. King John, had abandoned his first expedition to secure his mother, Eleanor of Aquitaine's lands, but now in the early summer of 1206 he set forth with a great number of barons and several hundred ships, for the port of La Rochelle. John had eight large transport ships made for his use and had personally rallied support for his enterprise in Yorkshire, Cumberland, Lancashire and Cheshire. Vessels were commandeered in the ports of southern England and were ordered to report on the eve of Whitsun at Dartmouth. In the Channel Islands recruiting officers went into the shipping lanes to coerce the sailors to respond to the king's need for their services. Reynold de Mohun I seems to have played quite an important part in these proceedings for the sheriff of Devon, his father-in-law, Sir William de Briwere/Brewer was given instructions to provide him with a ship at King John's expense.

In 1210 Reynold was one of the knights who accompanied King John to Ireland. The great army was composed of knights who were bound by the feudal obligation to render military assistance when required but there were also several companies of Flemish mercenaries. Although this expedition was said by the king to have been planned to catch Matilda de Briouze/Braose/Briouse and to punish the Irish barons for protecting her family, it was actually King John's intention to bring Ireland to heel and firmly under his control. The chronicler, Roger of Wendover, recounts the story that Matilda had provoked the king who had demanded hostages from her husband William. She had tartly made this reply to the messenger: "I will not deliver up my sons to your lord, King John, because he basely murdered his nephew Arthur, whom he ought to have kept in honourable custody."[82] Arthur was the son of Geoffrey and Constance of Brittany, and had Geoffrey not died in 1186, as the next eldest brother of Richard I, he would have succeeded to the English throne. William de Briouze fled to France and died at Corbeil in September 1211 and Matilda de Briouze and her eldest son disappeared and were probably imprisoned at Windsor and were never seen again.

Reynold de Mohun I made a notable marriage to Alice, the fourth daughter of Sir William Briwere/Brewer[83] and, in 1233 she was the co-heiress of her brother William Briwere, the younger.[84] Her father had lands in many shires, particularly in the west country and he founded the Premonstratensian abbey of Torre, near Torquay, the Cistercian abbey of Dunkeswell, an Augustinian priory at Mottisfont and a hospital at Bridgwater.[85] In spite of all these religious foundations as sheriff of Devon and Somerset, he was so hated that the men of the west country paid 1,200 marks in 1210 to get rid of him. King John readily accepted this money mistakenly regarding it as a mark of William's worth to them for he regarded his henchman highly and enjoyed such confidence in him that he would have happily entrusted him with twice as many shires. King John and William Briwere were also mutually loyal friends and enjoyed hunting together and, at least on two occasions, John displayed enormous support for his friend. When William de Briwere, the younger, fell into French hands, John, with typical generosity, helped to pay the ransom. He also sought to bring Geoffrey de Mandeville, earl of Essex to justice when during a squabble over lodgings while the royal court was at Marlborough he had slain a servant of William Briwere. This brought forth a strong remonstrance from Geoffrey de Mandeville's father-in-law Robert FitzWalter, lord of Dunmow, John's arch-enemy, who exclaimed: "You will not hang my son-in-law! By God's body you will not. You will see two hundred laced-helms in your land before you hang him!"[86] FitzWalter was more than "good as his word" since when the king put up the case for trial he appeared at King John's court, not with two hundred armed knights but with five hundred.[87] The accused Geoffrey de Mandeville was the son of Geoffrey Fitz Piers who by virtue of his marriage to Beatrice de Say, became earl of Essex. Beatrice de Say was a descendant of Beatrice de Mandeville who had married William de Say in the 12th century. In 1212 Maud FitzWalter died childless and Geoffrey de Mandeville married King John's divorced wife Isabel, Countess of Gloucester.

In February 1214, King John set forth for France on an ill-fated expedition aimed at recovering his lost territories. He left the realm in the charge of Peter des Roches, the Poitevin bishop of Winchester. This prelate, on the death in 1213 of Geoffrey Fitz Piers, earl of Essex, had become the justiciar. The chief justiciar was an officer first appointed by William, the Conqueror. He was the king's right hand man, the head of his council and, since our kings were often abroad fighting in France or elsewhere, he acted as the king's viceroy. In 1232 this office came to an end with the dismissal of Hubert de Burgh. None other than William de Briwere was appointed to assist Peter des Roches. Alice de Briwere's nephew, William de Braose, the son of her sister Graeca and her husband Reginald de Braose, lord of Abergavenny and Builth, was publicly hanged for intriguing with Joan, the wife of Llywelyn whose prisoner he had been. He had been released from captivity on the understanding that he gave Builthas as a marriage portion to his daughter, Isabella, on her marriage to Llywelyn's son David. A year passed before Llywelyn discovered William de

Braose's treachery. He took his revenge and William died at the hangman's rope. Reginald de Braose married twice and his second wife was Gwladus Ddu, the daughter of Joan and Llywelyn, the mother of his young step-mother.[88] William de Briwere was in 1216 one of the executors of King John's will. The others were the papal legate, the bishops of Winchester, Chester and Worcester, (where King John was buried), William Marshal, earl of Pembroke, Ranulph, earl of Chester, William Ferrers, earl of Derby, John of Monmouth, Savari de Mauléon and Fawkes de Breauté.[89]

Alice de Briwere's husband, Sir Reynold de Mohun I of Dunster, was only thirty years of age when he died in 1213 and their son and heir, also Reynold was a minor. Alice and her son went to live at Whichford and when her second husband, William Paynell of Bampton in Devon, a Crusader, died in 1228, she returned to Whichford where the church was possibly enlarged for her.[90] Whichford had been Alice's marriage portion and dower. There were other manors belonging to the inheritance which were held by her, or by Lucy de Mohun, her mother-in-law, widow of William de Mohun IV. Lucy had for dower seven of William's fees in Cambridgeshire and these were held by her in 1201.[91]

Apart from Reynold de Mohun II, the heir, Alice and Reynold de Mohun I had three sons. William, who was a benefactor of Cleeve abbey and the instigator of the foundation of Newenham abbey. He married Juliana de Vernon and died at Norton in Cornwall in 1265. He was buried near his elder brother Reynold at Newenham. During his lifetime he had been granted an annuity of £10 13s out of the manor of South Tawton (Devon) by Roger de Tony, who was presumably his wife, Juliana's grandfather. The third son of Alice and Reynold was rector of Brinkley in 1261.[92] Five years later he was presented by the abbot of Newenham to the living of Luppitt in the Hundred of Axminster but he only remained there for a year and vacated the living in 1267. The fourth son, Richard is only known to us because he is mentioned in Oliver's *Monasticon Dioeceses Exon*[93] and nothing further seems to be known about him. Alice de Briwere succeeded to a great estate in the west of England on the death of her brother, William de Briwere, the younger. Through her the Mohuns inherited the manors of Torre, Ugborough, Cadleigh, Bradworthy, and Axminster in Devon and Ile/Isle Brewer in Somerset and various knights' fees elsewhere.[94] The effigy in the church at Axminster is attributed to Alicia or Alice de Mohun but I think it is more likely to be that of Isabel, the second wife of Reynold de Mohun II.

Reynold de Mohun II

On the death of Reynold de Mohun I in 1213, Dunster castle fell into the hands of the Crown for the third time within thirty eight years. Reynold de Mohun II was but fourteen years of age and he became the ward of Henry Fitz Count (Henry of Almain), the natural son of Richard of Cornwall, King of the Romans, the brother of the future King Henry III.[95] Richard did not become King of the Romans, or Germany, until 1257 and he too was illegitimate being the natural son of King Henry II. Peter de Maulay now enters the Dunster arena. He was a Poitevin who, with Fawkes de Breauté had been the protectors of the royal family and royal treasure in Corfe castle after King John had died in 1216. The future king was a boy of only nine years and all was turmoil in the land for there was another claimant to the throne other than John's son, Henry. This was Prince Louis, the son of Philip II of France who claimed that through his wife Blanche, a granddaughter of Henry II, he had a claim to the English throne and that moreover he was the choice of the English barons. However, not all the barons supported Louis for many of them remained loyal to King John to whom they owed their all. In May, 1216, Prince Louis invaded England. He held London and controlled the Channel and the ports as far as Portsmouth. Hubert de Burgh, the chief justiciar of England, was one of those barons who remained loyal to King John's memory and he held Dover castle against the French between July and October 1216.[96] Peter de Maulay had become a fully integrated member of feudal society in the household of the late king and in 1220 King Henry III, who had good reason "to be grateful to him, had an area specifically referred to as the 'forest of Dunster' transferred to him to be safely kept by him during pleasure."[97] Peter de Maulay's descendants became a very important baronial family in Yorkshire until Richard II came to the throne.[98]

In 1222, Reynold de Mohun II's guardian, Henry Fitz Count died and his grandfather, William de Briwere, sheriff of Devon and Somerset became his guardian and also had the wardship of the demesne of Carhampton and the knights' fees but the castle and the borough of Dunster remained in the hands of the Crown.[99] By royal order of King Henry III, horsemen and archers protected the castle and two cross bowmen named Vilers were among their number and were on the pay-roll.[100] The little town of Dunster had grown up in the time of Reynold de Mohun I and by 1199 it was described as a borough which yielded £20 a year to the lord.[101]

In 1222 an attempt was made to establish a market at Watchet but it was a move promptly suppressed by the king's government. It was thought that it would be a threat to the market at Dunster.[102] The market at Dunster was in existence in the reign of William "Rufus," and is mentioned in William de Mohun's charter for the church made between 1080-1100. The earliest dated charter known is under the seal of Reynold de Mohun II, the year he came into legal possession of his lands and must be dated to c.1227, the year he was knighted and for this he had letters to his tenants to give him an aid on his being accorded this honour. The charter for the market is as follows:

"Know all men present and future that I, Reynold de Moyhun, have given, granted and by this my present charter confirmed to Hugh Rondevin and Robert Luci and Robert the Hunter *(venatori)* and Roger Pryer and Robert Chipera and Simon Coc, my burgesses of Dunster, and their heirs, the right of having and for ever possessing of me and my heirs a market and fair in the same in North Street *(in eodem vico del nord),* freely and quietly and wholly, and without removal and impediment of me and my heirs. On account of this gift and grant to be held of me and my heirs by them and their heirs for ever, the aforesaid burgesses have given to me a tun of wine of the price of forty shillings as an acknowledgement. In assurance of this, I have affixed my seal to this writing; these being witnesses: - Sir John de Regni, Roges, son of Simon, William Everadd, Richard of Holne, Roger Pollard, Robert of Cogstane, Geoffrey of Kytenor (Culbone), Geoffrey of Luccombe, and others."[103] (The North Street referred to is the present High Street, also called Market Street or Eststrete.)

Reynold de Mohun II rescinded the agreement of William de Mohun II whereby it had been an obligation of various tenants who had been granted manors on the usual terms of feudal service, that they should assist in the repair of the walls of the castle when required to do so. He allowed three military tenants to be released from this obligation and to compound for this service by paying a fine levied once and for all. The writer of the Mohun Chronicle recorded that the money deriving from this fine was applied to the building of the Lower Ward. *"Qui quidem Reginaldus fecit inferiorem castrum de Dunster, et pluribus tenentibus suis qui tenuerunt per feodum militare et solebant kernellitare in superiori castro, affirmare et facere cum necesse fuerat, remisit concessionem ad affirmandum castrum, ut dictum est, et hoc fecit pro inferiori castro faciendo."*[104]

To this Reynold may be ascribed the gateway in the Lower Ward which is surmounted by a low dropped arch; a pointed arch with a span greater than its radii. The vertical jambs are plain and chamfered, Lyte remarked: "it shows no traces of any former portcullis, and it can never have had a drawbridge."[105] Flanking this gateway are two semi circular towers which, with their three loops for the arrows of the cross-bowmen would have afforded some defence of the recessed gateway. On the ground floor of these towers there are vaulted chambers but the upper ranges no longer exist Lyte describes the remainder of the military buildings of the Lower Ward: "About sixty-six feet to the west of the tower on the right, and connected with it by the old curtain wall, there are the remains of a small semicircular tower, the bottom of which was approximately level with the first floor of the gateway, by reason of the slope of the ground. How much further the curtain wall formerly extended westward it is now impossible to say...There was certainly one other tower beyond, long known as 'Dame Hawis's Tower', and clearly identical with the 'Fleming Tower'. It probably stood on the western end of the Lower Ward, overlooking the vale of Avill, not far from the point at which the wall began to turn southwards and upwards in order to join the older wall of the Upper Ward."[106] These towers would have been roofed with thatch or wooden shingles. Precisely at this time, in 1248, Henry III ordained that rooms at Kennington and Woodstock should be roofed with shingles.

The domestic buildings erected by Reynold II were at the opposite end of the Lower Ward, to the left of the gateway but they also were fortified so that on their southern front he caused two towers to be erected. These towers projected from a lofty wall of variable thicknesses from 4ft. 8in. to 6ft. Lyte describes: "Two small pointed windows of his time, belonging to a closet, still remain. While the western end of this pile was partially excavated out of the native rock, there was at the eastern end a basement on a lower level, the ground sloping steeply in that direction."[107] Countless alterations to the fabric of the castle have taken place over the years, but Reynold de Mohun II's walls are distinguished by reason of their extreme thickness. It is not known when the castle chapel of St Stephen on the summit of the Tor was first built but in 1254 we have definite evidence of its existence.

In May 1230, Sir Reynold accompanied King Henry III overseas in what was to be an unsuccessful attempt to recover what his father, King John, had lost of the great Angevin Empire which had come to the English Crown through the marriage of Henry II to Eleanor of Aquitaine. In 1231 he was off again, this time to Wales with the king.[108] From the beginning of the reign in 1216, Hubert de Burgh, earl of Kent and the king's justiciar had held three castles, Grosmont, Skenfrith and White Castle, between the rivers Usk and Wye in Upper Gwent. These strongholds were known as "the castles of the justiciar."[109] Hubert had been associated with the Crown in the previous reign and had held the office of chamberlain to King John. He became the castellan of Chinon, sheriff of Norfolk and justiciar to John and his son.[110] Although he served the Crown well and believed that strong centralised administration was the key to success, he was always ambitious and in 1223 he added the castle and honour of Montgomery to his holdings. Montgomery castle was strategically important since it gave protection to Shropshire and posed a threat to the cantrefs of Powys.[111] The cantrefs were districts of approximately one hundred townships. Hubert's inordinate acquisitions were furthered in 1229 when he gained great power in Cardigan and Carmarthen where he held castles of importance by the service of five knights. The honours of Cardigan and Carmarthen also held sway over the Braose lordship of Gower.[112] Hubert de Burgh had also climbed the social ladder through his marriages. He was of the local gentry in Lincolnshire and had married successively a daughter of the Earl Warenne, Isabella, countess of Gloucester, the divorced first wife of King John and the widow of Geoffrey Fitz Peter, and thirdly Margaret, a daughter of William the Lion of Scotland, who had originally been destined at the age of fourteen to marry the future Henry III who was then but two years of age.[113] In 1223 Hubert de Burgh launched an unsuccessful campaign against Llywelyn and in 1231 Llywelyn himself took the offensive and his success demanded the assistance of the English feudal army and one of their number was Sir Reginald de Mohun II. Llywelyn laid claim to Paincastle in Elfael and was supported in his claim by his friendly neighbour, the earl of Chester. It seems the English host was kept kicking its heels in the district of Elfael, north of the Wye, and by November a truce was signed with Llywelyn which was to last a year.[114] Hubert de Burgh fell from grace due to the manipulative intrigues of his third wife, Margaret of Scotland, of which, it was said, Hubert was unaware. The couple had planned to marry their daughter, Meggotta, a child, to the young Richard de Clare who was Hubert's ward. Richard's father, the earl of Gloucester had died in Brittany in 1230 and Hubert had then amassed more power and had gained control of the late earl's Marcher lordships in the valley of Glamorgan and had become the heir's guardian. So far, he was party to the intrigue involving this marriage but he was apparently unaware that Margaret had, in fact, effected a secret marriage while both were children in sanctuary at Bury St Edmunds. These facts emerged when Richard became the king's ward and the desirability of finding a wife for him was discussed in 1236. Margaret's *fait accompli* must then have been discovered and Hubert finally fell from favour in 1236/9. Had he not done so, his earldom of Kent and the possession of other lands held by him and his wife in England and Wales, would have united the earldoms of Hereford and Gloucester.[115]

It is difficult to see how Sir Reynold de Mohun II fulfilled his office of justice of the Common Pleas for he seems rarely to have been in England, let alone Dunster. He acquired this position in 1234, the year when he is known to have been in debt to the Jews.[116] A year earlier, in 1233, we know he had a house in Streatley in Berkshire which had come to him through his first wife Hawis.[117] In 1242 his destination was Gascony and he was to have two good ships provided for him to follow the king across the sea to Gascony. The investiture of Alphonse, brother of Louis IX as count of Poitou at Poitiers in July, 1241, sent shock waves through all who feared the growing power of France. Hugh de La Marche, Hugh de Lusignan was outraged by the summons to do homage to Alphonse and he formed a party in Poitou allied to the seneschal, cities and towns of Gascony. A combined attack was planned on La Rochelle coming from land and sea. In January 1242 the English barons received the news of this plan with disapproval; had not the truce with France only just been renewed! They wanted nothing to do with the idea. Henry, however, was determined to support this enterprise against the French Crown and to support his mother. Money was his chief concern and this he raised in several ways. He levied loans, he levied fines, he collected scutages, or shield money, from those knights who for one reason or another could not, or did not wish, to attend him. He exploited the Jews and he ordered a complete investigation into the knights' service in England and, as was his right, he summoned military aid in accordance with feudal custom. Some were prepared to accompany him to Poitou, among them Reynold de Mohun II. The king sailed for Saintonge with his queen, Eleanor of Provence and his brother, Richard of Cornwall. On 8 June 1242, on the grounds of breaches made by the French, he denounced the truce made with Louis IX of France.[118] It is evident from the foregoing that, far from sitting in his castle at Dunster, and directing local affairs, Reynold de Mohun II, like all his contemporaries, really moved about more than is usually recognised. Properties were far flung to disperse power in any one place and military assistance was rendered to the king in exchange for lands. Many, many hours must have been spent on horseback and the endowments made to the priories and abbeys founded by the baronial class must have provided them with a network of "hotels" at their disposal.

In 1240 there was a disagreement between the monks of Bath and Sir Reginald de Mohun II. The monks claimed a tithe of the hay at Caremore, a large field in the lord's demesne in the parish of Carhampton. They also laid claim to a tithe of the pasture of Waterletes in the parishes of Dunster and Carhampton, tithe of a windmill at Kilton and tithe of his pigs at Dunster, Carhampton and Kilton. The question was referred by the pope to the dean of Salisbury; and to the precentor and succentor (precentor's deputy) of Salisbury. These persons heard both parties in the Lady chapel at Glastonbury and an elaborate agreement was arrived at which mentions for the first time Marshwood Park which was the most important park belonging to the lords of Dunster and was at Blue

Anchor about a mile and a half to the east of the castle.[119] An undated charter is a confirmation by Sir Reynold de Mohun II to the church of Dunster, "and to the monks there serving God" of the endowments granted to them by Sir Reynold de Mohun I, his father, and by his ancestors. This charter, "follows almost word for word the charter of the third William de Mohun, and makes no mention of Shurton or Kersham."[120] He gave fifty marks to the Benedictine monks of Dunster and two acres of land at Caremore, near the sea and, by another charter, he granted to the prior of Dunster and his monks and their successors in perpetuity every tenth pig "live or dead" belonging to him at Dunster, Carhampton and Kilton. These concessions were the result of a compromise arrived at after the meeting at Glastonbury in 1240. He also released them from obligations concerning the court of his Hundred at Minehead which had not been entirely absorbed into the Hundred of Carhampton.[121] In the 13th century that the Benedictine monks of Dunster rebuilt and enlarged the chancel of the entire church at the east end in the contemporary Early English style.

In 1245 Sir Reynold de Mohun II was away again serving King Henry III in Wales.[122] His brother William, who was the instigator of the foundation of Newenham abbey, seems to have favoured the Cistercians for he was a benefactor of the Cistercian abbey of Cleeve and Newenham was also a Cistercian house. He was prepared to exchange some of his lands with Sir Reynold if he could provide a suitable site. The three manors of Minehead, Ottery Fleming and Axminster were readily offered by Sir Reynold and Axminster was chosen by the abbot of Beaulieu and assigned to William in September 1245. The conditions were that the foundation of the abbey should be sanctioned by the king and by the Cistercian order within eighteen months. The king's approval was gained in July 1246 by the intercession of John Goddard one of the monks of Beaulieu, who was elected the first abbot. Richard of Cornwall, the brother of Henry III, seconded the proposal[123] and Sir Reynold provided 100 marks towards the new building. The abbot accompanied by twelve monks from Beaulieu and four lay brothers made the journey from Hampshire to Devonshire and according to Lyte: "The little band arrived at the site of the new colony on the feast of the Epiphany, chanting Salve Regina, in the presence of the founder, his; brother, and a great concourse of people."[124]

The formal charter for this abbey was issued by Sir Reynold de Mohun II and eventually confirmed by royal authority.[125] In 1248 the new monastery, called Newenham, enjoyed the pope's approval and received his protection and many privileges. Sir Reynold de Mohun II favoured three orders of monks: the Benedictines at Dunster, the Augustinian canons of Bruton and the Cistercian monks at Cleeve, but he is chiefly remembered for founding of Newenham abbey. His grandfather, William de Mohun IV had increased the endowments at Bruton with the gift of the church and mill at Minehead and Reynold de Mohun II helped to establish the vicarage there.[126] He renounced his rights as patron of Minehead, during any periods when the priory at Bruton had no prior. He also showed the Augustinians favour by bestowing land at Mariansleigh and the advowson of the church there upon the Augustinian house at Barlinch in Somerset on the Devon border. In the 15th century we still hear of Barlinch when, in 1474, Anne Watts, widow, the legitimate daughter of Mary and Richard Watts, gave some land at Wellow (Vellow) and money to the priory of Barlinch for the remembrance of the souls of her mother and her illegitimate brother, Richard Luttrell, constable of Dunster castle 1430-1449, the son of Sir John Luttrell, KB the last of the direct line of the Luttrells of East Quantoxhead who died *sans prole*. To the Cistercians of Cleeve abbey he gave some land at Slowley (Slaworthi), near Luxborough, to be held by service of an eighth part of a knight's fee.[127] Both Richard of Cornwall and William de Mohun, Reynold de Mohun II's brother, were benefactors of this abbey. In 1265 William de Mohun died at Norton in Cornwall and was buried near his brother before the high altar at Newenham abbey.[128] He had married Juliana Vernon, whose probable grandfather, Roger de Tony, granted an annuity of £10 13s to William.

Perhaps in return for his services when he accompanied Henry III to Poitou early in 1242, in April of that year he was appointed chief justice of the forests south of Trent where in 1252 he was appointed keeper of the royal forests south of Trent with one hundred marks per annum for maintenance and also keeper during the king's pleasure of Sauvey castle in the county of Leicester.[129] In 1259 at the Premonstratensian abbey of Torre, near Torquay, founded by William de Briwere, Reynold de Mohun II built a private chapel at his courthouse exclusively for family use, or for his guests or his servants. The monks of Torre abbey agreed to the chapel on the understanding that baptismal rites should not be administered in the chapel and further that they should be given half the offerings made there. An elaborate agreement was made between the abbot, the convent of Torre and Reynold de Mohun II.[130] There is no evidence of their courthouse today but the old form of the place name Tormoham, now corrupted to Torre, preserves the memory of the Mohuns. In 1253, Sir Reynold de Mohun II, obtained for himself and his heirs a grant of free warren (the right to take the rabbits) at Dunster, at Whichford and at Ottery in Devon, with licence to hunt the hare, the fox, the cat and the badger in Somerset and one other county.[131]

Between 1254 and 1258 the following charter was granted by Reynold de Mohun II to the burgesses of Dunster:

To all the faithful of Christ to whom the present writing shall come, Reynold de Moyun, greeting. Know ye all that I have granted, released and quit-claimed for ever for me and my heirs and all others who after me shall in any way be lords, or guardians, or bailiffs of Dunesterre, that the burgesses of that town or their heirs shall in no wise hereafter be made reeves, or farmers of the sea-port or of the toll of the borough or of the mills of the same town, against their will. I have also granted to the same burgesses and their heirs that they shall be quit of yearly tallage, so that no tallage according to the custom of other boroughs of England shall be exacted from them save for reasonable and due cause. I will moreover and grant for me and my heirs and all who shall be lords, or bailiffs, or guardians of Dunesterre, that the said burgesses and their heirs shall have common on Crowedon [Croydon] without any claim or impediment, as good for their use as they were wont to have in the time of any of [my] predecessors. And that buyers or sellers in the market of Dunesterre shall be quit of toll, unless their buying or selling exceed twelve pence. Likewise all fishermen and cornmongers shall be quit of toll in the said market for ever. I will moreover, granting for me and my heirs, lords, guardians and bailiffs of Dunesterre, that hereafter we shall not be able to make prise *(captionem)* from the brew of anyone in the same town beyond twenty-four gallons, that is to say four gallons for a penny. If, however, we shall wish to have more ale from that brew, it shall be bought at the rate at which buyers of the country *(patrie)* buy of the same. And that nobody hereafter shall make in the town of Dunesterre that ale which is called Reeve's Ale *(Cervisia Prepositi)*. If, however, it shall have been made, the brewers *(pandoxatores)* of the same town shall not for that reason cease from brewing and making ale and selling as they ought if that ale had not been brewed. And that if [the burgesses] shall fall into mercy for any offence, they shall be quit for six pence, except for laying hands upon the lord, or the lady, or any of the household of the Castle. And that after the buyings of the lord at the sea-port or in the aforesaid market have been made, [the burgesses] shall forthwith be able to buy' whatever they may wish to buy without objection *(querela)* or hindrance, and that others of the country *(de patria)* shall not be able to do their buying before them. And if they shall find a rabbit hurtful to them, they shall kill it and bring the skin to the Castle, and so be quit thereof. And also that they shall openly use the same customs at the Hundred [court] and elsewhere as they were wont to use in the time of any of my predecessors. All these things I have granted to the said burgesses and their heirs for ever, for the soul of John de Moyun, my firstborn son, of, happy memory, and for twenty marks which the same burgesses have given to me. Wherefore I will and grant for me and my heirs the lords, guardians and bailiffs of Dunesterre, that this is my grant, release, and quit-claim shall remain valid and unshaken for ever. And lest I Reynold, or my heirs or any other lord, guardian, or bailiff of Dunesterre, shall be able to contravene this in any respect, for the greater assurance hereof, I have affixed my seal to the present writing. These being witnesses: Sir Simon de Ralegh, Sir Roges of Porlok, Sir John Bretasch, Sir William le Bret, Philip of Lucumb, Richard Aylerd, Richard of Cloudesham, Hugh of Avele, Richard of Lincoln, and many others.[132]

It will be noted that the charter confirms the limits of the fines to 6d. with the exception of a case of assault on an inhabitant of the castle.[133] Lyte suggest that the paragraph concerning the rabbits may imply that the rabbits on Conigar Hill had so multiplied as to become a nuisance to the townsmen. During the minority of Reynold de Mohun II's grandson, who was his successor, and after the battle of Evesham in 1265, one Alun Plugenet was in command of the castle and Conigar became ordinary pasture and part of the castle estate and in 1266 the rabbits were exterminated. In subsequent centuries the flat ground, near the sea, a little to the east of Minehead, became the rabbit-warren of the lords of Dunster.[134]

Sir Reynold de Mohun II married twice and with Hawis/Hawise/Avice he had at least four children, the eldest was John, a knight, known to have been alive on 29 June 1253, but who died in Gascony 1253/4. In 1250 Gascony, led by Gaston de Béarn, a cousin of Eleanor of Provence, Queen of England, had rebelled against Simon de Montfort who had been sent there as King Henry III's lieutenant. In 1251 the king sent commissioners to Gascony to enquire but after a meeting with adjudicators appointed by the four courts of Gascony, no decisions appear to have been made and hopes of peace receded. In January, 1252, King Henry summoned the leaders of those opposed to Simon to London and the representatives from Bordeaux and six other towns, together with other barons and churchmen, met at a trial in the refectory of Westminster Abbey which opened on 9 May, 1252 and went on for several weeks. Simon de Montfort was well supported but amid the storm of recrimination nothing was settled. The king declared a truce and announced that either he or his son Edward, would go to Gascony the next year. In the event, Simon de Montfort, determined to restore order himself, returned to the scene of unrest and continued the war. This was in contravention of the truce Henry had imposed and the Gascons were told that their obedience was to the king alone. Simon capitulated and surrendered Gascony to Prince Edward as future lord.[135]

John de Mohun I's death in this fracas was a great sadness to his father Sir Reynold de Mohun II, who had his body brought back to England where he was buried at Bruton priory in Somerset. His heart was buried before high altar at Newenham abbey of which Sir Reynold laid the corner stone in 1254.[136] John had married Joan, the fifth daughter of William de Ferrers, the youngest sister of Reynold de Mohun II's second wife, Isabel de Ferrers.[137]

A paper endorsed "For the Castell Masse" provided for masses to be said for this dearly beloved son. It was an elaborate agreement made in 1254 between Reynold de Mohun II and the Prior and Convent of Bath whereby: "Certain masses were to be said for the benefit of the soul of his eldest son John, then deceased, of his own soul [he was to die c.1257/8] and of the souls of his wives, his ancestors and his successors. The monks thereby undertook that mass should be celebrated daily to the "end of time" by one of their own number attached to the Priory of Dunster, or by a respectable secular chaplain, in the "upper chapel" of Dunster Castle dedicated to St Stephen, unless prevented by war, by ecclesiastical interdict, or by order of the castellan, in any of which events it was to be celebrated in the chapel of St Lawrence belonging to the Priory below (inferius). To ensure due performance of this, they gave Reynold de Mohun right of distraint upon their land at Alcombe. He on his side granted to them fifty marks for the purchase of rents and undertook that the necessary books, vestments, lights and ornaments should be provided by himself and his heirs, owners of the Castle. Although the Prior's deed is dated at Ottery, in Devonshire, the witnesses came from the neighbourhood of Dunster.[138]

It is strange that reference is made in this 1254 agreement to Sir Reynold de Mohun's "wives." Hawis, his first wife was dead by 1253 but Isabel lived until 1260. John de Mohun I left at least two, possibly three, children by his wife Joan de Ferrers. John, his heir, became the next lord of Dunster, John de Mohun II. The next child was Robert who perhaps had an older brother Reynold.[139] Joan de Ferrers was a co-heiress with her sister Isabel de Ferrers, the second wife of Sir Reynold de Mohun II. Joan was the fifth daughter and much younger than Isabel and after John de Mohun I's death she married again and she chose to marry Robert Aguylon in contravention of the King's grant of her marriage to Peter de Chauvent. Since her late husband John de Mohun I was a tenant-in-chief in right of his wife, on his death, the king could grant her marriage to a man of his choosing and the great inheritance of the de Ferrers, earls of Derby was, no doubt, in his mind. This appears not to have been to Joan's liking, and as a result, the man of her choice, Robert Aguylon had to pay a forfeit of 200 marks to the grantee of the marriage, the king.[140]

Apart from John de Mohun I, Sir Reynold de Mohun II and his first wife, Hawis, had three daughters, Alice, named after her grandmother, the richly endowed Alice de Briwere. Her grandmother was thereby in a very favourably assured state when, as a mere child, she was married to William de Clinton, the younger, who generously settled land on her to the value of £40 a year. Her second marriage is of greater interest locally for she married Robert de Beauchamp, the younger, of Hache (Hatch), hence Hatch Beauchamp. This Robert was the son of Robert the first sheriff of Dorset and Somerset in 1162/3 and again in 1175/6-1181/2. Robert the younger was subject to the feudal aid, or tax, levied on his 17 knights' fees, held of King John as count of Mortain, on the occasion of the prestigious marriage of Isabella king Henry III's sister, to the emperor Frederick II. By law, the king could levy aids on his vassals under various circumstances such as the raising of a ransom, should he be taken prisoner, the knighting of his eldest son, or on the marriage of his eldest daughter. In this case, it was the marriage of his sister in 1235. Julianna was the second daughter. She married William de Lisle. On them Sir Reynold de Mohun II bestowed an estate at Walton in Northants which was part of the great Briwere inheritance.[141] The youngest daughter of Sir Reynold de Mohun II by his first wife Hawis, was Lucy who married John de Grey of Codnor.[142]

Around 1243, Sir Reynold de Mohun II married his second wife Isabel de Ferrers. Isabel was the daughter of William de Ferrers, earl of Derby, and his first wife Sibyl, with whom Isabel was co-heir. Sibyl was the daughter and co-heir of William Marshal, earl of Pembroke. "With Isabel, Sir Reynold de Mohun II received in frank marriage ten hides of land at Mildenhall, Wiltshire, and afterwards a share of the great inheritance of her maternal uncles the Marshals, successive earls of Pembroke. She died in 1260."[143]

Before she married Sir Reynold de Mohun II, Isabel de Ferrers married Sir Gilbert Basset, lord of Wycombe in Buckinghamshire, who was disseised "by the king's will" of a manor in Wiltshire in favour of Peter de Mauley, formerly castellan of Corfe, who was given "the forest of Dunster" by Henry III. Sir Gilbert predeceased her and there were no children of the marriage. With her second husband, Sir Reynold de Mohun II, Isabel had two sons and a daughter. William, the eldest son, was born in 1254 and he was therefore only six years of age when his mother died and only three or four years of age when his father, Reynold de Mohun II, died on 20 January 1257/8. King Henry III sold his wardship and his marriage to William la Zouche for 200 marks.[144] We know that through his mother, Isabel de Ferrers, he inherited: "the manors of Mildenhall, in Wiltshire, and Greywell, in Hampshire, lands at Sturminster Marshal, in Dorset, and Magor near Monmouth, and a larger estate in Kildare and Kilkenny."[145]

William married Beatrice, daughter of Reginald Fitzpiers, and their children were Eleanor/Elinor, Margaret and Mary, who died under age, also a son Reynold, who also died underage in 1284. Eleanor was born at Stoke Fleming in August 1281 and she was married to John de Carew. Lyte adds: "Sir Nicholas Carew had acquired her marriage for his son, in February 1295, from her aunt Isabel de Fienles, who had in turn acquired it from the Queen Mother." The Queen Mother, Eleanor of Provence, Edward I's mother, was given the wardship of Reynold, the heir (d.1284) and after his death that of the co-heirs. Mary, who was born posthumously, married Sir John of Meriet before she was fourteen years of age.[146] Beatrice de Mohun was widowed on the death of Sir William de Mohun in 1282 and in 1288 she paid £100 for royal licence to marry again. It appears that Sir Reynold de Mohun II of Dunster did not give all his Devon lands to Sir William for he alienated (transferred ownership of) his land at Holditch to Henry de Broc.[147] Lyte says that William's half nephew, John de Mohun II, Sir Reynold de Mohun II's grandson and heir, was the grantee. "He also obtained from his half-nephew, John de Mohun of Dunster, the manors of Galmton, Stoke Fleming and Ottery called afterwards Ottery Mohun, and other property in Devonshire, all, however, subject to the over lordship of the head of the family."[148] In his "Collections towards a Description of the County of Devon (1635) Sir William Pole refers to Sir Reynold de Mohun as the grantor of the Devonshire lands (barring Holditch) to his son William.

Sir William de Mohun was involved in the Welsh wars and was personally summoned in 1277 to engage in military operations which had begun in November 1276. In November 1277, the treaty of Conway was signed whereby the power of Llywelyn, Prince of Wales, was curtailed to the point of humiliation and in 1280 William went on pilgrimage to Santiago de Compostella. He died at his home at Ottery Mohun on 17 August 1282 and was buried in the choir of Newenham abbey, near his father, Sir Reynold de Mohun of Dunster.[149]

Apart from William, Sir Reynold de Mohun II, had, by his second wife, another son James and a daughter, named after her mother, Isabel. James was pursuing his ecclesiastical studies at Oxford in 1267 where he eventually gained his Master's degree. He was the recipient of a royal grant of two oaks from Shotover for his fuel.[150] Much greater facts have doubtless been lost to history but here the minutiae of everyday life has curiously survived. He was instituted to the rectory of Walkhampton in Devon in 1276 when only a subdeacon[151] and may have moved on to the parsonage of Brompton.[152] He was the owner of a small estate in Devonshire, at Horswell and South Milton and of a messuage near Newgate in London. He is known to have been alive in December 1322,[153] but he must have died very soon afterwards because his will was proved early the next year. He left the Newgate property to the prior and convent of St Bartholomew's, Smithfield, "in order that they should provide two chaplains to say mass daily for his soul, one in their own church and the other in the church of St Sepulchre."[154] Presumably their remuneration was provided by the rents gained from the messuage, or dwelling house in Newgate. The only fact which appears to be known about Isabel, his sister, is that she is said to have married Edmund Deyncourt.[155] This ends the account of the four children of Sir Reynold de Mohun

II of Dunster by his second wife Isabelle de Ferrers. Sir Reynold de Mohun II died in 1257/8 at Tor Mohun in Devon,[156] and his widow Isabel de Ferrers died before 26 November 1260.[157]

The account of the last days of Sir Reynold de Mohun II was possibly provided later by Walter de la Houe, the Cistercian abbot of Newenham Abbey. John Osberne, referred to by Lyte as "the untrustworthy chronicler of the Mohun family,"[158] was constable of Dunster castle in the 14th century. He wrote his account of 1350 in "a sort of Latin." It was a supplement to a more extensive work written in French by Walter de la Houe. This supplement "a professedly historical work,"[159] also written in the 14th century, was dedicated to Lady Joan de Mohun, the wife of John de Mohun V who died in1375. It is therefore an account written over a hundred years after the death of Reynold de Mohun II. The abbot goes back to William de Mohun I, whom he describes as "the noblest man in the whole army of William, the Conqueror."[160] Both the abbot and the constable appear to have been of an ingratiating nature. The constable's rendition fails to mention Lady Joan's husband, and he describes himself as: "the clerk and servant" of this "most excellent and most beneficent lady, the daughter of the most illustrious, active and noble knight, Sir Bartholomew of Burghersh, the elder."[161] It is possible that this very grandiose court lady, who seldom visited the gloomy fortress at Dunster, may have initiated this glowing account of her husband's ancestry and it may be that this apparently fawning constable was only too willing to accede to her request. It is however an illustration of the remarkable position of Lady de Mohun, during her husband's lifetime, that a royal grant of wardship was made to her while she was a *femme couvert*.

Sir Reynold de Mohun II of Dunster was buried at Newenham abbey in front of the high altar on the left hand side.[162] His date of death is given by Lyte as 20 January 1257/8 but according to the *Complete Peerage*[163] quoting the obits of Newenham abbey, the date was "3 Kal. Feb."[164] Walter de la Houe wrote:

...When the aforesaid Sir Reynold was seized with severe illness at Torre, he sent and summoned a Friar Minor named Henry, a learned man who was at that time ruling a school of theology at Oxford. The aforesaid Friar came to him at Torre on the Wednesday before the death of the aforesaid Reynold, and heard his confession, and, as it seemed to him, he confessed his sins truly, contritely, devoutly and fully. After this, at daybreak on the following Friday, the said Friar Henry came to Reynold where he lay, and Sir Reynold said to him: "I have seen a vision this night in a dream. I imagined myself to be in the Abbey Church of the White Monks and, when leaving it, I met a venerable person clad as a pilgrim, and he said: "Reynold, it is left to your choice either to come with me now in safety, and without peril, or to wait here until the week before Easter next, in danger." I replied: "My lord, I will not wait, but will follow thee forthwith, and indeed, I was fain to follow him." He said: "Thou shalt not follow me now as thou desirest, but thou shalt come to me in safety on the third day." And he added: "This was the dream I saw." The aforesaid friar, after many words of consolation, returned to his bed, lay down there, and slept a while, and it seemed to him in his dream that he was in the aforesaid church of the Cistercian order, and he beheld a venerable man, clad in a stately white robe, leading a boy fairer than the sun and in a garment brighter that the clearest crystal, from the font to the altar, like a child newly baptized. To him he said: "Good Lord, who is the child?" And the man answered: "This is the soul of the venerable Sir Reynold de Mohun." And when he woke, the aforesaid friar understood that his dream was a token in corroboration of the dream of Sir Reynold and had the like meaning. The third day having now arrived, Sir Reynold said to the aforesaid friar Henry: "Repeat to me Prime and Tierce, for my hour is very near at hand." Now it was his wont to hear the whole divine service daily, and the friar consented. The said Sir Reynold said: "For God's sake speak quickly for my hour is at hand." This done, the aforesaid friar went to the church to celebrate mass. The introit of the mass was *Circumdederunt me,* etc. as for one deceased, and all things were in like form. Mass being ended, the aforesaid friar returned in his sacred vestments carrying the Body of the Lord, in order to strengthen the said Sir Reynold by the receiving of the Body and Blood of the Lord. On his entering the chamber, the aforesaid Reynold wished to rise from his bed, but he could not, by reason of his exceeding weakness. About ten persons were standing around, and to them he said: "Alas! Why do ye not suffer me to meet my Saviour and Redeemer?" These were his last words. Henry then gave him the Communion and afterwards anointed him. Then the aforesaid friar, with the other priests and clerks there present, began the Commendation. After this, as Sir Reynold was still alive, they began to say the Commendation again, and when they recited the words: 'All ye saints, pray for him' he fell asleep in the Lord, without a groan or any apparent pain, with his body laid out and straightened, and his mouth and eyes closed, without help of anyone such as is wont to be given to men after they have breathed their last."[165]

About 75 years after the event a narrator adds the following information: "When the pavement of the presbytery was laid, his body was found in his sarcophagus, whole and in no wise injured, and his remains to this day incorrupt, exhaling the most fragrant odour. This very body I have seen and touched and for three days it lay open to public view in the year of Our Lord 1333."[166]

John de Mohun II

John de Mohun II, the son and heir of John de Mohun I, who had died in Gascony in 1253/4, was a minor at the time of his grandfather's death in 1257/8. King Henry III was at Windsor when he heard of the death of Sir Reynold de Mohun II and he forthwith granted the wardship and marriage to his queen, Eleanor of Provence.[167]

The year 1259 is when we first hear about a fulling-mill at Dunster. The rent of 13s.4d. went "to the lord of the manor."[168] This is a little unclear because, in fact, in that year there was no lord of Dunster; the heir not having yet come into his inheritance. Fulling was a process of scouring and pressing whereby woollen goods were cleansed of grease and thickened into a compact finished material. "The object of fulling is to work the fibres so that the surface may not show the naked transverse threads, but form a felted mass, fulling being only a kindred process to felting."[169] The cloth-making industry was one Henry III had deliberately fostered but by 1265, this peaceful industry was not the only activity in Dunster.

On 1 August 1265 an unruly band of Welshmen headed by William de Berkeley, landed at Minehead with the intention of ravaging the county. Their plans went sadly amiss for they were intercepted by the redoubtable warden of the castle at Dunster, Adam de Gurdon, who sallied forth and put them to the sword. They fled and it is recorded by the chronicler William Rishanger that "those who escaped the sword were drowned."[170]

Adam de Gurdon threw in his lot with Simon de Montfort and gathered round him in Dunster, adherents to the cause of the insurgent barons. Their leader who in 1265, had established his famous parliament, was slain at the battle of Evesham on 4 August of that year and Adam de Gurdon was supplanted as warden of the castle by Alan Plugenet. Soon after this the lands of the Mohuns were transferred from the wardship of Queen Eleanor to that of Richard, earl of Cornwall, King of the Romans, Henry III's brother, and benefactor of Cleeve Abbey.

Before John de Mohun II came into his inheritance in 1269, a valuation, known as an "extent" was made in 1266 and the Mohun cartulary contains a description of the castle at that time. The Upper Ward comprised a hall with a buttery, a pantry, a kitchen and a bakehouse to the south of it, a fair chapel, a knights' hall, three towers containing various rooms, and a prison. The hall is described as having two "posts," two "couples" and two "pignons" or pinnacles. The Lower Ward comprised three towers, of which that known as the Fleming Tower was a prison, and also a granary. The gateway must evidently have been reckoned as one tower and the irregular pile at the end of the Lower Ward must have been reckoned as another. The cow-house and stable, with accommodation for a hundred beasts, the dovecot, and the dairy lay below the Castle near the river.[171]

In this "extent" of 1266 we see that Henry III's fostering of the cloth trade was succeeding in Dunster. There was a dyer named Adam, Walter, a weaver or webber (from the German 'weben') who was referred to in the "extent" as a "textor" (from the Latin for weaver). Alice and Christina were weavers (textrix) also. So, although the grander folk preferred imported cloths, the "dunsters" made in this small town, were well under way, and became, like the "tautons" made at Taunton, quite famous.

In 1269, John de Mohun II did homage to King Henry III. He had reached his majority and came into his inheritance in the October of that year. In 1277 he was summoned for military service against Llywe1yn, who had assumed the name of Prince of Wales in 1258,[172] in the company of his brother Robert and one Thomas de Pyn, also known as Thomas de Payn. He attended the muster at Worcester and Carmarthen and served under Edmund, earl of Lancaster, known as "Crouchback," the second son of Henry III in west Wales.[173] Edmund, earl of Lancaster received the gift of the palace of Savoy from his mother, Eleanor of Provence. This palace had belonged to Peter of Savoy, the queen's uncle, who left it to the hospice of the Great St Bernard in Savoy in 1246. Eleanor bought it from the hospice and gave it to her son. It is, apart from the re-built chapel of the Savoy, no longer in existence having been destroyed, being then in the possession of the hated John of Gaunt, in the Peasants' Revolt in the reign of Richard II. The present Savoy hotel stands on the site. In the spring of 1277, Edmund took control of three military commands with the aim of restoring the defences, commanding military troops sent to them and the local militia, and to enlist and "make terms with local Welsh lords" and to organise Welsh foot soldiers. Their success was phenomenal and by the spring of 1277, Edmund took over all the lands which Llywelyn had conquered in the Marches from the Cheshire border to Cardigan Bay. John de Mohun II did not long survive his expedition to Wales and died in 1279 little more than thirty years of age.

It is therefore with some assurance that one may say that the charter granted to the burgesses of Dunster must date between 1269 and 1279 since he came into the possession of his lands in 1269 and died on 11 June, 1279. The terms of the charter are as follows:

"To all the faithful of Christ to whom the present writing shall come, John de Moyun, greeting in the Lord. Know ye all that I have granted, confirmed and quit-claimed forever, for me and my heirs, to all the burgesses of my town of Dunestorre and their heirs all the liberties of the same town which Sir Reynold de Moyun, my grandfather, at any time gave and granted by his charter to the said burgesses and their heirs, as that charter witnesses in all points, without any claim to be made thence hereafter. I have also granted to the said burgesses and their heirs [the right] to find yearly a suitable and faithful bailiff, to receive, present, and faithfully answer for all attachments- made within the borough. And if the same bailiff for the time being shall in anyway misbehave against the lord or the said burgesses or their heirs, he and the same bailiff shall make amend to his lord, according to the custom of the borough; and in his place the said burgesses shall put another bailiff suitable for the lord's work. For this grant, confirmation and quit-claim the said burgesses have given to me twenty shillings in hand. In witness wherof I have affixed my seal to the present writing. These being witnesses: Sir John de Brytasch, knight, Philip of Luccomb, Richard of Cloudesham, John of Holne, Geoffrey of Kytenare, Geoffrey le Tort, William Everard, William Pyrou, Robert de la Putte, and others."[174]

The right of the burgesses to elect the bailiff eventually reverted to the lord of Dunster because the burgesses were ineffective and ceased to act together as a corporation. The bailiff or bedel "was an outsider appointed by the lord" to look after his interests.[175]

Edward I, like his father Henry III, encouraged the cloth-making industry. The ownership of fulling mills was a profitable investment and at the date of John de Mohun II's death in 1279 and that of his successor John de Mohun III in 1330, the rent of the fulling mill was 13s 4d. Fulling mills first made their appearance in the reign of King John but only two are documented and customarily the craftsmen and their servants performed the task of "foot-fulling." The introduction of fulling mills was a threat to the livelihood of these fullers and the substitution of water power in places where there were fast-flowing streams, was, though a simple form of automation, a cause of much discontent. In the 18th century the mechanization of spinning and weaving was to cause similar disruption. The guilds sought to protect the fullers and in 1323 Henry the Walker, so named from his trade of foot fulling, defied a merchant gild of Leicester's regulation of 1260 which stated that "no gildsman should keep a fulling-mill outside the town." Nearer to Dunster, at Bristol, as late as 1346, it was forbidden to take "raucloth" out of the town to be fulled.[176]

John de Mohun II married Eleanor, the daughter of Sir Reynold Fitz Piers. After she was widowed she then married William Martin, Lord Martin. John de Mohun II's step uncle, the son of his grandfather by his first wife, had also married a Fitz Piers, Beatrice. When John de Mohun II died on 11 June 1279, he held the manors of Dunster, Carhampton, Cutcombe, Minehead, Kilton and Ile Brewers in Somerset, Whichford in Warwickshire, Bradworthy, Torre Mohun, Cadleigh and Ugborough in Devonshire and Luton in Bedfordshire.[177] His name and that of his wife, Eleanor Fitz Piers was remembered in 1276 in the Lucy mass when Walter Lucy arranged with the monks of Bath that a secular chaplain should say mass daily at the Altar of the Holy Rood, after Matins for his soul and the souls of his wives Margery and Lucy, Robert Lucy and Agnes, his wife, Roger Lucy and Sir John de Mohun and Eleanor his wife.[178] At that time this altar was on top of the rood loft between the western piers of the tower.

John de Mohun III

John de Mohun III was born in the second half of the 13th century and lived into the first half of the 14th century. His tenth birthday was only twenty four days after the death of his father and he appears not to have had any brothers or sisters. This John was to become the great benefactor of Dunster church and priory and he is represented as the donor figure at the feet of the Blessed Virgin Mary on the "Palme Crosse," which was seen everyday by the townspeople passing by. During his minority, the custody of his lands was granted to various people to whom the king, Edward I had made promise of annuities. Among them was Franciscus Accursius, or Francesco d'Accorso, a jurist and learned civilian to whom Edward accorded the manor and castle of Dunster. However, by June, 1281, he had lost his prize to John de Vesci, lord of Alnwick, one of Edward I's companions in his early years and a first cousin of the deceased John de Mohun II. John de Vesci obtained a definite grant of Dunster castle and other lands until the heir, John de Mohun III, reached his majority.[179] The abbot of Cleeve and the prior of Dunster were made responsible to John de Vesci for the arms and armour necessary for the defence of the castle at Dunster and these they kept temporarily in their respective houses.[180]

John de Vesci undertook various repairs to the castle and in 1284 Edward I sanctioned an enquiry both into the repairs already completed and those which were required to be done. A report emerged which is of great interest since it conveys to us details of the buildings then existing but unfortunately gives no indication of their location. Reference is made to the "oriel over the gate, the bakehouse over the oven, a garderobe near the bakehouse, the tower near the bakehouse, another tower called the Fleming Tower, the tower near the gate, the new tower over the great chamber, the children's chamber, the great hall, the saucery, the kitchen and a chamber between the same, the chapel, a certain knights' chamber and armoury, the lord's chamber, the oriel of that chamber, the bell-turret, the great knights' chamber and various embattled turrets. While the towers and certain buildings were roofed with lead, the hall and others were to be covered with wooden shingles."[181]

The young heir had a tutor John Launceleve and, whilst the custody of the lands had been granted to others, he personally was a ward of Edward I[182] and the accounts of the royal wardrobe record payments made on his behalf for saddles, bridles, leggings and spurs.[183]

On his father's death, his marriage was granted immediately to Robert Tibetot/Tiptoft/Tyebtot.[184] Robert Tibetot was the justiciar of west Wales and since he had a daughter, Ada, it was of advantage to the family to marry her to John, and she became his first wife in or before 1299. John de Mohun III was indeed a great "catch," possessed of vast lands. The manor of Whichford had come to him through Agnes, the wife of William de Mohun II and Ile Brewers had been inherited by Alice, the widow of Reynold de Mohun I. This lady's holdings were vastly increased on the death of her brother, William Briwere the younger when she inherited Torre, Ugborough, Cadleigh, Bradworthy and Axminster in Devon and Ile Brewers in Somerset all of which passed to the Mohuns. During John de Mohun III's minority, Whichford and Ile Brewers were committed by Edward I to Amaury de St Amand. When John de Mohun III came of age he received livery of his lands.[185] It was sensible and a course usually pursued that when great lords inherited far flung lands their policy was to endeavour to consolidate their scattered estate. Therefore John de Mohun III made over to the king all his share of the Marshal inheritance in Kildare in exchange for Long Compton in Warwickshire which adjoined his own manor of Whichford. The Marshal connection went back a long way for it was John de Mohun III's great grandfather, Reynold de Mohun II who had married as his second wife, Isabel, daughter of William Ferrers, earl of Derby and widow of Sir Gilbert Basset. The Marshals were the maternal uncles of Isabel and were successive earls of Pembroke. It is also believed that John de Mohun III exchanged the manor of Ile Brewers in Somerset, twenty four miles from Dunster, for that of Goring in Oxfordshire separated from his own manor of Streetley only by the river Thames.

He received his earliest summons for military service in Wales when only thirteen years of age when Edward I made war on Llewellyn, lord of Snowdonia, for refusing to pay him homage. More frequently, John de Mohun III was engaged in military service in Scotland where Edward was endeavouring to defeat the rebellious John Balliol whom he had chosen in 1292 to be king of Scotland and was also engaged in defeating the rebellion led by William Wallace in 1298. Sir John de Mohun III lived to be sixty one years of age and throughout what was considered to be a long lifetime, he was constantly campaigning in Gascony and Flanders as well as Wales and Scotland. The summons to arms of September 1298 addressed him among the barons but by 1318 he was numbered among the major barons and in June 1322 he was summoned to the muster at Newcastle as a banneret from the county of Oxford. The troops were raised by indenture, array, or voluntary enlistment. The commanding officers were the leading members of the aristocracy and were joined by captains of lower rank who had won renown for their acts of bravery. All were knights but their varying stations were rewarded accordingly so that a duke or an earl whose titles originally had military significance, were the highest paid. A duke received 13s. 4d a day, 6s. 8d for an earl and then came the bannerets who normally received 4s a day and were chosen from the body of knights. To be a banneret the knight had to exhibit military skill and be capable of sustaining the expenses incurred in converting the knight's pennon into a rectangular banner.

Strategy was carried out by the dukes and earls in consultation with the king, but Sir John de Mohun III, as a banneret, commanded retinues in the field of battle, arrayed contingents and was possibly called upon to garrison a castle and to act as a general staff officer. As a knight of the "armigerous" class, his arms, his personal armour and that of his great warhorse were indicative of a knight of great wealth and standing.[186] He was present at the brief siege of Carlaverock castle in 1300 which gained undeserved prominence simply because a poem written by Harris Nicolas in 1828 commemorated the arms of the earls, barons, and knights present. It is an important contribution to the history of heraldry.[187] It is from this time that the arms of Mohun change from the ermined maunch to the engrailed cross. Sir John was summoned to parliament by writs directed to Johanni de Mohun from 6 February 1299 to 23 October 1330, whereby he is held to have become Lord Mohun.[188] This summons was not entirely fulfilled because Sir John died on 25 August 1330. The title of Lord did not, in fact, exist in his day and, although he was one of the greater barons of the realm, a writ of summons did not, at that time, confer any title upon the recipient. He would have been addressed as John de Mohun, lord of Dunsterre as he was in the famous letter to which his seal, with its new arms, was appended, which was sent to Pope Boniface by the English barons in 1300/1.

Between 20 November 1300 and 19 November 1301 Sir John de Mohun III granted a charter to the burgesses of Dunster. It is the first charter bearing a specific date.

To all the faithful of Christ who shall see or hear the present writing. John de Moyun the Third, lord of Dunsterre, greeting in the Lord. Know ye all that I have granted and confirmed for ever for me and my heirs to all the burgesses of my town of Dunsterre and their heirs all the liberties of the same town which Sir Reynold de Moyun, my great-grandfather, gave and granted by his charter to the same burgesses and their heirs. I have also granted to the same burgesses and their heirs the estate and liberty which they had by a certain writing made to the same burgesses of Sir John de Moyun, my father. I have furthermore granted to the same burgesses and their heirs for ever, on account of the love which I bear to the same burgesses, that they shall have furze, whorts, turves, fern, and heath, sufficient for their fuel on my hill of Croudon, for ever. Provided that by reason of this grant nobody sojourning within the borough of Dunsterre shall in any wise have or hold the aforesaid liberties or grants except the burgesses and their heirs or those who hold a whole burgage in the same borough. And that this is my grant and confirmation may remain approved and valid forever, I have affixed my seal to the present writing. These being witnesses: Sir Andrew Loterel, knight, William Osberne then constable of Dunsterre, Gilbert de la Putte, Roger Arundel, Ralph Fitzurse, Robert of Bratton and Ralph le Tort. Dated at Dunsterre on Thursday before the feast of the Annunciation of Our Lady in the twenty-ninth year of the reign of King Edward, AD 1301."[189]

One of the witnesses was Sir Andrew Loterel of East Quantoxhead, who was the grandfather of Sir Andrew Luttrell of Chilton whose widow, Elizabeth Courtenay bought Dunster castle in 1376 from Lady Joan Mohun, the widow of the last de Mohun lord of Dunster, John de Mohun V. The hill of Croudon/Croydon was referred to in 1571 as Croydon common which contained two thousand acres "very commodious" to the town of Dunster "for the necessary fuell, heath and turfe growinge there."[190]

John de Mohun III issued a further charter which was granted between 20 November 1306 and 7 July 1307 when King Edward I died, in the thirty-fifth year of his reign.

To all the faithful of Christ which shall see or hear the present writing. John de Mohun, lord of Dunsterre, greeting in the Lord. Know ye all that I have granted and confirmed for ever for me and my heirs to all my burgesses of my town of Dunsterre and their heirs and all who hold a whole burgage that they shall freely dig and at their pleasure carry away slime for improving their lands, in the whole of my marsh between the road that leads to the sea-port of Dunsterre and the marsh of Richard of Avele; and that they shall have common of pasture with all their plough-cattle at every time of the year, except in my several marsh which is call Estmersh, [so] that they shall neither dig there and carry away, nor have common there with their plough cattle. Provided that by reason of this grant nobody sojourning within the borough of Dunsterre shall in any wise have or hold the aforesaid liberties or grants except the burgesses and their heirs or those who hold a whole burgage in the same borough. And that this gift, grant and confirmation may remain approved and valid for ever, I have affixed my seal to the present writing. These being witnesses:- Sir Henry of Glastonbury, knight, William Osbern, steward, Geoffrey of Loccombe, Gilbert de la Putte, Roger Arundel, Robert of Bratton, Ralph le Tort, and others. Dated at Dunsterre on Friday next after the feast of St James the Apostle in the thirty-fifth year of King Edward."[191]

The original charter was formerly preserved in a chest in Dunster church. It was then sent to the castle where it became part of Dunster Castle Muniments until the National Trust took over the castle in 1976 and these muniments were sent to the Somerset Archives and Record Office and retained their original numbers. The Dunster Church Book papers were, however, renumbered. The date of the charter is questioned by Lyte who observes that "Edward the First died on the 7th July 1307, and the feast of St James was on the 25th of the month."[192] The thirty fifth year of the reign of Edward I was 20 November 1306 – 7 July1307. The Friday next after the feast of St James would therefore have been in the reign of Edward II his first regnal year being 8 July 1307 to 7 July 1308.[193] Lyte points out that in the 16th century, George Luttrell questioned its validity "on the ground that the burgesses of Dunster were not a corporation" and added "it may be useful to note here that the East Marsh, as above, then comprised about forty acres used as a rabbit warren and commonly known by the name of Coleborrowes."[194] In both charters quoted John de Mohun III's burgesses who held a whole burgage were also entitled to the liberties and grants described. In Dunster, the land on either side of the streets had been cut up into narrow strips, "each strip of normal size was known as burgage and was held of the lord by the free tenure of that name."[195] The size of the strip was sufficient for the erection of a house leaving enough ground for a garden or a yard. The rent for such a burgage was usually a shilling a year. Medieval tenure was of two kinds, free and non-free, according to whether the services attached were becoming or unbecoming to a free man.

Apart from tenure in chivalry involving either knights' service or grand sergeantry, that is to say honourable services such as the right to carry the king's banner, or the lord's cup-bearer, there was also free socage, which was a non-military form of tenure involving a service such as ploughing the lord's land, or paying a fixed rent such as the shilling a year paid by the burgesses of Dunster for their burgage. This was apparently quite a high rent little less than the actual value of the burgage when first acquired. The tenements on the eastern side of the High Street were separated from the Hanger Park by a continuous paling or wall and those opposite were similarly separated from the Priory Green. In some parts of the town, the arrangement was not quite so symmetrical.[196] "Under the Feudal System no man had the absolute ownership of land. In return for his services he held it of some lord, who himself held it of a higher lord, while the King was the lord paramount, above the owner, subject to the rights of the tenants."[197] Much depended on local custom and there were varieties of socage, or feudal tenure, other than knight service. "Petit sergeantry" applied only to lands held directly of the King in return for a particular gift each year, e.g. a sword. Principally in Kent, another kind of socage prevailed. This was called "gavelkind" whereby on intestacy the land descended not to the eldest son, but to all sons equally; "borough-English" involved descent to the youngest son on the tenant's intestacy.[198] Should there be no sons, the youngest brother inherited. Ecclesiastics who provided spiritual services were given land in return, for example, for the celebration of an annual Mass for the soul of the overlord which was known as "frankalmoin."

"The burgess was a freeman with considerable independence and he could deal with the burgage as he chose. Although, when originally allotted there was one burgess to one burgage, the situation changed because the burgess had the right to bequeath his holding to the person of his choice. Thus the number of original burgesses diminished and those who remained in possession were a limited and concentrated band. The only way the lord could get an escheat was in the case of the forfeiture of the burgage by reason of a bastard tenant dying intestate. Should the burgess's tenancy be on agricultural land, he did, however, have to fulfil the usual obligations of villein service. The term burgage covered a variety of holdings. For example, it might straightforwardly mean a house inhabited by a burgess. On the other hand it could mean a barn or an empty plot of land, or there could be two dwelling houses on one burgage and even half-burgages are mentioned. The medieval meaning was lost in the 17th century. A successful trader and burgess could buy an adjacent burgage and thus enlarge his premises. Sales were also transacted between burgesses and investors who, seeing the increasing value of the tenure, could let them at a larger rent than that which was the obligatory and fixed rent owed to the lord. It was of no moment who occupied the premises for the owner alone was answerable to the lord and should he fail to pay the rent, the lord could seize any personal chattels to be found on the premises.[199]

We hear more of the first prior of Dunster, Martin (1257-74) for of the total number of burgages of which an escheat of 1266 shows that there were 17½, twelve of them belonged to this Benedictine prior. Robert of Galloxswell owned seven, all of which were beyond the river Avill. One of the main approaches to the town of Dunster was via the street we now call Park Street but which was described in 1323 in the time of John de Mohun III as "la Waterstret" and in the time of John de Mohun V as "Gallokystret." Both names were used as late as 1800 but generally the southern part across the river was known as Gallocks Street and the northern part leading from West Street to the bridge was known as Water Street, "the spring from which it took its name is mentioned in the reign of Henry VII" (1489-1509).[200] Gallocks Street led up to the site of the gallows where four roads met and it was the road leading west to Frackford. One of the four roads, a Roman road, led to the village of Carhampton but after the creation of the Deer Park in the late 18th century it became no more than a footpath. So seven of the 176½ burgages mentioned in a writ of 1266 were presumably in the aforesaid area, although Richard of Gallokswell could have been of Galloxwell but owned the burgages elsewhere within the borough of Dunster. Lyte gives the names of other burgesses whose surnames indicate their occupations. Thus we read about: Mazun (Mason), Smith, Carpenter, Poter, Baker, Cok (Cook), Webber, Fuller, Corour, Tannere, Glovere, Chepman, Miller, Gardiner, Fisher, Hunter (ventator), Wake (vigil), Clerk and Chaplain. Others, he says "took their names from the places at which they dwelt, the Marsh, the Bridge, the Bar, the Corner, the Well and the Churchyard."[201] He points out that "Roger Wyschard may be mentioned as a representative of the Norman element in the population, and John Portman of the English."[202] He also mentions the more curious names of burgesses such as William le Nywecomesone, Maud le Dublesterre, Nicholas Bukkehorn, Alice Stoukedostre and Joan Cockeslop. A few of the burgesses had only one name recorded, such as "Stou, Wyncestre, Cheftynge, Hunygod, Couleman and Scherpe."[203] Although the lord's rent was one shilling, in 1381 when some new burgesses were admitted they only obtained their burgages for life[204] perhaps because of the complications of obtaining the rent from subsequent buyers perhaps unknown to the lord, or the injustice of the fixed rent of 1s for the lord and the increased rents obtained by investors who had purchased the tenures from the original owners. If the burgage came into the lands of the lord of Dunster by forfeiture (escheat), by purchase, or by surrender, he could change the conditions of tenure. Also when a burgage was transferred, the lord was entitled to receive a small pecuniary sum and in all cases where the new owner was not already a burgess.[205] Sir John died in 1330, but in the later middle ages several burgages in Dunster were in the possession of the abbot and convent of Cleeve, the prior of Dunster and the guilds of St Lawrence and the Holy Trinity whose chantry chapels were within St George's church.

In December, 1307, Sir John de Mohun III was appointed joint keeper of the peace in Somerset[206] and four years later in 1311 a ship going from Ireland to Wales was wrecked at Dunster and the people, presumably Sir John's tenants, carried away the cargo. As early as 1182 the lords of Dunster had claimed the right known as "wreck of sea."

The coronation of King Edward II took place on 25 February 1308 and John de Mohun III was one of the 138 principle nobles and officers of state who with thirty-two ecclesiastics were summoned to attend the ceremony. In October, 1313, as an adherent of Thomas, earl of Lancaster, who was the king's cousin, John de Mohun III received a pardon after he and others consented to make a public apology in Westminster Hall,[207] for his participation in the death of the king's favourite, Piers Gaveston, and the disturbances which ensued.[208] Failing the approval of parliament the earl of Lancaster and three other earls refused to obey the King's summons to military service against Scotland where in 1314 the English suffered the crushing defeat of Bannockburn. The House of Lancaster had been built upon the confiscated estates of the De Montforts after Simon de Montfort was slain at the battle of Evesham. The earl of Lancaster wielded much power and possessed five earldoms and an immense private army, so the King became a puppet in his hands until the arrival of the Despensers.

The great greed and ambition of the Despensers, father and son, favourites at the Edward II's court, was the cause of resentment among the other Marcher lords and in 1321 they combined with Thomas, earl of Lancaster to force Edward to exile the new favourites. Sir John de Mohun III was among those forbidden to attend any illegal or treasonable assemblies, and again, in November, he was forbidden to attend the 'counte parliament' which Lancaster had summoned to meet at Doncaster. Although Edward forbade this meeting there appears to be no direct evidence that it took place. By the end of 1321 both the elder and the young Despenser were recalled from banishment through the medium of the archbishop of Canterbury, Walter Reynolds, and Edward secured for the convocation of Canterbury a condemnation of the moves against the Despensers and on the feast of the Epiphany in 1322 he came to a formal peace with the Despensers. The king then assembled the levies at Coventry, and Sir John de Mohun III was one of those summoned to the muster of the forces marching against the earl of Lancaster. However, he did not attend the muster personally and, in his place, his son and heir, John de Mohun IV performed the service. In this year, 1322, Edward II exhibited more resolution than he had ever shown before and, supported by moderate opinion, he attacked the Marchers in Wales and forced them to submit. Lancaster was isolated and made a treacherous mistake by asking Robert Bruce to come to his aid with a Scottish army. This was too much for the long-suffering men of the north and they re-acted with hatred against Lancaster and, at the battle of Boroughbridge in March 1321/2 they defeated the remnants of Lancaster's great private army.

In 1324 Sir John de Mohun III turned his attention to Dunster and issued a further charter as follows:

To all the faithful of Christ who shall see or hear the present writing, John de Mohun, lord of Dunsterre, greeting in the Lord. Know ye all that I have given and granted for me and my heirs and all other lords, guardians, [or] bailiffs of Dunsterre to all the burgesses of my town of Dunster continuing for ever twenty gallons of ale out of the twenty-four gallons of ale formerly due to me from every brew. I will also and grant for me and my heirs and all lords, guardians and bailiffs whomsoever, that hereafter we shall not be able to make or have prise of the brew of anyone in the same town, except four gallons of ale from a brew as I had them and was wont from the past term, and those of the ale which the bailiff found on sale on the day of the search. And I, the aforesaid John de Mohun, and my heirs will warrant, acquit and defend for ever to the aforesaid burgesses and their heirs and all who continue in the aforesaid town the aforesaid twenty gallons of ale against all mortals. In testimony whereof I have affixed my seal to this present writing. There being witnesses:- Sir Henry of Glastonbury, knight, Ralph le Tort, Geoffrey of Loccumbe, William of Kytenore, William of Holne, Robert Everard, Geoffrey of Avele, and others. Dated at Dunsterre on Sunday after the feast of the Purification of Our Lady in the seventeenth year of the reign of King Edward, the son of King Edward."[209] [Edward II 1324]

There must have been a good deal of brewing at Dunster at this period, for, some six years after the date of the foregoing charter, the Lord's prise of ale in the town was valued at £2 13s 4d. a year.[210]

In January 1325 Sir John de Mohun III was appointed one of the chief supervisors of array in Somerset and Dorset but he was superseded in April, perhaps on account of infirmity. The commissioners of array were appointed by the Crown to survey: "the able-bodied men between the ages of sixteen and sixty in each hundred, township, and liberty within the shire and, under the authorization of the Statute of Winchester of 1285, selected the best of them to serve at the king's wages, the cost of initial equipment being borne by the localities.[211] The commissioners themselves were normally men of the knightly class, sometimes members of the king's household, experienced staff officers who knew what they were looking for and may be presumed to have chosen well."[212] Sir John was excused personal attendance in parliament and service with the army in April 1329; again perhaps in consideration of his age or infirmities.[213] He was sixty years old in 1329 and he sent his second son Robert, his heir, John de Mohun IV, probably having died by this time (he himself was died the following year). This substitution seems to have been an acceptable practice for in 1333, John Cobham attended parliament on behalf of his father, and a son could be summoned with his father as were Richard and Gilbert Talbot between 1333 and 1334.[214]

Robert de Mohun married Elizabeth, the daughter of Simon de Roges of Porlock, who was murdered under suspicious circumstances towards the end of 1331. He had not enjoyed a happy marriage with Elizabeth and, when she was widowed, she and her mother were both suspected of involvement in the dastardly deed. The chief suspect implicated in this affair was John of Luccombe, a neighbour, but little more is known for certain about the circumstances except that very soon afterwards, Elizabeth married Sir Robert of Stockhey.[215] The date of her death is unknown but, in 1353, a John de Mohun of Porlock, knight, is mentioned. He is described as son of Sir Robert de Mohun and he must have succeeded Elizabeth.[216] The Mohuns of Fleet in Dorset claimed to have been descended from this John.[217] In 1329, Sir John de Mohun III, having sent Robert to represent him, was busy with affairs at home in Dunster. It was only a year before his death. There is little information regarding the castle in the 14th century. No documentary evidence exists but Lyte thought that one of the later Mohuns had lengthened the principal building of the lower ward by adding a tower and some rooms at the western end of it on a narrow strip of ground close under the eastern end of the upper ward,[218] so this work may have been done in the time of John de Mohun III or John de Mohun V.

Ever since 1086 there had been two corn or grist mills belonging to the lords of Dunster. They had been good investments and their value had increased from 10s a year in the time of William de Mohun I to £2 13s 4d in 1279, the year John de Mohun II died. Now in 1329 his son decided to convey the leases of these two mills to one of his burgesses, Walter Rughe at a rent of 24 marks.[219] In 1405 the conditions changed.

John de Mohun III married twice and by his first wife, Ada who died in or before 1324[220] he had seven or eight sons and one daughter. The heir John de Mohun IV died in the lifetime of his father and it was his son John, who succeeded to the lordship eventually and was the fifth of that name. Robert was the second son and Baldwin, the third son, was an interesting character. According to Lyte: "He received the first tonsure from the Bishop of Bath and Wells in 1315, but he did not obtain any preferment in the west of England, and there are some grounds for supposing that he married a lady of the Clavering family."[221] The "first tonsure" was the custom in 4th- and 5th-century monasticism which was introduced into the west from the east as the form of admission to the clerical state.[222] In 1342 Baldwin was working in a secular capacity and as a local magnate he served on several commissions in Warwickshire;[223] presumably this was the period when he married. He then reverted to the church and, having powerful patrons, in the persons of Edward II's queen Isabella and Henry, earl of Lancaster, he was recommended by the pope for a canonry.[224] However, in 1344 he was the incumbent of the church at Whichford which was in the gift of John de Mohun V, his nephew. He was later at Fordingbridge[225] and in 1348 he was presented by Edward III to the prebend of Warminster in the cathedral church of Salisbury,[226] but he died before 1350. Payn, of whom we first hear in 1323 was John de Mohun III's fourth son. In 1323 Payn received Episcopal licence to choose his own confessor.[227] The next year he was again in touch with the bishop. His concern was that his father should be compelled to give him 50 marks and a cope adorned with gold and relics which his mother Ada Tibetot had bequeathed to her three younger children.[228] Payn was very concerned about the murder of his brother Robert and made great endeavours to bring the culprit to justice.[229] He received from his father the manor of Cutcombe, but this was limited to his lifetime only.[230] In 1344 and 1345 he went with Henry Bolingbroke, earl of Derby, the son of John of Gaunt and Blanche of Lancaster, the future King Henry IV, to Guienne and to Auberoche where, in October 1345 Henry defeated the French. Perhaps it was judicious for Payn de Mohun to leave Somerset in 1344 since, with his brother Patrick and their nephew, Sir John de Mohun V and others, he was indicted for a variety of felonies in Somerset.[231]

In 1346, Edward III defeated the French at the battle of Crécy on 26 August. Three armed men from the town of Dunster had been called upon to serve. In 1350 the English defeated the Spaniards off Winchester and that year one man was demanded from Dunster. The fifth son of Sir John de Mohun III was Sir Reynold, the ancestor of the Mohuns of Hall and Boconnoc in Cornwall.[232] The sixth son was Patrick, also involved with Payn and John de Mohun V in the aforesaid felonies. He received from his father the manor of Bradworthy in Devon for life.[233] He apparently acted as receiver for the widow of Sir John de Mohun V (d.1375), Lady Joan de Mohun (d.1404). She allowed him to live at Marshwood and her elder daughter, Elizabeth, then Lady FitzWalter, ratified this arrangement. She, however, claimed the reversion, or right to future possession, but she was never successful.[234] The seventh son was Hervey and for him Lady Blanche Wake, the daughter of John of Gaunt and Blanche of Lancaster, obtained an annuity of 10 marks from the Crown[235] and Henry of Lancaster, earl of Derby, her brother, gave him an annuity of £10. His nephew, Sir John de Mohun V appointed him bailiff of the Hundred of

Carhampton.[236] Hervey died in 1349 probably of the plague since the Black Death was raging.[237] His appointment as bailiff was, in some ways, no sinecure for the bailiff had to make good, out of his own pocket, any loss due to the production target set for each manor not being attained.

According to McKisack: "the grain crop was required to be x times the amount of seed sown, the wool fleeces to average a prescribed weight, each cow and ewe to yield milk for so much butter and cheese, each breeding female animal to produce the right number of young."[238] The auditors kept a keen eye on: "what money was yearly made by sale of the locks, belts and tags of the Sheep (as well as of the fleeces) of the hearbes of the garden, stubble from off the Corne lands, crops and setts of withy'es, of Osier rods, the Offall wood of old hedges, of butter, cheese and milke, dunge and soile, of bran, nuts, wax hony, and the like."[239] It is true that the bailiff received certain perks and we learn that in Norfolk: "At Forncett the bailiff received, 52s a year, a robe worth 20s, stabling and a daily peck of oats for his horse; his dwelling was kept in repair at the cost of the lord, the earl of Norfolk."[240] The last and eighth son of Sir John de Mohun III was Lawrence about whom nothing is known except that he is stated to have been the ancestor of the Mohuns of Tavistock.[241] It is indeed not certain if he was the eighth son, since the Register of Newenham abbey states that John had only seven sons and then proceeds to enumerate eight, the 'et' before the name of Lawrence, Lyte suggest, should perhaps be a 'vel'.[242] The only daughter of this prolific marriage was Eleanor who in 1324 married Sir Ralph of Wellington.[243] Sir John de Mohun III's second wife was Sibyl, the widow of Sir Henry de Lorty.

In February 1325, a priest named Robert of Plympton was appointed confessor to Sir John de Mohun and Sibyl. In June 1330, two months before he died, Sir John entered into a recognizance, or bond, by which he engaged before a court, or magistrate, to pay Bartholomew of Burghersh the then enormous sum of £10,000. The intention is not stated, although it was probably connected with a matrimonial project since Sir John de Mohun III's grandson, and heir, married Joan, the daughter of Sir Bartholomew of Burghersh (Suffolk). Sir John de Mohun III died on 25 August 1330 and Sybil outlived him by seven years and was buried at Curry Rivel on 13 November 1337.[244]

Sir John's was the first known burial in the priory church at Dunster. In 1330 Sybil was assigned by the Crown the dower comprised of the castle and manor of Dunster. The castle was the "caput" of an ancient barony. Sibyl also enjoyed later a third of the knight's fees pertaining to this caput.[245] Lyte writes: "It is repeatedly laid down in books on law that the widow of a baron shall not have dower out of the *caput baroniæ* of her late husband."[246] She had however considerable difficulty in establishing her rights.[247] In 1335 it was reported to the King at Alnwick that she was dead and no time was lost in disposing of the lands which she held in dower, but the report of her death proved false and she was certainly living in 1337.[248] There is nothing further known about her except that she kept a domestic chaplain, presumably at Dunster.[249] John de Mohun IV, the eldest son and heir of John de Mohun III and his wife Ada, died in the lifetime of his father. He was on the side of King Edward II against Thomas, earl of Lancaster at the battle of Boroughbridge in March 1321/2[250] and his name appears on the Battle Roll (see also chapter V). He died in Scotland before 1330.[251] Lyte says: "A statement that he was buried in the church of the Grey Friars at York rests upon very questionable authority."[252] Philip Chatwin maintains that he was buried at Whichford: "his body was brought back to Whichford and was buried in the south chapel, where his stone coffin, with his coat of arms carved on it is still to be seen."[253] He married, in May 1305, Christian, the daughter of Sir John Segrave and Christian, the daughter of Sir Hugh du Plessis, when they were both minors. Had John de Mohun IV outlived his father he would have succeeded to property valued at £600 a year.[254] In 1309 an expedition against truce breakers was being discussed and Sir John

Segrave went to the border and made a private agreement with Robert Bruce to suspend hostilities, and advised Edward II to postpone operations until the summer.[255] The marital arrangements were that in consideration of Sir John Segrave's fortune of £400, Sir John de Mohun III would undertake to maintain the young couple and to give to Christian a dower of 100 marks a year if she survived her husband, which she did. Christian must have enjoyed this dower for she survived Sir John de Mohun III and died during the 1340s. In 1335 she was referred to as "the widow at Minehead." It is most probably Christian who lies in effigy under a canopied wall recess on the south side of the Priory chancel , whilst her father-in-law, Sir John de Mohun III lies opposite, below ground level; the place of his burial being marked by a small arched aperture at the base of the door leading into the de Mohun Chantry Chapel. Sir John de Mohun IV and Christian were the parents of: John de Mohun V, the last de Mohun of Dunster Castle, whose widow Joan de Burghersh sold the castle to Lady Elizabeth Luttrell, also a widow. Their daughters were Margaret, who married John de Carew, and Elizabeth who died without issue.

John de Mohun V

The last de Mohun lord of Dunster, was John de Mohun V and his wife, Lady Joan de Burghersh, a grand court lady, who lived during the reigns of Edward III and his grandson and successor, Richard II. It is a story of John de Mohun's military career in the reign of Edward III and of a couple living beyond their means. Lady Joan served at the court of Richard II's first queen, Anne of Bohemia, and of her husband's role as a founder member of Edward III's Order of the Garter. Lady Joan de Mohun and her husband survived the Black Death of 1348, which broke out immediately after the ceremony of the inauguration of the Order of the Garter, and its recurrence in 1361. Of their three daughters, two made illustrious marriages to the duke of York, who was slain at Agincourt in 1415, and to the earl of Salisbury. No less a place than the crypt of Canterbury cathedral sufficed as Lady Joan's final resting place in 1404 and there in the cloisters may be found the shields of the families associated with her. Anne of Bohemia was the sister of the Emperor Wenceslas and Richard married her in 1382. The court was one of great brilliance where the mystique of monarchy, ostentation, pomp and vainglory were carried to excess. As with most of England's foreign queens, Anne was, at first, unpopular, but, in spite of her plain looks the king was passionately devoted to her and she was seldom out of his sight. A pious and well educated lady, she was poor, and she was bought at great cost; her dowry being £4,500 supplemented by additional grants.[256] As time passed she gained acceptance and her virtues became evident. She had been accompanied to England by some of her countrymen who were instrumental in obtaining Bohemian horses for the king.

The early details of Sir John de Mohun V's life relating to Dunster includes the first charter of 1341 which was made when he had first attained his majority and had freed himself from the shackles of his guardians, Henry of Berghersh, Bishop of Lincoln and chancellor of England and later the guardianship of Sir Bartholomew of Berghersh, whose daughter Joan he married. This 1341 charter was granted to the Benedictines of Dunster priory and embodied a general confirmation of the gifts of his ancestors to the church of St George and the monks and specified all the endowments previously made with some additions. These were: "pasture called Fowlermarsh, land called Frackford (situate between Dunster and Avill, a ferling (or 12 acres) of the manor of Cutcombe at Chaldewell, another ferling between Stentwill and Cowbridge mill, several burgages in Dunster and the tithes of Combe and Codford."[257] The second charter of August 1342 added to the monks' benefactions. John de Mohun V remitted to them: "a yearly rent of 8s 6d due to him from burgages, which they had acquired in the town of Dunster and a yearly rent of 1lb of pepper from Kilton. He also gave them common of pasture at Croydon for all their beasts at Cowbridge, pasture on Grabbist, and twelve cartloads of windfall wood for fuel from

Marshwood Park, and the foreign woods of Dunster, provided that the carts should not be too large to be drawn by two horses."[258] His third charter was merely a confirmation of the second.

There was no male heir of John de Mohun V's marriage to Joan de Burghersh and she sold the castle to Lady Elizabeth Luttrell in 1376. The reign of Edward III was a long one from 1327 to 1377 and it was in the second half of the 14th century that the native woollen industry of England really flourished. The industry had been encouraged in the reigns of Henry III and Edward I but although Edward III had attempted to advance its interests, the industry was in decline. This was partly due to the great demand for raw English wool in the German, Flemish and Italian markets and this export precluded the expansion of the native industry and indeed threatened its existence so that the large cities and centres of cloth making were disastrously affected. Cloth-making in the smaller centres did not suffer the decline experienced in the larger towns and cities of the realm. The proliferation of fulling mills ordained the locations demanded. It was necessary to have swift running water and most urban centres were near slow-moving water in lower lying places. Hilly areas also provided an abundance of wool from the sheep which grazed the uplands and little evidence points to alien immigration in the south west. A lord erecting a fulling mill would sometimes seek to establish a monopoly but normally he leased the mill to a tenant and the weavers and fullers found little difficulty in recruiting labour, more cheaply than in the towns, from the younger sons of the tenantry or from the women and small-holders. At Dunster in 1376, the rent of the fulling mill had not increased since 1259 and remained at 13s 4d, but that year the reeve of Dunster accounted for 12d. A second fulling mill had been erected and the 12d represented the new rent of William Taillour at Hocktide and Michaelmas for a fulling mill which the said William had erected over the lord's watercourse.[259]

CHAPTER THREE

THE BENEDICTINE MONKS OF DUNSTER, PRIORY AND CHURCH

FOR OVER 350 years there was a little band of Black Monks at Dunster who followed the Rule of the Italian abbot St Benedict. When St Benedict wrote his Rule for the monks at Monte Cassino, he based it on the Italian Rule of the Master written by an unknown abbot in one of the monasteries south of Rome soon after 500 AD. He derived from the Rule of the Master not only most of his basic principles and organisational details, but also some of the most famous passages in the his Rule, such as the chapter on obedience and the grades of humility, were taken over verbatim and many other passages were transplanted with little change. In fact, all the essentials of St Benedict's Rule are to be found in the works of his unknown predecessor, who, to judge by the liturgical instructions, was writing some forty years earlier. It was not considered plagiarism, but a mark of humility and deference to a greater wisdom and it would have seemed perfectly natural for him to model his Rule on a treatise composed by some other acknowledged veteran of the ascetic life.[1]

The Benedictine monks were in Dunster possibly from the 11th century and certainly from 1177 and they did not depart until the dissolution of the monasteries in 1539. Martin, the first recorded prior was in office from 1257 to 1294. The respond in the southern arcade (c.1500) in the parish church bears on its capital the letter 'M' which may be a remembrance of this prior. St Benedict wrote that the monastery ought if possible be so constructed as to contain within it all necessaries, such as water, mill, garden and various crafts "…so that there be no occasion for monks to wander abroad, since this is no wise expedient for their souls." His Rule was to be read aloud in the community, "…so that no brother may excuse himself on the grounds of ignorance."[2]

St Benedict's Rule was one of great understanding and tolerance which discouraged excessive austerity and the whole is marked by a spirit of prudent leniency. It was decreed that architecture, painting and all branches of art were taught and that there ought always to be reading while the brethren were at table. "At the meals of the brethren there should not fail to be reading; nor should the reader be anyone who may chance to take up the book; but let there be a reader for the whole week who shall enter upon his office on a Sunday. Let this incoming reader, after Mass and Communion, ask all to pray for him that God may preserve him from the spirit of pride. He shall intone three times in the oratory the Versicle: '*Domine, labiat mea aperies et os meum annuntiatiato laudem tuam*' which shall each time be repeated after him by the choir. And so, having received his blessing let him enter upon his reading. And let there be the greatest silence, so that no whisper, and no voice but the reader's may be heard there. But for all the things that they need as they eat and drink, let the brethren so supply them to one another, that no one shall need to ask for anything. If, however, there be any need, then let the thing be asked for by means of some sign rather than by speech. Nor let anyone venture there to ask questions about the reading or anything else, lest it give occasion for disorder. However, the Superior, if he thinks fit, may say a few words for the edification of the brethren. Let the weekly reader be given a little bread and wine before he begin to read, on account of the Holy Communion and lest the fast might be hard for him to bear. Let him have his meal afterwards with the kitcheners and servers of the week. The brethren are not to read or sing each in his turn, but those only that give edification to the hearers. If there be craftsmen in the monastery, let them practice their crafts with all humility, provided the abbot give permission. But if one of them be puffed up because of his skill in his craft, supposing he is conferring a benefit on the monastery, let him be removed from his work and not return to it, unless he have humbled himself and the abbot entrust it to him again. If any of the work of the craftsmen is to be sold, let those who have to manage the business take care that they shall not be guilty of dishonesty. Let them always remember Ananias and Saphira, and take care lest they, or any others who deal dishonestly with the property of the monastery, should suffer in their souls the death which they endured with their bodies. And, as regards the price, let not the sin of avarice creep in; but let the goods always be sold a little cheaper than they are sold by people of the world, that in all things God may be glorified."[3]

Much time was devoted to reading and manual work. Benedictine monks also played an important role in the development of stained glass in early medieval times. It is said that stained glass adorned the abbey at Monte Cassino as early as 1066 and was a medium of teaching as well as decoration, as was wall painting.[4]

The Rule for the Divine Office, Opus Dei or Work of God in St Benedict's words provided the basic framework for the day and consisted of eight offices that were recited in common at certain hours of the day. It began in the hours of darkness with the singing of the office of Vigils or Nocturns later called Matins. The Rule for this Divine Office at Night tells us that: "in Winter, that is from the first of November until Easter, prudence dictates that the brethren shall rise at the eighth hour of the night (2a.m.) so that their sleep may extend for a moderate space beyond midnight, and they may rise with digestion completed. Those brethren who need a better knowledge of them, should devote the time that remains after Matins to the study of the psalms and lessons. From Easter to the aforesaid first of November, let the hour of rising be so arranged that there be a very short interval after Matins, in which the brethren may go out for the necessities of nature, to be followed at once by Lauds, which should be said at dawn. The office of Prime followed at sunrise. Then the monks processed out of the choir and set about their daily work. There were short offices during the day which concluded with the evening office of Vespers and finally with the brief office of Compline which was sung at sundown."[5] At Dunster these services may have been conducted in the chapel of Our Lady and from the adjoining northern transept, styled the "dorter aisle," a flight of steps presumably led up to the "dorter" or dormitory. The night service was the most onerous, being: "the longest and most elaborate of the services. Nocturns was divided into parts each of which consisted of six psalms and four lessons together with responsories, or meditative verses, relating to the subject of the lessons. On Sundays and feast-days, the night office contained three Nocturns, and it must have taken nearly two hours to complete."[6]

The Rule concerning sleep stated: "Let them sleep each one in a separate bed. Let their beds be assigned to them in accordance with the date of their conversion, subject to the abbot's dispositions. If it be possible, let them all sleep in one place; but if their numbers do not allow this, let them sleep by tens or twenties, with seniors to supervise them. There shall be a light burning in the dormitory throughout the night. Let them sleep clothed and girt with girdles or cords, but not with their belts, so that they may not have their knives at their sides while they are sleeping and be cut by them in their sleep. Being clothed, they will thus always be ready, and rising at the signal without any delay may hasten to forestall one another to the Work of God; yet this with all gravity and self restraint. The younger brethren shall not have their beds by themselves, but shall be mixed with the seniors. When they rise for the Work of God, let them gently encourage one another, on account of the excuses to which the sleepy are addicted."[7]

The Rule which deals with sick brethren says: "before all things and above all things care must be taken of the sick, so that they may be served in very deed as Christ himself, for he said, 'I was sick, and ye visited me' and 'what ye did to one of these least ones, ye did it unto me'. But let the sick on their part consider that they are being served for the honour of God, and not provoke their brethren who are serving them by their unreasonable demands. Yet they should be patiently borne with, because from such as these is gained a more abundant reward. Therefore let the abbot take the greatest care that they suffer no neglect. For these sick brethren let there be assigned a special room and an attendant who is God-fearing, diligent and careful. Let the use of baths be offered to the sick as often as may be expedient, but to the healthy and especially to the young, let them be granted seldom. Moreover, let the use of fresh meat be granted to the sick who are very weak, for the restoration of their strength, but as soon as they are better, let all abstain from fresh meat as usual. Let the abbot take the greatest care that the sick be not neglected by the cellarer and attendants; for he must answer for the deed of his disciples."[8]

The Rule also set out that: "At the gateway of the monastery let there be placed a wise old man, who understands how to give and receive a message, whose years will keep him from leaving his post This porter should have a room near the gate, so that those who come may always find someone to answer them. As soon as anyone knocks, or a poor man hails him, let him answer, *Deo gratias* or *Benedic*. Then let him attend to him promptly, with all the gentleness of the fear of God and with fervent charity. If the porter need help, let him have one of the younger brethren." The porter near the gate was a different person from the doorkeeper, the *"ostiarius"* whose task was to prevent the heathen from entering and disturbing the services, of keeping the laity and the clergy separated, of keeping men from women in the church, of guarding the church and its contents, of opening the church and sacristy at certain hours, and of opening the book for the preacher. This doorkeeper was concerned with activities within the church and as an *ostiarius* he was a member of the lowest of the Minor Orders of the Church.

The Rule laid down that: "Every man hath his proper gift from God, one after this. manner, and another after that. It is therefore with some misgiving, that we determine how much others should eat or should drink. Nevertheless, keeping in view the needs of weaker brethren, we believe that a hemina of wine a day is sufficient for each. But those upon whom God bestows the gift of abstinence, should know that they shall have a special reward. But if the circumstances of the place, or their work, or the heat of the summer require more let the superior be free to grant it. Yet let him always take care that neither surfeit nor drunkenness supervene. We do, indeed read that wine is no drink for monks; but since nowadays, monks cannot be persuaded of this, let us at least agree upon this, to drink temperately and not to satiety: for wine maketh even the wise to fall away. But when the circumstances of the place are such that the aforesaid measure cannot be had, but much less or even none at all, then let the monks who dwell there bless God and not murmur. Above all things we do give this admonition, that they abstain from murmuring."[9]

St Benedict's Rule concerning the Measure of Food took account of individual preferences for health reasons and it was laid down that there should therefore be a choice of dishes. "We believe it to be sufficient for the daily meal, whether that be at the sixth or the ninth hour, 12 noon, or 3pm, that every table should have two cooked dishes, on account of individual infirmities, so that he who perchance cannot eat of the one, may take his meat of the other. Therefore let two cooked dishes suffice for the brethren; and if any fruit or young vegetables are available let a third be added. Let a good pound weight of bread suffice for the day, whether there be one meal only, or both dinner and supper. If they are to have supper, let a third part of the pound be reserved by the cellarer, to be given to them for their supper. But if their work chance to be heavier, the abbots shall have the choice and the power, should it be expedient, to increase this allowance." Above all things, however, gluttony must be avoided, so that a monk never be surprised by a surfeit; for there is nothing so unfitting for a Christian, as surfeiting, according to Our Lord's words: "Take heed lest your hearts be overcharged with surfeiting." Young boys shall not receive the same amount of food as their elders, but less; and frugality shall be observed in all circumstances. "Except the sick who are very weak, let all abstain entirely from the flesh of four-footed animals."[10]

At Dunster, the small community of five monks and a prior were well provided for, for William de Mohun I gave to the priory of Dunster, two fishing places, one of which was in Dunster and the other in Carhampton. This grant was confirmed by William II ("Rufus") and by Edward III. Apart from fish, pork also would have been served at the refectory table for we know that Reynold de Mohun II granted to the prior and monks of Dunster and their successors in perpetuity every tenth pig 'live or dead' belonging to him at Dunster, Carhampton and Kilton, in accordance with the terms of the compromise of 1241. In 1240 there had been a controversy between the monks and Sir Reynold in which, among other things, they claimed a tithe of pigs at the aforesaid places and they won the day. The pigs caused some concern, however, and the burgesses of Dunster and the prior were frequently fined for allowing these pigs to roam at large although, it must be said, they would have fulfilled a needful role as scavengers. Apart from pork and pigeon, no doubt rabbits also, and a well to supply fresh water, the supplies of the priory were further enhanced by gifts of wheat. In 1358, John de Mohun V directed the bailiff and provost of Dunster to deliver four quarters of wheat to the monks of Dunster. The vegetables were grown in the prior's garden part of which adjoined the churchyard to the east. It was a productive garden for at Christmas time 1405, Lady Catherine Luttrell, who was celebrating her first Christmas at Dunster, was presented by the prior with a bushel of green peas. The garden was a secluded one and was not allowed to be overlooked. Between 1261 and 1290 Walter de Anno, prior of Bath, granted John le Barre a piece of ground next to the prior's garden. The rent was to be 8d. and the ground was to be about 40ft x 16ft but it was expressly laid down that the house which was to be built on this land should have no doors or windows towards the prior's garden.

Pigeons were consumed by the Benedictines in great numbers and provided the monks with a constant supply of fresh meat. Rev. Alderson states that until "Turnip" Townsend introduced root crops in 1730, sheep and oxen could only be fed in winter in very limited numbers and at Michaelmas those that were big and fat enough were slaughtered and either eaten or salted. Pigeons, apart from wood pigeons, who only bred twice a year, provided an almost constant supply of fresh meat because of their exceptionally short breeding cycle. Every six weeks for nearly the whole year, they lay a pair of eggs, hatch them out, fatten up two 1lb squabs "on pigeon milk," and then lay two more eggs. This cycle they repeat contentedly for the whole seven years of their useful breeding life together. Nor do they mind their young being taken after they have laid their next pair of eggs, as in any case, they push the fledglings out of the nest to make them fly. As both parents are fully occupied rearing their young and stay together as a pair for life, pigeons can live together peacefully at close quarters and in large numbers 1,000 or more. To maintain the numbers at full strength indefinitely, it is only necessary to keep back one pair from each nest every seven years. The Dunster dovecote could produce every week up to 200 three-week-old squabs, enough to supply the Castle and Priory with pigeon pie twice a week. Preb Hancock dates the dovecot to the 13th century and says: "A little to the west is the prior's dovecot, a building of 13th-century date. The door and jambs are of great antiquity, and within may still be seen one of those revolving ladders which were used to take the young pigeons from the nests. A terrible tragedy is on record with regard to this dovecot. It is related that when one spring it was full of birds, old and young (it would contain quite two thousand) someone shut up and forgot to open the window which gave the pigeons egress to obtain food for themselves and their young and that all the occupants were starved to death!"[11]

Alderson describes the dovecote: "at first its lovely conical roof was open at the top to allow the pigeons to fly in and out, but it was later given the present closed one to protect the revolving ladders from rain. Ash wood if allowed to get wet, soon begins to rot. At the same time an opening was made high up in the wall to enable the pigeons to forage for food in the surrounding country." It is the type of circular columbarium standard in the late Norman period. The roof was kept in good repair first by the monks and later by the Luttrells of Dunster Castle, but nearly all dovecotes were abandoned as soon as it became easy to get fresh meat throughout the year. There appears to have been another dovecote in Dunster for in 1266, "the cow-house and the stable, with accommodation for a hundred beasts, the dovecot, and the dairy lay outside the Castle, far below, near the river."[12]

Among the endowments given by William de Mohun to the monks of Bath before the year 1100, was the tithe of his vines at Dunster which would not have been mentioned in his charter unless accounted of some value. The cellarer was in charge of the supplies for the monastery and all guests. He was to keep the keys, and sample the wine. "As cellarer of the monastery let there be chosen out of the community a man who is prudent, of mature character, temperate, not a great eater, nor proud, nor headstrong, not rough spoken, not lazy, not wasteful, a God fearing man who may be like a father to the whole community. Let him have charge of everything; let him do nothing without the abbot's orders but keep to his instructions. Let him not vex the brethren. If any brother happen to make unreasonable demand he should not vex him with a contemptuous denial, but reasonably, and humbly refuse the improper request. Let him keep guard over his soul, remembering always the saying of the apostle that he that hath served well, secured for himself a good standing. Let him take the greatest care of the sick, of children, of guests and of the poor, knowing without doubt that he will have to render an account for all these on the Day of Judgement. Let him look upon all the utensils of the monastery and its whole property as upon the sacred vessels of the altar. Let him not think that anything may be neglected. Let him neither practise avarice, nor be wasteful and a squanderer of the monastery's substance; but let him do all things with measure and in accordance with the instruction of the abbot. Above all things, let him have humility, and if he have nothing else to give, let him a good word in answer; for it is written. 'A good word is above the best gift'. Let him have under his care all those things which the abbot has assigned to him, but presume not to deal with what he has forbidden to him. Let him give the brethren their appointed allowance of food without any arrogance or delay, that they may not be scandalised, mindful of what the scripture saith that he deserves, 'who shall scandalise one of these little ones'. If the community be a large one, let helpers be given him, so that by their assistance he may fulfil with a quiet mind the charge that has been committed to him. Let those things which have to be asked for and those things which have to be given, be asked for and given at the proper time; so that no one may be troubled or vexed in the house of God."

One of the guests at the prior's table was the lord's "faithful granger" who appeared at threshing time. In the Mohun cartulary there is a treatise on husbandry which was written for the benefit of the lord of Dunster in the first half of the 14th century. The treatise was written in clumsy French, the first half of it is missing, but the remaining portion deals with the arrangements subsequent to the harvest. The crops were to be gathered into the barns and were to undergo three valuations before they were threshed. The first was made by the sworn "homage" men, presumably chosen at the court baron of the manor. The writer of the treatise dismissed this valuation as the "members of the 'homage' might be fearful of being held responsible if the yield should not come up to expectations." The second valuation was to be made "by the bailiff, sworn upon the book of the Gospel." The third valuation was made by the auditors of the lord's accounts, or if they were unavailable, by the steward or constable, with two or three reliable neighbours with experience in this field, and two or three of the old threshers who were acquainted with the barns and well able to estimate the yield of every sheaf and stack. At the conclusion of these valuations the lord would be in a position, with the assistance of his council, to decide on the household requirements so that the remainder could be sold. The treatise then ordains that a faithful "granger" be appointed. He was to be supplied with a horse and it was considered un-necessary to appoint more than one granger for the manors of Dunster, Minehead and Kilton, all of which belonged to the Mohun demesne. If the lord or his lady was in residence at the castle he took his meals at their board but if they were absent, he was expected to eat at the Benedictine priory, or failing that, in the house of some respectable townsman. The houses of the reeve and bailiff were "out of bounds" because it was thought that the granger might be tempted into dishonest ways if he took food at their tables, although, in any case, if the lord was staying at the castle, the reeve also had his food there. The granger had to swear that when he came to Dunster to superintend the threshing we would securely lock and seal the doors of the barns every evening and not being trusted with the custody of the keys, he was required to deliver them, duly sealed to the constable of the castle, or to the prior. When he stayed at Minehead or Kilton, he resided with the vicar who, though independent of the lord of Dunster, was nevertheless expected to receive and be responsible for him and it was to the vicar of these parishes that the granger was expected to deliver his keys every evening. This fascinating treatise refers on several occasions to a "chariour e bernbrutte," who appears to have had some authority over the threshers. There seems to have been much suspicion and frugality to the point of meanness for we read: "even if a man employs his own brother as a thresher he must watch him with eyes before and behind." The husks had to be re-threshed if necessary and no residues were permitted to be given to the destriers or war-horses, to the palfrey, or to the steward's horses, or to those of the constable, the bailiff or the reeve. Placed in a separate store house, they would be useful to the lord's capons, chickens or pigeons. The bailiff was to see that during the threshing every tenth or twentieth sheaf of corn should be set aside, as a criterion of the amount that the entire crop should yield. It was also laid down that when it came to distributing or selling the grain, the bailiff and the "chariour e bernbrutte" were to abide by the standard bushel sanctioned by royal ordinance "without heap or cantle." Finally the treatise advises that, "the 'launds' at Marshwood Park should be ploughed and sown" and that "the remainder of it should be enclosed to contain the deer." There were four hundred acres at Marshwood and the writer of the treatise voiced the opinion that if cow houses and storehouses were established there, Marshwood might be made to yield more profit than all the demesne of Dunster.[13] In August 1342, John de Mohun V granted to the monks: "twelve cartloads of windfall wood for fuel from Marshwood Park, and the 'foreign' woods of Dunster, provided that the carts should not be too large to be drawn by two horses."[14] He also remitted to them a yearly rent of 1lb. of pepper from Kilton and gave them common pasture in Croydon for all their beasts at Cowbridge and pasture on Grabbist.[15]

The vicar of Dunster was subordinate to the prior and his income so small in the Middle Ages that he often resigned. Richard, the chaplain in the reign of King John, was vicar of Dunster and his successor Robert de Vaus was given the "perpetual vicarage" of Dunster and he was promised that he should have free food at the monastic table, food for his groom or servant and forage for his palfrey.[16] As the monks were not necessarily in priest's orders and were liable at any time to be recalled to the mother house at Bath, it was convenient that the care of souls and the maintenance of services for the lay folk, should be entrusted to a secular vicar by the prior of Bath and to some extent dependent upon him, but instituted, as a benefice by the bishop of the diocese and liable to be removed without good cause. An ordinance of 1512 maintains the same requirement of free food for all at the priory. The bishop of Bath and Wells, Cardinal Hadrian de Castello, decreed: "that the Vicar should receive free meals in the monastic refectory, sitting at table below the Prior and brethren but sharing in their food and in the refreshments provided by the fireside in the winter evenings." He also assigned to the Vicar a small meadow, a rent of 2s. from a fulling-mill and the rent of the former vicarage, the Prior being required to provide for him a room adjoining the graveyard.[17] The "sting in the tail" was that the provision of all these things resulted in his yearly stipend being reduced from £8 to £4.

In 1330, Sir John de Chueberri, chaplain, had also received a grant from the prior of Bath of a corrody out of the funds of the house at Dunster and in 1357 John Osebern received a similar corrody. Always, the prior of Bath is paramount; signing leases and all contracts of importance even engaging the officials of the priory, such as the gate-keeper. In 1345 the prior of Bath, borrowing from his priory, pledged the prior of Dunster for £32 of silver. He granted rooms in the priory buildings at Dunster and board and lodgings in the priory seemingly without any reference to the prior of Dunster. Simon de Wynton was granted a corrody and lodgings in his house at Dunster 'as long as he lived'.

SERVICES

In the 14th century an agreement was made between John de Mohun V and the prior, Richard de Childeston, the monks and the parishioners with regard to the services of the church, the provision of lights, and the repair and maintenance of the aisles and the central tower.[18] The agreement, in clumsy French, is dated "in the 13th [30th] year of the reign of King Edward, Friday next after the feast of St Wulstan," is as follows:

1. On festivals and Sundays, the prior and the monks shall begin their service at such a time that high mass may be said in summer, between Easter and Michaelmas, by the hour of tierce (nine o'clock), and in winter, between Michaelmas and Easter, by twelve o'clock at latest. The monk who is to perform the high mass shall bless the water, and shall sprinkle it throughout the church if the Vicar be not ready to do so. The Prior, the monks, and the Vicar shall unite in one procession, after which the high mass be begun at the altar of St George. There the parishioners shall make their offerings four times a year. On festivals, the Vicar may begin to say mass privately at the altar of the Holy Rood for his parishioners after the reading of the gospel at high mass.
2. At Christmas, Epiphany, Easter, Trinity and the feasts of St John Baptist and Sts Peter and Paul, the parishioners shall provide two candles, and the Prior a third to burn on the altar of St George at vespers, at matins, at the high mass, and at the second vespers, and at these festivals the parishioners shall provide candles for the choir as necessity may require. On the three days before Easter, the parishioners shall provide all the lights for the hearse except the "Judas" which the Prior and the monks shall provide, and the parishioners shall provide candles for the choir, any remains being saved. The parishioners shall provide one half of the Pascal Candle, and the monks the other half. After the feast of the Trinity, any of the wax of the Pascal Candle remaining over shall be divided evenly between the monks and the parishioners. The parishioners shall provide a lamp to burn before the altar of St George at night for ever, and the monks shall provide another lamp to burn there by day. For other lights, the parishioners shall give to the Prior and monks, two pounds of wax at Michaelmas yearly for ever.
3. The Prior shall repair and roof the tower suitably without defect, and shall receive from the parishioners 8 marks in three instalments. He shall roof, and for ever maintain the

chapel of Our Lady and the dorter aisle. The parishioners shall for ever maintain the chapel of St Leonard and the aisle between the chapel of St Lawrence and the tower.[19]

Although, it will be seen that relations greatly deteriorated and reached a climax at the end of the 15th century, at this time, in the middle of the 14th century, whilst some rivalry existed, there was also a good deal of co-operation between the prior and the monks and the Dunster parishioners. The rivalry centred round the differences between the regular and secular clergy; the latter being supported by the laity whose vicar was only permitted to say the low mass in the nave of the church. The visible expressions of co-operation were shown in the combined forces of the prior, the monks and the secular vicar, processing as one body, and in the fact that the parishioners not only made their offering four times a year at the altar of St George at the extreme east end of the church, but they also provided candles and the night light for the high altar to which the monks had an exclusive right. The prior and the monks were, it would appear from the 1357 Agreement, responsible for the maintenance of the priory chancel, where in all probability they had their stalls. Less probably they were installed beneath the tower, then a squat Norman tower which did not assume its present appearance until the middle of the 15th century. The high mass was conducted at the altar of St George. The deacon and sub-deacon would have occupied the sedilia which was, as is the present Victorian one, on the south side of the chancel, and music and holy chanting would have reverberated throughout the great building.

On festivals, the vicar said low mass at the altar of the Holy Rood, on top of the rood screen which, until it fell into decay, existed between the two western piers of the crossing. On other occasions low mass was conducted in the nave of the church, the maintenance of which was the responsibility of the parishioners. We have to imagine no 1498 screen, altar or choir as we see them today, and only the altar of St James at the base of the south west pier, apart from other side altars. The low mass, we are told: "grew up in the Middle Ages when the practice of each priest saying a Mass daily became common and the elaborate ceremonial and considerable number of assistants traditionally required for the liturgy, were no longer practicable. In a Low Mass there are no ministers to assist the priest except a single server; there is no choir; and no part of the service is sung by the celebrant. The celebrating priest, therefore, in the absence of both the sub-deacon and deacon reads the Epistle and Gospel himself."[20]

The parishioners were never entirely excluded from the priory church and in 1539, after the monks had departed and the observances of the Roman Catholic church were discontinued in the reign of Edward VI (1547-53), they recovered their rights in the chancel of the priory church. In 1498 when relations between the prior and monks and parishioners had reached a low ebb, the parishioners built the new screen 25 feet west of the decayed former rood-screen and formed their own choir. Some of the terms used in the 1357 Agreement are of interest. The "hearse," for example, was "an elaborate frame of wood or metal fitted with prickets for candles, which recalled the teeth of a harrow."[21] The triangular frame and the 15 candles it bore were, at Dunster, provided by the parishioners. Its use during the service of Tenebrae was a most dramatic evocation of the death of Christ and His descent into Hell. The service of Tenebrae – the Matins and Laud of the last three days of Holy Week – were actually sung on the three preceding evenings. Tenebrae literally means "darkness" and during this most solemn of services the lights of the church were extinguished one by one; the only flickering light being provided by the "hearse." Gradually the descent into Hell was further evoked by the extinction of each of the 15 candles, again one by one at the end of each successive psalm. Finally at the conclusion of the Benedictus the last candle died, and in utter darkness and desolation, the Miserere was recited. The day which commemorates the resting of Christ's body in the tomb was called Holy Saturday. On that day preceding Easter Sunday, the Pascal candle was placed on a large separate candlestick on the north side of the sanctuary and was lit, from the new fire, with great solemnity, by the deacon. The candle would have exuded an aromatic scent, for five grains of incense were inserted into its stem. The singing of the Exultet – or "Pascal Praise," sung to one of the finest chants in the Latin liturgy, reverberated through the church. The great candle burned, especially at liturgical functions during; Eastertide, until its extinction, after the reading of the Gospel, on Ascension Day.[22] A wonderful sense of drama, of darkness and despair followed by light and joy was engendered by these medieval practices, which must have had a powerful impact on the towns people of Dunster whose lives were bounded by the church, their lord, the demands of crops and animals, the ever present rumblings of wars and tumult, near and far, and from 1348, coming from Dorset, the horror of the Black Death.

An explanation of vespers is : "The Evening Office…together with Lauds is the oldest of the 'Day hours', but it was originally part of the Night Office, also called 'lucenarium'… because candles were lit at its celebration. From the time of St Benedict the office was recited earlier in the evening, before dark, and since the Middle Ages, in the afternoon and in Lent even before midday."[23] The reference to the second vespers accords to this day with the Roman Rite when all Sundays and feasts of double rank, having both a first and second vespers.

There was little congregational participation in the church services and no hymns were sung. The laity attended mass and it was obligatory to partake of the Lord's supper at Easter time. They knelt in the pewless and cold churches and they knelt in the street when the priest passed with the Host on his way to administer Extreme Unction to the dying. Until 1672 and the Declaration against, transubstantiation, the belief that at the Eucharist the bread and wine were converted into the whole substance of the Body and Blood of Christ, was a belief universally held by the church. The priests were only semi-literate and the people rarely heard a sermon, but they, themselves were simple and deeply superstitious. They took their pleasures in the processions, the plays, the church ales and in the pageantry provided by their lord and their church. All these rituals knit together the fabric of medieval life. With the coming of the Reformation, England was never the same again; her sense of religious and social integration was dealt a blow so severe that the country people must have felt devastated and bereft of all that they and their forebears, had known and enjoyed communally. The coming of the church house, possessed by many parishes by 1500, meant that the activities which had formerly taken place in the nave of the church, could now be accommodated elsewhere. The nave of the church could now acquire pews and seats and the fund raising events found a home in the church house of which there is a splendid example at Crowcombe. There, for a hundred years the large meeting-room served as a centre for social gatherings and wedding feasts. Then came the Reformation and the rising, puritanical ideas of the late 16th and early 17th centuries which put an end to the traditional merry-making of England in its medieval form. The church house at Yatton was started as early as 1445 and Dr Bettey gives a list of its very useful contents: "A chettyll (kettle) 2 grett crocks 2 lyttl crocks 4 pannys a botum for a panne a brandyce 5 tun vats 2 kyve vates 2 trowys (troughs) 9 stands barrellys 21 trandyllys (trendles) 6 borde cloths (table cloths)."[24]

PRIORY ORGANISATION

We read in the *County History of Somerset* that the church and property was so far from Bath that they could not be managed and served from the mother priory, and there must have been, from the earliest times a cell found there. This reference to the "earliest times" may relate to the charter of William de Mohun I which contains the earliest mention of the church at Dunster. Although not dated, it was issued during the episcopate of John de Villula in the reign of William "Rufus" and may certainly be ascribed to the period between 1090 and 1100. The first specific reference to a religious house in Dunster occurs in 1177 when the bishop of Winchester, as guardian or the heir of William paid 54s. "to the monks of St George, Dunster, for tithes...etc." The see of Bath and Wells dates from 1242. In 1262 a prior of Dunster is referred to and this would have been Prior Martin who held that office between 1257 and 1274. The Bath records show very clearly that the revenues of Dunster were administered at Bath, leased lands were made out in the name of the prior of the mother convent, and though we read of the prior's garden and his vineyard, yet the cell had no separate existence with its own prior and family of monks until the 14th century. It is doubtful if this small cell had any definite organisation at this time. In the 1380s there was a dispute concerning the tithes of Shurton in the parish of Stogursey which had been given to the priory of Dunster but which were claimed by the monks of Stogursey. The Prior of Dunster is mentioned in the proceedings but he takes no part in the litigation. The Prior of Bath is the plaintiff and the Prior of Stogursey the defendant and judgement was given in favour of the monks of Bath as the owners of the priory of Dunster.[25] The priory of Stogursey was the only alien house which was not made a denizen of Somerset and was a cell of the Norman abbey of Lonlay. Preb Hancock gives the dates as 1282/3 and not the 1380s. He quotes from the Bath Cartularies (No. 842) and says: A long dispute arose between the prior of Bath and the vicar of Kilton on one side, and the prior and monks of Stogursey on the other, concerning the tithes of Shurton (a hamlet in the parish of Stogursey). Henry de Lyncombe is attorney for the prior of Bath, Henry de Cumba for Robert de Camyng, vicar of Kelveton, and Geoffrey de Tynnoch for John de Mulecote, prior of Stogursey. The case was tried at Canterbury at great length, and decided in the favour of the prior of Bath, the prior of Stogursey receiving five marks from the prior of Dunster, and acknowledging aforesaid tithes to be the right of the prior of Bath and the vicar of Kilton from the foundation of the priory of Dunster.[26] Further information in the *County History of Somerset* reveals that: "In the Taxatio of Pope Nicholas IV, 1291, the priory (of Bath) is valued as enjoying an income from lands and rents of £5 13s 3d, and from churches and ecclesiastical dues of £13 7s 4d." The spiritualia came from the churches of Dunster and Carhampton, and pensions due to the prior from the churches of Stogumber, Cutcombe and Luxborough. The, temporalia were derived from lands etc. at Doverhay, Timberscombe, Wynard, Kyrington, Wylales, Cowbridge Cutcombe, Kenwardston and Lollokesworth. With regard to the spiritualia, in Lyte's words: Under an arrangement made between 1290 and 1301, the prior and monks of Dunster used to pay 20 marks (£5 8s 4d) a year to the mother house at Bath for the two churches of Carhampton, of which half a mark was due to the chamberlain on the feast of St Carantoc and a like amount on the anniversary of Martin prior of Dunster.[27] In the *County History* there are two versions which concern the appointment of Robert de Sutton to the priorship of Dunster. These are: "On the death of Prior Clopcote, 26 February 1332, the convent proceeded at once to elect Robert de Sutton on 7 March 1332 as prior (of Bath) but the election appears to have been irregular, for the resignation of Clopcote or a promise to that effect had been forwarded to the pope and the people's acceptance of it had not arrived in Bath when he died. The pope, therefore claimed to appoint to the priorship and Thomas Crist was chosen by him, and on 24 September 1332 Bishop Ralph of Shrewsbury confirmed Crist in his appointment as prior. To compensate Sutton he was made Prior of Dunster and that distant property became a dependent priory rather than an isolated cell. He was granted also a pension of £20 and permission to have with him at Dunster such friends as he desired. If any of them should prove troublesome Sutton had only to complain and the offender would be removed to Bath, (et alius magis quietus et maturas loco sul rogetur)."

The second version of the appointment of Robert de Sutton as a prior of Dunster is in the chapter on Religious Houses contained in the same volume. The appointment of Robert de Sutton, Prior of Dunster in 1332 of which the announcement was made by the Prior of

Bath to Ralph de Shrewsbury, Bishop of Bath and Wells, marks probably the beginning of the existence of Dunster as a distinct priory, dependent on Bath but able to a certain extent to manage its own affairs. Robert de Sutton had been elected, by the monks of Bath as their prior in succession to Robert de Clopcote, who died in March 1332 (the first version gives the date of death as 26 February 1332). It would seem that Clopcote had forwarded something like a deed of resignation to the pope when he unexpectedly died at Bath. Whatever had actually occurred, Pope John XXII claimed the right to appoint the new prior, and appointed Thomas Crist. Provision had therefore to be made for Robert de Sutton, who had been so hurriedly elected prior and so unexpectedly removed from office. So he was appointed by Crist as Prior of Dunster. He was allowed an income of £20 and to have such companions (socios) as he chose. If any of those sent him at Dunster should prove himself troublesome or should not be pleasing to the prior, he was to be recalled and another sent from Bath in his place. When Prior Sutton became old and infirm he might return at any time to Bath. Such terms were, of course, only personal and would not apply to future priors. Robert Clopcote is mentioned as having been rebuked by Bishop Drokensford for maladministration in 1321 and again in 1331. As Robert de Clopcote's resignation was made at the Roman Court of Avignon, the pope, Clement VI (this should probably be Pope John XXII) in accordance with a usurpation of immemorial antiquity, appointed his successor, annulling the election of Robert de Sutton (to Bath), who, on 24 October 1332, received from the convent a pension of £20, and the office of Prior of Dunster." The pension appears to be made up thus – from Bridgwater, £5, from Shurton, £2 15s 0d., from the portions of chamberlain and pitancer, £7 6s. 8d., from Bampton 18s. 4d, and from the common fund £4. On 24 October 1332 Robert de Sutton received 18s. 4d. from Bampton but by 11 November 1332 there seems to have been a remarkable increase for the letters of the Prior: to Master Roger Hussee, clerk, rector of the church of Baunton (Bampton) commanding him to pay Robert de Sutton during his life fifty shillings annual pension which the Prior ought to receive from the church at Baunton. Dated, Monday next after the feast of St Martin the Bishop (November 11) 1332.[28]

Hancock tells us: "In 1330 the foundation of the priory appears to have been remodelled and prior Robert of Bath declares by charter that the cell of Dunster, founded by Sir John de Mohun and Ada, his wife, and where the said Sir John is buried, shall consist of a prior and four brethren."[29]

LIST OF PRIORS

1257-74	Martin	Cartulary of Mynchin Buckland; D.C.M. VIII, 2; XVII, 1
1301	R	Two cartularies of Bath, L 580
1308	Walter	Two cartularies of Bath, L 560
1332	Robert de Sutton	Dugdale's *Monasticon*, Vol. II, 259
1337	Adam de Cheddar	Two cartularies L 780
1355	William Thouer	Assize Roll No. 772, m27
1376	John Hervey	D.C.M. I, 4
1411-17	William Bristow	D.C.M. XI, 1; D.C.B., No.71
1423	John Buryton	D.C.M. XII, 1
1425	John Henton	D.C.B., No.81; Weaver's *Somerset Incumbents*, 361
1437	William Cary	D.C.M. XVIII, 6
1443	Thomas Lacock	D.C.M. XII, 3
1449	Richard	D.C.M. XII, 3
1463	William Hampton	Brit. Mus. Add. MS. 25887
1470	William Bristow	D.C.M. XII, 3
1489-94	John Abyndon	Weaver's *Somerset Incumbents*, 326

1498	Thomas Browne	Prior at time of 1498 Agreement
1504	Richard Pester	*Somerset Medieval Wills*, Vol. II, 61
1509	Thomas	D.C.M. XIII, 1
1535	John Griffith	D.C.M. XIII, 4; *Valor Ecclesiasticus*, Vol. I, 220
		He signed the deed of surrender in 1539.

DUNSTER PRIORY

On entering the priory gate, whose iron fittings still exist in the wall outside the Georgian house of that name, the scene on the right when Priory Green turns to the left, would have been of rolling pastures where the sheep and cattle belonging to the priory grazed on the green. This was the Priory Farm which led down to the dovecot, none of the present houses being then in existence, and to that hub of activity known in 1431 as the Barnecourt and shown on the 1771 estate map as "the Yard." Here was the probably 16th-century tithe barn which may have replaced an earlier barn, with its three straw houses and flanked on its northern side by a cart-house. Behind the dovecote or pigeon house there was a barn, a shippen for housing cattle and a linney or linhay where mown or "lain" hay was stored. These three buildings were backed by the rising ground on which the Victorian rectory was built. Along the wall of the present rectory garden there was a further linney. Flanking this wall was the priory garden which contained a melon garden and a stable located in the corner before the springing of the arch which makes the exit from the priory into St George's Street. Opposite the house known as Melon Garden is a limehouse of great antiquity. Its windows are probably 14th-century and would have had wooden shutters rather than glass which was not made in any great quantity before the end of the century. Next to it is a small opening, now padlocked, which formerly housed the funeral bier. In the "Cloyster Garden," now called the Remembrance Garden, a further linney ran north-south along the eastern boundary. The prior's dwelling next to this garden is now known as the Old Priory. This, after the Dissolution of the Monasteries, became a farmhouse for many years.

It is likely that the site of the church at Dunster was preceded by a Saxon church and before it was one of pagan worship. Springs and wells are associated with pagan worship and when Christianised became holy wells. St Leonard's well 'under Grobbefast' was mentioned in 1375.[30] The prior of Dunster was responsible for the maintenance of Conduit Lane[31] which leads steeply up the north side of Grabbist, where there is the little 15th-century building which encloses the well. Pipes have been found underground leading from this well to the Old Priory. In St George's Street is a fountain marked now by a grill in the wall and pipes go from the Old Priory through the churchyard to the conduit in Church Street. According to Hancock: "The water of this spring was brought down in early times to supply the priory and the castle. …It is possible, therefore, that a trough or pump at which the villagers could obtain water, was situated here."[32] The conduit, 'le cundyte' is mentioned in the reign of Henry VI. The pipes conveying the water passed close or under the recess which is also said to be 15th century. This recess was known as the 'bow' or 'shoop under the Churchyard wall'[33] in Church Street, and in 1680 it was let out by the churchwardens at 1s. a year to John Pleasway. The rent later went up to 15s. to three persons. In 1682 the churchwardens accounts show that: 'It is agreed that William Pleasway is to have and enjoy ye shoop under ye Churchgate walle for his naturall life after his father.[34] It is possible that a lavatorium existed along the side of the priory cloister. There is a gully along the base of the wall of the north aisle of the church which then goes underground to a medieval stone culvert in the present Luttrell burial ground. It is possible that a lavatorium existed here, alongside the priory cloister. This was the monks' washing place and a good deal of hand washing was decreed in the routine of the cloistered monk.

Just in front of the principal door of the prior's dwelling is a well, now filled up, which is said to have been sixty feet deep.[35] The supply of water to the priory was of great importance and the monks would also have been adept at diverting and channelling streams to bring water and to carry away refuse.

CLOISTER

The square cloister garth is of great interest at Dunster. Hancock says: 'A cloister ran from the priory along the north side of the church, perhaps as far as the chapel of St Lawrence (now re-named the de Mohun Chantry Chapel.). The garden, into which the door in the north transept opens, is called in Mr. Luttrell's estate maps, "The Cloister Court," and one old map shows what appears to be a row of pillars running parallel with the church.[36] The reference to "a row of pillars," however does not apply to the 18th-century map which shows, in fact, a depiction of the buttresses of the north and south aisles.

Dr. Francis Eeles in his excellent guide, *The Church of St George. Dunster* (1940), disagrees with Hancock concerning his remark "perhaps as far as the chapel of St Lawrence," for he says: There is nothing to suggest that the cloister was east of the transept, as at Rochester, and there are no remains of a dorter, chapterhouse, frater or anything else, save only a house on an L-plan partly on the north side of the blank wall of the nave, partly beyond the line of the west end of the church which was the Prior's lodging.[37] He also says: "On the direct evidence of the old estate maps the cloister would have been on the north side of the nave [I think to be strictly correct he means 'north side of the north aisle'], immediately to the west of the north transept, out of which a doorway opens westward. But the range of large windows in the north aisle of the church makes it impossible that any south cloister walk was attached to the church in the usual way, and a raggle on a high level at the east end of the aisle wall indicates a roof on a high level running north and south along the west side of the transept."[38] Today, I feel certain that I have, through a key clue revealed by the estate map, been able to solve the mystery of the exact location of the cloister. The map shows that there is a "Cloyster Court" in the situation indicated by Dr Eeles but it is in the east wall of the Remembrance Garden that the answer lies. This wall, as it exists today, separates the grassy paddock-like area, (formerly, before it was the site of the Luttrell greenhouses, one of the priory gardens which leads to the Village Garden), from the Remembrance Garden. On the "paddock" side the wall is dated 1771 but the map reveals that prior to that date, a wall ran in that position from the western end of the transept only as far as the point where it met, at right angles, the wall of the "paddock" running east and west. It then continued east of the 1771 wall but parallel with it and then, about half-way along its length, it made a right-angled turn and continued even further east parallel with the 1771 wall until it returned at right-angles to the tithe barn. In front of the last range of the wall on the Remembrance Garden side, supports shown on the map indicate the position of a former linney. At the south-eastern end of the paddock which, as I have said, was a priory garden, lay George Poole's garden and also, at that time, the Village Garden was Robert Thomas's garden. The length of the north aisle is exactly the same as the length of the wall of the Remembrance Garden up to the point where it meets the east-west "paddock" wall. A perfect square is formed and lines up with the end of the range of the prior's dwelling on the other side of the west wall of the Remembrance garden. This square was the site of the former cloister.

We know that the most primitive type of cloister was roofed with a wooden lean-to and this was supported on the courtyard side by arcades of coupled columns set at right angles to the line of the arcades so as to give greater strength to the thrust of the roof, and the dorter aisle (actually the north transept) would have had a stair leading to the dorter, or dormitory, of the monks.

The former cloister would have had a sloping roof forming a covered arcade which the prior and his monks emerging from the prior's dwelling, would have used to reach the north door. When considering this cloister, probably a wooden construction, it is interesting to remember that the concept of St Benedict, was of a community of monks living as a family round one patio, or cloister, under one roof, indeed a villa monastery. We read: "the classical lay-out of the Benedictine abbeys and priories of the Middle Ages was descended from the plan of the Roman country villa of late antiquity."[39]

The churchwarden's accounts for Dunster in 1701 give us the following: "John Horman towards ye timber in ye Closter Courte. 20s.0d."[40] This seems to have been for a repair job. A sum of £11 per quarter was paid by 167 ratepayers in 1700 "for the repairing of the psh [parish] Church of the said psh."[41] It would seem that the church was at this time in a bad state of repair. John Hossome and Robert Strickland were the churchwardens at the time. In 1703 a further entry relates to the Cloister Court: "Paid for bringing the Timber out of the Cloister Court into the Church 1s 6d."[42] Preb Hancock refers to these accounts and observes: "In the churchwardens' accounts for the year 1701 (he means 1703 according to the entry above quoted) is the significant entry, "Paid for hauling the timber out of the Cloister Court," as though, even at that date, the dismantling of the priory and the cloister was still going on. The 17th-century fireplace over the priory door of the church looks as if an upper chamber had been constructed over the cloister after the buildings had been secularised. I do not believe that the "upper chamber" was constructed after the building was secularised in 1539, because the January 1357 Agreement refers to "la ele dortur."

OLD PRIORY

The "Old Priory" was formerly the prior's dwelling and the monks took their meals here. Geoffrey Webb says that Benedictine refectories generally lay east and west parallel to the church along the side of the cloister,[43] and that the western side of the cloister was used for a variety of purposes such as the prior's lodging.[44] The shorter side, running east and west parallel to the church and along the side of the cloister, appears to Hancock to have been the refectory, or principal room of the priory. It was designed, evidently, to be open to the roof which is waggon shaped and has timber of massive oak planed to show.[45] A typical plan of buildings of this Order has the refectory was generally parallel to the nave, while the dormitory was on another side with a stair leading to the church for night services.[46]

A little north-west of the old priory is the prior's barn, a large, possibly 16th-century building, with massive door jambs. Unfortunately it has of late years to be re-roofed.[47] The monks left in 1539 and if the barn is of the 16th century it was only in use by the monks for a few years and probably replaced an earlier barn. If after the 2005 survey it is proved to be 16th century, it is more probable that when Dame Margaret Luttrell obtained possession of the Priory in 1560, this barn was erected. It was used by Mr Luttrell at a later date as the estate workshop.

The roof of the prior's dwelling is of three-tiered wind-brace construction. The hall of the present "Old Priory," now has a lowered ceiling to provide bedrooms above. The leaded stone mullioned window of three lights in this room is said to be not later than c.1380 and therefore of the reign of Richard II. The ogee-headed lights may well substantiate this date. The fireplace, of somewhat later date was only "recently found," according to Hancock writing in 1905 and was said to bear "traces of colouring and gilding."[48] I would describe the fireplace as having within its rectangular surround, a three-centred arch or "anse de panier" basket arch. Within the spandrels of the arch are quatre-foiled circles flanked by trefoil headed panels. The panel motif, which is simply arched but with the arch cusped is the "signature" of English Perpendicular and is ubiquitous in the parish churches of England and is found notably in window tracery but also in blank wall decoration. This style started *c*.1330 but, in spite of the intervention of the English Renaissance exemplified in the Florentine Pietro Torrigiani's tombs of Henry VII and his wife Elizabeth of York in Westminster Abbey of 1511 etc. and later Henry VIII's favour, it persisted for 250 years. This makes it extremely difficult to date the fireplace but in view of the re-building of *c*.1500 in Dunster church following on the Glastonbury Agreement of 1498. I would suggest it, may be earlier 16th century, but this is open to debate and may belong to the early 15th century as suggested by Lyte. There is no trace today of colouring or gilding visible to the naked eye.

The room to the west of the refectory which itself is divided into two, was probably the prior's parlour. Viewed from the exterior, it is evident that the window of this room which opens into the churchyard, was originally of higher dimensions; the remains of a square-headed Perpendicular window can still be traced. The building running north-south adjacent to the main dwelling may have been uses as guest accommodation or offices. An example of more permanent occupation was the granting by Thomas, prior of Bath (1290-1301) to Simon de Wynton of a lodging in 'his house of Dunster as long as he shall live'.[49]

The priory at Dunster did not lack means; for example in 1392 Peter de Bratton gave some lands at Sparkhay, Porlock to the priory. In 1417 Canon Richard Bruton of Wells left 26s 8d to the prior and convent of Dunster.

COFFIN LIDS

One of the priors of Dunster is still remembered by virtue of his coffin-lid, inscribed Adam De Che and bearing a foliated cross, which is to be found in the south transept. Adam de Cheddar was appointed prior of Dunster by Thomas prior of Bath, on 5 July 1337 in the reign of Edward III and during the lordship of John de Mohun V of Dunster. His appointment was ratified by the papal nuncio in England of Pope Benedict XII, Bernard Cysta' in the August of that year. In 1345 there is mention of the sumptuous buildings erected by Adam de Cheddar but since he was chamberlain of the great Benedictine house at Bath, it is unknown whether this is a reference to Dunster or to Bath. Sir H. Maxwell Lyte thought that Adam de Cheddar might have had something to do with the erection of the great piers connected with pointed arches that carry the central crossing tower of St George's church. The coffin lid of Adam de Cheddar was discovered by John Long in Dunster Post Office where it had served as a fireback. John Long, during the Victorian restoration of 1874/6 fashioned the alabaster columns which support the 13th/14th century priory altar slab. More of these ancient coffin lids are illustrated in the *Gentleman's Magazine* of 1808. Hamper, in his article "History and Antiquities of Dunster" says, "here is an antient slab with a cross." He had written previously about slabs then in the nave with a variety of inscriptions and later he wrote about, "two antient slabs with crosses the memorials probably of some of the priors, removed from the other part of the church." Brian Kemp in *English Church Monuments* writes about coffin lids. He says: "the Anglo Saxons were in the habit of erecting memorial crosses and gravestones in the open. The continuous history of English church monument making begins after the Norman Conquest and, in particular, after the beginning of the twelfth century, from which time, the earliest extant examples, in the form of carved coffin lids and grave slabs have survived. The practice is associated with the burial of notable persons inside churches. Gradually the right extended to others though most people could never expect more than a graveyard burial."[50] In this connection I would add that gravestones were not used in churchyards until the 17th century. Sometimes a wooden cross was erected but the land was dug and re-dug and used again and again. The bones were kept in charnel houses in the churchyard. The carved lids of stone coffins were left exposed to provide a lasting memorial of the person interred (the 14th-century one of Adam de Cheddar is quite late in date). The practice grew up in the late 11th century and there are extant examples of 12th-century date. A variety of motifs were carved on these slabs which were usually, but not in this example, of tapering shape. The 12th-century coffin lids show the "green man" with foliage springing from his mouth and this fertility symbol, like the grotesque beasts and signs of the Zodiac, bore little relation to Christianity or to burials but it was the language well-known to the people of the period. Nevertheless, the cross was the dominant motif and persisted into the 14th century.[51] The coffin lids illustrated in the *Gentleman's Magazine* are now missing.

CHESTS

In St George's church we still have the very unusual chest with a sloping lid which was probably used by the monks for writing in the cloister. Originally, it stood higher so that one could sit at it. It is made of elm and Dr. Eeles thought that it might be unique and emphasises this view by saying: "the church possesses some unusual treasures. A large wooden desk, long used as a chest is considered to be the only surviving example of the desks at which monks sat and wrote in cloisters."

In 1958 the *West Somerset Free Press* reported that "the monk's chest had been converted into a collecting box, and had been placed in the south porch." The proceeds were to be given to the Fabric Fund. One writer says that it may have been the one in which the treasure of Ralph le Tort was stored when it was stolen in the year of grace 1225 by William Fauder and John Portman, and the town of Dunster was fined for having harboured such rogues within its jurisdiction. Hancock's version of this episode is that in the year of grace 1225, William Fauder and John Portman were suspected of robbing the church of Dunster and taking the money of Ralph le Tort, stored presumably in the church for safety. They were found to have lived in Dunster without frank-pledge. "Therefore it is in mercy – And because they are suspected of many thefts let them be exacted and outlawed. They had no chattels."[52] Hancock continues: "It would have gone hard with William Fauder and John Portman if they had been caught, and no doubt the burgesses of Dunster were smartly fined for their carelessness in allowing such vagabonds to live in their midst without having given security for their good behaviour."[53] Ralph le Tort was witness of the charter of John de Mohun III, dated 1301, to the burgesses of Dunster and to a charter of a few years later and one in 1324 by the same lord.

We now come to the two chests in Dunster church. The sloping desk is thought to be the oldest of the three pieces. "The early 'dug-out' chest, perhaps 12th century," according to Dr Eeles.[54] This date is confirmed by the Reverend G.D. Dunlop who allocates it to the reign of King Stephen (1135-1154). This would be during the lordship of William de Mohun II, earl of Somerset. The other chest Dr Eeles refers to as "early chest, probably 13th century."[55] This chest the Reverend Dunlop specifically allocated to the reign of Henry III (1216-1272) and therefore during either the guardianship of Sir Reynold de Mohun II or later during his lordship. In 1958 a report on the annual vestry and parochial church meetings which appeared in the *West Somerset Free Press* contained, under "Vicar's Impressions" (Rev. Michael McCormick) a reference to the chests: "Even the 12th and 13th century chests in the church are not merely to be looked at. Their keys fit, their locks work and their lids still open comfortably and easily on their hinges to reveal the chalice or ciborium or parish record book, when it is required." We have two Victorian locks and one medieval lock on these chests. I am told that the second medieval one was stolen in 1988. In the plan of the church made before the 1874/6 restoration by Mr Street's assistant, C. H. Samson, F.R.I.B.A., No. 9 indicates the position of the two ancient chests in the front of the parclose screen separating the Lady Chapel from the north transept. From this position they were moved to the wall of the south-eastern chapel but in 1715 they were in the tower. From the overseer's accounts 12 October 1715 we read: "The keyes [sic] to the chests in the middle loft in Dunster Tower the first is as you enter the loft the others in order. 1 William Blackford Esq. his key. 2 William Question (ye 3rd of that name), his key. 3 William Blake Esq. his key. 4 Thomas Chilcot, his key." It is noted that references made at various points to D.C.B. are to "... the former contents of one of the three ancient chests in the church now represented by a volume of indifferent transcripts made in 1716, which is in the possession of Mr Luttrell."[56] This was in 1909. D.C.B. stands for Dunster Church Book. In the *Gentleman's Magazine* "Antiquities of Dunster" (1808) by Mr Hamper we find: "In the chancel are three antient chests, two of them strongly bound with iron."[57] Their progress through the church seems to have been from the tower to the chancel, to the west of the screen separating the chapel of Our Lady From the north transept and finally to the south-east chapel.

To sum up, the artefacts in the church of 12th, 13th and 14th century dates are as follows:

PAGE 256

1 The stone cross – the top of the churchyard cross in the de Mohun chantry chapel (13th, possibly 14th cent)
2 The stone altar slabs in the above chapel and at the altar of St George (13th, possibly 14th cent)
3 The medieval floor tiles (14th cent)
4 Partly exposed Early English window opening (13th cent)
5 The sloping desk (12th cent)
6 Tomb-slab of Prior Adam de Cheddar (14th cent)
7 The processional cross acquired in 1896 (13th/14th cent, with 17th-century additions)
8 Stone fragments of effigy of Sir John de Mohun III (d.1330)
9 One chest (13th cent)
10 Another chest (14th cent)
11 Top of arch between south transept and south-east aisle (13th cent)
12 Effigy of probably Christian de Mohun (alive 1335) relict of John de Mohun IV (d. before 1330)
13 Early English pointed arches of crossing (14th cent)

AISLE

There was as we know, an adjunct on the north side from the earliest times and the chapel of the Holy Trinity, which I believe to have been in the north aisle received its first known bequest of a parclose screen in 1348. The aisle was rebuilt in the 16th century and if one views the west end of the north aisle from the exterior, it is very obvious that when the rebuilding took place it was squashed in at its western end between the existing walls of the priory dwelling. Particularly is this noticeable in respect of the most westerly window.

CHURCH ARCHITECTURE

We have a central crossing tower but the possibility of apsidal eastern ends must be addressed. Lyte says: "Whether the chancel was square or apsidal it is impossible to say."[58] On the other hand, Hancock says, the presbytery or Priory church "formed the chancel of the original Norman church. It had, as first built, no aisles but probably was terminated by an apse, of which no traces are now left."[59] It is possible that at Dunster there were apses off the eastern sides of the transepts, and that the chancel terminated in an apse. To quote Professor Freeman: "Yet the Transitional arch leading from the south transept into one of the present aisles shows that something was attached to the east of this transept, perhaps an apse, perhaps a square chapel not opening at all into the presbytery, as at Ewenny, or opening only by a low arch, as at Brecon. Whatever it was, it was swallowed up by the Perpendicular aisle...."[60] We may deduce the existence of these apsidal ends from the contemporary church of St Andrew at Stogursey also a Benedictine foundation which was suppressed 101 years before Dunster, in 1438, after the great Hundred Years' War with France, when its estates were used for the endowment of the College of St Mary at Eton. This church was granted by William de Falaise and his wife Geva, in the time, of Henry I (1100-35) to the church of St Mary at Lonlay, 4 miles west of Domfront in Normandy (although the earliest Norman work at St Andrew's is dated to the last quarter of the 11th century.) We may see there the excavations conducted by the Rev. Basil Tucker in the 1940s and his conclusions concerning the position of these apsidal ends off the chancel and two eastern terminations of the north and south transepts. St Andrew's like St George's has a tower over the crossing, albeit, no western towers in these more modest parish churches. The Norman tower at Dunster was of squatter proportions; the two upper storeys being added c.1443.

Although the Romanesque style was brought to England by the Normans and acquired thereby the name of Norman architecture, it was, of course, a harking back to Roman architecture and it is therefore not surprising that it was in northern Italy that the earliest architectural experiments were conducted, chiefly in Benedictine monasteries, and date back to c.875. This is not the place to explore the spread of the style from Dalmatia, on the Adriatic coast of Croatia to France or to Catalonia but the First Romanesque style, evident in the part Spanish and part French region of Roussillon, also penetrated north along the rivers Rhone and Rhine and is exemplified at St Philibert de Tournus and St Bénigne at Dijon. It was at Cluny II, which replaced the original building, that the 'Benedictine plan' was used before 981 AD., and it was introduced into Normandy from Burgundy by William de Volpiano who built St Bénigne. Eventually reaching England, this plan enjoyed a great vogue during the Romanesque period and was taken up in Switzerland also (Payerne). A Cluniac Order was established at Lewes by William de Warenne, earl of Surrey, and his wife Gundrada who visited Cluny on a pilgrimage to Rome in 1077. It is said that although all English Cluniac priories enjoyed sumptuous decoration, their style, judging by the remaining ruins, was Anglo-Norman. The effect of Cluny III was also great in England.[61]

To return to Dunster the only Norman work which remains today is the northern wall of the nave, the central part of the western wall of the nave, in which a Norman doorway was discovered during the Victorian restoration and the attached Norman columns of an arch which formerly stood between the eastern piers of the crossing tower. The idea of this Norman arch was revived soon after 1838 but it was no longer part of the integral structure of the tower and served no useful purpose and was removed 1874/6. There is also some evidence of Norman masonry embedded in the eastern and western piers of the Perpendicular arches now supporting the tower. It was Lyte's opinion that "the nave, which measured internally about 80 feet in length by 26 feet in breadth, had no side aisles... etc., etc."[62] However, the usual arrangement, according to Sir Bannister Fletcher, consisted of: "a square cloister having on one side an aisled church of cruciform plan, a transept of which one side bounded the cloister."

The chantry chapel of the Blessed Virgin Mary which is now the Vestry would have been suppressed in 1548 but since it had been re-built in the middle of the 15th century, it remained, although its altar would have been removed or demolished. In the middle of the 16th century it was connected with the intervening chancel or presbytery of the priory church by piercing apertures in its northern wall. By a will dated and proved in 1369, Gilbert Scutt of Dunster directed that 3lbs of wax should be made into two candles to burn by his corpse, on the night and the day of his burial, and afterwards to burn respectively before the altar of the Holy Rood and in the chapel of Our Lady. The chantry chapel of St Lawrence, on the southern side of the priory chancel was connected by similarly pierced arches. Pillars, carrying two arches of a debased character thus caused these lateral chapels to become aisles to the priory chancel.

Lyte says that: "In the reign of Henry the Third (1216-72), the Benedictine monks rebuilt and enlarged the chancel of the church of Dunster, in the prevailing style known as Early English or First Pointed. It measured internally 50 feet in length by 22 feet in breadth, being somewhat narrower than the Norman nave. In the eastern wall there were three lancet windows, the central one higher, as usual, than the other two. There was a row of simpler lancets in the south wall, where the sedilia occupied the usual position."[63] Eeles says: "The eastern portion of the church seems to have been lengthened in the 13th century, and there was abundant evidence found when the restoration (of 1874/6) was going on, that there had been Early English work there. He adds a note to the effect that, the church is 156 feet long; rather shorter than St Asaph."[64] However, Freeman wrote in 1885: "the entire dimensions of the whole building are about 180ft, or a little more than the length of St Asaph's."[65] St Asaph's in Flintshire is the smallest cathedral in England and Wales, smaller than many parish churches.

The Early English style is the first phase of the Gothic style and it lasted until the end of the 13th century when it was superseded by the Decorated style with its ogee curves, highly decorated, diapered surfaces, stylised foliage and unexpected vistas. The Benedictines had favoured the central apse and radiating chapels, but these were superseded by a cardinal feature of the Cistercian order, the rectangular east end, typified in St Bernard of Clairvaux's abbey at Fontenay in Burgundy. There are indeed many similarities between Fontenay and Dunster church. The guide book on Fontenay says: "the body of the Church is austerely beautiful. It is shaped like a Latin cross and consists of nothing but straight lines. It has a nave and two side aisles, a transept that scarcely juts out at all beyond the line of the walls, and a chancel with a flat chevet. To the north of the transept is a door onto the graveyard."[66] Dunster's north door, of course, leads into a garden. Fontenay acquired its square east end between 1139 and 1147 and this hall-mark of Cistercian architecture gained great popularity in England and by the time the third building was completed at Cluny in c.1120, the influence of the Cluniac order, an offshoot of the Benedictine order, was on the wane and the Cistercians came to prominence.

The Gothic style is said to have been the invention of the designer of the choir of St Denis, near Paris, whose foundations were laid in 1140, under the inspiration of Abbot Suger, the mighty counsellor of two French kings. The well known features of the style are the rib vault, the flying buttress and the pointed arch, but the pointed arch has an earlier history and is to be found in the early Romanesque architecture of Burgundy, notably at Autun. The first English house of the Cistercian order was Waverley in Surrey founded in 1128. Here the arrival of the Gothic style was manifest in this early form of Gothic with a Burgundian flavour. The Cistercians in England went Gothic very gradually, for example, at Roche in Yorkshire where the Gothic transepts are the chief remains of this abbey. The first fully Gothic building in England exhibits a French influence and this is exemplified by the east end of Canterbury cathedral. The east end of Canterbury has a corona, and Wells and Lichfield cathedrals have polygonal terminations. It is at Wells c.1180 that a thoroughly English Gothic begins and although it has this polygonal Lady chapel, its retrochoir has a square high gable. Both Wells and Lincoln display a greater stress on horizontals than is found in France. At Dunster the bias towards horizontal lines in the Early English style still lingers and can be observed in the string courses at sill level below the present lancet windows which continue at the same level on the north and south walls of the chancel. In 1855 Freeman observed: "The eastern limb contains some vestiges of Early English work, in a string course at the east end, continued along part of the south side."[67] The Early English lancet windows of the early 13th century were used in the form of stepped lancets at the east end above the high altar, or altar of St George, and in the north and south walls of the presbytery of the priory church. Evidence of these windows was found when the Victorian restoration took place and the specification states: "the present east window to be taken out and the old three light lancet window rebuilt stone for stone from the old fragments which have been discovered." The east window the Victorians removed was a 16th-century Perpendicular window matching that at the west end. Traces of 13th-century windows were also revealed when the plaster work was removed from the walls on the north and south of the presbytery of the priory church. The three in the south wall and the two in the north wall were restored. The specification reads: "The wall above the 'Mohun Monument' (actually the monument on which the effigies of Sir Hugh and Lady Catherine Luttrell now lie), to be rebuilt with two lancet windows, copied from the old remains here and in the south wall." The position of a half lancet window to the west of the three lancets on the south wall is a much 'tidied up' original 13th-century opening. Below the lancet windows in the south wall a sedilia with Early English arches occupied its accustomed place in the 13th century. The Victorian specification reads: "the old sedilia in the South wall of the Chancel is to be most carefully restored by preserving all the old stones possible, and by inserting new wrought and moulded stones corresponding with adjacent existing stones where the work is much decayed and otherwise to be restored according to the particular instructions of the Architect. The old Piscina in the South Wall to be restored etc." The upper part of the so-called "shouldered" arch between the south transept and the south-eastern chapel is also of the 13th century, c.1240, and the original de Mohun chantry chapel was probably built at that time though it was virtually rebuilt in the 19th century. An interesting exposition concerning the subject of the sedilia was put forward by C.L. Kirch of West Kirby, Merseyside; he wrote that he had: "watched with interest the series of programmes on Jerusalem for the week of 24-30 March on BBC-1 in which Ronald Eyre raised the question as to why Jesus died within a few hours, whereas people lasted from between two to seven days on the cross. He asked: could the answer lie in the possibility that Jesus resisted the temptation to put himself upon the little seat (called a sedile) that the Romans fixed to the cross to prolong the agony?" He continued: "If the seat wasn't used, the crucified person would die within a few hours of suffocation, due to the weight of the body through the arms pulling down on the chest. Further, he wrote: It was essential to fulfil the prophecy "no bone of his shall be broken." The two robbers had used the sedile, and hence their legs were broken to prevent them pushing upwards and making further use of its comfort: death followed promptly, so that all three were dead before the start of Passover, as was required by Jewish law.[68]

The *Dictionary of the Christian Church* states that the sedilia are: "The seats of the celebrant, deacon, and sub deacon, on the south side of the chancel, usually three in number. They were introduced in England in the 12th century and are used during those parts of the Eucharist and the Divine Office at which the ministers are allowed to sit: at the singing of the Kyrie, Creed and Gloria and while the Psalms and Lessons are chanted. In England they were usually stone benches built into a niche in the wall whereas on the Continent and in modern English churches, wooden seats (scamna) are more common. In the Middle Ages they were often richly carved and surmounted by arches or canopies."[69] The priory church has, since the middle of the 15th century, been flanked by square ended Perpendicular chapels. Professor Freeman, writing about the arcading ... which connects the chancel of the priory church with these chapels of Our Lady and St Lawrence says: "It is also clear from the masonry that the Perpendicular. arches on each side have been cut through an earlier and more massive wall. Hence it appears that the original presbytery or eastern limb, was without aisles," strictly so called.[70]

By the 16th century, therefore, the full blossoming of the light ethic had burst and the 13th-century stepped lancets over the high altar were replaced by the large Perpendicular window already mentioned.[71] The side chapels were also bathed in the joyous new light. However, at some time later, the windows in the side chapels of Our Lady and St Lawrence were blocked up. They were opened up again in the Victorian era.

DUNSTER ENVIRONS

At Yeovil stall-keepers at the weekly market paid to be allowed to erect booths against the churchyard wall.[72] Perhaps William Pleasway was lucky to be able to erect a booth under the protection of the "Bow." Close to the "Bow" were some steps leading from the street to the south western corner of the churchyard, Sadly, now "la scala," as it was known, no longer exists, and we have a safer, if history-effaced, sloping path. The original "scala" may be seen in John Buckler's south view of the church (Piggott Collection of 1839) which also shows the "Bow" and the draper's shop. There was a well, known as St Benet's which was eastward of the castle bayley on the way to "the Hanger Park," and to the Barton, or home-farm of the medieval lords of Dunster.[73] Lyte tells us that, in 1406, there was "practically no home-farm at Dunster,"[74] and the name Hanger Park is one given to what was known in 1279 as "the small park." It acquired the name of Hanger by 1330 and was so-named until 1752 or later.[75] It appears to have boasted a fish-pond which occupied an acre and to have been situated: "close to the back-yards or gardens of the houses on the eastern side of High Street [or Market St] separated from them by a wooden paling, afterwards replaced by a stone wall."[76] The accounts for 1417 show: "To Philip the carpenter and his fellow for cutting stakes (paludes) for enclosing the stews (stagnis) in the Hanger (park), in part payment, 18s. 4d."[77] The situation of what is now known as the Deer Park, altered considerably over the centuries, but in 1428 when Sir Hugh Luttrell, the first Luttrell to live at Dunster castle, died, the Hanger Park comprised a hundred acres of pasture and wood.

The fishpond is mentioned in 1426 in the accounts for that year: "In nails bought for mending 'le store hous' in the keep (castello) in which my lord's armour is placed, 1d ... In two carriages of timber from 'le Fysspole in le Hanger', towards my lord's said stable, without board, 2d."[78] After the Dissolution of the Monasteries, the abode of the priors became a farmhouse and is known today as the 'Old Priory' and in 1708 seven hogsheads of water were supplied weekly to this dwelling. A hogshead was a large cask holding approximately 50 gallons. This was nearly 170 years after the priors and monks had left Dunster. This water came from two springs one of which was called the Heart's Well or Hart's Well. They were near a spring called Galloxwell mentioned in the reign of Henry VII (1485-1509), which gave its name to Galloxwell Lane, so named in 1756. This lane led westward to Frackford, on the way to Avill, from Gallocks Cross where four roads meet close to the park gate beyond Gallocks Bridge. These two springs were demised, or conveyed, to Caleb Spurrier, a glazier, by Colonel Alexander Luttrell (1663-1711) in 1708.

There was a "Glasier's House" mentioned in 1647 and again in 1648 and this was situated where the thoroughfare, High St or Market St turns westward opposite the Cage House (now Shakespeare & Hall, the booksellers). Spurrier was to lay leaden pipes from the two springs to cisterns at the High Cross (at the southern end of the High Street) and the Corner or Cage House. From Gallocks Cross a public road, dating from the time of the Roman occupation of Britain, formerly led upwards in a south-easterly direction near Holway House, the exact situation of which is forgotten, to the village of Carhampton. Since the creation of the Deer Park, this "has become a mere footpath." A third road from Gallocks Cross went north-eastwards by Avelham Corner, Henstey, Skibberciff, and Gilt chapel close to the junction of Saltern Lane with the present main road from Carhampton to Minehead. The prior of Dunster was responsible for the repair of this road.[79] In the 14th century Gallocks Bridge was known as "Doddebrigge" and had acquired the former name by the reign of Henry VII when it was referred to as "Gallockisbrigge." The street now known as Park Street was in 1323, described as "la Waterstret" and by 1342 it was referred to as Gallokystret and the names were interchangeable. By 1800, in common parlance, the northern portion of the road was called Water Street and beyond the river the southern part was called Gallocks Street. "A footpath, no longer public, connecting this street with the road to the grist-mills was known in the 14th and 15th centuries as 'Colyerslane' or simply 'le Lane'.[80] In 1760 there is a mention of 'Ye footpath garden' in Water Street." The road to the grist-mill is Mill Lane and the footpath connecting it with Water Street is now public. The stream over which the Gallocks Bridge passes was known as "le Oldstreme" and the ford at the side was used by carts coming down Water Street. The bridge is a medieval one of two spans. Beyond the bridge at the top of the hill were the gallows of the early lords of Dunster connected with the bridge by Gallocks Street, now a footpath. Various crosses existed in Dunster and the most important was obviously the High Cross or "ye Cross in High Street" which was also called Market Cross and later the Butter Cross presumably because butter was sold here by country women seated on its steps.

According to local tradition, the shaft of a medieval cross, raised on several steps, at Rockhead, was removed thither in 1825, from the junction of High Street and Church Street. It is accordingly marked in the Ordnance Survey as the "Butter Cross."[81] While the tradition may be true enough, with regard to the existing remains, or part of them, a number of workmen were employed by Henry Fownes Luttrell in 1776 in "levelling the ground around the cross at Rockhead" and gravelling the road towards Conigar.[82] In the *Gentleman's Magazine* of 6 June 1808 its original position is described: "The Fore Street is close built, paved, and of a tolerable breadth, but blocked up in the middle by an old market cross and a long range of ruinous shambles. Many of the houses are good, being built with wrought stone (of these the Luttrell Arms, an excellent inn, is most conspicuous); but the greater part are low, rough stone, thatched buildings, with old penthouses over the door and windows, and chimneys towards the street. The Market is on Friday; and a Fair is held on Whit-Monday."[83] Fore Street is yet another name for the High Street which was also known as Market Street, North Street, East Street or "Chepyng strete." The name North Street (vicus del Nord) is mentioned in the charter of Reynold de Mohun II in the reign of Henry III. In the reign of Edward III and in the lifetime of the last de Mohun lord of Dunster, John de Mohun V, it was called Chepyng-strete, rendered in Latin as "Vicus Foralis." In 1478 it was known as "la Market Streete" and in 1489 as "Eststrete" (East Street).[84] By the 17th century it was referred to as "the markett streete of Dunster called the High Streete"[85] and by 1830 it is described by James Savage as "Fore Street."[86] Another cross, named Spear's Cross is known to have stood in West Street, at least, since the 15th century. West Street was known by this name in the 13th century and the cross was at the intersection of that street with St George's Street and the castle bailey. In 1486, "the cross opposite the dwelling-house (mansionem) of William Sper" is mentioned. The cross is also referred to earlier in 1413 as "la crosse in la Westerstrete."

There was, incidentally, a chaplain in Dunster named John Spere who seems to have been a rather violent fellow, for on 16 March 1411: "John Spere chaplain drew a knife against John Loty, contrary to the peace. Therefore he is in mercy, 6d And John Loty drew a dagger – forfeited to the lord – against John Spere chaplain. Therefore he is in mercy 6d."[87] The "lord" was Sir Hugh Luttrell, whose effigy lies in Dunster church. The third cross in Dunster, apart from the cross in the churchyard, was the "Corn Cross, mentioned in 1705 as close to the Wheat Market." This was a little south of the Ball and to the east of it was a building with a curious name, the Tub House. It would appear that this was where the tubs for the market were housed: "Conditions of a survey held on Thursday the 29 September 1763, at the Ship Inn (now the Luttrell Arms) in Dunster in the county of Somerset for setting (sic) the Cornhouse, Markethouse (now called Yarn Market,)

Tubhouse and butchers' shambles in Dunster aforesaid, together with the reasonable use of all the tubs, pecks, and other measures, boards, trussels, poles, beams, scales and weights that now are in or belong to the Markethouse and market aforesaid, and all tolls and other advantages, emoluments, profits and privileges of the market and fair to be holden and kept in Dunster aforesaid, and which to the clerk of the market of Dunster aforesaid do or may belong and of right appertain, except all the inclosed shops and other rooms taken out of the Markethouse, for the term of seven years."[88]

CARE OF THE SICK

It was customary to have a hospital or infirmary in a Benedictine complex in the south-east corner adjacent to the churchyard. Of course the terms "hospital" and "infirmary" are too grand for this small cell of Bath abbey which, no doubt, did possess these amenities. However, the mother house used the priory of Dunster as an escape from the ills of Bath and as a place where the sick could recover their health. "Licence to him who is a priest, and who, on account of infection and the unwholesomeness (intemperiem) of the air at Bath, cannot reside continuously, to leave his said priory whenever he falls sick, and reside in one of its dependent cells at Dunster in the said diocese, or Waterford, in that of Lismore, without requiring licence to anyone." This information appears in the Calendar of Papal Registers Vol. V, 414,[89] and the licence dated 6 November, 1406, came from Rome giving Robert Hyndeman, a Benedictine monk of the priory of Bath, permission to leave Bath and to reside temporarily at Dunster or at Waterford Ireland where the priory of Bath had estates.

We do not know where the Benedictines of Dunster cared for the sick but in the 18th century there was a range of poor houses belonging to Henry Fownes Luttrell adjacent to the 16th-century timber-framed house, known at that time as John Thomas's house. The "poor houses" were in existence in 1780 behind a stone wall with a lean-to wooden loggia (see south view of Dunster church, *Somersetshire* 1780. It is likely, since the position is in accordance with the Benedictine plan, that these houses or an earlier building on this site, was the so-called "hospital" or "infirmary" of the monks before they left in 1539. The wall which formerly ran from the timber-framed cottage up to the priory church was demolished during the 1874/6 restoration when railings were erected.

No building exists between the timber-framed house and the gateway to the present Luttrell burial ground but I contend that it would have been a natural progression, after the Reformation, to have turned the house where the monks cared for the sick into a poorhouse/houses.[90] The timber-framed house is said, by Lyte, to be 16th-century and to have "pertained to the monks." If this is so, they only held it for 39 years presuming it to have been built at the earliest in 1500. The subsequent history of the house appears chronologically later. The churchyard in the pre-Reformation period came to the notice of the court which made various ordinances for the good government of the borough. These ordinances included prohibitions regarding the use of the churchyard in the 15th century: "And it is ordained likewise by the court, with the assent of the twelve jurors and the other officials (aforesaid) that no man shall henceforth shoot with his bows (arquis) and arrows in the churchyard of Dunster, or unlawfully practice games there under pain of 40d." There were no gravestones in the churchyard until the 17th century, therefore there would have been plenty of room for practising games and shooting with bows and arrows. Other ordinances, not connected with the churchyard but with the town include: "1472. act 19. That nobody shall henceforth use or carry swords, lances, 'gleyves', or other defensible and unlawful arms, contrary to the statute of our lord the king [Edward IV] in this respect, under pain of forfeiture of the same and 6s. 8d for every offence of this sort, to be paid to the lord as often as the discovery shall be made."[91] Incidentally, it is difficult to say who the lord of Dunster was in 1472 since the estates were at that time held by the Crown.

Probably the fines were paid to Philip Beaumont who had been appointed by the king as constable of Dunster castle and steward of all the lordships and lands.

REMAINS OF THE EFFIGY OF JOHN DE MOHUN III AND HIS BURIAL

Preb Hancock was of the opinion that: "the old half-buried tomb in the priory church was the resting place of this Sir John, great benefactor as he was to Dunster church and Priory and that the fragments of the effigy near by are the remains of the figure that lay upon it."[92] Later he says. "Half covered in by the tomb, and evidently built when the floor of the church was of a lower level, is a plain arch of a 13th- or 14th-century date, beneath which, no doubt, once lay a recumbent figure. Here may have reposed the Sir John de Mohun of whom Savage speaks, and the helmeted head and the feet lying on Sir Hugh Luttrell's tomb, and found some years ago in the churchyard, may well be all that is left of the effigy. At all events the helmet is of that date."[93] The Reverend Doré and I found the stone remains of the sollerets, or sharp-toed armour clad feet, resting on a lion at the foot of the remains of the alabaster effigy of Sir Hugh Luttrell (d.1428), the first Luttrell to live at Dunster castle. The observant rector noticed the difference in the materials. The head was missing and, at the time, we thought we were looking for a fully helmeted head. Later, I found the head, in the stoke-hole whither, for some reason, it had been relegated. I had failed to associate it with Sir John de Mohun III since it was minus its helmet, but on examination traces of the lines of the camail were discernible. The camail was a tippet of mail, chain or banded, laced to the bascinet, (or pointed steel cap), and covering the neck and shoulders.[94] This head I believe to be that which John Leland referred to in the 16th century, when he wrote: "In the north part of this (chirche) was buried under an arche by the high altare one of the Luterelles, or, as I rather thynke, of the Moions, for he hath a garland about his helmet, and so were lordes of old tymes used to be buried."[95] John Leland (c.1506-52) was an English antiquary who was educated at St Paul's School and at Cambridge and Oxford. He was made chaplain and later antiquary to King Henry VIII in 1533. He went on a ten-year tour to collect material for a projected "History of the Nation" and his materials were used in his *Itinerary* and *Collectanea*. The extract concerning Dunster priory quoted above comes from the edition of the *Itinerary* published in 1907, p.166.

It is important to establish that we are here discussing Sir John de Mohun III (d.1330) since Preb Hancock speaks of a plain arch of 13th- or 14th-century date.[96] The Sir John de Mohun who died in the 13th century was Sir John de Mohun II (d.1279). Hancock seems quite confused about this, because he says: "It seems probable to the writer that the 13th century arched tomb beneath the doorway of the chapel may have been the tomb of Sir John de Mohun the third, who was a boy of nine years of age, succeeded to the Honour of Dunster in 1279. He was a great soldier, and served in the wars which Edward waged in Flanders and in Scotland. He was also one of the signatories to the famous document despatched to Boniface VIII, in AD 1300 by the barons of England in which they declared that the king should be independent of the authority of the pope."[97] Hancock was writing about Sir John de Mohun III but he must have meant the 14th-century tomb and not the 13th-century tomb, since this Sir John died in 1330. The seal of Sir John de Mohun III attached to the famous letter of the English earls and barons to the pope gives his new shield, adopted by 1300 with a lion on either side and an eagle above; the legend around the seal is, "S JOHANIS de MOUN." The heraldic shield shown on the seal may also be found among the medieval tiles and Victorian tiles in Dunster church. The Augustinian priory of Bruton and the Cistercian abbey of Newenham, both foundations of Sir John de Mohun III's forebears, also adopted his arms which may be blazoned thus: Or a cross engrailed Sable.

Lyte says of Sir John de Mohun III: "He had been more interested in the Benedictines of Dunster than in the Augustinians of Bruton or the Cistercians of Newenham and he was buried in their church, possibly on the north side of the chancel."[98] In February 1877, the Rev. Richard Utten Todd wrote in the *Parish Magazine*: "during the past month the Old Chantry or Mohun Chapel which is henceforth to be used as a Sacristy, has been paved with some of the old tiles found in the Church Two crosses in St George's church and churchyard belong to the period covering the life-time of Sir John de Mohun III. One is the churchyard cross and the other is the processional cross, although the latter did not come into the possession of Dunster church until 1896. Since this Sir John was so significant in the history of the establishment of the priory, it is conceivable that the churchyard cross, of which the uppermost portion is in the Mohun chantry chapel, was erected in the churchyard during his lifetime." Indeed whilst it is referred to as a 13th-century cross, it was the opinion of Mr Jeffrey West of the Council for the Care of Churches in 1988, that it could be 14th century. Either way, it comes within the period of Sir John's lifetime since he was born in 1269 and died in 1330. Also, the donor figure at the feet of the Blessed Virgin Mary, depicted on this cross is, I believe, Sir John de Mohun III. (See the fuller account in Chapter 1)

PROCESSIONAL CROSS

The processional cross of St George's also comes from the same period, although it has later additions and was not known in Dunster church, as far as we know, until 1896. In October of that year, the 20th anniversary of the re-opening of the church after the 1874/6 restoration, took the form of a dedication festival. The account in the *Parish Magazine* says: "There were special evening services on the actual anniversary, the 13th September and on the 20th September and on both occasions there was a solemn procession round the church… A very beautiful 13th century Processional Cross presented to our church as a 'birthday gift' was used…The cross, which is now the property of our church at Dunster is a really ancient one, being described by a leading authority at the British Museum, as probably dating from the 13th century, and is therefore very appropriate for use in our ancient church…" The writer, presumably Rev. Wynell-Mayow M.A., vicar of St George's said: "The use of the Processional Cross, was like many other laudable practices of the Christian Religion discontinued in the 'dark ages' of the last century in England, but we are glad to say that it has now been restored in several of our Cathedrals and hundreds of Parish churches throughout the land. A quite erroneous account of the processional cross appears in *The King's England. Somerset, County of Romantic Splendour*, edited by Arthur Mee and first published in 1941. Not knowing that it was, in fact, a gift to the church in 1896 the writer says: "We found by this old altar (i.e. the 13th/14th century altar in the Mohun chantry chapel) a processional cross carried here five centuries ago. In the centre on one side is an engraved portrait of Christ with the emblems of the Passion, and at the four corners are angels and a pelican; the other side has a cross in the centre and gems of colour in enamel representing the Four Evangelists. It is all 14th century and perhaps the rarest small possession of Dunster."

The Rev. Wynell-Mayow was succeeded by Preb F. Hancock who, in his book *Dunster Church & Priory* (1905) says: "The parish church possesses a processional cross of late 14th century date and of Flemish manufacture." Of the Alcombe cross he says: "Preserved at Alcombe is a very beautiful cross of English work, once silver gilt, and perhaps of not later date than the beginning of the 15th century. It was found at Dunster, and there probably is little doubt that it was the processional cross of either the prior or the vicar of Dunster."[99] It therefore seems that while our processional cross at Dunster was a gift in 1896, our true and ancient cross is at Alcombe, which place belonged to the Benedictine monks before the Dissolution and was in the same parish of Dunster until 1953. In 1948 the then vicar of Dunster, Reverend G.D. Dunlop, wrote in his Christmas Notes, a report on the Dunster cross as follows: "This was in very poor condition in 1946. The wood in a rotten state one of the arms half broken and badly fixed to a cheap deal staff. In the Autumn of 1948 I sent it up to Mr A.E. Erridge, Craftsman of St John's House, St John's Wood and he took it to pieces and remounted it on good oak and he also made an orb below the Cross head and provided a good English Oak staff. In answer to my question as to its age and period he wrote: 'Regarding the age of the Cross (although I am in no position to certify) it seems to be a mixed bag of periods; in my opinion the enamels do not belong to the original Cross and were applied when the cross was first restored. I say first restored because the Central Squares are, to my mind, the only bits of the original cross (back and front). The repousse work in these two squares has a character that might well be of the 14th century. The scroll work on the arms and the upright of the Cross are too formal in detail and suggest the use of a die or some mechanical device for stamping. The angels on the reverse side also have this very detailed resemblance. Notice that every little contour is in each Angel the same. This same characteristic applies to the scroll work and on the arms and upright of the Cross as well as the 'flory' terminals. The date of this work may be late 17th century. I doubt if it is earlier and may well have been copied from fragments of the original Cross; the Central Squares, front and back being the only pieces (to my mind) of the original. Please accept this opinion with my reservations. Signed A B. Erridge'. Mr Erridge's opinion then, amounts to this: 'The Cross is of no particular period. It has probably been restored time and time again. But the central squares may well be of the 14th century of the period of Chaucer and William of Wykeham – outside the squares there is work probably of the 17th century and there are later additions'. Signed G.D. Dunlop, Christmas 1948." In March 1949 the parochial church minutes for 14 March inform us that, the "Vicar reported on the repair of the Processional Cross and it was agreed that the cost of the repair, £28 10s.0d. should be paid."

The Cross is brass with a high copper content or it may have received a copper sulphate base preparatory to being silvered. The metal is thinly applied, to both sides of an oak base. It is an adorned Latin cross fleurée and the front of it is embellished with four enamels of roughly triangular shape with red backgrounds. They depict four Apostles all of whom have yellow nimbuses outlined in gold. The triangular shapes are set in quatrefoils applied to the cross within 'flory' terminals. Below the vertical terminal St Matthew is depicted, attired in green, the folds of his garment being picked out with gold lines. He wears a black skull cap and his features are outlined in gold and his beard and the cross on the black bible open before him, are also gold. A gold ribbon encircles the bust upon which is written S. MATHIEU in black. Saint Mark is shown below the right-hand 'flory' terminal. Apart from the fact that he is bare-headed, the figure is identical to that of St Matthew. The gold ribbon bears the name, S. MARC. Saint John occupies the area below the left-hand 'flory' terminal. He is red headed and attired in blue. He holds a white cross in his right hand. The name S. JEAN appears on a ribbon. Saint Luke also in blue holds a black open book and a white quill. The ribbon bears the name S. LUC. Below the figure of St Matthew, the initials INRI (JESUS NAZARENUS REX JUDAEORUM) are on a band superimposed on the cross. The central square is of repoussé work as is the stylised scrollwork of the entire cross. The square contains a cross placed over and extending beyond two concentric circles, the inner circle scalloped and the upper and side arms of the cross terminating in stylised elongated lilies. The circles are surrounded by minute stars. In the top left hand corner a circlet of ten outward looking birds, with one bird in the centre; perhaps intended to be the doves of the Holy Spirit. In the top right-hand corner a female face in profile, the head draped, possibly the Virgin Mary. The reverse of the cross shows four applied quatrefoils below the 'flory' terminals, which are of fleur-de-lys form. The quatrefoil below the upright terminal of the cross and that to the right of the left-hand terminal show angels bearing scrolls. The quatrefoil to the left of the right-hand terminal is the winged ox of St Luke also bearing a scroll. The quatrefoil above the lower 'flory' terminal shows the pelican in her piety. Richard Goddard wrote a fascinating and very comprehensive article on 'the pelican in her piety' entitled Nostro Pellicano.[100] He says he was astounded to discover in a footnote to a learned paper that "...in its piety is a modem invention unknown even to Guillim...the earliest use...which we have noticed is in Edmondson's Complete Body of Heraldry, 1780.[101] Mr Goddard remarks that he was prompted to investigate: "both the use of the symbol in general and the development of its heraldic description in particular (since) clearly the image of the pelican, on her nest and pecking at her breast was of much earlier provenance."[102] However, he concedes that perusal of other works did appear to support the view that Edmondson's "is the first printed instance of the phrase as a piece of specifically English usage" but that fifty years earlier than Edmondson, Boyer had written: "the Pelican on her nest, vulning herself to feed her young, is called, by the French, Piety."[103] Edmondson had written: "The Pelican is usually drawn in heraldry with her wings disclosed, her neck bent, and with her bill wounding her breast; from whence issue drops of blood: but sometimes she is borne standing in her nest, feeding her young; this is blazoned by some a Pelican in her Piety.[104] Mr Goddard, amidst a wealth of enthralling detail, concludes that: "What is certain is that the pelican and its attendant legend became a very potent symbol in the early Middle Ages after a Christian gloss had been grafted onto the fable set down in the Physiologus, that work composed in or near Egypt in the 2nd century AD, and which formed the kernel of all subsequent bestiaries."[105] In nature the pelican feeds its young by regurgitation. During this process the head and neck of the young bird might completely disappear into the parent's throat.[106] In addition the Dalmatian pelican develops a reddish spot over the crop and the gular pouch during the breeding season, and this might be interpreted as a wound.[107] Mr Goddard's Note 12 says: "Nature is mirrored by Art in Lincoln Cathedral where one of the supporters of a misericord shows a mother pelican literally 'biting the head' off an importunate fledgling." Note 13 reads: "and in the Proceedings of the Zoological Society (1869) a Mr A.D. Bartlett reported that he had obtained some of the coloured fluid from a flamingo...was little else but blood (and briefly that) ...it may be that in the translation the habit of one bird had been transferred to the other." Mr Goddard, to whom I am indebted[108] for this abundant information quotes Eve: "such imperfect remembrance of a partially seen fact, combined with the credulity of the times, may be answerable for the pelican in her piety. The observer not getting near enough to see the pouch beneath the bird's bill, but seeing the contents extruded from it by pressure on the breast, imagined that the young ones were indeed fed from the breast itself."[109]

To revert to the processional cross – the central square on the reverse shows Christ in Majesty with his feet on the orb of the world. Surrounding the Christ figure are the emblems of the Passion, the ladder, the hammer, the crown of thorns shot through with the sword and staff, the nails and some coins (tokens of the thirty pieces of silver) the pillar and cords, the scourge and the seamless robe. There also appears to be a flail, the sponge is missing and there are possibly pincers. The orb is 20th-century and the cross was repaired in 1949. The original processional cross of Dunster, at Alcombe, would have played an important part in the late medieval processions held in Dunster. Dr Bettey writes: "Processions, both inside the church and around parts of the village or parish, were always popular, and the bench-ends at Trull near Taunton show a complete procession including a cross bearer, taper-bearer, a man with an open book, another carrying a shrine and a priest in a cope." The churchwardens at Yatton (Avon) in 1499 spent the enormous sum of £18 on a cross to be carried at the head of processions, while at Croscombe (Somerset) during the 15th century the main source of income for the churchwardens was from collections made each year while processions went round the parish.[110]

On Palm Sunday the Dunster procession doubtless started at the "Palme Crosse" in the churchyard. Item 5 of the 1498 Glastonbury Agreement lays down: "That the Vicar and the parishioners should be free to make processions from their choir in the church or in the graveyard on any day of the year except on thirteen important festivals, to wit those of Christmas, Epiphany, Palm Sunday, Easter, Ascension Day, Whitsunday, Trinity Sunday, Corpus Christi, the Purification, St George, the Assumption, All Saints, and the Dedication of the Church, on each of which there was to be a joint procession to the church or in the graveyard according to season and weather. On these days the little band of monks "coming through the middle of their own choir" was to be met by the rest of the congregation as they began to issue through (egredi) "the door (hostium) on the north side" of the new parochial choir. Then the bearer of the monks' cross and the bearer of the parish cross were to walk side by side, followed by the clerks, the Vicar, the monks, the Prior and the lay folk. On their return, the two bodies were to separate at "the same door," the monks passing through (ingredientibus) it and the Vicar and his clerks returning to their choir, to finish divine service.[111] Dr Bettey reminds us that: "The regular round of processions and celebrations which marked the passage of the year was also intimately associated with the parish church. The processions such as those on Palm Sunday, Corpus Christi and Rogationtide were obviously religious in purpose, though often accompanied with considerable horse-play and merry-making. But events which were essentially non-religious or even pre-Christian in origin also came within the sphere of influence of the church and churchwardens in most country parishes and contributed money to the church coffers. Such events varied widely in different parts of the country, but they included well-dressing, rush- strewing, the feast of fools on the feast of the Circumcision, carolling and wassailing, Plough Monday (first Monday after Epiphany) ceremonies and dancing and other revels at Hock-tide (second Monday and Tuesday after Easter)."[112] Dr Bettey also refers to the part the guilds played, to their importance in late medieval communities as organisers and participants in the processions already discussed and to the other varying activities such as miracle plays, pageants, bonfires and drynkys.

All these artefacts have been addressed with the exception of the 13th-century arch, the top of which still remains. The St Lawrence Chapel led out of the south transept through an arch, the top of which still remains. It stands on shafts which Professor Pevsner rather quaintly likens to "hoses bent outward to allow for a wider arch. This is suggested as a Late Perpendicular adjustment."[113] Just above, and on the right of the arch, is the base of an early cross built into the wall.[114] Lyte says: "The small sacristy on the north, which retains its ancient stone altar, may also date from the 13th century although its doorway and windows are of a much later date."[115] However the 13th-century chapel – named "sacristy" in the Victorian period – was practically re-built during the Victorian restoration of 1874/6. He continues: "Another specimen of Early English work may be seen in the upper part of the curious opening between the southern transept and the south-eastern chapel. He adds. "To the desire of the laity for practical convenience unattended by unnecessary expense is probably due the extraordinary opening between the south-eastern chapel and the transept. Here there is a moulded arch of the 13th century, supported by jambs of the 15th century, which bend outwards immediately below the capitals, a standing puzzle to architects and antiquaries." The solution now offered is that, after the suppression of the chantries, an ingenious and economical builder united the ancient arch with the later jambs by inserting one stone on either side so shaped as to give a wider opening below than the former would have had. The communion table then became visible from the southern transept.[116] It would appear that fewer than ten persons per week participated in the communion service at Dunster after the Reformation. Lyte writes: "A return of the second year of Edward the Sixth (i.e. 1549) gives the approximate number of partakers of the Lord's Holy Sooper (sic) in Dunster as five hundred."[117] It is impossible for the jambs of the arch to be 15th-century as Lyte suggests, and also to date the alteration to "after the suppression of the chantries," which was in 1548. I think he must have meant 16th century since Professor Nikolaus Pevsner also refers to "a Late Perpendicular adjustment." Both dates are supported by Dr Francis Eeles who, in 1940, dated the widening of the arch to c.1540 with which I agree. He dates the 13th century upper part of the arch more precisely to c.1240. He also dates the arcades between the priory chancel and its adjacent chapels to c.1540; these also made the communion table more visible before the screens were installed during the Victorian restoration. The combination of the 13th-century arch with the 16th-century jambs forms an ogee outline which is characteristic of the "Decorated Style" which began in the late 13th century and lasted into the second half of the 14th century. This probably caused Preb Hancock in his book to draw the following conclusion: "The curious character of the arch which opens into the southern aisle of the priory church, at once strikes the observer. Its history is probably this. When, towards the end of the Decorated Period (to which the arch, belongs, 1277-1377) the services of the church became more ceremonious and stately, it was found that this arch as it was originally built was too narrow for the processions then in vogue. What was to be done? The arch was too good an one to be wantonly destroyed, so the architect called in to advise hit on the bizarre device of leaving the head of the arch in situ and setting back its jambs on two shouldered corbels, thus widening the opening."[118] Preb Hancock speaks of "the arch as it was originally built." I presume this is a tacit acknowledgement of its Early English, 13th-century, origin. I further conclude that he was of the opinion that the setting back of the jambs which he thought were part of the original 13th-century arch, were set back on the two shouldered corbels in the Decorated period which followed the Early English style, thus denying that the jambs are 16th century. It is neverthless quite obvious that the jambs are 16th century as their roll mouldings are of a quite different character from the mouldings of the 13th-century arch.

It is interesting to note also the human faces on the apex and at the sides of the arch. Perhaps we have here a 13th-century prior, vicar or, less probably, a lord of Dunster. Fragments, obviously originating from the church and of a similar nature were incorporated by J. Hole in 1864 or 1866 into a house which he built at that time called "Earlham," now "Higher Orchard," in St George's Street. Scratched on a window of the cottage in the grounds are the words "I am James Hole, 1865." One wonders if James was the father of Thomas Hole to whom Hancock refers. He says: "Some twenty years later, (i.e. 1850) the roof of the priory church began to fall in, and it was restored by the father of the late Mr Thomas Hole of Dunster, who himself carved many of the existing bosses in the roof, which he copied from old and decayed ones which had been taken down."[119]

In church architecture the late 13th century marks the change in style from Early English, used in this century for the rebuilding of the priory church, to Decorated as used in the monument probably of Christian de Mohun. This Decorated style lasted into the second half of the 14th century when it was superseded by the English Perpendicular style. The foremost characteristic of the Decorated style is the ogee, or double "S" curve, found chiefly in arches and window tracery. The other main characteristic is a maximum of decoration covering surfaces in a variety of diaper patterns and the encrustation of arches, gables and the like, with leaves of a stylised and knobbly form. Outside specific decoration, the Decorated style also favoured unexpected vistas, often seen diagonally. In the west country the principal examples are the east parts of Bristol cathedral (begun in 1298) and Wells (c.1290-1340). Elsewhere the Lady chapel and the famous octagon at Ely (1321-53) and the screens at Lincoln, funerary monuments such as the funerary monument to Edward II in Gloucester, the Percy tomb at Beverley and the stalls at Exeter. It is said that "no other country had anything as novel, as resourceful, and as lavish as the English Decorated style."[120]

The Middle Ages saw the development of canopied monuments much grander than that of Christian de Mohun, but nevertheless her monument, like the others reflects the same architectural language of the 14th century whilst never achieving the elaboration reserved ironically for a murdered king, Edward II. The tomb chest on which her effigy lies is to be found on the south side of the priory chancel and it is very evident here that the original floor levels were much lower. It is relevant to point out here that: The term "tomb chest" is misleading since it (apparently) does not contain a coffin and is only a form of monument. Tomb chests first appeared in the early 13th century.[121] It is thought that they were inspired by the shrines of saints who were buried in structures resembling chests above ground level. Christian de Mohun was married to John de Mohun IV and was the daughter-in-law of John de Mohun III (d.1330), that great benefactor of Dunster church whose last resting place is marked by a small arched aperture at the present ground level beside the doorway into the de Mohun chantry chapel, and the remains of whose stone effigy lie at the foot of that of Sir Hugh Luttrell (d.1428). The monument, on the south wall of the choir of the priory church is fashioned in Ham stone procured from southern Somerset and is dated c.1330. The date c.1325 is given by Dr Eeles who writes: "On the south side; effigy of a lady, probably Christian Segrave, wife of Sir John de Mohun IV, c.1325, under a much restored canopy."[122] This was two years before Edward II was murdered at Berkeley castle on 21 September 1327. Christian was almost certainly a widow by this time since her husband fought at the battle of Borough bridge in 1322 and died before his father who died in 1330. Lyte refers to "Lady de Mohun, the widow at Minehead" and talks about "her dower in 1335"[123] but it is a little unclear to whom he is referring. Earlier[124] he had written about Sibyl, Lady de Mohun, the second wife of Sir John de Mohun III (d 1330) who, he says, "was certainly living in 1337." There is nothing more to be said about her except that she kept a domestic chaplain, presumably, at Dunster.[125] If one assumes that he had really completed his information concerning Sibyl, the later reference must apply to the younger widow, the wife of Sibyl's step-son, John de Mohun IV If this is so Christian was alive in 1337 but, in spite of the rather misleading way in which this information was presented, I do believe that Lyte was still referring to Sibyl as being alive in 1337. Sibyl, or Sibilla, like Christian, was also a daughter of Sir John Segrave,[126] so father and son married two sisters. This seems to have been quite a custom among the de Mohuns for Reynold de Mohun II's second wife was the elder sister of his son John de Mohun's wife, both being the daughters (Isabel and Joan) of William de Ferrers, earl of Derby. With regard to the attribution of this effigy to Christian de Mohun, certainly Lyte thought that it was she, since No 6 in his ground plan of the church (see Chapter 1) shows "Monument of Christian de Mohun." Dr Francis Eeles in his 1934 and 1940 church guides also concurred with this attribution. However, From the 16th to the 20th centuries there have been varying views on the subject of the identity of this effigy. In the *Gentleman's Magazine* we read: "Under an arch below lies another figure, but I cannot agree with Collinson (or his co-adjuter Rack who supplied the Church Notes), in supposing it the monument of a domestick, it is most probably the 'Image of one of the Everardes', mentioned by Leland Itin. vol ii fol. 62 (and from him by Collinson), as having once been there, but removed into the church-yard: whence it may have been reinstated in its former situation."[127] This attribution persisted into the 19th century, with reservations, for the plan of the church before the Victorian restoration, by C.H. Samson. F.R.I.B.A. shows No 5 as "early tomb ascribed to the Everard family, but more probably to a member of the Mohun family." The *West Somerset Free Press* of 13 September 1876, however, latched on to the Everard attribution and said: "The fine monuments of the Luttrell and Everard families have been completely restored and several pieces of that of the Everards were found under a floor and were replaced." An error occurs on p.43 of Lyte's history where he refers to Christian, as the mother of John de Mohun III. The mother of John de Mohun III was Eleanor Fitzpiers. This was obviously an oversight on Lyte's part because elsewhere he rightly gives Eleanor Fitzpiers as the wife of Sir John de Mohun II (d.1279)[128] and the parents of John de Mohun III. Eleanor, when a widow married Sir William Martin. Lyte also states correctly that Christian was the wife of John de Mohun IV and the mother of John de Mohun V.[129] Four years before Lyte published his *History of Dunster* (Parts I & II), Preb F. Hancock in *Dunster Church and Priory* (1905) gave an account where he concludes by agreeing with Lyte that it is a monument of the de Mohuns but ascribes it to Avice, or Hawis, de Mohun and not to Christian de Mohun: "Within the priory church itself is the effigy of a woman lying beneath a beautiful canopy of the Decorated Period." Much controversy has arisen about this tomb. Tradition assigns it to the Everard family. Leland says of it "... thereby lay an image of one of the Everardes, gentlemen, first there set up by the Moions, yn token whereof they had a parte of the Castelle to defende by service: the image lyeth now bytwixt ij arches or Boteres in the Churchyarde." Collinson mentions it as "the figure of one of the domestics of the Luttrell family," a fanciful conjecture which has neither proof nor likelihood. He also, copying apparently from Leland, speaks of it as lying between two buttresses or arches in the churchyard. Collinson could hear in his day of no tradition even of an Everard monument in the churchyard, nor is it likely that a monument would have been erected between two arches there. Walcot tells us in support of the Everard ownership of this tomb "On the south side is a beautiful Late Decorated canopy over the effigy of a lady of the family of Everard, probably the one mentioned in the indenture, March 5, Henry VI, 1427, made with John Henton, prior of Dunster, to maintain the anniversary of Patrick Everard and Joan his wife, on the morrow of St George the Martyr, from the rents of an acre of ground called Pitaker, on the north side of the Prior's apple orchard, and a cottage and a court, and a half-acre of land in Mensthetown, by Dunster: every monk present at the service was to receive 4d; the clerk of the church for the knell 1d; and the town-crier (*praeco*) for proclaiming the anniversary through the town, 1d." (Dunster MSS., No. lxxxi). But that eminent antiquary Sir H.M. Lyte, is probably right in considering the monument to have been erected to the memory of one of the family of de Mohun, perhaps to that of the Lady Avice or Hawys de Mohun, the wife of Reginald de Mohun, Earl of Somerset who (the earl) died in 1257. One of the towers of Dunster Castle was still called "Dame Hawis Tower" in the 15th century.[130] It is questionable whether this de Mohun, Reginald de Mohun II was ever Earl of Somerset.[131] The information already briefly mentioned as having been supplied by Dr Francis Eeles in 1940 is now fully quoted because it contains a note which leads the investigation to a paper written in 1917. Dr Eeles says: "Against the south wall of the choir of the Priory church is a large Ham Hill stone canopy of the 14th century, much restored, beneath which lies the effigy of a widow. There has been much controversy as to her identity. Long believed to represent an Everard, the strongest possibility is that Christian Segrave, widow of Sir John de Mohun IV, is represented. She was alive in 1325 but the effigy is of a rather earlier character."[132] Note 1 refers to the *Proceedings of the Somersetshire Archaeological Society*, lxiii (1917) p.16 which is as follows: Person Represented. A lady of the de Mohun family. Lyte in his *History of Dunster* conjectures it may be to Hawis, wife of Sir Reynold de Mohun, or to Christian, daughter of Sir John Segrave and wife of Sir John de Mohun IV. This is not probable as Prof E.S. Prior dates the effigy to *c*.1315; and the first lady died in 1260 and the second was living in 1320. It is surmised that it may be to Eleanor widow of Sir John de Mohun II, whose second husband was Sir William Martin of Compton Martin, or to Ada, wife of Sir John de Mohun III. It is possible, however, the effigy is to some favourite daughter of the family of de Mohun who died young. Lyte tells us, "Sir Reynold de Mohun married two wives, the first of whom was unquestionably Hawis."[133]

He does not give her date of death but the date of death of 1260 is allocated not to her by Lyte, but to the second wife Isabel.[134] The references are of course, to Sir Reginald de Mohun II and his date of death is 1257/8. The attribution of this effigy to either ladies is, I think, improbable since the Decorated style of architecture had not come into effect during the lifetime of whichever lady died in 1260 and as Sir Reynold died in 1257/8, it must have been his second wife Isabel, who died in 1260.

Collinson's comment, "the figure of one of the domestics of the Luttrell family" is incorrect since the Luttrells did not acquire Dunster castle until Lady Elizabeth Luttrell, née Courtenay, purchased the property in 1376 and it was her son Sir Hugh Luttrell (d.1428) who was the first of his family to live at Dunster castle in 1405. Earlier Luttrells are unlikely to have had monuments in Dunster church. Also only persons of eminence were buried in church. Stylistically the monument is much earlier than this. The effigy is six feet long. The lady wears a kirtle with long tight sleeves under a side1ess cote-hardi and a mantle caught up under each arm. A wimple or gorget is worn round the neck, hiding the sides of the face. Upon the head is a coverchef or kerchief, in this case a widow's veil which descends to the shoulders. The hands (mutilated) are raised in the conventional attitude of prayer and the feet rest on a long eared reclining dog who keeps his back warm under her skirts. Her head rests on two cushions, the lower one rectangular (1ft 8in x 11in x 2in) the upper one is set diagonally (10½in x 10½in x 1¾in) The slab (6ft 8in x 1ft 8in x 3in), effigy and canopy (12ft 2in) are made of Ham stone. The Decorated wall canopy, in the form of a single crocketed gable of ogival form springs from a pair of ascendant side shafts and terminates in a crocketed finial. The upper sides of the arch are almost straight and give a bold angle at the point to which the finial is fixed. The side shafts continue beyond the spring of the arch in the form of pinnacles. Enclosed between the soffit and crocketed mouldings of the steeply rising arch is a pierced trefoil. The inner, slightly pointed, arch is decorated with open cinquefoil cusping which terminates in heads of knights and ladies re-cut in the 19th century. Perhaps, these represent members of the de Mohun or Segrave families.

In discussing the position of hands, Brian Kemp says: "…apart from knights drawing swords or bishops in the act of blessing, the position of the hands on the effigies in general is far from standard. On effigies recumbent and not at rest, the closing of the hands, in prayer became increasingly common but some ladies, for example, were shown clutching at their garments and other figures appeared holding symbolic or devotional objects, frequently a heart. more rarely, and by charming variation, a later 13th-century lady of the Mohun family at Axminster (Devon) has between her hands a tiny Virgin and Child."[135] The second wife of Reginald de Mohun II was Isabel, whose effigy I believe this to be, although the church in Axminster attributes it to Alice de Mohun, wife of Reginald de Mohun I.

Christian de Mohun married John de Mohun IV in May 1305. John de Mohun III was given Christian's marriage portion of £400, in return for maintaining the young couple and giving Christian a dower of 100 marks a year if she survived her husband, which indeed she did. Had he not died before Christian he would have inherited £600 a year. Does this point to Sir John de Mohun IV's death as taking place in 1324/25 when his father married the older sister and thus made sure of benefiting from the inheritance?

John de Mohun IV and Christian made their home at Whichford (Warwickshire) and after he died in Scotland before 1330, having fought in the battle of Boroughbridge in 1322, his body was brought home from Scotland and he was buried in the south chapel of Whichford church "where his stone coffin with his coat of arms carved on it is still to be seen."[136] The manor of Whichford had been brought to the Mohuns by Agnes, the wife of William de Mohun II in the 12th century. John de Mohun IV and his wife Christian left a son, John de Mohun V, the last de Mohun lord of Dunster.

CHAPTER FOUR

THE LUTTRELLS OF DUNSTER

THE NAME of Luttrell does not appear in Domesday Book but in the reign of Philippe Auguste of France, an Osbert Lotrel had the farm of Arques in Normandy and he held this farm in 1180 and 1198. In 1419 a certain John Loutrel of Dieppe is mentioned as a subject of the mad French king, Charles VI, whose daughter Isabelle had been the second wife of Richard II of England. In 1422, the year the French king died, a Robert Loterel was presented to a church near Bayeux.[1]

The progenitor of the house of Luttrell was Sir Geoffrey Luttrell (died c.1216) who married Frethesant Paynell (or Paganel) whose ancestor Ralph Paynell held East Quantoxhead in the reign of William the Conqueror. Their son, Sir Andrew of East Quantoxhead (c.1208-65), with his wife Pernel had three sons Sir Geoffrey (c.1235 - 70), the ancestor of the Luttrells of Irnham in Lincolnshire and Alexander of East Quantoxhead (d. c.1273). (It was the grandson of this Sir Geoffrey Luttrell also a Sir Geoffrey Luttrell of Irnham (1276-1345) who commissioned the famous Luttrell Psalter). The third son was Robert, who in 1262 was presented by his father to the church at Irnham. He deserves a mention as the founder of three chantries at Irnham, Stamford and Sempringham in 1303. He became a canon of Salisbury and died in 1315.

Sir Hugh Luttrell (d.1428), the first Luttrell lord of Dunster was descended from the younger branch of the Luttrells of East Quantoxhead known as the Luttrells of Chilton. He was the first Luttrell to live at Dunster Castle and his effigy and that of his wife, Catherine Beaumont, may be found in St. George's church. The senior line of the Luttrells of East Quantoxhead died out with Sir John Luttrell, KB., who died without issue in 1403. The small seal bears his arms and the legend: *SIGILL JOHIS LOTERELL.*

Sir Andrew Luttrell of East Quantoxhead (died c.1326) and his wife, Elizabeth de Raleigh, had two sons: Sir Alexander (c.1285-1354) who carried on the senior line and Sir John of Chilton who was the ancestor of the Luttrells of Dunster castle. Sir John of Chilton owned land on Lundy Island and in 1337 he was dubbed a knight by Edward III and he then acquired the Chilton property in Devonshire. It was the son of this Sir John of Chilton in the parish of Thorverton, Sir Andrew Luttrell of Chilton, who married Elizabeth Courtenay, the widow of Sir John de Vere, son of the earl of Oxford. The king awarded them an annuity of £200 for life in order that they should maintain their social position.[2] It was Hugh, the son of Sir Andrew and Lady Elizabeth who became the first lord of Dunster.

The senior line was maintained for only three generations. Sir Alexander was killed at Watchet, together with Alexander Montfort and John Strechleye; Several persons were found guilty of murder and others were declared to have been present and assisting.[3] He had married twice and with his first wife Mary, (the daughter of Sir Thomas Trivet) he had a son, Thomas. Secondly he married a Lucy. Thomas married twice also and with his wife Joan Palton,[4] he had a son, Sir John, but apparently no children with his second wife Denise. Sir John, KB, married Joan Kingston and he died *sans prole*. He directed that: if he should die without lawful issue before returning to his mansion at East Quantoxhead, the manor and the advowson of the church there and his lands at Alfoxton and Watchet should, after payment of his debts, be conveyed by his feoffees to his cousin Sir Hugh Luttrell [of Chilton] and the heirs of his body, or, failing them, to the heirs and assigns of John Venables.[5] It is unknown who John Venables was, but the interesting phrase: should he die before returning to his manor at East Quantoxhead was indeed fulfilled for he possibly died possibly at the battle of Shrewsbury on the 21 July 1403 where he took up arms on the King's behalf to oppose the rising of the Percies, the Mortimers and Owen Glendower, to resist the malice of a certain Sir Henry Percehaye, knight.[6]

At the coronation of Henry IV in 1399, John Luttrell was created Knight of the Bath and in March 1400, this first king of the House of Lancaster, took John Luttrell into his permanent service and gave him an annuity of £40 out of the issue of the county of Somerset.[7] In 1401, the king further rewarded John and granted him a further annuity of £16 payable at the Exchequer, and confirmed to him an annuity of £10 granted by John of Gaunt, out of the revenues of the Duchy of Lancaster. Sir John Luttrell was Sheriff of Somerset and Dorset for a year beginning in the autumn of 1401.[8]

His cousin, Sir Hugh Luttrell of Dunster (d.1428), the grandson of Sir John Luttrell of Chilton, was for a time an esquire in the household of John of Gaunt, duke of Lancaster. The eventual triumph of the House of York was disastrous to the Luttrells who had been attached to the House of Lancaster ever since the days of John of Gaunt. With the death in 1403 of Sir John Luttrell KB, without issue, the main line of the Luttrells of East Quantoxhead ended.

It was Sir Andrew Luttrell of Chilton, the son of Sir John Luttrell of Chilton, who established the fortunes of his family by his marriage to Elizabeth Courtenay, a lady of illustrious lineage. Her beautiful seal shows the arms of Luttrell: *Or a bend between six Martlets Sa. impaling those of Courtenay: Or three torteaux in chief a label of three points Az.* The engrailed bordure Sable differentiates this shield of the Luttrells of Chilton from those of East Quantoxhead. Mounted on a double rose the legend encircling the seal is *'Sigillum Elizabeth Luterell'*.

Lady Elizabeth Luttrell purchased Dunster castle from Lady Joan de Mohun who outlived her. She was the daughter of Hugh, 2nd earl of Devon (d.1377) head of the noble house of Courtenay, a companion in arms of Edward III and one of the original founder Knights of the Order of the Garter. Her mother Margaret, whom the earl married on 11 August. 1325,[9] was the first surviving daughter of Humphrey de Bohun, earl of Hereford and Essex, Constable of England, the flower of Knighthood and the most Christian Knight of the World who was slain at the battle of Boroughbridge in 1322, and Elizabeth Plantagenet, the daughter of Edward I.[10]

The contract for the marriage of Margaret and Hugh was made in 1314/15. The 2nd earl of Devon had been made a Knight Banneret on 20 January 1327,[11] an order of knighthood conferred on the field of battle as a reward for distinguished service or for a deed of valour. This was the exact date Edward II resigned the throne and was succeeded by Edward III.[12] The earl repulsed the French descent on Cornwall in 1339. He was summoned to parliament on 23 April 1337 by Edward III[13] and since the writ was directed to 'Hugoni de Courteney [sic] juniori', he, at that date became Lord Courtenay.[14] He succeeded to the earldom three years afterwards. He received livery of his lands on 11 January 1340/1, was Joint Warden of Devon and Cornwall in 1352 and Chief Warden of Devon in 1373.[15] This remarkable man lived to be seventy three years of age and fathered eight sons and nine daughters.[16] He died on 2 May, 1377 and was buried in Exeter cathedral. Margaret, his extremely fertile wife, died on 16 December 1391 and was also buried in the cathedral. She was at least 76 years of age.[17] The monument represents the likeness of the grandparents of Sir Hugh Luttrell (d. 1428), the first Luttrell lord of Dunster.

Sir Hugh's uncle, the eldest brother of his mother Elizabeth, Sir Hugh Courtenay K.B., was the son and heir of their father and was born on 22 March 1326/7. He attended Edward III in his expedition to France in 1364, and was present, in the following year, at the siege of Calais, in the company of his uncle William Bohun earl of Northampton. After the surrender of Calais he probably returned in the royal suite to England. Late that year he was at Eltham, where there was a royal palace, and here he distinguished himself at a tournament, and received from the king, as his guerdon, or reward, a hood of white cloth, buttoned with large pearls, and embroidered with figures of men in dancing postures.[18] He died at the age of 22, before 2 September 1349, twenty-eight years before his father, the redoubtable 2nd earl, and was buried at Forde Abbey. This Sir Hugh Courtenay, with his wife Elizabeth, the daughter of Sir Guy de Bryan of Tor Bryan, Devon, had a son also named Hugh de Courtenay who was the grandson of the 2nd earl and nephew of Elizabeth Luttrell née Courtenay. He served in the wars in Spain and was knighted by Prince Edward, the Black Prince,at Najara where Henry of Trastamara was defeated and Peter the Cruel was restored to the throne of Castile.[19] He married Margaret, daughter of Sir Guy de Bryan.[20] Although, the note in the *Complete Peerage* queries the fact that his mother Elizabeth was a daughter of Sir Hugh de Bryan and suggests that there was a confusion with Margaret also a daughter of Sir Guy de Bryan, this is not impossible. There are many instances of fathers and sons during this medieval period marrying the eldest and the youngest daughters of a knight and this may be the case here.

Margaret died shortly after 1361 and his second marriage was to Maud, the daughter of Thomas de Holland, earl of Kent and Joan, daughter of Edmund, earl of Kent. This is Joan, the Fair Maid of Kent of the Order of the Garter fame. She married the 2nd earl of Salisbury as her second husband and it is said that it was at the ball at Calais that the Countess dropped her garter which was retrieved by her cousin, Edward III who declared *Honi soit qui mal y pense*, the insignia of the Order. She thirdly married Edward, the Black Prince who died on 20 February, 1373/4 and their son was King Richard II. Joan then remarried for the fourth time at Windsor in 1380, Waleran de Luxemburg, count of Ligny and of Pol. She died before 13 April 1392/3.

So, the eldest brother of Elizabeth Luttrell née Courtenay, Hugh de Courtenay (d.1349) and his son, her nephew, Hugh de Courtenay (d.1373/4), both died during the lifetime of their father/grandfather the 2nd earl of Devon (d.1377). Elizabeth Luttrell's brother, Edward de Courtenay of Goodrington in Devon, was the third son of their father, the 2nd earl of Devon and he died between 1364-72 also during the long lifetime of his father. He married Emmeline, the daughter and heir of Sir John Dawnay. She died before 20 September 1372 and it was their son Edward who became the 3rd earl of Devon.

Edward, the heir of his grandfather, the 2nd earl, was still a minor on 14 August 1377. He served in the Scottish war and was knighted by Edward III's seventh son, Thomas of Woodstock, earl of Buckingham in 1380. This 3rd earl of Devon, Lady Elizabeth's nephew lost his sight and was known as the blind earl. He may have had some sight in one eye for he was nevertheless very active. He was one of the suite that conducted Anne of Bohemia from Gravelines to London in 1381 for her marriage to King Richard II.[21] Between 1383/5 he was Admiral of the West. The period between the battle of Sluys in 1340, when Edward III won a naval victory over a combined French and Genoese fleet, and the treaty of Calais in 1360 gave Edward the advantage at sea. The court of admiralty evolved to keep the king's peace at sea and to deal with piracy claims. Two admirals were appointed regularly in time of conflict but only on a temporary basis. In peace time the clerks of the king's ships were in charge of naval matters. These two admirals were drawn from the knightly class and Sir Walter Manny and Sir Bartholomew Burghersh were appointed admirals in August 1337.[22] One admiral controlled the coast northwards from the Thames[23] and the 3rd earl of Devon controlled the Thames westwards. He was a member of the King's Council in 1395 but he is said to have acted against the statutes of Edward III and Richard II. These were designed to prevent perversions of justice such as bribery, maintenance (the unlawful upholding of another's suit by word, writing, encouragement or other act), embracery (the attempt to influence a jury by money, promises, threats or persuasion), and champerty, (maintaining of a suit in consideration of receiving a part of the land, damages, or chattels recovered).[24] However, might seems to have triumphed over right and statutes went by the board and a session of the commissioners of *oyer et terminer* could be broken up by a knight invading the hall with drawn sword and seizing one of the justices by the throat.[25] One earl is specifically mentioned as an offender: this Devon himself sent a message to a justice of the peace telling him 'that he was false and that he should answer with his body, that he (the earl) knew all the roads by which he must come and go and that he should not escape the hands of the said earl who was sure of him'.[26]

He married Maud, daughter of Thomas, Lord Camoys, but their son Edward did not succeed to the earldom since he died shortly after August 1418, during the lifetime of his father who died on 5 December 1419 and was probably buried at Ford Abbey where his uncle Sir Hugh de Courtenay, Elizabeth Luttrell's eldest brother, was also buried. The only other brother of Elizabeth Luttrell (née Courtenay) who had issue, was Sir Philip de Courtenay of Powderham, Devon, KG, the ancestor of the present earl of Devon. He served Edward III in the Spanish war and was lord lieutenant of Ireland and steward of Cornwall. Two other brothers of Elizabeth Luttrell who reached positions of distinction were William de Courtenay who became the archbishop of Canterbury (1318-1369) and Sir Piers de Courtenay KG who was a highly distinguished soldier and died in 1409.

Elizabeth's sisters also made notable marriages. Margaret married John, Lord Cobham, a man of wide military and administrative experience who, as one of a great continual council, was appointed to hold office for a year in 1386. This great continual council had comprehensive powers over all matters of state and over Richard II's household and servants. Another of Elizabeth Luttrell's sisters married firstly William, Lord Harrington, and secondly Sir Thomas Engain.

Elizabeth was the second daughter of Hugh, 2nd earl of Devon and his wife Margaret de Bohun. Margaret's cousin Humphrey de Bohun, Earl of Hereford and Essex was the father of Mary de Bohun who was the first wife of Henry Bolingbroke, Earl of Derby, the son of John of Gaunt, Duke of Lancaster. Bolingbroke was to become the usurper of Richard II's throne and became the first Lancastrian king, as Henry IV, five years after Mary's death. Their eldest son became Henry V.

For some time, Elizabeth Courtenay was in the service of her cousin Edward, the Black Prince, and in the service of Joan, countess of Kent, his mother. In 1359 she married Sir Andrew Luttrell and in 1361 she and her husband set out on a pilgrimage to Santiago de Compostella. There were several routes to this famous shrine of St. James, from Paris, from Vézelay in Burgundy and from Le Puy. These all joined at St Jean Pied de Port and a little further west of this combined route the pilgrims from Arles joined the main route at Puenta la Reina. Here there is a statue of St. James wearing a hat with a scallop shell. Sir Andrew and Lady Elizabeth had set out with twenty four men and women and as many horses[27] and no doubt landed at Bordeaux and joined the Paris route to St. Jean Pied de Port and over the Pyrenees by the Roncevalles Pass (famous for the story of Roland and Oliver) and through Burgos and Leon to their ultimate goal at the extreme north east corner of Spain. In the window in the north aisle of Dunster church is a fragment of probably 14th-century stained glass which remains from a depiction of St James of Compostella with scallop shells in his hat. This may have been commissioned to commemorate the pilgrimage of 1361 and the complete depiction may have been intact until 1808. Scallop shells had the practical use of conveying food and drink to the mouth or even for the purpose of washing. The complete glass is depicted in the *Gentleman's Magazine* of 1808, figure 3.

Elizabeth Luttrell was an astute businesswoman who acquired valuable properties. She acquired the reversion of the manor of Feltwell in Norfolk. In Suffolk she did likewise at Moulton, Debenham and Waldingfield[28] and a charter of free warren at these places was issued to her in 1373.[29] This illustrates the importance of rabbits in the medieval diet. Lady Luttrell also obtained the right to appoint two of the canons of the priory of Flitcham.[30] In 1378 her annuity of £200 was confirmed by Richard II and renewed in her favour in 1381, her husband having died in the interval.[31] In 1374. Lady Joan de Mohun arranged to sell the reversion of the castle and manor of Dunster, the manors of Minehead and Kilton, and the hundred of Carhampton to Lady Elizabeth Luttrell.[32] The reversionary clause proved to be very important since Lady Elizabeth Luttrell died in 1395 and Lady Joan de Mohun outlived her and did not die until 1404, and therefore Elizabeth never obtained actual possession of this valuable property for which she paid five thousand marks.[33]

Lady Elizabeth died at Bermondsey on 7 August 1395 and was buried, by her own desire, in the Benedictine church of St Nicholas at Exeter.[34] The then bishop of Exeter, Edmund Stafford, in August of that year, ordered public prayers to be offered throughout his diocese for the souls of Margaret Cobham and Elizabeth Luttrell, sisters of the Archbishop of Canterbury, and, by way of encouragement, promised an indulgence of forty days for the faithful who should pray for them.[35]

This Lady Elizabeth Luttrell should not be confused with a later Lady Elizabeth Luttrell of Powderham who died in 1493. Both ladies were, before their marriages, Elizabeth Courtenay and both had sons named Hugh. The later Lady Elizabeth Luttrell was the widow of Sir James Luttrell (d.1461) and she was buried before the high altar, the altar of St. George, in the priory church. Her tomb slab was removed from there and may now be seen at the east end of the south aisle of the church at Dunster.

Sir Hugh Luttrell (d.1428)was the second son of Sir Andrew Luttrell of Chilton and his wife Lady Elizabeth Luttrell and his eldest brother John died soon after his grandmother Dame Joan Luttrell (d.1378). Sir Hugh became the heir to the small paternal property of Chilton in Devonshire but he did not actually possess it until 1385 when he was, in fact, abroad in the service of Richard II.[36] The Hundred Years' War between England and France raged between 1337 and 1453 and was in progress throughout the lifetime of this first Luttrell lord of Dunster. Born in the reign of Edward III he lived throughout the reigns of Richard II, Henry IV and Henry V and died during the protectorate of Humphrey, duke of Gloucester, the future King Henry VI being then only nine years old. John of Gaunt, the father of the usurper Henry IV, was a very powerful but loyal supporter of Richard II who was nevertheless suspected of ulterior motives. He lived in regal state in his great palace of the Savoy in the Strand which was fired in 1381 by rioters led by Wat Tyler in the uprising known as the Peasants' Revolt. As a member of his household Sir Hugh Luttrell would have frequented this palace.

At the beginning of 1390, Sir Hugh is mentioned as a knight having influence at court and he took part in some jousts at St Inglevert, near Calais.[37] At this time King Richard II, having reached the age of twenty two years, decided to rule as a monarch of full age and made changes in his household. There was opposition to the conduct of the court which was voiced by the Merciless Parliament of 1388, dominated by the five Lords Appellant but things returned to a semblance of normality and peace after the failure of de Vere's royalist rising, and his defeat at Radcot Bridge. In 1391 and again in 1395, Sir Hugh received annuities from Richard II in consideration of his services. The first annuity of £20 came from the confiscated English property of the Priory of St. Nicholas at Angers,[38] and the second, of £40, was granted provided that he remained in the King's service for life.[39]

He became keeper of the forest of Gillingham and constable of Leeds castle in Kent during the reigns of Richard II and Henry IV, who added £5 in lieu of the constableship of Leeds Castle. In 1404 letters patent to this effect were cancelled when Henry IV remitted to Sir Hugh £482 8s. 11d. due to the Exchequer in respect of lands farmed by him in Kent. In 1395 Sir Hugh's mother, Lady Elizabeth Luttrell, died, and after bitter wrangling with the Mohuns, he came into possession of his inheritance.[40]

In both 1349 and 1399 Sir Hugh was one of the military knights who accompanied Richard II to Ireland,[41] and in 1400 Sir Hugh is known to have been at Calais but his role is not specified. In 1403 his receiver in the west of England sent 22 marks by the hands of John Luttrell, son of Richard Lutrell [sic] at his coming from Calec, at the feast of the Nativity of St John in the fourth year, that is to say at midsummer 1403.[42]

Earlier in 1400 Owen Glendower had quarrelled with his English neighbours. It was a local affair which flared up into a national revolt when Henry IV's erstwhile supporters, the Percies, joined in the fray. Henry Percy, known as Hotspur, nursed grievances against the king concerning the ransom of the earl of Douglas which the king had denied him. The Percies had defeated a Scottish army carrying out one of its customary raids, at the battle of Homilden Hill in 1402 but they were defeated at Shrewsbury and it was probably at this battle on 21 July 1403 that Sir John Luttrell KB of East Quantoxhead, son of Thomas and Joan Luttrell, was slain. He may alternatively have been killed at Cardiff in October 1403 when urgent messages were dispatched to ship troops from Somerset to come to the relief of the besieged castle. Sir John died without issue and his cousin Sir Hugh Luttrell of Chilton, lord of Dunster, inherited his estates.

Calais and its March was of supreme importance to King Henry IV and he was faced with the ravages and despoliations wrought by the Flemish pirates. An embassy was set up in Calais to ensure that Bruges, Ghent, Ypres and the 'French territory', known as the Four Members of Flanders, observed the truce with France. This treaty was to be renewed and every endeavour was to be made to ensure a settlement resulting in a more lasting peace. This embassy was composed of Sir Hugh Luttrell, Sir John Croft, Dr Nicholas Risshton and John Urban.[43] Later, Sir Hugh was also one of the ambassadors appointed to treat with the commissioners of the overlord of the Flemings, Philip the Bold, duke of Burgundy. After the duke's death, his duchess, Margaret, endeavoured to advance the settlement but in face of hostile raids conducted by Flemings, Bretons and French on the English coast and reprisals, little progress was made until 1407 when a commercial agreement, renewed annually, was made and reinforced in July 1416 by a treaty of 'abstinence from war'. Thus the route to Calais was safeguarded against Flemish raids. In preserved official letters Sir Hugh Luttrell is described as lieutenant of Calais,[44] and for two years between 1404/6, Mayor of Bordeaux, an appointment made by royal authority.[45]

During this period he was present as one of the knights of the shire of Somerset in the parliament which met at Coventry on 6 October 1404, when he was 'paid for forty-six days personal attendance'.[46] Two days earlier, on 4 October 1404, Lady Joan de Mohun died and Sir Hugh put forward his claim to the estate of which his mother, Lady Elizabeth Luttrell had bought the reversion twenty-eight years previously. His title to Dunster, Minehead, Carhampton and Kilton was challenged by the co-heirs of Sir John de Mohun V and Lady Joan de Mohun, viz. Edward duke of York, and his wife, Philippa (de Mohun), and Elizabeth (de Mohun), countess of Salisbury, (daughters of the deceased), and by Richard, lord Strange of Knockin, grandson of Sir John and Lady Joan de Mohun and the son of their youngest daughter Maud who had married Sir John le Strange of Knockin who had died in 1397. Maud also predeceased her mother. This formidable opposition to Sir Hugh's title began legal proceedings in an endeavour to recover the estates. King Henry IV lost no time and by 17 October 1404, the escheator intervened on behalf of the Crown and the king, aware of the complications which were bound to ensue, gave a temporary lease of the Mohun property to William Grene and John Lawrence for a considerable rent. They remained in occupation until 17 February 1405 when it is presumed that Sir Hugh Luttrell obtained possession. Nevertheless, the case dragged on into 1406 and contention persisted right up to 1430, two years after Sir Hugh's death and the year his heir, Sir John Luttrell, died. Philippa, duchess of York died in 1431.

On 14 May 1405, the king appointed nine special commissioners, who included two chief justices and the chief baron of the exchequer to take an assize of 'novel disseisin' in the matter. In other words, they were to inquire into the question of illegal possession. However, by 28 June Sir Hugh Luttrell was probably already established at Dunster. The account taken from Lyte has been reassembled in chronological order. The household accounts read: June 28. In. 14 fowls (*pullis*) 16d.; July 1. In. 4 gallons (*lagenis*) of milk 4d.; In. butter, 7d.; July 2. In. two quarters of a calf, bought 10d.; In divers spices 8d.; In. 12 conger eels (*congres*) 4s. of the custom of the manor of Minhede; In. 12 *milwelles* 3s. of the same custom; July 3. Paid by order of my lord for the expenses of a varlet of my lady, the Countess of La Marche, sent with her letters to my lord, as in his horse being in the town 15½d.[47] It is unclear to which Countess of March this entry refers. Eleanor Holland, the widow of Roger Mortimer died in 1405. It may refer to her or her daughter-in-law, Anne Stafford, the wife of her son Edmund Mortimer, earl of March. July 8. Paid by order of my lord for the expenses of the horses of the Earl of Pembroke riding toward the King. 20d.[48] (Lyte appends a note to the effect that there was no Earl of Pembroke in 1405 and that the person so styled was probably Lord Grey of Ruthyn.[49]) The last Earl of Pembroke, John Hastings II, left no legitimate heir.[50]

Year after year Sir Hugh made an allowance to Dan John Buryton, one of the monks at Dunster, probably for the masses celebrated in the castle chapel of St Stephen. In 1405 when Sir Hugh took up his abode at the castle, he had a steward of the household who was paid £5 per annum, a chamberlain at £1 6s. 8d., a cook at £1 13s. 4d. and fifteen other men who received wages ranging from 13s. 4d. up to £2. There was also a constable of the castle who appears to have lived in the town. That year Sir Hugh's advisory council granted a lease of the two mills for sixty years at a rent of £10 upon condition that the tenants carried out all the repairs. Any timber required for this purpose would be supplied. The mills belonged to the lord and it was obligatory for all his tenants to bring their corn to be ground at these mills but the charges levied for this service went to the tenant who did the work.

The year before Sir Hugh Luttrell died the lessee of the two mills, William Person, erected a third mill, adjoining the lower mill. This lower mill which is the one in existence today was originally called Nethermylle and the higher mill, no longer in existence, was called Overmylle. They were called Higher and Lower Mill in 1620. The third mill was erected under the same roof as the lower mill and because William Person had expended so much money in building it his rent was reduced and fixed at £2 6s 8d. By 1739, the rent of the water grist-mills was raised to £22 and in 1777 it was £35 10s. In 1909 Lyte observed that: 'The Lower Mill, with two wheels, was partly rebuilt in 1801 upon the old site, and perhaps to some extent according to the old design, some of the windows being pointed … the grist-mill of Dunster has long been a favourite subject with artists and photographers…in 1886, just eight hundred years after the compilation of Domesday Book, the rent of the mill was fixed at £40, eighty times the nominal amount of its value in the reign of William the Conqueror … A quaint little bridge, just below the mill, considerably altered by Henry Fownes Luttrell in the 18[51] century, may represent the Millbridge mentioned in medieval records'.[51]

The household accounts at the time of the lordship of Sir Hugh Luttrell and his wife, Lady Catherine, in 1405 show that she had a damsel in attendance on her and a laundress for the whole establishment for 6s. 8d. The accounts also include: 1405. July 17. 'In. shoes, hose, shirts and breeches (braccis) delivered to William Russell, my lord's 'henxteman', 20d. 1405.... August 25. For the making of two 'dowbletes' for William Russel and Robert the keeper of my lord's horses, together with breeches and spurs bought for them by the hands of John Hunt, 2s. 6d.

On the same day there was cause for alarm. A messenger arrived in Dunster with letters from King Henry IV ordering Sir Hugh to 'hasten towards the parts of Wales'. The messenger received the gift of 3s. 4d. from Sir Hugh. The French had landed in South Wales to assist Owen Glendower in accordance with an alliance he had made with France on 14 July 1404. Sir Hugh paid 3s. 5½d. on 25 August for the expenses of the horses of the Earl of Pembroke returning from the King and those of other stranger's.[52] Just over a fortnight elapsed before Sir Hugh was ready to depart and, in the meantime, the household expenses included: 1405. September 6. In 8 dozen geese bought in Alliremore by Henry Baker, 22s.[53] Ninety-six geese seems a very large order until one realises that by 11 September Sir Hugh was already in Wales and that a cart carrying victuals from the castle went to the haven, towards my lord who was in Wales and that the cost was 6d for the transportation. Also on the same day paid for six standards of my lord's arms delivered to divers ships of Minhede carrying victuals to my lord in the parts of Wales, 2s.[54]

Also paid in the expenses of my lord and his household riding towards the King who was at Leicestre and absent for four whole weeks £4 15s. 8d. Also paid to John Cotes at his lodging at Henyngham, my lord being there, as more fully appears in indentures made between my lord and him, £4 13s. 4d ... 1405 September 12. Paid to two armourers cleaning my lord's armour for fourteen days and a half, at 14d. a day, both for them and for a servant who waited on them for the same time, 16s. 11d ... . 1405. October 2. In. bread and ale bought for certain seamen who were in the ship Howell sent to the parts of Wales to get news of my lord who was there in the retinue of the King, 12d.

Sir Hugh Luttrell was back in Dunster by 23 October for the accounts show: In. horse bread bought for the horses of my lord who was at Dunstre, 22d.[55] My lord dined off salmon that day and there appears to have been somewhat of a celebration to mark his return from Wales. October 23. In. 2 salmon bought at Le Merssh 12d. In 15 live pigs bought wholesale, 42s, of which 6 were sold for 20s. 4d. and 9 became bacon.[56] Then my lord went to his favourite chapel, no doubt to give thanks for his safe return from the hazards of the Welsh uprising.

With reference to the entry on October 26 Delivered to my lord going on pilgrimage to the Chapel of the Holy Trinity of Bircombe, 12d,[57] Lyte remarks that: The chapel thus mentioned may probably be identified with a small ruin now known as 'Burgundy Chapel', standing a little above the sea in a secluded valley on the west side of Minehead, not far from Greenaleigh Farm. Sir Hugh evidently held it in special honour, for in several subsequent years he gave considerable funds to a chaplain celebrating in the chapel of Byrcombe on his account. After Sir Hugh's campaign in Wales his armour needed attention so we read: November 13. To two armourers cleaning my lord's armour for eleven days at 4d a day apiece, 7s. 4d. In fresh lard for the same 7d.

Lady Luttrell's mother, Lady Beaumont, lived at Saunton and she had reason to wish to communicate with her and so a messenger was despatched to Devonshire: 'November 13. In the gift of my lady to Thomas Kynge riding towards Saunton as her messenger, 8d'. Lady Catherine had apparently just returned from London for, on the same day, Sir Hugh made a gift to John, the charioteer 'for bringing my lady from London to Dunsterre, 20s. and for certain expenses incurred and paid by him, as he stated, 15d.' Perhaps Lady Luttrell had gone to London to make special purchases for Christmas. Two special 'candles called Paris candles' were to illumine the knight's hall so that we read: November 20. In a bundle of 'macchernes' (wicks) for making Paris candles, 3s. 4d ... December 18. In 11½ 'ronnes' of wick thread (fili lichenii) bought for torches, 6s 1d. In. the costs of a man bringing the same from Brigewater to Dunster 2s. 2d ... December 20. In the gift of my lord, by his order, to two servants of the Prior of Dunsterre who presented to my lady twelve capons, two little bacon pigs and four bushels of green peas, 16d.[58] It is interesting that green peas are mentioned as being produced in December. This Christmas of 1405 was an occasion to be specially celebrated, the first Luttrell Christmas of many which were to be celebrated at Dunster. The scene can be envisaged: the castle was strewn with rushes and the feast was prepared, the servants were given Christmas boxes and my lady and her daughter had new apparel for the festivities.

The accounts also show: December 20. For hose and shoes necessary to William Russel and Robert, the keeper of the horses because of the approach of Christmas, 20d... In paid for fur of six gowns of my lady and her daughters, against the same feast, 4s 10d. Sir Hugh and Lady Catherine had three daughters, Margaret, Elizabeth and Anne. Also, on December 20 we read that Sir Hugh gave John Clifton's servant a gift, or tip, for his trouble in bringing two bucks from Gillingham: 'in the gift of my lord to a varlet of John Clifton bringing two bucks from Gillingham, 20d.'[59] Sir Hugh Luttrell had been given the reversion of the keepership of the forest of Gillingham and at the same time, in 1395, the constableship of the castle of Leeds in Kent.[60]

On Christmas Eve rushes were bought to strew in the hall and chambers and these cost 6d. On Christmas Day In. offerings of the servants of the household distributed in the church by order of my lord, 2s. These gifts were not, it seems, distributed in the castle chapel of St. Stephen but in the parish church. Much building went on in Dunster church towards the end of the 15th century and beginning of the 16th century, but in 1405 there would have been two screens under the crossing between the eastern and western piers and much else would have been structurally different. The next day, the merrymaking at the castle was in full swing; it must have been a joyous time; their lord had returned home unscathed from the Welsh wars. The castle, which had been rarely used by Lady Joan de Mohun, was once again open and feasting, music and dancing in the light of the 'Paris' candles continued until Twelfth Night. These festivities would have taken place on the summit of the Tor in the donjon, where there was a knights' hall connected to the chapel of St. Stephen. Sir Hugh gave 3s. 4d to three tenants of John Cobleston who played before him and dancing was provided by 'several children of Minhede who danced before him' and for this his gift was 20d. By 27 December the wine seems to have run out for the accounts read: December 27. In wine bought and conveyed from Taunton on account of the feast held by my lord, 7s.[61] There is an entry for 1406 with no day or month; it reads: 1406. Five gallons of white wine bought at Brigewater to fill up a pipe of wine somewhat diminished, 3s. 4d. Christmas and New Year had probably taken their toll of the wine supplies.

There was a shadow overhanging all these festivities for Sir Hugh's title was still not settled and allusions are made on 3 and 5 January 1406 to this suit against the formidable array of Mohuns and their marital connections already enumerated. 1405 July 10: 'For expenses incurred by my lord himself and strangers who came to him at Yevelchestre (Ilchester) because his adversaries intended on that day to have arrained the assize against him, 67s 11d...1406. January 3. Paid for four quires of paper bought, 2s ... Paid for twelve skins of parchment on which to write the evidences of my lord, at Briggewater 2s. 8d ... In the expenses of John Bacwell [the steward of the household] about the writing of the said evidences and other affairs of my lord, who was there for six days, 12s ... January 5. In the expenses of my lord who came to Brigewater for certain causes touching his plea, 3s. 1d. And in his gift to a lawyer, a kinsman of Richard Popham, 6s. 8d[62] ... January 5. In the gift of my lord to two servants of my lady of Pawlet who brought the carcase of an ox and a boar and a live grue and presented them to my lady, 6s. 8d; and in the expenses of their horses that were in the town for a night 17d ... Also on the same day in the gift of my lord to a servant of William Godwyn who brought a boar and presented it to my lady against Christmas, 20d ... Also in the gift of my lord to the Clerks of St Nicholas, 12d.'[63]

It seems that on Twelfth Night in spite of the roasting of the ox, the boar and whatever procedure was followed to cook the 'live grue', Sir Hugh had to go to Bridgwater on urgent business. William Godwyn, whose name so frequently occurs, had married Anne, the third daughter of Sir Hugh and Lady Catherine in Midsummer 1408. He held various responsible positions under the Luttrells. On their marriage, William Godwyn, the elder, settled land on the young couple to the annual value of £20, subject to his own life interest. The bridegroom undertook to provide the same sum and Sir Hugh undertook to pay 100 marks in instalments.[64]

The Clerks of St Nicholas, were: 'probably boys connected with the Priory of Dunster, of whom one, styled the "boy bishop" was, by irreverent custom, allowed to perform certain religious functions in church between the feast of St Nicholas and that of the Holy Innocents, in the month of December.'[65] The *Dictionary of the Christian Church* says of Boy Bishops: In medieval times it was a widespread custom, in many English monasteries, schools and country parishes, to elect on St. Nicholas' Day, 6 December, a boy who should execute till Holy Innocents' Day, 28 December, various functions in church ordinarily performed by a bishop. The practice was abolished by Henry VIII, revived by Mary, and finally abolished by Elizabeth. The intention was to express in dramatic form the reverence for childhood shown in the Gospels.[66]

In 1406 there was practically no home farm at Dunster. All provisions had to be purchased, with the exception of venison, game, fruit and vegetables and according to the custom of the manor of Minehead, the lord had the right to buy fish at wholesale prices. The consumption of fish in the medieval period was prodigious. February 12. In. 130 'haques' bought at Bristuyt (Bristol), the haque at 2½d and 120 for 100, 31s 3d ... In. 500 'scalpines' bought at 2s. 6d. the hundred, 12s. 6d ... .March 7. In. fresh 'melet' bought, 1d ... March 10. In mussels bought, 1d.[67]

Easter Day fell on 19 April in 1406. Elizabeth, the second daughter of Sir Hugh Luttrell married William Harleston in 1406 and John Bacwell, the domestic chaplain and steward was sent to Bridgwater to bring back a friar, John Somer. The entry in Sir Hugh's accounts is as follows: On the eve of St Mark (24 April), in paid for the expenses of John Bacwell sent by order of my lord to Brigewater for John Somer, a friar, to come to Dunsterre because of the marriage to be made between a daughter of my lord and William Harleston, 2s.[68]

Lyte gives an account of the subsidiary suit brought by Sir Hugh Luttrell against Thomas, Prior of Christ Church, Canterbury, in Easter term 1406:

> ...for the delivery of the sealed chest which Lady de Mohun had deposited in his charge two days before her death. He was opposed by the co-heirs of Mohun, but, after full argument, the chest was opened in the Court of Common Pleas, and adjudicated to him, the contents being title deeds to property of which he was in actual possession. Some weeks later, a novel arrangement was made for the determination of the main controversy. On the 19 June 1406, the House of Commons sent up a petition praying that the suit concerning the castle and manor of Dunster, the manors of Minehead, Kilton and Carhampton, and the hundred of Carhampton, with their appurtenances, should be referred to the award and judgement of four lords of the realm and all the justices. To this the Duke of York, on behalf of himself and his parceners agreed, stipulating only that the lords selected and the justices should swear before the King in Parliament to settle the matter

according to the laws of the realm before a certain day, without showing favour to either party. The plaintiffs accordingly nominated two laymen, the Lords Roos and Furnival, and the defendant nominated the Bishops of Exeter and St. David's. The 1 November was moreover fixed as the latest day for their decision. The Bishop of Exeter and the two lay lords took the stipulated oaths on the spot, and Parliamentary authority was given to the King's Council to receive the oaths of the other arbitrators during the recess then about to begin. Seven of the judges were sworn before the King and the Bishop of Durham, then Chancellor of England, at the house of the latter on 3 July, William Gascoigne, the Chief Justice being absent. It was not, however, until 22 October that the court was fully constituted, the Bishop of St David's then taking the oath, together with Laurence Drue who had been substituted for the Bishop of Exeter. The arguments seem to have been continued, by consent of the parties, beyond the date originally fixed for the decision, but without any result, no definite issue having been joined, and the parties being still en travers (in disagreement). At some unspecified date in November or December, the Commons, took up the matter again on behalf of Sir Hugh Luttrell, who sat among them as one of the members for Devonshire. Contrasting the 'poor estate of the said Hugh', with 'the great estates' of his adversaries, they prayed that the special assize should be repealed, unless concerned with evidence already produced, and that no fresh commission for a special assize should be issued. They further prayed that if a suit should be instituted for trial by the country in the normal manner, nobody should be put on the jury who had not £40 a year in land, and they ended by observing that the estates in question were of great value and the parties powerful persons, so that 'mischief and riot' might easily arise unless special precautions were taken. To this the King replied that the statute made should be observed, and that the Sheriff of Somerset should be sworn before the Council to empanel the most sufficient and impartial persons in his bailiwick.[69]

The case was duly heard, most probably at Ilchester in the Michaelmas term, by special commissioners nominated earlier in the commission of 14 May 1405. This was obviously a most important hearing at which it is probable that the whole judicial bench was present. It is certain that William Hankford C.J.K.B and John Markham C.J.K.B (later dismissed by Edward IV for too great leniency), and the Chief Baron and other judges were present, together with a great array of sergeants and counsel. The de Mohuns disputed the validity of the transactions which had taken place following the settlement of the succession of the property, or entail of 1346.[70] Their case was conducted by Robert Tirwhit). The entail of 1346 had been a source of concern to Sir John de Mohun V and his wife, Lady Joan as they feared that one day their proceedings might be challenged, as indeed, at this time, they were. In 1369, seeking to secure their position, and especially that of Lady Joan de Mohun, they had brought out the big guns and had selected most influential persons of high social standing to be the trustees of a conveyance: Simon of Sudbury, bishop of London, Sir Aubrey de Vere, knight, and Sir John de Burghersh, knight, were nominated. By letters patent of 6 July 1369 the manor and hundred of Carhampton were conveyed to these three trustees and they were further empowered to dispose of them by alienation, gift, or demise, in fee simple or otherwise, according to the pleasure and order of the lady, conveyance in mortmain being alone forbidden.[71] The conveyance of 1369 was duly recognised by Sir Baldwin Malet of Enmore and other military tenants of the Honour of Dunster and Sir Baldwin made a deposition to this effect on 30 December 1406.

An undated list of the principal men of Somerset classified as knights; esquires with 100 marks at the least, and esquires with £40 at the least. The dots against the names of twelve persons of the second category suggest that they were to be empanelled as a jury.[72]

These were therefore the powerful men who backed the de Mohun cause whose case was conducted by Robert Hill. The report submitted by the two lawyers, Tirwhit and Hill ends abruptly with an adjournment, and all that we know further about the matter is that Sir Hugh Luttrell remained in possession.[73] Arguments of prolonged length dealing with intricacies of the law of a highly technical nature had taken place but Sir Hugh's case seems to have rested on the questionable transactions conducted after the entail of 1369. The dispute between the de Mohuns and the Luttrells persisted and was still unresolved two years after Sir Hugh's death in 1428.

The household accounts continue in 1408 with reference to fines imposed on fisherman who sold their fish privately, May 8. John Diere, a common fisherman, went away with his fish, in prejudice of the town and contrary to the custom of the borough. Therefore, he is in mercy, 4d. 1424, October 23. Walter Phelp, Walter Stone, Philip Cras, John Oldley, tenants of the lord. sold their fish to strangers before offering (protul) it in the lord's court at the Castle, contrary to the ancient ordinance. Therefore, they are in mercy, 6d, 4d, 6d, 3d.[74] Butchers likewise were in trouble if they attempted to sell their meat at home, instead of bringing it to the market for sale. It was an offence to skin the slaughtered beasts and to sell their hides separately.

Fines were imposed on Ellen Watkyns and Geoffrey Taillour for pilfering in the first case and for night-walking and causing a disturbance in the second; the reason for the night-walking is not divulged. Whether it was for the purposes of stealing or for amorous adventures we do not know: 1408, May. Ellen Watkyns is a common 'holcroppe' of diverse things and a common scold and disturber of the peace. Therefore she is in mercy, 4d ... Geoffrey Taillour is a common night-walker and a disturber of the peace. Therefore, he is in mercy, half a mark.[75]

There are no entries for 1410, but in that year Sir Hugh was Steward of the Household of Queen Joan of Brittany, the second wife of Henry IV, who was accused of witchcraft practiced against her step-son, Henry V. Sir Hugh was appointed by her to the offices of constable of Bristol Castle and keeper of the forests of Kingswood and Fulwood for the term of her life.[76]

In 1086 there were two mills at "Torre" which yielded 10s a year to William de Mohun. By 1279 their value had increased to £2 13s. 4d. In 1329, Sir John de Mohun rented his two corn mills to Walter Rughe for £16 and in 1405 Sir Hugh Luttrell leased them for 60 years to tenants for £10 on condition that repairs wre undertaken by them. The upper mill has disappeared but the lower mill remains and was partly rebuilt in 1801. In 1886 the rent of this corn mill was fixed at £400.

In 1411 the first fulling mill which had yielded a rent of 13s 4d from 1259 was referred to as le tokyng mill.[77] The precise definition of tucking is to dress or finish woven cloth and to stretch it on tenters. Since in 1418. Thomas Touker was paying the rent of 13s 4d, which had never changed, it is perhaps established that his fulling-mill under Grobhurst [sic] was the original mill of 1259 and was actually at Frilford or Frekeford, now known as Frackford. The second fulling mill, known to have been in existence since 1376, is in 1418 described as being near le Colverhay but there was also, at this time, a third and a fourth mill; the third near Barlebienshay [sic] which provided a rent of 2s to Sir Hugh Luttrell and the fourth was owned by the abbot of Cleeve and was in West Street. This latter mill was rented by Thomas Touker, the younger, from the abbot. This Thomas Touker's name crops up earlier in 1413 in the court-roll of the borough: To this court comes Thomas Touker the younger and he gives to the lord 12d. as a fine for having estate and entry in a burgage on the south side of Grobbefast - pathe, which William Jone lately held, to hold according to the custom of the manor, rendering therefor and doing the same rents and services as the aforesaid William was wont to render and do. And he will build a new house of one couple and two inschydes upon the said burgage within two years, according to agreement. And he was admitted tenant and did fealty.[78]

Professor Salzman wrote: The normal roof may be taken to be composed of wall-plates, tie-beams, principals and purlins, common rafters, collars and ridge-pieces. The principals are sometimes called 'couples', which we have seen originally applied to all rafters, and houses are occasionally defined by the number of couples, or bays which they contain - as in a lease made at Henley-in-Arden in 1446, when the lessee undertook to build a hall containing two couples. Similarly at Dunster in 1413 Thomas Touker was admitted to a vacant burgage on condition that he should, within the next two years build a house with one couple and two 'inschydes' (i.e. gables).[79] In Sir Hugh Luttrell's time and in the reigns of Henry IV and Henry V, the continuation of West Street towards Frackford was understandably known as Toukerstrete, since it linked the mills run by father and son. Here there was the requisite running water, still evident today. After a few years there is no mention of the mill near le Colverhay and the existing ones were under Parbienshay or Barlebienshey, and the one in West Street and the one at Frackford. Towards the middle of the 15th century a Robert Touker built a fulling mill on the eastern side of the Castle but presumably far below it.[80]

Margaret Luttrell, the daughter-in-law of Sir Hugh Luttrell was widowed on 30 June 1430. It was necessary to observe the seemly practice of mourning, and so the widow's servants must be attired in black livery. The material was bought in Dunster market in the white and dyed black.

In six douseynys of white cloth bought for the livery of my lady at divers prices this year, 37s. In ten douseynys of white cloth woven for the said livery, this year, of Robert Northam, 5s. In fulling the same ten douseynys paying 4d per doseyne, at 3s. 4d. In dyeing all the aforesaid cloth, together with a piece containing twenty yards, to a black colour, by John Dyer, by the view of William Warderoppe, paying l2d per doseyne, 7s 6d, and paid to Thomas Touker of Clyve/Cleeve for shearing all the aforesaid cloth 4s.[81]

These expenses occur in the accounts for September 1430/1 and also cover the purchase of material for a new gown for the widow. In. five yards of 'fustyan' bought in the market-place of Dunsterre for a double gown of my lady, 2s 11d.. And in a quarter of a yard of 'tarterys' bought for the same gown, 10d.[82] Fustian was a general term for a large category of linen and cotton, but fustians, probably made partly of wool were imported into England under the name of the places where they were manufactured, Amsterdam, Augsburg, Milan, Naples, Prussia, Venice, Ulm and Genoa. In England from about 1336 Norwich made a worsted fustian and became the most flourishing city in all England, by means of its great trade in worsteds, fustians, freezes and other woollen manufactures.[83] So it may be that Lady Margaret's gown was not of a locally made cloth. Apart from a new gown the widow ordered new furnishings: And paid to John Dyer for dying a bed-cover, 'tapytes, curteynes, costerys, bankerys' and 'guysshenys [cushions] both for my lady's hall and for the chamber and the chapel at Karampton, 7s..[84]

The same account mentions James Luttrell, the son of Margaret and the late John Luttrell. They were married in 1422, so James could only have been, at the most seven years of age and little material was required to clothe him. Thus only two yards of linen cloth, called Braban·(perhaps from Brabant) was bought for James, my lady's son and this cost 14d, and a yard and a half of russet cloth was also purchased from a William Stone again for the young James. The little boy dressed in russet was later to die of wounds in 1461 but in 1459, just a year before the outbreak of the Wars of the Roses, life in Dunster was proceeding peacefully. It is recorded that a fuller was given permission to place a rack on the Castle Tor on a piece of ground 63 ft by 18 ft on which to dry the cloth that he had fulled or tucked. Presumably the racks, when covered with cloth, resembled tents and hence, in the muniments of the castle they are referred to as tentorum or more generally tenters and a rack as le reek. We next hear of the wool trade in 1467 when Dunster, famous for its woollen Dunsters, had also attempted to make linen and an order was made concerning this by the borough court. That nobody shall henceforth make linen cloth of 'flockys', and if it be proved by anyone that then the cloth so made shall be forfeited to the lord.[85] Flokys or flock, was powdered wool or cloth used to thicken cloth. Here the wool refuse was being used as a substitute for flax. We know much about wearing apparel in the 15th century from the Sumptuary Act of 1463 but the prime reason for the act was to establish social status, which was to be easily identifiable by dress. In the Paston letters edited by Roger Virgoe the example is given that: labourers were forbidden to wear cloth valued in excess, of 2s a yard. This, in any case, was probably dictated by the labourer's inability to afford more since in the 15th century he would have earned as an agricultural labourer about 4d a day and as a building worker 5d to 6d a day. To be permitted to wear a doublet padded with wool one had to aspire to the rank of a gentleman, a rank between a yeoman and an esquire. Only lords wore jackets, gowns or cloaks of extreme brevity. Short cloaks were forbidden and long piked shoes were worn only by the highest in the land. This attempt to differentiate social status by identifiable apparel was covered by this rarely enforced act. Some doublets were made of fine worsted but at the court imported silks and velvets of brilliant hue, variously patterned and lined with fur for greater warmth were preferred. Various furs are depicted by heraldry and not only cold draughty living conditions necessitated their use but the very cold, wet climate of the 15th century, said to be colder than previously, dictated their use.

At this time there were several fullers using Grobfaste to erect their racks and dry their cloth and one is known by name, John Cok, who paid 6d for the privilege; the others paid jointly 2s. 6d. This money was collected by the bailiff of the borough who himself seems to have set up racks on the castle Tor and on Grabbist for he debited himself with 7s new rent for tenters set up in these places. It must have been remarkable to see all these tent-like structures on the hill sides. In April 1491 an embargo on the manufacture of cloth on a Sunday was enforced. That no fuller shall henceforth allow his mills to make cloth from the time of evensong on Saturday until after vespers on Sunday under pain of 6s 8d, whereof 40d to the lord and 40d to the church.[86]

The next year fines were imposed on three people for polluting the river between Dunster and Dunster Hanger (Dunster Hanger extended beyond the wooded hillside behind the Luttrell Arms and the houses on that side of the High Street to the other side of the river Avill, a much more wooded and hedged area than the 18th-century Deer Park made in the time of Henry Fownes Luttrell). The order read: That no dyer shall henceforth put or throw 'le wodewater' in the lord's stream before eight o'clock at night, under pain of 40d every time.[87] Why was it permissible to pollute the water with blue woad after 8pm? Finally at the end of the 15th century this entry appears and points to the fact that the Dunster cloth makers were still trying to get away with it. 1494. William Morgan has unlawfully made his cloth mixed with 'flokkes', to the detriment of his neighbours, and contrary to the statute issued on his behalf. Therefore he is amerced 40d…John Lechelond unlawfully makes his cloth with cardes (thistles), contrary to the statute. Therefore he is amerced 3d.[88] We next hear of the cloth industry in Dunster in the 17th century, but in Taunton in the second half of the 16th century specifications for the measurements and weight of a broadcloth were established.[89]

In 1412 Sir Hugh Luttrell purchased a horse from John Slugge for £4.[90] The next year Henry IV died of a mysterious illness that his contemporaries called leprosy which had pitifully oppressed his last years. Enguerrand de Monstrelet, the 14th-century chronicler wrote: he had been a most valiant knight, zealous and cunning against his enemies. It was he, who, as is explained in other histories, used improper and dishonourable means to obtain the crown from his first cousin Richard who had been the King of England for twenty two years.[91] Henry of Lancaster died in the Jerusalem Chamber in the abbey of Westminster. The following story comes from Enguerrand de Monstrelet's contemporary chronicle but it is now said to have been one of his own inventions which was passed onto Holinshed and so to Hall. It occurs in Shakespeare's *Henry IV Part II*.[92]

> In the last few days of his illness he was quite helpless. One day those who were looking after him, seeing that he had stopped breathing, thought he had indeed died and covered his face with a cloth. Now it is the custom in that country when the king is ill, to place his crown on a couch near the bed so that his eldest son and heir can take it as soon as he is dead. This had been done and the eldest son readily took it when the attendants gave him to understand that his father was dead. But soon after this the king sighed deeply, uncovering his face, and his mind suddenly became clear. He looked to where the crown had been, and not seeing it asked where it was. His attendants replied: Sir, my lord the prince your son has taken it away. The king asked for him to be sent for, and he came. Then the king asked him why he had taken away the crown, and the prince replied: My lord, those here present had given me to understand that you had departed this life, and since I am your eldest son and your crown and kingdom will belong to me when you have gone from this world to the next I took it. Then with a sigh the king said to him: Fair son, what right have you to it? - for I never had any as you well know. My lord, replied the prince, as you won and kept it by the sword, so shall I keep and defend it all my days. Do as seems good to you, said the king, I leave everything else to God and pray him to have mercy on my soul. Soon afterwards, without speaking again he died.[93]

After his accession in April 1413 Henry V had the support of Church and the nobility. He had proved his military capability in Wales and his reputation stood high. In 1414 Sir Hugh Luttrell was returned to two Parliaments as member for Somerset. In 1415 Henry V began his campaign in Normandy besieging Harfleur and Sir Hugh Luttrell was involved in its surrender. It seems he was sent there to act as one of the councillors of the Governor of Harfleur,[94] and after the surrender it is likely that Sir Hugh Luttrell was among those who returned for we do not hear of him being in France again until 1417, and he seems to not to have take any part in Henry V's great victory at Agincourt in 1415.

Sir Hugh had ridden to Southampton and his horses were brought back to Dunster by Thomas Hody his receiver-general and John Bacwell, who seems to have fulfilled the roles of steward and chaplain. They were accompanied by three servants and their expenses to collect three horses at Southampton were 9s 9½d. In their lord's absence Hody and Bacwell were lodged at the castle for some weeks. There were numerous entries in the household accounts concerning the horses of Sir Hugh: 1416. In the cost of a groom travelling from Dunster to Taunton three times for the cure of a horse of my lord, there sick, 15½d...To Robert Hylwen, a groom of my lord, for his expenses with two other grooms, and for seven horses of my lord from Dunster to London, 13s 4d ... In 17 horse-shoes bought, to be put on my lord's horses 2s 10d...In 14 'revets' for the same 7d ... In a 'sadel housse' bought for my lord's saddle and other necessaries bought for other saddles and horses, 3s....To John Hunte, master of my lord's chariots for his expenses with regard to my lord's horses and chariots, by a tally of which the counterfoil is not produced, £6 13s 4d.[95]

In February 1417 Sir Hugh Luttrell was accompanied by his son Sir John Luttrell and by William Godewyn, his son-in-law, when he joined Henry V's second expedition to France. The company composed of one knight, nineteen esquires, and sixty-seven archers, forty-two of whom were mounted and twenty-five of whom were on foot was under the command of Sir Hugh Luttrell and the second in-command was Sir Geoffrey Luttrell of Irnham, the head of the Luttrell family.[96] The troops assembled at Southampton and the arrangement was made that Sir Hugh should serve the king for one year in France for the sum of £286. None of the company was a military knight of Dunster. Sir Geoffrey was not long to survive the French wars for he, the last of the Luttrells of Irnham died without issue on 3 January 1418/9 at the siege of Rouen. By August 1418 the English had gained control of lower Normandy including Rouen which finally succumbed in January 1419, being starved into surrender. Sir Geoffrey was the overlord of Sir Hugh Luttrell who nominally held the manor of East Quantoxhead under him by military service. This Sir Geoffrey was the great-grandson of the Sir Geoffrey Luttrell, who had commissioned the Luttrell Psalter, the now famous manuscript which is illustrated by numerous scenes of everyday life and religious images.

On 7 July 1417, when Sir Hugh went to France again, the household accounts read: For the expenses of my lord travelling to the sea, on 8 July £7 11s 4d. In the passage of my lord, paid for meat taken for my lord's hawk and expenses up to the same time 16d.[97] It is interesting to conjecture if the meat was taken for a hawk which was going to France with Sir Hugh or if he was having meat transported for a hawk he kept in France! Another entry reads: 1417. In. the provender of the horses of my lord and my lady for three weeks, 19s. 4d. After the departure of my lord, in 2 halters bought for my lord's horses going out of Mersswode (Marshwood) and placed in ward, 2d. Also in ointment bought for their feet, 2d. In a 'horscombe' bought 3d. In canevass for the pads of the saddles and collars, 3s 4½d. Also in 9 double girths for my lord's horses, 16d. Also in woodwork of 7 saddles for the carriage, 2s 10d. Also in 20lb 'flokkis' for the stuffing of the same, 18d. Also in cords called 'teugropis' (traces), 8d. Also in divers cords bought for my lord's chariot. 14d. Also in cords for the whip, 2d. Also in cords for driving the horses of the chariot, 2d. Also in 2 pair of 'steroppis' for the saddles of the carriage and 7 'polys' and 3 'reynes' and 8 'contre single boucles' for the aforesaid saddles of the carriage, 4s. Also 'takkys' and nails (clavi) for the chariot, 1s. 5d.... Also in the repair of two 'ronges' for the chariot, 2d. Also in 'teughookys'.7d. Also in 7 'teugys', 12d. Also in 7 pads for 7 'semesadils' at 8d apiece, 3s 4d. Also in a 'strake' (rim) and 'dowlys' for the wheels of the chariot weighing 12lb of iron, 16d. Also in 'vertgrese' for a horse of my lord that was sick, ½d. Also in white wine for the same. 1d.[98] 1417. In expenses incurred in taking of four couples of coneys and birds sent to John Merchaunt of Taunton at the purification of his wife, 2d.[99] 1417. To Philip the carpenter and his fellow for cutting stakes for enclosing the stews (*stagnis*) in the Hanger [park], in part payment, 18s. 4d.[100] 1417. Two pipes of wine from Gascony bought for the use of my lord £4 13s 4d, also in the carriage of the same wine to the Castle 5d.[101] 1417. Paid to three Breton prisoners going into Brittany for their ransoms and those of their fellows, for their expenses, 10s. In the expenses of a French friar for six weeks, at 20d a week, 10s. Also of six Bretons and a page, captives, of whom three for thirteen weeks, at 10d a week, and three for four weeks, and the page for ten weeks, 50s 10d. Also of a man of Portugal for seven weeks, 8s. 2d. Of another from Portugal for two weeks 2s. 4d.[102]

Sir Hugh had a barge called the *Leonard* which was his means of transport to France and in the same year of 1417 there is an entry: The account of Philip Clopton, master of the barge of the noble lord, Sir Hugh Lutrell, knight, lord of Dounstere, as for a voyage made by her from the port of Mynhede to Bordeaux and back in the fifth year of the reign of King Henry the Fifth. The same answers for £42 10s received for the freight of the wine of divers merchants for the aforesaid voyage. In paid for food, drink, planks, nails, wages of workmen, and other necessaries bought and expenses, as in the repair of the said barge, in part by the survey of the reeve of Minhede, as appears by a shedule £4 10s 10d. And in 6 pieces of 'tielde' bought for covering of the ship, 13s 4d. In 2 rolls of 'oleyn' bought for repairing the sail 42s. In old anchors repaired, 6s. 8d. In canevas bought for repairing the aforesaid sail, 7s. In empty pipes and barelles bought for placing flour in, together with grease bought for rubbing the same barge, 11s. In 7 broad planks bought for 'alcassyng' of the same, 6s 8d. In 5 live oxen bought at 12s apiece, deducting 5s for hides sold 55s. In 2 pipes of ale and other barelles bought, 36s. The total gross cost of the voyage amounting to £42 3s 1d.[103]

In the summer of 1418, Lady Catherine Luttrell was at Dunster with her mother, Lady Beaumont who had come from Saunton. Sir Hugh saw to it that they were well provided for and the accounts tell us that: In the expenses of my lady being there partly at the end of June and partly in the month of July, for five weeks in all, as appears by a paper exhibited at the account, 33s. 5d ... In a pipe of wine bought for the use of my lady and her mother by my lord's order, as of his gift, 49s 4d.[104]

Sir Hugh was engaged in France in 1418 and was lieutenant of Harfleur in 1419 with authority to treat with the captains of different Norman towns that were willing to capitulate to the English. At the siege of Rouen we know that the seal Sir Hugh Luttrell used was one which bore a shield blazoned: *Or a bend between six martlets Sa. within a bordure engrailed of the same.*[105] This was the seal he used during the greater part of his life, for legal, official purposes in England and in Normandy. Proud of the Bohun blood that ran in his veins, he placed over his shield a swan, the well-known badge of the Bohun family. The legend encircling the shield reads: SIGILLUM HUGONIS LUTRELL MILITIS.[106] The engrailed bordure is a cadency mark and it is doubtful if he used this seal after 1419, the year Sir Geoffrey Luttrell of Irnham, the head of the house of Luttrell died and Sir Hugh became the male head of his family. He had another seal which omitted the engrailed bordure but which in other respects was the same. The seal which shows a single martlet and two sprays of foliage was used for less important letters and for informal papers. His wife, Dame Catherine Luttrell, used a signet bearing a Catherine Wheel, a pun on her names.

The following accounts refer to Sir Hugh's involvement at Harfleur: 1418. In cleaning my lord's baselard and knife 4½d...In divers victuals bought for my lord and sent to him at Harflete by the hands of Richard Arnolde, in money delivered to the same Richard upon a tally, £104 13½d.[107] In the expenses ... of two prisoners...each at 10d a week for twelve weeks, 20s ... of one prisoner at 10d, for nineteen weeks 15s 10d.[108]

In 1419 Sir Hugh was also sent: In 4 casks of 'allec' bought and sent thither, 60s...In paid for the freight of 25 quarters of beans, 1 pipe of salmon,1 pipe of 'skalpyn', 1 pipe of green peas, to Arflue, 63s ... In 13½ dozens of 'leynges' and 'melewell' bought, at 3s the dozen, 40s. 6d ... In carrying the same from Mynheade to Dunster and thence to Hampton (Southampton) 46s. 2d ... In 100 'hakys' bought and sent to my lord at Arflue, 30s... In expenses incurred in the household of my lord there (at Dunster) from Sunday next before the feast of All Saints in the sixth year of King Henry the Fifth until the feast of the Assumption of St. Mary next following (15 August 1419), that is for forty-one weeks, three days, and then my lord was at home ... £14 3s 6d.[109]

In the expenses of my lord coming home from Hampton on Thursday next before Christmas and being at Dunster for a certain time and then travelling to Saunton, all reckoned by William Person, 12s 11½d... In the expenses of the same lord at his next coming from Saunton to Dunster and being there for a certain time at the Priory, 6s 1d ... In the expenses of my lord who was at Domerham, Hampton and Portysmouth, as appears by a bill under the signet of my lord dated the 10th day of February in this the seventh year of King Henry the Fifth, £64 8s... In paid to the reeve of Domerham for the expenses of my lord who was there, as appears in a bill under the signet of my lord, 55s. 8d...In certain victuals bought by Robert Ponyngys, knight, for the use of my lord and sent to Arflu, as appears by an indenture dated the 7th day of April in the eighth year, under the signet of my lord and the signet of the aforesaid Robert, £10 4s ... In twelve dozens 'myllewell' and 'leyngys' bought and sent to Arflu at the request of my lord, at Mynheade; and they were sent by Roger Kyng, by indenture, 36s. In twelve 'coungerys' bought and sent thither by the same Roger, 8s.[110]

The marriage of Henry V to Catherine de Valois, daughter of Charles VI had first been negotiated in 1413 and was solemnised in Troyes Cathedral on 2 June 1420. Sir Hugh became the steward of Queen Catherine's household. His accounts show that the purchase of certain supplies was made by Sir Hugh's son-in-law, William Godwyn and a Richard Arnold of Bruton and that Arnold delivered them to Roger King of Minehead who was at Poole harbour and, that King transported them to Sir Hugh in Harfleur.

Having returned home on 10 September 1419, Sir Hugh Luttrell had returned to France in February 1420. The next entry was written at Poole on 20 July 1420: "This beth the parcell, of the costages that beth makid by Williham Godewyn and Richard Arnolde of Bruton aboghte diverse vitailles the wheche the forsaide Richard hath delyvered to Rogger Kyng of Mynheade, shipman, at the havin of Pole, to the use and the profitez of my lorde, Sir Hugh Lutrell, as hit is specyfyed in endenters bytwixt hem therof maked; Forst, in 18 quarteres of whete boght by Godewyn, pris the bushelez 10d, £6...Item in 23 quarteres, 2 bushelez, whete, pris the bushelez, 8d, summa, £6 4s. Item paied for cariage of the same from the contre to the ship 5s...Item in 10 quarteres of barly malt boght by Godewyn, pris the bushelez 10d, 66s 8d ... Item in 54 quarteres of barly malt, pris the bushelez 9d, £16 4s ... .Item in 6 bobos (oxen) pris of 103s...In 30 motons pris of 45s...Item in 2 quarteres 3 bushelez salt for the same flessh, 7s 6d ... Item in 3 pipes for the same flessh, 1 hoiggeshede for otemele and 1 barell for candelles, pris in al 4s...Item in 6 bushelez of otemele, price the bushelez 16d, 8s ... Item in 9 dosyn pondez of candelles, 10s. 6d. In reward of the lardyner for syltyng (ie.salting) and dyghtyng (ie. dressing) of al the flessh, 20d. In 1 quarter 3 bushelez of cole, pris the bushelez 3½d, 3s. 3d ... In 1 pipe for the same, 10d. ...Item payed for beryng of whete from the house of W. Waryner into the ship, 16d ... Item in mattys and nailles boght for to make a caban in the ship for savyng of the corne and of the malt, 3s. 7d ... Item in caryng of 13 dosyns of fyssh from Dunsterre to the Pole 12s ... .This was write at Pole in Ingelonde the 20 day of July the 8 yere of the reignyng of Henry oure Kyng the 5th ... .In a pipe of ale bought for my lord, 6d ... In carrying divers victuals, that is to say flesh, flour, oats, candles and divers other victuals from Sheftysbery to Pole, 10s ... In carrying the fish to my lord from Mynheade to Dunsterre, 4d ... .In delivered to my lady, by appointment of my lord, by tally £133 6s 8d ... In paid the same lady, of my lord's loan, to give to my lady's workmen of Saunton, by appointment of the same, 6s. 8d ... In delivered to the same lady for wine bought for her use and that of my lady her mother, against a payment made by my lord for the same, 6s. 8d ... In the expenses of Richard Arnold travelling from Hampton to Dunster and taking two horses of my lord, 5s...In carrying to Dunster certain things of my lord that were at Mynheade having come from Arflue in charge of Roger Kyng, 3d...Paid to Roger Kyng 'shipman' for carrying divers victuals of my lord from Pole to Harfleu this year, £11 ... In a man hired to carry fish from the Master of Bruggewater to my lord's stew at Dunster, 3s. 9d ... To a certain servant of the rector of Aller, likewise carrying fish, of my lord's gift, 20d."[111]

One of the most attractive entries in the accounts is a letter which was found attached to the roll of accounts from Michaelmas 1420 to Michaelmas 1421. It concerns Sir Hugh Luttrell's servant to whom he refers with obvious affection as "littil Will." This letter written on 18 October 1420 from Harfleur is addressed to his receiver, Richard Arnold at Dunster and tells of his concern for Will, it reads: Dere frende, y charge yow that ye take litill Will oure servant 20s for his fee of the last yer, and yif hit so be that he compleine to yow of his monoie that y take him be spendid in my servise, that ye take him whanne he departith fro yow to come to me resonable despenses; and this cedule signed wyth my signet sall be yowr warant. And in al manere wyse thenkyth on my stuf of fich ageyns

Lentin. Writ at Harfleu the xviijt daie of Octobre. Hugh Lutrell, knight, lord of Dunsterre and senescall of Normandie. Unto Richard Arnold oure resseviour at Dunsterre."[112] Later "littel Will" received 10s. "In paid to William, called Lytelwille, my lord's servant, for his expenses at Pole and elsewhere on my lord's affairs, this year in the month of December, 10s."[113]

The ruins of Burgundy chapel on North Hill in Minehead concern Sir Hugh Luttrell who served Henry V as senschal of Normandy. In France, due to the insanity of Charles VI, rival factions arose for control of the royal council and the kingdom. The Orléanists favoured the dauphin while the Burgundians, allied to England, supported Henry V's claim, sealed by the Treaty of Troyes, and strengthened by his marriage to Catherine of Valois, the king's daughter. England was also deeply affected commercially because Philip of Burgundy ruled Flanders and much of the Netherlands which imported massive quantities of English wool and clothing. It is therefore most probable that Sir Hugh named this chapel to which he made pilgrimage, Burgundy Chapel.

On 1 December 1420 Henry V entered Paris[114] and at Christmas time the young couple took up their residence in the Louvre and there presided over a court of great luxury where feasting and ceremonies far outshone the court of Charles VI and his queen Isabelle of Bavaria at the Hotel de Saint-Pol. It must have been most humiliating for Frenchmen to see their old enemy belittling their king, who was only visited by servants or persons of lesser degree, and for them to endure this period of English domination. Charles VI "le Fol" was not capable of governing and an item included in the Treaty of Troyes stated "Since we are for the most part prevented from attending to the cares and government of our kingdom, the practice and exercise of governing and ordering the public weal shall for the duration of our life be given over to our said son Henry, with the Council of Nobles and wise men who are in our obedience."[115] Henry was seemingly all powerful and we read: "Subjects of the noble kingdom of France came from all parts in the greatest humility to do the king honour. From that time King Henry began to undertake the government and administration of the affairs of the kingdom of France, and to appoint officers at his pleasure in the place of those who had been appointed to the posts many years ago by the King of France and the late Duke of Burgundy."[116] Certain taxes were renewed, notably the "gabelle" or salt tax which had been first levied on the whole of France by an ordinance of 1341. The importance of salt to preserve fish and meat in this period cannot be over-estimated and the "gabelle" together with quarter-taxes and other levies were renewed in 1420, excepting only a tax on grain.[117]

De Monstrelet tells us that Henry V made the following appointments: "He gave to the Earl of Kent the position of captain-general of the town of Melun. with an adequate garrison of men-at-arms and of archers; his cousin, the earl of Huntingdon was made captain of the Bois de Vincennes; while the Duke of Exeter was ordered to remain in Paris with five hundred fighting men."[118]

King Henry V, the queen, the duke of Clarence, the king's brother and his heir presumptive, and his next brother, the duke of Bedford, then departed for Rouen, After consultations concerning further details regarding the government of France had been worked out, the royal party sailed for England returning in February 1421.It was necessary for Henry V to re-assert his personal authority in England and his new queen had to be crowned. Together they made a triumphal progress through the realm and enjoyed acclaim on all sides. Henry had pledged, in the Treaty of Troyes , to avenge the murder of the duke of Burgundy and to wage war on the dauphin who held sway south of the Loire and controlled most of France in that area. Aware of this commitment, Henry was not slow to make capital out of his triumphant tour and sought to secure loans to finance a further war in France. He realised that his support lay only in Burgundian France. Then tragedy struck, the duke of Clarence, his heir, had been slain at Baugé on 22 March 1421 and the English forces had suffered defeat. Henry found that the royalists reinforced by Scottish contingents, were more powerful than he had supposed. He landed at Calais and sought to confirm his power in Picardy and eastern Normandy, in the area north east of Paris. This proved to be a tall order, not easily achieved, and Meaux and Compiègne held out until June 1422. Dysentery stalked the ranks of his army at the siege of Meaux, and the king, whose prospects of reuniting France and England had seemed so promising, himself fell victim to the sickness and died on 31 August 1422 at Vincennes. Sir Hugh had been feeling unwell. The date of the following letter, written to Henry V, is given as "1420, four days after his marriage to Catherine de Valois," thus 6 June.

Wel excellent, and myghtyfull Prince, my redoubtabel and souverain Lord, I yowr meke and trewe lige recommande me unto yowr heye and soveraine noblesce as mekely as I can or may. Unto the whyche lyke to wyte that wyth all lowlynesse I have yreceyved yowr worshipfull lettres, the whiche of yowr benigne grace ye have enclyned yow to sende unto me, not having reward unto my simplenesse of my persone but to the exaltation of yowr heye discretion, in also much as I am unworthy therto; be the which I have undurstonde that the Creatour of all thyng of Hise heygh pourveance hath used yow in herte to bryng yow unto the conclusion of perpetual pes betux the two remes (realms) that ever owt of mende of ony cronicles han ben in discention, schewyng yow fortune to conclude and bring at an ende that noo mankynde myght hyr bifore have iwroght; thankyng God wyth meke herte that He bath isend unto me that grace to abyde that tyme for to seye hyt, as for the gretist gladnesse and consolation that ever come unto my herte, not dredyng in my self that He that hath send yow that grace in so schort a tyme schal send yow moch more in tyme commyng. And as towchyng my simple persone yif yow lyke to wyte, at the makyng of this lettre, I was desesed of my persone be the hond ofowre Creatour, in so moch that I may not exerce myn office as my will were, as yowre trewe knyght Sir John Colville and Maister Pierres your phisicien (Piers de Alcobasse) schall enfourme yow more playnely than I may write unto yow at this tyme; wheruppon I have isend yowr men that were in my company unto my Lord of Salsbery, for to do yow service ther, as most neth ys as this tyme, for in this sith in the bailliage of Caux, ne in the march of Picard, blessed be God, there ys no steryng of none evyl doers, saf byonde the rivere of Sayne toward the Basse Normandy of certaine brigaunts. And whan God of His grace fowchsaf to bryng me owt of Hise prison, I schal gouverne me in the excercise of myn office at yowr worship, and as I am ihold for to doo. And as towchyng my worshipfull lord the Duke of Bedford, yowr brother, atte hyse arrivayl I rood agayn hym to the Kyef de-Caux, and told hym the poverte of this countre. Wheruppon he gouverned hym and all yowr men in hise company in swych maner that all are thyse countre blesseth hym and hyse meyny (retinue) in swych wyse that I have ihad noo complainte of ham eftir hyse partyng . Wherfore be my simple discretion he ys thankworthy, the which I remete unto yowr hygh ' discretion.More can not I say at this tyme, but I pray unto God of Hys grace encresce yow in worship, prosperite, and perfit joye, and send yow good lif and long lastyng, I write at yowr town of Harefleu this vjte day of June. Yowr meke lyge Hugh Luttrell. A treshault et tresexcellent Prince nostre tresedoubte et tressouverain seignur le Roy de France et d'Engleterre.[119]

Sir Hugh would not have had such quantities of food sent to him at Harfleur without the appointments for his board. The splendour of his table was calculated to impress the French. Plate, gorgeous apparel, jewels were the status symbols of the Middle Ages and in the display of his plate, Sir Hugh was making a statement that here was a man of rank and standing. Part of his collection came from his grandmother, Margaret de Bohun, countess of Devon and possibly some came from his uncle, William Courtenay, archbishop of Canterbury,[120] who must have been a man of considerable wealth since he had been able to provide Richard II with a substantial loan of £1000 for his Irish expedition of 1394/5.

One of the first items in Sir Hugh Luttrell's inventory was "a coppe with a park,"[121] a cup depicting a stag within a park paling, which as the white hart was one of the badges of Richard II.'[122] The "park" or paling occurs on a coconut cup in Oxford and is probably better as a reference to the mystical garden, a powerful medieval concept symbolising heaven as opposed to a wasteland. Other items include, "a coppe with a sterr" (a cup with a star probably chased in the bowl).

A coppe with a perle in the pomell (knop)
A coppe withoute pomel
A coppe with an egle ygylt in the pomell (gilt eagle)
2 coppis with eglis of silvyr in the pomell (i.e. a knop in the form of a silver eagle)
3 tre coppis will coverclis
2 coppis with 2 okurlis (oak orles, or wreaths) of silvyr in the pomell
2 flatte pecis with coverclis.
A vat ycoveryd. (like tun or can, originally a large wooden vessel here made in silver as a novelty.)
An hie coppe ycoveryd with fetheris yplomyd. (A standing cup and cover, probably engraved with plumed feathers from the crest of Courtenay and Luttrell).
A coppe ynamyd Bath
A coppe ynamyd Courtenay
6 flatte pecis withoute coverclis.
A note, a spice dissch, 3 eweris, 2 sponis And all this ygylt
A peyr doble baceynys
3 sengle bacynys with 3 eweris therto
A galon potte. (an all purpose jug or drinking vessel, probably bellied)
2 potell pottis, 4 quart pottis
An ewer with 10 coppis withynne hym and 3 coverclis
A round coppe ycoveryd and 8 withynne hym
3 grete pecis ycoveryd, and 17 rounde coppis and a tastour and an ewer for water.
A... spone and a verke fore grene gyngyver and 15 flatte pecis and 3 coverlis
4 chargeris (large plates often with a raised boss in the centre)
2 doseyn disschis and 23 sauceris
23 sponis of on sort and 17 sponis of a lasse (lesser) sort and 3 grete saucerys with 2 coverclis and 5 flatte saleris (salt cellars) and an ymage of Synd Jon of silver and gylt, and an horne ygylt, and 4 candelstikkis of silver.[123]

In 1415 Sir Hugh paid £54, a vast sum, to the executors of Sir Ivo Fitzwaryn's estate for some silver vessels, many of which Sir Hugh used in France: "Of the whiche somme above saide my lord hathe with hym to Harflu 2 chargeris, 12 disschis, 12 sauceris of silver, 2 coppis and a ewer ygylt, an hie coppe and 8 withynne, a gret flat pece with a covercle, 7 flatte peces and on covercle, a basyn and an ewer, 11 sponis, 2 salers with a covercle and the chapell hole (i.e the whole of the chapel silver), 2 quart pottys, and an hie coppe with a covercle ygylt, and 6 littel sponys, and 2 candelstykys of sylver."[124] Not only in a knights' hall but during the celebration of the mass at Harfleur Sir Hugh's standing was proclaimed by a display of the entire chapel silver transported from Dunster. The "chapel hole" is shown as: "Item por le Chapelle and comprises the following inventoried items: In primis, a litil chaleis (chalice) ygylt. A pax bred ygylt 2 cruetis of silver A corperas A peir of vestymentis 2 towelles A lytil masboke (Mass book) 2 parelles for the auter and a superaltar."

The earliest references to Sir Hugh Luttrell's occupation of the castle appear in accounts for 1406: "In a key bought for the door of the tower over the gate, 2d. In hinges, staples, haspes, and a bolte of iron for the deal placed in the gate, 12d ... In a lock, a key, a haspe and a staple bought for the tower towards the west in 'le Dongeon' 8d... In a lock and key bought for the door of the closet (latrine) at the end of the hall, 6d."[125]

Again in 1406 the accounts show, "In paid for two bushels of lime bought, 2d ... In a hundred 'lath nailles' bought, 4d.[126] Lath-nails were the most commonly used nails for roofing. In 1222 they cost 12d to 14d a thousand. Prices varied over the years and in the 15th century they cost 10-11d a thousand. The work continued with: In a workman covering the slope 'penticium' of the tower over the angle of the 'Dongeon' towards the west for two days, 4d ... In a carpenter making the said slope for three days, 6d ... For three 'bordes' of 'pipler' bought for the garderobe of my lord, 2s. In paid to two 'masones' working on the chapel in le Dongeon for nine days and a half at 2d apiece by the day, 3s. 2d... In paid to three workmen carrying earth for the same, at 3d apiece by the day, for one day 9d ... In paid for two quarters of lime bought at Wachet, together with 2d for the carriage of the same, 18d ... on the same day, in paid to a carpenter for fourteen days and two carpenters for two days, at 2d apiece by the day, working 'cippes, bordes, tresteles', and windows and doors in the upper and lower castle. Also on the same day, in two hundred nails (clavis) at 4d; in a hundred and fifty nails at 6d; in a hundred nails at 6d., 16d. In twenty-two pounds of iron wrought in 'twystes, hokes', and other necessaries at 1½d the pound, 2s. 9d."[127] This entry is a little difficult to understand. The "two hundred nails at 4d" are referred to as "clavis" but this means a key, a clave being a keystone. "In a new lock with two keys, and the mending of the locks of the doors of the pantry, the kitchen and the oats house, 10d. Also the same day in paid for cleansing the house within the gates, full of filth, 4d...In paid to John Corbet, smith, for a 'wexpan', two 'wexirens', a 'wexknyfe' an 'iren rake', a 'pikeys', a 'matok', thirty-six 'hoques' for hanging bacons in the kitchen, two 'twistez' for the door in the tower over the angle of the 'Dongeon', and little bars for the glass windows in the hall, 6s. 8d. Also on the same day, in paid to a glazier making glass windows in the hall and my lord's chambers at 2d by the day, for twenty-one days, 3s. 6d. Also on the same day in paid for two 'hoques' and two hinges for the shutters of the glass windows at the end of the hall, 2d."[128]

The use of glass goes back to Roman times but in the Saxon period it disappeared so that in the second half of the 7th century when St Wilfrid, bishop of York (634-709), restored King Edwin's church at York "in the windows light came through linen cloths or a fretted slab; he made glass windows."[129] This window glass would have come from the continent for Benedict Biscop sent agents to Gaul to bring over glassworkers, a craft hitherto unknown in Britain, to make the windows of his chancels, chapels and cells.[130] They were to work on his monastic church at Wearmouth and they disseminated their skills and taught the English their craft. It did not become commonplace for a thousand years and then only for important houses. Greased paper or linen cloth was used as late as the first half of the 16th century. Churches had glass windows from the second quarter of the 12th century.

On the same day that hooks and hinges for the shutters were purchased for 2d, two carpenters were paid 2s. They had made chests for Lady Catherine Luttrell and also 'lez rakkes' in the gate. For this they were paid 2d apiece a day and worked for six days. Two hundred nails were required for the chests and these cost 1s and the three hinges for the same came to 4d. The final entry follows: "In two hooks and three great nails for the said 'rekkis', 2d. In a new padlock and the mending of another, 4d. Also on the same day, in paid for the making of an earthen wall below the tower over the gate, 2d. And for the making of a door with a 'lacche', in the same, 3d."

The accounts for 1416 also include: "In four thousand pounds of lead, at 5s 6d by the hundred, £11. In the carriage of the same lead from Wellys to Dunster, 8s. In expenses for buying the said lead, 2s in 'bordes' and 'nailles' bought for the covering of the towers in the Castle, 23d. In nine pounds and a half of solder bought, 14½d... In the salary of a plumber for four weeks, 10s."[131] (An allowance of 14d a week for food was to the plumber who also presumably enjoyed the usual free lodging in the Castle).

In 1417 the accounts show: "In four hooks for the door of the chapel in the hall, 2d."
A chapel of St Stephen

was probably on the summit of the Tor and there was a chapel adjacent to the hall below. These buildings documented in the 15th century may have been part of the de Mohuns' castle but it difficult to attribute the earliest known date. In 1427 the fact that this hall and chapel were adjacent is proved by the following entry: "Thomas [Pachehole] was hired there to make 'le enterclos' and 'hachys' (the screen and aforesaid door) between my lord's hall and the chapel there, for two weeks, at my lord's board, receiving 18d by the week, 3s...In paid to Thomas Smyth for six pairs of hinges for 'lez hacchys' in the chapel there, 2s."[132]

Also in 1417 repairs were made to the gates of the lower castle. These were presumably those which still hang under the archway of Sir Reynold de Mohun II's gateway. These gates are described by Lyte as follows: "Their framework is a massive grating of oaken bars four inches thick, four inches and a half wide, and four inches and a half apart, covered on the outside with vertical bands of the same material an inch and a half thick. These planks are held together by external iron bands, spiked to the internal bars of oak by great nails with diamond-shaped heads. In the right valve there is a wicket four feet four inches high by two feet one inch broad, fastened with a huge iron lock in a wooden shell."[133] The repairs undertaken were: "To a carpenter on the repair of the gates of the Lower Castle, for seven days at 3d by the day, 21d. Also in iron work for the same gates, viz. eighty-seven pounds at 1¼d by the pound, in nails, plates, and bands, 9s ¾d. Also in little nails (clavis) bought, with a key (clavi) for the door of the chamber of J Bacwell, 4d. Also in a key for the chamber of the garderobe and in a key for the door of the barn of the barton of Dounsterr, 4d."[134] John Bacwell was steward of the household. The barton was the home farm of the medieval lords of Dunster; it stood under the shadow of the Tor near the Barnbridge over the river, a little to the north of the grist-mills.[135] This is presumably the bridge rebuilt by Henry Fownes Luttrell in the 18th century.

Reverting to the gates: "Also in the repair of two iron bands with the nails necessary for the same for the principal gate in 'le Dongeon', 4d. Also in the cutting of a wicket in the same gate, 3d. Also in iron hinges for the same wicket with the nails necessary, 4d. Also in a 'hagodeday' with a 'lacche' for the same wicket, 3d. Also in a mason making a chimney in the porter's lodge for five and a half days, 11 d. Also in the carriage of a stone for the keystone of the said chimney given by the Prior of Dunsterre, 1d. Also in the repair of two locks on the chamber of the outer gate of the Castle with a key for the bakehouse, 5½d. Also in plates [and] nails with a knocker on the inner gate of the Castle, weighing 104lb at 1¼d by the pound, 10s 10d. Also in the expenses of a 'mason' coming from Brigewater to see my lord's hall in the Castle which is to be rebuilt, 3s 8d." This entry concludes the 1417 accounts and reveals Sir Hugh Luttrell's intention to build the Gatehouse referred to as his 'new building', now called the Tenants' Hall.

In 1418 the accounts only show one entry available to us: "In a tiler for two days at my lord's board for the bakehouse, 4d. In a mason for five days at my lord's board for certain chambers to be mended in the Castle, 10d. In a lock of the outer gate of the Castle repaired, 3d."[136]

The household accounts for the year 1420/21 show that Sir Hugh Luttrell's intention to build the gatehouse had begun in earnest. The role of the castle was changing from one of defence to the home of a man who had served Henry IV and Henry V well and desired to make life more comfortable and to entertain his family more commodiously. His receiver's accounts had a separate section devoted to the enterprise of the 'new building': "The new building in my lord's castle. In divers workmen hired for pulling down old walls, both a part of the walls of the hall and a part of the wall of the Castle, and laying the foundation of the new building close to the said hall, and for removing to a distance the old timber of the hall when pulled down, and for hauling great stones and carrying the said stones, with sand and timber, together with the purchase of free stone at Bristol and the carriage of the same by sea and lastly by land, and the carriage of water. and for making 'hurdelles', together with the purchase of ropes, cords, and divers other necessaries for the work, and likewise in the hire of men for burning lime in the pit near the Castle, with the making of the same pit, and coal and fuel for the same, with the shoeing of my lord's horses and oxen for carriage, and making and repairing divers iron implements. to wit, 'crowes, mattokkes, pycoyses, wegges, spades', and 'schovelles', and 'sleigges', all reckoned together, as appears in a paper made thereupon and examined at the audit, £45 15s 10d. In 2379lb of iron bought and wrought, that is to say for hinges, 'kacchers' for 'lacchis' for doors and windows, and also for putting iron work in the lights of the windows, £14 17s 4½d. In 141 quarters, 4 bushels of lime bought, at 8d for the quarter, £4 14s. 4d. Also paid to Thomas Hydon, mason for making walls, in part payment of a greater amount, £11. Also paid to William Boulond, free-stone mason beyond 100s received by him last year from Thomas Hody, as appears in the account of the same Thomas Hody, in part payment of a greater amount, £20. Also paid to Thomas Pacchehole, carpenter, beyond 60s received last year from Thomas Hody, in part payment of a greater amount, 20s, in 13 quarters of coal bought wholesale for burning lime. Total £98 2s. 10½d."[137] This was not. however, the final total.

During the year 1420/21, Lady Luttrell visited her mother in Devonshire and they were, as we know, well supplied with wine from Dunster. The accounts show that a pipe (i.e. 2 hogsheads, or 105 imperial gallons, 477 litres) was bought of Roger Kynge of Mynheade. "Also in a pipe of wine for my lady, who was at Saunton, bought of Roger Kyng of Mynheade, for the household of my lady, this year, 46s 8d."[138] One imagines that having the builders in was too uncomfortable an experience for her and she stayed away during the first year the gatehouse was under construction. Sir Hugh had also been away: "Paid to George, my lord's chaplain at Gyllyngham for the expenses of my lord there on his return from London, 15d."[139] Sir Hugh Luttrell was keeper of the forest of Gillingham hence it would have provided a good stopping off place during his long ride from London to Dunster. In 1421, before the feast of St. Denys on 9 October, 17s. 9½d. was paid to John Taunton, keeper of my lord's horses, for oats and horse-bread bought for my lord's horses.[140] There were also new 'reckis' and 'mangers' made by Thomas Pacchehole for the stable below the castle on the north side.

The same year Sir Hugh had two new gowns and the reeve at West Quantoxshead received material for his apparel. "1421. To Laurence Taillor of London for making two gowns of my lord. They were of 'felewet' and cost 13s. 4d ... In 4 yards of russet cloth bought and delivered to Thomas Pury, reeve of Estkantok, at 18d the yard, 6s."[141] The same year a bag at a cost of 3d was purchased to hold the roll of accounts. At this time the steward received £5, the receiver general £3, and £1 6s 6d was paid to an auditor of the accounts and an attorney and a clerk received £1 each. In 1423 it became necessary to re-stock the fish pond and 4s was paid for the carriage of live fish from Woolavyngton to Mynheade to stock my lord's 'vivaria'. In 1423 the household expenses increased when Elizabeth came to stay, "because Elizabeth Harleston, my lord's daughter, was in the aforesaid household with five men and seven horses at the costs and expenses of the said household for seventeen weeks."[142] The servants were all re-liveried in red and green, for that year the household accounts show: "In certain red and green cloth bought for the livery of the staff of my lord's household this year, £4 15s. 4d."[143]

The new gatehouse was nearing completion and in this year Sir Hugh enjoyed the rewards of his arduous life in the service of the Crown. He had two new velvet gowns, his servants were newly liveried, he had a splendid new gatehouse and his daughter brought friends to stay. The next year the colour of the livery was changed from red (sanguinio) and green to blue, perhaps his daughter did not care for the red and green and suggested blue would be more desirable. So in 1424 the accounts show: "In five dozens of blue cloth bought at Benehangre for the livery of the staff of my lord's household this year, with the expenses of carrying the purchases, 103s. 4d. In five pairs of embroidered wallets for my lord's five gentlemen for their livery … 16s. And in seven pairs of embroidered wallets for my lord's yeomen for their livery …15s. And in two embroidered wallets for two grooms, this year for their livery … 2s. 2d."[144] In 1426 the livery colours reverted to red and green.

Now Sir Hugh's aunt wanted to see what was afoot at Dunster and she came to stay for some months in 1424. Lady Elizabeth Harrington was his mother's sister and although Lady Catherine, Sir Hugh's wife, might see that her husband's aunt was provided with rabbits,[145] nevertheless a visit was quite another matter. Whether it was a lesson learned after the 1423 expense of his daughter's visit, or not, in 1424 Lady Harrington 'paid handsomely for board'. Margaret, Sir Hugh's daughter-in-law also came with her gentlewoman and paid 5s for their one week's stay.[146] The work was not quite finished, for in that year of 1424 Thomas Pacchehole, the carpenter was boarded at the castle for nineteen weeks. He had an assistant or two with him and Thomas Hydon the mason, also had his assistant with him and they spent eleven weeks completing work on the gatehouse. In all the total cost in the five years amounted to about £252.[147] In order to erect this building, which was outside the encircling walls of the original castle, it had been necessary to demolish part of the curtain-wall and two of the arrow-slits in the semi-circular tower to the right of Sir Reynold de Mohun II's gateway had had to be closed.

The following details from the accounts of 1426, refer to the gatehouse which appears to have been tiled and to have had a screen and mantelpiece. "For 'twystys', 'yemeaux', and nails bought of Hugh Lokyer for the screen and a new door in my lord's hall, 3s. 10d. And to John Burgh for two carriages of timber from 'le lymekyll' to the Castle for the said screen in my lord's hall, 2d … In a thousand tile-pins bought, 3d. In two thousand tile-stones bought of Henry Helver, 20d. In the carriage of the said stones from Treburgh to Dunster Castle, 3s. 4d. In paid to John Eylysworthi, tiler (regulatori) there hired to repair my lord's chamber and the constable's chamber, for three days at my lord's board, 9d."[148]

Attention was paid to Dame Hawis's tower at this time. It was cleaned out and a new lock was fitted. In a great key bought by Hugh Lokyer and in the mending of a lock for 'Damhawys Towre', 4d. …In John Bowman hired for a day to cleanse 'Damhawys Toure', at my lord's board, 2d. … Also to Thomas Pacheholl with his man there hired for a day and a half to make three 'gestys' anew in the keep by 'le Portcoleys', at my lord's board, 7½d."[149] With reference to the "portcoleys," Lyte wrote that Sir Reynold de Mohun II's gateway in the Lower Ward showed "no traces of any former portcullis" and that "it can never have had a drawbridge."[150] There was a store-house in the keep, referred to as "castello" in which my lord kept his armour. The entry occurs for the same year, 1426. "In nails bought for mending 'le store hous' in the castello in which my lord's armour is placed, 1d. In two carriages of timber from 'le Fysspole in le Hanger', towards my lord's said stable, without board, 2d. In ten thousand tile stones (petris tegulinis) bought for my lord's store, that came from Cornwall to the Haven of Dunsterre, at 2s. 7 d. by the thousand, sum total, 25s. 10d. In carrying the aforesaid stones from the ship to 'le slymvat', 4d."[151]

In 1426 the livery colour seems to have reverted to red and green. Sixty-six yards of each colour were purchased and one imagines that the shade of red was a little different and inclined towards a purplish-red since it was referred to as "rubeo." This cost £7 11s 6½d and was sufficient to clothe four gentlemen, eleven yeomen and four grooms in the household. This sum included expenses and carriage. In respect of the history of liveries around 1450: "Soldiers returned from the French wars and trained in nothing but killing, were unable to find employment. They roamed the countryside in armed bands, plundering travellers and holding villages to ransom. Others took service with a great lord, wearing his livery, and acting as his private army. As the practice of livery spread, the magnates became a law unto themselves. Many were now so rich and powerful that no man, certainly not the mild and pacific Henry VI, could control them. The Percys and the Nevilles were the real rulers of northern England; the Dukes of Norfolk and Suffolk held sway over East Anglia; while the Duke of York's word was law in South Wales. Magistrates dare not condemn, juries dare not punish. the man who wore a great lord's livery. In 1455 the Earl of Devon took an army to plunder the cathedral at Exeter."[152] Henry VII made a concentrated effort to cut down the hired bands of liveried retainers acting as private armies and in an effort to restore good order to his realm he presided over his councillors acting as judges in the Court of Star Chamber. Here defiant noblemen ignoring the courts of common law, or persuading men to wear their livery, were dealt with. The practice of livery, stripped of its potential threat, relaxed into a fashionable status symbol of the notable families of the realm. Liveried servants were readily recognised by all as the servants of a particular great lord.

The 1427 accounts specifically refer, among other things, to mantelpieces. "Also paid to John Myryman of Wylyton for two mantelpieces bought of him for two chimneys to be newly made in the keep (*castello*), 3s. Thomas Pacheholl was hired by order of Thomas Bemont at the keep for pulling down the old kitchen in 'le Donyon' for a week at my lord's board, 18s. And Thomas Pachehole was hired there to make a 'whelberwe' for a day at my lord's board, 3d.[153] Henry VIII's antiquary, John Leland, visited West Somerset c.1542 and he wrote about the second Sir Hugh Luttrell (d.1521) and said, "The Moions buildid the right goodly and stronge Castelle of Dunestorre. The Dungeon of the Castelle of Dunestorre hath beene fulle of goodly building; but now there is but only a chapelle in good case. Sir Hugh Loterelle did of late dayes repaire this chapelle."[154] It was this second Sir Hugh Luttrell who planned the heraldic tablet on the gatehouse. Lyte says (of the first Sir Hugh): "The gatehouse … was divided into distinct sections by a transverse wall reaching from the ground to the roof, and it does not appear that there was any internal communication between them. The lower part of the eastern section is pierced by a passage open to the air, 10ft 6in. broad, with a plain wagon vault and at each end a pointed arch. There can never have been a portcullis, but there was formerly a pair of large gates adjoining the outer, or lower, arch, which has moulded jambs continued round the head. Close to the inner, or southern arch, there is a small pointed doorway giving access to a room and also to a spiral staircase leading to a larger room on the first floor, to a similar room on the second floor, and lastly to the roof. In the western section there were three rooms on as many floors, connected with each other and with older buildings behind by a spiral staircase. The two upper rooms in this section were rather lower down than those on the other side of the transverse wall. Each of the six rooms in the Gatehouse had a simple fireplace…and a small dark closet. Such of the original windows as remain are square-headed but cusped, and in some cases divided by mullions and transoms."[155] This gatehouse was altered in 1765 and Salvin also made alterations in the 19th century.

The seal of Sir Hugh Luttrell was the one he used during the last few years of his life. It was copied from the seal which Hugh Courtenay, earl of Devon affixed to the deed by which he granted his badges to his cousin, Sir Hugh Luttrell in 1421. On both, the crest is composed of a large panache, or plume of feathers. rising out of a coronet which encircles the helmet and both bear, as supporters, a pair of swans, collared and chained, as born by the family of Bohun. The grant referred to '*a Boar passant - Argent; armed Or charged on the shoulders with a double rose of the second*'. The boar was never used as a crest or badge by the Luttrell family of Dunster but Sir Hugh's mother Dame Elizabeth Luttrell did use the double rose on her seal many years before the grant of 1421. The double rose was remembered by the Luttrells in the 16th century, when Sir John Luttrell had a 'lytell and open' ship called the Double Rose. Sir Hugh Luttrell rejected the silver boar, mentioned in the grant but he did adopt the crest and supporters of the head of the Courtenay family. The swans were derived from the marriage of Sir Hugh Luttrell's grandfather, Hugh Courtenay, second earl of Devon to Margaret de Bohun whose tomb chests in Exeter Cathedral show effigies with rather dejected swans.

From the 14th to the 16th century royal badges are found more frequently than the royal arms in many forms of decoration; they even make their appearance on the coinage. But the heyday of the badge was the age of livery and maintenance, and perhaps the best known of all such devices. along with the Prince of Wales's feathers, are those associated with the houses of York and Lancaster during the Wars of the Roses. Many of these derive from devices in use in the 14th century. The Lancastrian Swan badge was used in the 14th century by a number of English families, the Tonys, the Bohuns, Beauchamps and Courtenays, who were proud of their descent from the Swan Knight of courtly romance.[156] Mary and Eleanor de Bohun were second cousins of Lady Elizabeth Luttrell, the mother of Sir Hugh Luttrell, and their father, Humphrey de Bohun was Lady Elizabeth Luttrell's first cousin, her mother Margaret de Bohun, Countess of Devon, the wife of Hugh Courtenay, 2nd earl of Devon being the sister of William de Bohun, earl of Northampton. Eleanor inherited a psalter, the clasps of which were decorated with enamelled white swans.[157] It is not surprising that Sir Hugh Luttrell was proud of his de Bohun ancestry and that he adopted the swan supporters which still form part of the full achievement of the Luttrell coat of arms.

In 1420 3 bushels of oats were bought for the sustenance of my lord's swans at a cost of 10½d.[158] In the 16th century Sir Andrew Luttrell and his son Sir John Luttrell owned swans which were kept in the Mere at Glastonbury. The Dunster Castle Muniments included small memorandum on parchment with regard to swan-upping. The beaks of the swans were made to show their ownership by Sir John and Sir Andrew respectively. The Puritan pamphleteer William Prynne remarked in the mid 17th century "These were the markes which theise men above written had upon the beeles (beaks) of their swanes belonginge unto the Castell of Dunster by inheritance and always kepte at the Mere by Glastonberrye. Yt is good to renewe yt. S.L."[159] The initials S.L. refer to the savage sentence imposed on William Prynne by the Court of Star Chamber for distributing Puritan propaganda: he lost his ears, was condemned to stand in the pillory and was branded on both cheeks with the letters S L for seditious libeller.

Sir Hugh Luttrell died on 24 March 1428 at the age of 64. He was succeeded by his son John, who had accompanied his father to Normandy in 1417. William, his younger son, was probably the rector of Birch Parva in Essex from 1441-3.[160] There were four daughters and when Margaret, the eldest daughter married John Cotes, esquire, in July 1402, Sir Hugh covenanted to supply the young couple, their two servants and their two henchmen with suitable meat and drink for the first year after the marriage, and to give his daughter a sum of £20 'pour sa chambre'.[161]

Elizabeth, the next daughter, married William Harleston in 1406, and after his death she married John Stratton, esquire, of Norfolk, with whom she had a daughter also called Elizabeth. Then followed Anne who married William Godwyn who accompanied Sir Hugh to France in 1417 and held various posts in the Luttrell household. The youngest daughter,

Joan, was a nun at Shaftesbury.[162]

The effigy of Sir Hugh, and that of his wife Lady Catherine Beaumont who died in 1435 lie between the chancel of the priory church and the de Mohun chantry chapel. Lyte asserts that both the effigies were relieved with gold and had been sadly mutilated and that it was doubtful if they occupied their original positions.[163] Today there is no evidence of gilding; the mutilation may have occurred in the reign of Edward VI when monumental effigies were as vulnerable as religious statues to destruction and damage; or they may have suffered damage when acts of vandalism were committed during the Commonwealth of Oliver Cromwell. Alfred Fryer shared Lyte's opinion and said: "It is probable that this is not the original tomb and that the structure, except for the alabaster figures, was an Easter Sepulchre of the time of Henry VII."[164] He thought they were "formerly on a table tomb in the centre of the chantry of St Lawrence [now the Mohun chantry chapel] which was more in accordance with medieval practice."

Lyte described the effigies: "They now lie under a canopy carved in stone in an arched opening between the chancel and the little projecting sacristy which was almost rebuilt in the 19th century. The shields below them, likewise carved in stone, bear no arms; there is no inscription; and the whole structure, except for the figures, may be an Easter Sepulchre of the time of Henry the Seventh."[165] Later Dr Eeles voiced the opinion that it was probably an Easter Sepulchre.[166] The arms of Luttrell appear in many places in St George's church and are also to be found in the great cloister of Canterbury cathedral. The dating of the structure to the reign of Henry VII, 1485-1509, places it at least fifty years after the death of Lady Catherine Luttrell. With regard to a lack of inscription Lyte writes: "It might have been expected that the name of the Great Seneschal of Normandy, the first Luttrell lord of Dunster, the builder of part of the Castle, would have been so well known on the spot that there could be no question as to the fact that he and his wife were the originals of the two alabaster figures." Yet every writer down to 1879 who has mentioned them has described them as representing Sir John de Mohun and his wife. This deep-rooted error appears to have arisen out of an exaggerated respect for a hesitating opinion of the old antiquary, John Leland, who, in his account of Dunster Church, says: "In the north part of this was buried under an arche by the high altare one of the Luterelles, or as I rather thynke, of the Moions, for he hath a garland about his helmet and so were lordes of old tymes usid to be buried."[167]

It may well be that when John Leland, antiquary to Henry VIII, undertook his ten year tour of England between 1534 and 1544 for a projected History of the Nation, the effigy of Sir John de Mohun III was complete and occupied the position very soon to be occupied by Sir Hugh and Lady Catherine Luttrell. Sir Hugh would have received great acclaim in Dunster. The plate armour worn by Sir Hugh Luttrell is of the 15th century and is not the chain-mail which would have been consistent with the period of Sir John de Mohun III. Lyte comments on this armour: "Although the arms and legs of the knight have alike disappeared, his costume, the orle, or wreath, around his basinet, the 'demi-placcates' covering his breast, the sword-belt hanging diagonally across his body, the six overlapping 'taces', or plates, round his waist and hips and the tuiles that protect his thighs, show clearly that he lived in the first part of the 15th century. Furthermore the official collar of S.S. round his neck mark him out as a person attached to the service of a Lancastrian king. No lord of Dunster except Sir Hugh Luttrell answers to this description."[168] The collar, on a narrow band on the effigy, is of special interest. The great gold S.S. collar belonging to Henry V was pledged as security to the City of London against a loan of 10,000 marks when Henry planned the invasion of France in 1415 which culminated at Agincourt. The origin of the collar of linked esses is obscure: it may have been worn by knights and esquires before its adoption as a badge by Henry IV to represent the initial letter of his motto "souverayne"; it sometimes had the de Bohun swan attached as a pendant.

At Dunster, the tomb chest with its canopy and cusped arches forms a screen between the sanctuary of the priory church and the Mohun chantry chapel. It is possible that the tomb chest, which would not have held any mortal remains, originally displayed the stone effigy of Sir John de Mohun III[169] who is buried probably on the north side of the chancel.[170] The stone fragments of this effigy were discovered by the author in the 1980s in the stoke hole and remain to this day. They are to be found at the foot of the alabaster effigies of Sir Hugh and Lady Catherine Luttrell, which were probably placed there in the first half of the 16th century.[171] In the early 13th century quatrefoils contained figures and heads but later in the century they had been adapted to contain shields of arms, though there are neither at Dunster. The shields here are all 19th-century with the exception of the cusped shield within a square panel on the north side of the monument which may date from c.1350, and it would appear that this monument, or Easter Sepulchre, was most probably the place where the full effigy of John de Mohun III lay before its disintegration. Of the Easter Sepulchre Dr Bettey writes: "The Sacred Host was taken from the altar on Good Friday and laid in a specially prepared tomb, generally situated on the north side of the chancel. Here it was watched over by men of the parish during Good Friday and Holy Saturday until at mass on Easter Day the Host was ceremonially restored to the high altar with the dramatic Quem Quaeritis ceremony. This ceremony, symbolising the death, burial and resurrection of Christ, was very popular and was universally enacted in parish churches."[172]

Sir Hugh is wearing the plate armour of the 15th century as would have been seen on the battlefield of Agincourt and Orleans. Plate armour was a new departure, in that no chain mail was mixed with it except that sometimes, though not in the case of Sir Hugh Luttrell, a fringe was to be found on the lowest tace, or wide hoop of steel. There are however pendant decorations suspended from the tace, or more correctly from the tuile. The tuile is the correct name for what were originally small plates buckled to the lowest tace of hoops of the skirt of lames. At first they were much deeper than the hoops but they gradually became longer until they almost touched the knee pieces, called genouillières. At Dunster the tuile is deeper than the taces and seems to be made of one plate only. Sir Hugh wears a gorget, which would also have been made of steel, to protect his neck. This was the replacement for the camail made of chained or banded mail. This was longer than the gorget and protected the neck and shoulders and was attached to the basinet. The form of the helmet also changed and Sir Hugh's helmet is rounder and lower than the pointed basinet. Around this helmet are the words Jesus Nazarennus. Sir Hugh wears a broad sword belt which appears to be a bawdric. This is usually associated with the earlier camail period when the sword was fastened to it on the left side and worn over a very short tunic called a jupon. During the Lancastrian period of Sir Hugh Luttrell the narrow transverse belt which is also present was the usual way in which the sword would be fastened on the left.[173]

Lyte used the term "orle" or wreath around Sir Hugh's basinet.[174] It is not truly a basinet since it is not pointed and the term "orle" which pertains to heraldry is "a narrow border running parallel to the edge of the shield but not adjacent to it."[175] Also, the wreath or torse is a band of twisted strands of material worn about the helmet as a decoration, or to conceal the base of a crest where it was laced or bolted to a tournament helm. In the coat of arms the wreath is conventionally depicted as having six visible twists.[176] In the case of Sir Hugh Luttrell it is a wreath or torse worn as a helmet decoration. The arm defences consist of épaulières (epaulets), protecting the shoulders, here of three plates one above the other, known as brassarts, coutes and vambraces. The armpits had, at first in the Lancastrian period been protected by roundels but gradually gave way to oblong palettes. These can be seen in this effigy. Demi-placattes cover the lower part of the cuirass, broad at the bottom, and tapering upwards to a point between the placattes.[177]

There are many references to the fact that the effigies of Sir Hugh and Lady Catherine Luttrell are made of alabaster; a material which was first used for funerary purposes in the early 14th century and during the medieval period it came from Derbyshire and Staffordshire. The skills of late medieval carvers are most effectively displayed on monuments in alabaster and nowhere better than on alabaster monuments of knights and ladies.[178] Savage says: these effigies of Sir Hugh and Lady Catherine are of alabaster procured from the beds of that stone near Watchet.[179] This statement was refuted by Preb Hancock, who said: The material is very unlike the Blue Anchor alabaster...In fact...the Blue Anchor alabaster was not worked until the beginning, or middle of the 17th century.[180]

Sir Hugh had been made constable of Bristol Castle in 1410. The accounts for 1420 show: " In. the expenses of John, son of my lord, and William Godwyn travelling to London for the patents of my lord concerning Bristol, and for other business of my lord, in going and returning, for sixteen days, in all 40s. [William Godwyn was Sir John's brother-in-law, married to his sister Anne.] Paid to the clerk of the Pipe for searching for evidence and record of the receipts of the constable of Bristol and of the dues coming to him, 3s. 4d." In 1421, "of £20 received from William Godwyn of my lord's fee from the castle of Bristol."

In the accounts for the year of Sir Hugh's death the following entry appears: "Paid to John Bien of Shaftesbury by the hands of William Godewyn for spices bought of him for the burial of the said Hugh, 19 August, 44s. 1d ... To Thomas Wylhams for white cloth bought of him at the funeral of the said Hugh, £6 4s... Also paid to John Slug for providing oats against the burial of the said Hugh, 11s ... Also paid to William Stone for white and black cloth bought of him, together with the making of sixteen gowns and the like number of capes for sixteen poor people at the time of the burial of the said Hugh, 74s."[181] In 1430, the anniversary of Sir Hugh's death was observed: "Paid to Sir Robert Kent, chaplain, by order of my lord, to distribute among the chaplains, who were here on the day of the anniversary of Hugh Lutrell, knight, on the last day of March, 2s 9d."[182] The accounts for 1432 show that, four years after his death, the anniversary was marked by what would appear to have been a kind of celebration of his life: "Paid to William Stone of Dunster for six gallons, one pottle and one pint of white wine bought of him on the day of the anniversary of Sir Hugh Luttrell, knight, by order of my lady, paying 6d. a gallon, 3s.4d."[183]

Lady Catherine Luttrell was the daughter of Sir John Beaumont of Devonshire.[184] Her mother was Joan, the heiress of Robert Stockhay who had married the heiress of Robert Crauthorn/Crawstone. Before Lady Catherine married Sir Hugh Luttrell she had been the wife of John Streeche whom she married at Christmas time 1376 but her husband died during his father's lifetime and there were no children of the marriage. She and her second husband, Sir Hugh Luttrell enjoyed the life interest she obtained in the manors of Wolston in Devonshire and Sampford Arundel in Somerset.[185]

Catherine had two brothers, Sir William, who married Isobel, the heiress of the Willington family of Umberleigh, and Thomas, who figures in the Dunster castle accounts. He is known as Thomas I and is mentioned in various documents as 'son of John' and 'of Santon' (Saunton), as feoffee in several transactions, particularly in one of 1398, when co-patron of Parkham, as one of the feoffees of his brother William, son of Sir John Beaumont. He was co-patron of Landcross in 1406, and Sheriff in 1412, 1419, 1422 and possibly 1428. His nephew, son of William, was styled 'Thomas junior' and known as Thomas Beaumont II.[186]

Thomas I appears in the accounts for the year ending Michaelmas 1420: "Paid of the reward made to William Franceys, my lord's esquire, by John, my lord's son, Thomas Beaumont, and others of my lord's council, who were at Dunster on the 2nd day of

September, and were there on my lord's business, 20s. In the expenses of John, my lord's son, Thomas Beaumont, Hugh Cary, and others of my lord's council who were at Dunster in the month of August on my lord's business, 9s. 5½d. In the expenses of the horses of Thomas Beaumont at the same time, 2s. 4d. In the expenses of the horses of Hugh Cary at the same time, 2s. 9d."[187] Again in 1427, Thomas Beaumont is mentioned in connection with work undertaken at his instruction by Thomas Paccehole, the carpenter at Dunster castle: "…Thomas Pacheholl was hired by order of Thomas Bemont at the keep for pulling down the old kitchen in 'le Donyon' for a week at my lord's board, 18d."[188] In 1427, the year before Sir Hugh Luttrell died, his brother-in-law, Thomas Beaumont, with Sir John Luttrell, the heir, had taken over responsibility for the building operations undertaken at the castle.

During her widowhood, Lady Catherine Luttrell was assigned as dower the manor of Minehead and East Quantoxhead and the advowson of the church at the latter place, but she relinquished these advantages and exchanged them for an annuity of £100.[189] The family of Beaumont appears again in the history of Dunster castle when in the reign of Edward IV the first of the Yorkist kings, Philip Beaumont, esquire, was made constable of the castle and steward of all the lordships and lands that went with it.[190] The arms of Beaumont appear in the Victorian armorial window (south wall, south aisle) where they may be blazoned: Vairé Az and Arg overall two bars Gu. (Visitations of the County of Devon).These arms also appear in the second compartment from the left in the heraldic tablet over the western arch of Sir Hugh Luttrell's gatehouse at Dunster castle. This tablet was added by the second Sir Hugh Luttrell. Burke's *General Armoury* gives Gu and vair and over the gatehouse the bars are not restricted to two as in the windows. Naturally there are no tinctures here. It would be easy to assume that the medieval tile in the Mohun chantry chapel also refers to Beaumont but these tiles are 13th/14th century and, in any case, simply show Vair with no bars. Although it is impossible to be certain since there are no tinctures, this tile most probably refers to Beauchamp of Hache (Hatch). These arms also, appear at St Decuman's church, Watchet and at Cleeve abbey. In the 13th century Alice de Mohun, the daughter of Sir Reynold de Mohun II married as her second husband Robert Beauchamp, the younger of Hatch. A William Beauchamp of Wellington had a daughter who married a John Bedlisgate. Their daughter married Richard Wydeville who succeeded Sir Hugh Luttrell as Seneschal of Normandy, the father of Elizabeth Wydeville who married Edward IV.

Lady Catherine Luttrell died on 28 August 1435 and was presumably buried at Dunster.[191] Lyte describes her effigy: She is represented in a sideless dress, through the openings of which may be seen the girdle of her kirtle, and overall a mantle fastened in front by cords which pass through open fermeules, or loops; a long veil hangs down from the top of her head. Her feet rest on an animal now headless.[192] She wears a crespine headdress; the hair being gathered in bunches at each side of her face and enclosed in jewelled nets, or cauls. The loose veil is thrown overall and hangs down behind. It gives the impression of a hat since it rests on the crown of the head and on the top of the bunches and overhangs them like a brim. A brass of the same period, that of the wife of Nicholas Carew (d.1432) at Beddington (Surrey) is almost identical to this effigy except that the cauls are not jewelled.

The son and heir of Sir Hugh and Lady Catherine Luttrell was John Luttrell who was born in 1394 in the reign of King Richard II. There are many references to him during the lifetime of his father but he only outlived his father by two years and died on the 30 June 1430, and appears to have spent most of his time in west Somerset attending to the affairs of his father, who was so often in France either fighting or carrying out various duties as lieutenant of Harfleur and seneschal of Normandy. Sir John Luttrell's main residence was Marshwood in the parish of Carhampton where, after his death, his widow Margaret also resided.

In 1419/20 while Sir Hugh was acting as one of the councillors of the governor of Harfleur, he wrote a letter on 18 October to his son John and reprimanded him and Richard Arnold, his receiver at Dunster, for not restoring his goods to Philipot Stronge:

[Right] well beloved son, I greet you well with Christ's blessing and mine. Doing you to wit that I am certified that notwithstanding my [wi]ll and commandment by my letters that Philipot Stronge is not restored to his goods. Whereof I marvel me that my commandment may not stand, but whatsoever they be some men play the Lord, endure as long as they may, for by the grace of God sometime shall I, and then they would peradventure they had done my commandment, for when they grudge in so little a thing and considering it cost them nothing, no marve[l that] though they perform not my will in greater matters. But what between you and Richard Arnold this my letter and will i...nd y...it be executed whatsoever any man say there against, and that I have no nede to write. Therefore no more and think that thanked be God...alive and by the grace of him shall come home, and that rather than some one would. Wherefore take before you Wille Parson and...mine by his oath on the book if he had paid and what for that cause to my Receiver, and pay it him again, and that be del[ivered] to Philipot his goods the last pennyworth that he can ask at him, and that ye see this be done [in] all things. Last, dear friends I can ne...but the Holy Trinity have you in his keeping. And Richard Arnold this shall be your warrant upon your account of the pa...Written at Harfleur the eighteenth day of October. Also dear friends I charge you that ye send me in all goodly haste fish sufficient for my household and forget it not in no manner wise. Your father Hugh Lutrell, Knight, Lord of Dunster, and Great Seneschal of Normandy [Endorsed] Unto my right well beloved son John Lutrell and Richard Arnold my Receiver at Dunster delivered.[193]

Sir Hugh was obviously a man of generous instincts backed by ethical judgement. His generosity will be remembered in the letter, previously quoted, concerning his servant "litill Will" and how he is disturbed by his son's and his Receiver's failure to restore Philipot Stronge's goods to him.

In 1422, or before, Sir John had married Margaret, a member of the local aristocracy, the daughter of John Tuchet of Nether Stowey Castle and of his wife Isabel. Margaret and John Luttrell had two sons, John who predeceased his father,[194] and James, his successor, an infant at the time of his father's death in 1430.

When Sir John succeeded his father in 1428, his father's lands were mostly in the west of England; in Somerset, Dorset, Devon and Wiltshire but also in Suffolk. His first task was to arrange for inquisitions, or investigations, to be conducted regarding them. In Wiltshire expenses in this connection were incurred by John Stourton, knight, who wished to be paid promptly because he was going overseas and needed the money. His letter to Sir John says: "My ryght worshipfull and with all myne herte welbelovid cosyn, y recomaunde me to yow beseching yow that ye woll be remembrid of the litell money that I dude paie by the hondis of Robert Colyngborne whiche ys toward me in your name, as for the speed of your diem clausit extremum in the counte of Wiltes, and by advys of your cervaunt whiche laborid for hit in your name at that tyme, which drawith in all to the summe of iiijli. ixs. jd:, whiche y praie yow that ye do sende me in as hasty tyme as ye godely may, consideryng my nede ate this present hoeure that I have for my goyng obir see. And the holy Trinite yow evir conserve to his plesaunce and your ryght greet joye and confort, Your cosyne John Stourton, knyzght."[195] As a result "the litell money" was paid by John Luttrell and the following reply was sent to Stourton: "To John Stourton, knight, by the hands of Henry

Helyer, a yeoman of William Wadham, for taking a certain inquisition in the county of Wiltes concerning the death of Hugh Lutrell, knight, as by letter of the said John Stourton addressed to the said John Lutrell £4 9s 1d. And paid to Henry Helyar for his reward because of his pains, by order of John Lutrell, 20d."[196]

In the same year the accounts show: "To John Gregory, escheator of our lord the King in the county of Somerset, on the 10th of June, for the assessed portion of the lands and tenements which were of the said Hugh Lutrell in the aforesaid country, £12."[197] Sir Hugh died on 24 March and between April and September 1428 Sir John invested in a new barge; the modern version would perhaps be a new car on the strength of a new found inheritance. "To Thomas Touker of Wayssford for a barge bought of John Foughler of Ireland for my lord's use, as for a quarter of the same barge, £20."[198] John Stourton, knight, may have gone abroad but his son was here in England and was to be entertained by Sir John and given a repast of fish. The household accounts show: "To John Mathu for a 'burthyn' and a half of salt fish bought of him for John of Stourton, the younger, and William Carent, by order of my lord, 16s. To John Foughler of Mynhede, by the hands of the vicar of Mynhede, for wine bought for my lord's household at Karampton in the previous year, by order of my lord, 66s 8d."[199]

When Sir John Luttrell left Marshwood in Carhampton and came to live in Dunster castle, as anyone else would, he wished to entertain his family and friends but, according to medieval custom they paid for the privilege. Accordingly, when his mother, Lady Catherine Luttrell came to stay during the first five months of his residence in the year 1428, she paid £10 5s. 2½d for her board and that of her servants. Similarly, Sir William Palton paid £17 19s. 4d for his board and that of his household. Sir William was a wealthy landowner and he paid more than William Cornu who, for similar benefits, only paid £5 4s. 10d. The children were not invited and both men were married.

William Cornu's wife had, at this juncture, outlived two husbands. Her first husband was Sir John Malet, eldest son of Sir Baldwin Malet of Enmore, and in accordance with medieval usage she was known by her first married name of Malet and, in spite of her second marriage to John Luttrell of Carhampton, constable of Dunster castle, she was always known as Dame Joan Malet. This John Luttrell is not to be confused with Sir John, son of Sir Hugh Luttrell and there were no children by his marriage to Dame Joan.

Apparently Sir Hugh Luttrell's gatehouse, which had cost £252, was not fully completed, for in 1428 Sir John had to have the roof of the room over the gatehouse completed. Thus the accounts show: "To John Eylesworthe, tiler, hired for three and a half days to roof the chamber over the gate house near my lord's stable, at my lord's board, receiving 3d by the day, 10½d."[200] In the 15th century the stable probably occupied the same site as the 17th-century stables, still extant.

The amount of salt required for the preservation of fish and meat was prodigious and a whole house was required to contain it. In 1428 "this house by the outer gate" was plastered and the accounts record: "Also in the wages of John Eylesworthe, tiler, hired to plaster the house by the outer gate of the Castle, in order that salt might be put therein, for a day and a half at my lord's board, receiving 3d by the day, 4½d."[201]

Between September 1429 and his death on 30 June 1430 Sir John Luttrell was conferring with a Walter Portman, who appears to have been a lawyer. The dispute between the Mohuns and the Luttrells concerning the legality of the ownership of Dunster, and all that it entailed, dragged on. Almost to the end of her days Philippa (named after her godmother Queen Philippa of Hainault), the second daughter of John de Mohun V, and the widow of Edward duke of York, sought to establish her rights and before she made her will at Carisbrooke castle in 1430, Walter Portman visited Dunster. The accounts record: "To Thomas Couke for the provender of the horses of Walter Portman who was at Dunster three times to confer with my lord on his matter between him and the Duchess of York,

3s 6½d."[202]

The household accounts for 1429/30 record the visit of Elizabeth Courtenay to Dunster which poses an interesting question. It is almost certain that the visit was made by Elizabeth Courtenay, the daughter of Walter, Lord Hungerford, who had married Sir Philip de Courtenay of Powderham in 1426.[203] She may already have been the mother of the Elizabeth Courtenay of Powderham who in 1450 was to marry Sir James Luttrell, and had come to Dunster to arrange a marriage between the then infants. By 1433 her husband was the guardian of Sir James. The actual entry in the accounts is as follows: To the aforesaid Thomas Couke for the provender of the horses of my lady Elizabeth Courtenay who was at Dunsterre for a day and a night, 7s 11d.[204]

In Sir John Luttrell's time the parker, or keeper of the park, was Benedict Tolose. The office was granted for life and the annual salary was 40s. One of Benedict's tasks was to kill the rabbits, or coneys, at the warren for the table at the castle or for the purpose of presenting them as the gifts of Sir John or Lady Margaret.[205] At Marshwood in Carhampton the parker was John Blaunche and his terms of employment were the same.[206]

In 1430 it became necessary to buttress the eastern end of Sir Hugh's gatehouse (the present Tenants' Hall) and the accounts show: "To John Joce hired to gather stones on Croudon for 'les botreaux' by the gate of Dunsterre Castle, for one day at my lord's board, 2d ... To John Stone of Wotton, 'mason,' hired to make two 'botreaux' by the gate of the Castle, at my lord's board for two weeks, receiving 18d by the week, 3s. And paid to John Thresshe of Wotton, 'mason', hired to work with the said John Stone at the aforesaid 'botriaux' for two weeks, receiving 14d by the week, 2s 4d. And paid to John Joce, hired to wait upon John Stone and John Thresshe, the aforesaid 'masons,' for two weeks receiving by the week 11d, at my lord's board, 22d. And paid to John Burgh, hired with his cart and four horses to carry stones from la Hangre to the gate of the Castle for making the aforesaid botriaux for one day at my lord's board, receiving 12d by the day, 12d."[207]

Sir John Luttrell died on 30 June 1430, less than two years after his father, and was apparently buried at Bruton priory. Nearly two hundred years earlier between 1252/4 John de Mohun, who had died in Gascony, was also buried at this priory, although his heart was interred at Newenham abbey before the high altar. The fathers of both these lords of Dunster were responsible for buildings which are still extant at Dunster castle. Sir John de Mohun's father, Sir Reynold de Mohun II built the 13th-century gateway and Sir John Luttrell's father, Sir Hugh Luttrell, built the gatehouse.

At Bruton there is a table tomb in St Mary's church which today bears a notice indicating that this is the resting place of Sir John Luttrell. There seems always to have been a great link both with the Mohuns and the Luttrells with the priory of Bruton; a house of Austin canons established by William de Mohun II, who had granted Dunster church its first charter between 1090 and 1100. The last Mohun lord of Dunster, John de Mohun V, left his bones to the secular canons of that place.

Four months after Sir Hugh Luttrell died we first hear about his daughter Joan and an exchange of visits between her and her brother John. "1428. Paid to Robert Draper, by the hands of Thomas Kynggestone, for the banquet of my lady Joan Luttrell, a nun of Shaftesbury on the 27th day of July, by order of my lord, 40s...To the same lord, on the 30th day of July, when the same lord rode towards Shaftesbury to the banquet of my lady Joan Luttrell, his sister, to be held there, 106s 8d."[208] Now in 1430, after her brother had died on 30 June, she was back in Dunster on 19 July. Lyte writes "the nun had apparently been allowed to revisit her old home in order to see her brother on his death bed."[209] "1430. Paid to Robert Draper for the expenses of my lady Joan Lutrell, and her sister, a nun of Shaftesbury, riding thence to Dunster and there on 19th day of July, 12s."[210] This last entry is a little misleading since it was Joan who was apparently the nun. She had three sisters Margaret, Elizabeth and Anne.

The day of Sir John's burial is shown in the accounts: "To divers men for divers necessaries and the chapel on the day of the burial of John Luttrell, esquire, 12s 2¾d."[211] The anniversary of his death was marked the next year and the accounts show that the widow, Lady Margaret, was presented with a bill in September: "To Robert Drapere for divers expenses incurred for the anniversary of Sir John Luttrell, knight, by order of my lady, at Bruton, as in wax and other things bought for the same, as appears by a bill exhibited before my lady Margaret Lutrell on the 6th day of September in the eighth year (rectius ninth), 14s 11d ... And paid for divers expenses made with regard to holding the anniversary of Sir John Lutrell, knight, at Bruton, on the 6th day of August in the 9th year of King Henry VI, as appears by a bill exhibited at the audit of this account and attached to this account, 33s 3d."[212]

The exact details of the expenses are set out as follows: "In primis in six pounds of wax bought for making thereof five round candles at 5d a pound, 2s 6d. In wicks bought for the same, 1d. In making of the same, 1d. In four pounds of wax bought, as in four 'torchis' hired from the sacristan of the church there, paying 5d a pound, 20d. In a gift to four poor men for holding the said 'torchis' at the obsequies and at the mass, to each of them 4d., 16d. In a gift to the beadsman for proclaiming the anniversary in the town, 1d. In offerings, 2d. In bread bought as well for the Prior and the Convent as for others who came to the obsequies, 15d. In fourteen gallons of good ale bought for the same, 2s 4d. In one gallon of ale bought for the Prior there, 8d. In the distribution made to the Prior and Convent there, that is to say to the Prior, 40d, and the fifteen canons, 12d to each, 15s. Item, to two secular priests, 12d. Item, to two clerks, 4d. Item, to six poor folk, 3d. Item, for ringing the knell, 8d. Item, paid to Thomas Sartrye, late sacristan of the Priory of Bruton, for five pounds of wax bought of him, with the making, on the day of my lord's anniversary, at 6d the pound, 2s 6d. Sum total 33s 3d."[213]

An extract from Margaret Luttrell's accounts shows that the king's escheator had to visit Dunster to arrange the assignment of the dower. Paid to Walter Paunsefote, escheator of our lord the King, by the hands of Walter Portman, being here for the assignment of dower to my lady Margaret Luttrell, together with a reward made to W Bouchell his clerk, by my lady's order, 53s 4d. And in the expenses of the said escheator of our lord the King, of Walter Portman, of William Cloutesham, and others of my lady's council, together with the expenses of twelve jurors who were at the same place for the assignment of dower, together with the expenses of the said escheator by the way in going and returning, with a reward made to the said escheator's servant, 17s 10½d.[214]

Dame Catherine Luttrell, widow of Sir Hugh Luttrell was still alive at this time and it had been arranged that a third of the Luttrell estates was to be assigned to her. Now, Dame Margaret was to be assigned a third of the remaining two thirds. Lyte tells us: "Although it has been generally held that a widow could not have dower in the 'caput', or head-place, of a barony, it is certain that this Lady Luttrell received in this respect a third of Dunster Castle, comprising the new gatehouse (which Sir Hugh had built), and the older gateway adjoining and land on the Castle Tor."[215]

A detailed account of Dame Margaret's third share demonstrates a change occasioned by the peaceful conditions which prevailed locally at the time. Earlier, military considerations would have been paramount and such divisions of the heart of a feudal honour between mother and daughter-in-law would have been hotly contested by the lawyers. "Two gates at the entrance of the same castle of Dunster, together with all buildings situate over the said two gates, together with a certain old kitchen immediately adjoining the said buildings, and also a certain tower nearest to the said two gates on the western side of the same, and a certain garden lying between the said tower and a certain other tower called Hayveystoure, to hold to the same Margaret as a third part of the aforesaid castle of Dunster, saving, however, to the heir of the aforesaid John Luttrell, or to whosoever shall for the time have two parts of the aforesaid castle, free entry and egress to the said two parts of the castle whenever necessary or expedient."[216] The widow, Margaret, also received for the term of her life: "Three acres of pasture and an acre of wood around 'le Castel Torre', which three acres of pasture lie next on the western side of the entrance of the aforesaid castle of Dunster, and the aforesaid acre of wood lies on the eastern side of the same castle at the northern end of the wood there growing, with free entry and egress over 'le Castel Torre' aforesaid to the said acre of wood whensoever expedient to the same Margaret."[217]

Lyte enlarges on this information and writes: "The pasture assigned to Lady Luttrell was more suitable for goats or sheep than for cattle, as it was on a steep, narrow strip of ground between the outer wall of the Castle and the back-yards of the townsmen living in West Street below. The outlying acre of wood must have been on the precipitous side of the Tor overhanging the river and difficult of access. Her four acres constituted a third of twelve acres known as 'Casteldichepasture', a name which suggests that there was an artificial ditch round part of the Tor below the curtain wall." The moat of Dunster Castle is mentioned in 1318, and in 1381, a certain William Garland was admitted tenant for life of a burgage in "la Baleye," between the ditch and the king's highway, and consequently on the north side of it. The actual lease of this curtilage was given "de souz la mote du chaztel de Dunsterre en part de su e le ewe que court vers Daiynsbrigge en part de nortz."[218] Lyte remarks, "little or nothing is known about the condition of the Castle and its immediate surroundings for a considerable period after the death of Sir John Luttrell." He then refers to the Herberts and to the fact that they "did not spend an unnecessary penny upon the place during their temporary occupancy of it,"[219] during the Wars of the Roses when civil war broke upon the English countryside in 1460.

Dame Margaret Luttrell died on 1 June 1438, fifteen years before England lost the majority of her French possessions. She was a widow for close on eight years and in spite of receiving a third of Dunster castle as her dower she did not live there but at Marshwood. In 1431 she came to Dunster to take part in an archery match. Her companions were the local gentry and neighbours and one of these was Thomas Bratton. "In the expenses of my lady Margaret Lutrell and others coming with her on Sunday the first day of July, who were at Dunsterre to shoot with   and others, 2s 5d."[220] In the 14th century Robert of Bratton had been a witness to two of John de Mohun's charters.[221] John Bratton,[222] husband of Joan, daughter of Richard Chichester of Arlington, who later married John Loty III, appears in the history of Lower Marsh. Nicholas Bratton of Bratton, esquire, seems to have been a lawless character for in 1487 he and others were guilty of sheep rustling. They broke into the pound fold of a later Sir Hugh Luttrell situated at Nether Marsh. They stole twenty ewes and on the same day "certain other persons," not named, were charged with having lain in wait for John Loty of Nether Marsh with intent to murder him.[223]

After the Dissolution of the Monasteries, John Luttrell, rector of Dunster, Henry VIII's agent and the brother of Sir Andrew Luttrell, rendered a series of annual accounts showing the profits of the manor of Alcombe, divided under seven sub-headings. The rents of three freeholders are mentioned first and Nicholas Bratton of Bratton's rent in respect of land at Sparkhayes in Porlock is shown as 8s., the others being John Sydenham of Brympton who was liable for 10s. in respect of land known as Wyneard and Pytte, and the heirs of Bythemore who were liable for 4s. in respect of land at Wythycombe called Wilaller.[224] Thomas Bratton, Dame Margaret's archery companion, Lady Elizabeth Harrington, Dame Joan Malet and Thomas Copleston are amongst those whose names appear in the accounts of the reeve of Carhampton Barton for 1431 as recipients of gifts of rabbits taken at the warren by the parker of Dunster Hanger.

James, the second son of Lady Margaret and Sir John Luttrell is first heard of in the accounts for 1431 when a purchase was made on his behalf. "In two yards of linen cloth called 'Braban' bought for James, my lady's son, 14d. And in a yard and a half of russet cloth bought of William Stone for the said James, 9d." His mother had a new gown at the same time. "In five yards of 'fustyan' bought in the market-place of Dunsterre for a double gown of my lady, 2s 11d. And in a quarter of a yard of 'tarterys' bought for the same gown, 10d." The account continues: "Paid to Joan Noryce, my lady's nurse, for her wages in arrear, by the hand of William Percare, chaplain, of Wales, and William Warderoppe, 6s 8d. In six douseynys of white cloth bought for the livery of my lady at divers prices this year, 37s. In ten douseynys of white cloth woven for the said livery this year, of Robert Northam, 5s. In fulling the said ten douseyns paying 4d per doseyne 3s 4d. In dyeing all the said aforesaid cloth, together with a piece containing twenty yards, to a black colour, by John Dyer, by the view of William Warderoppe, paying 12d per doseyne, 17s 6d. And paid to Thomas Touker of Clyve for shearing all the aforesaid cloth, 4s. And paid to John Dyer for dyeing a bed cover, 'tapytes, curteynes, costerys, bankerys and 'guysshenys' both for my lady's hall and for the chamber and the chapel at Karampton, 7s."[225]

The following payments refer to the period between September 1431 and March 1432. In December 1431 a meeting lasting for ten days took place at Taunton. It was called a "love day" which is a term applied to a day or days appointed for the amicable settlement of a dispute. "In the expenses of William Bonvyle, knight,[226] Edward Seynt Jon, Thomas Bratton, John Lauerance, Walter Portman, and part of the household of my lady Margaret Lutrell, who were at Taunton with thirty-six horses, from Monday the 10th day of December until the Wednesday next following after dinner, for a certain love-day between my lady Catherine Lutrell on the one part and my lady Margaret Lutrell of the other part, together with rewards made to the cook of the aforesaid William Bonvyle, knight, and other servants who were then there, £4 15d. And paid to John Lauerance who was at Taunton for the aforesaid day, of the council of my said lady Margaret Luttrell, by assent of Walter Portman one of the council of my said lady Margaret, 13s 4d. And in the expenses of Robert Ryvers sent to London by my lady Margaret Luttrell, to confer both with the Bishop of Bath and Walter Portman about the said love-day and about the payment there of the farm of Dunsterre in part, to wit that of the month of November, and to do other business there of my lady, in going and staying there and returning, for three weeks and four days, 33s 10d. To William Wardropere, by order of my lady, to distribute to priests for the soul of John Lutrell, knight, on the 17th day of January, 2d."[227]

It certainly seems as if Dame Margaret "lived it up" after Sir John Luttrell's death in 1430; her expenses outran her income and difficulties ensued with her receiver-general, Robert Ryvers. She was even driven to sell her bed and clothes and some of her silver to him and in the accounts for the six months ending in March 1432, he credited the following amounts to her. "The same Robert has received of the same Margaret, as in silver vases bought of her, £20. And the same has received of her, as in the silver cups bought of the same Margaret, £7 5s. And the same Robert has received of the same Margaret, as in a silver pot bought of her, 58s 9d. And the same Robert has received of the same Margaret, as in a white bed of half 'worstede' with other clothes bought of her and received in part payment of his aforesaid excess, 33s 4d."[228] She still owed more than £90.[229]

As we know, Margaret lived at Marshwood and in the three months between Michaelmas (29 September) and Christmas the steward of the household there bought 246 gallons of good ale from various tenants at Dunster. It cost 1¼d per gallon and, in addition, he purchased 619 gallons at 1d per gallon. This must have been for the staff or, perhaps, for the lesser guests, for it was second class ale. Pigeon must have been a very popular ingredient of their pies at Marshwood for in only one year 632 were consumed and of these 124 came from the dovecote in the Barnecourt at Dunster, 504 were purchased from the reeve at East Quantoxhead and 4 were gifts. Earlier in Sir John's lifetime, 10s 8d was spent on "great and small eels" supplied by the reeve at Woolavington who, on capturing a stray swan received a reward of 4d.[230]

When the widow of a tenant-in-chief wished to remarry it was obligatory to obtain a royal licence. This injunction the wayward Dame Margaret ignored and she married, as her second husband, Robert Coker. For this a pardon was extended to the offending couple. Their marriage remained valid but the pardon was expensively won, for they had to pay the Crown the very large sum of £40.[231] In accordance with medieval custom she retained the surname of Luttrell and the rank of her first husband. She died on 1 June 1438 and after her death Robert Coker was charged with having committed waste in two thirds of the Castle of Dunster and in the manor of Carhampton.[232] "Committing waste" is a term used in law to denote damage to an estate caused by neglect or unauthorised action, especially by a life-tenant.

As so often happened in this family, James, the son and heir was only three or four years of age when his father died. He initially became a ward of the Crown but within a very short time, two-thirds of the late Sir John's lands were committed to John, bishop of Bath and Wells. This bishop was numbered among the king's council operative during Henry VI's minority. He was keeper of the privy seal, later treasurer and chancellor and between 1443 and 1452, archbishop of Canterbury and a close friend of the Luttrell family. The two thirds were not committed solely to John Stafford but also to his brother, Sir Humphrey Stafford, and Sir Philip Courtenay a cousin of the heir whose daughter Elizabeth was to become the wife of Sir James. In 1431 the following payment is recorded: "In the expenses of my lady Margaret Luttrell riding with eight horses to Hoke (in Dorset) to confer with Humphrey Stafford, in going and returning, for four days, 12s 10½d."[233] In July 1433 the king, Henry VI, sold the right of tendering in marriage to James Luttrell a lady of suitable rank to Humphrey, earl of Stafford, and paid 400 marks for this right. Soon afterwards the earl made it over to Sir Philip Courtenay of Powderham.

Sir Philip was the great-grandson of Hugh de Courtenay and Margaret de Bohun whose daughter Elizabeth Courtenay had married, as her second husband, Andrew Luttrell. Sir Philip was the great-nephew of Elizabeth and Andrew. It is, therefore, not surprising that he was interested in the Luttrell estates and that he sought to gain ascendancy over their divided lands. He made his first move in 1437, a year before Dame Margaret Luttrell died and again in 1439. He obtained a demise, or conveyance, of the manor of Minehead and rented it for 100 marks annually. This rent was afterwards reduced by £40. He obtained a fresh demise of two-thirds of her late husband, Sir John's, lands at a yearly rent of £100 and after Dame Margaret's death, in 1438, he obtained a demise of the lands she had held at a yearly rent of £83. This rent was fixed by the Lord Treasurer which office was held by John Stafford, bishop of Bath and Wells, keeper of the privy seal and treasurer. Sir Philip was also the chief trustee, or feoffee, invested with the advowson, or right to appoint the priest at East Quantoxhead. In 1445 he managed to get his rent reduced by 40 marks[234] on the grounds that the liabilities of the estates outweighed the advantages. He maintained that the wardship of James Luttrell and the bestowal of royal grants intended to benefit him were of no value, since the true annual value of the estates did not exceed £183 for which he was liable.

The time came for the young Sir James to take over his estates and in July 1447 John Stafford lately bishop of Bath and Wells but now archbishop of Canterbury, and Humphrey Stafford, lately earl of Stafford and now elevated to dukedom of Buckingham, petitioned Henry VI. The king promised that James should come into possession at Michaelmas, on 29 September 1447, without proving that he had reached his majority or petitioning for a legal claim to them[235] as was the usual practice. In February 1449 James Luttrell made a legal settlement and for the first time we hear of his "cousin," one Richard Luttrell who was a bastard for whom James appears to have felt some obligation. "In February 1449,

James Luttrell obtained royal licence to convey the castle and borough of Dunster, the manors of Minehead, Carhampton, and Kilton and the hundred of Carhampton to feofees, in order that they should be settled on himself and the heirs of his body, with remainder to his 'cousin' Richard Luttrell and the heirs of his body and ultimate remainder to his own heirs general."[236]

Richard Luttrell had been constable of Dunster castle from 1430, at least up to 1449, and perhaps after that. He lived in a house on the site of the present Luttrell Arms Hotel and we know that he owned property in Dunster. A small diversion here concerns not the grand people but the servant of one William Bedewyn who, for his unseemly activities, was fined 3s 4d. "1443, April 8. John [Towker, coryser, servant of William Bedewyn] is a common spy or listener at the windows of the neighbours and likewise a common night-walker and eavesdropper. Therefore he is in mercy, 3s 4d."[237]

The executorship, or administration of the lands at Kentsford and Iveton caused a local fraças with Alexander Hody, who was one of Sir James Luttrell's feoffees. Alexander Hody's wife issued a bill of complaint and she avowed that James Luttrell had sent a man to enquire of her husband's whereabouts and that she, in all innocence, told him where he could be found for the next three days. Thereupon one of Hody's servants was abducted in order that he should not divulge to his master what was afoot. James Luttrell is said to have taken the servant.

> and putte hym in his castell of Dunster by the space of a nyghte, so that the seyd servaunt shuld not make knowliche to the seyd Alisaunder of the unfeythfull disposission of the seyd Jamys.[238] The account continues: In the mornyng thereupon, the seyd Jamys with the nombir of xxxv persones and moo, with bowys beyng bente and arowys in ther hondys by hym unlawfully gaderyd, wente to the house of Thomas Bratton, squyer, fadir in lawe to the seyd Alisaunder, where and atte which tyme she saide her husbonde would be, and there sowght hym, purposyng to have murderyd and sleyne the seyd Alisaunder. Item, the seyd Jamys and his servaunts to the nombir of xxiiij te persones, arrayyd with dobelettes of defence, palettes, bowys, arrowys, gleyvys, and speris [went] to Ca . . ., and ther John Toker, servaunt to the seyd Alisaunder, bete and woundyd, so that the seyd John was in dispeyre of his lyfe. Item, the seyd Jamys with his servaunts and othir to the nombir of xliiij te persones and moo, of grete malice forthought purposyng to murdyr and slee the seyd Alisaunder, entryd the castell of Taunton and ther the constabillarye of the same, and all the dorys ther brake and entrid, serching after the seyd Alisaunder, and vij sponys of silver of the seyd Alisaunder and v ivery komys and other godis of the seyd Alisaunder toke and bare aweye, and apon the wyfe of the seyd Alisaunder asaute made, bete, and with here daggers manassyd to slee, and so would have do her, by grace of God, one of ther felishipp lette hit, and Water Peyntore, servaunt to the seyd Alisaunder, cowardly nye to the dethe smote, and apon Sir Robert, preste to the seyd Alisaunder, asaute made and hym by the here to the grounde pluckyd, betyng hym with the pomellis of ther swerdis. Item, the seyd Alisaunder askyth of the seyd Jamys a c. marke in money of the dette of Richard Luttrell, whos administrator of godis and catall the seyd Jamys ys. Item he askyth of the seyd Jamys xvijs. and vjd. remeynyng unpayyd for pottes of silver and gilte, for a gretter summe of moneye by the seyd Alisaunder to him sold.[239]

Lyte remarks that some of the allegations made, for example those concerning the bows and the dire perils of John Toker, were manufactured with the object of bringing the controversy to court. Lesser allegations would not have come under the jurisdiction of the court and thus the whole story was embroidered. A compromise was reached in February

1458 and we read that "Alexander Hody gave a general release from all personal actions to James Luttrell, Simon Milbourn and John Loty, jointly and severally."[240]

In 1450 Sir James Luttrell married Elizabeth Courtenay of Powderham, daughter of his former guardian, and cousin, Sir Philip Courtenay, in the private chapel of Powderham castle. Sir Philip's grandfather, also Sir Philip, a younger son, had inherited Powderham from his mother Margaret, second countess of Devon. It then passed to this Philip's son, Sir John de Courtenay and his wife Joan, and thence to their son Philip who married Elizabeth Hungerford. These two were the parents of Sir James Luttrell's bride. Much confusion has arisen between her and the Elizabeth Courtenay who was the wife of Sir Andrew Luttrell, the parents of Sir Hugh Luttrell, first lord of Dunster.

Sir James Luttrell espoused the Lancastrian cause and had been implicated in the death of the duke of York in 1460 at the battle of Wakefield. When eventually the Yorkists were triumphant and Edward IV became king, the Luttrells' fortunes suffered and the late Sir James was attainted and held to have been a rebel. Not so on the day of the battle of Wakefield for this was a momentous and proud day for Sir James who was knighted on the battlefield by the duke of Somerset who himself was in 1465 attainted, captured at Tewkesbury, tried and executed.

Sir James gloried in his knighthood for forty-nine days, for at the second battle of St Albans on 17 February 1461, he received a wound from which he died five days later. He left two sons and at least two daughters. His heir Alexander died before 1481 and his second son Hugh became his eventual heir. His only named daughter Jane married George Stewkley.[241] Sir James had not neglected to provide marriage portions for his younger children and shortly before his death, James Luttrell charged some of his lands in Suffolk and Devonshire, and others which he had acquired in Somerset, with a payment of £50 a year to John Loty upon trust that the money should accumulate in a chest to be sealed by him and Elizabeth Luttrell, in order to provide marriage portions for the younger children.[242]

The sheriff and the escheator in Somerset and Dorset seized all the possessions of the dukes of Exeter and Somerset, the earls of Devon, Wilts and Northumberland and the possessions of the late Sir James Luttrell and Sir Alexander Hody, one of his feofees, in those counties.[243] Again, Sir James Luttrell's lands were threatened. This time by Sir William Herbert, Thomas Herbert, John Herbert and Hugh Huntley who were commissioned to take possession not only of the lands of Sir James but of the lands of the earls of Pembroke and Shrewsbury, who were all singled out as rebels.[244] Further the king granted to Sir William Bourchier the wardship and marriage of Alexander Luttrell, the infant heir.[245]

A sweeping ordinance was passed by parliament, which sat in November 1461, against the chief supporters of Henry VI. Sir James Luttrell was therein named amongst those who "with grete despite and cruell violence, horrible and unmanly tyrannye, murdered the late Duke of York at Wakefield, and who were consequently to stand and be convycted and attainted of high treason, and forfett to the King and his heires all the castles, maners" and other lands of which they were or had been possessed.[246] Between February and November 1461, Lady Elizabeth Luttrell had been left to enjoy the benefits of the lands which had been settled on her at her marriage. This tacit permission soon came to an end when the king's representative took over her lands. Vainly she protested that she was a loyal subject of the Yorkist king which was surely quite a volte face for a lady whose husband had died in the Lancastrian cause and who had killed the duke of York. An enquiry took place in September 1462 but it did not avail her much satisfaction.[247] Finally, in June 1463, the axe fell. The King granted to Sir William Herbert, and the heirs of his body, the honour, castle, manor and borough of Dunster, the manors of Minehead and Carhampton, the hundred of Carhampton, the manors of Kilton, East Quantoxhead and Iveton, and lands at Kentsford, Watchet, Exton, Vexford, Rixen, Stogumber, Wibwell, Huish by Highbridge and Cothelston, in Somersetshire, the manors of Chilton and Blancombe in Devonshire, the manors of Stonehall and Woodhall in Suffolk, and all other lands and profits to which Sir James had been entitled in possession or in reversion.[248] Although the king was not crowned until June, his regnal year is counted from his acclamation on 4 March 1461, but the grant made to Sir William Herbert stated that he was to receive all the issues as from 1 March 1461, the day that, in fact, the soldiery had raised their voices for the king. Four years later, in March 1465, the grant was renewed and additional land was included, at Little Carhampton and Radlet and the grant was set back to 30 December 1460 which Lyte gives as the date of the retrospective attainder of Sir James Luttrell.[249]

In 1464 Edward IV thwarted the ambition of his cousin Warwick, the "kingmaker," and instead of marrying a French princess to seal a treaty of friendship between Louis XI and England, he had married Elizabeth Woodville who, unlike all Edward IV's other conquests had demanded no less than marriage in return for her favours. In 1466 her sister, Mary Woodville, married or a marriage was arranged between her and Lord William Herbert's infant eldest son, William, then aged five and a half. Indeed, four of the queen's sisters were betrothed to eminent magnates of the kingdom and the rise of the Woodvilles was a source of displeasure to Warwick. Not only Elizabeth and her younger sisters but her father, Richard Woodville, also achieved notability and became treasurer of England and was created Earl Rivers. William of Worcester relates that when the marriage between the infant William Herbert and Mary Woodville was negotiated at Windsor, the king dubbed the boy a knight and also created him "Lord of Dunster," again to the displeasure of Warwick and the other magnates.[250] However, there is no official record of this creation although "the younger William Herbert is styled 'Lord of Dunster' in some royal letters patent issued during the lifetime of his father."[251]

Between 1463 and 1485 the Herberts were in possession of the Honour of Dunster and seven months after the marriage of the infant, so called, Lord of Dunster, the following ordinances for the good government of the borough were made by the court. "1467 April 20. That nobody shall henceforth put dung, straw, or other nuisances in the water running to the lord's mills at any time of the week, save after one o'clock after noon on Saturday; and that the whole 'flodeyate' standing in the same water shall be open by the aforesaid hour; under pain of all those who can be found in default of 6d to be paid to the lord."[252] Also in 1467, "That nobody shall henceforth make linen cloth of 'flockys', and if it be proved by anyone that then the cloth so made shall be forfeited to the lord."[253] "1472 October 19. That nobody shall henceforth use or carry swords, lances, 'gleyves,' and other defensible and unlawful arms, contrary to the statute of our lord the king provided in this respect, under pain of forfeiture of the same and 6s 8d for every offence of this sort, to be paid to the lord as often as discovery shall be made. And it is ordained likewise by the court, with the assent of the twelve jurors and the other officers (aforesaid) that no man shall henceforth shoot with his bows and arrows in the churchyard of Dunster, or unlawfully practice games there, under pain of 40d. And it is ordained likewise by the court, with the assent of the twelve jurors (aforesaid) that nobody in the borough shall henceforth play at dice or cards, under pain of everyone who shall be found in default thus of 6s 8d. And that nobody shall allow games of this sort to be practised in his house, save during twelve days at Christmas, under pain of 10s."[254]

When the young William Herbert was around eight or nine years of age he became a ward of the Crown. His father, Lord Herbert, earl of Pembroke and his uncle Richard Herbert were beheaded in 1469 and an inquisition was taken at the earl's death. It did not mention lands in Somerset, Devon or Suffolk although Lyte writes: "it is stated elsewhere that he died seised of the forfeited inheritance of the Luttrells.[255] He observes that: it is not necessary to suppose that either of the Earls of Pembroke ever lived at Dunster Castle. Their main possessions lay on the north side of the Bristol Channel."[256] When the care of the young William Herbert's lands was entrusted to his mother, in recompense of her dower, the property of the late Sir James Luttrell in Somerset and Devon was specifically excepted. The King, moreover, appointed Philip Beaumont, esquire, to be constable of Dunster Castle and steward of all the lordships and lands that went with it.[257] So again, in 1472, the King appointed a certain John Gogh to be bailiff of Dunster and keeper of Marshwood Park.[258]

Earlier in that year the keeping of Minehead, Kilton, Iveton and East Quantoxhead, with the advowson of the latter, and lands at Exton, Vexford, Rixen and Stogumber, during the minority of the young William Herbert, earl of Pembroke, were committed, free from rent, to Lady Elizabeth's four Courtenay brothers, Peter, who was Edward IV's secretary, Sir William, Sir Philip and John and to her brother-in law, Sir Thomas Fulford.[259] These manors and lands were those she would have held in jointure if her late husband, Sir James Luttrell, had not been attainted for the murder of the duke of York in 1460. Apart from the four brothers and Sir Thomas, another of the trustees was George, duke of Clarence, Edward IV's brother and Lady Elizabeth's patron and it was probably due to his influential standing that Lady Elizabeth, known as the "farmer of the manor of Minehead"[260] could really attribute her success. Indeed, four years later, in 1476, she stood godmother to Richard, the short-lived son of George, duke of Clarence.[261] Richard was christened at Tewkesbury; a place which must have held poignant memories for her since it was here that her second husband, Sir Humphrey Audley, was beheaded.[262] It is remarkable to us that Lady Elizabeth's patron was the son of the duke of York who was murdered by her late husband and others. However, in spite of Lady Elizabeth's royal patron, things did not go all her way for in December 1472 Lady Herbert, the widow of Sir William (d. 1469) and the mother of young William, succeeded in obtaining a grant entitling her to keep the honour, castle, manor and lordship of Dunster, and of other possessions of the attainted late Sir James Luttrell. All this at the annual rent of £90.[263]

In 1475, Lady Elizabeth judiciously laid claim to the lands and manors that had been settled on her during the lifetime of Sir James. She feared that on attaining his majority the young earl would eject her. Her plea rested on a clause in the act of attainder which stated that the wives of those attainted, if born within the realm, should enjoy their own hereditaments. Since she was a native of Exeter she requested that the inquisition which benefited the Herberts should be ignored. It seems that a commission of enquiry was appointed and a Somerset jury endorsed her statements. The convening of the commission and the endorsements point to the probable success of her suit. She did not, however, achieve complete ascendancy over the Herberts because the young William Herbert came into his inheritance at the early age of fifteen years in 1476 and he enjoyed Dunster, Carhampton and other Luttrell estates as earl of Pembroke from 1476 to 1479 and as earl of Huntingdon from 1479 to 1485, relinquishing them only when Richard III went down fighting at the battle of Bosworth Field in 1485.

In 1479, Edward IV wishing to make his own son earl of Pembroke, conferred the earldom of Huntingdon on William Herbert, the younger, in lieu. In 1477, Lady Elizabeth's patron, George, duke of Clarence, was tried for high treason and drowned in a butt of Malmsey wine.

Before 1481 the heir of the late Sir James Luttrell and Lady Elizabeth Luttrell died and their second son Hugh (d. 1521) became the heir. This Hugh Luttrell, with the death of the Yorkist king, Richard III in 1485, like other Lancastrian supporters, sought re-instatement. He petitioned King Henry VII, the first Tudor king, who by his marriage to Elizabeth of York, daughter of Edward IV united the Houses of Lancaster and York, and his petition set forth that: "his father had been attainted for the true faith and allegiaunce which he owid unto the right famous prince of the moost blessed memory, then his soveraine lord, Henry late King of England the sixth," and praying that the act of attainder should be repealed, and consequent letters patent made void. His petition was readily granted and the agents of the Earl of Huntingdon made way for the rightful lord of Dunster.[264] The Herberts had cared little for Dunster Castle and Sir Hugh concentrated on East Quantoxhead where he mainly resided and built a large part of the existing manor house.

At the coronation of Henry VII's queen, Elizabeth of York, Hugh Luttrell was created a Knight of the Bath. His mother, Lady Elizabeth Luttrell, lived on until 1493. After Sir James Luttrell died at the second battle of St Albans, Elizabeth had married, as her second husband, Sir Humphrey Audley He was taken prisoner at the battle of Tewkesbury and beheaded. So this tragic lady lost two husbands to the Lancastrian cause within eleven years. Her third husband, Thomas Malet, does not figure to any great extent in Lyte's *History of Dunster*. The only information he gives is that Sir Hugh Luttrell had serious trouble with him and Sir Hugh's mother, Lady Elizabeth. It concerned: lands which she claimed to hold in jointure, and some jewels, plate and household stuff, valued at 800 marks, which Sir James Luttrell had bequeathed to his eldest son.[265] However, the parties reached a compromise resulting in Lady Luttrell's retention of East Quantoxhead and Hugh undertaking to pay his mother "80 marks annually for the manor of Minehead during her lifetime."[266] It all seems to have been fairly amicable for Lady Luttrell and her husband then delivered to him: "two basons of silver, two ewers, two gilte cuppes covered standyng, two pottes of silver and gilt with a pot of silver, two saltes with one cover, three bolles with one cover, a chafyng disshe of silver, two doseyn spones, a chaleys, a masse boke, a peir of vestementes," and a list of other goods that should pass to him at her death.[267+]

Although she died as the widow of Thomas Malet of Enmore in Somerset, in accordance with medieval custom she retained the surname of her first husband, Sir James Luttrell. She was buried before the altar of St George, in the priory church where her tomb slab was originally placed. The floors were undoubtedly laid with medieval tiles and tomb slabs and the level of the floors was lower until the restoration of 1874/6. The inscription on her tomb slab given by Lyte, and his translation, is as follows:

> "Orate queso pro a a dñe Elizabeth Lutterell que obijt primo die mensis Septembris Anno dñi Milliõ cccc nonages o tercio. Nunc X˜re te petimus miserer' q˜s qui ve sti redim˜e pditos noli dampnare redemptos."
>
> "Pray I beseech you, for the soul of the Dame Elizabeth Luttrell, who died on the first day of the month of September in the year of Our Lord 1493. Now, O Christ, we pray thee be merciful; we beseech thee have mercy, and do not condemn the redeemed whom thou camest to redeem when lost."[268]

Lyte describes: "An incised stone slab, which has since been removed to the south aisle of the chancel, shows her attired in a sideless dress faced with ermine, and a mantle lined with ermine, the neck bare, and the head covered with a veil falling below the shoulders. Two angels support a pillow, and there is the usual dog at the feet." The little dog is amusing; his head and forelegs being hidden to view as he burrows and frolics in the hems of her garment. Her pose is conventional and most dignified. Dr Eeles expressed the opinion that the alabaster slab was probably transported from Chellaston in Derbyshire and that it is a type common in the Midlands but rarely found elsewhere.[269] Whilst this tomb slab was placed before the high altar of St George, when Lady Elizabeth was buried in 1493, it is not inappropriate that it was, in the 19th century, placed at the east end of the south aisle, the site of the pre-Reformation chantry chapel of St Lawrence, which like the Chapel of Our Lady at the east end of the north aisle was rebuilt in 1450, the year Lady Elizabeth married Sir James Luttrell in the chapel of Powderham Castle. shows the nine holes punctured into the slab. It appears that the tombstone of this great lady was regarded with little respect during the years when the priory church was regarded as simply a burial vault for the Luttrell family and was neglected and uncared for until the Victorians came to the rescue. Here it appears that the youths of Dunster, accustomed to amuse themselves wherever they wished, played the old English game of "Nine Holes." As Preb Hancock says "sic transit gloria mundi."

SIR ANDREW LUTTRELL

Around 1514 Sir Andrew Luttrell chose Margaret, the daughter of Sir Thomas Wyndham of Felbrigg in Norfolk as his bride. Had Sir Andrew preferred one of her sisters that would have been agreeable to her father. The agreement is dated 31 March 1514 and is as follows: "Androw Luttrell, sonn and heire apparant of the saied Sir Hugh, by the grace of God, shall mary and take to his wiefe Margaret one of the doughters of the saied Sir Thomas or any others of the daughters of the saied Sir Thomas suche as the saied Androwe shall best lieke byfore the Wonysdaie next after Lowe Soundaie next commynge after the date of this presentes, after the cosdom and lawe of holye churche, if the said Margaret or such of her sisters as the said Androwe shall best lieke therunto will agree and the lawe of holye churche it wyll permytt and suffer."[270] Sir Hugh Luttrell KB and Sir Thomas Wyndham were determined that one of the former's sons should form an alliance with one of the latter's daughters for, although there were only four weeks between the date of the agreement and the last day allowed for the solemnisation of the marriage, it was agreed that if Andrew Luttrell should die during that period, his next brother John should marry one of the daughters of Sir Thomas before Whitsuntide.

There is even a clause in the agreement which relates to the apparell of either Andrew or John whichever might survive the ensuing four weeks: "The said Sir Hugh, at his proper costes and charges, shall apparell the said Androwe or John that shall happen to mary with one of the doughters of the said Sir Thomas at the saied daie of maryage as shalbe convenyent for his degree."[271] Sir Thomas Wyndham undertook to "apparell" his daughter for the wedding and to pay half the costs of the dinner and other expenses occasioned by the wedding. Margaret's marriage portion of seven hundred marks, (£466 13s 4d), was to be paid to her father-in law in instalments. Sir Hugh's obligations were to settle £40 a year on the young couple and to guarantee that Andrew would duly inherit the bulk of his landed property. Both bride and groom were at that time minors and it was agreed that Sir Thomas Wyndham should have the "rule and governance" of Andrew and Margaret pending Andrew's coming of age.[272] It seems that, between the two fathers, the young couple had little access to money. The marriage took place on 22 April 1514 and the legal settlement followed in May. In later years the bride's family, the Wyndhams, acquired much property near Dunster.[273]

In about 1527 Andrew Luttrell was knighted[274] and in November 1528 he was appointed sheriff of Somerset and Dorset.[275] Dame Walthean, did not regard her stepson so highly. Sir Hugh Luttrell had died on 1 February 1521 and was buried at East Quantoxhead and after his death, his widow, in reply to a bill filed against her in the Star Chamber stated that after the death of her husband, Andrew Luttrell "in Lent last past, of his wilfull and cruell mynde, without any cause resonable, took her goodes and catalles, not levying her dische, pott, nother panne" and that she and her children and servants had "stood in daily perell of their lyves," until she went up to London, leaving only a certain Lewis Griffyth and an "impotent, power" almsman, eighty years of age, to look after her interests at East Quantoxhead. She professed, moreover, to have instructed her agent to offer no resistance if Andrew Luttrell or anyone on his behalf should attempt to eject him from the manor house. In such an event, she intended to have her remedy at law. A serious affray, however, occurred in her absence. Two versions of it have been preserved.[276]

It seems, according to one of Andrew Luttrell's servants, John Gay, that Lewis Griffyth did not obey his mistress's injunction to offer no resistance, for John Gay made a complaint to the King's Council to the effect that: "on the 7 of June, 1521, Lewis Griffyth and several other evil-disposed persons assaulted him at East Quantockshead, shot eleven arrows at him, one of which pierced him through the left arm, while others 'grevosly strake hym in dyvers places of hys body, so that and yff socoure of trees hadde nott byn, they hadde kylled and murdered hym oute of hand'. He also said that he had received 'a grette wonde in the shilder' with a forest bill."[277] The case made by Griffyths was quite different and more detailed. He said he was in the park at East Quantoxhead: "with his bowe and his shaffes under his gyrdell, going abought to recover a dere, being hurte, in a place called Blakwell."[278] Here he met Gay and two other men. All were armed, Gay having "a longe peked staff" said to be seven feet in length and his companions bearing great axes. They said Sir Andrew had commanded them, "to take sixty trees for posts" but Griffyths would not allow them to do this unless they had a warrant from Dame Walthean, who held the manor for her lifetime. To add weight to this he "to fere the said John Gay and his felowes, shot an arrowe wyde of them." Gay was obviously alarmed by this and asked Griffyths "to holde his hand" whereupon Griffyths "took his cap in hand and desyered and tenderly prayed them to departe." That was not the end of it, for Gay and his companions "wente into a place withyn the said towne and ther harnyssed them, and called to them two idell persons." They all returned to the park, two of the party "havyng forest billes," Gay "having the said longe pyked staff, a hanger and a shorte dager," the remainder "having grete axes in their hands." They duped Griffyths by felling "an olde lying tree" and the sound, so near the manor house, caused Griffyths to imagine that they were indeed felling trees. He came out and he and "a chylde of sixteen" were attacked. It is possible that Gay was injured and Griffyths and the boy were taken to the abode of Lord Fitzwarren, three miles distant for Griffyths had not only been knocked down but had received injuries to his head and hand caused by the forest bill. Lord Fitzwarren dealt with them, it would seem, somewhat harshly for he had them "fetered" and for two hours confined in the porter's lodge from which place they freed only "on payment of a fee to the porter."[279] Lytes quotes the story from Star Chamber Proceedings, vol. xvi, ff, 20-22, and concludes: "It is impossible to say whether Gay's version or Griffyth's was the more truthful."

Lyte describes as "somewhat mysterious" a letter Sir Andrew Luttrell wrote on 16 July 1537 to Thomas Cromwell: "Acordyng [to the] request made unto me by your late letters yn the favowr of Mons. Pynto for the transportyng of a sertyn lady owt of Portyngale hither, I have, as muche as yn me ys furnysshyd your sayd desyre, in suche sorte that she ys here aryvyd yn safete wyth her gooddes, wyche is extemyd to be of noo small summe. Nevertheless, for as myche that y have percevyd, as well by conveans of her sayd goodes by nyght, as also the receyving of her person and company certyng dystance from the common porte that y was apoynted to, that suche secrett thyngkes wrought yn her sayd conveance, that nether my shipe nor maryners herafter can use there trade of merchandise thither without danger, etc."[280] Sir Andrew asks for Thomas Cromwell's advice and assistance: "yff any trobell shall chanyce unto me or myne."[281] Apparently, a few weeks later, another Portuguese lady of rank and wealth, wishing to go to Flanders, thought it prudent to sail in the first instance to an English port, thus avoiding the northern coast of France. She too had the assistance of the same Pinto, a Portuguese merchant.[282] In the same year of 1537 Lady Margaret received from her mother's sister, Elizabeth, countess of Oxford, "a legacy of a tablet of gold,"[283] and the next year, a year before the surrender of Dunster priory on 1 January 1538 Sir Andrew Luttrell died and was buried at East Quantoxhead.[284]

CHAPTER FIVE

THE CHURCH

T HE CENTRAL crossing tower, the heart of the church, is usually a mark of a Benedictine foundation. At Dunster the tower is a plain, well-built Perpendicular structure supported on great piers connected with pointed arches. The plan made by C.H. Samson FRIBA before the Victorian restoration shows that the two eastern Perpendicular piers are supported by angle buttresses which project through the chancel into the former chantry chapel of the Blessed Virgin Mary on the north side and on the south side into the former chantry chapel, shown in this plan as that of the Holy Trinity or St George, but more probably the site of the chantry chapel of St Lawrence on the south side. The plan shows small areas of Norman work round these eastern piers. The two western piers appear in this plan to have been built against far more extensive Norman work flanking the area which, before 1874/6, was the site of the parish altar. The plan also shows smaller Norman areas round these western piers below the present ground level. As these piers are built against the massive earlier work, they occupy a larger space than the eastern piers. The existence of Norman masonry in all four piers points to the fact that before the building of the existing Perpendicular pointed arches, there would have been round-headed Norman arches supporting a squat Norman tower.

Central towers, often lantern towers, were very popular in England as opposed to the dome over the crossing in some continental Romanesque buildings. It may be that these central towers owe their existence to the lasting monastic influence over English architecture. In monastic churches the monks' choir occupied the crossing and the eastern bays of the nave. At Dunster the nave of the church originally ran straight through the entire building from east to west. Eeles wrote: "There was almost certainly a broader and lower tower on the site of the present tower with a small choir for the monks beyond it."[1] When the very dark Norman churches were later enlarged, aisles with lighter arcading and additional, larger apertures were made to receive windows, which reduced the lateral support for these massive Norman towers making them liable to crumble and fall. Until that time the piers of the tower, the nave and the transepts had provided sufficient support and the church was of true cruciform shape. The attached columns and capitals of one of the former Norman arches remain attached to the two western piers and the base of the northern attached column is about 8inches below the present level of the floor. The capital of this column bears a rudimentary volute beneath which is an enchanting carving of a juggler or reveller, on his back, his neck grotesquely large and his legs, one behind the other, flung into the air, and from his neck a scrip is suspended. The figure was re-cut during the Victorian restoration. The southern attached column is topped by one and a half sides of a cushion capital. Drawings made by J.C Buckler, in 1842 indicate the form of the church at that time and the meaningless chancel arch, serving no structural purpose, connecting the two Norman attached columns of the western piers of the tower.

According to Prof Freeman: "The Priory of Dunster was originally founded towards the close of the eleventh century, and some small portions of the church, which was doubtless built soon afterwards, still exist. A little to the west of the western arch of the present lantern a large Norman arch spans the nave and connected with it on each side is a portion of masonry, that to the south showing a small fragment of a Norman pillar. The Norman church then had a nave and aisles, doubtless of the same proportion in point of width as the present ones, for the nave is extremely wide, and the aisles unusually narrow. Of its probable length I cannot undertake to speak."[2] There is also a Norman pillar on the north side. Lyte disagreed and said that the nave "had no side aisles" (Lyte H.D.Part II 387). Freeman speaks of a Norman arch: "the Norman arch across the have has clearly been tampered with, its inner order or orders taken away; but I could see no sign of its having been removed from its original place. From its position, it might be either a mere chancel-arch if there was no central tower, or the western arch of a lantern…, if there was one. But as a Transitional arch leads from the south transept into the south aisle of the monks' choir, I think we may safely infer that the original church was cruciform, with a lantern tower, of considerably greater massiveness than the present one."[3] The reference to a Norman arch must be explained. This was deemed to be a "mock" Norman arch and was removed in 1875. Freeman also observes that "The lantern itself, with the transepts, formed a noble vestibule to the church of the monks, who had a private entrance in the west wall of the south transept." There is no evidence of the entrance today. The reference to a lantern at that date is inaccurate for, if ever Dunster had a lantern tower, it was in existence before the 1443/6 tower was built and would have surmounted the Norman tower. A lantern is "a small circular or polygonal turret with windows all rounds crowning a roof or dome."[4]

East and west of this neutral space, the monks and the parishioners appear to have remodelled their respective portions, without much regard to each other's proceedings and there is a wide difference in the details employed in the two. As the Priory of Dunster was a cell of Bath abbey, one might expect to find some approximation in its architecture, to the magnificent, if anomalous, reconstruction of the mother church which was going on much about the same time, but there is little or no resemblance.

Prof Freeman refers to a "transitional arch" leading from the south transept into the south aisle. However, this is not an arch built during a period of transition between two styles of architecture, but a 13th-century arch, widened with 16th-century jambs. Although it gives a superficial appearance of a work of the Decorated Period by reason of its overall ogee shape, a mark of this style, the mouldings of the upper portion belong to the 13th century and the entire arch was not conceived as an entity but was widened later and adapted to suit altered circumstances. "This Transitional arch should be noticed on account of the extraordinary shape of its shafts, which curve inwards below the capitals, so as to give the whole an approach to the trefoil form. The arch is pointed, with Early English mouldings, but the *abaci* are square."[5]

The present four-centred arches which support the tower may be dated to the middle of the 14th century or the early 15th century. Lyte considered: "Adam de Cheddar may have had something to do with the erection of the great piers connected with pointed arches that carry the central tower of the church. From the fact that there are four such arches, uniform in size and design, it is clear that the building was intended to be cruciform at the time of their erection in the middle of the 14th century or soon after."[6] Adam de Cheddar was appointed prior of Dunster in 1337 by Prior Thomas of Bath. He was succeeded by William Thouer in 1355, by Richard de Childeston in 1357 and by John Hervey in 1376. In the Bath Cartularies (No 876) the following entry appears: "Octave of S. Mich. 1345. John, prior of Bath, grants to Adam de Cheddr, chamberlain of the church of Bath and prior of Dunster, in consideration of the sumptuous buildings he has made and the many and notable good works that he has done, an annual rent of 50s per year for an anniversary.[7] It is uncertain whether these "sumptuous buildings" were at Dunster or at Bath. The repair and maintenance of the tower is mentioned in the 1357 Agreement. This agreement was made between Richard de Childeston, prior of Dunster, and the monks on the one side and the parishioners on the other and was made in the presence of the last de Mohun lord of Dunster, John de Mohun V. The third section states: "The Prior shall repair and roof the tower suitably without defect and shall receive from the parishioners 8 marks in three instalments. He shall roof and forever maintain the chapel of Our Lady and the dorter aisle. The parishioners shall for ever maintain the chapel of St Leonard and the aisle between the chapel of St Lawrence and the tower."[8]

In 1419 there was talk of a new bell tower. "William Pynson, by his last will, dated the Wednesday in the feast of St Valentine the Martyr 1419, bequeaths his body to be buried in the Church of St George the Martyr at Dunster before the image of St Christopher, and 40 shillings towards the new Bell-tower, and 20 shillings towards one of the new bells, with 6s.8d. towards the new Rood-loft in the said Church." The bells are first mentioned in 1419. The same year: "Joan Wedmore of Dunster, widow, gave the bells of Dunster 8d." [9] William Pynsoun desired that "his body should be buried before the image of St Christopher."[10] Prof Bettey says: "groups of people continued to pay for statues. Most churches had several such statues of the most popular medieval saints, the Virgin, St John, St Peter, St George, St Christopher and many others which were the object of veneration and devotion.[11]

The date of the Tower is more certainly known, from a coaeval agreement found in the Church a few years ago, endorsed by a recent hand: "The building of the Tower of Dunster in the 21st year of the reign of King Henry Sixth, 1443. This building was undertaken by John Marys of Stogursey, Somerset, and an engineer from Bristol; to be completed in three years." The endorsement was copied in 1716 at the discovery of this curious document; the Agreement itself was originally in the chest in Dunster church, but has unfortunately been mislaid. Although the two upper storeys of the tower were built between 1443 and 1446, Lyte ascribes the first stage above the roof to c.1419: "The lower stage of the tower above the roof of the church has a window of two lights on each of the four sides, and was clearly built about this period."[12] Lyte also writes: "The absence in this elaborate contract of any allusion to the lower stage of the tower may fairly be taken to show that it was already in existence. On the other hand the reference to the 'gras tabyl' as a level from which measurements could be taken is worthy of notice."[13]

Jon Maryce/Marys seems to have enjoyed the full confidence of the churchwardens who arranged this communal undertaking, for they only required that the work was done "after reson and gode proportion" and the parish was prepared to offer muscle power if required since there was little assistance of a mechanical nature save a crane. The materials used are New Red Sandstone with Doulting or Dundry freestone dressings. This local sandstone erodes rapidly and has been the cause of much re-building in the area. Peter Poyntz Wright remarks: "Dunster is one of the less elaborate towers, ... the tower is small... the pinnacle arrangement, parapet, merlons, window format, and buttresses are all features shared with the small West Somerset tower of Combe Florey with which Dunster should be compared."[14]

The contract for the building of the tower reads: "Thys beth the convenants betwyne the paroch of Dunsterr and Jon Marys of Stokgursy in the Schere of Somerset. That is to seyng for the making of a towre in the paroch church of Dunsterr. That the sayd Jon Marys schall make suffycyantly the seyde towre with iiij french botras and a vice in the fowrtt pyler in stede of a botras fynyng at the Altertabyll*. And in the fyrst flore ij wyndowys On yn the Sowth and another yn the North everych of on day with iiij genelas yn the hedd of every wyndow And iiij wyndowys at the bell bedd of ij days with a trawnson and moynell according to the patron ymade by the avyce of Rychard Pope Fremason Allso the sayde Jon Maryce schall make suffycyantly the batylment of the sayde towre with iiij pynacles the fowrth pynacle standing upon the vice after reson and go de proportion Acordyng to the same worke And the sayde schall be embatyle Allso the sayde Jon Maryce schall make iij gargylles in thre corners of the sayde towre And the wall to be iiij fote thykk and a halfe yn to the bell bedd And from the bell bedd ynto the batylment iij fote and a halfe suffycyantly to be made undyr the forme forsayde And the sayde paroch schall bryng all suffycyant materials withyn the palme crosse of the sayde Church And he to have for the workemanchyppe of every fote of the sayde towre xiij.s iiij.d And the sayde worke to be full endyd withyn iij ere nexte folowyng aftyr the date of this present wrytyng And rather yf hit may be by the power of the sayde paroch And the sayde Jon Maryce schall be redy aftyr the stuffe of matyr at all tyme by the warnyng of xiiij days and the crane at all tyme necessary for the same worke with ropys polys wynchchys schall be removyd at the cost of the paroch forsayd with help of Ion Maryce and his mayny Allso the sayd paroch schall fynd all syntarnys for the same worke with ropes poleys winchchys and all other thyngys necessary to the sayd work The towre conteynyng yn heyth from the gras tabylll an hundred fote Allso the sayd Ion Marys schall be payd for his labour lyk as he doth his work other ellys at the most xxs. byfore as hit aperyth yn work Also the sayd paroch schall fynd an howse for the sayde Johon Maryce to sett therein his tole and other necessarys Allso if there be any stone ywrozyte of such quantyte that ij men at most may not kary hym the sayde paroch schall helpe hym Allso the sayde Johon Maryce schall receive of the sayde paroch xxs. for the pynaclys of the same towre. Into the whych wytnys y put thereto my seelez I give and y wrytte at Dunsterr in the fest of Seynt Mychaell the yere of King Herry the vj aftyr the conquest xxi."[15] (*The term "Altertabyll" implies a moulding that allows the water to trickle down the wall,[16] and "tabling," or "tablements" or "ledgements" were stone slabs that marked out the walls horizontally. The edges were sometimes carved, as in early string courses, or moulded.[17])

Lyte's account states: "In 1443, the parish of Dunster resolved to complete the work, and accordingly entered into a contract with a certain John Marys of Stoke Courcy for the addition of the two upper stages." According to the terms of this interesting document written in English, the tower was to be a hundred feet high above the "gras tabyl" or plinth. There were to be three "French" buttresses, that is to say angle-buttresses "fining" or diminishing (the buttresses are steeply stepped and set diagonally) at the "water-table," or string-course, and three "gargylles," one at each angle. In the fourth angle there was to be a "vice," or spiral staircase. The top of the tower was to be adorned with "batylment" and four "pynacles," one of which was to be placed "upon the vice, after reson and go de proportion." On the first new stage, called "the first flore," there were to be two windows, one on the north side and the other on the south, each of one "day," or light, with four "genelas," or cusps. At the "bell-bedd" there were to be four windows each of two "days" separated by a "moynell" or mullion, and further divided horizontally by a "trawnsom" designed by a freemason named Richard Pope. The main walls to be built by Marys were to be 4 feet thick (the transcript says 4½ feet) up to the "bell-bed" and 3 feet 6 inches thick above.

The parish undertook to provide all the material and the necessary appliances, such as "ropes, poleys, winchchys," and the like, and to pay Marys 13s 4d per foot for "workemanchyppe" with 20s extra for carving the pinnacles. He had apparently only one or two assistants, and he was allowed three years for the completion of the work.[18] The contract for the building of the tower was made between the mason and the parishioners. The parish was heavily involved and provided local labour to bring all the necessary materials to the churchyard referred to in the contract as "withyn the palme crosse." The parish provided the centrings, ropes, winches and parishioners helped shift the crane and stones which were too heavy for two or three men to handle. It is probable that at Dunster the sand required for building works came from Dunster beach. Only sand washed by the winter rains would have been suitable, since summer sand would have had a heavy salt content which would have rendered it unsuitable for building operations. After the lime was burnt, it was stored in the Lime House Lime, the product of the burning of chalk or limestone, could be bought ready burnt, or could be burnt in kilns specially constructed in the neighbourhood of building operations. The burning of lime was comparatively well paid, skilled work including night work, as the furnace had to be kept burning.[19] Apart from actual building operations, it was customary to lime wash churches inside and outside once a year. Walls were lime-plastered in the medieval period to receive biblical fresco paintings. In 1842, in the *Ecclesiologist* (no. xviii, Jan. 1843) we read, "lime is no longer burned in the lantern."

Although the contract is for two windows, one in the south and one in the north, each of one "day" with four cusps in the head of every window, it appears that only one was inserted on the south side which, today, has a small clock face below it. It has also two louvred lights, or "days," and not the one specified. The number of cusps is three or five and not the four specified. Rev. Utten Todd writing in the *Parish Magazine* in 1882 commented: "nor do the windows quite correspond to the specification of 1443." Hamper, in 1808 wrote: "the Tower is 90 feet high, embattled at the top with low broken Pinnacles at the corners and contains a clock, chimes (which play the 113th Psalm-tune at the hours of 1, 5 and 9) and eight bells, the oldest of which bears date 1668 and the newest 1782."[20]

The fourth pinnacle which was to stand "upon the vice after reson and gode proportion" was apparently either never placed there, or supplanted at some later date by a weather-vane which rises above the battlemented stair-turret, or vice, above the main tower. Reference is made to the weather-vane in 1674 when the churchwardens' accounts record: "Paid Robert Ashford and his men for fitting up the Vane 3s 4." "For taking down the Vane and for beere for the workmen 2s 0d." This seems a contradiction but perhaps it was not satisfactorily put up the first time. In 1710 there is another reference to the vane: "For Iron and work about the vane and Thomas Morcombe for setting up the vane and John Wilkins for cullering it, £1 5s."

Some of the money for the building work came from bequests, donations, fund-raising and from church ales. Bettey writes: "From the 14th century churchwardens' accounts survive, and by the latter part of that century, it is known that the church ale played a prominent part in providing funds for the parish church which, by this time had acquired its role as the focal point of village life. One of the interesting accounts given by Dr Bettey belongs to the second half of the 15th century. He writes: "There are many examples of parishes going to considerable trouble to make their ales as grand and attractive as possible, even hiring the regalia and choirs from other parishes to swell their own processions which were often a popular and important part of the proceedings. For example, the processional cross, banner, vestments and other regalia from the affluent church at Yeovil were hired for 1s 6d by the parish of Sturminster Newton some 15 miles distant, in 1457, for use at their patronal festival and church ale. At Yatton in Avon the 15th century churchwardens' accounts show a regular annual profit of more than £4 from church ales, as well as similar annual sums received from hiring out the church-house and its utensils for parish functions, especially for wedding feasts."[21] There is little documentary evidence that church ales took place in the church but that the nave, where they are thought to have been held, was the responsibility of the parishioners. Dr Bettey quotes one example which provides extant evidence that at St Lawrence, Reading, in 1506 church ales were held within the church, for they paid "to Macrell for makyng clere of the Church agaynst the day of drinking to the said Church 4d."

In 1602 Richard Carew, in his Survey of Cornwall refers to one of the purposes of church ales... "to defray any extraordinary charges arising in the parish."[22] "For the church-ale, two young men of the parish are yerely chosen by their last forerunners to be wardens, who, dividing the task make collection among the parishioners of whatsoever provision it pleaseth them voluntarily to bestow. This they employ in brewing, baking and other acates (i.e. provisions bought or provided), against Whitsuntide, upon which holidays the neighbours met at the church house and there merily feed on their own victuals, each contributing some petty portion to the stock, which by many smalls groweth to a meetly greatness; for there is entertayned a kind of emulation between these wardens, who, by his graciousness in gathering, and good husbandry in expending can best advance the church's profit. Besides, the neighbour parishes at those times lovingly visit one another and frankly spend their money together. The afternoons are concerned in such exercises as olde and yonge folke (having leysure) doe accustomarly weare out the tyme withall. When the feast is ended, the wardens yeeld in their accounts to the parishioners; and such money as exceedeth the disbursement is layd up in store to defray any extraordinary charges arising in the parish, or imposed on them for the good of the countrey or the prince's service."[23]

John Aubrey, the Wiltshire antiquarian, later in the 17th century said of church ales: "There were no rates for the poor in my grandfather's days; but for Kington St Michael (no small parish) the churchale of Witsontide did the business. In every parish is (or was) a church-house to which belonged spits, crocks, etc., utensils for dressing provisions. Here, the housekeepers met, and were merry, and gave their charity. The young people were there too, and had dancing, bowling, shooting at butts, etc., the ancients sitting gravely by, and looking on. All things were civil and without scandal."[24] However, things were of a more puritanical nature at Dunster. William Prynne, who had been apprehended on 25 June 1650 "for writing and practising against the Commonwealth," was a puritan who wrote that, "the main purpose of church ales was to enable the common people to dance, play, revel, drink and profane God's Sabbath."[25]

Thomas Luttrell, along with the justices of the peace, in 1633, protested against the revival of church ales, clerk ales and revels.[26] Thomas Luttrell was a Parliamentarian and was married to Jane Popham of Littlecote in Berkshire, who came from a notable Round-head family. Church ales had existed, at least from the middle of the 14th century and were probably a valuable source of funds for the building of Dunster church tower in 1443.

THE ALTARS UNDER THE TOWER

The earliest reference to the altar of the Holy Rood occurs in 1276. It is recorded in the cartularies of Bath (L. 368) that Walter Lucy arranged for masses to be said daily at this altar. The arrangement that he made with the monks of Bath laid down that a secular chaplain should perform this duty and that the masses were to be said for the benefit of his soul, the souls of his two wives Margery and Lucy, and for Robert Lucy and Agnes, his wife, Roger Lucy and for the lord of Dunster, Sir John de Mohun II and Eleanor, his wife. In 1276 Walter Lucy provided £40 but there was no separate endowment. There was a chantry chaplain who received 20s annually but for some reason by 1333 his allowance was reduced to 13s 4d per year and soon there was no special chaplain and the masses were said by the vicar who served the parish or by one of the secular priests connected with the church. There was a petition made by William Harwood and John Atwood, churchwardens, to the chancellor, Sir Thomas Audley. It appears that, in the name of the parishioners they were requesting Sir Thomas to provide a chaplain or priest to celebrate the Lucy mass which had been instituted in 1266. It had lapsed owing to the ruinous state of the roodloft between the western piers of the crossing tower. They said that thirty years earlier (c.1500) they had erected a new screen and roodloft, "with an altar before the Rood for a priest to say mass" but William, the prior of Bath, having been approached on many occasions, had failed to send anyone.

In the presence of Sir John de Mohun V an agreement was made in January 1357, between the prior of Dunster, Richard of Childeston, and the monks and the parishioners. In the first section of this agreement the altar of the Holy Rood is mentioned: "On festivals and Sundays, the Prior and the monks shall begin their service at such a time that high mass may be said in summer, between Easter and Michaelmas, by the hour of tierce (nine o'clock), and in winter, between Michaelmas and Easter, by twelve o'clock or later. The monk who is to perform the high mass shall bless the water, and shall sprinkle it throughout the church if the Vicar be not ready to do so. The Prior, the monks and the Vicar shall unite in one procession, after which the high mass shall be begun at the altar of St George. There the parishioners shall make their offerings four times a year. On festivals the Vicar may begin to say mass privately at the altar of the Holy Rood for his parishioners after the reading of the gospel at the high mass."[27]

In 1369 a Gilbert Scutt directed that: "3lb of wax should be made into two candles to burn by his corpse on the night and the day of his burial, and afterwards to burn respectively before the altar of the Holy Rood and in the chapel of Our Lady."[28] The altar of the Holy Rood, according to the 1357 Agreement, appears to have been the parochial altar. It is mentioned in the 1420 will of John Batelyn of Dunster in which he bequeathed a pair of cruets to three altars, that of the high altar, the parochial altar and that of St Lawrence, altars at which he is thought to have worshipped on particular days or at particular hours. It is obvious from the foregoing agreement that the high altar was served by the prior and his monks and that the secular vicar served the parochial altar, or altar of the Holy Rood. The altar of the chantry chapel of St Lawrence had its own chaplain. The altar of Our Lady was probably served by the monastic brethren and did not have its own particular priest. The first duty of Richard Baker, the secular chaplain in the last decade of the 15th century, was to celebrate the mass at the altar of the Holy Trinity for its founders and trustees, but he was also obliged to join the other priests and proffer assistance on Sundays and holy days in the choir of the parochial church.[29]

The four-centred doorway on the south side of the north-western pier leads off the spiral staircase leading to the bell-chamber and the roof. It formerly gave access to the roodloft which, according to William Pynsoun's will, dated it to 1420. He bequeathed 6s 8d to the work of the new loft of the Holy Rood. The position of the open screen below it is marked by notches on the western archway of the tower. Lyte surmises that: "The roodloft and this screen were probably connected by a deep cove, purely ornamental, but giving an appearance of support to the upper part of the lofty structure."[30] It is probable that the remnants of this were incorporated with the Victorian screen leading to the then Lady Chapel (now the vestry).

It is thought that when the 1498-9 screen was completed in the early part of the 16th century, the great rood, the figure of Christ on the crucifix, flanked by the figures of Mary Magdalene and St John, was removed from the roodloft between the two western piers of the tower to this new roodloft. The original roodloft decayed and the parishioners who built the new screen erected it some twenty-five feet west of the earlier one and thus made a choir for themselves. It was not placed there to divide the monastic portion of the church from the parochial portion: that was the original purpose of the two screens under the tower. A second screen, dating from the first half of the 15th century, which was formerly between the eastern piers, was a choir screen. It was removed from that position to the eastern arch of the south transept at the time of the 1874-6 restoration. Lyte writes: "The oaken screen which now stands under the shouldered arch…was placed there about thirty years ago at the time of the restoration of the church. Before that, it stood under the eastern arch of the tower, giving access to the chancel."[31] At the time of its removal to its present position, it was reduced in height, and the cornice was freely altered.[32] This screen in the south transept is referred to by Pevsner as having "an uncommonly broad frieze of foliage in the cornice."[33] The frieze is three dimensional and in the early 19th century, it was whitewashed

Eeles shared the idea that this screen may have been a choir screen between the two eastern piers. He had made reference to Wm Pynsoun's 1420 bequest of 6s. 8d. for the work of the "new rood loft": "The new rood loft went across the western arch of the tower where the doorway leading to it from the tower staircase is still to be seen. It must have been a structure of some size, for in it was placed the altar of the Holy Cross. Beneath it, no doubt, a screen of openwork, while another openwork screen with central doors crossed the eastern arch of the tower at the entrance to the monks' choir; this is now in the arch on the east side of the south transept."[34] He also says: "Just behind the arch from the south transept to the Priory church is an earlier straight headed screen finished with modern cresting believed originally to have been placed across the eastern tower arch at the west end of the monks' choir. Its design is sufficiently open to allow the parishioners to follow the services held eastwards of it in accordance with the agreement of 1357."[35]

Kenneth Lindley wrote to the vicar of Dunster on 1958 and quotes from *The English Abbey* by F.H. Crossley as follows: "The quire of the monks was separated from the nave by a double screen, having central doorway with altars on either side of it on its western face. This screen was called the pulpitum; from it at stated times the epistle and gospel were read, and the organs were housed upon it." The main screen was erected after the Glastonbury Agreement of 1498, which also mentions an "altar of St James the Apostle which is on the south side of the door which leads from the choir of the monks into the nave of the church."[36] The only chancel at this time was the chancel of the priory church and before the erection of the 1498 screen, the two screens under the tower separated this original chancel from the nave. Eeles comments on the erection of the 1499 screen: "A peculiarity of this arrangement was that no power was given to the parishioners to build a new high altar or to make that of St James central to the church, and directions for processions which follow seem to emphasise the fact that nothing of the kind was intended in the award, notwithstanding that very little space was available for the new choir."[37]

It is presumed that the high mass celebrated by the Vicar in the western part of the church, was celebrated at an altar in the roodloft of the 1499 screen. Lyte states: "The existing roodloft, which stretches across the nave and both aisles, has a projection in the centre of the eastern side large enough to accommodate an altar of moderate size, and is known to have been set up in pursuance of an award of 1498 to the effect that the vicar and parishioners should make a new choir for themselves 'in the nave of the church'. The discontinuance of the masses for the Lucy family and others thus synchronises with the erection of the new roodloft. Although the churchwardens state that the parishioners had recently 'buylded' the roodloft with an altar before the rood, they do not give a hint that its position had been moved some twenty-five feet westwards."[38] This shows that the main screen was not erected to divide the church into monastic and parochial areas as is so often erroneously stated, but to make a new choir for the parish. The division was created by the two screens under the crossing tower or lantern and, even when that which was between the western piers of the tower decayed, there was still the choir screen between the eastern piers of the crossing tower. Freeman says: "The lantern itself up to this time ... with the transepts, formed a vestibule to the monks' church."[39] Lyte continued: "Nor are ... .the churchwardens quite accurate in suggesting that the original deed contained a specific mention of a roodloft. It says, 'Si contingat quod predictum altare alico [sic] casu fuerit interdictum, vel quod navis ecclesie aliquo infortunio ruinam patiatur, ob quod idem capellanus ibidem celebrare non possit, tune predicta missa ad altare Beate Virginis per eundem capellanum celebretur donec predictum altare Sante Crucis in pristinum statum revertetur'."[40] Hamper wrote: "The Chancel is divided from the Nave by a truly rich screen of oak, about 11 feet high, formerly supporting the Rood-loft containing 14 arches of elaborate tracery, one of which is imperfectly represented. The upper part is painted white and yellow, and has a very good general effect...The stairs leading to the Rood-loft are in a turret on the South side of the Church; the doorway now walled up." The light of the Holy Rood was also known as the light of the High Cross.[41]

There was trouble between the prior and monks and the parishioners before 1497. The differences were resolved, to an extent, by the Glastonbury Agreement of 1498 which had long-term consequences for the church at Dunster. The prior of Dunster, probably William Bristow, must have complained to the Prior of Bath who took steps and instituted proceedings by making application to the privy seal for "remedy of certain wrongs" that the Prior of Dunster said had been done to their brethren at that place. The most important grievances were:

(1) That, whereas the Prior had been wont to receive a fee of 6s 8d "for breking of the grounde" in the church "for every sepulture there made," certain persons had taken upon themselves "to breke the said grounde" without his "licence or favour," and without payment to him.
(2) That the parishioners had caused holy water to be "halowed within the bodie of the churche, contrarie to tholde custome and to there composicion."
(3) That they had withdrawn their customary offerings to the Prior "at wedynges and at buryynges, as was wele shewd at the buryying of the modre of Maister Loty, gentilman."
(4) That they would not suffer any citation or privy seal "to be executed there within a certeyn brigge."
(5) That "to fulfill and satisfie theyr croked appetites, thei toke up the bell roopis and said that the Priour and Convent there shuld have no bellis there to ryng."[42]

The parishioners, who were the subject of the complaints, had apparently been encouraged by their vicar, Richard Harris, who, contrary to his duty, had condoned their behaviour. The Star Chamber Proceedings, Hen VII, No.122 record the principal names of the offenders but seems to have confused the vicar's name with that of a clerk, who was probably a chantry priest, one William Harris, who is named in a local court-roll of 1509.[43] This information comes from parish registers and churchwarden's accounts of the priests who, between 1313 and 1528, served the cure of Dunster.[44]

The extract from the Star Chamber Proceedings is as follows: "Sir William Harries, vicary there, wiche hathe cure of there soules, and shuld move and councell them to be of better condicions to Goddes pleasure, [but who] contrary to his dewtie comfortethe them in theire ill doinges and wulnot that they shuld be refourmed to a better and more godlie way; Thomas Upcote, merchaunt; Thomas Kodogon, yeoman; John Withur, baker; Adam Wilkyns, clothemaker; William Crasse, bocher; Symond Pers, yoman; John Greyme, yoman; John Philippis, tanner; John Paynter, barbour; John Morgan, parker; Martyn Glover."[45]

The reply of those who had banded together and caused offence is unknown, but no doubt they would have exonerated themselves by claiming that the vicar of the parish conducted the weddings and funerals, as well as other services, in the part of the church to the west of the chancel where the monks had their stalls and recited their offices. As far as the bells were concerned they hung in the upper part of the crossing tower for which the parishioners had provided the funds and the access to the tower was from the nave which was always the responsibility of the parishioners. We know that several of the men, who had been the subject of the complaints made by the prior and the monks, were interested in their church and indeed in the early years of the 16th century they bequeathed money to the Prior of Dunster, notwithstanding the censures levied at them.

More disputes arose between the monks and the parishioners of Dunster and it was decided to put the whole matter to arbitration. The monks were represented by the prior and convent of the cathedral church of Bath, the impropriators of the church of Dunster and Dan Thomas Browne, Prior of Dunster from 1498 and the convent of the cell of Dunster, the latter being explicitly described as removable at the pleasure of the superior authority at Bath. The laity was represented by William Bond, vicar of the parish church of Dunster and Sir Hugh Luttrell who represented the inhabitants of the town. The arbitrators were Richard, abbot of Glastonbury, Thomas Gilbert, a doctor of canon law and Thomas Tremayle, one of the king's justices who owned 8½ burgages in Dunster and died in 1509.[46] The outcome of their deliberations was an agreement made at Glastonbury on 4 April 1498 which was: ...ratified by the five seals of the prior and convent of Bath, the prior and convent of Dunster, the vicar of Dunster, Sir Hugh Luttrell and the parish of Dunster.[47]

The terms were as follows:
(1) That the Vicar, renouncing all previous endowments, should receive from the Prior of Dunster an allowance of £8 a year, paid quarterly, and should continue to occupy the house in which he then lived, upon condition of keeping it in repair, and, if necessary, of rebuilding it.
(2) That the Vicar should have all offerings made by devout lay folk for the celebration of obits, trentals, anniversaries, private masses, and prayers, known as "the bederaele penys," the Prior and Convent continuing to receive other ecclesiastical payments due to them as impropriators of the church.
(3) That the Vicar should have a choir independent of the Prior and monks, to be made and maintained at the cost of the parishioners "in the nave of the church, that is to say at the altar of St James the Apostle, which is situate on the south side of the door which leads From the choir of the monks into the nave of the church."
(4) That in this choir the Vicar, having the cure of souls, should, without interference on the part of the Prior and monks, administer the sacraments and celebrate sacramentals, to wit the hallowing of water, bread, candles at the Purification, ashes on the first Wednesday in Lent, flowers and boughs, and the consecration of fonts, receiving the customary offerings on behalf of the Prior and monks.
(5) That the Vicar and the parishioners should be free to make processions from their choir in the church or in the graveyard on any day of the year except on thirteen important festivals, to wit those of Christmas, Epiphany, Palm Sunday, Easter, Ascension Day, Whitsunday, Trinity Sunday, Corpus Christi, the Purification, St George, the Assumption, All Saints, and the Dedication of the Church, on each of which there was to be a joint procession in the church or in the graveyard according to season and weather. On these days, the little band of monks "coming through the middle of their own choir" was to be met by the rest of the congregation as they began to issue through "the door on the north side" of the new parochial choir. Then the bearer of the monks' cross and the bearer of the parish cross were to walk side by side, followed by the clerks, the Vicar, the monks, the Prior and the lay folk. On their return, the two bodies were to separate at 'the same door', the monks passing through it and the Vicar and his clerks returning to their choir, to finish divine service.[48]

Under this new system, the parishioners were released from any obligation to attend mass in the chancel, and the Vicar was empowered to celebrate high mass in the western part of the church, even on the principal festivals of the ecclesiastical year."[49]

The vicar figures largely in the 1498 Glastonbury Agreement and in the first clause his salary is an allowance of £8 a year, paid quarterly. A few years later these arrangements were altered and his annual stipend was reduced from £8 to £4 by an ordinance of 1512 issued by the bishop of Bath and Wells, Cardinal Hadrian de Castello. There were to be compensations, however, since it was decreed that he should receive free meals in the monastic refectory of the priory, "sitting at table below the prior and brethren" but "never getting higher." He was to share in their food and "in the refreshments provided by the fireside in the winter evenings." He was also assigned a small meadow, a rent of 2s from a fulling-mill and the rent of the former vicarage. The prior was required to provide a room for him in the priory adjoining the graveyard. Furthermore, the payments made by the laity for the publication of the "Bedrolle" after the gospel at high mass and for the offerings made by them when going to confession in Lent were specifically to be made over to the vicar.[50] The bishop, in other words, decided that the vicar of Dunster should have a "corrody," in the monastic refectory; the room running east and west and parallel with the nave.

It is probable that the 'room in the priory adjoining the graveyard' was in the picturesque building at the south eastern corner of the church yard near the south transept. In a deed of the reign of Elizabeth, it is simply described as the 'stone-healed' house'. Richard Harris was vicar from 1485 resigned in 1494 and was presented to Carhampton. The same thing happened to the next but one vicar, William Bond, who was the vicar at the time of the 1498 agreement. His successor was appointed in 1507, when Bond also went to Carhampton. The resignations were constant.

The bill of 1533-38 throws much light on the earlier rood screen, which before 1498, stood between the western piers of the tower and on the main screen erected after the Glastonbury Agreement of 1498. It was reproduced in *Somerset and Dorset Notes and Queries*: [51] 12. DUNSTER CHURCH. The following bill was filed (E.C.P. 826 / 10) between 1533, when Sir Thomas Audley was appointed Lord Chancellor, and 1538, when he was raised to the peerage: "To the right honorable Sir Thomas Audley, Knight, Lord Chancellor of England. In moost humble wise showen unto your good lordshippe your dayly oratours William Harwood and John at Wood, churchewardeyns of the paryshe of Dunster in the counte of Somersete, for and in the name of the paryshens of the seyd paryshe, that wher in the yere of our Lord God a thousand cclxvj. *(sic)* one Water priour of Bathe and the covent of the same place then havynge respect to the good devocyon whiche Water Lucye and his predecessors had to the sayd howse of Bathe, and for the grett benefites don by the sayd Water unto the sayd howse of Bathe, and also to the howse of Dunster, beyng a celle of the sayd pryory, by one assent and consent graunted to the sayd Water Lucye that one seculer chapleyn lefully should be founde with the costes and charges of the sayd howse of Dunster successyvely for ever to celebrate and saye dayly every yere one messe for them that be departed owte of this worlde and for the sowll of Margery Ivans, late wyfe to the sayd Water, and for the sowlles of Robert Lucye and Agnes his wyfe, and for the sowlles of the sayd Water and Lucy his wyfe, and for the sowlles of all them of whoys go odes the sayd Water enythynge toke, and for all Christen sowlles, at the alter of the Holy Crosse in the paryshe churche of Dunster comenly called the Rodeloft, after the matyns don in the sayd churche, and if hit fortune that the sayd alter by any chaunce to be enterdyted or that the sayd bodye of the sayd churche happen to be in rewen and dekey so that the sayd chapleyn for the tyme beyng could not celebrate nor saye messe at the sayd alter in the Rodeloft of the said churche that then the sayd chapleyn to saye messe at the alter of our blessed Ladie the Virgin in the sayd churche untyll suche time as the sayd alter of the Holy Crosse be amendyd and repayred, with diverce and many oracions and prayers to be sayde by the sayd chapleyn at the sayd messe, as by certeyn wrytinges shall appere, for the contynuance wherof the sayd Water Lucye, among dyverce benefitz and goode dedes that he dyd to the sayd monestary, gave unto the priour of the same then beyng to the use of the sayd howse xl. poundes of good and lefull money of England,accordyng to the whiche grant a chapleyn hath byn found from tyme to tyme at the costes and charges of the sayd monestary and don the devyne servyce at the sayd alter in the Rodeloft above the space of cc. yere untyll aboute XXXti yeres last past that the sayd Rodeloft was in suche extreme rewen and dekye that no messe myght be convenyently sayd nor song theryn, and by necligens of the rulers of the sayd paryshe yn not callyng upon the priors of the sayd howse for the tyme beyng the sayd servyce hath remeyned undon. But so yt ys, right honorable lord, that the paryshens of the sayd paryshe att ther costes and charges have amended, buylded, and repayred the sayd Roodeloft and made hyt a mete place and convenyent to saye devyne servyce withyn the same, with an alter before the Rode for a prest to saye messe therat, and have dyverce and many tymes required William now prior of Bathe, havyng the sayd celle of Dunster in his hands, to fynde to the sayd paryshens an honest prest orchapleyn to saye masse at the sayd alter with suche other prayers accordyng to the grant made by his predecessors, whiche From tyme to tyme he hathe not only deferred and delayed and woill yn no wyse fynde the sayd chapleyn to saye messe at the sayd alter nor at any other alter withyn the sayd churche, ageyn all reson, equite, and good consciens, but also hath gotten in to his possession, custody, and kepyng certeyn wrytinges and bokes wheryn is made mencion of the fyndyng of the sayd chapleyn with the contynuance of the same. And forasmoche as the sayd graunt was made to the sayd Water Lucy unto whom the sayd compleynantes be but estraungers, they can meynteyn non accion at the commen lawe for the redresse of the premisses, of the whiche wrytinges and bokes your sayd oratours have dyverce and many tymes required the sayd priour to make delyvere, which to delyver he at all tymes hath denyed and yet doyth, ageyn all ryght and consciens, and forasmoche as your sayd oratours knowe not the certeyn nomber of the sayd evydences, dedes, and wrytinges, theffect of them wheryn they be conteyned, they arre withowte remedye by the courtes of the commen lawe, yt may therfore please your good lordshippe, the premisses concedryd, to graunt a commission to be dyrectyd to certeyn discreet and sufficient personages of the sayd counte gevyng them auctorite for the same to cause the sayd part yes personally to appere afore them at a certeyn daye by them to be lymyted, there to examyn the sayd matter and all the cyrcumstances therof, and to make and order and elide theryn if they can, and if they cannot elide the same to certefye the king in his chauncere by a certeyn daye what shall happen them to doo theryn, there to be orderyd as by your good lordshippe shalbe thoght moost expedient and necessary in this behalf. "And your sayd oratours shall dayly pray for the preservacion of your good lordshippe longe to endure."

The bill of 1533-38 may be interpreted as follows: "Your daily orators William Harwood and John Atwood, churchwardens of the parish of Dunster in the county of Somerset most humbly bring to the notice of your good lordship, on behalf of the parishioners of the said parish, that in the year of Our Lord 1266 *(sic)* Water, prior of Bath and the convent there, having respect for the devotion which Water Lucye and his predecessors had for the house of Bath and for the great benefits given by him to the houses of Bath and Dunster, a cell of Bath, with one assent had consented to grant to Water Lucye, together with the costs and charges incurred by the house of Dunster, that one secular chaplain should be lawfully found to successively and forever celebrate and say daily every year one mass for the departed and for the soul of Margery Ivans, late wife of Water and for the souls of Robert Lucye and Agnes his wife and for the souls of all from whom Water had derived anything *(i.e. his benefactors),* at the altar of the Holy Cross in the parish church of Dunster, commonly called the Roodloft, after matins and if it came to pass that by any chance the said altar should be debarred or that the body of the church should chance to be in ruin and decay so that the chaplain could not celebrate nor say mass at the altar in the Roodloft for the time being that then he should say mass at the altar of our blessed Lady the Virgin until such time as the altar of the Holy Cross be amended and repaired, with various and many orations and prayers to be said by the chaplain at the mass, as by documents shall be shown, for the continuance whereof Water Lucye among various benefits and good deeds he did for the monastery, gave to the then prior of the house £40 of good and lawful English money, according to which grant a chaplain has been found from time to time at the cost and charge of the monastery to perform divine service at the altar in the Roodloft for the past two hundred years until about thirty years ago when the Roodloft was in such a state of extreme ruin and decay that no mass could be conveniently said or sung therein, and by the negligence of the rulers of the parish in not calling upon the priors of the said house for the time being the service has not been performed. But now, right honourable lord, the parishioners at their cost have amended, built and repaired the Roodloft and made it a suitable and convenient place to say divine service within, with an altar before the Rood for a priest to say mass, and they have on various and many occasions requested William, now Prior of Bath, being responsible for the cell of Dunster, to find for the parishioners an honest priest or chaplain to say mass at the said altar with such other prayers in accordance with the grant made by his predecessors which from time to time he has not only deferred and delayed and will no way find the said chaplain to say mass at the said altar or any other altar within the Church, against all reason, equity and good conscience, but also has in his possession, custody and keeping certain documents and books wherein mention is made of the finding of the said chaplain with the continuance of the same. And for as much as the grant was made to Water Lucye, to whom the complainants are strangers, they are unable to maintain any action under the common law for the redress of the foregoing matters since the documents and books your spokesmen have on a variety of occasions requested the said prior to hand over, he has at all times failed to do, against all right and conscience and for as much as we do not know the exact number of testimonies, deeds and documents and the implications contained in them, they have no redress in the courts of common law, it may therefore please your good lordship, the aforesaid matters considered, to grant a commission to be directed to certain discreet and adequate persons of the said county giving them authority to make the said parties to appear personally before them on a certain date to be stated, then to examine the said matter and all the circumstances appertaining and to make and order and settle and if they cannot settle, to certify to the king in his chancellery by a certain date, which action they shall be requested to make according to what shall be thought most expedient by your good lordship."

There is documentary and architectural evidence that a roodloft was erected in Dunster Church in about 1420, and that it stood between the two western piers of the tower. The existing roodloft, which stretches across the nave and both the aisles, has a projection in the centre of the eastern side large enough to accommodate an altar of moderate size, and it is known to have been set up in pursuance of an award of 1498 to the effect that the Vicar and parishioners should make a new choir for themselves "in the nave of the church." The discontinuance of the masses for the Lucy family and others thus synchronises with the erection of a new roodloft. Although the churchwardens state that the parishioners had recently built the roodloft, with an altar before the rood, they do not give a hint that its position had been moved some twenty-five feet westwards. Nor are they quite accurate in suggesting that the original deed contained a specific mention of a roodloft. Lyte comments: "The Prior of Bath might perhaps have argued that the parishioners of Dunster had nullified the old arrangement by removing the altar of the Holy Rood, or, more generally, that he and his convent had, after the award of 1498, ceased to have any concern with the services conducted in the western part of the divided church. Unfortunately, his answer, as drawn up by a lawyer, gives no information whatever. It begins by saying that the churchwardens' bill in Chancery was 'contryved, imagyned, and fayned, to thentente to putt the sayd Prior to cost, troble and vexacion', and proceeds to declare that he knew nothing about the alleged grant by his predecessor Walter, or about Lucy's alleged gift of £40 to the monks. If, however, he had so chosen, he could easily have obtained information, for a chartulary of his own house at Bath contains copies of the deed of 1276 cited by the churchwardens and three other documents relating to the perpetual chantry of Walter Lucy."

Before Lyte was apparently aware of the bill of 1533 he had stated that: "The altar of the Holy Rood presumably stood at the end of the nave, close to the north-western pier of the tower, and almost under the crucifix from which it took its name."[52] Again, later he reiterates the same idea concerning the site of the altar of the Holy Rood. It has been seen that the award of 1498 directed the vicar and parishioners to make a new choir in the nave of the church at the altar of St James: "a very handsome oaken screen of fifteen unequal compartments stretching, like others in this county, right across the building, and surmounted by a loft or gallery. A small head of St James may still be seen in one of its spandrels facing westward. There are three pairs of doors in the screen, one opposite to the centre of the north aisle, the second opposite to the centre of the nave, and the third approximately opposite the centre of the south aisle. Over the middle pair of doors the gallery projects eastward, and it has been suggested that the additional space there provided was intended for an organ."[53] It is possible that, on the completion of the screen in the early part of the 16th century, the great rood was removed to it from its former position on a beam between the two western piers of the tower.[54] Clearly Lyte was unaware that the bill of 1537/38 stated that the 1499 screen had "an altar before the Rood for the priest to say mass." Whether, at some post Reformation date, this projection over the middle doors was ever used for a small organ, is not known. Certainly by the 18th century a gallery had been built at the west end of the church to accommodate musicians.

The transcription of the original bill of 1533-38 makes one wonder how the former roodloft between the western piers, if it was erected around 1420 could have been in "a state of extreme ruin and decay" as early as c.1500. The will of William Pynsoun refers to the new loft of the Holy Rood "ad opus novi solarii Sancte Crucis" to which in 1420 he bequeathed 6s 8d. As the Lucy mass had been celebrated since 1276 "at the altar of the Holy Cross in the parish church of Dunster commonly called the Roodloft," it is reasonable to suppose that by 1420 this roodloft could have been in a sorry state and all the authorities so far quoted have believed that the bequest was for a new roodloft between the western piers of the tower. However it may be that Pynsoun left his money, not to a new roodloft in the former position between the western piers, but that he was an early benefactor to the already envisaged roodloft which, with its screen, was not achieved until 1499 after the 1498 Glastonbury Agreement, and when Dunster not only delighted in their beautiful new screen but celebrated the return of the rightful lord of Dunster, Sir Hugh Luttrell (d.1521) and the departure of the Herberts.

Lyte states that the list of Vicars and Curates of Dunster from Richard the Chaplain, followed by Robert de Vaux in c.1213, up to Frederick Hancock is: "the fullest that has yet appeared of the priests who successively served the cure of Dunster." It seems to be continuous from 1313 to 1528, but according to Hancock no Curates were instituted by the Bishop between the dissolution of the Priory and 1821.[55] For nearly three centuries, therefore, the parish registers and the churchwardens' accounts are the main source of information. A further list[56] given by Preb Hancock gives, over the period 1313 and 1528, the reasons why the incumbencies were vacated and the references to the bishop's register. In all cases between those dates the patron was the prior and convent of Bath. He also gives the names of the patrons from 1821 to 1898 and again the references to the bishop's register. John Ryce (Ryse or Rice) died in 1561 and thereafter definite appointments seem not to have been made. The prior and convent had formerly presented vicars to the bishop for institution as to a benefice. From the time of the suppression of the monasteries the vicarage was suppressed and the lay impropriator, Hugh Stewkley, the first lay rector, had to provide a stipendary curate who did not require to be instituted and was removable at his pleasure. This was the case until the mid 18th century when the curate ceased to be removable 'at pleasure'.

****

LIST OF VICARS AND CURATES OF DUNSTER

	Richard the Chaplain	
[c.1213]	Robert de Vaux	
1313	Thomas Cote	*He exchanged for Timberscombe*
1319	Ralph of Gloucester	*Resigned*
1333	John of Cherbury	
1333	Richard of Keynsham	
	Robert of Ichestoke	*Resigned and was presented to Carhampton*
1362	Robert Drayton	
	Robert Ryvers	*He died as Vicar*
1406	John Corbyn	*He exchanged for Little Wittenham*
1409	Roger Holford	*He died as Vicar*
1415	William Drayton	*He exchanged for Oare*
1417	Thomas Prydle	*He died as Vicar*
1418	John Bacwell	*He died as Vicar*
1421	Thomas Barry	*Resigned*
1434	Thomas Russell	*Deprived*
1446	William Robbs	
1447	John Sloo	*He died as Vicar*
1451	William Russell	*He died as Vicar*
1476	John Lucas	*Resigned*
1485	Richard Harris	*Resigned and was presented to Carhampton*
1494	Thomas Kyngsbury	*Resigned*
1495	William Bond	*Resigned*
1507	Richard Davys	*Resigned*
1512	Robert Williamson	*Resigned*
1514	John Fymores	
1515	William Hooper	*Resigned*
1528	John Thomas	
[1535-61]	John Rice (Ryce)	*Vicar at time of Dissolution. Buried September 1561*
[1582]	William Hodgson	
[1592]	James Listone	
c.1598-1600	Christopher Williams	*Vicar in 1598. Buried April 1600*
1600	David Williams	
[1603-38]	Thomas Smith	*Buried April 1638*
[1639-40]	Robert Browne	
[1641-42]	Robert Snelling	
[1661-62]	Richard Savin	
[1673-1704]	John Graunt	*Buried February 1704*
[1704-29]	William Kymer	
[1731-38]	Thomas Question	
[1741-43]	Robert Norris	
[1743-45]	Jeremiah Davies	
[1746]	William Cox	
[1747]	Richard Bawden	

[1748-51]	James Gould	
[1752]	Richard Bawden *(again)*	
[1753-55]	James Gould *(again)*	
1755	John Smith	
1755	Thomas Cooke	
[1756-58]	Richard Bawden *(again)*	
[1758-59]	John Anthony	
[1759-73]	William Camplin	
1773	George Henry Leigh	*Died August 1821*
1821	Thomas Fownes Luttrell	*Died December 1871. Formally instituted by Bishop*
1872	Richard Utten Todd	*Died June 1886*
1886	Geoffrey Barrington Simeon	*Resigned*
1894	Arthur Wynell Mayow	*Resigned*
1898	Frederick Hancock	

This is the last entry given by Sir H.C. Maxwell Lyte[57]

1920	William Tofield Reeder	*Instituted 3 June 1920. Resigned due to age Easter 1935*
1935-38	Arthur Burnel Burney	*3 May 1935. Resigned 24 June 1938*
1938-45	Austen Humphrey Balleine	*5 October 1938. Resigned October 1945*
1945-57	George Gerald Derne Dunlop	*October 1945. Resigned 30 September 1957*
1957-67	Michael Edward McCormick	*26 October 1957. Resigned 15 March 1967*
1967-82	Christopher Derek Alderson	*29 April 1967. Resigned 23 February 1982*
1984-93	Robert Edward Doré	*16 December 1984. Retired 31 July 1993*
1994-2006	Michael Paul Grantham	*29 April 1994 (by Bishop of Taunton)*
2007-	Lee Brant	*21 April 2007 (by Bishop of Taunton)*

* * * * * * * * * *

NORTH AISLE

The history of the north aisle is an on-going one for there was probably an adjunct to the church on this side from *c.*1177 and the chapel of the Holy Trinity which was "almost certainly the north aisle" goes back to 1348.[58] The "north transept and north aisle of the priory church" are dated by Dr Eeles to the mid 15th century.[59] He refers also to the fact that, "There was certainly a north aisle beside the eastern part of the nave, probably with a lean-to roof.[60] There is definite proof that the north aisle was referred to at the beginning of the 16th century as, "the new aisle there to be built or repaired." The north aisle is not to be confused with "*la ele dortur*" the dorter aisle which is the north transept for which, together with the Lady Chapel, east of the north transept, the Prior was responsible. "La ele dorter" was so named because a flight of steps presumably led up to the "dorter," or dormitory, just inside the north door. The actual words from the January 1357 agreement made in the presence of Sir John de Mohun V, the last de Mohun lord of Dunster, between Richard of Childeston, Prior of Dunster and the monks on one side and the parishioners on the other side actually records: "He shall roof and for ever maintain the chapel of Our Lady and the dorter aisle."[61] Both the north transept and the Lady Chapel were re-built in the mid 15th century. Even though the north aisle is dated to the mid 15th century, certainly the north aisle to the west of the north transept which flanks the north side of the nave, was re-built in the early 16th century with larger windows. In 1504, Thomas Upcot of Dunster bequeathed ten tons of iron to the fabric of the church of St George: "that is to the new aisle there to be built or repaired on the north side," on condition that the work should be undertaken within three years.[62] "Thomas Upcote, merchaunt" was one of those parishioners, together with "John Greyme, yoman" and others, headed by the vicar, Sir William Harries, who were the butt of the grievances made by the monks before 1498. In 1517 the widow of John Gryme of Frackford left money specifically for the repair of the aisle of the Holy Trinity.[63]

This north aisle was always truncated by virtue of the constraint laid upon it by the "Old Priory" which probably dates to the end of the 14th century. In 1537 the aisle of the Holy Trinity was referred to as being "in the parochial church." The northern arcade which separates the north aisle from the nave is early 16th century also. It is composed of four Perpendicular arches resting on three pillars with capitals of an ordinary type. The four bays are narrower than those of the south arcade and they are not symmetrical and, if they had been, it would not have been possible to gain access to the rood-loft over the screen. Prof Freeman writes: "the rood-loft crosses the church in a singular way, passing close to a pillar on one side, but not on the other."[64] The eastern respond of this arcade is foliated and is referred to as: "a debased capital testifying to the lateness of the work."[65] The compound piers are of standard section with four hollows. They have capitals to their shafts with the exception of the most westerly one, which does not bear a capital.

SOUTH EAST AISLE

The south-east aisle, the site of the former chapel of St Lawrence, is sometimes referred to as the south aisle of the priory church for Eeles dates this area and the south transept to mid-15th century.[66] Lyte makes a slightly different statement and writes: "the chapel of St Lawrence on the east side of the southern transept seems to have been enlarged and re-built in the later part of the 15th century,"[67] a slightly later date. Eeles sums up the work and writing about the 1498 Agreement, states: "The immediate result of this award may be seen in the great screen which crosses the structural nave and which enclosed the choir thus erected by the parishioners. But more was done than enclosing a choir, for the parishioners must also have reconstructed the nave. New arcades were made, the chapel of St Lawrence was included as part of the south aisle.[68] The south arcade, like the north arcade, is also c.1500 and is composed of six bays. The compound piers are of the standard section of four hollows with octagonal capitals only to the shafts. The eastern respond of the south arcade is, like that of the north aisle, foliated but also bears a capital 'M', probably a 16th-century remembrance of Prior Martin (1257-74), the first recorded Prior of Dunster.

AISLES – CHAPELS - TRANSEPTS

Eeles writes: "The detail of the rood-loft staircase, and the aisle wall east of it, is different from and later than that of the western, part of the aisle and it contains windows of which one at least is of much earlier date and was probably made for the previous building. This is evidence of a rebuilding here subsequent to the main work done about 1500."[69] The chapels of Our Lady and St Lawrence were probably originally of apsidal form. They were enlarged and given square ends in the middle of the 15th century. The arcades which connect these former flanking chapels with the chancel of the priory church, or Luttrell chapel, were erected soon after 1548. They have four-centred, or depressed arches and the piers have, in their diagonals, two wave mouldings. When these arcades were built it was the intention to open up the priory church to the parishioners. Similarly the "shouldered" arch, with its Early English upper arch, was widened in the 16th century and again was not screened off. Eeles writes: "After the dissolution of the monastery in 1539 the parishioners recovered the use of the high altar and appear to have abolished the distinction between the two parts of the church. John Leland in his *Itinerary*[70] wrote: "The hole chirch of the late Priory servith now for the paroche church. Aforetymes the monks had the est part closid up to their use."[71] Of the ensuing demise of the priory church Lyte says: "there is no indication that any religious services, except the office for the burial of the dead, were performed in the eastern limb of the church between the middle of the 17th century and the later part of the 19th century."[72] The Stewkleys, who were lay rectors responsible for the priory chancel after the Reformation, migrated to Hampshire and the Luttrells apparently obtained exclusive rights there at the end of the 17th century. Gradually the priory church fell into a state of ruin and was bricked off.

With regard to the vestigial transepts, the north transept was rebuilt in the mid 15th century shortly after the completion of the two upper storeys of the tower, c.1446, and does not appear to have been altered after the 1498 agreement. Eeles[73] dates both north and south transepts to the mid 15th century as does Prof Pevsner[74] and writing specifically about the south transept Eeles states: "During the 15th century, the south transept was rebuilt as it is at present and very soon afterwards the south choir also: the great similarity of architectural detail may here be noticed. These must have been provided by the parishioners, but the similarity of the architecture of the north transept and the north choir aisle shows that the monks carried out a similar reconstruction in these parts of the building at the same time."[75] Preb Hancock thought that both transepts probably occupied the same position as those of the Norman period.[76] Of the four western bays of the south aisle Lyte says: "there is some attempt at symmetry of plan, but even there the work shows signs of haste. On the whole it seems probable that both the aisles were largely composed of old materials put together without much skill. Fragments of round shafts, possibly relics of a Norman clerestory to the nave, may be recognised in the south wall, and the stonework of several windows may have come from demolished chapels of the 15th century."[77]

PORCH

The embattled south porch is of less distinction than the earlier entrance which graces the south transept, an entrance of great presence and dignity with its canopied niches supported by now fragmentary angels and with its great Perpendicular window surmounting the entrance. Freeman considered that: "externally there is a pleasing effect about the south transept front; it has a pretty, simple, elevation, consisting of a tall, well proportioned window, with a niche on each side, and a doorway below."[78] This entrance is impressive from the roadway below, but is only used during flower festivals. This was the main entrance built in the middle of the 15th century probably on the site of an earlier entrance leading to the south transept of the Norman period. It would have been built at least fifty years before the south entrance to the west of it which is now regarded as the main entrance. Lyte dates the south porch at its earliest to 1509 and at its latest to 1625. Eeles dates it to c.1500 when all the other post-1498 agreement alterations took place.

FONTS

There are two fonts in Dunster church. One in the south transept is a round Norman font acquired by the Reverend Reeder in the 1920s. In the south aisle, there is a font which possibly dates from the later part of the 15th century. Eeles dates it to 1538 or a little earlier,[79] referring to it as: "font of c.1530 with delicate carving of the Five Wounds and instruments of our Lord's Passion."[80] Pevsner describes it as: "Perpendicular, octagonal, panelled stem and bowl with quatrefoils containing shields, flowers, the wounds of Christ, etc."[81] Its original position in the church is not known, but in the 19th century it was moved from the corner between the south and west walls of the aisle, raised on a double pedestal and placed so that all could see the baptismal ceremonies. The oak canopy is also 19th-century and replaced an 18th-century canopy.

ROOF

The nave roof is another example of the work which was undertaken after the 1498 Glastonbury Agreement when the Norman walls of the nave were lowered to receive it. There must have been, at least, three roofs in successive periods over the nave. Preceding the *c*.1500 wagon roof, the higher walls of the nave were covered by the flat, massively coffered roof with carved bosses, now over the south aisle which is dated to before the middle of the 15th century and, of course, there must have been an earlier roof, or roofs. Eeles writes: "the existing waggon roof was placed on the nave, while the central part of the earlier nave roof seems to have been used to cover the aisle, where it can still be seen, without wall plates or cornices. The span of the nave was perhaps too great for the roof and it is probable that the wall plates had become damp. The sound portions were no doubt re-used in what may have been a somewhat hasty scheme of reconstruction."[82] Lyte describes the south aisle roof as: "A flat wooden roof divided into panels and enriched with carving fits the aisle badly, having no wall plate on the north or on the south."[83]

Eeles says of the *c*.1500 nave roof: "the heads and quatrefoils alternating in the bosses on the side purlins, giving place to richer bosses east of the screen: this proves the roof to be of the same period as the screen."[84] Kenneth Wickham writes: "In West Somerset these wagon roofs are especially finely carved: a rich trellis runs along the wall plates and is relieved, as at Watchet and in the beautiful church of Selworthy, by an array of shield-bearing angels. Wootton Courtney, Sampford Brett, Old Cleeve and Dunster are other examples."[85] At Dunster the wall plates are plain and the term "wagon roof" has been described as having: "closely set rafters with arched braces, the appearance of the inside of a canvas over a wagon is achieved. Wagon roofs can be panelled or plastered or left uncovered. Also called a cradle roof."[86]

DUNSTER BOROUGH ORDINANCES

In 1486 the borough court of Dunster made various public injunctions, namely: "1486 April 17. That nobody shall henceforth put or throw any ashes with fire on any "donghill" within the town under pain of *40d* ... .That nobody shall henceforth break the palings of the lord's park or carry them away, or have any gates or footpaths in the lord's park, without licence, save the parker of the same, under pain of *40d*.[87]

In 1488 Sir Hugh Luttrell was sheriff of Somerset and Dorset for a year and was granted the office Master of Poundsford Park, near Taunton by his mother's brother Peter Courtenay, bishop of Winchester and with the grant went an annuity of 10 pounds for life. He was also a borderer of Exmoor.[88] The same year among the various ordinances ordained by the borough court of Dunster for the better government of the borough, was the following:

"1488 April 29. That nobody shall henceforth winnow *(ventulat)* his grain in 'le Castell Bayly' and at 'le Barrys' unless he forthwith remove the chaff arising therefrom, under pain of every one delinquent therein of *12d.* every time."[89]

"1489 May 11. That nobody dwelling beside the lord's water between the tenement of William Symes and the lord's mill shall throw any dirt or straw into the water there during the week, save on Sunday after two o'clock after noon, under pain of every one delinquent therein of *12d.* every time."[90]

"1489 October 22. That nobody of the country *(patrie)* shall henceforth buy any grain in the market before ten o'clock, under pain of 40d."[91]

"1489. October 22. That nobody shall henceforth sell any loads of furze called 'trusses' beyond 2½d. under pain of *12d* of the seller and the buyer alike."[92]

"1489 October 22. That nobody shall henceforth keep to his service any Irish servants, save one, under pain of 10s."[93]

By 1490 the ordinance of 11 May 1489 was changed: "1490 October 22. That nobody shall henceforth throw any dirt into the water running to the lord's mill, save only on Saturday after twelve o'clock, under pain of 40d."[94] The day and time had changed and the fine increased by 28d.

"1491 April 25. That nobody resident *(manens)* in the borough, who is not a burgess, shall henceforth cut or dig heath on Crowdon for sale, but only for his own use, under pain of 40d; and that no stranger resident without the borough shall henceforth cut or dig heath or turf on Crowdon, unless he be hired by burgesses of the aforesaid borough, under pain of 6s. 8d."[95] Crowdon was, of course, Croydon Hill.

"1491 October 24. That nobody shall henceforth play at dice or cards in the borough, save only during ten days at Christmas, under pain of everyone who shall so play of 40d every time, and of every one of those who shall allow such games in their houses of 6s.8d."[96]

"1492 May. That nobody shall henceforth keep greyhounds *(leporarios sive leporarias)* in the borough unless he can spend 40s. of yearly income *(redditus)* under pain of 6s. 8d.[97]

"1493 October 21. That nobody in the borough shall henceforth make a fire outside the chimney, in any house covered with thatch *(stramine)*, under pain of20s."[98]

By 1496 the fine for polluting the lord's water, having started at 12d. and then increasing to 40d., was now reduced for some inexplicable reason to 3d.

"1496 October 24. That nobody shall henceforth put or throw any dirt or dung in the water to the lord's mill save only on Saturday at the second hour after dinner, under pain of 3d as often as anyone shall happen to be found in default herein."[99]

1496 October 24. That no baker in the borough shall henceforth buy grain in the market, or go into the market to buy any grain therein before eleven o'clock, under pain of 6s. 8d. one half to be paid to the lord and the other half to the church."[100]

In Hancock's *Medieval Wills* is mentioned a Thomas Upcot, a dealer in iron and a man evidently of considerable means, who died in 1504 and left his "body to be buried in holy grave in the church of St George of Dunster," and bequeathed: "To the fabric of the said Church, that is to the new aisle there is to be made or repaired in the said Church in the North part 10 tons of iron coming in a ship of John Cokkys if the parishioners of Dunster begin to repair the said aisle within three years otherwise the 10 tons of iron shall remain in the hands of my executors for other works of charity to be done in the said Church. To Richard Pester prior of Dunster, 20s."[101] There is also: "To a certain honest priest celebrating for one whole year £6. Sir Richard Pester, Prior of Dunsterre 20s. March 25, 1504."[102] In 1511 Thomas Cadogan bequeathed 6s 8d to the prior,[103] and on 22 July 1511 the will of Thomas Codogan was proved. He left: "My body to holy grave in the Church of St George of Dunster. To the light of the high cross 20d. To the light of the dead 20d. To the light of the Blessed Mary 20d. To the light of St George 20d. To the Prior of Dunster for tithes forgotten 6s.8d. Sir John Holcomb 3s.4d." Thomas Kodogan's name is variously spelt as Kodogan, Codogan or Cadogan. He, with Sir John Holcombe, curate of Dunster and many others were witnesses to the will of Robert Loty. Symonde Pers, yeoman, left a will dated 15 May 1514 He left: "my body to be buried in the churche of Dunster, in the diocese of Bathe and Wellis. To the Prior of Dunster for my tythynges forgotten or witholden 5s. To the Rode lyght 20d. To the Dedde lyght 20d. To the vicar of Carhanton for forgotten tythynges 20d. If it shalt please Master Luttrell *(Sir Hugh Luttrell)* to se that my wyfe have no wrong, to have for his labour *20s*. To Robert Dovell under hym to see the execucion of the same *10s*. To John Greme, scholar, my best doblet, my cote, my best gowne. To John Greme, servant to John Cockes my violet gowne lyned with bokerhm, my black doblet of chamblet. To John Thlude my gowne furred with foxe. To Johan my wyffe all my other goodys moevable and unmoevable, she to dispose for my soule and heris as she shall seme best, and I make her my sole executrix. These wytnesse, Sir John Holcomb, Sir Denyster, Thomas Juyn, JohnWright and dyvers others. Proved at Lambeth, January 26 1515."[104]

John Greyme/Gryme in 1509 left: "my body to be buried in the Churchyard of St George of Dunster. To the fabric of the parish Church of Dunster £6 *13s. 4d* to the light of the high cross *20d.*, the light of the dead there *20d.* To the prior of Dunster for tithes forgotten *6s. 8d* Sir John Asshely Monk *12d* Sir John Holcomb my confessor and curate there at that time *6s. 8d*. The will was proved on 21 February 1509. No remnant of a habitation now remains at Frackford." There were three monks who benefited by the will, (Sir) John Wykys, (Sir) Thomas Kagnesah and (Sir) John Assheley and they received *12d.* each.[105] Non-graduate priests were conventionally given the honorific title "Sir" or in Latin "Dominus" this was a form of respect which by the 16th century could sometimes carry undertones of irony, as a street vendor nowadays might call his customers "squire." "Sir John Lacklatin" the ignorant country priest was a conventional figure of fun.[106]

John Wythur/Withur, the baker, had a wife named Agnes and a son also named John. Apart from being one of those parishioners who had offended the prior and his monks, little is known about him except that in 1448 he was amerced for buying corn in Dunster market before 9 o'clock.[107] The effigies of John and Agnes are engraved on a brass at the west end of the south aisle of Dunster church and the inscription refers to them and also to their eldest son who had the brass placed to the memory of his parents and himself around 1520.[108] The date is deduced from the costume and the style of engraving but since the inscription is extremely difficult to decipher there are varying opinions about the date of John Wythur's death which may be 1487 or 1497. There is even doubt whether the inscription refers to the figures depicted. John Withur, the younger, drew up his will in 1532 but the date of his death is unknown since he failed to leave room for its insertion to be added.[109] Lyte quotes the Latin inscription which shows the date as 1487,[110] while Hamper, Savage and Connor give it as 1497.[111] Connor describes: "Effigies of John Wyther, 1497, in civil dress, and Agnes, his wife; also their eldest son John, with foot inscription Brass engraved circa 1520…The two figures and the inscription have been re-laid in a new stone on the floor at the west end of the nave, north of the font. The original stone has disappeared."[112] Two effigies of a common type slightly turned towards each other. John Wyther is represented clean shaven and with long hair, wearing over his doublet a fur-trimmed gown with deep full sleeves, and on his feet large round-toed shoes. His wife wears the pedimental head-dress with plain lappets, a close-fitting gown with fur cuffs and fur round the neck and the hem of the skirt. Round the hips is a plaited girdle, ending in a metal tag with beaded end. Her shoes are also large and round-toed. Below the figures is a four-line inscription in black letters, which Lyte renders as: "Of your charite pray for the soules of John Wyther and Agnes his wyf et John Wyther their eldest sone, whose bodys restyeth under this stone anno domini millesimo cccclxxxvii penultimo die Septembris expectando generalem resurrecconem mortuorum et vitam aeternam, amen." [113]

REFORMATION AND DISSOLUTION OF THE MONASTERIES

The Reformation Parliament began its deliberations on 3 November 1529 and over the next seven years undermined the authority of the pope in England.[114] Henry became Supreme Head of the Church of England, a national church which nevertheless retained its medieval organisation but lacked a firm confession of faith.[115] During this time, in the year 1530, Sir Andrew Luttrell, who had some hereditary rights in the poor priory of Flitcham in Norfolk, sanctioned an arrangement whereby this impoverished house should be united to the mother house at Walsingham. The prior and convent of the larger and more well known house of Our Lady at Walsingham, in 1530, "admitted him and his wife to their fraternity, making them partakers in all their prayers." Further they "undertook to provide an anniversary mass for their souls after death, and to maintain a canon who should celebrate daily on their behalf at Flitcham." Finally they promised to supply them with board and lodging for two days and nights every year if they should wish to go to Walsingham, a noted place for pilgrimage.[116] On 25 January 1530, Archbishop Cranmer passed judgement at Dunstable that Henry's first marriage had been null and void from the beginning. Anne was crowned queen at Westminster abbey at Whitsun and one of the servitors at this coronation was Sir Andrew Luttrell.[117] It had been his father, Sir Hugh Luttrell, who was one of the seven knights and gentlemen of Somerset who were selected to escort the now divorced Catherine of Aragon from Crewkerne to Sherborne[118] when she came to England in 1501 to marry, not Henry, but his elder brother Arthur. Arthur died of consumption at Ludlow on 2 April 1502. To preserve the Spanish alliance, Henry, then aged 12, was betrothed to the widowed Catherine.

When the future Queen Elizabeth was born in September 1533 at Greenwich[119] the bells would customarily, if they were repaired in time, have rung forth at Dunster, but the year before we know they were in need of attention. In June 1532 John Wether of Dunster left money for their repair in his will: "to be beryd yn chyd of Dunster Ch of Wells ijd - iij lyghts of the Ch of Dunster and to the reparyng of the bells, my gowne - dowter Jone ij platers ij pongers ij sawcers ij chandelers ij sylver spones, a basyn and a crocke - same to dowter Alys - my wife shall geve to the vycary iijs vjd for to say a trentall yf he wyll say it, els to some other priest. Ref - Agnis my wyfe. Witn - Sir John Ryse, Will Owen, Thomas Joyce."[120] It seems to have been a custom to leave one's gown for the repair of the bells. In 1533 For the year of Elizabeth's birth we read: "Adam White of Dunster leaves to the reparacyon of the bells of Dunster and 4 lights my gowne." In the same year Rich. Holcumbe of the "towne of Dunster" leaves "to the bell 12d." Robert Sankyn, also of Dunster, makes the same bequest in the same year, as well as 4s 4d to the vicar of Dunster and Joh. Hooper of Dunster, "leaves to the reparacyon of the bells a gowne so that 4s of the price of it be geven to the 4 lights of Dunster." John Whyte of Dunster in March 1534 left "to the reparacyon of the bells 6s 8d."[121]

The Act of Supremacy was passed on 15 August and this was the final severance of the Church in England from Rome. The clergy had to submit to the king and Luther's translation of the whole bible was complete. In 1535 a new prior, named John Griffith, was appointed at Dunster and in that year a valuation of the estates of the priory, called the *Valor Ecclesiasticus* was made. It begins: "Declaration of the extent and annual value of all and singular the lands and tenements and other possessions, with the tithes, oblations, and other issues, of divers benefices and chapels belonging to the priory of Dunster, in the name of John Griffith, prior of the same, by Sir Andrew Luttrell and Hugh Malet, esq, the King's commissioners, and Hugh Trotter and John Plompton, auditors."

LIST OF REVENUES

	£	s	d
Demesne Lands			
Annual value of the demesne lands in the hands of the prior			
for the use of the priory, and valued by four lawful men	3	10	6
but of which there is paid			
In alms annually distributed to certain poor persons for the soul of			
Sir John Mohun, Knt. [Sir John de Mohun III (1269-1330)]		6	8
	3	3	10
Manor of Alcombe			
Annual rents there	11	12	0
Out of which there is paid			
The fee of William Machyn, steward	1	0	0
The fee of J. Gryme, bailiff	1	0	0
In alms annually distributed to divers poor persons by			
gift of the founders		8	0
Clear	9	4	0
Perquisites of the courts and other casualties		10	0
Marsh			
Annual rents there		13	4
Frakeford			
Annual rent of two tenements there	1	0	0
Cutcombe			
Annual rent of two tenements there		9	4
Luxborough			
Annual rent of two tenements there		10	0
Out of which there is paid			
For an annual rent to the lord of Luxborough		2	0
		8	0
Cowbridge			
Annual rent of a tenement there	1	6	8
Dunster			
Annual rent of nine burgages there	2	10	6
Wyllaller			
Annual chief rent of the heirs of			
By the more there		4	0
Minehead			
Annual rent of a mediety of the demesne lands			
and agistments of the park there	1	10	0

Value of the spirituals undermentioned:

Rectory of Dunster

Personal tithes with other casualties

			17	5	8
Out of which is paid					
To the bishop for procurations				7	5 ½
For an annual stipend to the vicar there			4	13	4
To the archdeacon for synodals				2	10 ½
		=	5	3	8
	Clear			12	2 0

Rectory of Carhampton

Predial tithes and other casualties			14	6	8
Out of which there is paid					
Annual pension to the prior and convent of Bath			8	10	0
Annual pension to the cathedral church of Wells			5	0	0
		=	13	10	0
				16	8

Rectory of Kilton

Predial tithes and other casualties		2	16	4

Stokegomer

A pension from the vicar there			7	0

South Wales Abbey of Neath

A pension in Exford, in the County of Somerset, per annum			3	0
Sum total of all possessions aforesaid, as well temporal as spiritual	37	4	8
Tenths	3	14	5 ¾

According to Hancock: "The total revenue of the priory would, therefore, at its dissolution have amounted to about £800 of our money."[122]

There had been rumblings against the monasteries as early as 1348 when the Black Death had started in the coastal towns of Dorset and the priesthood ministering to the dying had been decimated and reports filtered through of a monastic decline. Ecclesiastical visitors observed over-rich and indulgent foundations in debt; whilst many monasteries housed souls of deep devotion they also harboured persons of disorderly conduct. Cardinal Wolsey made some endeavours to stem the tide of corruption and suppressed twenty-one monasteries and used the proceeds to endow new colleges at Oxford and Ipswich. Later in 1536 the king dissolved nearly four hundred smaller monasteries with endowments less than £200. The dissolution of the monasteries was enacted by Parliament on the nominal grounds that: "manifest sin, vicious, carnal and abominable living is daily used and committed amongst them". The position of the monasteries was weak; they were hopelessly in debt, the discipline was slack and disorder abounded, but one sixth of the cultivated land in England belonged to them and their treasures were fabulous.

In 1525 William Tyndale had translated the New Testament. In England, smuggled copies of this were collected and publicly burnt, and in 1535 Tyndale, remembered for his lovely and immortal translations, was arrested and executed by the Catholics near Brussels.

Dunster castle from the Deer Park.

A view of Dunster church from the castle. (Geoffrey Lancaster)

The 13th-century churchyard cross, which stood at one time on the west gable of the church. (Geoffrey Lancaster)

In 1954 the churchyard cross was moved into the church and is shown here placed on a 13th/14th-century altar. The figures are those of the Blessed Virgin Mary and the Christ Child. (Geoffrey Lancaster)

A sketch by Hamilton Aidé (1868) of a view in Dunster churchyard. (Lyte, *Dunster and its Lords*)

West view of the church, 1845. (SANHS, Braikenridge Collection)

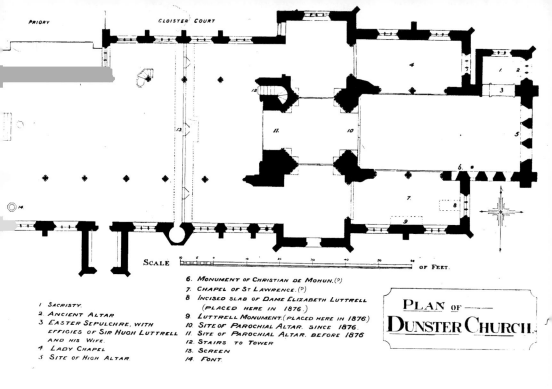

PRIORY CLOISTER COURT

SCALE of FEET.

1 SACRISTY.
2 ANCIENT ALTAR.
3 EASTER SEPULCHRE, WITH
  EFFIGIES OF SIR HUGH LUTTRELL
  AND HIS WIFE.
4 LADY CHAPEL.
5 SITE OF HIGH ALTAR.

6. MONUMENT OF CHRISTIAN DE MOHUN.(?)
7. CHAPEL OF ST LAWRENCE. (?)
8 INCISED SLAB OF DAME ELIZABETH LUTTRELL
  (PLACED HERE IN 1876.)
9. LUTTRELL MONUMENT.(PLACED HERE IN 1876)
10. SITE OF PAROCHIAL ALTAR. SINCE 1876.
11. SITE OF PAROCHIAL ALTAR. BEFORE 1876.
12. STAIRS TO TOWER.
13. SCREEN.
14. FONT.

PLAN OF
DUNSTER CHURCH.

Plan of Dunster church. (Lyte,
A History of Dunster)

The High House, Dunster, by
F.F. Lyte.

Dunster,1845. (SANHS, Braikenridge Collection)

Lower Marsh Farm in the 1980s. (Geoffrey Lancaster)

Eastern respond, foliated and with a capital "M", southern arcade, Dunster church.
(Geoffrey Lancaster)

The dovecote before
restoration.

St Leonard's Well.
(Geoffrey Lancaster)

The Old Priory. (Robin Downes)

The Old Priory. A stone fireplace of the early 15th century. (Geoffrey Lancaster)

A very unusual chest in Dunster church, with a sloping lid which was probably used by monks for writing in the cloister. (Geoffrey Lancaster)

An early "dug out" chest, of perhaps the 12th century. Dunster church. (Geoffrey Lancaster)

A slightly later chest, probably of the 13th century. Dunster church. (Geoffrey Lancaster)

High Cross, also called the Market Cross and later the Butter Cross. (Geoffrey Lancaster)

Detail from the Processional Cross, showing St John. (Peter Tudball)

The tomb of Christian de Mohun, née Segrave, after 1335. (Geoffrey Lancaster)

Opposite: Thirteenth-century upper arch widened in the 16th
century, Dunster church. (Geoffrey Lancaster)

Stone remains of the effigy of Sir John de Mohun III (1269-1330) of Dunster. (Geoffrey Lancaster)

Effigy of Sir Hugh Luttrell (d.1428). (Geoffrey Lancaster)

North-east view of
Dunster church by John
Buckler, 1839, showing
the Perpendicular
window and sloping roof
the de Mohun Chantry
Chapel before its
restoration. (SANHS,
Pigott Collection)

Stone wall shutting off
the south transept and
screen under the eastern
arch of the crossing
tower, Dunster church.
(Alfred A. Clarke, from
Freeman, *Dunster Priory
Church*)

Seal of Sir John Luttrell KB (d.1403), last of the main line of the Luttrells of East Quantoxhead. (Geoffrey Lancaster)

Seal of Elizabeth Luttrell née Courtenay (d.1395). (Geoffrey Lancaster)

Fifteenth-century glass in Dunster church, of which only the hat now remains. (*Gentleman's Magazine*, 1808)

The "Lower Mill", Dunster. (Robin Downes)

The entrance gateway to Dunster castle, north front, 1845. (SANHS, Braikenridge Collection)

Gateway of Dunster castle, south front, 1845. (SANHS, Braikenridge Collection)

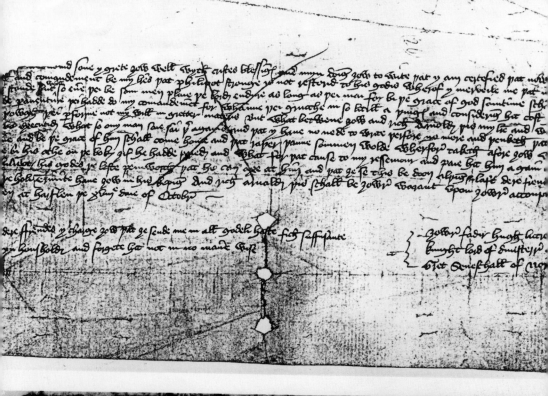

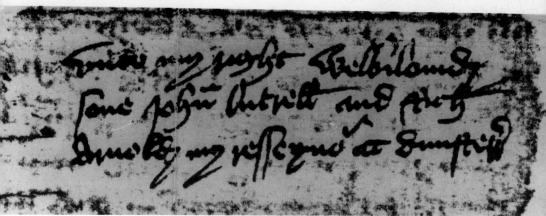

Letter from Sir Hugh Luttrell (d.1425) to his son John, reprimanding him and his receiver Richard Arnold, for not restoring his goods to Philipot Stronge. (*Journal of the Archaeological Institute*, Vol.xxvii, 1870. Ref: DD/L, 1-16)

Opposite: Tomb slab of Lady Elizabeth Luttrell of Powderham (d.1493), Dunster church.

(Geoffrey Lancaster)

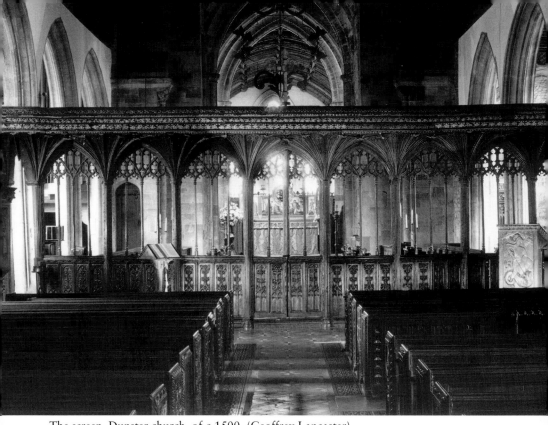

The screen, Dunster church, of c.1500. (Geoffrey Lancaster)

Detail of roof and bosses, Dunster church.

Dame Margaret Luttrell, née Wyndham, d.1580. (Geoffrey Lancaster. By kind permission of the National Trust, Dunster castle)

The allegorical portrait of Sir John Luttrell, c.1519-51, by Hans Eworth. (Geoffrey Lancaster. By kind permission of the National Trust, Dunster castle)

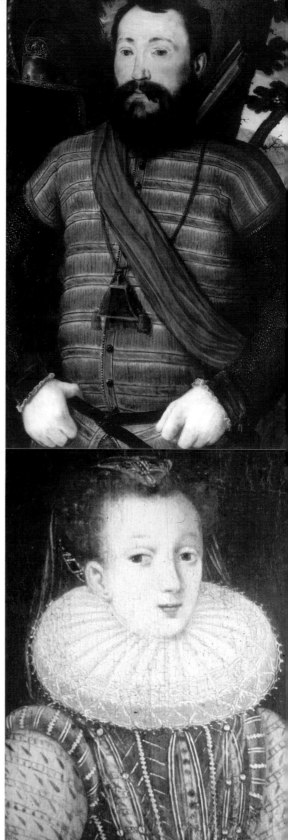

Thomas Wyndham (1510-53), by Hans Eworth. (Private collection. Photograph, Courtauld Institute of Art)

Margaret Edgcumbe (d.1607), daughter of Sir Andrew Luttrell (d.1538). (By kind permission of the National Trust)

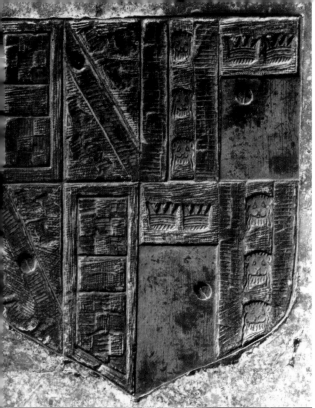

Brass of Elizabeth Stewkley, mother of Joan first wife of George Luttrell. (Geoffrey Lancaster)

DEA ILLVS TRI VIRO D THOMA DE COPLEI ORDINIS EQVES TRIS MILITIE
ICANE BARONE DE WELLES ET DE HAW DOCTE COMPOSITA EST ET
OCTORES THEOLOGOS ACADEMIE PARISIENSIS APPROBATA ANNO 1580 NE
ERD IOANAM D D DE COPLEI PRIMOGENITAM SED VNICAM INSIGNIS
TAN EID PETRI DE MARTIGNI EQVITIS GALLOBELGE DOMIN DE STEVELS ET
PIVILLE GVBERNATORIS CONIVGEM IN MELIOREM QVAM ANTEA FORMAM
TA EX VT QVILIBET MENTE COLENS QVOD CERNIT IN IPSA ORTVM

The allegory of Sir Thomas Copley, whose wife Catherine was the eldest daughter of Sir John Luttrell. (National Trust Photographic Library/John Hammond)

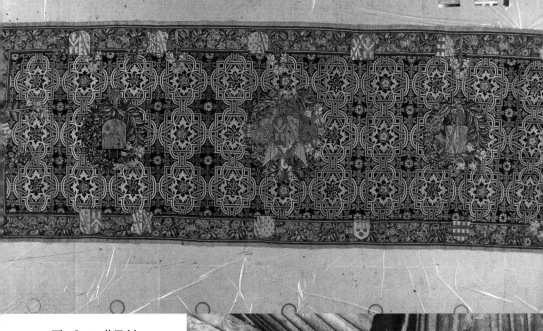

The Luttrell Table
Carpet. (By kind
permission of Glasgow
Museums, The Burrell
Collection)

Opposite: The
monument to Thomas
and Margaret Luttrell,
and George and Joan
Luttrell, erected
between 1621-29, in
Dunster church.
(Geoffrey Lancaster)

Detail of the effigies of
Thomas Luttrell (1525-
71) and Margaret
Luttrell née Hadley
(d.1607).
(Geoffrey Lancaster)

Joan Luttrell née Stewkley (d.1621), first wife of George Luttrell (d.1629).
(Geoffrey Lancaster)

George Luttrell (1560-1629), son of Thomas and Margaret Luttrell. Being alive in 1621 when Joan his wife died, he is shown facing west. (Geoffrey Lancaster)

Detail of the Luttrell tomb, showing the feet of Thomas Luttrell and the folds of Margaret Luttrell's dress. (Geoffrey Lancaster)

The seal of George Luttrell (d.1629) - a plume of twelve feathers.

Overmantel in the Luttrell Arms, depicting Diana and Actaeon. (Geoffrey Lancaster)

The Luttrell Arms Hotel, Dunster.

George Luttrell when 34 years of age
in 1594.
(From Lyte, *History of Dunster*)

Detail of the arms of Luttrell (dexter) and of Sylvestra Capps (sinister) on the porch of the Luttrell Arms Hotel, Dunster.

Thomas Luttrell (1584-1644). (Geoffrey Lancaster. By kind permission of the National Trust, Dunster castle).

In 1538 archbishop Cranmer had bibles containing these translations placed in parish churches but for some reason it was not until 1548 that a large bible and a copy of the Paraphrases of Erasmus were bought for Dunster church. One half of the cost was borne by the parishioners of Dunster and the other half by the king as rector, or patron, in accordance with royal injunction. Although much in the field of the visual arts was lost, much was gained in the immortal cadences of John Merbecke or Marbeck's plain chant which was adapted to Edward VI's first liturgy. This plain chant was dropped summarily at Dunster church after the departure of the Rev. Doré but from 1550 it had reverberated from the walls of St George the Martyr, in Dunster, then already, in part, four hundred and fifty years old.

In January 1539 most of the Somerset religious houses were suppressed. Muchelney, Keynsham, Bath and its cell Dunster, were surrendered. In February Athelney, Buckland and Sororum, Taunton, and its annexed priory at Stavordale, Witham, Montacute and Hinton ceased and on 1 April, the Austin Canons at Bruton were suppressed...the houses for Benedictine monks in Somerset were all, with the exception of Dunster, which was a cell of Bath, of great antiquity and importance.[123] Lyte says: "No inventory has been preserved of the furniture, ornaments and books found in the Priory, but it would be possible to trace in detail the subsequent history of its most valuable possessions."[124] From *Dugdale's Monasticon* Lyte obtained information concerning endowments: "The endowments were in the first instance divided into three sections and committed to laymen, to be made profitable to the Crown. One section, consisting entirely of temporalities, comprised the manor of Alcombe and various lands in the parishes of Dunster and Cutcombe that had been let out to farmers. A second section, consisting entirely of spiritualities, was limited to the rectory of Carhampton. The remaining section, consisting partly of spiritualities, is the only one of which it is proposed to treat in this place. It comprised the site of the Priory, with its demesnes and the rectories of Dunster and Kilton, all of which were committed to John Luttrell, a younger brother of Sir Andrew Luttrell of Dunster Castle, then lately deceased"[125] John Luttrell acted for the Crown at the Dissolution of the Monasteries and the surrender of Dunster Priory on 1 January 1539 and became lessee of the Priory.

The Dissolution of the English monasteries had begun in 1536 and in 1538 shrines and relics were destroyed. By 1539 the task was completed and the great English monasteries were dissolved. In Dunster on 27 January 1539, the deed of surrender was signed. John Griffiths, the prior, was the third to sign this document in the presence of the prior of Bath, the sub-prior and the monks of Dunster. Many corrupt practices, such as the selling of indulgences, the cult of relics, which relied so much on superstitions, all ceased but so did much of the merry-making. The processions, pageants, bonfires, miracle plays and "drynkys," events organised by the gilds, all ceased and England, in the years which followed, fell under the censorious rigidity of emerging Reformed thought and practice. Whether the people were truly religious or not, the church had been the centre of medieval life and to its multifarious and colourful practices the people brought their gifts, their enthusiasms and their traditions, often traditions rooted in pre-Christian, pagan symbolism.

CHAPTER SIX

THE DISSOLUTION AND ITS AFTERMATH

THE DISSOLUTION of the Monasteries in 1539 and the signing of the deed of surrender at Dunster in the January of that year did not mean that catholic doctrines and practices were immediately abandoned and indeed it was not until the reign of Edward VI that England became unequivocally protestant. After the surrender of Dunster priory John Luttrell, 'the elder' became the crown agent and at Michaelmas, 1539 he rendered an account. John 'the elder' was the second son of Sir Hugh Luttrell and the ancestor of the Luttrells of Kentsbury and Spaxton. His brother, Sir Andrew Luttrell, the heir had died in 1538 and was succeeded by his eldest son, named John after his uncle, John "the elder."

By 28 October 1539 this agent for the Crown had been granted a lease for twenty-one years at an annual fixed rent of £3.13s 4d. This rent was based on John Luttrell's account which deemed the nett revenue to be £13 15s 7d of which £3 was payable in respect of the rectory of Kilton. Apart from this John Luttrell rented for his £3 13s 4d yearly: "the site of the late house, or priory, or cell, of Dunster now dissolved, with all houses, buildings, barns, yards, orchards, gardens, land and ground within the precinct of the same," land called Waglondes, a close under "le Conynger," a close above the highway, a close at the head of the same, and lands called Le Dene, Hyllyberes, Lower Hillebouer, Alger, Gille-chappell, Clerkelome, Foxgrove, Lynche, les Hams, Awcombe Meade, and Birchehame, all situate in Dunster and recently in the occupation of the Prior."[1]

Waglondes refers to the glebeland behind the present Priory Court, formerly the Victorian rectory. Le Dene persists as Dene Close at Alcombe, and Birchehame as Bircham Road. The Crown reserved all large trees growing on the property thus demised, but undertook to provide timber sufficient for necessary repairs. It is likely that the lessee managed to get rather more out of the land than it was yielding when he first entered upon it. Furthermore, he got the empty buildings of the Priory, on the north side of the church, as a residence for himself and his family.[2]

In 1539 John Luttrell's wife was Elizabeth Reynolds. He had formerly been married to Joan Flamank and they were divorced before 1528. John had the rectories of Dunster and Kilton committed to his charge and his lease of 28 October 1539 included specifically the rectory of Dunster as opposed to the priory and its lands. For this he paid a rent of £7 2s 3d, the nett amount they had yielded in 1538 when John Luttrell was only the agent for the Crown and before he became the lessee in 1539. The conditions concerning the rectory of Dunster were that John Luttrell should be responsible for the vicar of Dunster's salary of £8 a year and for a yearly rent of 10s 9d to the archdeacon of Taunton 'for procurations and synodals'.[3] The Crown accepted liability 'for all other expenses incident to an impropriate rectory'.[4] The twenty-one year lease in 1539 granted to John Luttrell for twenty-one years also assigned certain titles and other advantages to him as follows: "the tithes of sheaves, wool and lambs, and all other small tithes of Avill, Ellicombe, Alcombe, Staunton and Medyet,. of the demesne lands of Minehead, Lophall [sic], Skyllacre, and Dunster fields, and of the mill of Dunster, the Lordesfeld, and Exford. The rent for these was fixed at £7. 2s. 3d, being the nett amount which they had yielded in the previous year, when John Luttrell was merely agent for the Crown."[5] The rectory of Dunster is not to be confused with the priory and its lands.

Regarding the priory church Lyte says: "It is difficult to say what would have happened at Dunster if John Luttrell had wished to secularize the non-parochial part of the divided church. He might have contended with force that the chancel, having been adjudged to the monks in 1498, was legally one of the conventual buildings, like the tithe-barn and the dovecot. On the other hand the parishioners had rights in the southern transept, and in the central tower which they had built in the previous century. They seem also to have had rights in the chapel on the eastern side of the southern transept. Furthermore it is necessary to observe that even if the whole of the eastern part of the church had belonged to the monks, John Luttrell could not have pulled it down, as he never was the owner of the priory. For the first year after the Dissolution, he was merely an agent of the Crown, and afterwards he was a lessee. In point of fact there were good reasons why John Luttrell should not claim rights in the chancel at Dunster more extensive than those which he had in the chancel at Kilton, the right that is to say of the representative of the lay rector," (the king was lay rector). Whatever his theological views may have been, he could hardly have wished to desecrate wantonly a building in which his grandmother and other ancestors lay buried.[6]

Lyte maintained that: "The late Mr Freeman was wont to refer to Dunster as a typical place where there were two churches under one roof, the eastern church monastic and the western church parochial. Many instances have been cited to show that lay grantees of the sites of suppressed monasteries and colleges had the right to secularize and even to demolish buildings, which, from the architectural point of view, formed integral parts of parochial churches.[7] He further points out: "Many of the lay-folk living in 1539 could remember the time when they were not wholly excluded from the chancel, and we may readily credit them with a desire to recover their ancient rights: notwithstanding all changes, the original high altar of the undivided church had a special sanctify. Private sentiment and local opinion might alike be gratified by the opening of the gates of the screen under the tower."[8]

John Leland in his *Itinerary and Collectanea*, visited Dunster and wrote: "The hole chirch of the late Priory servith now for the paroche chirch. Aforetymes the monks had the est part closid up to their use."[9] John Leland was educated at St Paul's School and at Cambridge and Oxford. He was made chaplain, and later in 1533 he became antiquary to Henry VIII and his ten year tour took place between 1534-1544. In 1540 he made reference to the church at Alcombe. John Luttrell, the lessee of the rectory, claimed 32s.10d from the Court of Augmentations. Repairs had been undertaken to cottages in Alcombe which were in a ruinous state and this claim included the repair 'of the chancel of the church of that place.'[10] Alcombe was then part of the parish of Dunster. The next year John Luttrell's claim of 59s was 'for repairs at Dunster, specifically to the chief mansion of the manor to the window of the chancel of the church. In 1546, however, he claimed allowance of 3s.5d from the Crown for repairs to the chancel which he stated were 'very ruinous'.[11]

Once the king acquired the monastic lands he sold them with great alacrity, as Lyte says: "Although the confiscated monastic property yielded a considerable revenue, the Crown was generally willing to sell outright, a lump sum of money in hand being preferred to a rent, however regular. Thus, when a very small part of John Luttrell's term had expired, the King, in March 1543, arranged to sell the rent and also the reversion of the Priory demesnes of Dunster. The purchaser was Humphrey Colles, gentleman, who undertook to pay close upon a thousand pounds, a very large sum at that time, for these and other monastic possessions in the west of England. The property at Dunster conveyed to him was that specified in the lease of 1539, the only reservation to the Crown being a rent of 7s. 4d., which was exactly a tenth of the rent payable by John Luttrell. An examination of the proceedings of Humphrey Colles, after the issue of letters patent in his favour, makes it perfectly clear that in most cases he was merely an agent for persons who thought that they could purchase monastic property on better terms through him than in their own names. Each of the principals got his or her pre-arranged share. Within a few days of the date of the grant to Colles, he obtained a licence to transfer his rights at Dunster to Dame Margaret Luttrell, the relict of Sir Andrew and the mother of the actual lord of Dunster."[12] Lyte adds a note that: "Colles may have been a solicitor. He was party to a fine for the settlement of Lady Luttrell's dower in 1542."

Preb Hancock has also written about the Colles transaction and quotes from Lyte's earlier book, *Dunster and its Lords*: "The Luttrell family, as Lyte suggests, were unwilling 'that a building which adjoined, and apparently included within its precincts, the monastic chancel in which several of their ancestors lay buried', and an estate which lay contiguous to and intermixed with the Dunster Castle lands, should pass into the hands of strangers, so Dame Margaret Luttrell determined to buy H. Colles' interest in the priory. In the same year, 1544, H. Colles levies a fine to "Margaret Luttrell, widow, her heirs and assigns, of 6 houses, two lofts, one pidgeon house, two gardens, 100 acres of land, 40 acres of meadow, 100 acres of pasture, 12 acres of wood and 40 acres of furze and heath in Dunster and Carhampton belonging to ye priory of Dunster, for 100 marks of silver (£66. 13s. 4d) paid by the said Margaret Luttrell'."[13] Dame Margaret, in the same year does homage for the site of the priory or cell of Dunster (Rot. 62,63,64). Two years later, A.D. 1546 the king grants a licence of alienation for the consideration of 22s to Margaret Luttrell, widow, to alienate the priory of Dunster to feoffees in trust, to the use of herself for life, the remainder to Thomas Luttrell her second son, with other remainders. In 37 Hen. VIII (Origin, Rot. 84) it is stated that John Wyneham and others did homage for the site of the late house or priory of Dunster. Wyneham is no doubt meant for Wyndham, and this John Wyndham was probably Dame Margaret Luttrell's brother and one of the feoffees mentioned above. This lady survived her two elder sons, and we find her later remonstrating with her grandson, George Luttrell, the young squire of Dunster, who had been induced when a mere lad to agree to marry his cousin Joan, the daughter of Hugh Stewkley of Marsh, that if he should marry in defiance of her wishes, she would leave away from him the priory of Dunster, and so make a "poor gentleman of him." The young man, however, was obdurate and as soon as he left Cambridge he married Joan Stewkley at Dunster, and his grandmother, Sir H. M. Lyte relates, forgot her prejudices and forgave him and left him "the Priorie of Dunster and all the landes and other revenues and other profits belonging to the same."[14]

After Colles had transferred his rights at Dunster to Dame Margaret Luttrell: "John Luttrell rendered no account to the Court of Augmentations of rent payable by him for the site and demesnes of the Priory."[15] He only had to pay the 7s 4d tithe to the Crown. This he deducted from the rent which was now payable to his sister-in-law.[16] His sister-in-law was a most forceful personality and after the death of her husband, Sir Andrew in 1538 she became possessed of considerable wealth. Many of the Luttrell family owned vessels which they used to transport goods of great variety. Dame Margaret was one of them and in 1543 she was registered as the owner of a ship of 100 tons belonging to the port of Minehead when it was in London.

From 1543 Dame Margaret was responsible for all necessary expenses incurred by John Luttrell, as her tenant. The king, as lay rector, was responsible for the maintenance and repairs of the chancel which was now regarded as an integral part of the church rather than part of the monastic building. As his representative John Luttrell provided bread, wine and wax for the celebration of the masses at Dunster and Kilton, the usual charge being 6s. 8d for Dunster and 2s for Kilton. The parishioners responsibility was for the whole area of the church on the western side of the tower.

King Henry tried to steer a middle course. He had dissolved the monasteries because he needed the money for his French wars, and he had disposed of papal authority because he wished to divorce Catherine of Aragon who had not produced a male heir. As far as the practices of the church were concerned these were unaltered and at Dunster the various altars and chantries persisted until Edward VI came to the throne. However, in 1545 plans were afoot for the dissolution of the chantries and a few surrendered voluntarily. An act was passed stating that the possessions of the chantries were generally misapplied and they were vested in the king for the term of his life. Although commissioners were appointed to enquire into their property, none was actually suppressed during Henry's reign.

Although some chantries had been voluntarily surrendered in 1545, it was not until 1547 that they were suppressed by a new act and 2374 chantries and guild chapels disappeared...Where they had been educational centres and the guild chaplain had acted as schoolmaster as well as curate or chaplain, they survived and became the renowned Edward VI grammar schools. The term chantry was initially 'applied to the office or the benefice maintained to sing or say Mass for the souls of the founder and his friends, and also to the little chapel in which such masses were usually said.[17] Among other conditions, 'the erection of a chantry chapel in the later Middle Ages in England required a monetary endowment for its erection and upkeep',[18] and various permissions and consents also.

It was in 1545/6 that a return was made concerning the chantry of St Lawrence in Dunster church but it appears not to have been one of those chantries which voluntarily surrendered at the time because a further return was made in 1547/8 in consequence of the statute for the suppression of the chantries passed that year. The return of 1545/6 is as follows: "The Chauntrie of Saincte Laurence wtin the paryshe churche ther. Is yerely worthe in Landes, rente and hereditamente in the tenure of sondery psones as maye appere pticulery more at large by the Rentall of the same ix li. viijs iiijd. Whereof in Rente resolute paide yerely xxs. And so Remaynethe clere viij.li.viijs.iiijd. Plate and ornamente. A Chalice, a pax ij cruetts and too candelsticke of silu waying lxxij oz. Ornamentes praysed at ixs.iiijd. Memord. John Bayley clerke of the age of lx yeres, a singing man, incumbent ther."[19] In other words the value of the lands, rents and property of the chantry of St Lawrence which devolved on the heir at law but which was leased to the tenants came to £9 8s 4d. the rents resolute came to £1, thus leaving £8. 8s. 4d clear. The value of the ornaments came to 9s. 4d.

The return of 1547-8 is as follows:
"The Chantry of St Lawrence within the parish church there.
"The dwelling house with a garden to the same adjacent, per ann. iijs iiijd
"Alexander Voysey holds land and a tenement there and renders per ann. iiijs
"Roger Hoper holds land there and renders per ann. xiiijs
"Robert Goffe holds land there, and renders per ann. xs
"Thomas Joyner holds land there, and renders per ann. xiijs iiijd
"The same Thomas holds other land there, and renders per ann. iiijs
"John Sexton holds certain land there, and renders per ann. ijs
"Thomas Holcombe holds certain land there, and renders per ann. xjs
"The same Thomas holds other land there, and renders per ann. xvjd
"Edmund Stibbe holds certain land there and renders per ann. iiijs
"Troilus Hayne holds certain land there, and renders per ann. ijs
"Rise Gouffe holds land there and renders per ann. ijs

"Henry Crane holds land there, and renders per ann. vjs

"Walter———, clerk, holds a house there, and renders per ann. iijs

"The Wardens of the parish church there hold a house called the Churchhouse and render per ann. iijs

"Morgan Howell holds land there, and renders per ann. vs

"John Sutton holds land there, and renders per ann. .vijs viijd"

"Thomas Capner holds land there, and renders per ann. vjs

"Thomas Make holds land there, and renders per ann. iiijs.

"Katerine Lowdon holds a house there, and renders per ann. vjs viijd.

"John Borge holds land there, and renders per ann. xijs.

"William Hyndon holds land there, and renders per ann. viijd.

"John Lyolle holds land there, and renders per ann. vjs.

"William Lowlys holds land there, and renders per ann. xs.

"John Williams holds land there, and renders per ann. xijs

"David Arter holds land there, and renders per ann. iiijs.

"William Carran holds land there, and renders per ann. iiijs.

"John Mawhoude holds land there, and renders per ann. iiijs.

."John Cottrill holds land there, and renders per ann. vs iiijd.

"Christiana Sole holds land there, and renders per ann. vjs.

"Nicholas Browne holds land there, and renders per ann. vjs

"The heir of ———Bartelott holds certain free lands, and renders per ann. viijd.

Total £ix viijs iiijd (According to my calculations the total is £9.3s. and not £9. 8s.4d.)

"Deduct in Rent resolute to John Luttrell, Kt., chief lord there for free rent for the premises, per ann. xs.

"And remains over, per annum iijli. iiijd,"[20]

Since chantries were suppressed in 1548 it seems strange that Hancock refers to: "A paper MS. in the muniment room of Dunster Castle, undated, but evidently of 4 Elizabeth, gives the following list of part of the possessions of this chantry."[21] This paper would now be in the Somerset Record Office. Hancock's calculations are correct since Antony Wood (see below) held tenure for twenty-one years in H VIII 36 (1544/5) and when the list was made there were three years of his tenure to go. It would therefore appear that the list was dated to Elizabeth 14 (1561/2) or Elizabeth 15 (1562/3). The details are as follows:

"Dunster possessionum Cantur of Saint Laurence"

"John Were holds at will one tenement garden and backeside containing one rodd and pays vjs

"Morris Nicholes holds at will of the Queen one tenement with a garden and pays iijs

"Thomas Capener holds at will one tenement with a garden containing one rood and pays vjs

"Antony Wood holds by indenture for 3 years still to come as appears by indenture dated 4th September in the year H VIII 36 for the term of 21 years and pays..14s.4d one tenement and garden containing one rood and one acre of land in .Loxall xiiijs iiijd

"One piece of waste land lying in High Street (in alto vico) containing by estimation one rood in the tenure of John Saxon at will and he pays ijd

"The widow Miller holds at will one acre of land in Watchet and pays per year xijd"

"Parcel of the possessions of the late Monastery of Cleve.

"William Miller holds at will one tenement and one garden containing one rood and pays 6s 8d

"Roger Rowe holds at will one tenement and garden containing one rood and pays 10s

"Robert Gough holds at will one tenement and garden in Weste Strete and pays 16s

"Laurence ffemell holds at will 3 tenements together annex fut (adjoining the water trough?) one tectum (roofed building?) and small garden containing by estimation one rood and pays thence by the year 20s

"Thomas Edwardes als Evans holds at will one tenement and one garden containing one rood and pays thence per year 16s"[22]

The Royal Commission of February 1548 also reported on the chantry of the Holy Trinity at St George's church Dunster, as follows:

"Land and possessions assigned to the use and maintenance of a chaplain there, celebrating in the Chantry of the Trinity or St George.

"Divers persons hold ten tenements and five acres and a half of land there and render per ann. iiijli

"Total iiiijs

"Deduct in Rent resolute to John Luttrell Kt. for free rent for the premises, per ann. vijs

"And remains over, per annum. lxxiijs

"Land assigned to the use and maintenance of a Light perpetually burning in the parish church there——

"holds half an acre of land lying in Watchet and renders per ann. xviijd

"Deduct in—— Rent resolute to——Fulforde, Kt., for free rent for the same half acre of land per ann. vjd

"And remains over per annum xijd" *Som. Record Soc.,* vol 2.[23]

Prebendary Hancock writes about two more chantries apart from those of St Lawrence and Holy Trinity or St George, those of St John and St Mary. Lyte doubts that there was ever a chantry of St John at Dunster church. "At any rate one of the two quotations given in support of the theory refers neither to the Baptist nor to the Evangelist of that name, but to the lord of the neighbouring manor of Luccombe."[24] Hancock's account of this chantry of St John to R de Cogston, who died in 1348 and 'bequeathed towards the building of the new screen or parclose of the Holy Trinity 6s.8d'[25] Lyte also refers to the will of de Cogston as follows: "The Dead Light, called also the Light of Devotion.[26] It may be further identified with the Light of 'Wex Silver' which is mentioned in the will of Ralph of Cogston, executed in 1348.[27] In some parishes of Somerset, a similar light was called the light of All Souls."[28]

Hancock's detailed account of the supposed chantry of St John states: "There was also a chantry of S. John attached to Dunster Church, to which, or its chaplain at the time, occasional references appear in early wills. Thus, R de Cogston (will proved 1348) leaves a sum of money for masses to be sung for the rest of his soul on the anniversary of his burial, and for the ringing of a peal. The prior and convent appears to have had 10d of this sum, the vicar 2d for his services, the Church Clerk[29] for ringing the bell 1d, the town crier to pray for my soul round the whole town 1d, the Chaplain of St John's (Clericus S Johannis) 2d and to the parish church for the lights burning about his body 3s," (lying presumably in the church during the night preceding the funeral). Master Richard Bruton, canon of Wells, and sometime vicar of Minehead, in his long will, dated 30 March, 1417, alludes to "the preest beside Dunsterre which I helped to have a benefice which as I remember was the gift of S. John"[30]

Hancock gives details of a will which concerns the chantry of St Mary: "Gilbert Scut of Dunster, whose will is dated 42 Edward III (1369), leaves three pounds of wax to make two large lights, one of which was "to burn in the chapel of the Blessed Mary of

Dunsterre." He left, also, a vessel of brass to hire a man to go on a pilgrimage for the good of the testator's soul to some of the shrines of note mentioned above, viz., those of our Lady of Walsingham, Canterbury, Hayles (All Hallows), London, and the Cross of Northden. One John Hurlebusch, whose will was proved early in the reign of Henry VIII, leaves legacies to five chantries in Dunster Church, of which no doubt these two, St John & St Mary, and the chantry of St Lawrence formed three.[31] Scut's will follows: " 2 Edw III, 1369. Gilbert Scut of dunsterre. Body to cemetery. S George of dunsterre. To the prior of dunsterre for tithes forgotten 2s 6d. To the prior of Dunsterre to celebrate one trentall for my soul 2s.6d. To William Baldyngton Monk to celebrate 2 trentalls 5s for my soul. "To Master Richard the Chaplain of Dunsterre to celebrate one trentall 2s 6d. To Robert the Vicar of Dunsterre to celebrate one trentall 2s 6d. "To the Fratres Minores of Briggewater to be mentioned in their prayer To a certain monk of Clyve being in Holy Orders to celebrate for my soul 6d. To Robert the Vicar of Karhampton to celebrate for my soul 20d. To Master Robert parson of Wethicombe to celebrate for my soul etc. 20d. To Robert Vicar of Codecombe to celebrate etc 12d. I give 3 pounds of wax to make thence two lights to burn around my body on the night and day of my burial, and after my burial one light to burn before the Altar of the Cross of the Church of Dunsterre and another light to burn in the Chapel of the Blessed Mary of Dunsterre. I leave to the poor on the day of my burial, namely to each poor man coming to the distribution 1 farthing. To Adam Clerk of the Church of Dunsterre 2d. To Alice my younger daughter for her life all that tenement with its appurtenances situate in Dunsterre in High St in between the tenement of John de Bratton on the one part and my tenement on the other. After the decease of the said Alice the aforesaid burgage etc. to the burgesses of the town of Dunsterre in perpetuity. To William Pynson all that burgage of mine etc. situate in Westret held by WilliamTailloar and formerly by Thomas Thurlot. To have and to hold the said burgage etc. to the aforesaid William for his life after the death of Margery my wife - so that after the decease of the aforesaid Margery and William - the whole of the aforesaid burgage etc. shall go to the burgesses of the town of Dunsterre and their heirs in perpetuity so that the aforesaid burgesses shall have a chaplain for ever to celebrate in the Church of Dunsterre that the aforesaid burgages shall go towards the payment of the said Chaplain in the best way possible But if the aforesaid Burgesses shall have no such Chaplain that the aforesaid burgesses shall cause to be celebrated annually for my soul, those of Walter Scut, Elenor his wife, Beatrice Scut, Avice Scut and Margaret Scut my wives, John de Wylton and Marcell his wife, William Pynsonn and all faithful dead in the Church of St George of Dunsterre to the value of one mark for ever. To Alice my younger daughter towards her Mariage 60 shillings. To John my son 20s. To Alice of Wolfecote my da. 10s. To David Herneys toward the maintenance of his son the fourth of a chain of mine. To John my son 13s 4d. To David Herneys one velvet gown...one sword with its sheath one bow with its arrows. To John my son one bed and my plough. To Alice my younger daughter one bed one new brazen pot. To John my son one new brazen pot. My brazen pot to send a man on a pilgrimage toWalsingham, Canterbury, Hayles near London, to the Cross of Northden. To Thomas de Ryvers 40d. To be distributed for my soul on the day of the anniversary viz. the end of 4 weeks after my death to each poor man coming for the same one farthing. To be distributed for my soul on the day of the next anniversary after the next complete year after my decease to each poor person coming for the same obolus. Residue of goods not specially bequeathed my funeral expenses and debts paid, to Margery my wife to do for my soul as she shall be best to arrange. Proved at Taunton."[32]

When John Luttrell, the rector and lessee of the priory after the Dissolution, died in 1558, he directed in his will that he should be buried in the Lady chapel, adjoining his residence in the house now known as the Old Priory. It is thought that this chapel, before 1547 the chantry of St Mary, was re-established and refitted in the reign of Mary. There is no evidence today of his burial, nor of that of his son George, who was buried at Dunster 12 February 1586.[33]

A royal commission of enquiry was issued 13 February 1548 and the commissioners for the survey in Somerset were Thomas Speke, Hugh Powtell, John Rogers, John Seyntlow, Thomas Dyer, knights and William Morryce, George Lyne, Robert Kelway, Robert Metcalfe, esquires. In 1549, a royal commission paid a visit to Dunster and issued the following account with regard to the church: "Dunster. The Salerie of one prieste celebratynge wtin the paryshe churche ther Is yearly worthe in Landes tente and heredidamente in the tenure of sondery psones as may appere pticulerly more at large by the rentall of the same iiij li

Whereof in Rente resolute pd yerely vijs
And so Remayneth clere lxxiijs
Plate and ornamente Noone. Memord. (Nil)
Lyghte foundyd wtin the paryshe church ther
Ar yerely worthe in one half acre of lande lying in wachet gyven to the same
use xviijd
Whereof in Rente resolute paide yerely vjd
And so Remayneth clere xijd"[34]

It is incredible that Dunster church had no plate or ornaments in 1539 and Hancock suggests that the churchwardens, aware of the coming storm, had sold or perhaps hidden the church plate, vestments and other furniture before the commissioners descended upon them.

The first Prayer Book came into being when the act of Uniformity for public worship was passed on 5 June 1549. This enforcement of the reformation was ill received in the West Country and when the first prayer book was first used at Sampford Courtenay, Devon, on Whit Sunday, 1549, the hostility of the villagers forced the priest to don his vestments and to celebrate the Latin Mass. Soon the whole of the West Country was up in arms and demanded a return to the old religion and the abolition of the offending book which they likened to a 'Christmas game'.[35] Protector Somerset tried to cajole them saying "Content yourselves good people. Do not with this rage and fury drive yourselves to the sword, your wives and children to famine and hunger."[36] The King's Council did not take so conciliatory a view and the uprising was rigorously suppressed. Despite the change to the fanatical protestantism of Edward VI, the monks having departed in 1539 and papal authority having been entirely rejected, still the services went on much as usual and the numerous altars were still in use. John Luttrell, the representative of the king who was lay rector, provided the bread and wine and wax for the celebration of masses in the churches of Dunster and Kilton, at Dunster this cost 6s 8d and at Kilton 2s. In 1550 wax was no longer supplied for candles and the money allotted for the bread and wine was reduced to 1s 8d at both churches[37] In 1548/9, the second year of the reign of Edward VI the approximate number of 'partakers of the Lord's Holy Sooper' at Dunster was quoted as five hundred,[38] but we do not know over what period this figure was calculated.

Iconoclasm was rife among the reformers and was carried out savagely. Monuments were defaced, wall paintings disappeared under coats of whitewash, stained glass windows depicting subjects regarded as of a superstitious nature, were removed and saints' days no longer marked the passage of the year. Masses for the dead and other remembrances of the departed ceased and the newly translated Bible took precedence. A copy of the Paraphrases of Erasmus was bought for Dunster church. These paraphrases of the New Testament was begun by Mary, Princess of Wales and finished by Nicholas Udall.[39] Although we have no record of the exact date in the middle of the sixteenth century when side altars, crucifixes and images were removed from Dunster church we know that a large Bible and a copy of the Paraphrases of Erasmus were bought for the church in 1548. In accordance with royal injunctions one half of the cost was borne by the king as rector or patron and one half by the parishioners.[40] By January, 1552, the Second Act of Uniformity was passed and the Second Prayer Book came into being. The central message of the prayer book was that the Holy Communion was merely a commemorative rite and the doctrine of transubstantiation was entirely rejected. Early in the reign of Edward VI a Nicholas Gravener negotiated the purchase of the reversion of the rectory of Dunster. He appears to have been forestalled by John Luttrell, for his overtures came to nothing and John Luttrell, on surrendering his subsisting lease and on payment of a fine, secured a fresh lease to run for twenty-one years from 1552.[41] He died in 1558 and Elizabeth, his widow, appears to have relinquished her interest in the remaining fifteen years of the lease.

In 1560 the rectory and tithes for the remaining fifteen years of the late John Luttrell's lease were sold by the Crown to two brothers, John and George Fytz[42] who were lawyers of the Inner Temple. They were obviously acting for Elizabeth Sydenham because we find that shortly after the brothers had received their grant, the Sydenhams conveyed to Hugh Stewkley various houses, barns, orchards, lands and rents in Dunster, Carhampton, Minehead and Exford, common of pasture in Dunster, and also the rectory of Dunster with tithes of sheaves, hay, wool and lambs and other small tithes.[43] A fine in lieu of the rights was levied so that the Sydenhams and the Fytz brothers forewent any claim made by them or their heirs. As far as the Fytz brothers were concerned they were hardly likely to have had any ideas of retaining the tithes of a parish in West Somerset, and they almost certainly acted as intermediaries.

Hancock makes a rather extraordinary statement concerning Thomas Luttrell, Dame Margaret's second son, and the priory. He says: "It would be interesting to know if Thomas Luttrell converted the priory into a dwelling house and lived there, but in 1557 he succeeded to Dunster Castle on the death of his elder brother, Sir John, and the priory appears soon to have been dismantled, a great portion of it pulled down and the rest converted into farmhouse."[44] Firstly, Sir John Luttrell died at Greenwich 10 July 1551.[45] Secondly, according to Lyte, although Thomas was constantly at Dunster transacting business, he did not actually reside there. He is described as '"Thomas Luttrell of Marshwood" in some legal proceedings with regard to treasure-trove in the Hundred of Carhampton.'[46]

In, or before, 1561, Dame Margaret's youngest daughter died. She married firstly Richard Malet of Currypool in Charlinch. After his death in 1551, she had married, as his first wife, Sir George Speke, K.B. of Whitelackington.[47] The manor of Alcombe which up to the Dissolution of the Monasteries had belonged to the Benedictines of Dunster, and in 1539 had been owned by the Crown, was sold to Sir George. During the lay rectorship of Hugh Stewkley it is recorded that 'Sir George Speke's land lyeth on the west end, and the widow Foxe's land lyeth on the east ende, and the churchyard on the north side, and the highway on the south side adjoining.[48] He died in 1584 possessed of this manor and other lands in or near Alcombe, which also belonged to the monks.[49] It was in 1560/1 that Dame Margaret Luttrell obtained actual possession of the priory and, although Hugh Stewkley appears to have been a 'thorn in her side', nevertheless, she apparently did not quarrel with him over his rights in the church. At her death in 1580, it passed to her grandson and heir, George. Her eldest son, Sir John, had died in 1551, but had left only two daughters and her second son, Thomas, died in 1571. The priory was regarded as an integral part of the Luttrell estate and, on the cessation of her brother-in-law, John Luttrell's lease, the duty of collecting the rent of 7s 4d was transferred to the sheriff. Hugh Stewkley purchased the remainder of John Luttrell's lease before 1566 when this much disliked lay rector was the butt of a manifesto issued by fourteen of the inhabitants of Dunster. He could claim relationship with the Luttrells for his grandmother was Joan Luttrell who married into the Stewkley family and was the wife of George Stewkley (d 1508). There was a further alliance between the Stewkleys and the Luttrells when Joan Stewkley, the daughter of Hugh Stewkley, named after her great-grandmother, married George Luttrell. Joan Stewkley is shown as a recumbent effigy on the Jacobean tomb and therefore quite near to the tomb slab of her great-great- grandmother, Elizabeth Luttrell.

The office of lay rector as defined in the *Oxford Dictionary of the Christian Church* is: "In the C of E, a layman receiving the rectorial tithes of a benefice. By custom he enjoys the right to the chief seat in the chancel of the parish church for himself and his family and the freehold of the whole church, but this gives him no right of possession or of entering it when not open for divine service. He also has the duty of repairing the chancel, for the neglect of which he may be sued in the county court. He may compound for this liability, however, with the Board of Finance subject to the approval of the Diocesan Dilapidations Board."[50]

When Hugh Stewkley acquired the rectory of Dunster, he became responsible for the repair of the chancel, and correspondingly entitled to the chief seat therein.[51] Lyte wrote: "It seems that five members of the Stewkley family were buried in the chancel of the priory church. By a will dated January 1587 Hugh left the following instructions: "if he should die in Somerset, he should be buried in the Priory Church of Dunster over against his own seat or pew, or else in the church of Carhampton near his parents"[52] His death in Somerset is confirmed by the register and he was buried in Dunster church. There is a delightful heraldic brass to the memory of his wife, Elizabeth, who was also buried in the chancel. The three children of Hugh and Elizabeth Stewkley, George Stewkley of Dunster their younger son and their daughters, Margaret and Joan, wife of George Luttrell, all left directions that they should be buried near their parents. Joan's will was made in April 1613. Lyte writes: "she and her husband had doubtless been allowed to occupy a seat in the chancel."[53]

In 1571, Thomas Luttrell, the elder, died and his son and heir, George, then only eleven years of age, became the ward of Hugh Stewkley of Marshtown, near Dunster. It will perhaps be remembered that it was Hugh Stewkley who was given a day's grace to provide one demi-lance and two light horsemen at the Hundred of Carhampton muster during the 1583 preparations made in Somerset against the armada of 1588. Stewkley was required to supply this deficiency "havinge made defalt at this muster."[54] George Luttrell was not in default at this muster but was given one day to meet the same requirements as Stewkley. His mother had died three years before so the entry reads: "George Lutterell esq. who nowe ys, to supplie the place of the ladie Lutterell deceased."[55] In 1586 under the heading, 'the names of those persons charged to find horses at the West part of Somerset'[56] we again find the names of George Luttrell and Hugh Stewkley, referred to as armigers, and the same requirements as before.

There was no doubt a shortage of money in the latter half of the 16th century and that the clergy were reduced and impoverished. After the chantries were abolished the money and gifts provided by the guild members with such generosity for their parish churches dried up. After 1547 there was never more than one priest and in 1566 when the complaint was made against Hugh Stewkley, they had not enjoyed the services of any priest for five years. Lyte tell us that 'it seems doubtful whether anyone had received a definite appointment there since the death of John Ryce, the Vicar, in 1561'.[57]

In 1566 the difficulties which arose between Hugh Stewkley and fourteen of the inhabitants of Dunster were as follows: "We of the foresaid towne and borough of Dunster have in oure churche ben verie well and orderlie served with suche devine service as ought to be, untill that here of late one Master Hewgh Stuclie, gentilman pourchased of oure sovereyne ladie the Quine the personage of the same, being not so lytell worthe as one hunderethe marks by the yeare, to the whiche tythes and other duties of the churche are solie paied, and nothing reserved or allowed for the fyndinge of a curat to serve the cure but onlie eight poundes being paied out of the saide personage, which pention is not sufficient for the mayntenennce of a curat, so that by the same means the cure of Dunster aforesaide, being the hed churche of the Denerie and having heretofore thre curates continuallie therein serving, is now altogether unserved, to the infringinge of the Quine's majestie's prosedinge and great disquiet of us her lovinge subjects."[58]

Hugh Stewkley was, in fact, a grasping lawyer, who only allowed £8 per annum as a salary for a curate out of extensive holdings and tithes. This was not enough to attract an applicant and the Dunster people were aggrieved that formerly they had had three curates and now could not afford the services of one. The three curates referred to in the manifesto were the vicar and chaplains of the pre-Reformation chantry chapels of St Lawrence and the Holy Trinity and were the spiritual pastors offering guidance to the guilds of these chapels. The chantry chapel of St Lawrence being in the south-east aisle and that of the Holy Trinity in the north-west aisle. In1509 John Gryme of Frackford in Dunster described a certain Sir John Holcomb, who was not the Vicar of the parish, as his confessor and "curate" there.[59]

We do not know what Hugh Stewkley replied to the manifesto of 1566, it has not survived the passage of time, but it is highly likely that he questioned the assertion that the rectory was worth more than a hundred marks, or £66.13s.4d a year. In 1535 it had been valued at £17.5s. 8d gross. At the time the vicar's salary accounted for £4.13s.4d of this sum and two years after the surrender of the priory, in1539 it was valued at £7.2s.3d net when the vicar's salary had been ostensibly increased to £8 but he no longer received food gratis at the priory[60] as he had formerly done.

John Gryme bequeathed a considerable sum to the fabric of Dunster church and his widow left money specifically to the repair of the aisle of the Holy Trinity. Bettey explains the arrangements very clearly in his book *Church & Community*. He tells us that: "a chantry was essentially an endowment, generally of lands from which the income went to pay a priest to say masses every day for the repose of the soul of the founder and for the souls of all departed. The great majority of people, who were unable to afford the very heavy expenditure of founding a private chantry, could nonetheless participate in the benefits by joining a gild or association and sharing in the communal or gild chantry. Private gild chantries were commonly established inside parish churches or in chapels or aisles attached to parish churches…The number of altars which formerly existed in parish churches can often still be seen from the 'piscina' at which the priest washed his hands and cleaned the sacred vessels during mass, and which survive in many parish churches in side chapels, aisles and occasionally, in the nave or even in the tower."[61]

Procedure had dramatically changed since the suppression of the chantries and the prior and convent of Bath had retired from active participation. Formerly they had presented 'successive Vicars of Dunster to the Bishop for institution as to a benefice'.[62] Now the rector, as lay impropriator had the duty of providing a stipendary curate whose position seems to have been insecure for he was removable at the pleasure of the lay rector and was not instituted by the bishop. There was no residence provided for him and hardly any endowment.

The poor curate in charge of the parish had no vicarage and we read: "We have no vicaridge, neither hath there been any this many years. There is a little garden containing one yeard of ground or near thereabout. Sir George Speke's land lyeth on the west end, and the widow Foxe's land lyeth on the east ende, and the churcheyard on the north side and the highway on the south side adjoyning. There is one meadow containing three yards of ground or near thereabout lying near the Castle on the east side and a river of water on the other side. The Minister hath eight pounds per annum, beside the aforesaid meadow and garden, and not anything else."[63] As Lyte comments: "From the Curate's point of view, the only redeeming feature of the case was that, as Dunster was not accounted as an ecclesiastical benefice, he was free to hold another church without dispensation. In time, various small additions were made to the emoluments of the Curate."[64]

Dame Margaret Luttrell became a widow in 1538. Sir Andrew made a will dated 14 April 1538 and died a few weeks later on 4 May 1538. He was buried at East Quantoxhead since he was 'of the parish of East Quantock'[65] and resided at the manor house. The tomb erected on his instructions bears inscriptions to his memory and that of his father, Sir Hugh Luttrell K.B. The three shields on the lower part of the tomb are the Luttrell shield, the shield of Luttrell impaling Hill, for Sir Hugh Luttrell's first wife, Margaret Hill and Luttrell impaling Wyndham[66] for Sir Andrew's wife, Margaret Wyndham. When Dame Margaret died in 1580, forty-two years after her husband, she was of a great age. She too was buried at East Quantoxhead, beside her husband and her father-in-law. Her portrait hangs in Dunster Castle. In his will, Sir Andrew made many bequests. A silver cup was bequeathed to Thomas Cromwell, 'so that he should be "a good lord"' to the testator's wife and children,[67] and £5 for the purchase of a chalice for the church at East Quantoxhead. He left instructions that his body be interred in the chancel of the church, 'before the picture of Our Lady at the north end of the high altar, under the tomb and window to be made there.'[68] To the high altar he left 20s 'for tithes overlooked'. He also made bequests to Wells, London and Bridgwater, recorded by Lyte in the following terms: "He also left another 20s to the mother church of St Andrew at Wells, and 40s to the Carthusians in London for two solemn obits with two dirges. The Friars Minor of Bridgewater (sic) were to receive 20s a year for three years for solemn obits for his soul, the souls of his parents and the soul of a certain Hugh Trot."[69].

At East Quantoxhead, a trentall, or set of thirty masses for the repose of the soul of the departed, was said on the day of Sir Andrew's burial and thirty priests undertook the task. The poor were to receive money and this practice was to be repeated on the first anniversary of his death. Five priests were engaged for a year to sing mass every day for his soul, and Wednesdays and Fridays were devoted to special prayers. Each priest was paid £6 13s 4d annually and was provided with singing-bread, wine, candles, vestments and books.[70] Legacies were left to a godson and to servants of the East Quantoxhead household. Sir Andrew and Lady Margaret had four sons and four daughters. "To his eldest son, John Luttrell, he left all his raiment and his bows and arrows, and to his wife, Lady Margaret, all the rest of his goods, upon condition that she should surrender them if she should marry again. Each of his younger children was to have a fortune of 400 marks, the sons at the age of twenty-one and the daughters at eighteen."[71] These children were, Thomas, who succeeded his brother John, Nicholas of Honibere, in the parish of Lilstock who was born c.1532 and was the ancestor of the Luttrells of Hartland Abbey and Staunton Court, both in Devonshire, and the younger son, Andrew mentioned in his father's will. The girls were Margaret, who married Peter Edgcumbe of Mount Edgcumbe in Devonshire (d 1607), Honor who married Edward Barrow, Cecily (d 1566) who married Richard Rogers of Bryanston, Dorset, and Elizabeth (died c.1561), who married firstly Richard Malet of Currypool in Charlinch and secondly Sir George Speke, K.B. of Whitelackington. The third son Nicholas should have received money and plate under the will of his mother, Dame Margaret Luttrell who died 1580. This included a gilt cup and cover bearing the arms of Luttrell and Wyndham, but since his sister Margaret Edgcumbe and her husband appear to have purloined it, he was forced to bring a suit against them. Earlier he had also been involved in litigation concerning the manor of Honibere in the parish of Lilstock, which he eventually obtained from the Crown in 1562.[72]

CHAPTER SEVEN

SIR JOHN LUTTRELL
IN SCOTLAND
– THE ALLEGORICAL PAINTING
– THE LUTTRELL TABLE CARPET

THE SCOTTISH wars of the mid 15th century concerned the French king, Henri Deux's ambitions to make Scotland a province of France and it was Mary Stewart, daughter of James V of Scotland and Marie de Guise, who was the pawn in the political struggle. The question of her marriage to either Prince Edward, the only son of Henry VIII and Jane Seymour, or to the dauphin of France, was the crux of the dispute; each faction desired to secure a political advantage by a marital alliance. On 1 July 1543, the Peace of Greenwich was made between England and Scotland and it was agreed that Mary Stewart, who was but seven months old, should marry the aforesaid Edward. The baby's grandmother was Margaret, a sister of Henry VIII. The treaties were ratified at Holyroodhouse, one of which was a peace treaty and the other concerned the proposed marriage of Mary Stewart and Prince Edward. Henry, however, broke the peace and seized Scottish ships in the Thames. The Scots retaliated and by 11 December, their parliament repudiated the English treaties.[1] The king would not brook any threat to his suzerainty and by the spring of 1544, Edward Seymour, earl of Hertford, the brother of Jane Seymour was in Scotland and was instructed to obliterate all resistance by the sword or fire. The horrific result was the burning of Edinburgh, Holyroodhouse and Leith and the devastation of their environs.[2] It was at Leith that, in May 1544, John Luttrell was knighted by the earl of Hertford; this was immediately after the capture and burning of Edinburgh and was the last occasion on which a knighthood was bestowed on a member of the Luttrell family of Dunster until Sir Walter Luttrell was knighted in 1994.

There were West Country ties between John Luttrell and Edward Seymour, earl of Hertford, which concerned the manor of Avill whose lands lay contiguous with those of the barony of Avill. Between 1536-39 this manor was held by Edward Seymour and his wife Anne. Seymour's rival, John Dudley, Viscount Lisle, earl of Warwick and later duke of Northumberland, had in 1531 conveyed the manor to feofees; a temporary measure, it would appear, until it was sold to Sir Edward Seymour who was deposed in 1550 and executed in 1552. Avill had come to John Dudley through his mother Elizabeth Grey, daughter of Edward, Viscount Lisle by Elizabeth Talbot, his wife, who had married firstly Edmund Dudley, John's father. Edmund Dudley was speaker of the House of Commons, author of the 'Tree of Commonwealth' and was executed for treason in 1510. On Dudley's death, his widow Elizabeth married Arthur Plantagenet and he, through his wife, was created Viscount Lisle in 1523. The association with the Luttrells was made manifest in

1530 when Arthur, Viscount Lisle paid 50s to John Luttrell's father, Sir Andrew Luttrell, by way of a relief on half a fee.[3]

In 1547 Sir John Luttrell again crossed the Border with the earl of Hertford, now duke of Somerset, and was present at the battle of Pinkie where he led three hundred men in the vanguard of the English forces. A week after the battle he was also one of those chosen to remain behind and occupy a strong point. He was placed in command of the island of Inchcolm in the Firth of Forth and 'the Augustinian canons who inhabited it had to evacuate it, removing to Donisbristle.'[4] A contemporary satirical account of the substitution of soldiers for canons of the Augustinian order was written by the military judge, William Patten, as follows: "Sir John Luttrell, knight, having bene, by my Lordes grace and counsell, elect abbot, by God's sufferance, of the monastery of Saint Coomes Ins afore remembered, in the afternoon of this day (Saturday, 17th September) departed towards the island, to be stalled in his see thear accordingly; and had with him coovent of 100 hakbutters and 50 pioneers to kepe his house and land thear, and 2 rowe barkes well furnished with ammunition, and 70 mariners for them to kepe his waters; whereby it is thought he shall soon becum a prelate of great power. Ther perfytness of his religion is not alwaies to tarry at home, but sumtime to rowe out abrode a visitacion, and, when he goithe, I have heard say, he taketh alweyes his sumners in barke with hym, which are very open mouthed and never talk but they are heard a mile of, so that either for loove of his blessynges or fear of his cursinges, he is like to be souveraigne over most part of his neighbours."[5] The reference to 'sumners' is a pun, they were officers of courts of law, also pieces of artillery.

Sir John Luttrell did not have an easy time on the island of Inchcolm and the English commanders became anxious about the garrison then established in the old abbey. He became surrounded and beleaguered by Scottish ships and boats commanded by an abbot and one James Dogge, who were sure that they could capture the rock although they never actually made an assault. Nevertheless, Sir John was undermanned and impotent to face the onslaught of two warships of 80 tons. He deplored the fact that he could not attack and that thereby he lost prizes which would have paid the expenses of the garrison for four or five months. His ship, the Sacré, had been sent to England to obtain timber, coal and other necessities and on 2 November 1547 he wrote: "There ys nothinge, thatt grevys me so myche as that I cannott have on suyche shyppe, wythe my pynnays, as the *Wyllyby* ys … .wyche yf I had had, the prisys that I have lost wold have paid ther chargys for 4 or 5 monythys."[6]

The only ship he had was the *Double Rose* which was 'lytell and open'.[7] Also on 2 November 1547 Sir John Luttrell wrote to Protector Somerset and told him of a French two-masted ship, or, as he wrote, 'of 2 toppys' that had failed to reach harbour at low tide. He related that the pinnace from Inchcolm: "bett herr wyth herr artyllerye and shotte so often thoroghe and alongeshypp of the Frenche menne that they gave greate cryes wythynn borde and ranne herr ashore agaynst the chapyl att Lythe, where the pynnys bett herr still thorow wythyn poynte blancke, and had broft herr awaye yf hitt hadd nott bynne for the number of botys that laye under the Frenche mannys foreship."[8] Although the pinnace from Inchcolm had inflicted so much damage on the French ship and apparently terrified the crew, the Scots came to the rescue and 'mounted on the shore two pieces of brass and ten large iron pieces of artillery, and so drove off the pinnace and her boat.'[9] To Sir John's chagrin the French ship was towed into harbour at high tide and he was deprived of the booty which consisted of wine and other commodities with which the ship was laden, and which was destined for the Governor of Leith.[10]

One of the greatest hardships Sir John and his men suffered was cold and the lack of fuel and he somewhat sarcastically averred that: "I am macchyd wythe suyche stobborne neyhbors that yf I be a colde, they gyve me leve (to) blowe my fyngers, whose gentylnes, as I maye, I shall ryght well accquytt, and the better whenseover hitt shall please the Concell tapoynt me wherwytheall."[11] The intention to take revenge on those who told him to blow on his fingers is evident and in another letter he tells how he was driven to burn two boats for fuel: and then to skirmish on the Forth for more. He wrote: "I have bynne dryvenn to burne too botys, to cutt downe and burne 2 or thre lytell treys thatt grew aboute the howse, and yett yn thend have benn fayne to goo to the Fyfe syde to scyrmyshe wythe them for to gett owte some of theyr botes to burne, whe I have lost 2 of my menn."[12] On the arrival of an English ship he appears to have thought it wise to reduce his garrison, and he sent away all the pioneers and kept with him on Inchcolm only a few men to carry out repairs, 'to make doors, iron work and walls to support platforms' and some very "simple" soldiers.'[13]

The provision of supplies to Inchcolm was a precarious business and, although in November 1547 Lord Grey of Wilton, previously in charge of the cavalry beaten off by Archibald Douglas in the first flush of Scottish success before their annihilation at Pinkie, now ordered the master of ordnance at Newcastle to send certain specified munitions to Inchcolm. Some of them went astray before they reached their destination. An inventory of the arms on the island reveals a sorry state of affairs for an iron culverin is described as 'broken at the mouth' and a demi-culverin as 'full of honycombes and blow' so that 'none dare shute it.'[14] At the end of November, although the council made certain orders for the reinforcement of necessary supplies to Sir John he was, nevertheless, instructed to use his ship, the Double Rose to protect and fortify the western side of the island and, surely an unnecessary bequest, to 'economize his powder.'[15] The pessimistic view was that it was questionable if supplies could be sent from Tay to Inchcolm more frequently than once a month during the winter months.[16]

The military service rendered by Sir John in this desolate and ill-provisioned place was readily acknowledged by Lord Grey who wrote on 8 January 1548 to Protector Somerset as follows: "It maie please your Grace. It hath bene by dyvers showed unto me of the forwardnes of service of Sir John Luttrell. And having this present daie receyved from hym intelligence of his proceedinges in those parties, I thought good to signefie thereof to your Grace, whereby the same maie perceyve howe willingly he escueth idelnes, and dayly studdyeth for thannoyanceof his yll neighbours. Fyrst, he wryteth howe before Crystmasse, he sent a lytle boote he hath, wiche roweth with six oores, unto the north ferry, in the nyght, where he tooke the ferrie boote harde from the towne, wiche boote wyll lande well 80 men. He wryteth also howe twoo daies before Crysmasse, he landyd at Aberdoorie, skyrmyshed with them and burnt a house harde at the townes ende; but the contrey came so faste upon them that they war compelled to retyer. On Crysmasse daie in the nyght, he gave them a camysado at the north ferrye, and burnt all the towne, but most parte of the men fled, and for hast lefte ther geldinges behinde, whiche war slayne and burnt in a house they thought to kepe. The thirde daie after Christmasse, he landyd at Burnt Ilande and brent certayne bootes in the pyer and all suche howses as they had newe buylt there, where he had three prowde onsettes gyven by the Skottes; yet he repulsed them, and at the same (time) slewe 16 of them and, as he thinke, many hurte with shott; after the wiche he went to a castle that standeth on the weste part of the ilande, and out of the same there rendered unto hym a riche man and his sonne who dwelled in it, and hath brought them both with hym, and had the hoole spoyll of the house, and so retorned and mett with one hundred freshe Skottes wiche cam from Kynghorne, thinking to have putt our men from there bootes, but they safely embarked and with there shott hurte and slewe dyvers of the Skottes; and of our men twoo hurte."[17]

So much for our illustrious forebears who received accolades for deeds of wanton destruction and infamous cruelty. Doubtless, the Scots were no better and that this was the general conduct of war throughout Europe. Lyte remarks these 'details... are of some interest as illustrations of the manner in which the English were trying to subdue the

Scots.'[18] He wryly comments: "Thomas Wyndham, Sir John Luttrell's half-uncle, distinguished himself by burning a convent, and bringing away the nuns and the gentlemen's daughters who were at school there."[19]

In February, 1548, it was decided to abandon the stronghold of Inchcolm and the garrison left on the *Mary Hamborough* and, beset by storms, set forth for Broughty Craig. Before leaving Sir John carried out Somerset's instructions and destroyed the fortifications and the house leaving it useless to the enemy as a fort or habitation. On 1 March they arrived off the Tay with all they had been able to transport in the way of munitions, victuals, planks and timber. There was little storage space and Sir John was forced to abandon and burn timber and planks; to say nothing of biscuit, cheese and beer 'wyche yndede was suyche and so yll that no manne myght occupye'; (i.e. use it). He had suffered a set back because one of the 'hoyes', or small rigged sloops, used for the conveyance of goods and passengers along the waterways, which had been consigned for his use by the vice-admiral had taken off on another route to 'some part' of England and since it was one that could accommodate the greatest load, he was unable to remove all he had wished to take with him.

He wrote this letter in March 1548 to Somerset concerning the evacuation: "Accordinge unto your plesure by yowr late letters adresyd, I have ruynatyd the fortfycatyonne off Combys Ynche and the howse ther bothe in suyche sorte as thenymye shall by the same nether receyve comodyte ner force; and frome thence aryvyd yn thys ryver off Taye the fyrst of Marche, wythe suyche munytyon, vytayle, planke and tymber as I myght thenn transporte, havynge so lytell stoage for the same, for wher the vyz admirall here hadd apoyntyd certeyne plates or hoyes unto me for to shyppe the same, on the gretyst burdyn of thos toke another course ynto sume part of Ynglonde, by reason wheof I was enforcyd as well to burne suyche tymber and planke as I was ther dryvyne to leve, and a portyon of byscet, cheyse and bere, wyche yndede was suyche and so yll as no manne myght occupye."[20]

Sir John went with Sir Thomas Palmer to Dundee where he was to take command. The idea was abandoned because it was found to be impracticable to build a fortress dominating the town. Instead Sir John was given the command of a new hillside fort situated near Broughty Craig. Sir John seems not to have been dismayed by his new appointment and had little regard for the place to which he was sent. He only concerned himself to take trouble over the king's affairs and to please Somerset. He writes as follows: "…as on that nether have respecte to placys nor what paynys I take in cacys wher I do the Kinges majeste servys and content your Grace."[21] Again, two days later, he writes: "I truste I shall employe myselfe so yn settyng forwarde of the workes as shalbe to your Gracys contentatyonne, not dowting butt that I shall yelde a good accompt of the same, yf famyn do not more hurt thenne feare of other attemptes."[22]

To carry out all the tasks on the new fort near Broughty Craig, he needed supplies and on 11 April, 1548, he wrote a request to Sir Thomas Holcroft and Sir Francis Leake for 'biscuit, beer, butter, horses, carts, masons and money.'[23] On April 30 he wrote a very long letter to Somerset[24]: "Wheras hytt aperyd unto me by yowr Gracys letters addressyd unto me by my brother and beringe date the 22 of Februarye thatt artyffycers were comandyd hyther att that present, may hytt pleas your Grace to understand ther ys nott one aryvyd here as yett, besyde the want of whome the gretyst laccke of all ys nott as yett suplyed, wyche ys of vyttallys, spetyallye of byscett and drinke, I meane suyche proportyone as ys requysit for a somer's store, and, sondrye wyndes bringe overslypt, ther ys yett no hope of their aryvall herr untyll the last howre, and thenn how the wynd and passage shall prove yowr Grace know ys dowtfull. I cannot butt jugge a great fawt yn yowr Gracys mynesters and comysyoners of the northe part, wheryn yf remedye be no hadd, all my travaylle here maye lytell suffyce. Whatt commodyte is ther fownde yn the raysynge of the bulwerkes here and turfynge of the same, whenn, for the laccke of a few masons and nessessarys for them, the same fallys dayle downe and fyllys the dykes agayne, as even presently the ester part of the northe est bullwerke ys fallyn downe, with suyche abundance of yerthe that the powre of a hundrythe cannons could nott make a more perillus breache? The powre soldyers here ar enforcyd to suyche a nyghtlye wacche and dayle travayll withall as I darr saye yn tyme of seyge ytt canne be no whytt greater, by reasone wheref they fall dayle syccke, so as att thys present there ys ysn the fort and castell welner a hundrythe syccke and not able to come unto the wallys … Consyder the travayle of the powre menn having nothinge butt salt meates. As for my part, yf hytt wolde pleas yowr Grace tapoynt a ,amme pf suyche dyscretion as yow myght better trust, I wolde rather trayle the pyke agayne as a soldyer under hyme then havinge charge and wantynge credytt. Besyde the lose of fortyfynge for laccke wherwithall, I canne neyther have powder, ledd, not any other want supplyed thatt I have wryttenn for. As for herkebusys, here ys not thre able to serve nor one thatt wylbe sent. Macccche the powre menn have benne enforcyd to make of ther shyrtes, welnere thys 3 monythys, and not yett sent. Monytyone also for fyar worke nor cresset lyght I canne gett none, to se the dykes cleryd yn the nyght, werbye the Scottys come nyghtly ynto my dykes. I am suar yf yowf Grace knew how the powre soldyers here ar dyscoragyd with ther aforsayd travayle and myserye, yow wold bothe of yowr pryncelye goodnes pyte them, and dowt the ynconvenyence thatt may folowe of hytt. Thaye saye they have servyd 18 monythes and never hadd throghe paye, which ys a great tyme. I am, yowr Grace knowys, butt one manne amonges them, and nottwithstandinge thatt I have and do kepe them yn suyche awe and obedyence thatt thaye darr nott utter ther seccrett murmuringes, I am fayne to seme nott to hyar all, and, havinge myselfe the same want thay have, they ar content to take lyke paynys with me, for ther purse and table ys bothe furnyshyd as myne ys, and bycawse they se I am also partaker of ther wacche and travayle, they do the lesse complayne. I wold wyshe yowr Grace shuld send rather att the fyrst 200 menne to myche thenn so many to few. I juge 400 handsome soldyers, and all haccbuters were the lest, besyde on hundrythe masons, wheref 50 tesyde quaryers, and good store of pycckaxys, with style and ashe ynoghe for helvys, all manner of other monytyon lykewyse, as barows, bascekettes, crowys and 2 able fornyshed cartes with horsys, att the last 2 or thre hoyes also laden with strawe, with wyche I wyll rayse the utter part of the worke att lest 5 fote … .The Scottes and Frenchemenne here determyne to take hytt owt of hande. Thabbbott of Pasle came hyther with 2 anseynys of Frenchemenn from Jedworthe to scale the forte, and broght with hyme all hys adherentes off Fyfe, so thatt, as I exteme, with Frenche and Scottys, they were 2 thowsand fotemenn and 500 horse, which thaye preparyd to kepe the pasage betwyne the fort and the castell, to thend thatt whenn the powder here shuld have benne brent, ther myght no freshe relyfe be hadd from benethe. Whenn the howre apoyntyd came, I had preparyd 2 demy barrelles of powder, wich I fyryd yn the dyke, with wich then Scottys gave a sodenne showte; butt whenn they should have come to the sawt (assault), as farr as we withyn myught understand, thaye begann to stryve who shuld come fyrst and nott beinge agreyd therapponne thay thoght hytt better to retyre agayne with wett cotes thenn to cleme wallys, and so retyryd; my lorde of Dunkelles lordeshippe being myche ashamyd hys empryse (enterprise) toke no better succes. And yn ded I sent hyme suyche a moccke the same mornynge by my drome to Dunde thatt hys sprytuall patyence was myche ofendyd withall."[25]

At about the same time as Sir John Luttrell wrote this letter to Proctector Somerset, the English built up-to-date defences at Haddington which afforded them a vantage point only eighteen miles from Edinburgh. Somerset's victory seven months earlier, at Pinkie, far from furthering the terms of the Treaty of Greenwich and ensuring the marriage of Mary Stuart, queen of Scots, to Edward VI, had the effect of driving the Scots into the arms of France. In May, 1548 the French arrived at Leith with 6,000 armed men under the command of the sieur d'Essé. Their numbers were further increased by the Scots who joined them with 5,000 men under the command of James Hamilton, earl of Arran and the siege of Haddington was underway.[26]

On 20 June Sir John Luttrell reported to the Protector. He was in good heart and in answer to his pleas, supplies had been sent and his men had abundant victuals though the drink supply was questionable. Still, as he said, 'there was an abundance of good water![27] They had engaged the enemy which had arrived off the coast of Fife with sixteen galleys and 'a bryggandyn, havinge a lytell Scottyshe bote for ther gyde.'[28] So, the little Scottish boat had guided the sixteen galleys and Sir John gleefully reports that, "…he had greeted them with 'the fyrst salve, wyche the lykyd so yll' that they withdrew."[29] Daily harassments were made by 500 or 600 horsemen and such foot soldiers as the surrounding countryside could provide but Sir John and his men led them such a dance that they soon abstained from coming within a mile of the fort and, in spite of provocation, he refused to be lured into skirmishes with them. He had so heavily defended the fort that unless they brought ladders it was impossible to scale the new works which had been heightened with turves. On the water side of the castle he had erected a platform and encased its walls in a structure of lopped trees six feet thick. The turves required were considerable and since two "plowys and oxen" and eighteen horses …were constantly employed in carrying turf,[30] the size of the fort must have been extensive. Needless to say, the ploughs and oxen had been purloined from the, no doubt, aggrieved peasantry.

In his letter of complaint to the Protector of 30 April 1548 Sir John had written about the plight of the soldiery. He had said that he was sure that if his Grace knew how the poor soldiers were discouraged with their travails and misery, he would, of his princely goodness, pity them. He also seems to have warned the Protector of the troubles that might arise among the discontented men whom he said complained that they had served for eighteen months and had never been fully paid. He said he was but one man among so many and although he had kept them in such awe and state of obedience to him, so they dare not voice their inner discontent, he pretended not to hear their secret murmurings. He had the same needs as they had and they were contented to take the same pay. Their expenses and provisions were the same as his and because he shared in their watches and their misfortunes they complained less.[31] It seems that Lord Grey of Wilton disputed the question of the soldiers' pay for he wrote to the Protector as follows: "I have dyvers tymes requyred Sir John Luttrell that, in the depeche of his souldiours or laborers, he wolde eyther paie them throughly or sende me worde of the true debte unto them, so as nether the poore may be enwronged, nor the Kinges majestie further burdened then reason is, and yet now agayne here is arryved 30 or 40 poore laborers, syckly and weake, who saith they be not payd any one peny syns I sent them thither, nor bring with them any pasporte or other declaration of their due."[32]

Protector Somerset thought highly of Sir John Luttrell, in spite of Grey's complaints and he 'highly commended' his 'good service'. He was formally authorized to negotiate with the earl of Argyll who, it was thought, might be susceptible to English gold.[33] Edward Seymour relentlessly pursued his course and appealed to the German emperor, Charles V for help to further his designs against the Scots. This was a dangerous move because a military presence in the form of an advance guard was just what the emperor wanted in order to interfere in England as he was doing everywhere else on the Continent. As a result of Somerset's appeal to Charles V, German mercenaries were despatched to fight in Scotland. They were more reliable than the English who it was said were 'apt to fraternize with the Scots, and particularly, as fellow-peasants, to dislike firing their harvest and ripening crops.'[34]

Of the particular incidents associated with Sir John Luttrell recorded by Lyte who wrote: "In the autumn of 1548, Luttrell had several sharp skirmishes with Sir David Graham in

Fintrie and other neighbours, and killed a considerable number of the soldiers and townsmen who were holding Dundee. In one of his forays, he captured the eldest son and the nephew of the laird of Panmure, tenn hakbutters, nore than 700 "white beasts" and 120 "horned beasts."[35] On the 7th of November, some English ships in the Tay landed men at Dundee and, with assistance from Sir John Luttrell, drove out the townsmen. As soon, however, as the soldiers began to loot the place, James Dogge fell upon them and drove them out in turn, with a loss of thirty killed. The English recaptured the town the next day, but abandoned it very shortly.[36] On the 3rd of December, the Earl of Angus and the Rhinegrave, with 50 lances and 200 light horsemen, appeared before Broughty Craig, and Sir John Luttrell, "seeing that they sought some pastime," sallied out with thirty horse and some footmen. After some skirmishing, the Rhinegrave retired and tried to lead the English into an ambush. Luttrell had, however, forseen such a scheme and had stationed some signalmen in the fort, to watch the movements of the enemy. Duly informed by them, he retired to a hill and there gallantly defended himself against superior numbers until reinforcements, hidden behind the hill, came up. The enemy was thus caught in the trap which they had prepared for him. Panic-stricken they fled, and their leaders could not induce them to stop until they were safe within the town of Dundee. The pursuit would have been more effective if the English captain had had more than thirty horsemen, but nevertheless he had reason to be satisfied with the day's work. A young French gentleman was found dead on the field. Eighteen of the Germans met their fate in the River Dighty and many more on dry land. Sixteen of them and two Scots were taken prisoners. Many, including the Rhinegrave himself, were wounded. The details of this affair come, curiously enough, from a Spanish source.[37]

On 22 January 1549 Sir John Luttrell wrote to Edward Seymour, duke of Somerset and addressed the Protector in these words: "I have receyved, with the last convoye of victualles that cam hether, a letter from my mother,[38] wich I have sent yower Grace enclosed herein, to thend that, seing the good offer she hath made me for thadvauncement of my poore levyng, it might the rather please yower Grace's pryncelye honour to fordre me therein. Wich doing, I shall be the abler to serve the Kynges majestie and yower Grace, as one that dowteth not to shewe myself so as yower Grace shall perseyve both that and all the rest that I possesse shall be bent always unto his maister's servyce-so as it might please yower Grace to serve hyr fanceye and my commodyte at thys tyme for my commyng home presentlye. And because yower Grace shall the better perceyve the offer that she hath made me, may it please yower Grace to understand that the manor of Myniett (Minehead) that she promyseth me, is 120*l* by the yeere, besydes that hyr joynter is almost 300 marke with hyr demeynes, as I gesse it, wich wyll be, as yower Grace maye consydre, a great advauncement of my poore levyng, besyde the helpe that I shall procure at hyr handes, and my mother in lawes,[39] for the payment of my dettes, wich I shold not take now when it is offred me, I never loke to come unto it. For iff shee shold take a fancye in hyr head to marrye, I were utterlye undone!" "Notwithstandyng my busynes with my mother, I wyll in the meane tyme so furnyssh myselfe with horse and harnes that, in the begynyng of this somer, my trust is I wyll be in as good order to serve yower Grace in the feld as no gentylman, I trust, in all Ingland shall be better of my abyllyte and power. "Humblye desyryng yower Grace in the meane tyme to heere my humble sute, for, besyde the goodnes of my mother unto me, I have a great deal of monye to paye unto my creditours, for whome I must provyde payment, or otherwyse it wyll be more to my dyspleasure then I maye well beare."[40]

Sir John was requesting leave of absence for a few months in order to settle his debts and to see his mother who had promised him the manor of Minehead which was worth £120 per annum. This was to the detriment of his younger brothers and sisters since the late Sir Andrew it would appear had made a charge on the manor to their benefit. Although

Dame Margaret's letter has now disappeared this pecuniary liability was now to be removed. Dame Margaret was both powerful and rich and the provision made for her during her widowhood brought in 300 marks from the landed estates. She owned a vessel of 100 tons and had consolidated the holdings of her family by purchasing Dunster priory in 1539. Sir John also had expectations from his mother-in-law and it was imperative that he should 'strike while the iron was hot' for all would be lost if his mother decided to marry again. In the event Sir John was to survive only for another two and a half years and his mother outlived him by twenty-nine years and her husband by more than forty years.

Leave of absence was not granted. He had declared that he would return to serve Protector Somerset in the early summer of 1549 furnished with 'horse and harnes' and better able to serve his Grace in the field so that no gentleman in England 'shall be better of my abyllyte and power'. He was, however, valued as much as a diplomatist as a soldier and was one of two commissioners appointed: "to treat with the Earls of Argyll, Athol and Errol and others, with a view to the expulsion of the French from Scotland, and a marriage between Edward then Sixth and Queen Mary."[41] These negotiations were fruitless. Edward VI kept a journal in which he recorded that Sir John, in a raid "burned several villages and took prisoner a certain Monsieur de Toge."[42]

In June 1549 the French, under their new commander, the seigneur de Termes, appeared at Dumbarton with 1,300 men. "The English held on with tenacity, and though they slowly lost their strong-points, they kept Haddington until they deliberately evacuated it in September1549."[43] Although spasmodic warfare persisted, there were greater concerns to occupy the English, for war broke out between England and France on 9 August 1549. Haddington was deliberately abandoned and Broughty Craig fell. The Scots aided and abetted by their French allies, made a serious attack on the Craig early in 1550. The French were very experienced but the Scots were said to be "behind the age of both in raising and the besieging of fortified places."[44]

Lyte records the events which followed this attack, in the same year: "Monsieur de Thermes, with the assistance of the Governour quha accompaneit him in all his interprices, came forduarte to the toune of Dundie in the beginning of Fabruar; quhair having prepared sic thingis as wes necessar for the seiging of the fort, he laid the battre thairto apoun the south eist pairt thairof, and cuttit away all moyens, passages and intelligences betuix the fort and the castell of Broughtie, so the fort culd haif no kinde of ayd nor releyf frome the sey; and eftir the same was doung doun with gret ordinance, the assailt was gevin thairto, baithe with the Scottis and Frenche men the xx day of Fabruar; quhair the Inglismen maid resistance and defence at the first entering, bot thay war so curageouslie and stoutlie assailyet that thai war dung frome the wallis, and the most part of thame all quhilk was within the fort war slayne, and the rest taikin presoners. The nixt day, the Inglismen quha kepit the castell of Broughtie, fering the like to cum to thame, randerit the castell, having onlie thair liffis saif. So that haill cuntrey wes clenged of the Inglismen immediatlie."[45]

The behaviour of the Scots appalled even the French. They gave no quarter and three English chroniclers, Hayward, Kennet and Stowe, who place the fall of Broughty Craig, two months earlier than Lesley, state that 'the Scots slew all the defenders except Sir John Luttrell, whom they took prisoner.[46] Negotiations ensued over the ransom and release of Sir John. On 5 March 1550 the Warden of the East and Middle Marches was ordered by the council at Westminster: "to do what he can for the delyvery of Mr Luttrell, and, at his arryval, to helpe him with money for his cummyng wich shalbe repayed."[47]

The Scots in the East March had become 'sworn Englishmen'.[48] Following on the order, the Wardens issued a warrant for £400 'for the raunsom of Mr Luttrell and others taken at Browghty Crag'.[49] Hostages were in their turn hostages for the opposing side so that members of the Gordon clan were held firstly by the English for important Scotsmen. Presumably it was after the release of the important Scotsmen, that the Gordons were further held and were sent to Sir John Luttrell's half-uncle, Thomas Wyndham 'to be by him conveyed to Sir John Luttrell for his relief'.[50] This release was effected and Sir John was duly freed from captivity. He was rewarded for his services and was given lands to the value of 100 marks a year but it is not known where they were. The appropriate Patent Roll states: "That Sir John Luttrell, in consideration of the notable good service he hath doone unto the Kinges Majistie during all his warres, shall have landes to the value of 100 markes by the yere duringh his Highnes pleasure."[51]

Sir John had complained that his long suffering soldiers had not received their pay but now he was able to redress their complaints for he extracted from the government £3,200 for 'the waiges of himself and his souldiours in the Northe.'[52] Thus the defeated Sir John was duly recompensed for his unremitting service to the English cause in Scotland. After the Peace of Boulogne there was no war in which he could fight. The role of squire of Dunster was too tame for him but his half-uncle, Thomas Wyndham, was a pirate. This was more to Sir John's liking, and he determined to join, with several other like-minded adventurers in an expedition to Morocco under the command of his undoubtedly valiant and skilled sailor uncle. Ostensibly their aim was the furtherance and development of commerce but when the ship sailed from Portsmouth, Sir John was not on board. In London the sweating sickness was rife. A 19th century account describes the symptoms of this 'sweating sickness': "The sufferers were in general men between thirty and forty, and the stoutest and healthiest most readily caught the infection. The symptoms were a sudden perspiration, accompanied with faintness and drowsiness. Those who were taken with full stomachs died immediately. Those who caught cold shivered into dissolution in a few hours. Those who yielded to the intense temptation of sleep, though only for a quarter of an hour, woke only to die."[53] When the sickness struck Londoners left for the open fields, but Sir John was not one of those who escaped, for he succumbed to the disease at Greenwich on 10 July 1551, at the age of thrity-one. A Londoner described him as "a nobull captayne."

PORTRAIT OF SIR JOHN LUTTRELL

The allegorical portrait of Sir John Luttrell in Dunster castle by Hans Eworth has a counterpart in the Courtauld Gallery in London. Hans Eworth was an Antwerp painter working in London from 1545-49 to 1571.[54] According to Lyte he was resident at Southwark in 1552.[55] The painting at Dunster is in a less deteriorated condition than that in London and bears the date 1550 and the monogram HE. Sir John Luttrell returned from the Scottish wars to England in 1550 and Lyte suggests it is possible that both the pictures were painted by order of Dame Margaret Luttrell some time after 1550, in order to commemorate the valour displayed by her son and her half-brother in the war of that year.[56]

Dame Margaret' half-brother was Sir Thomas Wyndham, the incorrigible pirate who met his end by drowning when returning from Guinea. He and Dame Margaret were the offspring of Sir Thomas Wyndham of Felbrigg; he by the second wife of Sir Thomas, Lady D'Arcy and she by the first wife Eleanore Scrope.[57] It is therefore reasonable to suppose that the drowning man, with a large moustache, added to the painting of Sir John by George Luttrell in 1591 was Sir Thomas Wyndham. Blue Anchor must have been well acquainted with this competent sailor, but hardened plunderer, who engaged in the burning of a convent and the abduction of the nuns and their pupils, the daughters of gentlefolk, for he enjoyed the lease of Marshwood for sixty years at a nominal rent. When George Luttrell renewed the painting there was no problem about Sir Thomas being drowned off the north-west coast of Africa and being shown in the painting as drowning off the Firth of Forth since the entire concept was allegorical. George also added to the original inscription on the rock at the bottom left-hand side of the painting as follows:

"*Effigiem renovare tuam, fortissime miles, Ingens me meritum fecit amorque tui, Nam nisi curasses heredem scribere fratrem, Hei, tua contigerant prædia nulla mihi*. 1591. G.L." Lyte translates this as: "Your great desert and my regard for you, Cause me, brave knight, your portrait to renew. For had you not your brother made your heir, None of your lands had fallen to my share.[58]

The original inscription above the date 1550 and the monogram of the painter reads: "MORE THE THE ROCK AMYDYS THE RAGING SEAS, THE CONSTÄT HERT NO DÄGER DREDDYS NOR FEARYS, S.I.L."[59] Sir John Luttrell avers that more than the rocks amidst the raging seas, the constant heart neither dreads or fears any danger. His portrait was renewed by George, Sir John's nephew, some seventeen years after the latest date Hans Eworth was in England and therefore the suggestion that George Luttrell commissioned the Dunster version in 1591 realising that the original was deteriorating does not hold water. In 1591 as Lyte states: "Before very long, the picture at Dunster was slightly altered by the addition of the head of a drowning man and other minor accessories, with two Latin couplets on the rock."[60]

The painter's style is said to be "sensitive and nervous employing a great deal of delicately rendered detail, ultimately dependent on Holbein, yet without his robustness."[61] Holbein, Henry VIII's Court Painter was a straightforward painter but in Sir John's portrait of the reign of Edward VI, there is not only the delicately rendered details in the depiction of the female symbolic figures holding their attributes, but their underlying allegorial significance. The figure of Peace is a reference to the Treaty of Boulogne signed on 29 March 1550.[62] The two diminutive figures of Friendship, one of whom carries two money bags, alludes to the terms of the treaty whereby the town of Boulogne was immediately surrendered to the French for 400,000 crowns, payable in two instalments. This was a reversal of Henry VIII's triumphal state entry into Boulogne to celebrate the success of Charles Brandon, duke of Suffolk, who, on 14 September 1544, had, after six weeks achieved the capitulation of Boulogne. Subsequently, after war had been declared by England on 9 August 1549, the French quickly captured Ambleteuse and descended on the Boulonnais and partially succeeded in securing the defences of Boulogne itself. After four months of stout resistance, the English finally capitulated. The Peace of Boulogne marked the end of the struggle, for France was eager to settle its affairs with England before embarking on an attack on the king of Castile and emperor of Germany, Charles V. England was only too pleased to conclude the Treaty of Boulogne but what was far more serious was the English withdrawal from Scotland which was due to the outbreak of the war with France in 1549. In the 'next decade Scotland was in great danger of becoming a French province'.[63]

Sir John, whilst not disgraced, was defeated in Scotland though the resolution and defiance shown in his face in the portrait deny this and in spite of the restraining hand of Peace on his right forearm, his fist is raised to Mars, symbolised by the snorting horse of war. This refusal to admit defeat flows from his fist to his face and the bracelets he wears on his wrists tell us that he is not influenced by monetary reward, nor does a crisis shatter him, *nec flexit lucrum* and *nec fregit discrimem*. He rises symbolically above the turbulence, and in spite of the wrecked man-of-war besieged by lightning and flames, that is by natural causes and man-made fire, be god-like in his nakedness, and rides the waves above all misfortune.

In a cloud to the viewer's left and above the head of St John there is a group of female goddesses. The largest one is Pax and represents Peace with her attribute of the olive branch. One of the smaller figures represents Juno Regina, among whose several attributes is the peacock. There is also in the figure of Juno, a reference to Juno Lucinda who, under the name of Martialis, was the mother of Mars, the god of war, whose attributes were a cuirass and helmet and the sacred spears. Here the female figure wears a helmet and other figures hold a breastplate, a sword and the snorting horse of war. The man-of-war flies the cross of St George and round his upper arm, the red and white material wraps Sir John in this emblem of the saint and proclaims "England and St George."

Sir John Luttrell married Mary Ryce, the daughter of Sir Griffith ap Rhys and Katherine, the daughter of Sir John St John. After the death of Sir Griffith, Katherine married Sir Piers Edgcumbe who died on 14 August 1539. She died in 1553 at Cotehele (Cornwall) and bequeathed to her daughter Mary Luttrell: "all her household goods that she hath of hers at Dunster, which some time was Sir Griffith Ryce's, to her chaplains and servants, each a black gown and a years' wages; and the residue of her goods and chattels and her tin-works in Cornwall, to her executors, *viz* her brother Sir John St John of Bletshoe, and her nephew Sir Thomas Stradling."[64]

Mary Luttrell, on the death of Sir John in 1551, enjoyed as part of her dower or jointure, the castle of Dunster, and was apparently in residence in 1533. This was contrary to established feudal practice, as a widow did not normally benefit from the head place, or caput, of the Honour of Dunster. She, as was customary retained the surname of Luttrell until her death although she married secondly James Godolphin of Gwinear (Cornwall)[65] Just before Sir John Luttrell died, Edward VI authorized certain commissioners officially to declare a divorce between Sir John and Mary Luttrell on proof of her adultery[66] but it would appear this proof was never established, since she remained a legatee under the will of Dame Margaret Luttrell[67] her mother-in-law who died in 1580 and was buried with her husband, Sir Andrew at East Quantoxhead. Mary Luttrell went to live at Kilton subsequently, and when she died on 31 March 1588, she too was buried at East Quantoxhead.[68]

There were three girls of the marriage of Sir John and Mary Luttrell. The eldest, Catherine married Sir Thomas Copley of Gatton in Surrey in July 1558 in the last months of the reign of Queen Mary I. The marriage of the twenty-one year old bride took place in the fantastical palace of Nonsuch, at Ewell in Surrey. Though this palace was demolished in 1687, we still know from Wenceslaus Hollar's engraving what it looked like. The palace was built by Henry VIII who sought to emulate his rival François Premier's Chambord. Eleven years after Henry's death the marriage took place in this incomplete palace where foreign workmen had been employed to make the decorations.

There is a very strange story that Sir Thomas Copley, a very rich and highly connected man, wrote to the Master of the Revels asking for the loan of a mask for the wedding. He effected to deplore the arrangements and one wonders why he wished to hide his face. Was he, perhaps, disfigured by small-pox and so wished his bride not to see his face or, was it a prank? A tradition in the Copley family says that he refused the hand of a daughter of Lord Howard of Effingham, the Lord High Admiral, because he was so attracted to Catherine Luttrell's beauty and thus he made an enemy of the admiral.[69] Beautiful she may have been but she is described as 'very simple' and unfit to meddle with politics. Being a noted 'bigot' she was suspect and more than once committed to prison in her later life.[70] In 1563, Sir Thomas Copley became a Roman catholic.[71] In 1561 Queen Elizabeth, the upholder of the new state religion, stood god-mother to his eldest son. Sir Thomas fell from grace after his conversion and was fined and imprisoned in 1568.[72]

The fact that the queen was god-mother to his son made his conversion a more public affront to the queen who had dealt with the embracing of all her subjects, whether of the old or new persuasion, with consummate skill. She had avowed that 'all members of the state were *ipso facto* members of the state church'.[73] The most disastrous step Sir Thomas Copley took was to go abroad in 1570 without licence to do so and, as a result, his goods were seized by the government and his rents confiscated. He remained an exile and died in Antwerp in 1584, although his wife was allowed to return for a time and on his death she finally returned to England where she enjoyed 'the right of nominating two members for the little constituency of Gatton.'[74] Her husband had sat in several parliaments and had been knighted and created a baron by the French king, Henri Quatre after which honour he styled himself 'Sir Thomas Copley, knight, Lord Copley of Gatton'. He also claimed, without foundation, the English baronies of Welles and Hoo.[75] At Sutton Place near Guildford 'the arms of Luttrell occur in some fine heraldic glass which was removed from one of the seats of the Copley family'.[76]

Mr G.F. Luttrell in 1909 bought an oil painting of Sir Thomas Copley, his wife and their five sons and four daughters. It is a strange painting which hangs today in the Inner Hall of Dunster castle. It is in need of cleaning and difficult to decipher but it is said to show Sir Thomas wearing a tabard bearing the arms of Copley and Hoo quarterly which are blazoned : *Ar a cross moline Sa*. The arms of Hoo appear on this tabard because Jane, a daughter of Sir Thomas Hoo, a distinguished soldier in the reign of Henry III (1216-72), married Sir Roger Copley, Knt. The baronry became extinct in 1453. The daughters and co-heirs of Sir Thomas Hoo were Aleanore who married Sir Thomas Carew, Knt. of Bedington, Surrey, Jane already mentioned and Elizabeth who married Sir Thomas Devenish, Knt. Sir Thomas Hoo was descended from Robert de Hoo, of Hoo, co Bedford and Knebworth, co Hertford alive in the time of Edward I (1272-1307). The arms of Hoo may be blazoned : *Quarterly Sa and Ar; quarterly Ar and Sa; quarterly Or and Sa; quarterly Sa and Ar within a bordure erminois; and quarterly Sa and Ar a bend Or*.[77] These five variants were used at various times and by various branches. Sir Thomas Copley kneels on a faldstool with his five sons behind him. Lady Catherine Copley kneels opposite him and wears a mantle bearing the arms of Luttrell and Ryce alternately. She is attended by her four daughters.[78] The arms of Luttrell may be blazoned : *Or a bend betw six Martlets Sa*. Lady Catherine Copley's maternal grandfather was Sir Griffith ap Rhys whose arms may be blazoned thus: *Gu a chevron Ar betw three plates*.[79] In this picture the Ptolemaic system of astronomy is bent to an ecclesiastical meaning.

This sixteenth 'device' concealed cryptic meanings and was much to the taste of the emerging Elizabethans. As Lyte describes it: "The central part of the picture is intended to illustrate the progress of the human soul from earth to heaven. The flesh and the devil endeavour to hold it, but death cuts their gilded cords with his scythe and the soul ascends through thirteen concentric circles representing the Ptolemaic system. In the Empyrean Heaven above is the crucified Saviour attended by Saints, and in the circumference are Seraphim, Cherubim, Thrones, Dominions, Virtues, Powers, Principalities, Archangels, and Angels, according to the Dionysian arrangement which was followed by Dante and others. This 'device' of Sir Thomas Copley, having been approved by the theologians of the University of Paris in 1580, was engraved there in that year."[80]

The reference to Dionysius is apparently to 'Dionysius, the Pseudo-Areopagite (c 500) a mystical theologian' who combined in his extant writings Neo-Platonism with Christianity, one of which was 'The Celestial Hierarchy' 'which explains how the nine orders of angels mediate God to man.'[81] Dante (1265-1321) in the *Divine Comedy*, a trilogy composed of the Inferno, the Purgatorio and Paradise, describes in poetic form, 'the soul's journey from the state of separation from God to the Ultimate goal of the Beatific Vision.'[82] Dante is guided by Virgil, the representative of natural reason, and he descends into the inferno. Here in the depths of hell, he experiences in realistic vision, the torments of the damned souls. He is given the chance to denounce the vices of ecclesiastical ambition and corruption; the vices of his day. Next he is conducted to purgatory, to the to the 'seven terraces of the mountains of Purgatorio'[83] where the souls are purified and led to the Earthly Paradise. Virgil now departs and leaves Dante to the care of Beatrice, who repres-ents 'reason enlightened by Divine Revelation'. They journey together 'through the nine heavens peopled by saints and angels in hierarchial order up to the threshold of the empyrean'. Here Beatrice leaves Dante to St Bernard who represents 'mystic contemplation' and who introduces him to the Blessed Virgin Mary who intercedes for him and grants him a glimpse of the Beatific Vision.[84]

Catherine Copley had two sisters, Dorothy and Mary. These three girls were respectively fourteen, twelve and nine at the time of their father Sir John Luttrell's death in 1551, and, although their mother, Lady Mary Luttrell lived until 1588 the girls became wards of the Crown.[85] There was no male heir and they were their father's co-heiresses. They and their paternal grandmother, Dame Margaret Luttrell (d1580), inherited a third of Sir John's landed property. The relict of Mary Luttrell retained the castle and the borough of Dunster and the manor of Kilton during her lifetime. Thomas Luttrell, Sir John's brother inherited very little property but he did manage to buy up some of the rights of his sister-in-law, Mary and of her three daughters. The three girls inherited from their maternal grandmother, Lady Katherine Rhys, later Edgcumbe, the bequest to Catherine Copley née Luttrell being 'a chain of gold with a flower set with two diamonds and a ruby'.[86] Her sisters inherited a great bowl each and when their brother-in-law, Thomas Copley died in Antwerp in 1584 they inherited 'a gold ring with a death's head and enamelled motto'.[87] The sisters Dorothy and Mary married Humphrey White, a citizen and merchant tailor of London[88] and interestingly enough, Henry Shelley of Mapledurham, Hants, respectively. Henry Shelley was a cousin of Sir Thomas Copley and also a 'Popist Recusant'.[89] Dame Margaret Luttrell, the paternal grandmother of Catherine, Dorothy and Mary outlived her son and heir Sir John Luttrell and his brother and successor Thomas Luttrell. She died in 1580 and was only outlived by her third son Nicholas Luttrell of Honibere, in the parish of Lilstock, Somerset, ancestor of the Luttrells of Hartland Abbey and of the Luttrells of Saunton Court also in Devonshire.[90] He was buried at Lilstock on 23 March 1591/2.[91] Possibly she was also outlived by Andrew, her youngest son who was alive in 1551 but whose date of death is unknown.

THE LUTTRELL TABLE CARPET

The Luttrell table carpet must have been one of the prize possessions of Dame Margaret Luttrell for she left to her eldest daughter, Margaret, 'her best and largest carpet' a magnificent example of heraldic tapestry, measuring 18'3" by 6'7". Margaret had married in 1555, Peter Edgcumbe of Mount Edgcumbe in Devonshire and they were her mother's executors and residuary legatees.[92] Her father, Sir Andrew Luttrell had been a servitor at the coronation of Anne Boleyn and Margaret was maid of honour to Queen Elizabeth I.

Mr Julian Luttrell provided the following information: "The carpet is either of English or of Flanders origin - period 1520-30 but could possibly be after 1538 when Sir Andrew Luttrell died. The material it is made of is a mixture of wool, silk and metal and was woven for Sir Andrew to commemorate his marriage with Margaret, daughter of Sir Thomas Wyndham of Felbrigg, (Norfolk) in 1514. It was bequeathed in 1580 by Dame Margaret Luttrell to her daughter who married Peter Edgcumbe of Mount Edgcumbe. Whereby it passed into the possession of Lord Edgcumbe of Cotehele House, Cornwall. From there it was acquired by Mr. Howard Carter, the egyptologist, and was offered for sale at Christies on 13 July 1922, but was not sold. It was then on exhibition in 1927-28 in America at both the Pittsburg and Chicago art galleries, and it was then bought by Sir William Burrell. His account continues: "The Luttrell carpet is possibly the earliest known surviving example of an English table carpet; the only other one of comparison is the Lewknor table carpet of 1564, now in the Metropolitan Museum in New York. Though they both employed an utterly different vocabulary of design, they conform in so far as a general heraldic arrangement is concerned, both having three coats of arms for the central field of scrolling, flowering plants and twelve shields in the border. What is strange about the Luttrell carpet is not the overall disposition of the heraldry but the apparently irrational and erratic variations in detail. Whereas, for example, in the Lewknor the shields preserve a simplicity of shape and size and are placed at regular intervals along the border; in the Luttrell carpet the shields are of several different shapes and sizes and are scattered along the border in higgeldy piggeldy fashion. Another seemingly eccentric quality of the Luttrell table carpet is the number of repetitions that occur in the coat of arms of the three central shields, that of Sir Andrew and Margaret Wyndham in the centre is repeated twice in the border and that of his father, flanking it on the left, three times. The three central shields are accompanied by the initials of the Luttrells who bore them, joined by a lover's knot above or below the shields and the central coat of arms is surmounted by a cross, the white swan collared and chained, which is derived from the Bohuns through the Courtenay marriage. There is no motto, but we know that Sir Andrew's signet bore a French motto which may be read either 'Tous Sur' or 'sur tout' and it would be in order to surmise that when he or his widow ordered a carpet to put on or all over a table, they were not unmindful of its literal meaning."

Sir Hugh Luttrell married twice and in the carpet the shield surrounded by lilies and daisies, shows the arms of Luttrell impaled with those of Hill, with the initial 'H' reversed and 'M' standing for Hugh and Margaret, his first wife being Margaret Hill. The central shield shows the arms of Luttrell impaling Wyndham, with the initials of Sir Andrew Luttrell below. Between these initials is a lover's knot. The white swan, collared and chained relates to Elizabeth Courtenay, the wife of an earlier Sir Andrew Luttrell of Chilton. Elizabeth was the daughter of Margaret de Bohun, and Hugh, 2nd earl of Devon and Margaret herself was the daughter of Elizabeth Plantagenet, daughter of Edward I and her husband Humphrey de Bohun, earl of Hereford and Essex and Constable of England, who died at the battle of Boroughbridge. Elizabeth Courtenay had two cousins, Mary de Bohun and Eleanor de Bohun who were co-heiresses and they made illustrious marriages. Mary was the first wife of Henry Bolingbroke, earl of Derby, the future first Lancastrian king, Henry IV, Eleanor married the seventh son of Edward III, Thomas of Woodstock, earl of Buckingham and duke of Gloucester.

The son of Sir Andrew Luttrell of Chilton and Elizabeth Courtenay was Sir Hugh Luttrell who was the first Luttrell lord of Dunster and was very proud of his ties with the De Bohun family and the House of Lancaster and he adopted the swan supporters from that source. The central shield is flanked on the right by the shield of Luttrell impaling Courtenay of Powderham with the initials of Sir James Luttrell, great-grandson of Sir Andrew Luttrell of Chilton and the grandfather of Sir Andrew Luttrell of East Quantoxhead. The initials of Sir James are interlaced with a lover's knot surmounting the shield which itself is surrounded by a wreath of lilies and cherries issuing from a vase. Sir James married Elizabeth Courtenay of Powderham, daughter of Sir Philip Courtenay who was his cousin and former guardian. On the three principal shields, gold and silver threads represent the armorial metals *Or* and *Argent*.

Lyte's description of the table carpet is: "The ground of the central portion is black, ornamented with an elaborate geometrical pattern of yellow circles, interlaced with floriated yellow quatrefoils and green squares. In the centre of each circle there is a blue floriated cross radiating from a stiff yellow sunflower; in the centres of the quatrefoils and squares, Tudor roses alternate with honeysuckles. The border has a running pattern of honeysuckles and sunflowers on a red ground. At intervals, white lilies, growing in the border, impinge upon the central part of the design. The heraldic adornments of the carpet are very interesting and beautiful. In the centre, surrounded by a wreath of lilies, honeysuckles, and daisies, and hanging from the neck of a white swan, is the shield of Luttrell impaling Wyndham, with the initials of Sir Andrew Luttrell below.[93]

The border of the Luttrell carpet shows twelve shields placed at irregular intervals. They are of varying shapes and sizes. They represent the arms of:

i)   Luttrell impaling Beaumont. *Or a bend between six Martlets Sa., impaling Gu., and vairé.* Alternative blazoning *Or a bend, between six Martlets Sa., impaling barry of six vairé and Gu.;* Sir Hugh Luttrell, 1st Lord of Dunster Castle (c 1364-1428), the son of Sir Andrew of Chilton and Elizabeth Courtenay (d 1395) married Catherine Beaumont, the daughter of Sir John Beaumont of Devonshire.[94]

ii) Wyndham impaling Scrope, quartered Tibetot, *Az a chevron between three Leopards' (or Lions') heads erased Or. langued Gu., impaling Az., a bend Or quartered Arg., a saltire ingrailed Gu.;* (The quartering is 1 and 4 *Az* and 2 and 3 *Arg.* The arms of Scrope *Az, a bend Or,* refer to the marriages of Sir Andrew Luttrell and his younger brother Geoffrey, the sons of Sir Geoffrey Luttrell of Irnham, who married respectively Beatrice and Constance Scrope, two sisters who were the daughters of Sir Geoffrey Scrope, son of 1st Baron Scrope of Masham. Beatrice Scrope appears with her mother-in-law Agnes de Sutton, and the equestrian figure of her father-in-law, Sir Geoffrey Luttrell of Irnham, in the famous Luttrell Psalter (B.M.) The arms of Tibetot refer to the marriages of Roger, second Lord Scrope of Bolton and his brother Stephen le Scrope to Margaret and Millicent, the daughters of Robert de Tibetot, third baron and his wife Margaret, the daughter of William, Lord Deincourt. This Robert de Tibetot died in 1372, when his lands devolved upon his daughters as co-heirs. Apart from Margaret and Millicent he had a third daughter Elizabeth who married Philip le Despenser, the younger.

iii) Luttrell impaling Audley, *Or a bend between six Martlets Sa., impaling Gu., a fretty Or.* Alternative blazoning *Or a bend between six Martlets Sa., impaling Gu.,a fret Or.* The arms of Audley *Gu.,a fretty Or/ a fret Or* refer to the marriage of Margaret Tuchet, daughter of the 4th Lord Audley who married Sir John Luttrell, the son of Sir Hugh Luttrell and his wife Lady Catherine Luttrell née Beaumont. The arms of Audley also refer to Sir Humphrey Audley, the second husband of Elizabeth Courtenay of Powderham, who had married, as her first husband Sir James Luttrell, the son of Sir John Luttrell and his wife Margaret.

iv) Luttrell impaling Hill.
Or a bend between six Martlets Sa., impaling Gu., a saltire vair between four mullets Arg.

v) Luttrell impaling Wyndham. *Or a bend between six Martlets Sa., impaling Arg., a chevron between three   Leopards' (or Lions') heads erased Or langued Gu.*

vi) Luttrell impaling Hill (as before)

vii) Luttrell impaling Wyndham (as before)

viii) Luttrell impaling Hill (as before)

ix) Luttrell impaling Audley (as before)

x) Courtenay of Powderham. *Three torteaux in pile a label of three points each charged with as many plates or bezants*

xi) Beaumont *Gu., and vairé* Alternative blazoning. *Barry of six vairé and Gu.*

xii) Courtenay of Powderham (as above).

Lyte comments on the fact that: "there are no crests or mottoes on the carpet. It must have been made for the high table at Dunster or East Quantoxhead between 1514 and 1538 or at latest 1543."[95] It would therefore have been made in the reign of Henry VIII. Mr Julian Luttrell says however, that: "it is possible that the designer could have been the Flemish painter Hans Eworth who worked in England between 1545 and 1573." This is not possible if Lyte is correct in saying the latest date of manufacture is 1543, but he does not give the source of his evidence. Mr Luttrell continues: "he was a designer of considerable reputation and it was to him that Queen Elizabeth entrusted the costumes and décor for the fêtes to welcome the French ambassador, during the peace with France in 1572." It is debatable whether Hans Eworth would have designed a tapestry; presumably executing the cartoon, in which the shields were irregular both in shape and size; their position in the border chosen with careless abandon, with no regard for symmetry and one which displayed repetitious arms.

The 16th century Luttrell table carpet shows, in one of the shields, the earlier marital liaisons between the Scropes and the Tibetots and particular reference was made to the daughters of Robert Tibetot. The great great grandfather of Robert Tibetot was Henry de Tibetot who, in the reign of King Henry III was granted, in conjunction with Thomas Botterel, lands in the counties of York and Lincoln which had belonged to Adam Painel, 'who fought on the other side'.[976]Painel was among the names listed in the retinue which accompanied William the Conquerer to England. A Frethesant Paynell married Sir Georffrey Luttrell.

Sir Robert Luttrell of Irnham and Sir Andrew Luttrell of East Quantoxhead were cousins who were both wards of Edward I. Sir Robert was the son of Sir Geoffrey Luttrell (c 1235-70) the ancestor of the Luttrells of Irnham and was the overlord of Sir Andrew of East Quantoxhead. Sir Robert was a minor up to 1276 and Sir Andrew was a minor at the time of his father's death in 1273; his father being Sir Alexander Luttrell.[97] Sir Alexander and Sir Geoffrey were the grandsons of Sir Geoffrey Luttrell and Frethesant Paynell. When Sir Robert and Sir Geoffrey were wards of the king, he, in 1274 committed two-thirds of the manor of East Quantoxhead to Robert Tibetot (d 1298). Presumably Pernel Luttrell the mother of Sir Andrew received the other third.

CHAPTER EIGHT

TUDOR AND JACOBEON DUNSTER

THOMAS LUTTRELL, the second son of Sir Andrew and Lady Margaret Luttrell and heir to his elder brother, Sir John (d 1551), was born in 1525. He reached his majority at the end of the reign of Henry VIII, inherited the Dunster estates in the reign of Edward VI, saw the brief nine day reign of Lady Jane Grey and the reign of the catholic Mary Tudor and, when he died in 1571, Elizabeth I had been queen of England for thirteen years. In his forty-six years he saw England tossed between the beliefs of the Reformation to those of Roman Catholicism and back to a Protestant state. In legal documents Thomas, who unlike his brother, was never knighted, was known as 'Thomas Luttrell of Marshwood'.[1] Thomas Luttrell had served under his brother, Sir John Luttrell in Scotland and had assisted him by collecting men and money to further his martial endeavours in the Scottish wars.[2] A link between these two brothers is provided by the effigy of Thomas on the monument in Dunster church and the portrait of Sir John in Dunster castle.

The connection of Marshwood with Dunster goes back, at least to 1350 when the last de Mohun of Dunster, John de Mohun V and his wife Lady Joan de Mohun, conveyed Dunster castle, Carhampton, Rodhuish and Marshwood to her father and brother, Sir Bartholomew of Burghersh the elder and Sir Bartholomew of Burghersh the younger, Sir Peter de Veel, Sir Roger la Ward and Matthew of Clevedon. Although the rent was, for four years, only a nominal one of a red rose, after that time it rose dramatically to £400.[3] When Lady Joan became a widow in 1375 her late husband's uncle apparently became her receiver, and she allowed him to live at Marshwood. This arrangement with Patrick de Mohun was validated by Philippa de Mohun, Lady Fitzwater, the second daughter of Lady Joan, who was unsuccessful in her attempt to gain the reversion, or return of the estate to her at the expiry of her grant.[4] In the time of the early Luttrells, the great-great grandfather of Thomas Luttrell, Sir John Luttrell apparently lived at Marshwood, referred to in 1417 as 'Mersswode', until the death of his father,[5] when he moved to the castle. At that time Marshwood Park comprised two hundred and seventy acres worth 40s a year. In 1553 it comprised a hundred acres and maintained a hundred deer. In the Marshwood papers it says that: "subsequently the castle (i.e. the buildings on top of the Tor of which there is now no trace), fell into disrepair and the Lords of Dunster seem to have resided at Marshwood though transacting their business in Dunster."[6]

The property that actually passed to Thomas Luttrell in 1551 was very meagre and although Sir John had left him all his landed property, the law stepped in and maintained that a third of it should go to Sir John's daughters, Catherine, Dorothy and Mary and his co-heirs. Dame Margaret Luttrell the mother of Sir John and Thomas enjoyed for her lifetime the manors of East Quantoxhead, Iveton, Vexford, Radlet, Carhampton and Rodhuish. The manor of Minehead was administered by trustees whose task was to make provision for the younger children of Sir Andrew Luttrell and Dame Margaret from that source. We already know that Dame Mary Luttrell, Thomas's sister-in-law, had for her lifetime the castle of Dunster, its borough and the manor of Kilton which in 1553 was 'merely a wood of about a hundred acres 'well sett with okes and yonge ashes'."[7]

Thomas succeeded in increasing his lands by buying up the rights of Sir John's widow, Mary, since she re-married and her husband, John Godolphin was of Cornwall, she probably had no more interest in Dunster. Thomas also acquired the reversionary rights of her three daughters and their respective husbands.[8] In order to find the wherewithal to do this he sold Stonehall and Woodhall in Suffolk and various outlying estates in the west of England.[9] He consolidated his holdings by the purchase of Hopcot, between Wootton Courtenay and Minehead and when he granted a lease of Hopcot, we learn, "he reserved all hawks, pheasants and partridges"[10] for his own use.

In 1560 when Thomas was "lawfully married unto Margery Hadley" his fortunes dramatically improved and he acquired for himself and his successors a vast inheritance in the neighbourhood of Dunster. His bride was his cousin, the daughter and eventual heiress of Christopher Hadley of Withycombe. One of her direct ancestors had married the heiress of the Durboroughs of Heathfield and a previous Durborough had married a co-heiress of the Fitzurses of Williton and Withycombe. In 1350 a Durborough was a military knight of Dunster. Thus Margery (or Margaret) Hadley brought to her marriage the manors of Heathfield, Williton Hadley and Withycombe Hadley as well as a variety of lands in other parishes of West Somerset.[11] In the dairy of Marshwood Farm there is an overmantel bearing the arms of Luttrell and Hadley.

The legal proceedings, already mentioned, in which Thomas was referred to as 'Thomas Luttrell of Marshwood' concerned treasure trove found in the year 1559. "A certain Agnes Ellesworth, the wife of Richard Ellesworth the elder "of Imbercombe, husbandman," was delivered of a still-born child, in the month of May 1559, at Owl Knowle in the parish of Carhampton, a house which he presumably rented from Thomas Trevelyan. In digging a grave hard by, wherein to bury the body, she suddenly came upon a great quantity of gold coins sufficient, it was estimated, to fill a "wynne quart" less a quarter of a "wyne pynte." After giving a few to two female friends who were with her at the time, she put the rest ·into a "trene dysshe" (wooden dish) and so handed them over to her husband on his return. They consisted of "old nobles," "half-nobles," and "quarter old nobles," and Richard Ellesworth, reckoning the noble at 13s.4d[12] estimated their value at 107l.10s. When a report of their discovery reached Thomas Luttrell, he laid claim to them as treasure trove in his Hundred of Carhampton, but satisfied himself with coins to the value of 100l. The finder was not, however, suffered to keep the remainder, and they were handed over, in May 1560, to Sir Thomas Parry, Treasurer of the Queen's Household.[13] Then began tedious proceedings in the Exchequer, the Attorney General putting forward the right of the Crown and Thomas Luttrell defending his own claim, to be supported by extracts from court rolls and bailliffs' accounts. Eventually the case was set down for trial before the justices of assize at Chard in July 1564.[14] Here the story ends abruptly. There is no record of the judgment, which was to have been entered at the Exchequer in Michaelmas term. Perhaps the Crown withdrew its claim. Anyhow, the Luttrells have maintained theirs ever since, and it is interesting to note that there are now at Dunster Castle a number of nobles, half-nobles and angels,[15] of the reign of Edward the Fourth, which are presumably the remains of the hoard found at Owl Knowle in 1559.[16]

Thomas Luttrell married Margery Hadley twice. The first marriage is thought to have taken place in the reign of Edward VI. There were reasons for keeping the marriage secret; the couple had common ancestors. They were guilty of the ecclesiastical offence of con-sanguinity and if their marriage was known they faced excommunication from the church of Rome. Their common ancestors were Robert Hill and Elizabeth Courtenay of Pow-derham. Thomas Luttrell was the great-grandson of Robert Hill, his maternal grandmother being Margaret Hill, the daughter of Robert Hill and the first wife of Sir Hugh Luttrell (d1521). Margery Hadley was the great-granddaughter of the same Robert Hill, her father having married Anne Hill, the granddaughter of Robert Hill, who was a 'military knight of the honour of Dunster' and was buried in St George's church, Dunster.[17]

The couple's descent from Elizabeth Courtenay is through her two marriages. Thomas Luttrell was the great-grandson of Elizabeth and her first husband, Sir James Luttrell. Margery Hadley was the great-great-granddaughter of Elizabeth Courtenay, her great-grandfather having married Philippa, the daughter of Elizabeth by her second husband Sir James Audley. Thus in the case of the descent from Robert Hill, they were both related in the third degree of kinship and in the case of the descent from Elizabeth Courtenay of Powderham they were related in the third degree as far as Thomas was concerned and in the fourth degree as far as Margery was concerned. They seem to have become alarmed about the validity of their marriage in the reign of Mary Tudor and Philip of Spain, and they communicated with the papal authorities. The cardinal of St Angelo was the papal penitentiary at St Peter's and he presided over the penitentiary court and had power to absolve the couple which he did provided that they underwent a second public ceremony 'in the face of the church'. This papal dispensation was issued eleven days after the accession of Queen Elizabeth I, who ascended the throne on 17 November 1558. Nevertheless, Margery was in the eighth month of her pregnancy before the second solemnization of the marriage took place. The couple were married at East Quantoxhead on 27 August, 1560 and the register shows the rather remarkable entry in which the bride is designated as Mrs Margaret Hadley. Lyte remarks that the dispensation was: "probably one of the very latest documents of the sort that was despatched before the final breach between England and Rome."[18] The Hadleys and the Luttrells must have enjoyed a close relationship for Margery Hadley's godmother was Thomas Luttrell's mother Dame Margaret Luttrell.

In 1559 the town of Minehead received a charter of incorporation from Queen Elizabeth I. Charter and grants which recognised the privileges of the towns were gradually succeeding the feudal system which originated at the Conquest and which had been a blow to the burghal self-government. In the Middle Ages towns which enjoyed some measure of self-government were generally known as boroughs; a term that was applied generally and never strictly defined. The history of the borough is said to have begun with: "the Danish invasions of the eighth century., when the shires gradually developed around the *burh* or fortress, which in 960 was granted its own law-courts."[19]

Now the charter which the growing town of Minehead received would have included the privileges of holding a market and fair, of having separate jurisdiction, self-assessment and of having merchant guilds. The guilds were: "a great source of power, and with the new borough organisation under a mayor, laid the foundations for a large measure of self-government. By the seventeenth century, the governing powers of the guilds has been handed over to the borough corporation of an elected mayor, aldermen and councillors. These corporations became gradually more exclusive and less subject to the will of the ordinary burgesses.[20] However, in Minehead the government of the borough was, in 1559, vested in the portreeve and twelve burgesses. The portreeve, the official in charge of the port was, at Minehead in charge of a new quay or pier which Thomas desired to make with contributions to this end from 'his neighbours, friends and "well-wishers"' He urged them to accept his invitation to participate in the scheme which "would be very useful to the country."[21] There had been a small pier at Minehead in the early part of the sixteenth century built by Sir Hugh Luttrell (d1521) who had also "enlarged the harbour considerably to the great benefit of the little town."[22]

In 1563, for the first time, Minehead sent members to parliament and Thomas Luttrell was one of the two elected.[23] The autumn of 1570 saw him appointed as sheriff of Somerset.[24]

According to Professor Black the justice of the peace in the Elizabethan period was "the beast of burden on whose broad shoulders the government continuously devolved new tasks."[25]

Professor Black compares the office of the justice of the peace with that of the sheriff: "The office of the sheriff...was becoming more honorific, and was certainly less arduous than the justice-ship. As the immediate representative of the Crown in the shire, the sheriff was charged with the provision of hospitality in the event of a royal visit, or the sojourn of distinguished strangers from abroad, and the periodical visit from the justices of assize. He had also important financial responsibilities in connexion with the collection of debts due to the Crown and of fines imposed by the law-courts, either locally or at Westminster, together with the enforcement of the queen's right to purveyance. He had nothing to do, however, with the collection of taxes levied by the authority of parliament; but in the county court, over which he presided, he supervised what was by far the most important function of this decaying assembly, the election of members of parliament. In the same place he proclaimed the laws, published outlawries, decided civil suits involving less than 40s., and awarded damages for breach of contract and non-payment of wages. After the close of each parliamentary session writs were sent to him authorizing the payment of wages and travelling expenses to members of parliament, and these were assessed upon the hundreds and townships at the next meeting of the county court. The sheriff also attended the quarter sessions of the justices of the peace and the assize courts for the impanelling of juries, and the due presentment of prisoners from jail, whose safe keeping was part of his duty. These courts could not be properly constituted without his presence, nor could the sentences imposed be discharged without his co-operation; and all writs and summonses required his sanction. Certain other powers were also exercised by the sheriff, either on his own initiative or in conjunction with other Crown officials. Such were the suppression of riots and unlawful assemblies and the supervision of the county musters, but in these matters his responsibility was over shadowed by that of the lord lieutenant. The lord-lieutenant was, like the justice of the peace, a typically Elizabethan functionary."[26]

The common descent of Thomas Luttrell and Margaret Luttrell from Lady Elizabeth Courtenay of Powderham (d1493) is today emphasised, whether by accident or design, through the proximity of their respective memorials. Originally the tomb slab of Elizabeth Luttrell née Courtenay was placed where she was buried before the high altar, or altar of St George, in the priory church. When the large monument was erected it was placed on the south wall of the priory church just to the east of Christian de Mohun's effigy and on this monument lie, side by side, the effigies of Thomas and Margaret Luttrell.

Thomas and Margaret left three sons and three daughters. The sons were George, the heir, John of South Mapperton in Dorset and Andrew who was baptised at Dunster on 14 October 1569 and died without issue. The girls were Ursula, Margaret and Mary. Margaret Luttrell lived thirty-six years after her husband Thomas who died on 16 January 1571. She promptly married again as soon as the prescribed period of mourning was over. Her second husband was the aforesaid John Strode whom she married at East Quantoxhead on 28 January 1572.

Mary is the one about whom most is known. She was baptised at Dunster on 11 October 1567 and was mentioned in her grandmother, Dame Margaret Luttrell's will in 1580. She married, as his second wife, Sir Robert Strode of Parnham in Dorset;[27] who was the son of John Strode of Parnham, her step-father. John Strode died some ten years later and in 1587 she entered a third state of matrimony. This time her husband was Richard Hill. We do not know if he was a relation; her mother, grandfather and great-grandfather all bore this surname but Lyte refers to him as 'her "servant," probably her agent'.[28] In spite of all these marriages, she returned to her first husband Thomas as an effigy lying beside his effigy in Dunster church. George, their eldest son (1560-1629) erected the imposing Jacobean monument to the memory of his parents and that of his first wife Joan Stewkley. Joan Luttrell in April 1613, made a will with the consent of her husband, by which she directed that she should be buried 'in the Priory Church of Dunster, near her parents.'[29] Her father, Hugh Stewkley, lay rector of Dunster after the dissolution of the monasteries had been buried in accordance with the instructions left in his will made in January 1587. The terms were that: "if he should die in Somerset, he should be buried in the Priory Church of Dunster over against his own seat or pew, or else in the church of Carhampton near his parents."[30]

Elsewhere we find added information as follows: "In his will dated Jan...,1587, proved Feb 19 1588 (1588-9),by Elisabeth Stukeley, his widow, Hugh Stewkeley directs that he should be buried in St Sepulchre's, London, near his first wife Christian, and his son William, should he die in London; but if in Somerset, "then in the Chancel of the Priory Church of Dunster, over against my seat or pewe, or else in the Church of Carhampton, near my father and mother." He was buried at Dunster on 7 Feb. 1588.[31]

Joan Luttrell had many brothers and sisters two of whom,, George Stewkley and Margaret Stewkley also directed that they should be buried near their parents. Hugh Stewkley refers to them in his will and to all his other offspring. "He mentions "My daughters Susan, Margaret, and Ursula, not married. My wife Elisabeth. My godson Hugh, son of William Steynings. Tenement at Counyngar [*sic* for Conygar] Hill, which I had of the demise of Sir John Luttrell and Dame Mary, widow of the said Sir John. If my heir be under age at my death, I give to Lady Burleigh £100 to get the wardship of him. My son Thomas to apply his studies to the Law. My son George Stewkeley. Peter Stewkeley, my father decd, Lands in Marsh, Dunster and Carhampton, which I purchased of Hugh Smithe, Henry Dodington, and William Morgan Esqrs.,and John Morris, gent. My park, Mynehed Park, Manors of King Brimpton, Withypoole, Wootton Courtney, &c, to my eldest son Thomas Stukeley; my youngest son George, lands in Stokenheathe, Whitechappell, Fulham, &c.,Middx."[32]

Joan Luttrell's mother, Elizabeth Stewkley née Chamberlayne, died in 1598. The brass to her memory is now to be seen on the floor of the south-east aisle. Joan Luttrell predeceased her husband George Luttrell. and was buried on 22 November 1621 The inscription is within a rectangular frame with an outer debased and static seventeenth century strapwork and a faint allusion to a broken pediment. The inscription on the left of the tomb reads: "*Here lyeth the body of* Thomas Luttrell esquire *who departed this lyfe in sure hope* of a most *joyful* resurrection the 16 day of Jany, anno Dom. 1570, anno 13 of Elizabeth late Queene of England, being then High Sheriff of the countie of Somerset. *&* one of the youngest sones of Andrew Luttrell, knight: the sayd Thomas being lawfully married unto Margery Hadley daughter and sole heire of Christopher Hadley of Wythycomb esquire, by whom he had issue 3 sones and 3 daughters, George, *John,* Andrew...3 daughters *vizd* Ursula, Margaret and Mary, *the which* Andrew, Ursula and Margaret dyed without *any issue of* theire bodyes."[33] Lyte adds, "it is necessary to observe that the words printed in italics are purely conjectural, and that the actual situation of Thomas Luttrell's grave is quite unknown."[34]

EFFIGIES

Thomas lies on the plinth of the monument with his right hand folded over his breast and his left hand on a book, possibly the Bible. Margaret and her son George, are shown with their hands in the attitude of prayer and Joan, George's first wife, holds a book in her right hand while the left arm rests naturally across her body. All the recumbent figures are supported at the head on tasselled cushions and wear Elizabethan costumes with ruffs.[35]

The detail is remarkable and even includes the layers of leather which form the heels of their shoes. There is no evidence of colouring and indeed from around 1620 up to the end of the century, except for a little high-lighting in gilt which is sometimes found, colouring was reserved for heraldry. In their lack of colouring, the figures imitated the revived classical forms of the Renaissance, and were unadorned with colour which had been used earlier and which again became popular after 1700. This Dunster monument is in a sad state and even the figures are becoming detached and many pieces are loose or have fallen off. The removal of this monument from the chancel to the south-east aisle during the Victorian restoration could not have been beneficial to it.

The figures are of alabaster and the monument itself is composed of white marble with a red vein and of black marble and alabaster. After 1600 black and white was added to the traditionally used stone and alabaster which came from Derbyshire and Staffordshire until the seventeenth century. This monument was conceived as an almost free-standing canopied erection with a flat tester. It is not wholly free-standing since it is set against the wall and has been provided with an ornamented back-plate composed of two shallow recessed arches divided by broken pilasters from which spring a corbel on whose face is a winged-cherub's head; a representation of the spiritual world of immortality. This corbel supports the centre of the canopy which is further supported on its outermost corners by Ionic columns The Ionic order should bear a dentil cornice but this non adherence to classical Roman dictates is typical of Italian Mannerism, so popular during the Jacobean period. The columns, the entablatures, the rounded arched recesses are all classical elements freely used to create a composition which is substantially unclassical and includes Netherlandish ornament and brightly coloured heraldry but which has little in common with earlier Renaissance works.

In this monument, dating soon after 1621, we see the spirit of the later Elizabethan and Jacobean periods exemplified in a self-confident and assertive secularism. This was the age of the great architectural monument, many canopied examples reaching to the very roof of the church. Earlier, during the reign of Edward VI effigies had been suspect and had suffered acts of vandalism. These acts had ceased in the reign of the catholic queen, Mary Tudor (1553-58) but had threatened to be re-enacted in the reign of Queen Elizabeth (1558-1603) had she not intervened in 1560 and expressly forbidden such secular vandalism. Monuments became 'big business' and the worldly successful gave full play to commemorative ostentation. The Reformation brought, not the celebration of saints and religious imagery as heretofore but secular and, very often, though not in the case of the Dunster monument, antique pagan motifs passed on through the medium of the Renaissance.

The repertoire of classical Renaissance ornament which survived during the late Elizabethan and Jacobean periods shows how plain, for its period, is the Dunster monument, for such motifs as trophies of arms, acanthus scrolls derived from Roman sarcophagi, masks, mermaids and sea-monsters and, above all, the ubiquitous strapwork, lively in the Elizabethan period but becoming more static in the Jacobean period,, abounded. Although the Dunster monument exhibits a very poor example of strapwork decoration, it is perhaps worth saying that this decorative element originated from the shields, scrolls and the cartouches in early *cinquecento* decoration. It was developed by Rosso at Fontainebleau and soon found its way into Flanders where the engravers embraced it with enthusiasm and enjoyed to the full the writhing and curvetting leaps of this architecture in space cut, as it were, from parchment or leather. The architects employed strapwork in decorative stucco work; the carvers, in woodwork. At first using it in interiors of a festive nature and later in brick and stonework. It reached Elizabethan England via Antwerp and enjoyed enormous popularity and was to be found in the decoration of ceilings, screens, chimney pieces, funerary monuments and as a decorative element surrounding heraldic achievements.

Another ornamental device was ribbon-work which persisted as a decorative device down to the mid eighteenth century. Obelisks also abounded and these, derived from Egypt, symbolised eternity. Sometimes the obelisk bore a heart or a ball on its apex. Later symbolism made its appearance in the form of cherubs of which the Dunster monument boasts one. In the celestial hierarchy an angel was of the second order; the highest of the nine orders of angels being the seraph, especially associated with love. In funerary parlance they represented the spiritual world of immortality but, sometimes they were the representatives of death as they are shown resting on spades or extinguished torches. The Four Cardinal virtues of prudence, temperance, fortitude and justice vied with the Three Theological Virtues of faith, hope and charity and all appeared as female figures from classical antiquity and were there to reflect the virtues of the deceased.. Symbols of death were also epitomised by the urn which, when shown with flames emerging from it, represented, not death, but immortality. The burning lamp, on the other hand, was a symbol of faith and this entered the funerary repertoire in the 17th century. Death, immortality and the transitoriness of a mortal life had many manifestations such as skulls, bones, hourglasses, spindles and thread (an allusion to the fables of Greek mythology). Above all, Time appeared as an old man with a scythe.[36]

On the Dunster monument there is a skull on the lower right face and on a bracket attached to the back-plate a funerary helm; here a barriers' helm appropriate to the rank of a baron or knight and often made of wood. The spike would have held the carved, probably wooden, crest of the Luttrells and black velvet mantling would originally have flowed from this helm which would have been carried in the funerary procession. What is so interesting about this monument is that the bevelled black marble edge is decorated with a typical Netherlandish device of gadroons and single dots and this is considered to be the trade mark of Southwark workshops of which there are examples at Bottesford (Leics),for the earl of Rutland and at Holcombe Regis (Devon), Richard Bluett (d 1614). At Dunster the gadroons are strictly not correct since they diminish towards the top. Following the religious persecution and domestic upheaval caused by the Wars of Religion in the Netherlands and above all on the arrival of the hated Spanish duke of Alva in the Low Countries, many protestant refugees made for our shores. Among them were monumental masons who created some of our most important monuments.

In *Churches of Somerset* by the late Kenneth Wickham, the Jacobean monument is referred to in these words: "It may be of interest to note that of the monuments before 1600 only two, and those of the most important families, Paulet and Luttrell, are in alabaster."[37] He also gives, under Dunster, Thomas Luttrell 1570 (alabaster)[38]. In fact, whilst the inscription refers to the death of Thomas Luttrell in 1570, the monument was not erected until after 1621 when Joan Stewkley, the first wife of George Luttrell, died. The extract from Wickham continues: "In the seventeenth century more than twelve are in this material, including those of William Brewer 'phisitian'. By this time, it became a cheaper material;, and perhaps for that reason the supplies became exhausted. There is an outcrop of alabaster on the coast near Blue Anchor, and this is evidence to show that this was largely drawn upon in the seventeenth century."[39]

Thomas Gerard wrote 'A Particular Description of Somerset', and in speaking of 'Mynehead' he refers to the Dutchman who located the alabaster and said: "The Dunster monument was visited by Mr Hamper in the early nineteenth century and he wrote: 'On the S. side is a stately mural monument of various kinds of marble, whereon are recumbent the effigies of a man in armour, and two females; another man in a kneeling attitude, and in a religious vest. These are the memorials of the Luttrell family."[40] The reference to a 'religious vest', is somewhat misleading since George Luttrell never aspired to holy orders.

Professor Pevsner's entry regarding this monument follows: "Thomas Luttrell + 1571 and George Luttrell + 1629. S. chapel. Large Jacobean monument set up by George Luttrell after the death of his wife in 1613, for four persons, Thomas and wife and George and wife. George kneels, the others recumbent. The whole is treated as one composition, flanked by a column on the l. and the r. Not of special skill or elaboration."[41]

The heraldry surmounting the canopy of the monument is of interest and comprises three coats of arms.

On the left the shield of Luttrell within a cartouche. The arms may be blazoned thus: *Or a bend between six Martlets Sa.* The shield is oval and not within a bordure engrailed or a decorated quatrefoil as is sometimes shown in earlier Luttrell arms. For example, the quatrefoil of elaborate form shown in the seal of Sir Alexander Luttrell (fl 1318-1354) and the engrailed seal of Sir Hugh Luttrell (d 1428).[42] In the middle the arms of George's parents, Thomas and Margaret Luttrell née Hadley are displayed. They may be blazoned thus: Luttrell quartering Hadley. *1 and 4 Luttrell. Or a bend between six Martlets Sa. 2 and 3 quarterly 1 and 4 Gu on a chevron Or between three Cross-crosslets Sa for Hadley. 2 and 3 Or on a bend cotised Sa three Bears' heads Arg bridled Gu for Durborough.* This shield is surmounted by two confronted helms carrying crests, the otter and the panache of feathers and is on a cartouche with mantling.

ARMS

George Luttrell (d 1629) transformed Dunster castle from a medieval castle into its present form of a largely seventeenth century mansion and it was he who was responsible for the spider-web plaster ceiling in the Inner Hall. Here he caused the arms of Thomas and Margaret Luttrell, his parents, to be displayed over the fireplace with the Luttrell motto. *Quæsita marte tuenda arte* flanked by the swan supporters from the arms of Bohun and Courtenay from whom Elizabeth Luttrell née Courtenay (d 1395), the purchaser of the castle from Lady Joan de Mohun, was descended. These supporters were adopted by her son, Sir Hugh Luttrell (d1428), and the arms are also to be found on a plaster overmantel in the 'dairy' at Marshwood. Before discussing the arms on the right of the canopy, as you face the monument, the crests of the Luttrells, the otter and panache of feathers should be explained. The name Luttrell was originally spelt Luterel or Loterel and was derived from the French word for an otter *loutre,* and ultimately from the Latin *lutra.* It is thought that it was first used as a punning nickname. In 1180 and again in 1198 an Osbert Loterel farmed at Arques (Normandy) and in 1419 John Loutrel of Dieppe is mentioned as a subject of the French king, Charles VII. The device of the otter first appears on the small signet used by Sir John Luttrell (1394-1430), the son of the first Sir Hugh Luttrell (d 1428), Sir John's son, Sir James Luttrell (c1426-61) also used this device on a larger signet. It also appears with the arms of Luttrell and their motto in the plaster overmantel at East Quantoxhead. It continued to be used by several members of the family but was quietly abandoned in the eighteenth century by Margaret Luttrell and her husband Henry Fownes. The panache of feathers was used on a very fine seal by Sir Hugh Luttrell (d 1428) towards the end of his life. This crest was not used again until it was revived by George Luttrell (d 1629) who not only used it to surmount the arms of his parents Thomas and Margaret Luttrell on the canopy of the monument but also used it on his seal. Here the plume of twelve feathers is arranged in two rows rising out of a crest coronet unlike Sir Hugh Luttrell's panache which is triangular in form with interwoven feathers, flat and uncurled.

The panache crest also surmounts the arms of Luttrell impaled with those of Capps to be found in the hotel named the Luttrell Arms (see later). At East Quantoxhead George altered and enlarged the manor house for his second wife, Silvestra Capps. On George's death in 1629, Silvestra had for her jointure the manor of East Quantoxhead as late as 1655. The arms of Luttrell together with the otter crest and motto displayed on the plaster overmantel, already mentioned, belong to this period. It is a very strange thing that the arms of George's first wife, Joan Stewkley, who lies in effigy on the monument to the right of her in-laws, do not appear on the monument at all. The arms of Stewkley of Marshe were: *Chequy Arg and Sa a fess Gu with a bordure Az*. These arms quarterly were confirmed and crest granted to Thomas Stewkley of Marshe, Somerset by R.Lee Clarencieux on 21 June 1595.

The arms on the right as you face the monument are those of Thomas Luttrell (1584-1644), the eldest son and heir of George Luttrell and his first wife, Joan Stewkley, and of Thomas's wife, Jane Popham. The arms of Luttrell *Or a bend between six Martlets Sa* are impaled with those of Popham *Arg on a chief Gu two Bucks' heads cabossed Or with a crescent for a difference*. So while the monument shows no arms nor inscription for Thomas's mother, Joan Stewkley whose effigy lies on the monument, it does show the arms of her son and his wife whose effigies are not on the monument. Thomas married Jane Popham in 1621 and for the young couple, George, renowned for his building activities, renovated Marshwood where they lived probably until 1629 when George died and they went to live at the castle which George had turned from a range of medieval buildings in the lower ward into a comfortable manor house. All that remained of the earlier castle being the ruins on the Tor and Sir Reynold de Mohun's gateway below and the gatehouse of Sir Hugh Luttrell (d 1428), now known as the Tenant's Hall.

GEORGE LUTTRELL

George was born in 1560 the year the rectory and tithes of Dunster were sold, eventually to end up in the hands of Hugh Stewkley. This was of great material advantage to him as was the wardship of the then young George which he bought from the Crown soon after the death of George's father, Thomas, in 1571 when George was eleven years of age. As was so often the case, the object of securing a wardship was to marry off a daughter to an influential, or rich person to the advantage of the bride and her family. George did have the opportunity to choose between Hugh Stewkley's two daughters Susan and Joan, he chose Joan. A marriage was solemnly contracted between the fifteen year old George and the thirteen year old Joan. He took her hand and said 'I George take thee, Joan, to my wedded wife, and thereto I give thee my faith and my troth.' Hugh Stewkley was an astute lawyer and he made sure that there were witnesses to this contract and that they should sign 'a written memorial of it'.[43] As it turned out Hugh Stewkley was very wise in securing testimony of the event.

George started his education under the tutorship of a Mr Brebrooke; an arrangement made by Hugh Stewkley. In July 1576, George, then nearly sixteen, was admitted a fellow commoner at Caius College, Cambridge and was given a cubicle in the master's lodging. The next year he wrote from Cambridge a letter in which he stated his firm intention of marrying his betrothed. The couple were distant cousins since Joan, a daughter of Elizabeth Luttrell of Powderham (d1493), and her first husband Sir James Luttrell (1426-61) had married a George Stewkley (d 1508).[44]

George said that by announcing his intention he hoped to see the 'brablings' between her father, Hugh Stewkley, and his own grandmother, the redoubtable Dame Margaret Luttrell, at an end. George's father, Thomas, had been dead for six years and his mother Margery Hadley was now married to her second husband, John Strode of Parnham (Dorset). He too joined in the fray and all three opposed the marriage. Grandmother declared that her grandson would be 'utterly cast away' if he were to marry the daughter of a miserly lawyer who was a thorn in the side of the Luttrell family. She made threatening noises and declared that if her wishes were disregarded she would leave the priory of Dunster to someone else and thus render George 'a poor gentleman'.[45] Joan Stewkley certainly did not get a 'good press' from one Sir James fitz James who said she was,' a slutte and that she had no good qualities.[46] Sir James had 'an axe to grind' for he was desirous of capturing the young heir for his niece. This Welsh alliance did not materialise and George married his intended at Dunster on 25 September 1580, and in October 1580 he was admitted a member of Grays Inn and in 1584 was returned as one of the two members for Minehead.

In 1580, Dame Margaret relented and made a will in which she bequeathed to George the hanging arras that had been made for the parlour (the present dining-room) of Dunster castle, two bowls of silver gilt, a drinking cup of silver-gilt that had belonged to his father Thomas, two spoons and a salt and above all, that wise purchase she had effected at the dissolution of the monasteries, the priory of Dunster with all the lands and profits appertaining to it. She died on 7 July 1580, two months before the wedding and was buried beside her husband, Sir Andrew and Sir Hugh Kt. (d1521),her father-in-law, at East Quantoxhead.[47] In 1588, the year of the Spanish Armada, Dame Mary Luttrell, the widow of George's uncle, Sir John Luttrell (d 1551), died and he acquired Kilton and in 1607, on the death of his mother, he succeeded to the lands which she held in dower and to the Hadley inheritance. During her lifetime George had agreed to let her have, …"one fee bucke of season in the summer and one fee doe in the winter," from his park at Dunster or from that at East Quantoxhead at her choice.[48]

As soon as George Luttrell came of age, the ever avaricious Hugh Stewkley presented his son-in-law with a long list of his dues as lay rector. They were as follows:

1. Agistment of Dunster Park for all cattle feeding there, and the shoulder of every deer killed, on the ground that the South lawn had been under cultivation at the end of the reign of Henry the Eighth.
2. Agistment of the Park at the rate of a penny in the shilling on its value.
3. Tithe of the bailiff of Dunster, the keeper of the park, and all servants, at the rate of a penny in the shilling on half of their wages.
4. Agistment of Dunster mills at the rate of a penny in the shilling on the rental.
5. Agistment of the Waterlete and Caremore (near the sea). A fee of 53s.4d for the stewardship of the lands late of Sir John Luttrell, out of the manor of Dunster.
6. Tithe of the conies in the warren, and of the desmesne lands of the manor of Minehead between the Whitehouse and Minehead Lane, near the sea.[49]

He also claimed that three houses in the churchyard belonged to him as parson.

The reference to Minehead brings to mind the involvement of Hugh Stewkley in Minehead Park. During the lifetime of George Luttrell's uncle, Sir John Luttrell, Hugh Stewkley had foreclosed on a mortgage of Minehead Park which Sir John, in need of money to pay the soldiery in the Scottish wars, had secured from the crafty lawyer. This land had ceased to be a park in the lifetime of his grandfather, and his grandmother, Dame Margaret , had promised to pay off her son's debt but in spite of Hugh Stewkley being castigated as 'behaving dishonestly in the matter',[50] he held on to this valuable agricultural property of two hundred acres. George's grasping father-in-law also laid claim as lay rector to the ownership of 'three houses in the churchyard' which belonged to him, 'as parson'. There was a little financial respite for George who could offset, against the tithes demanded, the burgage rents due to him as freeholder.[51]

A vicar had served the people of Dunster up to 1561 when the incumbent John Ryce died. The customary procedure had been for the prior and convent of Bath to present to the benefice for institution their chosen candidate. After the dissolution of the monasteries this practice was considered to be unnecessary. However, Dunster appears to have slipped through the net for, although the priory was dissolved in 1539, Ryce remained. The position of the vicar of Dunster was indeed a parlous one. Unlike the lay rector, no tithes were assigned to him, no accommodation provided and scarcely any endowment. This resulted in the suppression of the vicarage and it became Hugh Stewkley's obligation, as lay owner of the benefice, to provide a stipendary curate. In spite of the people's protest of 1566 concerning the lack of a vicar, it took Hugh Stewkley sixteen years to fulfill their needs. In 1582 one William Hodgson was appointed. The people must have been greatly relieved when Hugh Stewkley departed this life in 1588. The portrait of George Luttrell, painted when he was thirty-four years of age in 1594 shows him dressed in black brocade with a metal belt, a large ruff and white cuffs. In the top right hand corner the shield show the arms of Luttrell.

George is said to have been. 'noted for his hospitality and general love and respect of his neighbours.' He was appointed sheriff of Somerset the year before the portrait was painted and hospitality was one of the obligations of his office. An office to which he was again appointed in 1609.[52] He was, above all, a lawyer engrossed in the minutia of the law. To ensure his legal rights in the Honour of Dunster , he is thought to have spent a considerable time in London poring over records; evidence to support his feudal rights. He engaged in suits against his father-in-law the lawyer Hugh Stewkley, against his aunt Mary Luttrell, the widow of Sir John Luttrell, and against his tenants, neighbours and tradesmen. He was a prolific writer of ill-written notes concerning rents, boundaries and such like 'bones of contention.'

It is thought to have been at George's instigation that a royal commission was appointed to enquire into maintenance of the port of Minehead and to discover if the portreeve and the burgesses had carried out their duties and obligations in this respect. The conclusion was that they had not and in the early part of the 17th century the charter was forfeited and the corporation dissolved. Although he was their member of Parliament his relations with the borough were less than amicable and he even wished the town to be disenfranchised. His building activities did, however, secure for Minehead in 1616, a pier known as 'the old Quay'. This he provided at a considerable cost of £5,000.

It is for his building achievements alone that George Luttrell is a notable figure in the history of Dunster. In October 1617 he engaged William Arnold also known as William Goverson, or William Arnold alias Goverson, to convert the irregular pile of medieval buildings in the lower ward of Dunster castle into a Jacobean house. William Arnold was living at Charlton Musgrove near Wincanton from c.1595. He was the churchwarden and his children were baptised there and finally on 12 March 1637 he was buried in this place only twelve miles from Montacute. Wadham College, Oxford, was founded in 1610 and Pembroke in 1624.[53] Arnold was referred to by Dorothy Wadham as 'an honest man' and 'a perfectt workman' and she engaged the practical stonemason and sculptor to design and build Wadham College. One of the Wadham trustees, Sir Edward Hext said he was 'wonderfully sought being in deede the absolutest and honestest workeman in Ingland'. He came of a family of craftsmen and was originally a stonemason and sculptor. Edmund and Thomas Arnold, who are thought to have been his brothers were employed as masons at Wadham college and his father, Arnold Goverson, was a joiner at Longleat in 1555. William was not, in the modern sense of the word an architect although he was capable of supplying 'plots' (plans) and 'uprights' (elevations) for his clients and had a reputation for 'great experience in architecture'.

He is thought to have designed Montacute by reason of a letter which Dorothy Wadham wrote to her brother Lord Petre in which she said that Arnold had been 'commended' to her by her 'good friend and lovinge neighboure Sir Edward Phelipps'. Here is revealed more than a local mason; a man of imagination who conjured up unforgettable fantasies such as the charming little lantern-crowned turrets at the corners of the balustraded parapets at Montacute. These have an airy delicacy by reason of their skeletal form and their domes are of an unusual ogee shape. For the earl of Salisbury Arnold designed Cranborne (Dorset) where the porch ties up with that of Wayford Manor (Somerset) and, at this latter place, the fireplace finds a twin at Montacute. His work can be traced in Dorset, Somerset, Wiltshire and Devon where details, not only of chimney-pieces and porches, but of tombs can be found.[54]

George Luttrell's building at Dunster lacks the imagination and fantasy of Montacute and Cranborne. This is the account given by Lyte: "George Luttrell, the first of that name, may from some points of view be regarded as the creator of the existing Castle. Dissatisfied with the irregular medieval buildings which he found at the eastern end of the Lower Ward he set himself to convert them into a mansion suitable to the requirements of a more luxurious age. Retaining at least two projecting towers and the thick outer walls on three sides, he inserted in the latter a series of square-headed windows, each divided by a mullion and a transom into four oblong lights. Furthermore, he entirely reconstructed the façade, giving to it as symmetrical an appearance as circumstances would allow. All his external masonry is laid in regular courses of red stone with quoins of a lighter colour. Within the Castle, his walls may be recognised as being thinner than those of the thirteenth century and thicker than those of the eighteenth. Owing to the slope of the ground and perhaps also to earlier arrangements, he found it difficult to establish uniform levels throughout the mansion, and so divided it into two sections, each comprising three storeys, the floors of the rooms in the southern section being several feet higher than those of the rooms on the northern side of the transverse wall. To him may certainly be attributed the ornamental plaster ceiling of the Hall, the frieze of the Gallery, the balusters of the part of the smaller staircase and at least two architraves within the existing fabric."[55]

The ornamental plaster ceiling of the Inner Hall is called a "spider-web" ceiling and it is far more delicate than the work done in the parlour, the dining-room in the time of Colonel Francis Luttrell. Over the chimney-piece may be seen the arms of Thomas and Margaret Luttrell dated 1589 and there is also a fireback bearing the arms and initials of Queen Elizabeth I. In 1617 George Luttrell entered into an agreement with William Arnold for "a house or parcell of building to be sett up and built within the castle of Dunster."[56] Arnold agreed to provide a "plot" or plan and an "upright" or elevation of the envisaged edifice and "to oversee the work until the completion of the roof."[57]

George Luttrell paid William Arnold £40 in instalments and his travelling expenses but perhaps his greatest reward was a toe-hold in Dunster in the form of a beneficial lease of lands called Burchams, the Hollingborrowes and Lyncroft situate in the north-western part of Dunster[58]. However, all ended in discord and Arnold had to apply to the court of chancery to get his money. George Luttrell contended that Arnold had substituted a fresh plan other than that originally approved and that the building he was erecting agreed with neither plan. Complaints about the wastage of materials, unduly protracted work not well executed and finally the cost which had been estimated at £462 was likely far to exceed that sum and be in the region of £1,200. "An allusion to stairs leading from the new building into the new cellar, and another allusion to a pre-existing back wall, seem to show that Arnold's addition to the Castle, comprised the central portion of the main façade.[59]

It was on 3 October 1622 that George Luttrell married his second wife, referred to in a quote of Lyte's as "an obscure person."[60] His first wife, Joan Stewkley died in 1621 and ten months later he married Silvestra Capps, the daughter of James Capps of Jews in the parish of Wiveliscombe, apparently of Welsh origin, and of his wife Maria, a daughter of William Lancaster, Esq., of Milverton, whose elder sister was the wife of Roger Sydenham of Skilgate.[61] George and Silvestra were married at East Quantoxhead which, together with the manor of Kilton, was part of the estate settled on her as her jointure.[62] She enjoyed this provision for the twenty-six years she survived her first husband. It was most probably for the newly married couple that the alterations were made. High up in one of the bedrooms on the first floor of the Luttrell Arms Hotel there is a shield commemorating the marriage. It is surmounted by the panache crest of George Luttrell. These arms also appear on the porch tower. They may be blazoned thus: *Or a bend betw six Martlets Sa* (for Luttrell) impaled with *Arg a chevron betw three trefoils slipped* (for Capps). The latter arms are given by Lyte who refers to them as "the reputed arms of Silvestra Capps...."[63] In Burke's *General Armory* we find Capps/Cappus (Kent) given as *Arg a chevron betw three trefoils slipped*.

Prebendary Hancock in *Wifela's Coombe* writes: "The family do not appear, however, in the Herald's Visitations of Somerset, except that the marriage of James Cappes with the daughter of Mr Lancaster is noted in the Lancaster pedigree in the Visitation of 1623 and that John Cappes,[64] gent, of Huish Champflower is returned as 'ignobilis' in the same Visitation, his application to have his coat of arms registered by the visiting Heralds , having been refused."[65] Further, Hancock says that James Cappes refers to himself as 'a gentleman of ancyente discente and lyvynge, answerable to his calling', but adds that 'his name is not registered in the Herald's Visitation of 1623.'[66] Wiveliscombe appears frequently in the Star Chamber proceedings and in 1558 the proceedings concerned a dispute between Anthony Stawell of Colthestone and Thomas Cappes, then the owner of Jews/Jewes.

In 1581 the Cappes or Capes family again figure in the Star Chamber's proceedings. They appear to have been a very quarrelsome family always in dispute with their neighbours. Hancock writes: "Their quarrel on this occasion was with "David Yea of Wyveliscombe, yeoman, John Yea and Christopher Hoyll of Wyveliscombe, and others, for dyvers vearye notable and owtragious ryotts and other misdemeanoures by them before that tyme committed and done"" "James Cappes of Jewes, Somerset, Esq.," is the complainant. The defendants answer that the accusation is untrue: "Whereas he did complain of a riotous assault made by certen of the defendants upon one John Slocombe his servante, and of a greate wounde and hurte then given to John Slocombe in his hedd and face by Jozyns Holcombe one of the defendants. The said Xtofer Hoyll did make his answer upon his othe, that the said Jozyns Holcombe with the wrong ende of a dagger gave Slocombe a small towche in the face and a little scratched him, as yt weare with the scratching of a Bremell (bramble), which the said Hoyll in that manner most falselye sett down in his said answere to thintente to excuse the ofence of Holcombe and of himself and other his confederates. Whereas in vearie deed Xtopher Hoyll did viewe and see the saide wounde and hurte, and did playnelye perceive and know the same to be vearye great wownde...Whereby the said Hoyll in his answer to this court did wilfullye perjure and forsweare himself....,.being thereunto directly suborned by David Yea and John Yea." "A committee was appointed to sit at Wilveliscombe and go into the rights of the case, consisting of Gabriel Hawley, Esq., William Lacy, Nicholas Strete, and John Worth, gents, who sat from "nyne o'clock in the forenoon until abowte eight of the clock att night of the same day, and a veary dilligent and carefull manner for the despatch of the witnesses." David Yea endeavoured to break up the proceedings, Cappes states, "well knowinge that the dew exs thereof would depely towche him... and presentlye grewe into vearye badd and unseemlye speeches and contemptuous behavyour in disturbance of the sd court, saying that your subject did lye, and called him 'knave' several tymes. Your subject beinge a Gentleman of ancyente descente and of lyveinge answearable to his calling, and the said David Yea att the beginning but a Husbandman and a days laborer in husbandrye for any man that would hyer hym to doe work, but had by happ a certen farme income unto him for terme of his lief onely." The commissioners appear to have come to no conclusion, and a fresh commission is appointed. David Yea draws his dagger upon Cappes, but is restrained by two of the commissioners; Yea then declares that Cappes "did then challenge hym into the feeld, sayinge that if he durste go with hym into the feeld he would then ende all matters of controversye between them." They were put out of the room, when Yea declared Cappes would have attacked him with his dagger, "had hee not been staied by the people that stood bye, and uttered very hard and lewde speeches against hym." Cappes denied having threatened or abused Yea, but the commissioners commit him to the Fleet[67] from whence he memorializes the Star Chamber. David Yea denies any violence on his part. He objected to one witness, John Woollcott, because he was a "lewd person and of small credite, and had been indyted dyvers times for felony, and had suffered paynes of death yf he had not had benefitt of his Clergie." Hereupon Cappes, he declares ," did revyle him, and used wordes of such disgrace and contempte as were far unmeete for the place, and not decente in any place. He asserts that he is contente with his callinge and had rather be the first gentleman of his kindred than the last, and an honest subject than an unquyet troblesome gentleman; and yet yf that were to the purpose he thinketh that many a husbandman and daye labourer hath bene better descended, and that without disgrace of gentrey, than the Plaintiff, though his lyvyng be answearable to his descent, with which he ought to be contented, rather than make such greate bragges thereof."[68] It would appear that Yea, of more humble origin than Capps was a far nicer person. Silvestra Capps, the daughter of James committed to Fleet prison, was as unpleasant as her father - as will be seen later.

Silvestra Luttrell was the mother of Sarah Luttrell alias Capps and Diana Luttrell alias Capps During his lifetime, their father, George Luttrell, provided generously for them and, on his death in 1629, he left £500 to each of them when they attained the age of twenty-one, or on marriage.[69] Sarah married Alexander Keynes and Diana married John Wogan of Pembrokeshire in 1634 at East Quantoxhead and secondly Alexander Lynde.[70]

George Luttrell by his first wife, Joan Stewkley had five sons and seven daughters so Sarah and Diana had many step brothers and sisters. They were:

Thomas, his father's heir

Hugh of Rodhuish, baptised at Dunster on 29 February 1587. He married at Charlton Makerel on 13 July 1629, Jane the daughter of Thomas Lyte of Lytes Cary in that parish. He was alive in 1656. He had property, not only in Rodhuish in the parish of Carhampton, but at Northridge and West Myne in that of Minehead.[71]

George, baptised at Dunster on 12 October 1590 and buried there on 30 December 1619.

John, baptised at Dunster on 5 January, 1592. Alive 1620

Andrew, baptised at Dunster on 6 June 1596 and buried there four days later.

Margaret, baptised at East Quantoxhead 11 October 1584,and married John Trevelyan of Nettlecombe at Dunster 3 August 1607.

Catherine, baptised at Dunster 18 April 1589. She married Lewis Pyne of East Down (Devonshire) the day after her sister Margaret on 4 August 1607.

Elizabeth, baptised at Dunster 23 March 1593, was buried there 21 May 1595.

Susan, baptised at Dunster 9 October 1594. She married John Francis of Coombe Florey at Dunster on 29 June 1612.[72]

There was a second Elizabeth by George Luttrell's first marriage. She was baptised just over three years after the death of her namesake. The ceremony took place at Dunster on 3 October 1598. Her mother Joan Luttrell née Stewkley died and was buried on 22 November 1621 and in the March1621/2,George Luttrell, her father declared that she should inherit the large sum of £1,400, bequeathed to her by her late mother, provided that she did not marry a popish recusant (that is a catholic who refused to attend the Church of England services) or, the son of such a person, or, for that matter, any other prospective bridegroom without his consent. He did not die until 1629 but nevertheless he also laid down that if she married after that event, she would have to gain the consent of Thomas Wyndham of Kentsford, John Francis and Richard Worth, or two of them. Should she see fit to disregard her father's wishes, the money was to be divided between her sister Margaret Trevelyan's children and her sister Susan's husband, John Francis.[73] In spite of the £1.400, such a large sum of money in 1622, her heart won and she married into a notable Roman catholic family, the bridegroom being Thomas Arundel of Chideock in Dorset. It seems extraordinary that her father could override his wife's will unless there was a clause covering the situation. It is apparent that Elizabeth must have been her mother's favourite, for Sarah, baptised at Dunster 3 April 1600 only inherited £200 from her mother and, in this case George did not make any stipulation concerning her choice of husband.[74] She married Edmund Bowyer of Beer, near Cannington[75] at Dunster 9 February 1625. She was buried at Stockland, on the 17 May 1664.[76]

The last child of this marriage was Mary and all we know about her is that she was buried at Dunster on 24 March 1608.[77] So with his two wives, George Luttrell fathered five sons and nine daughters. After his death his second wife, Silvestra Luttrell married Sir Edmund Skory, who does not seem to have liked her very much for, in his will, dated 4 May 1632 be bequeathed 20s 'to Giles Baker, my servant, who hath lived under the tyranny of my wife, to the danger of his life, during the spate of two years'.[78] He also bequeathed 'to Dame Silvestra Skory, my wife, whom I harteley forgive all her wicked attempts against mee, a praier booke called *The Practice of Piety* desiring that she better love and affect the same than hitherto she hath done'.[79] It appears that Dame Skory unsuccessfully endeavoured to establish that the testator was of unsound mind.[80] Undaunted by two seemingly unhappy unions, Dame Skory managed to prevail on a third unfortunate man to enter the state of matrimony with her and in 1634, at East Quantoxhead, she married Giles Penny.[81] Her stepson, Thomas, son of George Luttrell by his first wife, Joan Luttrell brought a suit against her for he alleged that she had damaged his deer and his timber at East Quantoxhead.

During her marriage to George he had materially altered the manor house. So much so that it is apparently difficult to trace the old plan. He enlarged the house and his initials together with those of Silvestra are to be found on a leaden pipe-head there together with the date 1628, the year before George's death. It is known that Silvestra was in possession of the manor house in 1655 and therefore she survived her step-son Thomas Luttrell who was buried at Dunster on 7 February 1644[82]. She also survived Alexander his son, who died in 1642 or 1643.[83]

The story of Silvestra Capps unfolded as a result of the building activities at the Luttrell Arms during the early years of her marriage to George Luttrell when it was not an inn. George's most celebrated achievement was the building of the Yarn Market, or Market House, erected for the sale of cloth. The exact date of its erection is not known but George died in 1629 at the age of sixty-nine years. Certainly cloth making had gone on in Dunster, at least as early as 1259 when there was a fulling-mill which yielded 13s.4d to the representative of the lord of the manor. At that time the heir was under age and Queen Eleanor was given the wardship by Henry III; presumably therefore the 13s.4d was paid to the Crown. Professor Powicke writes: "King Edward, from the first, showed an appreciation of the cities and boroughs as elements in the community, apart from their liability to immediate taxation.....in his first parliament after his return (Easter 1275), when the new duty on wool was granted "at the request of the communities of merchants," probably more cities, boroughs and merchant towns were represented, "than in any subsequent parliament before 1500." This parliament, however, had more than a mercantile purpose, which explains the presence of persons from little market centres which never or rarely were represented again; it was intended as a demonstration of Edward's good intentions and in this aspect reveals a new interest in the organs of corporate activity in the realm, not an intention to link the boroughs in parliament with grants of taxation.[84]

During the 14th century there was a rapid expansion of the cloth industry, until in the 15th century it was deliberately fostered by the government of Edward IV. It is said that he showed a keen interest in foreign trade and backed a number of successful commercial ventures as a merchant inhis own right.[85] In 1464 he forbade the importation of foreign cloth and in 1467 he 'prohibited the export of unfulled cloth.'[86] Professor Mackie has further interesting information to impart and says: "In his reign the export trade in wool, which during the Wars of the Roses had fallen to 35,000 cloths, rose to 62,000. The Tudors, in this as in other matters, followed the Yorkist precedent and encouraged the cloth industry by all means in their power. During the reign of Henry VIII the export figures showed a steady rise from about 85,000 cloths to over 120,000 and the average annual figure was upwards of 98,000. This export consisted almost entirely of plain undyed cloth, partly because the Flemings, who were great buyers, insisted upon dyeing themselves, but even so the expansion of the woolen trade spelt prosperity for many areas. Before long the trade became wholesale. In London, Blackwell Hall became the scene of a weekly market for cloth brought from the country, and in Norwich, Bristol, York, Southampton, Beverley, Coventry, Northampton and Winchester separate markets were reserved for the sale of cloth alone. A business so widespread and so prosperous soon burst forth from the simple organization of the gild and the narrow limit of the town. The "clothier" became a producer on a large scale who employed men engaged upon all processes of manufacture. Factories were not unknown." [87]

Abbeys such as Malmesbury and Osney housed a large number of looms, the former having been bought by Willian Stumpe from the king and the latter rented by him in 1546[88]. "Tucker of Burford, who employed 500 workers sought, in 1538, to establish himself in the abbey of Abingdon, and all over the country from Kendal in the north to the Cotswolds, Somerset and Wiltshire and East Anglia, wealthy clothiers began to flourish. From the evidence it is plain that their looms were often "in their houses."[89]

In 1529, Thomas Everard, the younger, paid a rent to Sir Andrew Luttrell (d1538) for "a clotherack caulyd the myddell racke upon Grobfast with a fullyng myll caulyd Frekeford."[90] The fulling mill at Frackford, variously spelt Frekeford or Frilford, was rented by Thomas Touker a few years after 1418 during the lordship of the first Luttrell lord of Dunster, Sir Hugh Luttrell. In 1533 a John Toker left his "toker's shears," (fuller's shears) which were "with Bernard Dovell, towards the building of the tower of Old Cleeve." According to Hancock: "John Toker in the same year (he had been writing about 1532) left the vicar (of Dunster) his 'best shears'"[91] In 1534 John Leland noted that, "the toun of Dunestorre makith cloth."[92]

The tucking-mill owned by the abbot of Cleeve in West Street before the Reformation was, in the reign of Queen Elizabeth I, demolished by the grantee named Colle, who erected, in its stead, two corn mills. These were a threat to George Luttrell who owned the anciently held manorial grist or corn mills and he sought to deprive Colle of the necessary water, by diverting a part of the water course. In reply Colle brought a suit against George Luttrell for 'breaking the head-water at Hurlpool'.[93] 'In 1589 George Howe of Dunster, clothier, built "one tuckinge or fullinge mill" of "two stooks" adjoining the eastern end of the "water griste mille," situate "under the Castell Torre, on the south parte thereof"[94]. For this George Howe had only to pay a nominal rent of 26s 8d. because he had been put to great expense to erect the mill. George Luttrell leased to him for twenty-one years and included much more than the mill, viz: "… a close called Culvercliffe containing two acres, with a rack standing therein "under Grobhurst "(Grabbist), two "rackromes" standing on the south-western part of Castle Tor, and a little plot called the "Hopkegarden," on the western side of the common ryne adjoining the grist-mill…[95]

Both the demolished fulling mill and George Howe's fulling mill were of two 'stooks', that is to say, there were two fulling-stocks or great beams which were set in motion by the water wheel to pound the cloth. Acts of parliament passed in 1601 and 1607 laid down that: "Dunster cotton hereafter shalbe by this present acte intended and taken to be of like length and breadth as Taunton and Bridgewater cloth."[96] The further enactment stated: "That every broad cloth commonly called Tauntons, Bridgewaters and Dunsters, made in the western part of Somersetshire, or elsewhere of like making, shall contain, being thoroughly wet, between twelve and thirteen yards, and in breadth seven quarters of a yard at the least, and being well scoured, thicked, milled and fully dried, shall weigh thirty pounds the cloth at least."[97]

We do not know the exact year George Luttrell built the Yarn Market but in 1571 a Richard Worth of Dunster left £6 13s.4d to assist young apprentices 'exercising the art of cloth-making in the borough'.[98] He must have been proud to see the business his building engendered as the cloth sellers stood back to back and bargained with their prospective buyers standing outside. Freeman said of this building:"The old Market Hall, can, indeed hardly be called in strictness a work of architecture, but its picturesque effect is about as perfect as may be[99] The grandson of George Luttrell, also George (1625-55) is remembered by the weather-vane on top of the Yarn Market. It bears the date 1647 and his initials. He, and his father Thomas were both Parliamentarians during the Civil War when the Yarn Market was damaged by a cannon-ball from the castle and it was probably then that the roof was renewed.[100]

So the cloth making went on in Dunster and in 1655 ' piece of waste land was beaten out of the rock at the lower end of West Street, adjoining the mill-stream, under a close called "Racke Cloase" wherein stood divers fullers' racks'.[101]

Francis Luttrell in 1657 received 35s for the rent of seven 'rack rooms', five of which were on the castle Tor. His extravagant son, Colonel Francis Luttrell did not do so well. There were two more rack rooms but the rent had fallen from 35s for seven to 30s for nine. Colonel Francis Luttrell died in 1690 and, at the beginning of the eighteenth century when his brother, Colonel Alexander Luttrell was lord of Dunster there were four hundred inhabited houses in Dunster and a large manufacture of Kersey cloth was going on. Kersey cloth was named after the village in Suffolk and was a coarse, usually ribbed cloth woven from long wool. George Luttrell is referred to in A History of Somerset: "In July 1596, George Luttrell brought an action against Robert Ragland for fishing in his several fishery at Carhampton and taking fish, viz flounders, soles, shrimps, salmon etc. The defendant pleaded not guilty, but there was a verdict for the plaintiff with damages and costs. It appears from the proceedings that there were at this time, seventeen weirs at Carhampton belonging to Mr Luttrell."

Among various memoranda written in the atrocious hand of George Luttrell, there appears an account of the Rogation Day processions. These processions were suppressed in England in 1547, but under Queen Elizabeth I the royal injunctions of 1559 ordered the perambulation of the parish at rogationtide. The 'Major Rogation' which is on 25 April is a Christianized version of the pagan Robiglia when processions through the cornfields took place and prayers were especially offered for the preservation of the crops from mildew. Historically it has no connection with the feast of St Mark instituted later and also observed on 25 April. The 'Minor Rogations' are kept on the Monday, Tuesday and Wednesday before Ascension Day.[102] According to Bettey: "the sole survivor of the multitude of processions in which the pre Reformation church had engaged, and combined the two functions of maintaining and recording afresh the parish boundaries, and offering prayers for seasonable weather and a successful harvest. The processions were often elaborate affairs, following a traditional ritual of meals, drinking, and horseplay, all designed to impress the route upon the memory of the participants and especially upon the children."[103] Where there were no natural boundaries such as broad rivers the delineation of the boundaries could be obscure, especially in afforested areas or in downland areas. There were no detailed maps and notwithstanding these processions, disputes often ensued which were costly and often long-drawn out. Accurate maps and enclosures did away with the necessity of such processions and, in some places, where processions had provided an excuse for over-eating and drinking to the ratepayer's cost, they were not sorry to see the practice die out.

The account of the Rogation Day procession in Dunster quoted by Lyte in his *History of Dunster* is: "The perambulacon of processyon in the weke caulyd Processyon weke, or Gayn weeke, or Rogacon weke, of the parysh of Dunster. The Monday in Rogacon weke, the parysh going [toward] Alcombe a gospell sayd by Skilaker by the west part of the waye that lieth at the south part of Deneclose where somtyeme was a crosse, and from thence to Alcombe Crosse and there was accostomyd to be sayd a gospell, and from thence to the Chapell of Alcombe and theare a gospell, and from thence backwarde downe by the water to Yllycombe to Pyne's house and theare a gospell, and theare the parysh were accostomed to have a dtynkyng, and from thence to Dene Lane, and so to Dunster Church. The Tewsdaye, upp St George Strete and through Dene Lane and thear torne west by the Pekyd or Threecorner close along in the Marsh, and so over the Fresse to Dunster Hawn, and so from thence over the felde to go to Salterne Lane, and so by Gyltchapell alonge by the parck [pale] under Henstye to a crosse by thollow elme, and from thence leving Holwaye Howse and grounde which W. Hart now holdyth upon the left hande, and so to Gallockes Crosse, and theare a gospell, and from thence over the stone brydge through Gallockes Strete and over the tymber brydge, and so home. The Wennysdaye, from the church through Weststrete over the sayd brydges through Gallockes Strete and by Jone Fynnes dore west in the way to Fayer Oke, and from thence to Avell and thear was accostomyd to be sayd servys in the chapell of Mary Maddaleyne and thear was a drynkyng for the parysh at Avell Howse, and then from thence the sayd parysh went over the water to Hurlepole path and so to the crosse that stoode by the est [of Fra]ckford Howse, whear the bowndes of the burugh of Dunster begann [and so] home."[104]

CHALICE

When George Luttrell was thirteen years of age the Elizabethan cup and cover was made. It bears the London assay mark for the year 1573 and the maker's mark I.P. Whilst it was made in that year it could, of course, have been acquired after that date. Many communion cups were made between 1563/79 by the maker I.P. whose mark is in a shaped shield[105] but his identity is unknown. The inventory pasted inside the 1920 minutes book of the parochial church council lists 'Elizabethan cup and cover 1573. 7$^{5/8}$" high'. Also in this inventory is listed under, 'other Document (if any) of value; Churchwardens' and Overseers' a/cs. 1655-1683. Churchwardens 1670'.[106] The churchwardens' accounts and overseers' accounts are quoted by Hancock. and the first entry given by him under the former is for 1670: "June5th. The Goldsmith for mending the challis...2.0s. Again in 1672: "April 10th One Silver Chalice with cover. Again in 1720 under "An Inventory of furniture belonging to the Communion Table and other things in and belonging to the parish Church of Dunster, Taken the 26th day of May. Anô Domî 1720, 'A Silver Chalice and cover for the wine'.[107]

The Reverend E.H. Bates mentions this cup and cover: "The parish still preserves its Elizabethan cup and cover, though now relegated to the Mission Chapel at Alcombe.[108] It is 7$^{5/8}$" high; and possesses all the characteristics of the work of I.P.: the bands of foliage divided at four points round the bowl; hyphen belt on knop and foot, and egg and dart moulding on foot. Marks: 2offic.; date-letter for 1573. I.P. The cover is of the usual pattern; and has 1573 on the bottom."[109]

In 1954 Alcombe, up to this time part of the parish of Dunster, became a separate parish and it is possible that this Elizabethan cup and cover were returned to Dunster at that time. Prebendary F. Hancock's description is as follows. He says: "The church also possesses an Elizabethan cup and cover of the customary design. The cup is 7⅝ *in.* high. The bowl is slightly bell shaped, and is decorated with two bands of the customary conventional foliage, each band being divided by upright sprays in four places. The knob of the stem is decorated with hyphens. The foot is moulded, and has a band of hyphen decoration near junction with stem, and around the edge a band of egg and tongue moulding. Marks: 2 office Maker's I.P. within shaped shield. Date letter 1573. Paten No II forms the cover to this cup, and is 3⅞ *in.* in diameter. On the button foot is inscribed 1573 within a fillet. On the cover itself is a band of foliage within double fillets corresponding to the bands on the bowl.[110]

Gerald Taylor[111] instead of referring to 'two bands of conventional foliage', says 'two panels of moresques enclosed within strapwork borders'.[112] The term 'moresque' (arabesque, moresque) is ' line ornament, usually of stylised scrolling and intertwining foliage and is derived from Near Eastern art'.[113] Hyphen decoration is referred to by Taylor as 'hit and miss ornamentation'.[114] The stem is called an 'hour glass stem'. It 'resembles a concave hour-glass with a large knop in the middle, very commonly found on the Elizabethan communion cups[115] The foot is a domed and stepped circular foot and the bowl is deep and beaker-shaped. George Luttrell would probably have taken his Communion wine from this cup.

The second object in Dunster Church pertaining to the period of George Luttrell is the memorial brass to Elizabeth Stewkley daughter of Richard Chamberlain/Chamberlayne , alderman and sheriff of the City of London relict of Hugh Stewkley (d 1588) of Marsh, in the parish of Dunster, and mother of Joan Stewkley, the first wife of George Luttrell (d 1629). The superscription over this most attractive small heraldic shield bears the following inscription measuring 8¾ in., by 31½ in.

HERE LYES BVRIED Y BODY OF THAT VERTVOVS GENTLEWOMAN ELIZABETH (THE WIFE OF HVGH STEWKELEY OF MARSH ESQVIRE, THE DAVGHTER OF RICHARDE CHAMBERLAYN, OF LONDŌ ALDERMAN, WHOE LIVED A WYDOWE 'X' YERES, & DYED Y XIX th OF SEPTEMBER, 1598. BEINGE OF THE AGE OF 56 YERES. LEVINGE BEHIND HER BY HER SAYD HVSBAND 2 SONNES, & 4 DAVGHTERS, THOMAS, & GEORGE THO; MARIED ELIZABETH SOLE DAVGHTER & HEIRE OF JOHN GOODWYN, ELDEST SONNE OF SR IO; GOODWYN WOOBORNE IN Y COVNTIE OF BVCKIN Ḡ: KNIGHT.IOANE Y WIFE OF GEORGE LUTTERELL OF DVNSTER CASTLE ESQVIRE SVSAN MARIED VNTO HENRY DRVRY OF HVGELEY IN Y COVTIE OF BVCKIN Ḡ. ESQVIRE, MARGARET & VRSULA VNMARIED.

The shield is 6½ in. x 5½ in. and is blazoned thus: QUARTERLY I and IV *Chequy Arg and Sa a fess Gu a bordure Az* STUKELY[116] II and III *Or a bend betw six Martlets Sa*[117] LUTTRELL. *Impaling.* QUARTERLY I and IV *Erm on a pale Sa three Lions' faces Or.*[118] CHAMBERLAIN II and III *Arg on a chief Az 2 eastern Crowns Or.* DOWNES[119] Although the inscription refers to four daughters there were in fact five. Anne pre-deceased her parents and is not mentioned. This brass was formerly in the chancel of the priory church where Elizabeth was buried[120] and is now to be found on the floor of the chapel on the eastern side of the south transept.

Elizabeth Stewkley had a sister named Margery or Margaret - the names are synony-mous, after whom Elizabeth named her unmarried daughter, Margaret. Margery/Margaret married Edmund Windham . She died in 1585 and is remembered by a brass in Stogumber church. Her husband died in 1616 and his memorial brass is in St Decuman's church at Watchet. Like her husband Hugh Stewkley, Elizabeth directed that if she die in London she should be buried there but in her case at St Olave, Old Jewry whereas Hugh, should he die in London was to be buried at St Sepulchre's, London, near his first wife Christian, and his son William. Both Elizabeth and Hugh died in Somerset, and were buried at Dunster on 24 September 1598 and 7 February 1588 respectively. Elizabeth mentions in her will: "My late Mother Ann Chamberlain. My daughters, Susan Drewrye, Margaret and Ursula. My daughter-in-law, Elisabeth Stukely. My daughter Joan Luttrell. My Brother Robert Chamberlain. My son, George Stukely. To Thomas Luttrell, my godson,[121] a chayne, at age of 21. Hugh Luttrell, 2nd son of my daughter Joan Luttrell, £20. To George, a jewell or tablet of gold. My sister, Margaret Windham, and her children, Thomas, Zacharias, Edmund, John, Francis, George, and Hugh Windham. Residue to Thomas Stukely.[122] The five daughters and two sons of Elizabeth and Hugh Stewkeley were:

1. Sir Thomas Stewkeley (b.1569 d 1639), married Elizabeth, only child and heir of John Goodwin. She died19 April 1649 ,at Hinton Ampner, Hants, where there is an inscription in brass to her memory.
2. George Stewkeley, married Elizabeth, dau. of Sir Humphrey Drewell
3. Joan, married, 1580, George Luttrell. She was buried at Dunster,22 Nov. 1621.
4. Susan married Henry (afterwards Sir Henry) Drury. She died 1640. A brass to her memory is at Penn, Bucks
5. Anne, born 1570, baptised at Dunster 26 Aug., buried at Dunster 5 Sept. 1585.
6. Margaret, born 1574, baptised at Dunster 15 June, died 1606.
7. Ursula, born 1576, baptised at Dunster 27 Sept., married Henry St John.[123]

Of the above George (2), Joan (3) and Margaret (6) all left directions that they should be buried near their parents, Hugh and Elizabeth Stewkley in the chancel of the priory church.[124] Elizabeth Stewkley also remembered the poor and the craftsmen to whom she left £26.13s.4d.

The arms of Stukeley (Farindon, Kene and Trent, co. Devon) are given as follows: *Az thrée Pears pendent Or.*[125] These arms are incorrectly attributed to Joan Luttrell née Stewkley, in the genealogical and heraldic table on the back oak staircase of Dunster castle, whereas they should be *Chequy Arg and Sa a fess Gu a bordure Az*. The arms *Az three Pears pendent Or* can be seen over the mural monument to Anne Luttrell née Stucley, wife of Francis Luttrell of Venn and daughter of Charles Stucley of Plymouth.

LUTTRELL ARMS

Alterations to the Luttrell Arms were also made during George Luttrell's time but before describing these, the history of this hostelry claims our attention. Appropriately enough in a deed of 1419, in the time of Sir Hugh Luttrell, the Dunster vineyard was, shown 'to have occupied the sunny slope at the back of the house now known as the *Luttrell Arms Hotel*.'.[126]

We first hear of houses on the site a little later in the 15th century when Richard Luttrell, constable of Dunster castle from 1430 to 1449, lived in the most southerly of three houses known to have been in existence in 1443. Richard Luttrell referred to as 'cousin of James Luttrell (1426-61), lord of Dunster, wished to acquire the two houses to the north of his residence which were owned by William Dodesham, the son and heir of Ellen, the daughter and heiress of Robert Homond. The northern boundary of their houses was the road leading towards Marsh . These 'two messuages on the east side of the Market Street of Dunster',[127] were duly conveyed to Richard Luttrell in 1443. Under an entail of 1449 Richard might have succeeded to the entire barony of Dunster but he died without lawful issue. He was, in fact, a bastard whose property at Kentsford, near Watchet, on his death, came to his overlord, Sir James Luttrell,[128] Sir James died in 1461 and in 1467, the property was in the hands of feofees.[129]

During the Herberts ascendancy in Dunster, Richard Luttrell's property was in the hands of feofees, but by 1499 the three houses, to-day forming the Luttrell Arms, were conveyed to Sir Hugh Luttrell (d 1521) and Margaret, his wife. The property remained in the ownership of the Luttrell family and was presumably an integral part of the desmesne of the lords of Dunster until the village was sold in the 1950's. In 1909, Sir H. Maxwell Lyte wrote: "The arched doorway, with quatrefoils in the spandrels, and the northern wing may perhaps be assigned to the early part of the sixteenth century. The exterior of the latter is richly carved in oak, having a double row of windows with panelling between them, not unlike that of the principal screen in the church. An open roof to the upper storey was until a few years ago hidden by a plaster ceiling.[130] The 17th century alterations date from 1622 to 1629 when the porch-tower and part of the adjoining buildings were built or very largely altered; they were altered again in the 18th century.

There is a further allusion to George Luttrell in the Luttrell Arms in the shape of a second plaster overmantel depicting the story of Diana and Actæon. This is also of seventeenth century date and may be associated with the alterations made at that time by George and Silvestra Luttrell. Within an oval strapwork frame, the story of the Greek hero, Actæon is depicted. He, while out hunting with his hounds, espies Diana bathing. She causes him to be changed into a stag to be chased and devoured by his own hounds. Surrounding the frame are putti and fruits flanked by richly gowned ladies who daringly reveal bare legs from their thighs downward. Surmounting the central scene and within a triangular moulded frame is a male figure which may represent George Luttrell. His hands rest on a cornice supported by the two caryatid-like figures of two ladies. The cornice projects on either side of the triangular frame and supports two lions bearing shields depicting the arms of England and France. Between the lions and the triangular frame there are obelisks on plinths decorated with cabochons and foliate relief decorations.

CHAPTER NINE

LIFE IN THE SIXTEENTH CENTURY

THE LIVES of Thomas Luttrell, the elder who had succeeded his brother Sir John, of George, the son and heir of Thomas, and of Thomas, the younger, named after his grandfather, together with the lives of their respective wives, encapsulate in their total life spans, a great swathe of English history to which this chapter is devoted. It is a remarkable thing that when one regards the monument in Dunster church one sees the effigy of Thomas, the elder, born in the reign of Henry VIII and dying in that of Elizabeth I, the effigy of his wife Margaret who lived on into the reign of James I, the kneeling figure of their son George, born in the reign of Elizabeth I and dying in that of Charles I and finally the effigy of George's first wife, Joan Stewkley who also died in the reign of Charles I, in 1621. Their son, Thomas, the younger, born in the reign of Elizabeth I and dying in that of Charles I and his wife Joan Popham, who lived on into the reign of Charles II, whilst both buried at Dunster, are to-day only remembered by their arms which occupy the right-hand position when facing the canopy which surmounts the monument which was first erected between 1621 and 1629. No doubt, the younger Thomas was regaled by his father George with tales of the bitter religious struggles which had riven England during his grandfather's time for Thomas, the elder, had lived through the religious upheavals which figured so largely in the reigns of Henry VIII, Edward VI and Mary Tudor and he died in the thirteenth year of Elizabeth's reign. Thomas Luttrell, the elder, is mentioned in this period 1569/70 and is recorded as having a park of two miles where he kept two mares. He was a "captayne" under the commissioner, Sir George Wyndham in the Hundred of Carhampton which could provide 206 able men who were "hackbutters."

During the years 1571/1580 George Luttrell was a minor and the ward of Hugh Stewkley of Marshtown, near Dunster and he was being schooled by a Mr Brebrooke. In July 1576 he became a Fellow Commoner of Caius College, Cambridge and in 1577 he wrote from Cambridge that he intended to marry his cousin, Joan Stewkley, to whom he had been betrothed in 1575. He was seventeen years of age in 1577 when a return of that year shows: "a muster in Somerset of 6,500 ablemen, *i.e.* men fit to serve. Of these 3,720 men were selected, 2998 being furnished and 300 trained. There were also 27 demi-lances furnished and 81 light horse furnished with pistols, and 58 furnished in "other manner." Able men unfurnished 3,500 and 9 captains. There in store 835 corslets, 479 callivers, 38 hand guns, 796 long bows, 796 sheaves of arrows, and 1,391 black bills.[1] Another return of this time adds 648 almain rivets, 122 sallettes and steel caps, 13 halberts or partysonnes, 93 wheelwrights, 208 smiths, and 2,163 pioneers and labourers.[2]

In 1580 there was a muster of the county of Somerset: "the whole of the able men in the "shere," with armour and weapons, was ordered to be mustered. From these 4,000 were to be selected to aid the adjoining shires on the sea coast, but as at that season, between summer and winter, the "horses were not in a state to make a commendable show," the muster was deferred until July. Several new men meantime were charged to find a horse, and the "men of worship," the gentlemen and others of the county, to "shewe their dewtyful devotion unto her Majestie's servyce and theire love to theire countery, set themsellves at a far higher rate than they could be pressed unto by Law."[3] The certificate of this muster is in two "plottes," one gives the number of men of each arm in each Hundred; the total now being 12,000 able footmen, 47 demi-lances, and 308 light horse;[4] the other gives the Hundreds and the weapons of the 4,000 men selected for service. The certificate is signed by the Bishop, Thomas Poulet, Morris Berkeley, Amias Poulet, George Speke, John Stawell, John Horner, Henry Portman, George Sydenham, John Bret, Edward Popham, John Colles, William Hyll, Nicholas Wadham, Thomas Malet, and Robert Hill. The total number over and above the 4,000 selected men being reduced into "bands" of hundreds, captains and other officers were appointed to lead and conduct them. The chief commands over these were given to Lord Thomas Poulet, the sheriff of the county, Sir Maurice Barckley, Sir George Speke, Sir George Rogers, Sir John Horner, Sir John Siddenham, Sir Henry Portman, Knts., and George Sydenham and Edward Popham, esquires."[5]

Because the horsemen were less than expected, orders were issued for the "careful breeding of horses."[6] "Mares and good stallions" were to be kept "in all parks, pastures and commons as by statute appointed."[7] The townships with commons were to keep the one stallion. Every lord was to determine what mares should be kept on the commons and should provide a stallion, apart from the stallion kept by the tenants. A stallion was to be provided for every person who kept mares. People were persuaded to have horses and mares of as "fayre and large a scantling as may be, and everyone bound to do so was to provide his mares before the end of February next."[8] Precise details were to be kept and the horses and mares were to be inspected by the deputy lieutenants in every county and were to record in a book the names of the owners and the parks, pastures and commons wherein they were grazed. These orders were to be carried out in Somerset by the earl of Bedford.

The Hundred of Carhampton consisted of:

> George Luttrell esq. who nowe ys, to supplie the place of the ladie Lutterell deceased, hath daye geoven to furneshe one d 1 and twoo 1h.
>
> Hughe Stewkleye esq havinge made defalt at this muster hath day geoven him to furneshe one d 1 and twoo 1 h.
>
> Phillipp Steyninge esq one l h named Phillipp Acoll, and for want of sufficient habilitie ys eased of the other which ys supplied by Willm Crosse in the Hundred of Cannington.
>
> Alexander Siddenham esq one l h named Thomas Toose, and for that hys not so well able to beare the chardge of one other, Roger Siddenham supplieth yt in Cannington Hundred.
>
> John Worthe gent one l h named George Tanner.
>
> Edward Stradlinge gent one l h named Wilm Baker.
>
> John Newton hath day geoven to furneshe one l h, and for his want of good habilitie John Hawkeswell ys ioyned with him.
>
> Agnes Harrisonne widowe and Alexander Nott are ioyned together to furneshe one l h in place of Walter Popham and hath daye (geven) for it.
>
> Hugh Crosse hath day geoven him to furneshe one l h with John Dunscombe for his want of a good habilitie to doe yt alone.[9]

Under the heading Parks are listed:

> Sir George Speake, knight, hath twoo parkes and inclosed groundes for deere

eache of them of one myle compasse and keepeth four mares according to
the statute.

George Luttrell esq hath two parkes the one at Dunster the other at Quan-
tockeshead eache of them one myle compas and keepeth four mares
according the statute.

John Coles esq hath one parke at Corypole in the right of younge Mallett
being one myle compas and keepeth two mares according to the statute.

Edward Stradling gent holdeth in lease from the said George Luttrell one
parke at Marshwood of one myle compas and keapeth two mare according
to the statute.

Sir John Stawell knight hath one grounde inclosed for deere at Cothelston of
one myle compas and keapeth twoo mares according to the statute.

Sir John Clyfton knight hath twoo parkes or inclosed groundes for deere,
thone at Staple being two myles compas and thother at Barington being
one myle compas and keapeth five mares according to the statute.

The La: Elizabeth Pawlett widowe hath one parke or inclosed grounde for
deere at Georgehenton of twoo myles compas and keapeth three mares
according to the statute.

Nicholas Wadham esq hath one parke at Merifeld and keapeth two mares
accordinge to the statute the same parke a little above one myle compas.

Edward Popham esq.[10] hath one grounde inclosed for deere at Huntworth of
one myle compas and keapeth two mares according to the statute.

Thomas Wrothe esq and five other of his brethren dwelling aboute London
have one parke at Petherton of four myles compas almost decayed but doe
keape no mares in yt.

Christopher Symcoxe esq dothe holde one parke at Sharpham of twoo myles compas
and keapeth three mares according to the statute.[11]

In 1580, 1500 Spaniards landed in Ireland but for attacking a country with which they
were supposed to be at peace, they were set upon and although they quickly perceived the
error of their ways and surrendered they were nevertheless slaughtered. In England a
proclamation was circulated specifically to cause discord and to encourage rebellion. It
declared that "the Pope, the King of Spain and other princes"[12] had agreed "to make a
great army to invade England and to dispose of it and the subjects of the realm at their
pleasures." To which the resolute Queen Bess replied and "declared her intention to keep
her people in the true profession of the Gospel and free from bondage to the Roman
tyranny."[13] Further she said: "With the help of the loving subjects, their bodies, lives and
substances, she would withstand both by sea and land all foreign power however mighty;
and to this end she had caused to be mustered and viewed the universal strength of her
subjects, so that, without doubt, she had a force that "never any king of this realm had had
ye lyke."[14]

In June 1581 a William Lytlestone of Barnstaple was in communication with Lord
Burghley and had told him of reports he had received from merchants of an English ship,
recently arrived from Spain. The merchants came from Bridgwater and Taunton and were
old acquaintances of Lytlestone and theytold him that in Bilbao and San Sebastian 10,000
Italian and other soldiers: "were ready to come from the "hye contrye of Spayne" by 500
or 600 at a time, and "yt ys geven outte in grett bravvtye of talke," that when shipping
arrived they with more would "go for Ireland out of hand."[15]

On 14 March 1586 under the names of the various hundreds of "the Easte parte of
Somerset Sheere" appear the names of those who "are sett at lances and lighte horses"
but, of more interest in this context are, "The names of those persons charged to find

horses in the West part of Somerset," of these only those of the Hundred of Carhampton and the Hundred of Williton Freemanors can find a place here. They are:

Hundred of Carhampton

	Demi-lance	Light horse
Hugh Steuckley ar. *(i.e carriage)*	1	ii
Geo. Luttrell, ar.	1	ii
John Worthe, gen.	..	1
Edward Stradlinge, gen	..	1
Peter Trevilian, gen.	..	1
Joan Wyndham, vid:	..	ii
Hugh Crosse	..	i
Philip Stayning, ar.	..	1

Again, we have under the headings of the various hundreds the names of the pikemen and shotte, those listed under Carhampton were:

Pikemen –	*Shot –*
Willm. Poole	Walter Frauncke, Corporall
Willm. Welche	Thos Elsworthie, Decenier
Covenaante Harris	John Uppington
Robt Syderfine	John Hill
Gregory Wydlake	John Dunscombe
John Chepman	Willm Pearse
Gregorye Bryant	Barnabe Saffine
Willm Baker	John Rooche
John Toconete	John Bryant
Anthony Craning	Mychaell Hensley
Willm Worthe	John Whyttenstalle
Alexander Smythe	Davye Whyte
Jonn Gilles	Hugh Stronnge
John Slowley	Henry Spurryer
Robt Holle	John Tayler
Richd Yarde	Thomas Pearse
Willm Holle	
Josephe Kente	
Androe Webber	
John Dallen	

(Signed) George Sydenham.[16]

The names of the CCC Shott and Pyckes trayned by Sir John Stawell, Knight, at Bridgwater the viijth of October in the xxviijth yeare of her maties Raigne, Anno Dom 1586.,[17]

In April 1588 George Luttrell contributed £50 towards a loan to the treasury. He was one of seventy listed under the title of "The Names of the Nobility" and others who have contributed to the defence of the country.[18] The queen had adopted the plan of borrowing to secure money for the imperial treasury. It had proved difficult to raise subsidies because of heavy costs already borne locally. Contributions varied from £25 to £100 and were mostly in the region of £25 to £50, the largest sums being contributed by Sir John Stawell, Kt., and Hugh Bampfeild of North Curry.

The port of Minehead is mentioned in 1419 when Philip Clopton, master of Sir Hugh Luttrell's barge the *Leonard of Dounstere* made a voyage "from the port of Mynhede to Bordeaux and back in the fifth year of the reign of King Henry the Fifth."[19] During the lifetime of the same Sir Hugh (d 1428) he "built a small pier and enlarged the harbour considerably, to the great benefit of the little town."[20] In 1543 Dame Margaret Luttrell (d 1580) was "registered as the owner of a ship of 100 tons belonging to the port of Minehead"[21] "In 1559, the growing town of Minehead received a royal charter of incorporation, the government being vested in a portreeve and twelve burgesses."[22]

CHAPTER TEN

THOMAS LUTTRELL

THOMAS LUTTRELL, the younger, was the grandson of that grasping lawyer and first lay-rector of Dunster, Hugh Stewkley, and was himself a lawyer and doubtless a puritan and certainly a parliamentarian,. The son of George and Joan Luttrell, née Stewkley, he was baptized at Dunster on 26 February 1584.[1] The likeness of this somewhat dour man, plainly dressed in a light green doublet with trunk hose and white linen collar and cuffs, may be seen in a possible portrait at Dunster castle. His dress is far removed form the later extravagant elegance of the courtier and cavalier of the royalist persuasion. Born in the reign of Queen Elizabeth when the ruff was almost *de rigueur,* he grew to manhood in the reign of King James I. Gradually the ruff was replaced by the plain, sometimes lace-edged collar, and here we can see a man who, while sporting the pointed beard and moustaches of his opponents, would nevertheless have scorned to wear the profusion of lace they favoured. He wore his hair long as did many Parliamentarians. Thomas Luttrell matriculated at Lincoln College, Oxford, in 1597, and became a B.A. in 1599.[2] Early in 1603 James VI of Scotland, the son of Mary, queen of Scots and Lord Darnley, came to the English throne and the next year the twenty year old Thomas was finding his way in the career chosen for him and he became a law student at Lincoln's Inn. Thomas was a man of his period who married the daughter of a leading parliamentarian at the age of thirty-seven.

The eldest son of Sir Francis Popham, John, died *sine prole* and the line was continued by Colonel Alexander, the second son. As one of the richest men in the West Country, securing the marriage of one of Francis's daughters was an advantageous achievement. This Thomas Luttrell did for he married one of his eight daughters, Jane Popham at Newington in 1621. Two of Jane's sisters, Mary and Katherine named after their aunts, married into Somerset families Mary married Henry Rogers of Cannington and Katherine married John Frauncis of Coombe Florey a grandson of George Luttrell (d 1629) the father of Thomas. John was named after his father for we know that Susan, one of the daughters of George Luttrell, who was baptized at Dunster 9 October 1594 married there on 29 June 1612, John Francis/Frauncis of Coombe Florey.[3] Thomas Luttrell married Jane Popham the year his mother, Joan Stewkley, died in 1621. The early years of their marriage were spent at Marshwood where they lived until George's death in 1629. In a bedroom the overmantel displays the arms of Luttrell impaling those of Popham. These are the arms of Sir John Popham of Hunstrete and Littlecote but here with a crescent for a difference. They may be blazoned thus: Luttrell. *Or a bend between six Martlets Sa.* impaling the arms of Popham. *Arg on a chief Gu two bucks' heads cabossed Or with a crescent for a difference.*[4]

George Luttrell (d 1629) left various memoranda belonging to the reign of Queen Elizabeth and King James. The perambulation of the parish of Dunster has already been given but since Sandhill is mentioned in the Carhampton perambulation it is here included: "The perambulacon of the processyon of the parysh of Carhampton in the Rogacon weke as followith:— "The Monday, from the parysh church to the crosse in the strete which stode uppon the strete and from that southwarde to a howse or tenement nowe in tholdyng of Lawrence Escott thear and from thence west along by Jeles Dyes howse to Aller styele where was wont to be a crosse and thear sayd a gospell, and from thence to Colstones Crosse whear was sayd another gospell, and from thence to Holwaye Howse now W. Harte's, and so to Holwaye [Hollow] elme at Henstye fote and from thence to Henstye hedd and thear another gospell, and so home. "The Tewysdaie, from the church to the wester [thester] church styele and from thence by Henry Lee's towards Webber's and so towardes Brethren Crosse and thear a gospell, and so upp by Hadley's howse and so towardes the parsonage of Wythicomb by Sanhill *(Sandell/Sandhill)* grounde to Laurence Escotte's and thear wont to be sayd a gospell, and thear was wont to be som refresshing for the pryst, and from thence to Rodehuysh by Chestershowse the wydo Doddrydg and to Georg Escotte's and thear a gospell sayde and thear they dranck, and so to St. Barthemewe's Chapell whear they sayd a gospell, and from thence to Harry Dowlle's howes whear they sayd a gospell and dranck, and from thence to Poppers [Pyppers] Crosse where also was sayd a gospell, and from thence to Okehowse (*now known as Oak*) whear was sayd a gospell and drank, and so to Harpers and a gospell and thear they drank, and from thence they goo to a crosse that goyth to Lokesborowgh and thear was sayd a gospell, and from thence to Everarde's howse whear was wont to be sayd a gospell, but now they goo without hys wawles homeward by Lawrence Escotte's, Rogers howse and so to the Hundred Elme wher the Sherow turne is kept, and from thence to the churche agayne.

"The Wennysdaye, westward along the towne to Dunsterward and at the fotewaye entry going to Hensty thear was wont to be a crosse caulyd Emmys Crosse alias Lanhey Crosse, and thear was sayd a gospell, and from thence by Gyltchapell to the lorde's feelde gate and so along the waye in the north part of the parck to Broklanefote over the brydge thear and so along by Chapman's howse and the wydow Hobbes [Holes] and so over to Marsshbrydge to Poynz' howse, and thear was sayd a gospell and was some refresshing, and from thence to Marchwaye estward along by all the Chesell and so to Marshwood and thear sayd a gospell and wear also was wont to be refresshed, and from thence towards Shilves and to a crosse that was wont to stande by est the styele that goyth into Rogers grounde caulyd South C[arhamp]ton, and so home alonge the depe waye to the churche."[5]

In 1625 when King Charles succeeded his father, the financial needs enumerated had compelled the immediate summoning of parliament. Among the members present were almost certainly Thomas Luttrell[6] and John Pym. Thomas was the representative for Minehead, Somerset and John, in 1625 was the elected representative for Tavistock in Devon; the constituency he served in all the future parliaments which met during his lifetime.

Thomas Luttrell's background was typical of the son of a country gentleman for, as we know, he had been sent to London over twenty years earlier to learn a little law at Lincoln's Inn. He participated in the English passion for litigation as had his litigious father George. This was a passion shared by high and low who observed an attitude of positive ownership towards the law which existed to serve and preserve against injustice every man in the station in which he found himself. It was a guard and not a master and was designed to provide fair and just, if not equal relations between all levels of society The only exceptions were "vagabonds and 'masterless men'…[who] were the only constant victims of the law and they were not always helpless."[7]

It was said of Thomas Luttrell having married into the Popham family, that he, subsequently seems to have used his influence in "in favour of different members of his wife's family, who, espoused the Parliamentary side in the reign of Charles the First."[8] Like his father before him he became sheriff of Somerset in 1631 And his sympathies were apparent when in 1633 he joined with other justices of the peace in their protests "against the revival of such practices as church-ales and revels."[9]

Before reviewing the background of that other Somerset gentleman, it is perhaps pertinent here to quote Miss Wedgwood's account of day-to-day administration of justice in the countryside and in the cities and its application to the local scene in Dunster in the seventeenth century.

"Justice was administered throughout the kingdom in a multitude of small courts, and the governors of England, in all that affected the daily life of the subject, were the local justices of the peace—small gentry in the countryside, aldermen in the cities. At Quarter Sessions the justices, gathered together in the county town, fixed the rate of wages and discussed the state and needs of the county. They were competent to try all crimes except treason or offences by the King's servants. These cases, together with a few which presented exceptional problems of law, would be reserved for trial by the King's judges at the Assizes. Between sessions the justices saw to the daily affairs of the village, apprenticed boys to trades, disciplined unruly servants, ordered idlers into the fields at harvest time, licensed or suppressed alehouses, punished rogues and vagabonds, put bastard children out to nurse, sent lewd women and incorrigible beggars to the house of correction, relieved the sick, poor and disabled, encouraged lawful and discouraged unlawful sports, and saw to the maintenance — such as it was — of roads and bridges. The innumerable petty disputes over boundaries and trespass, which occurred in the countryside very little enclosed and cultivated on the strip system, were mostly settled by the old manorial courts—the Court Leet or the Court Baron—both of which still survived. Here the lord of the manor or his steward sat in the chair of justice, to deal with trespass, poaching, and injury to park land, but also to rebuke eavesdroppers, scolds, drunkards and trouble-makers.

Neither lords of the manor, stewards nor justices of the peace in town or country were by custom or necessity deeply versed in the law, though many of them had been for a while at the Inns of Court in London. The little learning they had there acquired, and one of the many convenient handbooks specially written for them, gave them all the technical help they needed in a task in which experience and common sense were fully as important as knowledge of the law."[10]

Miss Wedgwood makes reference to the Court Leet, to eavesdroppers and scolds among many other things. In Lyte there is a reference to the Court Leet as follows: "In 1617 and the following year, the deputy of the Clerk of the Market of the King's Household attempted to exercise jurisdiction over the constables of the borough, but George Luttrell applied to the Exchequer for redress contending with truth that he and his ancestors, lords of Dunster, had been used 'to keepe courtes leete' there twice a year from time out of mind."[11]

The borough court lost much of its ancient authority in the reign of Charles II and in the nineteenth century the court leet and the court baron sat together and met only once a year. In 1443 reference was made in the household accounts of Dunster castle to an eavesdropper: "1443. April 8. "John [Towker 'coryser', servant of William Bedewyn] is a common spy or listener at the windows of the neighbours and likewise a common night-walker and eavesdropper *(ascultator)*. Therefore he is in mercy 3s 4d."[12]

The word coryser may be correctly coryza meaning an acute catarrhal inflammation or common cold. This would not be a surprising ailment for such a person.

In 1408 reference is made to a scold: "1408, May "Ellen Watkyns is a common 'holcroppe' of divers things and a common scold and disturber of the peace. Therefore she is in mercy 4d.....Geoffrey Taillour is a common night-walker and disturber of the peace. Therefore he is in mercy, half a mark."[13]

In 1493 two hundred husbands were ordered to keep their offending wives in order: "1493,August 5. "Order John Huyshe and Jerard Goldesmyth that henceforth they do not allow their wives to quarrel or to use opprobrious or scandalous words against their neighbours or them (seipsos), under pain of either of them delinquent in the matter of 20s , to be paid to the lord."[14]

George Luttrell at the end of Queen Elizabeth's reign "claimed a right to hunt the deer and other beasts and birds of the forest, chase and warren throughout the whole of the Hundred" [of Carhampton]. Neither Dunster, Carhampton nor Treborough had, it appears, ever been part of the forest of Exmoor and therefore the dispute which arose between George, lord of the Honour of Dunster and Hundred Carhampton, and Sir John Poyntz, warden of the Queen's Forest of Exmoor is difficult to understand. Sir John counter-claimed "exclusive rights over a large portion of the Hundred as being purlieu or,..., within the precincts and liberties of the forest."[15] Culbone, Oare, Stoke, Luccombe and Wootton were certainly within this category of purlieus for they had been disafforested in the reign of Edward I, but it is clear that Dunster, Carhampton and Treborough, were not.

In 1597 a case is recorded in the Court of Star Chamber in which the accused, Thomas Pearse of Minehead, a servant of George Luttrell killed a deer and took calves to stock his master's park at Dunster. The offence had taken place on several occasions at Oare, Luccombe and Wootton Courtenay. The real defendant should have been, of course George Luttrell. A fascinating extract from Sir John Poyntz[16] case made 'to the Queen's Moste Excellent Maiestie' follows: "that one Thomas Pears of Mynehedd in the said Countye of Somerset, not regardinge his dutye to your maiestye, nor fearinge the paynes penalties and punyshements provided ordeyned and vsed for the due correction of suche evell disposed persons as shall or have in any vnlawfull manner entred into any of your maiesties Forrests, Chases, parks, or the liberties or lymitts thereof, and there vnlawfully hunt, chase, take, cary away, distroye, or kyll any of your heighnes deare, game, beasts and fowles, he the said Thomas Pearse Combyninge himself with divers other persons like mynded, and endevoringe the spoyle of the said deare, game, beasts and fowles, hath often and sondrye tymes within three yeares nowe laste paste sythence your maiesties laste Free and generall pardon, in night tyme and also by daie procured and in verye riotuos rowtous and vnlawfull manner assembled and gathered vnto himselfe divers and sondrye of the lewid and evell disposed persons, some time to the number of three, fowre, five, sixe persons and upwards, and provided and armed themselves with forceable and vnlawfull weapons, and havinge then and there Crossebowes and arrowes, guns, dearestalles, engins, huntinge houwndes, gray houndes; And beinge so assembled and Armed did at everye of the said tymes riotouslie, forceiablye and vnlawfullye come and enter into your Highnes said Forrest of Exmore, and the boundes and lymitts thereof, and with theire said Crossbowes, gunes, engins, hownds, and grayhounds did then and there hunt, Chase, take, kyll, and carry awaye from thence divers of your Heignes deare, game, beasts and fowles of the Forrest, and very many younge Calfes of redd deare he the said Thomas Pears and his said Confederatts and Compaynions did then and there take and carry away alive; and particullerly he the said Thomas Pears accompaned with sondrye other his Confederatts whose names are vnkowen vnto your Heighnes Subiecte, beinge in that riotous manner armed and prepared and accompanyed as aforesaid, in or about the tenth daie of June last paste [1596] did vnlawfully, forceblie and riotouslie enter into, and vppon your Heighnes said Forreste of Exmore, and within the precyncts and lymitts thereof, and did then and there hunt Chase take and carry awaye soundrye deare, beasts and younge Calfes of redd deare of the said Forrest, and the same havinge secretly conveyed and putt into the parks and enclosed growndes of deare of divers gentlemen neare inhabitinge to the said Forrest, where the same ar yet keapte alive, and kylled, spoylled, and distroied divers and soundrye others of the said beasts and fowles to the great decrease and distruction of your Highnes said Forreste....etc."[17]

The reply of Thomas Pearse, defendant to the Bill of complaint of John Poyntz contains the following extract: "the saide defendant [*Thomas Pearse*] for answer thereunto, sayethe that one George Luttrell of Dunster in the County of Somerset, Esqiuer, the defendants maister, durynge all the time mencioned in the saide Bill And before was seissed in his demeasne as of fee, as the defendant thinckethe, of and in the hundred, Leete and libertye of Carhampton in Somerset, within whiche Hundred and Libertye the parishes of Culbone, Oare, Stock [*Stoke Pero*], Luccombe, Wotton, Dunster, Carhampton, Treborrow, and diuers other parishes are, and tyme oute of mynde haue beine. And the aforesaid Thomas farther sayeth that George Luttrell, and all those whose estaite the said George nowe haithe in the Hundred of Carehampton, from the tyme whereof the memory of man is not to the contrary have accustomed and vsed to huntt, kyll and take anye redd deare and the calues of them whiche haue happened to come or bee within the Hundred aforesaide durynge all the time aforesaid, whiche his Hundred and liberty is withoute the precinctt and bounds of the saide Forreste, as this defendt haithe beine done to vnderstande by the crediable reporte and Commone opynion of the Country there; And That in or aboute the monethe of June in the six and Thirtye yeare of the reign of the Quenes Majestie that nowe in [1594] the saide George Luttrell thene beinge sheriffe of the County of Somerset, this defendant, one John Bryant gent, William Harryson gent, and others whiche the saide defendant now remembreth not, for and in the behalfe of the said George Luttrell at Luccombe aforesaid, did huntt inpeaceable manner, and the saide John Briant did then and there in lyke peaceable manner and by his Commaundment or appoyntment with a Crosse bowe arrowe kyll one redd deare, whiche then laye and harbored within the same Hundred; And the said George Luttrell caused the same to be carryed awaye for his provision against the assises, which weir holden shortlie after in the said Countye of Somerset, And farther sayeth That att or neere the said tyme the said George Luttrell and the said defendant at Luccombe aforesaide did take vpp a younge hynds calfe, whiche was there calvede, and the same caused to be carryed home and putt into the parke of the said George Luttrell as lawfull was for them so to doe for ought this defendant knoweth to the contrarye. And sayeth That aboute Julye in the seven and Thirtye yeare of the Quenes Majesties reigne that nowe is [1595] the said George Luttrell, the saide defendant Andrew Bullock, John Stevens, and John Squirrell, and John Whitingstall, beinge servants of George Luttrell and then waytinge vppon hym, did lyckwise huntt at Wotton aforesaide within the said Hundred, and then and there did kyll a redd deere with a Crosse bowe arrowe, and did carrye awaye the same withe them to the use of the saide George Luttrell, as lawfull was for them to doe for ought this defendant knowethe to the Contrarye.....etc. etc."[18]

As has been stated King Charles I increased the royal coffers by £133 6s 8d and a yearly rent of £13 6s 8d in exchange for the titles of Somerset and Devon which he granted to George Cottington. In the same year (1633) the farmers who pastured their beasts on Exmoor for payment were, for the first time, liable to pay tithes to Cottington. This imposition caused litigation which went on for many years and also the numbers of sheep sent annually to the forest in March or June fell from 43,000 to 16,000. The forester Humphrey Venner, in 1637 increased the cost of pasturing of a score of sheep from 2s 6d to 3s 4d. and of pasturing cattle from 4d or 6d to 1s; the same for horses both in summer and winter. The charge made for cutting turf remained unaltered, nor was it affected by the tithe demand of Cottington. The increases were resisted by some but Venner maintained that they were forced upon him because of the decrease in the number of beasts pasturing and the demands of Cottington and the ensuing strife.

In Dunster, as in Porlock and other Somerset market towns, the early spring brought the forester's men to town. Also busy in the market towns of Devon, they came to "Cry the moor" and their proclamations would have been of vital import to the owners of sheep, cattle and horses. In March, and sometimes in May, the sheep were taken to the forest where they remained until shearing time.

The bustle and noise enlivened the little town of Dunster and one can imagine the vociferous resistance offered by the owners of the beasts when the cost of pasturage exceeded that charged the previous year. Here the tellers appointed by the forester counted and recorded in the Forest Book the numbers of sheep, their mark, the name and parish of the owner and woe betide any who gave less than honest answers for if, when they left the moor, there were more than had been paid for, they were charged double for the excess animals. After shearing, the sheep were returned to their forest pasturage and were again counted by the tellers. Here they remained until October. They could, for the same price, remain throughout the bleak winter months for the same charge, but few remained. We read, "two drifts for cattle, or rother beasts, as they were often called, were usually made in the summer before St James' Day."

Thomas Luttrell was buried at Dunster on the 7 February 1644.[19] His heir was Alexander who was born in 1622 and matriculated at Lincoln College, Oxford, in 1637. He was only eighteen when he became elected member of Parliament for Minehead, as his father, a lawyer, had been in 1625. It is not known whether he attended the Short Parliament, convened in the spring of 1640 or the Long Parliament convened on 3 November, 1640. His participation in the affairs of the land was however, short-lived for he died two or three years later and George, (baptised at Dunster on 12 September 1625) became Thomas Luttrell's heir.

Alexander Luttrell probably 'declared against the king' in the Long Parliament of 1640. His father Thomas and his next brother George were all parliamentarians. The Luttrells were therefore apparently in a minority in Somerset according to Davies and Kershaw. Davies quotes R. N. Kershaw, in the *English Historical Review, XXXVIII, 508*: "The richest and most populous part of the country (with the exception of Somerset) thus declared against the king ... It was the heart of England, in wealth, population, and progressive quality that appealed, through its chosen representatives against past oppressions and apprehensions for the future.[20]

In West Somerset, the Trevelyans of Nettlecombe were royalist and Thomas Luttrell had promised to assist George Trevelyan "if he would compound for his delinquency and not persist in his 'former disobedience unto the Parliament'."[21]

CHAPTER ELEVEN

DUNSTER CHURCH AND LIFE IN THE SEVENTEENTH CENTURY

IN 1642 at the beginning of the Civil War, Thomas Luttrell manifestly displayed his allegiance to the Parliamentary side when he committed Thomas Manwaring, bishop of St Davids' to prison in Minehead. This fugitive bishop had 'given offence by his advocacy of absolutist views'.[1] In 1633, the *Book of Sports*, first issued in the reign of James I in 1617, was re-issued and it was decreed that those who had already attended church on the sabbath, could legitimately take part in certain recreations afterwards. Every parson in every parish was instructed to see that the provisions of the book were thoroughly known. The belief that King Charles had commanded that it be read from the pulpit, brought forth opposition from one parson who followed the instruction by reading aloud the fourth commandment, 'But the seventh day is the sabbath of the Lord thy God; in it thou shalt not do any work, thou, nor thy son, nor thy daughter, thy manservant, nor thy maidservant, nor thy cattle, nor thy stranger that is within thy gates.'[2] He then addressed his congregation with the words," Dearly beloved, you have heard the commandment of God and Man; obey which you please."[3] In 1633 the *Book of Sports* would have been read from Dunster pulpit by the Rev. Thomas Smith who was vicar for thirty-five years from 1603 to 1638. He died in April 1638 and was buried at Dunster. He therefore served the parish throughout the entire reign of James I and during the first thirteen years of that of Charles I.

The interesting artefact in Dunster church relevant to this period, is a cupboard bearing the date 1634. This cupboard was in the possession of the Rev. Malcolm Ogilvy (d. 31.3.1962) who had strong reason for believing that it had been made from the Dunster pulpit of that date. He believed that it was replaced in the eighteenth century and it is true that Dunster church did possess an eighteenth century wooden pulpit which, according to a former rector, the Rev. Doré, was in the church of St Michael and All Angels, Alcombe before he secured its return to Dunster. The Rev. Boyd thought that the wood from the seventeenth century pulpit was used to make the cupboard which was bequeathed to him by an ancestor, an Ogilvy or an Adams. His executrice, Ruth Bird of Minhinick, Mary Tavy, Tavistock, Devon, wrote to the vicar of Dunster on 16 April 1962 to say that the Rev. Boyd: "wished me to ask, after his death, whether Dunster Church would like to have it, not to sell, of course, but to put it in the Church. If so, she said, I am to send it to you. You have, I believe, near the South Door, an alms box of the same date."

There is, in the earliest register extant started in 1598, an entry made before 1638 to which Thomas Smith's signature is appended. It is a reminder that in accordance with the ancient discipline of the church ' marriages were prohibited during Advent, Lent, and Whitsuntide. It reads:

De temporib in quid non licet
matrimonia Solemnizate
Solemnitas nuptiaum facienda non est Septuagesimo
in Octava Pasche et primo
die rogatione in mane danditur
illa Sollemnitas et Durat xhibitio ad
octaviam diem post Pentecosten
inclusionem et prima Die Domminica
Adventus usque ad Epiphaniam non Detent
nuptia Celebrari   Tho Smith.[4]

The terrier of the glebe lands of the vicarage of Dunster dated 19 August 1634 reveals the poverty of the Rev. Smith who received only £8 per annum in monetary terms. His other advantages were a little garden and a meadow.

Back in 1560, Hugh Stewkley (d 1588) had become the Lay Rector of Dunster and thus he received the rectorial tithes of the benefice. He had acquired from the Crown through various intermediaries and by a final grant to George and Elizabeth Sydenham: "various houses, barns, orchards, and rents in Dunster, Carhampton, Minehead and Exford, common of pasture in Dunster and also the rectory of Dunster, with tithes of sheaves, hay, wool, and lambs and all other small tithes.[5]

It was the obligation of Stewkley, as lay impropriator, to provide a stipendiary curate who did not require to be instituted and was removeable at his pleasure. After the suppression of the monasteries it was decided that it was unnecessary to present the vicar designate to the bishop for institution and the last vicar to be so presented was John Ryce (d 1561). The Vicarage was thus suppressed and the parlous position was that the poor clergyman had no house, little endowment and no part of the tithes.

In 1535 the rectory was valued at £17 5s 8d gross out of which the vicar received a salary of £4 13s 4d. In 1539, Dunster priory was suppressed and the value of the rectory was given as only £7 2s 3d nett. Because it was no longer possible to receive free food at the prior's table, the vicar's salary was raised to £8 per annum.

The complaint was made that: "We have no vicaridge[6], neither hath there been any this many years. There is a little garden, containing one yeard of ground near thereabout. Sir George Speke's land lyeth on the west end, and the widow Foxe's land lyeth on the east ende, and the churchyeard on the north side, and the highway on the south side adjoyning. There is one meadow containing three yards of ground or near thereabout lying near the Castle on the east side and a river of water on the other side."[7]

Since the Reformation tithes had either been commuted for money or, as in the following case, had been alienated to the lay rector so that in 1634 the poor curate/vicar had to subscribe together with the Church Wardens and sidesmen to the following spiritualities levied by the Stewkleys as lay rectors.

For offerings, 2d, both men and women.
For servants 2d apiece.
For corne, we tythe by the tenth stitch and for odde stitches one sheaf of a stitch.
For the tythe hay, we tythe by the pook or cock, the tenth pook at the first taking up.
For kine, 2d
For a summer cow 2d
For a winter cow, 1d.
For a heifer, 1d.
For the calves sold to the butcher, 1d of 1s.
For store calves ½d.

For a garden, 1d.
For wooll, the tenth in kind.
For lambs, the tenth, and for odde lambs ½d, apiece for the fall.
For apples, the tenth.
For piggs, the tenth at three weeks or before.
For weddings 10d.
For churchings 4d[8]
For hopps, the tenth.
For honey, the tenth.[9]

It therefore appears that the greediness of the Stewkleys countenanced no increase in the Curate's salary and it may be that the impoverished clergyman, perforce had to engage in other activities. We know that Thomas Smith had a meadow and although manual labour was frowned upon, nevertheless he would have had to work his glebe. Light is thrown on the situation by Miss Wedgwood who wrote: "The parson's status in the social hierarchy was doubtful, manual labour was frowned on but he had to work his glebe. Parishioners in one village complained because the parson played ninepins with the butcher, and in another, because he undertook odd jobs of thatching in his spare time. No doubt much depended on the reputation and general behaviour of individuals; many of these disappointed educated men, exiled in remote places, found solace in drink and low company, and thatching and playing ninepins with the butcher were only one part of the conduct which was felt to misbecome their office."[10]

Dunster was not an ecclesiastical benefice and so the poor curate was free to hold another church without dispensation. In some cases, through rich patrons, a clergyman could 'procure several livings for himself and delegate his religious duties to one or two poor curates hired at miserable wages.[11]

At Dunster Lyte suggests that, 'the communion table was removed from the chancel [of the Priory church] and placed lengthways east and west under the western arch of the tower, near the site of the parochial altar sanctioned by the arbitrators of1498.[12] This fifteenth century altar was "in the nave of the church, that is to say at the altar of St James the Apostle, which is situate on the south side of the door (hostium) which leads from the choir of the monks into the nave of the church."[13] The arrangement in the mid seventeenth century was very simple and, until the nineteenth century, it was most unusual to find a cross on the altar. The most one could expect to find was a pair of candlesticks. Now the emphasis was on the sermon and unlike the practices of the Early and Middle Ages, the Holy Communion service was celebrated only on a few special occasions during the Church's year. The altar, which was covered with a cloth or carpet in normal circumstances, was then, in addition overlaid with a fair linen cloth.

It appears from the foregoing that the Calvinist practice of placing that altar in the middle of the nave did not take place at Dunster immediately, if Lyte is correct in his surmise. It must be borne in mind that if it occupied an east west position under the western arch [under the southern pier of that arch] it was nevertheless in the nave which extended up to the choir screen between the eastern piers of the tower. In this choir screen was the door or hostium to the monk's choir.

In 1676 the Dunster Churchwardens' Accounts shew an entry, "Paid for Timber for the rayles about ye Communion Table £1.10s 0d. A later photograph of 1842 (John Buckler Pigott Colln) shews the interior of the church with eighteenth century box pews and with a simple wooden communion table, now placed north and south and protected by wooden rails. If these are the 1676 rails, they and the position of the communion table accord with Archbishop Laud's 1640 injunction. It would therefore appear that the one which was placed under the south-west pier of the crossing tower on the site of the pre-Reformation altar of St James, the Apostle, did not survive for long. In 1694 John Strong was paid 2s 6d for "one joynstule (joint stool) belonging to the Communion Table"[14] and in 1714 a William Strong made a "Joynt Stule" which cost "3s.0d.[15] Further furnishings include matting and covers for the Communion Table so that 7s was paid for "Making ye Matting Round ye Communion Table"[16] in 1703 and in 1720 an inventory was taken which included "A large velvet carpet to cover the Communion Table"[17] and "A large Holland table Cloth and two Holland napkins" and "Three long Cushions to place round the railes of ye Communion Table."[18]

There were difficulties peculiar to Dunster church, in adapting to the services laid down by the Church of England in the Book of Common Prayer, in compliance with the Act of Uniformity. The mid-seventeenth century arrangement at Dunster was a natural corollary following the introduction of the English Prayer Book in 1552 which was revised in 1559. The church had been organized for the services of the Roman catholic church and had had many altars serviced by the Prior and his monks, by the chantry chaplains and by the vicar for the parishioners, and endowments had been provided for the saying of masses. Then came the Act of Uniformity and the requirement to adhere to the Book of Common Prayer.

If services took place at the High Altar, or Altar of St George in the Priory Church, the priest ministering at the extreme eastern limb of the church could not be seen, nor heard by the congregation in the nave. The laity had recovered its rights in the chancel of the Priory Church after the departure of the Prior and monks in 1539 and was no longer confined to the use of the parish altar which had been sanctioned for their use by the Glastonbury Agreement of 1498. In 1540 they opened up the Priory chancel by building the arcades between it and the side chapels of Our Lady and St Lawrence adjacent to it on the north and south sides. The thirteenth century arch leading from the south transept into the former St Lawrence Chapel was also widened. Sermons had gained in popularity in the later Middle Ages and people could, at least, listen to them with some degree of ease as a result of the introduction of seats into the nave. Formerly, the congregation had stood and only the old and infirm were provided for and "went to the wall" or had seats provided round piers or columns. In the early Middle Ages the sermon was not a regular part of worship and the clergy, often illiterate, only attempted to instruct their congregations in the basic doctrines of the Christian faith.

In St George's Church the priest delivering his sermon from the pulpit in the nave could not be seen and certainly could not be heard by those in the chancel of the Priory Church, or by those in either of the eastern chapels. Thus with the growing importance of the sermon and the differently orientated services of the church, the division which had existed form 1498 to 1539 grew up again. This time between the "old church" as it came to be known, (which became in effect the Luttrell mausoleum) and the parish church. Between the mid-seventeenth century and the Victorian restoration of Dunster church only the office for the burial of the dead took place in the Priory church. The seats and monuments were however not neglected and were cleaned by Robert Coffin who, after 1731, was paid 5s a year for his work. It would appear that in the reign of Queen Elizabeth I and to about 1639 in the reign of Charles I, the chancel of the Priory Church was well maintained by firstly Hugh Stewkley, the first lay rector, who died in 1588 and then by his successor Sir Thomas Stewkley, who died in 1639. The chancel was entirely their responsibility.

As has been shown the Stewkleys were closely related to the Luttrells, a daughter of Sir James (c1426-61) and Lady Elizabeth Luttrell (d 1493), Joan married George Stewkley (d 1508) and Joan Stewkley, daughter of Hugh and Elizabeth Stewkley married George Luttrell (1560-1629). The Stewkleys were a great force in Dunster; they owned the ground on the three sides of the eastern limb of the church and many of their ancestors were buried in the chancel. It is thought to be extremely unlikely that the Stewkleys formally relinquished their rights in the chancel or that there was any legal undertaking on the part of the Luttrells to keep it in repair. The Stewkley family eventually migrated to Hampshire and before the end of the seventeenth century the Luttrells had to all intents and purposes assumed exclusive rights. This is apparent in the funeral directions of Thomas Luttrell (1584-1644), the son of George, who gave instructions that he was to be buried "in my isle" which suggests that the Stewkleys had ceded their rights to the Luttrells.[19] No longer did a Stewkley occupy the principal seat in the chancel, which was the right of the lay rector but to them and their successors in title, the rectory became merely a source of income and its upkeep was abandoned by them and left to others.

All interest in the "old church" evaporated when the communion table was removed from the chancel at the altar of St George or the High Altar and placed in the nave. As the years rolled by the wind blew through the broken windows, the east window was then a large window in the Perpendicular style dating to the sixteenth century. The parishioners made no demands that the chancel should be maintained as an integral part of the fabric and in fact, when the 1874/6 restoration took place many of the windows in the adjacent north and south chapels were blocked up. It seems to have been a place which produced materials for the parish church for in 1699 there is an entry in the Churchwardens' Accounts, which reads, "Paid for tills taken out of ye old Church 1 .6." Hancock remarks, "the tiles were no doubt the original heraldic and otherwise decorated tiles of which so few remain."[20] These tiles have suffered grievously and to ensure their survival they were in 1874/6 taken up and gathered with other fragments found under the floors and placed in the Mohun chantry chapel then known as the Sacristy.

In 1693 reference was made to the paving of the church which according to Hancock was probably laid with slate from Treborough. The entry reads: "Richard Wardle and his men 3 days and a ½ paving ye Church."[21] In 1713 the paving was still proceeding for, in that year, Hugh Stewkley's agent was paid 1s 4d "for paving stones for the church." The Stewkleys did not sell the rectory until 1790 when a descendant, Lord Stawell, sold it and his farm at Marsh and all lands to John Fownes Luttrell for £5,000.

Miss Wedgwood describes the state of ruination pertaining in many churches and draws a picture which in many respects finds a parallel at Dunster. "Lack of money and the disappearance of endowments had caused many churches to fall into decay and some altogether into disuse. Many were filthy, with unglazed windows, and mud floors like cow byres. Squatters took possession of neglected chapels; in Wiltshire several families were found camping in one, using suitable tombstones as cheese presses. The abhorrence of idolatry taught by the Puritans had degenerated into open disrespect for church buildings. The parish church was often the parish meeting place, not only for sober business but for dancing and drinking parties. Sporting parishioners brought their dogs and hawks to divine service and the poorer sort pastured their hogs in the graveyard. An indignant sexton in Suffolk found the local squire sheltering from a storm with his horse inside the sacred building. Much Communion plate had vanished at the Reformation and its place was often meanly supplied by wicker and earthenware bottles and vulgar tavern pots."[22]

A piece of social history is encapsulated in the alms box which may still be found just inside the south door of Dunster church. It has a brass plate ~ part of an earlier box ~ which was originally found in one of the church chests. The plate bears the following inscription:

HE THAT HATH PITY ON THE POORE LENDETH VNTO THE LORD AND THAT WHICH HE HATH GIVEN WILL HE PAY HIM AGAINE. PROV.XIX WHO SO STOPPETH HIS EARS AT THE CRY OF THE POORE HE ALSO SHALL CRY HIMSELF BUT SHALL NOT BE HEARD. PROV XXI M.H. 1634 I.G.

The initials are those of the two churchwardens Mathew Harte and John Giles who were churchwardens from 1633/4. This alms box prompts an investigation into the poor laws as applied by the overseers of the parish to Dunster itself. "Throughout the seventeenth century the relief of the poor was based on the Elizabethan statute of 1601."[23] This statute was "the final expression of Elizabethan statesmanship in the sphere of the poor law,"[24] and was a slightly amended version of the statute of 1576. In 1563 the need to impose 'a compulsory levy for the maintenance of "impotent, aged, and needy persons,"'[25]was recognised in principle. This category was divorced from the fraternity of vagabonds and beggars[26] whose begging brought little reward since 'private charity had grown cold since the dissolution of the monasteries. "A poor man" says Robert Greene, "shall as soon break his neck as his fast at a rich man's door."'[27] Robert Greene was a pamphleteer, dramatist and novelist who lived between 1560 and 1592.

George Luttrell (d 1655) bequeathed £40 to the poor of Dunster.[28] His father Thomas, who was buried at Dunster on 7 February 1644, left 50 guineas and his widow, Jane, continued to pay interest at the rate of six per cent[29] presumably for the next twenty-four years of her life. She died and was buried at Dunster in November 1668. In 1662 the parish had £353. 8s 10d in stock and it was decided that the sum of £245. 8s 10d should, "by the desire of the parish for better securing (be) in the custodie of ffraunceis Luttrell Esq"[30] brother of George whom he succeeded. This Francis was buried at Dunster 14 March 1666. The relief of the poor throughout the seventeenth century which is here detailed in relation to Dunster, depended upon the Elizabethan statute of 1601. The overseers of the poor were, at that time, nominated by two or more justices of the peace and were chosen from the churchwardens of the parish and from substantial householders. By 1670, in Dunster the system was changed and four overseers were appointed annually by the outgoing overseers. By 1681 the parishioners, for the first time, signed the election of the churchwardens and overseers. Their names are recorded as Michael Blake, Richard Bower, Walter Slocombe, Thomas Chilcott, Francis Shutt, Thomas Mickper and Jon Moffatt.[31]

Professor Davies recounts the duties of the overseers which were: "setting to work the children of paupers and all without adequate means and daily employment, with raising by taxation such sums of money as they thought necessary to provide a convenient stock of flax, hemp, wool, thread, iron, and other wares for the employment of the poor, with granting relief to the lame, impotent, old, blind, and such others as were poor and not able to labour, and with apprenticing pauper children. In the event of the able-bodied poor refusing to perform the tasks allotted to them, they might be sent to the house of correction. In order to provide dwellings for the poor, the overseers might erect houses on waste or common land within their parish. (with the leave of the lord of the manor). With exceptions for certain deserving classes begging was strictly forbidden. By another act the justices of the peace were to cause to be erected one or more houses of correction in every county or city in order that all rogues, vagabonds, and sturdy beggars might, after being whipped, be sent to a house of correction, unless the place of birth or residence for one year of the culprit was known, in which case he or she was to be sent from parish to parish until reaching the place of birth or last legal residence. Probably a mistake was made in fixing so small an area as a parish as the unit of poor relief, because the overseers were often more concerned to save their neighbours' pockets by restricting relief than to afford proper aid to the needy. Certainly the anxiety of overseers of the poor that new-comers should not become a charge on the parish often worked great hardship. Thus a labouring man born in a parish and working there all his life might find, on marrying a woman living elsewhere, that the overseers would not permit her to reside in the parish lest the expected family should become a charge on the poor rates. Sometimes the overseers would not allow a couple to continue to dwell in their own village after marriage. Such actions might well create vagrants out of hitherto self-supporting men and women, but the parish responsible for the social crime might be able to avoid maintaining them. More reasonable was the attempt to prevent the settlement of strangers by fining heavily landlords or lodging-house keepers who provided a roof for intruders In fact the first regulations against overcrowding were inspired as much by fear of increased poor rates as by dread of the visitations of the plague in insanitary tenements."[32]

This last paragraph regarding new-comers is borne out by an entry in the Dunster Overseers' accounts of 1667 when a warrant was issued "for warning strangers out of the towne." A further warrant was specifically aimed at the miller who lived just outside Dunster, at Avill. It was "to warne ye miller of Avill out of ye pishe."[33] Hancock writes "all through this period warrants are frequently obtained for the 'removal of strangers'. The danger of poor people from other parishes becoming chargeable on the rates was always jealously guarded against."[34] The miller of Avill was not to be budged and on his refusal to leave the warning 'having been ignored', an order was obtained "for sending ye Miller of Avill out of ye pishe."[35]

In 1676 two orders were issued "to remove the Wid Snow and ye Wid Skyner with two horses higher (hire) 6s."[36] Further "Paid for the higher of two horses to carry the Widow Snow and here child to treborow."[37] In 1695 William Craze declared his wish to live in Dunster, the town in which he was born. He stated that: "I William Craze Junior do hereby give notice in the parish Church of your said Towne of Dunster that I am come home to settle as an inhabitant of your said parish of Dunster being born there. In witness whereof I have hereto sett my hand this fourth day of September *Annoque Domini* 1695"[38] This declaration was: ..."published in the parish Church of Dunster by the Churchwardens and Overseers of the poor of the parish on Sunday Eveninge 15th daye of September after devine Service." On the 30th of Sept., however, Craze, under a warrant from Mr Palmer of Fairfield, was carried before "George Musgrave Esq., who there told him that he was a parishioner in Carhampton."[39]

There are no overseers' accounts for Dunster extant before 1654/5 and the first official appointment of overseers did not take place until 1665.[40] In 1654/5 the overseers had the sum of £259 10s for the benefit of the poor. Parishioners requiring loans could obtain them from this fund at interest. We read: "In this year there were no less than thirty-one persons holding portions of this stock, "all which bondes are in Mr Luttrell's hands."[41] The castle, and the family holding it, seem to have been always very naturally the resort of the parishioners when safety was required. The total expenditure for the year amounted to £69. The accounts are signed, May 1655, by George Luttrell, who we know died a young man of thirty in this year.[42]

The training of apprentices, again incorporated in the Elizabethan statute of 1598/1601 is referred to in the Dunster Overseers' accounts of 1656. It was customary for the overseers and churchwardens to pay a premium to those persons to whom children were bound out as apprentices. An example of this is the payment of £1. 5s made to William Meade and Andrew Worth who each took an apprentice in that year. The accounts were signed by John Turberville of Gauldon in the parish of Tolland and Thomas Siderfin.[43] Thomas Siderfin was lord of the manor of Exton, Hawkridge and Withypool.[44] He continued to sign the accounts in 1658 but now with Francis Luttrell (d 1666) successor to George (d 1655) and with George Trevelyan. The accounts for that year show that a pair of shoes cost 1s 6d and a shirt, together with the making 3s 9d.[45] In 1676 "Alexander Prole nine shillings with his apprentice besides close (*clothes*) to make out, twenty shillings."[46] The fee received for an apprentice had increased by 15s in 1688 so that "Wm Cross received £2 when he took John Crase as his apprentice and likewise Robert Briant received the same sum for ffrancis Newton. Parents who wished to apprentice their own children were assisted by the overseers, so that Joan Pullin received 10s "towards the binding of her son."[47]

According to Hancock the poor house was not established in Dunster until 1699 when the paupers and their furniture were removed to this establishment. He remarks: "The confinement and life under rule in their new quarters must have come as a great hardship to the paupers, who had been accustomed to live separate and free lives."[48]

Lyte identifies the location of this poor house/workhouse as being three small houses close to the school established by the Weslyans in 1825 near the corner of West Street and, in fact, in Mill Lane. They were between 1696 and 1699 let to the overseers of the parish apparently to serve as a workhouse which closed in 1836.[49]

Previous to the establishment of this workhouse, "the poor chargeable on the parish were either lodged out or placed in houses, the rent of which was paid by them."[50] In 1686: "Ye Widdow Morgan for keeping Burts a child for ye moneth 10s.[51] The widow Morgan received more than the usual 6s per month for her charge for some reason unknown to us. In 1692 "John Clements for keeping Antony Courteney for board for him 2s, fier (fire) in his chamber 2s 4d = 4s 4d."[52] Rents averaging from 10s *to* 16s per year were paid for nine paupers families in 1694. Fifteen years earlier one Andrew Hobs, for some misdemeanour not specified, had to give up his bed to William Watts the proceeds apparently being used to provide 2s 6d towards his rent.[53] The actual entry is : "1679. Given towards the redemption of Andrew Hobs bed unto Will. Watts for rent 2s 6d."[54] The poor received food and firing, rough and hard-wearing clothes. Doctor's fees were paid but, it must be said, the cost of their maintenance was reduced to a minimum so that in 1680 "John Burchams diet "cost no more than 1s 4d a week.[55]

In 1718 the poor house, now referred to as the Parish House, underwent a good deal of renovation. A master mason was employed by the overseers at the rate of 1s 4d per day and labourers at 1s per day. The work undertaken included re-thatching for which a "hundred of reed cost 7s., 27 hogsheads of lyme 14s and Messrs Samuell Chafyn and Gyles Escott received 4s 2d for "tyles stoanes" and 15s for "stoanes" respectively. Later in 1760 there is reference to "Ye Workhouse in West Street."[56]

A list of the rate payers of Dunster does not exist before 1667 but in that year on 23 April a rate was levied "for ye maintaynance of ye poor of the psh." It is headed with names of the two churchwardens John Leigh and Thomas Thorne[57] and of four "Overseers of ye poore of ye pish, Richard Bower, Edmond Burington, James Turner and Allexander Prole."[58] The names and amounts paid are as follows:

	£	s.	d.
The heires of Francis Luttrell, Esq	1.	10.	0
Sr Hugh Stewkley, Bart	1.	10.	0
Mrs Jane Luttrell		4.	0
Mrs Linde or occupyer		2.	0
The Heires of Tho. Trevelian, Esq		1.	0
Nicholas Blake, Gnt		1.	2
Anne Prole, Wid			9
Ambrose Moore			10
Allice James, Wid			4
Allex Prole		2.	4
Anne Kidner			3
Adrian Millet			4
Benjamin Blandon			4
Eliz. Everts,			4
Ephraim Lewis			10
Edmond Brimpton			4
Edward Shenton......................................			

	£	s.	d.
Edward Radford		1.	0
ffrancis Pearse, Gent.		2.	0
George Ashe			
George Bartlet		1.	0
Giles Punter..			
George Allderman.......................................			
Henry Dye...			
Henry Strong...			
Henry Berryman...		2.	0
Henry Prole...			
Henry Blandon			
Izot Shorland Vid			
John Dunn			
John Question			
John Strong			
John Strue			
John Clement			
John Brint			6
John Wright		2.	8
John Teingler			10
John Tirroll		2.	2
Jeremie Spurrier			9
John Leigh		1.	0
John Paggin		2.	8
John Mitchell		2.	0
James Wilkins		1.	2
John Trill			4
James Turner		1.	6
James Shute		3.	0
John Daunter		3.	0
John Blake		1.	0
John Bryant		12.	0
John Edmunds		2.	8
John Leigh		2.	8
John Skinner/ or o[59]		1.	8
James Ashford			4
John Raull			4
John Hosegood		2.	0
John Clement			6
John Pearce or or		3.	4
John Turrill or or.			2
John Long			4
Katherine Long, Widw		1.	3
Katherine Price			4
Lewis Sweetinge		1.	0
Lawrence Luckwill or or			2
Lawrence Thomas			2
Mary Mead, Vid		1.	4
Mrs Mitchell		3.	2
Mary Markes Vid			6

	£	s.	d.
Margeret Watts			4
Mrs Wescombe or or		2.	0
Mrs Downe for ye meddows or or		1.	6
Matthew Hooper		2.	6
Mary Giles, Vid		4.	6
Mary Crockford, Vid		4.	0
Mrs Downe for what was Stephens land		4.	0
Nicholas Ingrain or or			2
Peter Horman Jun			10
Peter Berryman or or			6
Peter Horman, Sen			5
Peter Kidner			6
Phillip Elston			6
Richard Bower...			
Richard Slocombe..			
Robert Courserer			6
Robert Marknes..			
Ralph Hill		2.	0
Robert Giles Sen			8
Robert Wilkins			8
Richard Escott or oc		1.	0
Robert Drew			4
Richard Starcorow			4
Richard Escott, Sen.., ye marsh			4
Richard Coocksly		1.	0
Richard Blackford		1.	2
Richard Moore or oc			8
Richard Escott for yt was Wilkin's ground			4
Silvester Allercot		7.	0
Samuell Crockford Sen., ye medd		1.	6
Thomas Chillcot		1.	0
Thomas Clement		1.	0
Thomas Dennis		1.	0
Thomas Mackness		1.	4
Thomas Dennis		1.	0
Thomas Beard			10
Thomas Wheaden			10
Thomas Hendly, Gent.		2.	4
The Wid. Bartlet		1.	10
The Wid. Chapman		1.	10
The Wid. Quirke		1.	0
Thomas Bampton...			
Thomas Blackwell.......................................			
Thomas Elston..			
Thomas Siderfin, Esq.		3.	0
The oc of Burcham's		6.	0
Thomas Evyhorn		2.	0
The Wid. Ewens..			
Thomas Beryman...			
Thomas Turner		4.	0

	£	s.	d.
Thomas Blackwell		4.	0
The Tenmt of Hopcot..			
Margaret Evet..			
The Wid. Knowles..			
The Wid. Batt		4.	0
The Wid. George...			
The Wid. Welch..			
William Shenton...			
Walter Slowcombe, Sen..		1.	0
William Hurford		1.	0
E. Vats		1.	0
Will. Bryant		1.	0
William Mowis		1.	0
Will. Coffin.			
Will Arsie..			
Will James... [60]			

Examples of expenditure on clothing for the poor follows:

1658 A pair of shoes	1s	6d
A shirt with the making of it	3s	9d
"A pair of stockings"		3d
1661 3½ yards of Irish Cloth and thread and buttons and canvas to make pockets	3s	8d
1665 "Base" for clothes for the poor	3s	3d per yard
"5 yards and one quarter twille clothe with baze and tape to make Elizabeth Braze a coate"	6s	8d
1667 8 yards of Irish cloth (at 1s 2d per yard) for "a coate waistcoat and galoons."	9s	4d

In 1667 a material called "carsie" (probably Kersey cloth) cost 2s 8d per yard, Irish cloth cost 1s 2d per yard. In 1668 dowlas was used for shirting and cost 10d per yard, and 4½ yards of "bays" cost 5s. Dowlas did not go up in price for in 1686: "Antony Courtney 8 yds of dowllas for 2 shurts 6s 4d." At the same time a smock was made for "ye Widdow Stone." In 1676 we first hear of calico being used. It is referred to as "Brod Calley Crow" and cost 12½d per yard. In 1690 "Pd for five yeards of cloth at 2s 4d. p. yed. for a Coat and breeches for Thomas Berryman and making 2s 8d, 16s 6d."[61]

Dunster had its wise woman in one Margaret Gardener who was paid "for curing Thomas Hellman's child for the Ricketts." According to country lore such persons, often the seventh child of the seventh child, were called upon to cure toothache, warts and the pains of childbirth and were said to be especially endowed with the healing touch.

The entry of 1668 concerning "George Ashforde's maidshead" is somewhat perplexing since it can hardly be a reference to maidenhead, it is perhaps a reference to an injury to George Asheford's maid's head, if so the treatment was horrendous. Two people were called in to deal with the situation, John Wright and Diana Worth. John was paid for "½ a yarde of canvas and turpentine to make plaisters for George Asheforde's maidshead which cost 1s 10d." This was unsuccessful and again John Wright was called upon and he received 1s 5¼d on several occasions "for turpentine canvass and rossin."

In 1674 Luke Hitchox received 10s "for couring (curing) Collimore's boys head" and Mr Question received £1. 5s. 0d "of curing John Dowent leedge." In 1678 Mary Badcoke was cured "of the itch" and this cost 8s and Doctor Handcock received £2 for "ye curing of Jane Welch" and a year later a Mr Rich, Gent, received the same sum "for curing Jane

Blindon's thigh." A further £1 was paid "for setting Joane Blindon's leg being broken" and in 1682 £1 15s was paid "for seting Thomas Gillse his leeg being broken in 3 places." Notwithstanding these individual fees for setting bones the doctors generally received a retaining fee of £5. 5s annually to provide ordinary attention and medicine. The poor were sometimes sent to Bath for the waters so that the second book of overseers' accounts shows that Anthony Courtney went there "to bee cured of bad eyes 10s." The expenses of paupers going to Bath to take the waters was automatically met by the overseers. Around 1690 a Mrs Devonsheir received 10s " for curing Widow Hemburys arms by ye consent of ye prishioners" and one Luke Pitcher, thought to be the local apothecary, received 2s 6d "for cures." When Mary Badcock was confined a variety of purchases were made but the cost is not given "for a yeard and a half of bayes and shuger and candels and one yeard of white bayes and more shuger and dyvers cordyal and hunie and oyl for Mary Badcock in her troble." Further "for the middwife and the weeming (women) that ware with Mary Badcock." The apothecary Pitcher received 6d the same year "for drawing a tooth for Porters mayle."

The provision of warmth for the poor often appears in the accounts so that in 1676: "Gave David Palle 3 boushells of Colles 1s 9d." In 1679 "Andrew Hobb and Willm Watte for Waking with Hoborn. A score of faggots – 3s." Here, it would appear that the vigil kept over the deceased Hoborn was a cold exercise and the watchers needed a fire. In 1693 Thirty faggots of wood cost 4s; and six "bushells of coles" 3s 6d.

Diverse subjects involving the overseers and warrants obtained from them follow:

1662. a warrant was obtained for bringing in "the Card-maker of Lyddeard before Mr Luttrell, Justice of the Peace."

1665. Mr Grant the vicar receives "the 6s 8d for a sermon upon Markes day accordinge to Doneer's will." In 1689 "A Sermon Markes Day 6s 8d."

1665. A traveller passes through Dunster under "a passe under ye Duke of Albemarle." (George Monck became duke of Albemarle at the restoration of Charles II.)

1676. "A warrant to distraine on severall persons that refused to paye ye poor rate with horse higher."

1679. "To Thos Hewey his charges for presenting Mary Perkins for murder and drawing his Indictment 13s."

1688. "Paid for two Mattins Books for hoopers children, 6d."

"7th Month "Pd for Beer and wood to make bonfires for the p'tended prince of Wales. £1. 16s."

1692. "For a bottle of Stirtick Water. 1s."

1693 "May ye 10th. Received of Mr William Sealey, 3s. 4d being moneys leveyed by the Justice on Mr Thomas Joanes A minister for being overcome with bear (*beer*) And give to the poor as ffolloweth."

1693. "December 12. Received Money Leveyd on Mr Bryant by ye Justice for his Gray hound given thus (13s.4d)."

Goods belonging to the poor were, on their decease, sold to compensate the funds for the money spent on their maintenance during their life times.

Examples concern one "Sander Rackley (whose) goods are sold for the good of the parish."

"The Crock wais 17 powne sold at 6 peince a powne comes to.....	8	9
platters wais 7 pownd and a quarter at 7 pens a pound comes to.....	4	2
the....and board and Coberd comes to	8	0
And to cofers and to platters comes to	2	1
"The holde of his goods comes to	£1. 3.	0

On 7 October, the goods of Joan Alderman, 'who had been maintained by the parish' were sold. Her possessions were:

"A Hamnell Coate		7s	
A green coate			2d
A black Coate			7d
A Wascote		1s	
1 drawer		1s	6d
1 Apron and hood			9d
Two kittles and a skillet		7s	6d
Ye bedsteed		5s	1d
2 sheets		5s	1d
2 blew rugs		4s	8d
Ye bolster		7s	
1 bolster, 1 pillow and bed 66 lbs at 7d	£1	18s	6d "

'The parish, however, was left in debt by the poor old soul.'
A similar sale of the goods of Ann Thomas comprised:

A pewter dish		4d
An "earthen platter and a plate of earth (earthenware)		2 ½d
A "blankett"	4s	4d

At this sale one Will Lang purchased a miscellaneous lot for £1 10s. It consisted of:

1 wascot
2 Coates   .
2 pewter dishes
9 spoons
1 hood 1 mantle
1 bolster
2 feather Pillos
2 bedtyes
2 bed steeds *(bedsteads)*
1 Caster
3 crooks
1 coffer
1 box and other things £1. 10s

Bequests were made and in 1686 the churchwardens acknowledged the receipt of £10, "beinge the gifts of Andrew Worthe, Gent., deceased."

Fourteen years earlier, Andrew Worthe's name is mentioned in:

"An accompt of the principall monies belonging to the poore of the pysh of Dunster an in whose hands the same are made up this 22nd of Aprill 1672
There is placed on the securite of Taunton deane lands in Taunton
  Castle   £200
There is due upon bond dated 15 April, 1659 from
  Mr Andrew Worthe   5
There is due from Mr Joseph Drake upon bond dated
  27 Apri 1658   10

There is due from Wm.Skynner in pte of 20*li* upon
bond dated 10 April. 1656   10

There is due from John Hayes upon bond dated
1 Nov. 1667   8

There is due from Thomas Macknees upon bond dated
22 May 1658   10

There is due from Thomas Clement upon bond dated
27 Dec, 1687   15

There is due from John Burt upon bond
dated 17 April 1659   3

There is due from Mary Giles widd. Upon bond
dated 16 Dec. 1658   4

There is due from John Ewens upon bond
dated 14 July 1668   8

There is due from Nicholas Pawlington, upon bond
dated 23 Nov. 1654   10

There is due from Wm Bryant upon bond
dated 8 Janu. 1670   5

There is due from Phillip Grandfield upon bond
dated 24 March 1663, which was pte of Mr
Thomas Luttrell's legacy   40
                                                               ————
                                                               £328

There is remayning in the hands of Mr
Horman pte of monies received by
him and paid into Taunton Castle as
pte of the £200 untill more monies
bee received to make a greate sume
to be there alsoe placed by the discretion
of Mrs Luttrell w th consent of the
Overseers.   18
So the whole monies belonging to the poore is......   346

There was 20s due from Wm Pullen and
There was 20s from Richard Cowlin both which
somes are lost there being noe pson
now to be found lyable to pay the same   2
Which makes up the auncient sume be-
longing to the poor   £348 [62]

A convoluted sentence concerns the practice of seizing sheep illegally imported from Ireland and selling them for the equal benefit of the poor and those who seized them. It runs as follows:

"An account to whome the money received for 24 and halfe Irish sheep which were sold for the poor the 14th of Aug. 75 being £7. 19s 3d was given."[63]

The money was disbursed between fifty-eight of the poor; each receiving a small sum. The following year "two pounds fourtine and a penny" was realised "for Irish sheep which was seased and sold according to law..."[64]

The law covered sheep and cattle and was "an act against importing cattle from Ireland and other parts beyond the seas."[65]

Although the act referred to the importation of cattle as "a common and public nuisance"[66] doubtless a vigilant watch was maintained along the English coast by those not only desirous of benefiting the poor but also of lining their own pockets with half the proceeds of the sales of cattle and vessels.

The overseers also held land for example the "Meadow at Gallick's Cross"[67] and they also sought legal advice concerning the purchase of land. "For drawinge the Case to advise with Councill for the byinge of Webbers land."[68]

In 1678 the rate was £84[69] and in 1680 one hundred and seventy-eight people paid poor rate.[70]

An extensive list giving the names of those liable for the poor rate in 1686 follows.

Hancock gives the sums paid by some, but not all, of the inhabitants of the parish. The names from Allercott to Woolcotts have been listed alphabetically for easy reference.

ffrancis Luttrell, Esq.	1.	19.	0
Sir Hugh Stewkeley, Kt and Barrt	1.	10.	7
the heirs of Knoll (of Mr Thomas Trevelyan)		1.	0
ffrancis Pearce, Gent		3.	0
Robert Allercott		3.	6
Grace Evans, Wid			4
Thomas Clymont		1.	0
of Hartnolls		1.	4
Henry Blundon			3
Edw Shenton			3
Geo Gregory			2
Thos Cross			

Joane Allercott, George Allercott, Henry Andrewe, Kathern Aprice, Wm Apsey, John Atkins, Widd Attawill, (occupier of what was Walter Slocombes), Thos Banton, George Bartlett, Peter Berriman, George Berry, George Blackford, Mr Blackford for Wescombe. Widd Blackwill, ffrancis Blake, George Blake, John Blake, Nich Blake Gent., Benj Blundon, Rich Bowers, Ambrose Bradford, Christian Briant, John Briant, John Burnell, John Burroes, Robt Burt. Edm Cade, Geo Chaplin, Wm Chaplin, Rich Chaplin, Widd Chapman, Eliz Chilcott, Tho Chilcott, George Clarke, John Clarke, John Clement Snr, JohnClement Jnr, John Clement for dauntsey, Geo Close, Honor Coffin, Eliz Coggan, Robt Courtt, Mr Sam Crockford for ye Shop, Mr Sam Crockford for Ellicombe (4s), Sam Crockford, William Cros, Thos Dennis[71] for ye Ship, Geo Dolbridge, Mr Downe for Hopcott, Widd Drew, Geo Edmond, John Edwards, William Elston, Ellen Escott, John Ewens, Rob Giles, Rob Griffith Robert Griffy, John Gunn, John Hernian, Rob Hosegood, Henry Hurford, Widd Hurford, Robert James, Widd James, Peter Kidner, Joane Knight, Bernard Knight, John Leigh, Willm Leigh, Ephraim Lewis, John Long, Katheren Long Rich Luckwill, Tho Mackness, Sam Matthews, Peter Meade, Tho Mercomb, Andrew Millett, John Milton, John Moffatt, Willm Moor, William Norrich, James Pears, John Perry, occupier of Phillips, Jenkin Philpott, John Philpott, Wm Pinn, John Plasway, Tho Platte, Henry Prole, Mr Prowse, Augustin Question, Rachell Question, Willm Reed, William Sealey, Willm Shepherd, James Shutt for Staunton (5s), Mr Siderfin, Tho Siderfin Gent., Wid Skiner, Walter Slocombes, Geo Speake Esq for Berrimans, Henry Stockham, John Strettinger, John Stride, Joan Strong, Robert Strong, Widd Stronge, Mr Sweeting for Haymarsh, Eliz Taylor, Abraham Thomas, JamesTurner, John

Turrill, Rich Wardle, William Warman, Wm Watts, John Way, John Widbourn, James Wilkins for Berrimans, Tho Wilkins, Tho Wilson, James Withicomb, Robt Wood, occupier of Woolcotts.

In 1690 the total rate was £140. 8s 6d and Hancock further detailed the outgoings which were:

Weekly payments to the poor	96.	10.	1
Burying	2.	4.	0
House Rent	5.	9.	9
Apparell	9	18.	10
Want and sickness	20.	4.	2
	£134.	6.	10 [72]

The overseers went about their business on horseback and the expenses they incurred record that in 1676 they, and presumably the offenders, had to attend Bath Sessions: "Charges at Bath Sessions with horse higher (hire) the same by thirty six shillings."[73] Warrants were served on those who failed to pay the poor rate by the overseers who, no doubt, visited outlying farms and homesteads. Thus "A warrant to distraine on severall persons that refused to pay ye poor rate with horse higher."[74]

In July 1685 when the battle of Sedgmoor took place, the Dunster overseers were John Clement, John Moffatt, John Blake and John Wilson. These men hunted down Monmouth's supporters living locally and denounced them to the Petty Sessions held at Stogumber in the August of that year. "Pd for expenses to ride to psent the Rebels at Stogumber. Horse hire and expenses 5s."[75]

If the rebels were found guilty by the justices they were sent to Taunton to face Judge Jeffrey's infamous assizes held in September 1685. It is known that, Henry Lackwell, John Geanes and William Sully, all Dunster men, faced execution and doubtless, were hanged on Gallox Hill. Prebendary Hancock paints a moving picture. "We can picture the mournful procession passing down Water Street (Park St), the three men, known to all Dunster, surrounded by their weeping friends and relatives across Gallox bridge, then up the steep ascent climbed in earlier times by those whom in the rough days of the twelfth and thirteenth centuries the De Moiones had condemned to death, till the top of the brown hill and the gibbets, which stood out against the skyline, were reached. But the refined cruelty of Jeffreys waged war even against the dead. He did not allow the dead bodies of his victims to remain in peace. They were taken down from the gibbets, and the limbs torn asunder and boiled in pitch to preserve them, were nailed to posts or hung on trees at various points along the highways as a terror to the foes of his most pious majesty James II. The cross way at the bottom of West Street perhaps claimed a share of these ghastly trophies."[76]

In the third quarter of the 17th century an entry concerning the payment of marriage fees occurs in the overseer's accounts. 1675 Paid Mr Grant (the vicar) for marrying Walter Watts and Jane Baker 1s."[77]

Hancock writes: "At this period, and still more later on, the arrangements for the poor were very unsatisfactory, and no doubt encouraged idleness. Whole families made no effort at self-support. The children of such families were brought up entirely on charity, clothed, fed and apprenticed, till finally the fees for their marriage were paid out of charity money as in the case above. Nor did the matter stop there, for after many years perhaps of wedded life, the couple could return to their parish, and if in need of help, be maintained by parish funds until they died, when the parish paid the cost of their funerals."[78]

When John Lacy died his hair was cut before burial. 1670 "Paid for cuttinge of John Lacy's haire. 1d."[79] Not only was it seen to that John Lang was buried in a seemly condition but 9d was paid for "two pound of Candles to wach with John Lacy."[80] Those who watched beside the corpse until burial were also a charge on the parish. In the same year, Grace Worth died and 1s 4d was "Paid for Beere and for Stretching forth,"[81] or for laying out of the departed Grace. In 1674 "a shroud and ringing cost 5s 2d; making grave 6d."[82] To assist the woollen industry in that year an act was passed decreeing that everyone should be buried in woollen stuffs and not in linen and the clergy had to make an entry in the register that "an affidavit had been made to them, within eight days after burial, certifying that the requirement of the law had been fulfilled"[83]. The law was generally ignored and had to be made more stringent in 1678 and in that year the Churchwardens paid 6d "for an act for the Burying in Wooling."[84] The penalties were heavy and any infringement resulted in a fine of £5 —50s of which went to the poor of the parish and 50s to the informer who had caused the information to be laid before the justices of the peace.[85] An example occurred in Dunster when: "Upon burying of Frances ye wife of Thomas Watts on ye 29th of November Anno. Dom. 1689 50s was paid because she was buried in linen and thus disbursed." Then follows a list of one hundred poor people who had each received sixpence.[86]

The next year Colonel Francis Luttrell died as did Elizabeth Hayman, the wife of Samuel Hayman. Both were buried in linen and their executors fined. "1690. Upon Burying of Francis Luttrill Esq. on the 4th of August, Anno. Dom. 1690, fifty shillings was paid because he was buried in linen and thus disbursed."[87]

The cost of a pauper's funeral was 7s 7d. The shroud was made from five yards of material at 11d per yard and this cost 4s 7d and 3s was paid for making the grave, ringing the bell and for the stretching out the deceased and for the affidavit stating that the shroud was made of wool.

CHAPTER TWELVE

DUNSTER IN THE CIVIL WAR

I T WAS William Seymour, earl of Hertford, created a marquess in 1640 and Sir Ralph Hopton who came to Somerset to organize the militia for the king. The marquess, later to become duke of Somerset[1] was a staunch royalist and governor of James, duke of York, the future King James II. His wife Frances Devereux must have been one of the many wives experiencing a dichotomy of loyalties for her brother was Essex, the commander of the opposing forces. Hertford was the lord lieutenant of Somerset and there he received his first set-back when he was driven out of Wells by Sir Edward Hungerford and forced to retreat to Dorset and then to Wales. He occupied Sherborne castle and here an unsuccessful attempt to dislodge him was made by the parliamentary forces under the earl of Bedford, Lord General of the Horse, who was accompanied by Denzil Holles, member for Dorchester who was in command of a regiment of foot. "When the Castle guns opened fire, the Parliamentary troops – country lads unused to such doings —"fell flat on their bellies" and were loath to move again. At nightfall they began to desert and Bedford was forced to retreat."[2]

Lyte takes up the story: "This place in turn he found to be untenable and while negotiating or pretending to negotiate for a surrender, he broke out with about four hundred followers on the 19th September, and directed his course to Minehead. The Earl of Bedford, commanding for the Parliament, at once issued warrants for the apprehension of any of the party, and sent off posts to Thomas Luttrell bidding him strengthen and make good his castle at Dunster. The order was promptly obeyed and Thomas Luttrell increased his garrison by a hundred men. Anticipating moreover that the Royalists would endeavour to cross over to Wales, he caused the rudders of all the ships in Minehead harbour to be removed."[3]

When Hertford arrived in Minehead he fortified himself in a "strong inn" *(possibly The Ship, now The Luttrell Arms)*and then took steps to gain possession of Dunster castle. He sent sixty of Sir Ralph Hopton's men to demand entrance. They had not reckoned on the formidable Jane Luttrell, the wife of Thomas, and their demands were met with a peremptory refusal. After some parleying they refused to leave and "Mistresse" Luttrell commanded the men within to "give fire."[4] In spite of a royalist urging them to ignore her, she persisted and further commanded them "upon their lives to do it, which accordingly they did."[5] The cavaliers were fired upon from behind the rampart and to Hertford's chagrin they beat a hasty retreat. The castle was considered to be impregnable and securing it would have been of great value. Hertford was mortified and later wrote a letter to Sir Ralph Hopton and accused his men of cowardice. Hopton, a professional soldier, understood the nature of civil war and the great reluctance of men to fire upon their fellows. He stoutly defended them and hastened to say that had the enemy been foreign they would never run or give one foot of ground. The much vexed Hertford wrote to Hopton as follows: "I have acquainted His Majesty of our disastrous fortune at Mineard and Dunster occasioned by the multitude of your countrymen's evil dispositions and cowardly behaviour in them, upon which I remembered a reverent speech of that worthy souldier, Swinden, who was General of Ostend in the time of the Infanta, Arch Duchesse of Flanders, who said that our English nation stood too much upon their owne conceit and valour, and that he would with a considerable army runne through our whole kingdome, knowing the vulgar sort of our nation to be fainthearted and unexperienced in martiall discipline. This relation of the Generall's happened to be true, for in our best actions and in the midst of our hopefull successe, Capt Digby's, Sir John Stowell's[6] and your owne souldiers ran cowardly away from us, insomuch that had it not been for the small number of my owne Horse and Foot we had lost our ordnances, hazarded our persons, and lost the honour of that daye's work. HERTFORD."[7]

To which the incensed Hopton made reply: "May it please your Lordship, with humble pardon, according to my weake ability I have considered your worthy advertisements, and vindicate myselfe and country from your Lordship's mistake. I shall now make it appeare that my actions and those under my command have bin concurrent to your Lordship's command and I have in briefe devoted myselfe to answere to every particular of your Lordship's letter. First, whereas your Lordship condemned our endeavours and cowardly behaviour at Mineard and Dunster, your Lordship may well remember and saw, three to one of the Earl of Bedford's forces forsake him, then those of our country under your Lordship's command had good successe considering the great odds (five to one). Secondly, that whereas your Lordship remembered one of the Generall in his speech at Ostend, that our nation stood too much upon their owne strength and valour and that he would with a few experienced soldiers run through our kingdome, My Lord the question herein is not disputable, for nature at home bindeth filiall affection, and one Brother or one nation to fight another is not warrantable by God's lawes, and in that respect there might be faintheartedness in our nation, but my Lord, let the Generall of Ostend or any other forraine Princes, invade this our land, I know that your Lordship believes that one Nation will not runne or give one foot of ground to such an enemy, for we are all sencible with whom we quarrell, the Father against the Sonne, and the Sonne against the Father, and if Alexander the Great or the Emperor of Persia were now alive, whose armies dranke Rivers of water, yet my Lord it would daunt the hearts of these gallants to destroy their owne bloud. Your Lordship's obedient Servant, RALPH HOPTON."[8]

Lyte remarks that, "as the Civil War progressed he (*Hopton*) must have found it necessary to modify his humane and peaceable sentiments."[9] Jane Popham of Littlecote in Wiltshire married Thomas Luttrell II in 1621 in the reign of James I. The ceremony may have taken place in the chapel at Littlecote. The present chapel of the Cromwellian period was formed out of the Great Hall and gave precedence to the pulpit which is elevated and replaced the altar at the end of the nave; all emphasis then being on the sermons rather than the sacrament. Jane was a redoubtable character, true to her family's loyalties she also echoed her husband's political sympathies and proved to be no mean opponent. She was the granddaughter of Sir John Popham of Littlecote and Wellington, lord chief justice of England, who had presided over the trial of Sir Walter Raleigh and that of Guy Fawkes. She was one of the six daughters[10] of the politically orientated Sir Francis Popham of Littlecote who during the Long Parliament of 1640 was one of nine out of the sixteen members from Somerset who had supported John Pym in damning ship-money and other excesses. One of these excesses, leaving aside ship-money and tonnage and poundage, was particular to Exmoor and concerned Exmoor tithes. The farmers in the unsettled state of the country had refused to pay these tithes and north Devon became strongly parliamentarian.[11]

To revert to Sir Francis Popham, he was a county governor and is referred to as "one of the Gentlemen of His Majesty's Privy Chamber"[12] and "a Colonel of a regiment of Foot in the County of Wiltshire."[13] He, like Essex[14] was one of those who voted for Strafford's attainder, or forfeiture of estate on death or exile. Although Sir Francis was buried at Stoke Newington church, three years later his body was exhumed and re-buried in the Mayor's Chapel of St Mark's in Bristol. In 1597: "Sir Francis was elected Member of Parliament for Somerset and between then and his death in 1644 successfully represented Wiltshire (1604/11), Marlborough (1614), Great Bedwyn (1621/22), Chippenham (1625/9) and Minehead (1640) sitting in every Parliament except the 'Short Parliament' of 1640. He was a Justice of the Peace from 1613, became Constable of Taunton Castle in 1620, and from 1625 was a Deputy Lieutenant of Somerset."[15]

Jane Luttrell's brother, the second son of Sir Francis, was Colonel Alexander Popham (b 1605) after whom Jane and Thomas Luttrell named their son Alexander (b 1622). Colonel Alexander is especially associated with Dunster since he played a prominent part in the campaign in the western counties from the beginning of the Civil War up to the surrender of Dunster castle in 1646. In 1648 he raised a troop of horse and it is thought that it was his cousin, Colonel John Popham of Bridgwater, who commanded this troop, and settled in Cork after the restoration of Charles II. At Littlecote Alexander is still remembered for there in the great hall hang the bandoliers, helmets, armour and swords, some of which he is said to have used.

Back in the January of 1643, the parliamentary party was much exercised about Dunster castle. It was feared that the royalists would make a surprise attack and gain possession of this commanding site and that if they succeeded, it would take ten thousand men to dislodge them. It was proposed that horse and foot should be raised to guard this stronghold "but the 'very thoughts' of such a measure caused the peaceable men of Minehead to give a very cold reception to Lord Bedford..."[16] Lord Bedford had been sent to pursue the royalist forces in the west and for a short time, quartered himself at the castle.

It was the Welsh who carried out a raid on Somerset in 1643. There are two accounts of this raid one given by Emanuel Green in 1880 and by Lyte in 1909. Their common source was *Special Passages*. This is Greene's account: "Early in January, 1643, the Welshmen gave trouble on the Somerset coast. Some blockaded Minehead, and preventing the entry of all boats or barques, kept back the supplies of provisions and coal. Others, about five hundred in number, under Captain Paulet landed there, 'invaded' the county, and 'constrained the inhabitants to yeeld to any taxation, and to submit themselves servants and slaves to every poore base companion, to save their throats from being cut' an operation daily threatened. This party attacked Dunster Castle, but Mr Luttrell being prepared, was able to defeat them and secure the town from plunder. In the attack, a shot from the castle killed some of Capt. Paulet's men, which 'moved him to wroth', and he vowed he would quarter the 'murderer' limb from limb and hang his quarters on the castle as food for ravens. Being thus unsuccessful here, he went on to Barnstaple with two hundred of his musketeers and forty horse,[17] and Dunster remained intact and held for the Parliament until after the fall of Bridgwater in this year. The royalist successes then added so much to their prestige that many began to think that victory must be a certainty for the king. Mr Luttrell, amongst others, seems to have been of this opinion and to have trimmed his conduct thereto, for Mr Francis Windham, at that time, having opportunities for conference with him 'found that he had good inclinations in him' to deliver up the castle; inclinations, however, in which he was 'much distracted and disturbed' by some persons near him, *i.e.,* 'Mistresse' Luttrell, his wife. But, by persistently pressing his advantage, Mr Windham so 'wrought on his fears' that eventually, with a fine of a thousand pounds, the castle was surrendered and garrisoned for the king."[18]

In May 1643 the month before the castle was surrendered Thomas Luttrell had issued a pass for his niece Margaret, the wife of George Trevelyan, to cross over to Wales. She was the daughter of his sister Margaret, who had married John Trevelyan of Nettlecombe at Dunster on 3 August 1607.[19] In his *History of the Rebellion* Clarendon writes of the surrender of the castle to the royalists. In the middle of June 1643 Taunton and Bridgwater had fallen to Hertford in three days. "Dunstar Castle, so much stronger than both the other that it could not have been forced, yet by the dexterity of Francis Windham, who wrought upon the fears of the owner and master of it, Mr Lutterell, was, with as little bloodshed as the other, delivered up to the King; into which the Marquis put in him that took it as Governor, as he well deserved."[20]

In the Dunster castle muniments there is a receipt for a large sum levied as a fine or as proof of his allegiance to the royalist cause. "xxxiito die Junii 1643. Receaved the day and yeare above written to his Majesties use by me Edward Kyrton, Esq. Treasurer for the army under the command of the right honorable the Marquesse of Hertford, Liftenant Generall of his Majesties forces in the west, of Thomas Luttrell of Dunstar Castle in the county of Somerset, Esq. the summe of five hundred powndes, in part payment of the summe of one thousand powndes which the said Mr Luttrell is to pay towardes the charge of the said army. I say receaved, Edw. Kyrton."[21]

We do not know if Thomas Luttrell was permitted to remain in his castle but he apparently survived for only eight months and, according to Lyte's first reference to his death 'he was buried at Dunster on 7 February 1644.[22] Much has already been written about his eldest son Alexander who served in one or both of the 1640 parliaments of Charles I and predeceased his father. His two brothers George, baptized at Dunster 12 September 1625, died 1655 and Francis, baptized at Dunster 1 November 1628, buried at Dunster 14 March 1666, successively inherited the castle. Francis was named after his grandfather, Sir Francis Popham. These two surviving brothers had a sister, Amy baptized at Dunster 26 June 1630, who married firstly Thomas Hele of South Pertherton and secondly George Reynell of Kingsbridge, Devon.[23] There is some confusion concerning the date of Thomas Luttrell's death. The fine of a thousand pounds was receipted on 23 June 1643,when Thomas was alive This makes the date of burial 7 February 1644 feasible. However, Lyte's second reference to Thomas's death is as follows: "Within a few days of the death of Thomas Luttrell, his relict was compelled to pay a large sum to the Crown, as appears by the following receipt:— '13th February 1643. Then received of Mrs Jane Luttrell the summe of fiveteene hundred pounds, as soe much due to his Majestie for the fyne of her selfe and her two soones; I say received for his Majestie's service the day and yeere above written the summe of 1500, by me Francis Hawley.'"[24]

Prebendary Hancock gives the date of Thomas's burial as extracted from the registers as "7th Feb.1643."[25]

The receipt for fifteen hundred pounds was given by an officer in the royalist army but in Lyte's opinion: "the payment might possibly be regarded as the purchase money for the wardship of the heir of the Dunster estate, who was a minor at the time of his father's death. A few weeks later there is another acquitance:—"25to die Marcii 1644, anno regni Regis Caroli 19o. Receaved then of Mistriss Jane Luttrell the summe of three score pownds in parte of payment of one hundred pownds which she was to pay by way of loane upon his Majestie's service I say receaved per me William Prowse, deput ' vicecomitis'"[26]

Lyte observes that Jane Luttrell must have been loath indeed to furnish money for the party which she and her relations had so steadily opposed.[27] Thomas Luttrell left instructions that "My boddie I will to be buried decently in the parish church of Dunstarr (*sic*) in my isle (*sic*) which is there."[28] Lyte observes: "The position of the aisle thus mentioned was so well known at the time as to need no further description. All that can now be said is that if this aisle was the old chancel, the Stewkleys must, tacitly or otherwise, have ceded their rights to the Luttrells before 1643. On the other hand, the place in question may have been one of the aisles of the chancel, and so quite independent of the lay rector. In any case Thomas Luttrell's aisle was "in the parish church," and not on his private property."[29]

Lyte's comment that the side aisles were quite independent of the lay rector is a telling one. The parishioners had always had rights in the south aisle and since these aisles were "quite independent of the lay rector" it follows that when the Stewkleys ceded their rights to the Luttrells, the aisles would still appear to have been independent. They were the sites of the pre-Reformation chapels of Our Lady and of St Lawrence. However, in 1876 the Luttrells established their presence in the south aisle and the tomb slab of Lady Elizabeth Luttrell of Powderham, and the Jacobean tomb were moved from the chancel into this aisle.

The castle being in royalist occupation in 1643 and East Quantoxhead being the residence of Jane's mother-in-law, the much disliked Silvestra Skory[30] who had married Sir Edmund Skory on the death of George Luttrell in 1629, had no option but to live at Marshwood with her three children George, the heir, Francis and Amy. She and Thomas had lived there during the first eight years of their marriage between 1621 and 1629 and Thomas's grandfather, also Thomas (d 1571) was referred to in some legal proceedings as "Thomas Luttrell of Marshwood."[31] In an upstairs room at Marshwood the arms of Luttrell and Popham are displayed on a plaster overmantel. LUTTRELL *Or a bend between six Martlets Sa* impaled with the arms of: POPHAM *Arg on a chief Gu two Bucks' heads cabossed Or with a crescent for a difference*. These arms may also be seen in Dunster church where they occupy the right hand position on the canopy surmounting the monument in the south aisle.

It would therefore not be irrelevant to mention here that Thomas Luttrell had a younger brother Hugh who was baptized at Dunster on 29 February 1587. He was the second son of George and Joan Luttrell (the first wife of George). He had property at Rodhuish in the parish of Carhampton and Northridge and West Myne in the parish of Minehead. He was alive in 1656 and married at Charlton Mackerel on 13 July 1629, Jane, the daughter of Thomas Lyte of Lytescary. Their arms are to be found in the chapel of the manor house of Lytescary. They were placed there in 1631 and may be blazoned:

LUTTRELL *Or a bend between six Martlets Sa* impaled with
LYTE *Gules a chevron between three Swans Argent*.

When the heir to Dunster castle, George Luttrell was twenty years of age he must have been aggrieved by the fact that the castle was occupied by royalists and that the fifteen year old prince of Wales was to pay a visit. It is said that "it may be safely assumed that his mother would not have allowed him to go to Oxford to mix with young Cavaliers."[32]

By the middle of May the prince of Wales had arrived at Dunster as nominal commander-in-chief in western England. He was only fourteen years of age when he was sent to Bristol in March 1645 and may have celebrated his fifteenth birthday in Dunster, since his birthday was 29th May. He was quite unaware of the risks he was running for when he was sent "to encourage the new levies"[33] it was "not known at Court that the plague, which had driven him from Bristol, was as hot in Dunster town, just under the walls of the Castle."[34] Bristol had experienced the dreaded Black Death more than forty years earlier when on 9 September 1603, 'The beginning of the pestilent plague' is recorded in the registers and is said to have started 'in the Parish of Little Sainte Augustine's in Bristoll'. In the May of 1645 the parish registers record that eighty victims were buried at Dunster and at Minehead the annual death rate for that year had increased five-fold. Following on the interment of the eighty Dunster casualties: "the entries stop altogether, as though the deaths were so frequent and so awful that the sufferers were no longer buried in the churchyard, or the burial service said over them. So infected was the air of the town, that such of the inhabitants who survived in one "long street in Dunster," probably West Street, "broke communications through the party walls of their houses, so that they might pass along without venturing out in the plague-laden atmosphere of the open street." The terrible affliction seems to have hung over the town during that summer and autumn, for history tells us that the parliamentary army which laid siege to Dunster Castle in the November of that year was greatly reduced by the ravages of the plague."[35]

The quotes were taken by Preb. Hancock from a 1681 account by Willis in *Of Feavers*. Like Bristol, Dunster had suffered from an outbreak of the plague earlier in the seventeenth century. It was 'so serious as to call for charitable aid from other places in the country.'[36] The year was 1611. The registers record the burial of soldiers. These were probably burials at Minehead since the list given by Hancock follows on his comment, 'Minehead was bitterly parliamentarian. The troops of the parliament swept the neighbourhood, and no doubt there were frequent small skirmishes. Thus in 1643 we find:

1643.	"Bartholomew a souldier buryed Marche ult"
1644.	"William Ashford a souldier buryed ffeb. 12"
	"Jenkin Jones a souldier buryed ffeb. 18"
	"Henry Stevens a souldier buryed March 18"
1645.	"David ⸺ a souldier buryed April 2nd."
	"Thomas Robinson a souldier buryed May 13th."
	"Steeven Tucke a souldier buryed May 10th "
	"Thomas ffowler buried May 28th"[37]

Although Minehead was fiercely parliamentarian, diplomacy prevailed and the royal visit of the Prince of Wales was marked by the ringing of the church bells. The ringers as was customary, had to be suitably refreshed. "Given the ringers in beere at severall tymes when the Prince and other great men cam into the towne, 14s."[38]

It is not disclosed why the prince's footman received remuneration but an entry records: "Paid the Prince's footman which he claymed as due to him for his fee 5s 1d."[39] The feelings of the people of Minehead were more truly reflected when four months later in September 1645, Bristol fell to the parliamentarians and the bells rang out again. "Paid the ringers when Bristoll was taken 3s."[40]

The May visit of the prince lasted for only a fortnight when he left Dunster and proceeded to Barnstaple. It is thought that he took the route used by John Leland, the antiquarian, who, in 1540 had also travelled from Dunster to Barnstaple. This highway 'by Exford, Simonsbath, Kensford Cross, 'the Spann' and Brayford....was a well-known highway in 1653, when it formed the boundary between the freeholds of the two purchasers of 'Exmoor Chace.'"[41]

After the battle of Langport, General Fairfax stormed Bristol which he took. He was gracious in his triumph and ever humane to his adversaries. He offered the defeated Prince Rupert honourable terms which were accepted but as the prince marched out of the city, the people, bearing him so much hatred cried out; "Give him no quarter. Give him no quarter."[42] Siege followed siege and in the winter of 1645 it was the turn of Dunster castle. There are almost identical accounts given by Emanuel Green and by Sir Henry Maxwell Lyte.[43] Here Green's account will be given together with his sources: "After the reverses of the royalist party at Langport, Taunton, and Bridgwater, in the summer of 1645, Dunster Castle remained the only place held for the king in Somerset, but, isolated as it was it was, harmless except as a means of annoyance to the district immediately around it. As it was desirable to stop even this power, Colonel Blake and Colonel Sydenham, taking a small party from Taunton, laid siege to it early in November,[44] and by the sixth had so completely blocked it that its surrender seemed certain, if it were not taken by surprise. Neither of these expectations were realised as the besieged held out, although by the end of the month they were said to be straitened for provisions and had suffered badly from want of water. It was reported that Colonel Francis Windham, the Governor, about the 20th November wrote to Lord Goring, then commanding the king's forces in Devon, that he could hold out but a fortnight or three weeks longer, and was only enabled to do that from having secured a good supply of water from some late heavy rains.[45] He at least wrote for aid, as in response, Goring sent some foot to Bideford intending to forward them to Dunster by sea, and a party of horse was got in readiness to march by land to protect them on arrival.[46] But, possibly not knowing their destination until they arrived at Bideford, and then not getting their promised pay, and finding they were to be out for more than the twenty days agreed for with Lord Hopton, they deserted there and ran. Sir Richard Grenville was quickly after them to bring them back but the plan for this time resulted in failure.[47] The design becoming known, Sir Thomas Fairfax placed a party to command the road and prevent or check the repetition of any similar attempt. Thus early in December when another party endeavoured to pass, the others guarding the roads being on the watch about Tiverton and Crediton, encountered them and compelled them to return."

Meanwhile Colonel Blake had repeatedly summoned the Governor *(Colonel Windham/Wyndham)* to surrender, but always receiving a curt refusal, he had pushed forward his approaches and batteries[48] and worked busily at his mines, as these were "next to determine the business."[49] A summons was again sent in, now with the threat to storm if it were refused. Colonel Windham replied as before, that as he had formerly announced his intention to keep his charge to his utmost, so he was still and would ever be *semper idem,* always the same.

About the 6th of January, 1646, Blake received a reinforcement of fifteen hundred horse, and these he quartered some five or six miles from the castle, to keep a sharp look out on the Exeter road...[50] As relief was constantly attempted and as often prevented, these troopers had a very harassing and hard duty to perform, and this, with the continuance of the siege and the dodging and perpetual activity thereabouts, drew the general attention towards Dunster.

At the very end of December, 1645, or about the 1st of January, 1646, a story was circulated by the royalist party at Oxford, on the reported authority of two men supposed to have come from Dunster, that the castle was relieved and the siege raised. The story was, that the besiegers, having taken prisoner the Governor's mother, sent in a summons thus—"If you will yet deliver up the castle, you shall have fair quarter, if not, expect no mercy; your mother shall be in the front, to receive the first fury of your cannon. We expect your answer." The Governor is supposed to reply, "If you do what you threaten you do the most barbarous and villainous act that was ever done. My mother I honour, but the cause I fight for and the masters I serve, God and the King, I honour more. Mother, do you forgive me and give me your blessing, and let the rebels answer for spilling that blood of yours which I would save with the loss of mine own, if I had enough for both my master and yourself." To this the mother is supposed to answer, "Son, I forgive thee for this brave resolution. If I live I shall love thee the better for it. God's will be done." The story adds that just at this moment there appeared Lord Wentworth[51] Sir Richard Grenville, and Colonel Webb, who attacking the besiegers, killed many, took a thousand prisoners, rescued the mother, and relieved the castle.[52] This report is here quoted from its original source; it has been often repeated, but was not true.[53] The siege was not raised, the castle was not relieved at this time, and the supposed chief actors in the affair were then in Cornwall or on the borders of Devon.[54] The Parliamentary party soon cried it down as "ale house intelligence and a feeble lie."[55] As the Governor seemed determined not to surrender, Fairfax wrote to Colonel Blake to proceed with the siege and to spring his mines.[56] This he did on the 3rd January, fully expecting to have blown up the castle. But they within, aware of what had been going on, had discovered one mine, and had spoilt it by countermining, another was not fired or did not spring, whilst the third, although it exploded fairly, destroyed but a part of the wall, causing a considerable breach, but yet making "more noise than execution."[57] The road opened by it was altogether too difficult for approach, and proved so inaccessible that the intended attack could not be made. Thus the hoped for opportunity was lost. For the defenders, however, now very short of necessaries, it proved a great annoyance, as they were put to double duty to keep their guards. In this emergency Sir Richard Grenville wrote to Colonel Windham to hold out yet a little longer and help should certainly come to him.[58] Intending this, two regiments were sent out on the 8th of January, ostensibly to relieve Exeter but really destined for Dunster. Their plan was either betrayed or assumed by their opponents, as some horse and foot were called from their winter quarters to watch them, and if necessary to go and strengthen Colonel Blake. Seeing their enemy thus prepared, and that relief was impossible, the Royalists once more retired, and the blockade of Dunster was continued without interruption until the end of January.

Towards the end of 1645 the king's army found itself cooped up in Devon, the Parliamentary forces gathering in Somerset and along the line of its retreat, in high spirits, cheerily concluding that at last the country had a chance of peace and that the royal troops were securely and certainly trapped. A report now came that Goring intended to break through this line and get his whole force away. Orders were at once sent for the reserves in the rear to be ready to meet such a movement, and Major-Gen. Massey immediately busied himself with preparations about Crewkerne.[59] Taking advantage of the attention of the Parliamentary force in Devon being given to this matter, a party of fifteen hundred horse and three hundred foot, sent by Lord Hopton under the command of Colonel Finch, managed to reach Dunster, and on the 5th of February relieved the castle with four barrels of powder, thirty cows and fifty sheep.[60] Having done this they spoilt the mines and destroyed the works thrown up by the besiegers and then returned to Devon, plundering several places as they passed. Finding the relieving party too strong for him, Colonel Blake on their arrival retired for protection into a strong house and remained there unmolested. As they left, however, he sallied out on their rear and took a few prisoners, but in turn got himself into an awkward trouble, from which he managed only with great difficulty to make an honourable retreat without great loss.[61] Colonel Luttrell, the owner of the castle, apparently regretting, under the altered circumstances of the war, his former surrender of it, now offered, by report, to raise a thousand men to help in any other attack, but[62] Blake determined simply to renew and continue the blockade, until he could be strongly reinforced from the main army. From his better information he may have judged that this would early be possible, as not long afterwards Exeter fell. Sir Thomas Fairfax then, with his usual energy, quickly moved off for fresh work, and on the 8th of April his army was camped around Chard, from whence he sent Colonel Lambert's regiment to strengthen the force before Dunster.[63]

Colonel Blake had gone to meet the general, when, on Thursday night, the 16th of April, those in the castle called to Captain Burridge, who commanded at the time, to know if it were true, as some of his soldiers had stated, that Exeter and Barnstaple had both fallen. Captain Burridge "hearkening" to what was said, they "tendered their desires" to be allowed to send to Barnstaple to get the news confirmed, and if it were true they would capitulate. The captain answered that he "would not by any false way or smooth language go about to beg their castle," and offered himself as hostage if they would send out one of like rank whilst they sent for intelligence, and if what he had said was not true he would forfeit his life, provided that they would agree to surrender on a day named if all were confirmed. Weak and reduced, and now barely able to defend more than the fort or keep, this conversation "wrought so much" upon the garrison that on Friday morning it was re-opened and a request again made for leave to go for intelligence. Notice having meantime arrived that Blake was returning and would soon be with him, Captain Burridge desired them to have a little patience and they should get an answer from the colonel himself. About noon Blake arrived, having with him Major-General Skippon's regiment and the remainder of his own. This force he drew up in two bodies on a hill facing the castle, and, in accordance with orders given by Sir Thomas Fairfax, sent in another summons for surrender.[64]

Deprived of all hope of relief, Colonel Windham, in reply, demanded a parley, the result being that after having sustained a close siege of about a hundred and sixty days, with a loss of twenty men, he surrendered on the 19th April on the following conditions:

1. That the Castle, together with the arms, ammunition, and other furniture of war (except what is hereunder excepted), be delivered up into the hands of Colonel Blake, for his Excellency Sir Thomas Fairfax, to the use of the King and Parliament.
2. That all Commissioners and officers in the Castle should march away with horses and arms and all other necessary accoutrements appertaining.
3. That common officers and common soldiers, both horse and foot, should march away with their arms and three charges of powder and bullet, and with three yards of match, for those that had matchlocks, together with colours and drums.
4. That Colonel Windham should carry with him all that was properly his own, and that what property belonged to Lady Windham should be sent to her.
5. That all officers and soldiers with all particular persons of the castle should march forth secure, as many as would, to Oxford, without delay, and those that were otherwise minded should lay down their arms and have "let passes" to their homes, or any other place they should desire, with protection against violence of the soldiers.
6. That prisoners to either party be released.
7. That the said Colonel Francis Windham and his soldiers march to Oxford in twelve days.[65]

Under this agreement the castle was delivered up on the 22nd April 1646. Six pieces of ordnance and two hundred stand of arms were all the booty found within it. Colonel Blake, writing from Taunton, 21st April, when reporting the event to the Parliament, remarked that, at the price of time and blood, he could no doubt have obtained very different terms, but he was induced to accept these, wishing to follow the exemplary clemency of his general.[66] A public thanksgiving was now ordered for the many and continued successes of the Parliamentary forces, Dunster being named in the list of places whose capture deserved especial emphasis.[67] Minehead, too, rejoiced that her disagreeable neighbour had fallen, and "gave the ringers when Dunster had yielded" four shillings and eight pence. With this surrender of Dunster the fighting ceased in Somerset. The "trumpet left off his summons, the cannon forbode his chiding," and all the county was hushed into obedience to the Parliament. The war was now virtually over. The royal army, defeated everywhere, was soon disbanded, and the king, a captive, bought and sold, was destined to remain a prisoner till the bitter end.[68] The surrender of Dunster castle on 22 April 1646 had been made by Colonel Windham to Colonel Blake and Major-General Skippon.

Addendum to Chapter Ten

THE HISTORICAL LINKS BETWEEN THE FAMILIES OF LUTTRELL AND POPHAM

(i)   Thomas Popham (c 1350/1412) married Dionysia, widow of Thomas Luttrell (c1324-?65) of Dunster. (Popham *West Country Family of Popham*, 18). This is incorrect, Thomas Luttrell was of East Quantoxhead. This Dionysia (called Denise by Lyte) was apparently the mother of the last Luttrell of East Quantoxhead in the direct line. (Lyte. *History of Dunster* Part I, 72). This was John Luttrell (d 1403), the cousin of Sir Hugh Luttrell (d 1428), the first lord of Dunster.

(ii)   The second wife of Thomas Luttrell (b c1324) was Denise Palton who survived him and married secondly Thomas Popham. (Lyte H.D. Part I 72 , Note 6)

(iii)   Sir John Luttrell (d 1403) cousin of Sir Hugh Luttrell (d 1428) conveyed the manor and advowson of the church at East Quantoxhead to Sir Hugh together with his lands at Alfoxton and Watchet. He made a supplementary will by which 'he directed that some land at Williton was to be conveyed to Thomas Popham for life, with remainder to his own maternal brother, Richard Popham, and the heirs of his body and, in default of such, to be sold for the benefit of his soul, the souls of his ancestors and the soul of John Fitzurse'. (Lyte. H.D. Part I 73/4)

(iv)   .. Sir John Luttrell's receiver paid "to the executors by the hands of Richard Popham, by indenture, 6 marks." (Lyte. H.D. Part I 79, Note 4)

(v)   January 5 (1406) "In the expenses of my lord (*Sir Hugh Luttrell d 1428*) who came to Brigewater for certain causes touching his plea, 3s 1d. And in his gift to a lawyer, a kinsman of Richard Popham, 6s 8d" (Lyte H.D. Part I 84) A tenuous connection between the de Mohuns, the de Ports and the manor of Popham follows: At the time of the Domesday Survey of 1086 the Manor (*of Popham [Hants]* was held of the Abbey (*of Hyde*) by Hugh de Port (Popham W.C.F.P. 3). Henry de Port was one of the witnesses to the charter of William de Mohun I for the church at Dunster. (Lyte H.D. Part II 383)

(vi)   In 1420 Richard Popham acquired the Manor of Alfoxden in Stringston from John Aythe and held also land and houses in Watchet and elsewhere along the West Somerset coast. In 1449 he obtained confirmation of his title to property in Dunster from Sir James Luttrell (d 1461) and his name appears with the names of Stradling and a Sydenham in a Deed of Attornment (*Transfer*) granted that year by Sir John Audley in respect of tenements held of Sir James Luttrell. Richard married Joan, daughter of John Orchard of Orchard Wyndham by whom he had two daughters Margaret and Joan; the latter married first, John Sydenham of Badialton and secondly John St Aubyn of Parracombe both of whom she outlived. In her Will (1498) Joan Sydenham mentions her lands and tenements in Alfoxtden, Wache (Watchet), Tuxe, Oldmyston, Tokingmill and Stogursey "which lands etc were the lands and tenements of Richard Popham." (See Popham W.C.F.P 2/3/4)

DUNSTER IN THE COMMONWEALTH

A GARRISON HAD been maintained at Dunster castle since the surrender of Colonel Wyndham to Colonel Blake in April 1646. In October 1649, this parliamentary force was to be increased and 'it was proposed to place 2,000 foot of Somerset in Bridgwater and Dunster castle.'[1] On 25 March, the Council of State first mooted the destruction of the castle and resolved: "That it will be referred to the Committee which conferrs with the Officers of the Armie to consider whether or noe Dunster Castle and Taunton Castle, or either of them, are fitt to be demolished, and to report to the Councell their opinion therein."[2]

The military governor of the castle was Major William Robinson who had, on 6 May, received twelve barrels of gunpowder issued "for the supply of Taunton and Dunster Castle."[3] He made a further demand for arms and ammunition on 25 May and this demand was referred to the Committee of the Ordnance.[4] It was decided that the fate of the castle was to rest with Colonel Desborough, Oliver Cromwell's brother-in-law, as is revealed by the following resolutions which appear in the order-book of the Council of State for 1650.[5]

6 June. "That a letter bee written to Colonell Desbrow[6], to let him know that this Councell leaves it to him to put in such number of men into Dunster and Taunton Castles as hee shall thinke fit to secure them."[7]

5 August. "That it bee refered to the Committee which meets with the Officers of the Armie to take into consideration the present condition of Dunster Castle, and to report to the Councel their opinions what they thinke fitt to bee done therein, either as to the making it untenable or repairing of it."[8]

It was decided because of the great cost of repairs, that the castle should be slighted and only the gatehouse of Sir Hugh Luttrell (d 1428) and the part in which George Luttrell (d 1655) lived were to be spared. Thus the conversion of the castle into a Jacobean manor house by the first George Luttrell (d 1629) was left intact though it must have been a distinctly uncomfortable abode for any Luttrell at this time.

10 August. "At the Committee for Marshall Affaires. Ordered that the Committee, haveing seriously considered the present state of the guarrison at Dunster Castle, and finding that the makeing of it every way teneable against an enemy will require a great summe of money which they conceive the Councell at present cannot well spare, conceive it necessary that the said guarrison be drawne to Taunton , and that the Castle be soe farre slighted as that it may not be made suddainely tenable by an enemy, and that it be referred to Major Generall Desbrow to the Commissioners of the Militia for the county to see this done and to send an account thereof to the Councell."[9]

Thereupon, a rate was levied in Somerset, "for pulling downe Dunster Castle."[10] On 27 August the work was well under way. A parliamentary newspaper, *A Perfect Diurnal* (no. 38) records that: "Here have been above two hundred men working at this Castle these twelve daies about sleighing the same, which is almost finished except the dwelling-house of Mr Luttrell and the Gatehouse, according to order of the Councel of State."[11] Work had been halted on 20 August by a resolution of the Council of State. This resolution had arrived rather late and read: "To write to Major Robinson that Dunster Castle be continued in the condition it is till further order of the Councell, and that there bee twenty or thertie chozen men there for the defence thereof."[12]

In his second volume Lyte gives additional details concerning the vicissitudes suffered by the castle. He writes: "Dunster Castle suffered some injury during the siege of 1645 and 1646, and it certainly lost most of its medieval character in 1650, when three hundred men were employed to dismantle its fortifications. The chapel of St Stephen and other ancient buildings on the summit of the Tor were then totally demolished, while the Lower Ward was laid open by pulling down at least two towers and all the curtain wall on the western side. Prynne also records the destruction of 'a fair new building', which cannot be located. There is no documentary evidence as to the date of the extensive stables belonging to the Luttrell family which stand below the Gatehouse, at the corner of the Bailey, afterwards called Castle Street. In an exposed position just without the *enciente* of the Castle, they can hardly have escaped considerable damage in the course of the long siege: their roof must have been renewed once or twice since then. The mullions of the windows are wood. The chief interest of the stables is, however, in the interior, where there are now twenty-eight stalls, exhibiting three varieties of design, but all apparently erected in the first half of the seventeenth century. Untouched by any modern 'restorer', they merit the careful examination of architects."[13]

William Prynne was imprisoned in Dunster Castle. Prynne had never been opposed to the king. He believed in the divine right of kings and heartily agreed with the original aims of the parliamentarians to defend themselves and rescue the king from his evil counsellors. His war was with the bishops and, in particular, with Archbishop Laud, who was the cause of his martyrdom. He was a strong presbyterian, opposed to the independents and he strongly objected to the religious toleration and social doctrines of Lilburne.[14] When the king was executed Prynne returned to Swainswick and he displayed his disapproval of the government, which he considered to be illegal, by failing to pay his taxes. On 30 June, 1650 he was arrested by soldiers who came to his home armed with a warrant issued by his former friend and fellow lawyer John Bradshaw. Bradshaw was the president of the Council of State which, together with the Rump had governed England since the execution of the king and the proclamation of a republic. Bradshaw had presided at the king's trial and it was against this trial that Prynne had launched two indignant pamphlets. The first accused Cromwell, Ireton, Sir Hardress Waller and Colonel Pride and nine others of high treason and demanded: "...that the said Traitors and every one of them may be forthwith apprehended secured and brought to Trial, before they ruine King, Parliament and the Kingdoms of England and Ireland and enslave them in their Tyrannie."[15]

Prynne considered that parliament had gone against its original intentions and that, in establishing a republic, it had infringed the basic laws and liberties of England. He believed that Cromwell and his generals were acting for the Jesuits and were re-enacting the unsuccessful regicide of the Gunpowder plot against James I, in the person of Charles I. In the end his house was searched and his papers removed. He was marched through Bristol and imprisoned in Dunster castle "where no one was permitted to confer with him except in the presence of his gaoler."[16] Lyte tells us about the activities Prynne, the ever meticulous lawyer, engaged in during his heartily deplored detention: "Finding that the muniments of

George Luttrell were in a 'confused chaos', he employed his time in making an arrangement of them according to localities, which has been maintained to the present time (*Lyte was writing in the first decade of the twentieth century*). He also compiled a general calendar of them, at the end of which there is a characteristic note that it was made 'by William Prynne of Swainswick, Esq. in the eight months of his illegall, causeless, close imprisonment in Dunster Castle by Mr Bradshaw and his companions at Whitehall, Feb 18, Anno Dom 1650, 2 Car.II'. The obstinacy of the man is shown by his reference to the regnal year of the prince in exile. From Dunster, he was that year removed to Taunton, and thence to Pendennis Castle. Soon after the Restoration, he was appointed Keeper of the Records at the Tower of London."[17]

While he was incarcerated in Dunster he wrote: "George, son and heire to Thomas, succeded him in his estate. His castle of Dunster and estate being in the enimies' hands at his father's death, he enjoyed little thereof till reduced. The walles of his castle of Dunster, Mount Stweevens and a fair new building therin were totally demolished and his gatehouse much defaced, by an order from Whitehall under Mr Bradshaw his hand, and another from the Malitica, without and before any notice, view or recompense, August 8, 1650, to about 3000*l*. dammages, to save the charge of a garrison, and his very mantioned house at first advise to be puld down by it Maliticia, but afterwards countermanded, and twenty souldiers put into his house to guard Mr Prynne close prisoner there. His wife is now pregnant. God send her a sonn and heir, a joyfull delivery and numerous happy posterity, to perpetiate the family and name with onner and happines, to God's glory and the publick welfare of the country and kingdom in their successive genarations till the second coming of Jesus Christ, which is the cordiall option and fervent prayer of the collector of this pedigree. Febr. 18, anno 1650 (1651).[18]   Will Prynne, Esq."[19]

An interesting entry made by Prynne and recorded by Lyte, refers to swan-upping. On a small memorandum on parchment are drawn marks[20] on the swans as a means of identifying those belonging to Sir John Luttrell (d 1551) and Sir Andrew Luttrell, his father (d 1538). Prynne writes: "These were markes which theise men above written had upon the beeles of their swanes belonginge unto the Castell of Dunster by inheritance and alwayes kepte at the Mere by Glastonberrye. Yt is good to renewe yt. S.L."[21]

Before leaving the subject of the Dunster castle muniments (now in the Somerset Archives and Records Office at Taunton), Lyte writes about muniments concerning, not the Luttrells, but the earlier owners of the castle, the de Mohuns. "In June, 1908, when the earlier part of the present book (i.e. *Vol I of his History of Dunster*) had been already printed, there was offered for sale by auction in London, a folio of 170 leaves of parchment catalogued as '*Cartularium et feodarium Dominorum de Mohun*'.[22] On inspection this proved to be a fragment of the important compilation made, in 1350, by John Osberne, Constable of Dunster Castle, as mentioned on page 49 and elsewhere. The originals of many of the documents transcribed into it had disappeared before Prynne's time, but it is interesting to note that such of them as still remain in Mr Luttrell's muniment-room are endorsed '*irrotulatur*', in evidence that they had been duly entered in the cartulary. I was not so fortunate as to secure this manuscript at the sale, and I have not been able to obtain direct access to it since. The present owner, however, who wishes to remain anonymous, has very kindly supplied me with full transcripts of some of its contents, notably the treatise on agriculture mentioned on page 321, and the agreement between the monks and the parishioners of Dunster... mentioned on page 393. I take this opportunity of thanking him." [23]

In March, 1651, the Council of State was uneasy about Dunster castle. The council had been informed of the royalist moves, and although there was no apparent enemy activity, the following letter shows the members concerns. It was written from Whitehall and addressed to the commissioners of the Militia of the County of Somerset. "Gentlemen.

Although there appeare not much at present of any stirring of the enemy, yet Wee have sure information that they have designes on foot at present of great danger to the Commonwealth and particularly in those parts; to prevent which Wee think it necessary that such places as are not yet made untenable should. have some strength put into them to prevent the enemyes' surprize. And Wee being informed that Dunster Castle, the house of Mr Lutterell, is yet in condition that if it be seized by the enemy might prove dangerous, Wee therefore desire you to appoint some Militia forces to prevent the surprize of it, till there may be some course taken to make it untenable, or that the state of affairs may not be subject to the like danger as now they are.

Whitehall, 25 March 1651."[24]

Nearly two months later, the Councell wrote to Major General Desborough: "Sir. Wee are informed from Major Robinson, Governour of Taunton and Dunster Castle, that the forces remayning in those garrisons are not sufficient to enable him to preserve the same for the service of the state. Wee therefore desire you to consider those places and the forces in them, and in what you find those forces defective to make supply thereof, that the Governour may be able to give a good accompt thereof to the Commonwealth.

Whitehall, 20 Maie 1651."[25]

A week later the Council sent a letter addressed: "To George Lutterell, Esq. of Dunster Castle.

Sir. Wee conceive it hath been some prejudice to you that your house hath been still continued a garrison, which Wee are willing that you should be freed from, soe as the Commonwealth may be assured from danger by it. And Wee doubt not but you will bee carefull to keepe the place from the enemies' surprise in respect of your interest in it. But that Wee may be able to give the Commonwealth a good accompt of that place upon the remove of that garrison, Wee hold fit that you enter recognizance before two justices of the peace with two suretyes to the Keepers of the Liberty of the Commonwealth of England, yourself in 6000*l* and 3000*l* each of your suretyes. The condition to bee that you shall not suffer any use to be made of your said house, of Dunster Castle to the prejudice of the Commonwealth and present Government, which being done, Wee have given order to Major Generall Desborow to draw off the men that are in the same castle and dispose of them as Wee have given order. Wee have had information of designes upon your Castle the prevention of the operation whereof hath occasioned our putting of a guard there; and having now put it into this way wherein Wee have had regard of your conveniency, Wee expect you to be careful of what besides your particular herein, concerns the interest of the publique

Whitehall, 27 Maii 1651."[26]

Major General Desborough received instructions the same day to remove the Dunster garrison of twenty men as soon as George Luttrell had met the requirements laid down.

In 1651 *The Ship* (the present *Luttrell Arms*) was valued at £16 a year. It had been an inn for a considerable time and was, no doubt, frequented by the garrison in spite of their puritan beliefs. In the spring of that year, an heir, yet another George, was born to George's wife, Elizabeth. Sadly, Prynne's "felicitous hopes for Mrs Luttrell's expected heir" were short lived, for the child survived for only eighteen days.

The sole entry in the registers for 1651 records his death and was entered by Peter Meade, one of the principal inhabitants of Dunster as shown in the rate made for the year 1686:

"Md that Elizabeth the wife of George Luttrell Esq. the xviiithth daie of April 1651 between two and three of the clocke in the morninge was delivered of a sone and heire apparent who was Baptised the sixth day of May followinge by Mr Clymson, Rector of Muncksilver and named George who the same at night dept d this life. Itã testatur Pet. Meade."[27]

His burial is recorded by Hancock as follows:

1651 "George the son of George Luttrell, Esq., was buried 9th day of May, 1651, being the same daye three weeks after his byrthe. Itã testatur, Pet Meade."[28]

In July Charles Stuart planned to march south to claim his inheritance in London but Cromwell exhibited his great skill as a general. He had overrun the lowlands and had inflicted a crushing defeat on the Scots at Dunbar in 1650, and by advancing to Perth, the source of supplies for the royalist army, he prevented the provisioning of the forces around Stirling. The inviting road to England was purposely left open and Charles and his Scottish army took it and advanced as far as Worcester. The English militia was reluctant to join an invading Scottish army but was happy to enlist with Cromwell and to fight with the old brigade of the New Model army. On 3 September, the anniversary of Cromwell's defeat of the royalists at Dunbar, Charles' army of thirteen thousand men was overwhelmed at Worcester. Cromwell reported to parliament that the battle: "...became an absolute victory...and so full an one as proved a total defeat and ruin of the enemy's army. It is...a crowning mercy."[29]

Robert Blake, the son of a Somerset merchant and, at the outset, himself a merchant, became M.P. for Bridgwater, a colonel, and one of England's greatest admirals. He won brilliant victories over the Dutch and the Spanish and died within sight of Plymouth after a successful blockade of the Spanish coast during the winter of 1656/7.[30] Cromwell honoured him by ordering that he should be buried in Westminster Abbey but at the restoration his remains were ignominiously dug up and thrown into a pit outside the precincts of the abbey.

In the spring of 1652 before the first Dutch war broke out in June, George Luttrell's first wife, Elizabeth died. The registers record: "1652. Elizabeth, the wife of George Luttrell of Dunster Castle, Esq. (and daughter of Nicholas Prydeaux, late of Soldon in the county of Devon, Esq. deceased), departed this life at the saide Castle on Saterday ye two and twentieth day of May about 8 of the clocke in the morninge in the year of our Lord 1652, who was buryed the same Saterday att night."[31]

Three weeks later, the parliamentary garrison left Dunster castle. The terms of their departure were the guarantee of two sureties of £3,000 and George's own recognisance of £6,000. It is no wonder that this saddened, and no doubt, worried man only a few weeks later found solace in the arms of his late wife's cousin, Honora Fortescue, the daughter of John Fortescue of Buckland Filleigh (Devonshire). Their marriage took place on 15.7.1652.[32] To mark the occasion the couple presented the church of Buckland Filleigh with a silver flagon bearing their arms. In November, 1652, the government 'became so well satisfied of George Luttrell's loyalty to the Commonwealth as to appoint him Sheriff of Somerset."[33] He lived for only three more years and died childless at the early age of thirty in 1655.

His widow, Honora, who lived at Exeter, gave him a funeral *par excellence*. Henry Prigg and Edward Foxwell, both of that city in which presumably George died, were paid respectively £101 for cloth and £159 for "wines for the funerall."[34] This George is memorable in the annals of Dunster for the weather-vane atop the Yarn Market, probably built during the lifetime of his grandfather, George (d 1629), bears the second George's initials and the date 1647.

These are some of the measures of the Barebones parliament as they affected Dunster.

On 24 August 1653 an ordinance was passed whereby the parish registers, formerly the concern of the clergy, were to be replaced by a register under the control of a civilian, chosen by the inhabitant householders of each parish, and to be known as the 'Parish Register'. In the case of Dunster the layman chosen was John Giles whose election was signed by the local justice of the peace. Details of the first and earlier registers dating from 1598 and composed of eleven books, may be found in *Dunster Church and Priory*.[35] Giles second register was of twenty parchment pages and the first reads:

"Dunster Entry for Marryages.
Bee it remembered that the five and twentieth day of October in the yr of our Lord 1653, John Giles of Dunster aforesaid was elected and Sworne Register there accordinge to the Act of Parliament in that case made and provided before me.
　　Tho. Siderfin"

He then divided it into three sections, headed Weddinge (as before)
Births thus:

"Dunster. Entryes of birthes of Chyldren from Sep. the 29th, 1653
By the register their."

Burials thus:
"Dunster. Entryes of Buryalls from September 29th, 1653.
By the register their."[36]

For every birth and burial Giles registered he was allowed to charge the ordained four pence but no more.

Back in 1640 England had been a baptized nation. Now in 1653 no fee was payable for a baptismal entry since the ceremony of baptism, according to the Book of Common Prayer, was only possible if the parents could prevail upon a minister to conduct the baptism in a private house and risk the penalties prescribed by law. The prohibition of the Book of Common Prayer deprived church men and church women of their accustomed rites of marriage, baptism and burial. Since burials took place publicly it was difficult openly to follow the rules laid down in the prayer book.

Even the late king was denied the funeral rites according to Anglican church tradition and we read: "When the body of Charles I was taken to Windsor for burial, the royalists accompanying it were anxious that Bishop Juxon should repeat the church service, but this was refused by Colonel Whichcott, the governor of the castle, who forbade the use of any other form than that of the *Directory*. Other authorities were sometimes less punctilious, for Evelyn records that on the death of his mother-in-law he obtained permission that she should be buried with all decent ceremonies, which had not been used in their chapel for seven years.[37]

The greatest deprivations, bitterly resented and frequently violated were the marriage regulations and a parliamentary debate took place at which a speaker declared that 'not one marriage in a hundred was made according to this act, and both the chief justice and the attorney-general denounced it.[38] A ludicrous situation sometimes arose when: "a conscientious man might be married thrice to the same wife; once before a justice of the peace; a second time by a minister, according to the *Directory*; and a third time by an Anglican minister."[39]

The act made no mention of the wedding ring which was commonly considered to be an emblem of fidelity. It was considered to be of heathen origin although the Roman betrothal rings were adopted by Christians at an early date. The 'zealots' seriously debated the prohibition of their use in the marriage service. There is an interesting entry in the *Dictionary of the Christian Church* as follows: "In England down to the end of the 16th cent., the bride wore the ring on her right hand. The present custom of wearing it on the third finger of the left-hand is explained by the practice of pronouncing the Trinitarian formula over the thumb and first two fingers, so that the third was reached at the 'Amen' which sealed the marriage rite."[40]

Marriages were more profitable propositions than births or burials. John Giles and all Registers were permitted to charge a fee of 12d which covered the entry in the register and the publication of the banns of marriage. These were to be published on three "successive Lord's days, at the close of the morning service, in the public meeting place commonly called the church (*Dunster church was used as a garrison and stables by Cromwell's troops),* or chapel or (if the parties preferred it) in the nearest market place on three successive market days."[41]

The requirement having been fulfilled, the couple took the certificate to the local justice of the peace where the simplest of formalities could then take place. The man was required to declare: "I A.B. do here in the presence of God the searcher of all hearts, take thee C.D. for my wedded wife; and do also in the presence of God, before these witnesses, promise to be unto thee a loving and faithful husband."

The woman made a like declaration except that she was required to promise to "be a loving, faithful and obedient wife."[42] Sometimes, as in the case of Cromwell's daughter, Frances, 'a godly prayer' was offered 'by one of His Highness's divines' and this was followed by the tying of the knot by the justice of the peace.[43] When Mary, another daughter of the Lord Protector, was married to the ex-royalist, Fauconberg, the ceremony was conducted according to the Book of Common Prayer.[44] Thirty-six civil marriages took place in Dunster between 1653 and 1656 and all were performed by Mr George Luttrell or Mr Thomas Siderfin. The first marriage was of: "Hopkin Williams of Dunster, glovier, and Anne Webber of the same, single woman, where three Lord's days lawfully published according to the Acte of Pliament, the first publication the thirtieth of October, 1653, and the next two Lord's days following."

> The 29 Day of December, 1653. Somst. Bee it remembered that Hopkin Williams of Dunster, Glovier, and Anne Webber of the same, Spinster, were married in the presence of Richard Blackford,[45] John Giles, Andrew Hobbs and others, according to the Acte of Pliament in that case made and provided, by Tho. Siderfin, esq., and of ye justices of ye peace within ye sayd county, the day and yeare above said. Tho. Siderfin.[46]

The last civil marriage which took place in Dunster was entered in the register on 6 December 1656. The last birth recorded on 17 May, 1654 and the last burial 27 May, 1654. 'From this date the registers are once more entered in the original church book and are so entered until 1666. In that year the vicar returned to the discarded Commonwealth Register and started to make his entries therein. It appears that by 1666 the church book was full and the vicar, being of a careful disposition was regardless of historical chronology.

ENDNOTES

CHAPTER 1

[1] Cross O.D.C.C., 180
[2] Hamper. G.M. HAD. 879
[3] Lyte H.D. Part 2, 406. (Note 3)
[4] Lyte H.D. Part 2, 393. (Note 1)
[5] Ibid. Part II, 393/5. Ibid. Part II, 395/6
[6] Eeles. C. 51. G. (1940), 9. Note 1
[7] Ibid. 8/9
[8] Ibid. 9.
[9] Ibid. 10
[10] Lyte H.D. Part I 30/31 (Note 1, 31)
[11] Lyte H.D. Part I, 31. (Note 2)
[12] Lyte H.D. Part II, 399. (Note 1)
[13] Hancock. D.C.P., 35
[14] Lyte H.D. Part II, 399. (Note 2).
[15] Hancock D.C.P.,14/15
[16] Lyte Part I. Preface. VII.
[17] Hancock D.C.P., 16/17.
[18] Ibid. 38
[19] Hancock D.C.P. 16/17
[20] Ibid. 66
[21] Hamper G.M. HAD., 879
[22] Lyte H.D. Part II, 400
[23] Lyte H.D. Part II, 399
[24] Eeles C. St G. (1940), 10/11
[25] Lyte Part II, 406 (Notes 1, 2, 3)
[26] Hancock D.C.P., 36/37
[27] Lyte H.D. Part II, 423
[28] Lyte H.D. Part II, 463 (Note 3)
[29] Lyte H.D. Part II, 389 (Note 2)
[30] Lyte H.D. Part II, 335
[31] Ibid.
[32] Ibid.
[33] Lyte H.D. Part II, 336
[34] Lyte H.D. Part II, 336 (Note 2)
[35] Lyte H.D. Part II, 336
[36] Lyte H.D. Part II, 336/7
[37] Lyte H.D. Part II, 337
[38] Ibid. 335, (Notes 4, 5, 6)
[39] Ibid. Part II, 338.
[40] Ibid. Part II, 338/9.
[42] Lyte H.D. Part I, 99
[43] Ibid. Part I, 307
[44] Lyte H.D. Part II, 458 (Note 1)
[45] Ibid. (Note 2)
[46] Ibid. 459 (Note 1). 458/9 (Note 2)
[47] Ibid. Part II, 459. (Note 2)
[48] Lyte H.D. Part II, 459 (Note 3)
[49] Lyte H.D. Part I, 117
[50] Lyte H.D. Part II, 459 (Note 4)
[51] Ibid. Part I, 303 (Note 1).
[52] Lyte H.D. Part II, 459 (Note 5)
[53] Lyte H.D. Part II, 459 (Note 6)
[54] Lyte H.D. Part II, 459 (Note 7)
[55] Ibid. 459/60 (Note 1)

[56] Ibid.(Note 3)
[57] Ibid.(Note 4)
[58] Ibid. 460
[59] Lyte H.D. Part II, 460/1
[60] Ibid. 460
[61] Ibid. 329
[62] Ibid. 461 (Note 1)
[63] Lyte H.D. Part II, 390/1 (Note 1, 391)
[64] Ibid. 461 (Note 2)
[65] Ibid. (Note 3)
[66] Ibid. 461
[67] Lyte H.D. Part II, 461
[68] Mackie ET (1485-1558),141
[69] Williams K.Q.E. The Tudors, 173
[70] Lyte H.D. Part II, 461
[71] Lyte H.D. Part II, 461/2
[72] Ibid. 462
[73] Ibid.
[74] Lyte Part II, 510
[75] Memoirs of the family of Poyntz by Sir John Maclean (1886), Chapter X, 263. quoting Westwood
[76] Hancock D.C.P., 101
[77] Memoirs of the family of Poyntz by Sir John Maclean (1886), Chapter XI, Note 3. Prob. P.C.C. 24 Jan., 1583/4
[78] Lyte H.D. Part II, 463
[79] Ibid. (Note 2)
[80] Scarisbrick H.E.8, 117/8
[81] Lyte H.D. Part II, 463 (Note 4)
[82] Ibid. 464 (Note 1)
[83] Ibid. (Note 2)
[84] Ibid. (Note 4), 58
[85] Lyte H.D. Part II, 464 (Note 3)
[86] Ibid. 465
[87] Lyte H.D. Part II, 465 (Note 1)
[88] Ibid. (Note 2)
[89] Ibid. 466 (Note 1)
[90] Ibid. (Note 2)
[91] Lyte H.D. Part II, 467 (Note 3)
[92] Ibid. (Note 4)
[93] Ibid. 466/7 (Note 1, 467)
[94] Lyte H.D. Part II, 467 (Note 3)
[95] Ibid. 467

CHAPTER 2

[1] Lyte, H.D. Part I, 2 (Note 2).
[2] Ibid. 2
[3] Ibid. 2
[4] Hutchins (HAD) 272
[5] Lyte. Part I, 3 (Note 3)
[6] Lyte Part I, 4
[7] Lyte H.D. Part II, 349
[8] Lyte H.D. Part II, 349
[9] Lyte H.D. Part I, 5. and Part II, 556. (Additions and Corrections)

[10] Lyte H.D. Part II, 383/4 (Notes 1, 3, 4)
[11] Ibid. 391 (Note 4)
[12] Ibid. 391
[13] Ibid. Part I, 324 (Note 2)
[14] Ibid. (Note 3)
[15] Ibid. (Note 4)
[16] Ibid. (Note 5)
[17] Ibid. 325 (Note 1)
[18] Lyte H.D. Part I, 325 (Note 2)
[19] Ibid. (Note 4)
[20] Ibid. 325 (Note 3)
[21] C.P. vol ix, 18 (Note d)
[22] Lyte H.D. Part II, 384/5 (Notes 1 and 2)
[23] Hancock D.C.P., 4/5
[24] C.P. vol ix, 18 (Note e).
[25] Ibid. (Note f)
[26] Lyte H.D. Part I, 5/6 (Note 1)
[27] C.P. vol ix, 18 (Note g).
[28] Lyte H.D. Part I, 8
[29] Lyte H.D., Part I 8. (Note 3)
[30] Ibid. 9. (Note I)
[31] Ibid. Part II, 385 (Note 1 in 9)
[32] Lyte H.D. Part I, 9 (Note 2)
[33] Lyte, H.D. Part I, 7.
[34] Chatwin, W.S.W. Birmingham Arch. Soc. *Trans.* Vol. 63 (1939/40)
[35] The Mohuns of Whichford (newspaper article, B'ham)
[36] Lyte H.D. Part I, 8 (note 2)
[37] Lyte H.D. Part I, 8
[38] Ibid. 9 (Note 3)
[39] C.P. vol ix, 18 (Note j)
[40] Lyte, H.D. Part I, 10 (Notes 1 and 2)
[41] Ibid. 10 (Note 2)
[42] Lyte H.D. Part I, 9 (Note 4)
[43] Ibid. (Notes 5-8)
[44] Ibid. Part II, 385-6 (Note 1)
[45] Ibid. 386 (Note 1)
[46] C.P. vol ix, 18 (Note 2)
[47] Poole DB-MC (*Domesday Book to Magna Carta 1087-1216*), 215, 328
[48] Lyte H.D Part I, 10 (Note 4)
[49] Ibid. (Note 5)
[50] Lyte H.D. Part II (Appendix A) 469 (Note 3)
[51] Lyte H.D. Part II (Appendix A) 470 (Note 3)
[52] Ibid. (Note 4)
[53] Lyte H.D. Part II (Appendix A), 470 (Note 5)
[54] Lyte H.D. Part I, 11 (Note 6)
[55] Ibid. Part II, 556 (Additions and Corrections)
[56] Lyte H.D. Part I, 11/12 (Note 1, p.12)
[57] Poole (DB-MC) 210/1
[58] Ibid. 220
[59] Lyte H.D. Part II, 386 (Note 2)
[60] Lyte H.D. Part I, 386
[61] Ibid. Part I, 11
[62] Ibid. 11/12
[63] Ibid. Part II, 386
[64] Ibid. (Note 3)
[65] Lyte Part I, 12 (Note 3)
[66] Ibid. 13 (Note 4)
[67] Lawrence M.M. (Medieval Monasticism), 142

[68] Lyte H.D. Part I, 13 (Note 1)
[69] Lyte H.D. Part I, 13 (Note 3)
[70] C.P. volix, 19
[71] Lyte H.D. Part I, 32
[72] Ibid. 277 (Note 1)
[73] Richardson., L.H.E. (*Local Historian's Encyclopaedia*),42
[74] Lyte H.D. Part I, 14 (Note 6)
[75] Ibid. (Note 7)
[76] Lyte Part I, 15 (Note I)
[77] Ibid. (Note 2)
[78] Lyte H.D. Part I, 15
[79] "Les origines et les premiers développements de la sculpture romane en Normandie," by Maylis Baylé.
[80] Lyte H.D. Part I, 14 (Note 2)
[81] Lyte H.D. Part I, 15 (Note 5)
[82] Warren, K.J., 186
[83] C.P. vol ix, 19 (Note h)
[84] Ibid. (Note l)
[85] Lyte H.D. Part I, 20
[86] Warren, K.J., 230
[87] Ibid. (Note 3)
[88] Powicke, *13c*, 395
[89] Warren, K.J., 255 (Note 1)
[90] Chatwin, W.S.W., B.A.S. *Trans.*
[91] C.P. vol ix, 19 (Note e)
[92] Lyte H.D. Part I, 17 (Note 5)
[93] Ibid. (Note 7)
[94] Ibid.
[95] C.P. ix, 19
[96] Powicke, *13c*, pp. 1, 3, 4, 8-15 and passim
[97] Lyte H.D. Part I, 18 (Note 2)
[98] Powicke *13c*, 22/3 (Note 1, p.22)
[99] Lyte H.D. Part I, 18 (Note 3)
[100] Ibid. (Note 4)
[101] Ibid. 277 (Note 1)
[102] Ibid. (Note 2)
[103] Lyte H.D. Part I, 277 (Note 3)
[104] Lyte H.D. Part II, 351 (Note 1)
[105] Ibid.
[106] Ibid. 351/2
[107] Lyte H.D. Part II, 352
[108] C.P. vol ix 19 (Note 11)
[109] Powicke, *13c*, 43
[110] Ibid. 23
[111] Powicke 13c,. 43
[112] Ibid
[113] Powicke 13c, 23 (Note 1)
[114] Ibid. 44
[115] Ibid. 43 (Note I)
[116] C.P. vol ix, 20 (Note a)
[117] Ibid. (Note b)
[118] Ibid. (Note b)
[119] Powicke 13 c. 100/102
[120] Lyte H.D. Part II, 387/8
[121] Ibid. 388 (Note 2)
[122] Ibid. 388 (Note 3)
[123] C.P. vol ix,20 (Note d)
[124] Lyte H.D. Part I, 21 (Note 1)
[125] Ibid. (Note 3)
[126] Lyte H.D. Part I,21, (Note 2)

[127] Ibid. Part I 12/20
[128] Ibid. 20 (Note 5)
[129] Ibid. 17 (Note 4)
[130] C.P. vol ix, 20 (Note t)
[131] Lyte H.D. Part I, 19 (Note 6)
[132] C.P. vol ix, 20 (Note g)
[133] Lyte H.D. Part I, 278/9 (Note 1)
[134] Ibid. 279 (Note 2)
[135] Ibid. Part II, 279/80
[136] Powicke *13c*, 112/3
[137] Lyte H.D. Part 1, 31 (Note 1)
[138] C.P. vol ix, 21
[139] Lyte H.D. Part I, 31 (Note 2)
[140] Ibid. (Note 3)
[141] Lyte H.D. Part I, 32 (Note 1)
[142] Hutchins. H.A.D. 339, and Powicke *13c* 32
[143] Lyte, H.D. Part I, 32 (Note 5)
[144] Lyte H.D. Part I, 32. (Note 6)
[145] Ibid. 32 (Note 7)
[146] Lyte H.D Part I, 33 (Note 2)
[147] Ibid.
[148] Lyte H.D. Part I, 34 (Note 1)
[149] Pole C.T.D.C.D.
[150] Lyte H.D. Part I, 33 (Note 3)
[151] Lyte H.D. Part I, 33 (Note 7)
[152] Ibid. 34 (Note 4)
[153] Ibid. 34 (Note 5)
[154] Lyte H.D. Part I, 34 (Note 6)
[155] Ibid. (Note 8)
[156] Ibid. (Note 9)
[157] Ibid. (Note 10)
[158] C.P. vol ix, 20 (Note k)
[159] Ibid. (Note l)
[160] Lyte H.D. Part I, 29
[161] Ibid. 49
[162] Ibid.
[163] Ibid. (Note 2)
[164] C.P. vol ix, 20. (Note I)
[165] Ibid. (Note k)
[166] Lyte H.D. Part I, 27/28
[167] Ibid. 29 (Note I)
[168] C.P. vol ix, 21
[169] Lyte H.D. Part I, 297. (Note 6)
[170] Montgomery. T.A. (Beck) 243
[171] Lyte H.D. Part I, 35. (Note 2)
[172] Lyte H.D. Part II, 353. (Note 1)
[173] Powicke 13c. 392,401
[174] C.P. ix, 21 (Note g)
[175] C.P. ix, 21 (Note h)
[176] Lyte H.D. Part I, 280. (Note 1)
[177] Ibid. 281. (Note 1)
[178] McKisack *14c*., 365. (Notes 1,3.)
[179] Lyte H.D. Part I, 36. (Note 1)
[180] Ibid. Part II, 389 (Note 3)
[181] Lyte H.D. Part I, 36 (Note 7)
[182] Lyte H.D. Part I, 36, 37. (Note 1)
[183] Ibid. 36
[184] Ibid. Part II, 353/4 (Note 1)
[185] C.P. vol ix, 21 (Note I)
[186] Lyte H.D. Part I, 37 (Note 2)
[187] C.P. vol ix, 21 (Note k)

[188] C.P. vol ix, 21 (Note m)
[189] McKisack *14c*. 237/8
[190] Powicke *13c* 693 (Note 2)
[191] C.P. vol ix, 22
[192] Lyte H.D. Part I, 281 (Note 2)
[193] Lyte H.D. Part I, 282 (Note 1)
[194] Lyte H.D. Part I, 282 (Note 2)
[195] Ibid. 282
[196] *Handbook of Dates*
[197] Lyte H.D. Part I, 282/3
[198] Ibid. 285
[199] Lyte H.D. Part I, 285
[200] D.E.E. (S-Z), 224
[201] Ibid.
[202] Lyte H.D. Part II, 342 (Note 1)
[203] Lyte H.D. Part II, 287
[204] Ibid.
[205] Ibid.
[206] Ibid. 287 (Note 2)
[207] Ibid. 287/288
[208] C.P. vol ix, 22 (Note e)
[209] McKisack. *14c*. 30.
[210] Ibid. (Note t)
[211] C.P. vol ix, 22
[212] Lyte H.D. Part I, 283 (Note 1)
[213] Ibid. 283/4 (Note 1)
[214] McKisack *14c*, 237 (Note 1)
[215] Ibid. 237
[216] C.P. vol ix, 22 (Note b)
[217] McKisack *14c*, 186 (Note2)
[218] Lyte H.D. Part I, 40 (note 1)
[219] Ibid. (Note 2)
[220] Ibid. (Note 3)
[221] Ibid. Part II 354
[222] Lyte H.D. Part II, 326/7
[223] C.P. vol ix, 22
[224] Lyte H.D. Part I, 40 (Note 4)
[225] Cross. O.D.C.C. 136617.
[226] Lyte H.D. Part I, 40 (Note 5)
[227] Lyte H.D. Part I, 40, (Note 6)
[228] Ibid. (Note 8)
[229] Ibid. 40/41. (Note 1)
[230] Ibid. 41, (Note 2)
[231] Ibid. (Note 3)
[232] Ibid. (Note 4)
[233] Ibid. (Note 5)
[234] Lyte H.D. Part I, 45 (Note 5)
[235] Ibid. 41 (Note 7)
[236] Ibid. (Note 8)
[237] Ibid. (Note 9)
[238] Ibid. 41/2 (Note 1)
[239] Ibid. 42 (Note 2)
[240] Ibid. (Note 3)
[241] McKisack. *14c* 318
[242] Ibid. (Note I)
[243] Ibid. 317 (Note 5)
[244] Lyte H.D. Part I, 42 also Appendix A. Part II, 495
[245] Ibid. Part I, 42 (Note 4)
[246] Ibid. (Note 5)
[247] C.P. vol ix, 23 (Note c)
[248] Lyte H.D. Part I, 43 (Note 2)

[249] Ibid. (Note 1)
[250] Ibid. (Note 3)
[251] Ibid. (Note 4)
[252] Lyte H.D., Part I, 43 (Note 5)
[253] CP. vol ix,23 (Note d)
[254] Lyte H.D. Part I, 39 (Note 3)
[255] Ibid. (Note 4)
[256] Chatwin, W.S.W.
[257] Lyte H.D. Part I, 39 (Note 2)
[258] McKisack. *14c.*, 33
[259] McKisack. *14c.*, 427 and (Note 1)
[260] Lyte H.D. Part II, 391 (Note 3)
[261] Ibid. 392 (Note I)
[262] Lyte H.D. Part I, 297 (Note 8)

CHAPTER 3

[1] Lawrence M.M.
[2] McCann, R.S.B.
[3] Zarnecki. R.A.
[4] McCann. RS.B.
[5] Lyte. Part II, 396.
[6] Lawrence M.M., 29.
[7] McCann. RS.B.
[8] McCann. R.S.B.
[9] McCann. RS.B.
[10] McCann. RS.B.
[11] Hancock. D.c.P., 44
[12] Lyte H.D., Part H, 353. (Note 1)
[13] Lyte H.D., Part I, 324
[14] Ibid. Part II, 392 (Note 1)
[15] Ibid. 392
[16] Ibid. 387
[17] Lyte H.D. Part II, 405
[18] Lyte HD. Part II, 393 (Note 1)
[19] Lyte HD. Part II, 394/5
[20] Cross O.D.C.C., 824
[21] Boase F.M.A., 397
[22] O.D.C.C. 486, 1020, 1331
[23] Cross, O.D.C.C., 1414
[24] Bettey C. and C., 59
[25] V.H.C.E. (Som.)
[26] Hancock D.C.P., 49/50
[27] Lyte H.D., Part II, 390 (Note 5)
[28] Bath Cartularies Lincoln's Inn M.S. 216/17 (for this information I am indebted to Tom McManamon)
[29] Hancock, D.C.P., 51, (B.C. 694)
[30] Lyte H.D. Part II, 340, (Note 1)
[31] Ibid. (Note 2)
[32] Hancock D.C.P., 129
[33] Ibid.
[34] Ibid. 173
[35] Hancock. D.C.P.,43/44
[36] Hancock. D.c.P., 44
[37] Eeles C St G (1940), 18
[38] Lawrence. M.M., 23
[39] Hancock D.C.P., 181
[40] Ibid.
[41] Ibid. 182.
[42] Webb A.R.M.A, 64
[43] Ibid. 59
[44] Ibid. 43
[45] Sir. Bannister Fletcher. HACM.
[46] Ibid.. 44
[47] Hancock. D.C.P., 43
[48] Hancock. D.C.P., 49
[49] Kemp. Rc.M., 11
[50] Kemp. E.C.M.,11 (Note 5)
[51] Hancock. D.C.P., 31 (Somerset Pleas S.R.S., 51)
[52] Ibid.
[53] Eeles (1940), Guide, 6
[54] Ibid.
[55] Lyte H.D. Part I, vii (Preface)
[56] Hamper G.M., (HAD.), 879
[57] Lyte H.D. Part II, 387
[58] Hancock D.C.P., 22
[59] Freeman D.P.c. Proc. S.A.N.H.S., 7
[60] Zarnecki F.M.A.C.O., 12/14. 52/54
[61] Lyte H.D. Part II, 387
[62] Lyte H.D. Part II, 388/9
[63] Eeles C. St G., (1934)
[64] Freeman D.P.C., (Proc S.A.N.H.S) 5
[65] Bazin and Pascal, F.A
[66] Freeman D.P.C., (Proc S.A.N.H.S) 7
[67] See letter to the *Radio Times*, April 1991
[68] Cross O.D.C.C., 1236
[69] Freeman D.P.C. (Proc S.A.N.H.S.) 7
[70] Freeman D.P.C. (Proc S.A.N.H.S.) 7
[71] Bettey C. and C., 53
[72] Lyte H.D. Part II, 338 (Note 3)
[73] lbid. Part I, 95
[74] lbid. Part II., 342/3 (Note 1)
[75] lbid. Part II., 343.
[76] lbid. Part I., 97 (Note 2).
[77] Lyte. H.D. Part II., 357/8.
[78] Lyte H.D. Part II, 342, (note 2)
[79] Ibid. 341, (Note 3)
[80] Hancock D.C.P., 163.
[81] Lyte H.D. Part II, 339.
[82] Ibid.
[83] Hamper G.M.H.A.D., 874
[84] Lyte H.D. Part II, 331 (Note 1)
[85] Lyte H.D. Part II, 331 (Note 2)
[86] Ibid.(Note 3)
[87] Ibid. Part I, 303 (Note 1)
[88] Lyte H.D. Part I, 293
[89] Hancock D.C.P. Appendix A
[90] Lyte H.D. Part I, 308
[91] Lyte H.D. Part I, 308
[92] Hancock D.C.P., 51, (B.C., No 698)
[93] Ibid. 90/91
[94] Macklin M.B., 62
[95] Lyte H.D. Part I, 104 (Note 1)
[96] Hancock D.C.P., 90
[97] Ibid. 24
[98] Lyte H.D. Part I, 42 (Note 10)
[99] Hancock D.C.P., 116
[100] Goddard C. of A. (NP), 209/220
[101] Ibid 209 (Note 1), C.J.P. Cave & H.S. London. 'The Roof-Bosses in St George's Chapel, Windsor', from *Archaeologia* Vol XCV (1935)

[102] Ibid. 209
[103] Ibid. 209 (Note 3)
[104] Goddard, C. of A., (NP), 209, (Note 2)
[105] Ibid. 212
[106] Ibid. (Note 12)
[107] Ibid. (Note 13)
[108] Permission granted by J P Brooke-Little on behalf of Richard Goddard (letter 28 Sept 1989).
[109] Goddard C. of A., (N.P), (Note 14)
[110] Bettey C. and C., 23
[111] Lyte H.D. Part II, 404 (Note 1)
[112] Bettey C. and C., 56/57
[113] Pevsner S.W.S, 155
[114] Hancock D.C.P., 13
[115] Lyte H.D. Part II, 389
[116] Lyte H.D. Part II, 424
[117] Ibid. 423 (Note 1)
[118] Hancock D.C.P., 13
[119] Hancock D.C.P., 126/7
[120] Fleming, Honour and Pevsner P.D.A., 107
[121] Friar N.D.H., 344
[122] Eeles C. St G. (1940) Guide, 6
[123] Lyte HD. Part I, 44 (Note 2)
[124] Ibid. 43
[125] Lyte H.D. Part I, 43 (Notes 4 & 5)
[126] Beltz M.M.N.O.G., 49
[127] Hamper G.M. (RA.D.), 877
[128] Lyte H.D. Part I, 35/36 (Note 3)/500
[129] Ibid. 39
[130] Hancock D.C.P., 87/88/89
[131] Lyte H.D. Part I,23/26
[132] Eeles C. St G. (1940) Guide, 16 (Note 1)
[133] Lyte H.D. Part I, 29
[134] Ibid. 32 (Note 1)
[135] Kemp E.C.M., 22
[136] Chatwin W.S.W. (B.A.S.Trans), Mohuns of Whichford

CHAPTER 4

[1] Lyte H.D.Part I, 59. (Note J)
[2] Lyte H.D. Part I, 76 (Note 4)
[3] Lyte H.D. Part I, 72. (Note 2)
[4] Lyte H.D. Part I, 72/73
[5] Ibid. 73/74 (Note I on 74)
[6] Ibid. 7
[7] Lyte H.D. Part I, 73 (Note 4)
[8] Ibid. (Notes 5 and 6)
[9] CP., vol iv., 324 (Note f}
[10] Lyte H.D. Part I, 76: C.P, vol v., 324 (Note g)
[11] CP., vol iv, 324.
[12] Steinberg, HT. 74.
[13] CP. iv, 324 (Note d).
[14] Ibid., (Note e)
[15] Ibid., iv, 324
[16] CP. iv, 324. (note h). (Beltz, M.M.N.O.G. says there were six sons.)
[17] Ibid.
[18] Beltz M.M.N.O.G., 52
[19] Steinberg H.T. 82.
[20] C.P., vol iv 325 (Note g)
[21] C.P. vol iv, 325.
[22] McKisack, 14c. 245 and note I
[23] Ibid. 245
[24] Ibid. 207.
[25] Ibid. (note 2.)
[26] Ibid. (note 3)
[27] Lyte H.D. P3I1 J, 76/77 (Note 1 on 77)
[28] Lyte H.D. Pali L 77. (Note 3)
[29] Ibid. (Note 4)
[30] Ibid. (Note 5).
[31] Ibid. (Note 2)
[32] Ibid. 50
[33] Lyte H.D. Part I, 77. (Note 6).
[34] Ibid. (Note 7)
[35] Ibid. (Note 8)
[36] Lyte H.D. Part I, 78 (Note I).
[37] Lyte H.D. Part I, 78 (Note 3).
[38] Ibid. (Note 4).
[39] Ibid. (Note 5)
[40] Ibid. (Note 6)
[41] Lyte H.D. Part I, 78 (Note 7).
[42] Lyte H.D. Part I, 79 (Note 3)
[43] Jacob 15c, 72.
[44] Lyte H.D. Part I, 79 (Note 6).
[45] Ibid. 79
[46] Lyte H.D. Part I, 80 (Note I).
[47] Ibid. 80
[48] Ibid. 80 (Note 3)
[49] Lyte H.D. Part I, 328.
[50] McKisack 14th Century, p.260
[51] Lyte H.D. Part I, 328
[52] Lyte H.D. Part I, 81
[53] Lyte H.D. Part I, 96
[54] Lyte H.D. Part I, 81
[55] Lyte H.D. Part I, 81
[56] Lyte H.D. Part I, 96
[57] Lyte H.D. Part I, 81
[58] Lyte H.D Part I, 81/2
[59] Ibid. 82
[60] Lyte H.D. Part I, 78
[61] Ibid. 82
[62] Ibid. 83/4
[63] Ibid. 82/3
[64] Ibid. 107
[65] Ibid. 83 and Note 2
[66] Cross F.L. D.C.C. 190
[67] Lyte H.D. Part I, 96/7
[68] Ibid. 107
[69] Lyte H.D. Part I, 84/85/ 86. (Also Notes 1 on 84, 85, 86)
[70] Lyte H.D. Part I, 86
[71] Ibid. 49/50 (Note I, 50)
[72] Lyte H.D. Part I, 86. (Note 2)
[73] Lyte H.D. Part 1, 86
[74] Ibid, 304
[75] Lyte H.D. Part I. 305 (Note 2)
[76] Ibid. 87 (Note 2)
[77] Ibid. 297 (Note 7)
[78] Lyte H.D. Part I, 287 / 8 (Note 1, 288)
[79] Salzman B.E., 213 (Notes 1 and 2)
[80] Lyte H.D. Part I, 298 (Note 4)

[81] Ibid. 115/6
[82] Lyte H.D. Part I, 115
[83] Montgomery T.A., 244
[84] Lyte H.D. Part I, 116 (Note 1)
[85] Lyte H.D. Part I 298 (Note 5)
[86] Lyte H.D. Part I, 299
[87] Lyte H.D. Part I, 298
[88] Ibid. 298-9
[89] Montgomery A., 361
[90] Lyte H.D. Part I, 98
[91] de Monstrelet H.Y.W., 264
[92] Jacob 15e., 116
[93] de Monstrelet. H.Y.W.,264/5
[94] Lyte H.D. Part I, 87 (Note 3)
[95] Lyte H.D. Part L 98
[96] C.P. vol viii, 289 (Note I)
[97] Lyte H.D. Part I, 88 (Note 4)
[98] Ibid. 98/9
[99] Lyte H.D. Part I, 99 (Note 1)
[100] Ibid. 97 (Note 2)
[101] Ibid. (Note 5)
[102] Ibid. 88
[103] Ibid. 88/89
[104] Lyte H.D. Part I, 89
[105] Ibid. Part II, 543 (Note 6), 89 (Note 1)
[106] Lyte H.D. Part II, 543 (Note 7)
[107] Ibid. Part I, 89
[108] Ibid. 90
[109] Lyte H.D. Part I, 90
[110] Lyte H.D. Part I, 90/91
[111] Lyte H.D. Part I, 90-92
[112] Ibid. 92
[113] Ibid. 92/93
[114] Steinberg H.T., 92
[115] de Monstrelet H.Y.W.,288
[116] Ibid. 289
[117] Ibid. 288 and note
[118] Ibid. 289
[119] Lyte H.D. Part II, 557/8 (Additions and Corrections).
[120] Ibid. 95 (Note 2)
[121] Ibid. 93
[122] Lyte H. D. Part I, 93 (Note 1)
[123] Lyte H.D. Part I,94
[124] Lyte H.D. Part I, 95 (Note 1)
[125] Lyte H.D. Part II, 354
[126] Lyte H.D. Part II, 354
[127] Lyte H.D. Part II, 354/5
[128] Ibid. 355
[129] Salzman B.E., 173
[130] Ibid.
[131] Lyte H.D. Part II, 355
[132] Lyte H.D. Part II, 356/8
[133] Lyte H.D. Part II,356/7
[134] Ibid. 356
[135] Ibid. Part I, 316
[136] Lyte H.D. Part II, 356-7
[137] Lyte H.D. Part II, 358/9
[138] Ibid. Part I, 93
[139] Ibid.
[140] Lyte H.D. Part I, 99

[141] Ibid. 99/100
[142] Ibid. 107
[143] Lyte H.D. PartII, Ibid.101
[144] Ibid. 101 (Note 2)
[145] Ibid. 116
[146] Ibid. 101
[147] Lyte H.D. Part II, 359 (Note 1)
[148] Ibid. 357
[149] Lyte H.D. Part II, 357
[150] Ibid. 351
[151] Ibid. 357/8
[152] Thorne, Lockyer and Smith, H.E., *200/1*
[153] Lyte H.D. Part II, 358
[154] Ibid. 364 (Note I)
[155] Lyte H.D. Part II, 359/60
[156] Payne (Medieval History) A.C.59
[157] Cherry (Jewellery) AC. 178
[158] Lyte H.D. Part I, 97
[159] Lyte H.D. Part I, 160/1 (Note 1 on 161)
[160] Ibid. 106 (Note 1)
[161] Lyte H.D. Part I, 106 (Note 2)
[162] Ibid. Part I, 108
[163] Ibid. 103
[164] Fryer, M.E.S. S.A.N.H.S. Part 10, Vol. LXX, 1924. Part 2,73/74
[165] Lyte H.D. Part I, 103
[166] Eeles C. St G. (1940),16
[167] Lyte H.D. Part I, 104. (Note I)
[168] Lyte H.D. Part I, 104
[169] Lyte H.D. Part I, 42 (Note 9)
[170] Ibid. (Note 10)
[171] Letter 9.12.1988 from David Bromwich, Librarian, Local History Library
[172] Bettey C. and C.
[173] Macklin M.B., 68
[174] Lyte H.D. Part I, 104
[175] Friar N.D.H. 260
[176] Ibid. 378
[177] Macklin M.B., 71
[178] Kemp E.C.M., 23
[179] Savage H.H.C.
[180] Hancock D.C.P., 89 (Note I)
[181] Lyte H.D. Part I, 103
[182] Lyte H.D. Part I, 103
[183] Lyte H.D. Part I,103 (Note I)
[184] Ibid. 104
[185] Lyte H.D. Part I,105 (Note 1)
[186] D.S.N.Q., 26 (1954/5),79/82
[187] Ibid. 108/9
[188] Ibid. Part II, 358
[189] Lyte H.D. Part I,105
[190] Ibid. 125 (Note 4)
[191] Lyte H.D. Part I, 105. (Note 3)
[192] Ibid.
[193] Journal of the Archaeological Institute, Vol XXVII (1870) Original Documents, 54, G.T.C. Reference DD/L, 1-16
[194] Lyte H. D. Part I, 114 (Note 3)
[195] Lyte H.D. Part I, 109
[196] Ibid. (Note 1)
[197] Lyte H.D. Part I, 110 (Note 1). Also further details

of the issues of the estate can be found on this page.

[198] Ibid. 110

[199] Ibid. (Note 4)

[200] Lyte H.D. Part II, 360

[201] Ibid.

[202] Lyte H.D. Part I, 111

[203] The History of Parliament. Vivian's Visitation of Devon.
Sources above supplied by David Bromwich M.A., A.L.A. Somerset Studies Librarian

[204] Lyte H.D. Part I, 111

[205] Ibid. Part II, 344 (Note 3)

[206] Ibid. (Note 2)

[207] Ibid. 361

[208] Lyte H.D. Part I, 30/3 (Note 1)

[209] Lyte H.D. Part I, 108

[210] Ibid.

[211] Ibid. Part I, 108 (Note 1)

[212] Ibid. Part I, 113

[213] Ibid.

[214] Lyte H.D. Part I, 113/4 (Note 1)

[215] Ibid. 114/115

[216] Ibid. 115 (Note 1)

[217] Lyte H.D. Part II, 362 (Note 1)

[218] Ibid. 362 (Note 2)

[219] Lyte H.D. Part II, 363

[220] Ibid. Part I, 115

[221] Lyte H.D. Part I, 218

[222] Lyte H.D. Part I, 47

[223] Lyte H.D. Part II, 460 (Note 2)

[224] Ibid. Part I, 456

[225] Lyte H.D. Part I, 115/6 (Note 1)

[226] For further information on Lord William Bonvyle/Bonville see Jacob (15c), 508, 524

[227] Lyte H.D. Part I, 116

[228] Lyte H.D. Part I, 117

[229] Ibid. (Note 1)

[230] Ibid. 117

[231] Ibid. 118, (Note 1)

[232] Ibid. (Note 3)

[233] Ibid. 118 Lyte's reference is to the earl of Stafford. A kinsman of this earl, Sir Humphrey Stafford represented Dorset in 1422, see Jacob (15c), 417

[234] Lyte H.D. Part I, 119 (Note 1)

[235] Ibid. (Note 2)

[236] Ibid. (Note 3)

[237] Lyte H.D. Part I, 305 (Note 3)

[238] Ibid.

[239] Lyte H.D. Part I, 121 (Note 1)

[240] Ibid. 122 (Note 1)

[241] Lyte H.D. Part I, 122 (Note 4)

[242] Lyte H.D. Part I, 122, (Note 5)

[243] Lyte H.D. Part I,122/3 (Note 1 on123)

[244] Ibid. (Note 2)

[245] Ibid. (Note 4) (see also p 123 for extra information)

[246] Ibid. 122/3 (Note 5)

[247] Lyte H.D. Part I, 124 (Note 1)

[248] Ibid. Part I, 124

[249] Ibid. 124 (Note 3)

[250] Lyte H.D. Part I, 124 (Note 4)

[251] Ibid. 125 (Note 1)

[252] Ibid. 306 (Note 2)

[253] Ibid. 298 (Note 5)

[254] Lyte H.D. Part I, 308 (Note 2)

[255] Ibid. 125 (Note 3)

[256] Ibid. 125

[257] Ibid. 125 (Note 4)

[258] Ibid. (Note 5)

[259] Lyte H.D. Part I, 126 (Note 1)

[260] Lyte H.D. Part I, 126 (Note 2)

[261] Ibid. 127 (Note 4)

[262] Ibid. 127 (Note 3)

[263] Ibid. 126 (Note 3)

[264] Lyte H.D. Part I, 129 (Note 1)

[265] Ibid. 129

[266] Ibid. 130

[267] Ibid. 130 (Note 1)

[268] Hancock D.C.P., 87

[269] Eeles C.St G. (1940), 15 (Note 2).
*Around this time [1450] the chapel of Our Lady in the north aisle of Dunster church and the chantry chapel in the south aisle were rebuilt. [p.31]

[270] Lyte H.D. Part I, 134

[271] Lyte H.D. Part I, 134

[272] Ibid. 135 (Note 1)

[273] Lyte H.D. Part I, 135 (Note 1)

[274] Lyte H.D. Part I, 137 (Note 2)

[275] Ibid. (Note 3)

[276] Ibid. 135/6

[277] Lyte H.D. Part I, 136

[278] Ibid.

[279] Lyte H.D. Part I, 136/7

[280] Lyte H.D. Part I, 137/138

[281] Ibid. 138 (Note 1)

[282] Ibid. (Note 2)

[283] Ibid. 135 (Note 3)

[284] Ibid. 140 (Note 1)

CHAPTER FIVE

[1] Eeles C. St G. (1940) 8

[2] Freeman D.P.C. (PROC S.A.N.H.S.) 6/7

[3] Ibid. 9

[4] Fleming, Honour and Pevsner, P.D.A., 191

[5] Freeman D.P.C. (PROC S.A.N.H.S.) 7

[6] Lyte H.D. Part II, 392/3

[7] Hancock D.C.P., 55

[8] Lyte H.D. Part II, 394/5

[9] Hancock D.C.P,. 68

[10] Ibid. 38

[11] Bettey C.&C. 44

[12] Lyte H.D. Part II, 397

[13] Lyte H.D.Part II, 398

[14] Poyntz-Wright P.C.T.S., 180

[15] Salzman B.E., 514/5

[16] Salzman B.E.,106. (Willis' Nomenclature, 35)

[17] Salzman B.E., 105/6.

[18] Lyte H.D. Part II, 397/8 (Note 1 398)

[19] Salzman B.E., 149-152

[20] Hamper G.M. (H.A.D.), 877

[21] Bettey C.&C., 51/52

[22] Bettey C.&C., 51
[23] Bettey C. & C., 50/51
[24] Ibid.
[25] Ibid. 93
[26] Lyte H.D. Part I, 180
[27] Lyte H.D. Part I, 393/4
[28] Ibid. 390. (Note 1)
[29] Lyte H.D. 399
[30] Lyte H.D. PartII, 396
[31] Lyte H.D. Part II, 424
[32] Lyte H.D. Part II, 560
[33] Pevsner S.W.S., 155
[34] Eeles C. St G. (1940), 9
[35] Ibid. 13,14
[36] Lyte H.D., Part II, 403
[37] Eeles C. St. G. (1940), 10 (Note 2)
[38] Lyte D.C. (D.S.N.Q.), 19
[39] Freeman D.P.C.(Proc.S.A.N.H.S.),9
[40] Lyte D.C. (D.S.N.Q.),19
[41] Hamper G.M. (H.A.D.),878
[42] Lyte H.D., Part II, 400
[43] Ibid. 401 (Note 1)
[44] Ibid. 553/4 (Appendix F)
[45] Lyte. H.D. Part II, 400. (Note 1)
[46] Lyte H.D. Part II, 402 /3
[47] Ibid. 403 (Note 1), 404 (Note 1)
[48] Lyte H.D., Part II, 404 (Note 1)
[49] Lyte H.D., Part II, 404 (Note 1)
[50] Ibid. 405 (Note 1)
[51] Lyte Dunster Church,D.S.N.Q. (Part C.L. 11. March1927., 17 /20.)
[52] Lyte H.D. Part II, 390.
[53] Ibid. 407 (Note 1)
[54] Ibid. 407
[55] Lyte H.D. Part II, 553 (Note 6)
[56] Hancock, *Dunster Church and Priory*(1905) p.130/131
[57] Lyte H.D. Part II, 553/555
[58] Eeles C. St. G., 194O, 11 (Note I).
[59] Ibid. 7
[60] Ibid. 7
[61] Lyte H.D. Part II, 394/5
[62] Lyte H.D. Part II, 405 (Note 2)
[63] Ibid. 406 (Note 1)
[64] Freeman D.P.C., 12
[65] Lyte H.D., Part II, 406
[66] Eeles, C. St G., 1940, 7
[67] Lyte H.D. Part II, 398
[68] Eeles. C. St G., 1940, 10 (Note 3)
[69] Eeles. C. St G., 1940, 10 (Note 3)
[70] Ibid. 11 (Note 3)
[71] Ibid. 11.
[72] Lyte H.D. Part II, 428
[73] Eeles C St G. 1940, 7.
[74] Pevsner S.W.S., 154.
[75] Eeles C. St G., 1940, 9/10.
[76] Hancock D.C.P.,13
[77] Lyte H.D. Part II, 407/8
[78] Freeman D.P.C., 10
[79] Eeles C. St G. (1940), 11
[80] Ibid. 1.

[81] Pevsner S.W. S., 155
[82] Eeles C. St G., (1940), 10
[83] Lyte H.D. Part II, 407
[84] Eeles C. St G., 1940, A Short Summary for Visitors, (Note 2)
[85] Wickham C.S., 51
[86] Fleming, Honour and Pevsner. P.D.A., 268
[87] Lyte H.D. Part I, 307
[88] Lyte H.D. Part I, 131 (Note 3)
[89] Ibid. 307
[90] Ibid. 306
[91] Lyte H.D. Part 1, 307
[92] Ibid.
[93] Ibid. 308
[94] Ibid. 306/7
[95] Ibid. 307
[96] Ibid. 308 (Note 3)
[97] Lyte H.D. Part I, 308 (Note 1)
[98] Ibid. 307
[99] Ibid.
[100] Ibid.
[101] Hancock D.C.P., 6 (Medieval Wills, 131)
[102] Hancock D.C.P., 35
[103] Ibid. 66/67
[104] Hancock D.C.P., 37/38
[105] Hancock D.C.P., 66
[106] Eamon Duffy, *Voices of Morebath*, p14
[107] Lyte H.D. Part II, 401 (Note 3)
[108] *Gentleman's Magazine* of 1808, pt ii, 878
[109] Lyte H.D. Part I, 401 (Note 3)
[110] Lyte H.D. Part II, 401 /2
[111] *The Hundred of Carhampton* by James Savage, 409
[112] Connor M.B.S., 5/6.
[113] Lyte H.D. Part II,401
[114] Williams K.Q.E. (Tudors), 183
[115] Williams K.Q.E. (Tudors), 183
[116] Lyte H.D. Part I, 138 (Note 3)
[117] Lyte H.D. Part I, 137 (Note 4)
[118] Lyte H.D. Part I, 131 (Note 6)
[119] Williams K.Q.E. (Tudors), 177/183, Thorne Lockyer and Smith RE., 231/5, Steinberg R.T. *ad passim*
[120] Hancock D.C.P., 38
[121] Hancock D.C.P., 68
[122] Hancock. D.C.P., 61/65
[123] *Victoria History of the Counties of England, A History of Somerset*
[124] Lyte H.D. Part II, 409
[125] Ibid. (Note 3)

CHAPTER 6

[1] Lyte H.D. Part II, 410
[2] Ibid. (Also Note 1, 410). The residence mentioned is now called the 'Old Priory'
[3] Lyte H.D. Part II, 412 (Note 2)
[4] Ibid. 412
[5] Ibid. 412
[6] Lyte H.D. Part II, 420
[7] Ibid. 419/20. He also quotes Freeman E.T.D 348/50

[8] Ibid. 420/1
[9] Lyte H.D. 421 (Note 1)
[10] Ibid. 412
[11] Ibid. Part II, 421/2
[12] Lyte H.D. Part II, 410/1 (Notes 1-2 411)
[13] D.C.M. Box 16 N° 10
[14] Hancock D.C.P. 59/60 (Notes 1 and 2 59 - Notes 1 and 2 60)
[15] Lyte H.D. Part II, 411
[16] Ibid. (Note 3)
[17] Ibid. 262
[18] Ibid.
[19] Hancock 25/26
[20] Hancock D.C.P. 26/28
[21] Ibid. 28
[22] Hancock D.C.P. 28/9
[23] Hancock D.C.P. 16/1
[24] Lyte H.D. Part II, 409 (Note 2)
[25] Hancock D.C.P. 14
[26] Lyte H.D. Part II, 408 (Note 2)
[27] Ibid. (Note 3)
[28] Ibid. (Note 4)
[29] Hancock D.C.P. 17 (Note 1)
[30] Ibid. 17
[31] Ibid. 20
[32] Hancock D.C.P. 20/22
[33] Lyte H.D. Part II, 510
[34] Hancock D.C.P. 31/32
[35] Thorn, Lockyer and Smith H.E. 256
[36] Ibid.
[37] Lyte H.D. Part II, 422
[38] Ibid. 423 (Note I)
[39] Williams K.Q.E. (The Tudors) 198
[40] Lyte H.D. Part II, 422 (Note 1)
[41] Ibid. Part II, 412 (Note 3)
[42] Lyte H.D. Part II, 413 (Note 1)
[43] Ibid. Part II, 413
[44] Hancock D.C.P. 61
[45] Lyte H.D. Part I, 161
[46] Ibid. 170
[47] Lyte H.D. 141 (Note 6)
[48] Ibid. 416
[49] Ibid. 457 (Note 2)
[50] Cross O.D.C.C. 792
[51] Lyte H.D. 424 (Note 3)
[52] Lyte H.D. 425 (Note1)
[53] Ibid 425
[54] Green S.A. 34
[55] Ibid.
[56] Ibid. 70
[57] Lyte H.D. Part II, 414
[58] Lyte H.D. 413/414 (Note 1, 414)
[59] Ibid. 414 (Note 2)
[60] Lyte H.D. Part II, 414/415 (Note 1, 415)
[61] Bettey C. & C. 29
[62] Ibid.
[63] Ibid. 417/418 (Note 1, 418)
[64] Ibid. 418
[65] Lyte H.D. Part I, 138
[66] Ibid. Part II, 140
[67] Ibid. Part I, 139
[68] Lyte H.D. Part I, 139.
[69] Ibid.
[70] Ibid.
[71] Ibid. (Note 1)
[72] Lyte H.D. Part II, 513 (Notes 3 &4)

CHAPTER 7

[1] Mackie E.T. 1458-1538, 407
[2] Ibid.
[3] Lyte H.D Part II, 439
[4] Lyte H. D Part I 142
[5] Lyte H. D. Part II142/3 also Mackie E. T. (1484-1558) 483 (Note 2)
[6] Ibid 143 (Note 4)
[7] Ibid 143
[8] Lyte H. D. Part 1, 144
[9] Ibid.
[10] Ibid. Part I, 144 (Note 1)
[11] Lyte H. D. Part 1, 144 (Note 2)
[12] Ibid. 144
[13] Ibid. 145 (Note 1)
[14] Lyte H. D. Part 1, 145 (Note 2)
[15] Ibid. (Note 3)
[16] Ibid. (Note 4)
[17] Lyte H. D. Part I, 145/6 (Note 2 146)
[18i] Ibid. 146
[19] Ibid. (Note 3)
[20] Lyte H. D. Part I, 147 (Note 1)
[21] Lyte H. D. Part I, 147 (Note 2)
[22] Ibid. (Note 3)
[23] Ibid. 147/8
[24] All the letters quoted from State Papers, Scotland Edward VI
[25] Lyte H.D. Part I, 148, 149, 150 (Note 1, 150)
[26] Mackie E.T (1485-1558), 485
[27] Lyte H.D Part I, 150
[28] Ibid.
[29] Lyte H.D Part I, 150
[30] Lyte H.D Part I, 150 (Note 2)
[31] This is not intneded to be an accurate translation of the letter but is the gist of the complaint
[32] Lyte H.D Part I, 151 (Note 1)
[33] Ibid 151 (Note 2)
[34] Irwin Y.B 155 ad passim
[35] Lyte H.D Part I, 151 (Note 3)
[36] Ibid 151 (Note 4)
[37] Lyte H.D Part I, 151/2 (Note 1)
[38] Dame Margaret Luttrell née Wyndham
[39] John's mother-in-law was Katherine Ryce who by her first husband, Sir Griffith ap Rhys bore Mary the wife of Sir John.
[40] Lyte H.D Part I, 152/3 (Note 1, 153)
[41] Lyte H.D Part I, 154 (Note 1)
[42] Lyte H.D Part I, 154 (Note 3)
[43] Mackie E.T. (1485-1558) 485
[44] Lyte H.D Part I, 154 (Note 4)
[45] Lyte H.D Part I, 154/5 (Note 1, 155). He quotes Lesley's History of Scotland, p231
[46] Lyte H.D Part I, 155 (Note 2)

[47] Ibid
[48] Mackie (1485-1558) 484
[49] Lyte H.D Part I, 155 (Note 4)
[50] Ibid.
[51] Lyte H.D Part I, 155 (Note 6)
[52] Ibid. 156 (Note 1)
[53] Lyte H.D Part I, 161 (Note 3)
[54] Murray D.A.A. 103
[55] Lyte H.D. Part II, 559 (Note 2)
[56] Ibid. Part I, 157
[57] Wyndham F.H. (1410-1688) Gen I
[58] Lyte H.D. Part I, 157
[59] Ibid 156 (Repetition of 'THE', is not an error. The original inscription shows the first 'THE' with a line above the 'E', denoting a contraction of the word 'THEN'.
[60] Lyte H.D. Part I, 157
[61] Murray D.A.A. 103
[62] Sir John was at Boulogne commanding over two hundred men in 1544.
[63] Ibid. 486
[64] For much of this information I am indebted to Mrs Campbell Culver, Chief Ranger and Park Manager of Mount Edgcumbe
[65] Lyte H.D. Part I, 162
[66] Ibid. 162 (Note 1)
[67] Ibid. 162 (Note 2)
[68] Ibid. 162
[69] Lyte H.D. Part I, 162/3 (Note I 163)
[70] Lyte H.D. Part I, 163 (Note 5)
[71] Ibid. (Note 2)
[72] Ibid. 163
[73] Black R.E. (1558-1603) 166
[74] Lyte H.D. Part I, 163 (Note 4)
[75] Ibid. 163 (Note 3)
[76] Ibid. 164 (Note 1)
[77] Burke G.A. 504
[78] Lyte H.D. Part I, 164
[79] See under Griffiths ap Rhys. B.G.A. 430
[80] Lyte H.D. Part I, 164 (Note 2)
[81] Cross O.D.C.C. 402
[82] Ibid. 408
[83] Cross O.D.C.C. 408
[84] Ibid.
[85] Lyte H.D. Part I, 162 (Note 5)
[86] Ibid. 162 (Note 6)
[87] Ibid. 165 (Note 3)
[88] Ibid. (Note 1)
[89] Ibid. (Note 2)
[90] Ibid. 141 (Note 1)
[91] Ibid. Part II Appendix 513
[92] Lyte H.D. Part I, 141
[93] Lyte H.D. Part II, 547/8 (Note 1 548)
[94] Effigies of Sir Hugh Luttrell (d 1428) and his wife Lady Catherine Luttrell (d 1435) may be seen in St George's Church Dunster.
[95] Lyte H.D. Part II, 548
[96] C. P. vol xii
[97] Sir Alexander Luttrell received from his father, also Andrew, (d 1265) a grant of the manor of East Quantoxhead and the advowson of the church there

at a yearly rent of a pair of gilt spurs or 6d at Whitsuntide: Lyte H.D. Part I, 66 (Note 5).

CHAPTER 8

[1] Lyte H.D. Part I, 170
[2] He was falsely reported as having met his death in a fight at Dundee in 1548 (Lyte H.D. Part I, 166)
[3] Ibid. 48
[4] Ibid. 41
[5] Lyte H.D. Part I, 110
[6] Papers gratefully provided by the present occupants of Marshwood.
[7] Lyte Part I, 160
[8] Ibid. 166/7 (Note 1)
[9] Ibid. 167 (Note 2)
[10] Ibid. 167 (Note 3)
[11] Lyte H.D. 167 (Note 4)
[12] But see glossary re value.
[13] 'Sir Thomas Parry was Comptroller of the Household in 1558'. Mackie E.T. (1485-1558) 650
[14] Lyte H.D. Part I, 171 (Note 1)
[15] Mackie E.T. (1485-1558) 604/8 for details of Tudor coinage from Henry VII to Elizabeth.
[16] Lyte H.D. Part I, 170/1
[17] Ibid. 132
[18] Lyte H.D. 168
[19] D.E.E. Vol 2 121
[20] Ibid.
[21] Lyte H.D. Part I 170 (Note 1)
[22] Ibid. 132 (Note 2)
[23] Lyte H.D. 169 (Note 2)
[24] Ibid. 170
[25] Black R.E. (1558-1603) 213 (Note 1)
[26] Black R.E. (1558-1603) 214 (Note 1)
[27] Parnham Dorset.
[28] Lyte H.D. Part 1 172 (Note 2)
[29] Ibid. 176 (Note 3)
[30] Lyte H.D. Part II, 172. (Note 1)
[31] Connor M.B.S. 8 (Brown's Somerset Wills)
[32] Ibid.
[*] (See Pedigree of Stewkley)
[33] Lyte H.D. Part II, 425/6
[34] Ibid. 426
[35] Thomas died during the reign of Elizabeth but Margaret and Joan died during the reign of James I.I
[36] Kemp E.C.M. 71
[37] Wickham C of S 74
[38] Ibid. 73
[39] Ibid. 74
[40] Hamper G.M (H.A.D.) 877
[41] Pevsner S and WS. 155/6
[42] See Chapter V
[43] Lyte H.D. Part I, 172 (Note 5)
[44] Lyte H.D Part I, 122 (Note 4) . The name is given as Joan in the pedigree of Stewkley. (see Lyte Part II 417)
[45] Lyte H.D. Part I, 173
[46] Ibid. (Note 2)
[47] Lyte H.D. Part I, 173
[48] Lyte H.D. Part I, 174 (Note I)

[49] Ibid. Part II, 415

[50] Lyte H.D. 159 (Note 3)

[51] Ibid. H.D. Part II, 415

[52] Lyte H.D. Part I, 175 (Note 2)

[53] Davies E.S. (1603-1660) 354

[54] For much of this information I am indebted to Mark Girouard's guide book, 'Montacute House (NT) 1961 (with additions)

[55] Lyte H.D. Part II, 365/366

[56] Lyte H.D. Part II, 366

[57] Ibid.

[58] Ibid.

[59] Lyte H.D. Part II, 366/7

[60] Ibid. Part I, 178

[61] Hancock W.C. H.P.W (General History) 23

[62] Lyte H.D. Part I, 178 (Note 4)

[63] Lyte H.D. Part II, 550 (Appendix E)

[64] John Cappes was the brother or cousin of James.

[65] Hancock W.C HPW. (Personal History) 218

[66] Hancock W.C HPW. (General History), 23

[67] Fleet Prison was a famous London prison which stood in Farringdon Street, on what was called Fleet Market from the River Fleet which flowed into the Thames. Its keeper was called the Warden of the Fleet: as far back as the 12th century the Fleet served as a royal prison. In the reigns of Mary and Elizabeth it was used for religious martyrs and political victims of the Star Chamber. It became a place of confinement for debtors and persons committed for contempt of court; and rapidly acquired a notoriety for every kind of brutality and extortion. It was several times destroyed and rebuilt, being finally abolished in 1842.

[68] Hancock W.C. (HPW) (General History) 21/22/23

[69] Lyte H.D. Part I, 178 (Note 2)

[70] Ibid. (Note 3)

[71] Lyte H.D. Part II, 531 Appendix C

[72] For further details see: Lyte H.D. Part I, 176/177 (Notes 1 and 2, 177)

[73] Lyte H.D. Part I, 177 (Note 3)

[74] Ibid. 177 (Note 4)

[75] Ibid. 178 (Note 1)

[76] Ibid.

[77] Ibid.

[78] Lyte H.D. Part I, 178/9.

[79] Ibid 179 George Luttrell's will refers to Dame Silvestra Skory, but she did not re-marry until nine months after his death.

[80] Ibid.

[81] Ibid.

[82] Ibid. . 183

[83] Ibid. 184

[84] Powicke 13c (1216-1307) 531/2 Notes 1 and 2 532

[85] K.Q.E. Cheetham The House of York 149

[86] Ibid. 462 (Note 2)

[87] Ibid. (Notes 3 /4)

[88] This information may also be found in Mackie, 462

[89] Mackie E.T. (1484-1558) 462 (Notes 5 /6)

[90] Lyte H.D. Part I, 299

[91] Hancock D.C.P. 7

[92] Lyte H.D. Part I, 297 (Note 4)

[93] Lyte H.D. Part I, 300 (Note 2)

[94] Ibid. 300

[95] Ibid.

[96] Ibid. (Note 4)

[97] Lyte H.D. Part I, 300 (Note 5)

[98] Ibid. 299/300 (Note 1 300)

[99] Freeman D.P.C. 14

[100] In 1996 the roof was again renewed.

[101] Lyte H.D. Part I, 301

[102] Cross O.D.C.C. 1172

[103] Bettey C. & C., 82

[104] Lyte H.D. Part II, 346/7

[105] Jackson EG edited by Pickford

[106] These documents are now in the Somerset Archives and Record Office.

[107] Hancock D.C.P. 168/185

[108] This is not so to-day. The Elizabethan cup and cover is safe-guarded by Dunster but its Victorian set is at Alcombe.

[109] Bates I.C.P. (Proc S.A.N.H.S. for the year 1900. Vol XLVI.) 155

[110] Hancock D.C.P. 114/5

[111] Taylor S. 90,91,102

[112] Ibid. 90 (Fig 18)

[113] Taylor S. 278

[114] Ibid. 91

[115] Ibid. 101 (Fig. 21)

[116] Connor M.B.S. 6/7 These arms (quarterly) were confirmed and crest granted to Thomas Stewkeley of Marshe, Somerset Esq. by R. Lee Clarencieux, 21 June, 1595; see Burke's General Armory under Stukeley, 984 (Henton, co Hants, bart, extinct 1719) for further details.

[117] The arms Az a bend between six Martlets Arg are given by Connor for Luttrell. These arms correctly refer to the Luttrells of Irnham (Lincs) and the arms of the Luttrells of East Quantoxhead are Or a bend between six Martlets Sa. However, it should be noted that the last hatchment in Dunster Church (N° 9) the hatchment of Francis Luttrell (1792 - 1862) and Emma Louisa Drewe, his wife, uses the Irnham shield. (see later)./ The arms of Luttrell appear on Elizabeth Stewkley's brass not only because her daughter Joan married George Luttrell (1560-1629) but because her husband Hugh Stewkeley was descended from George Stewkely (d 1508) who married Joan Luttrell, the daughter of Sir James Luttrell (d 1461) and Lady Elizabeth Luttrell (d 1493) whose tomb slab lies in the south eastern chapel with the brass in question and the Jacobean tomb.

[118] These are the arms given in Burke's General Armory, 182 under Chamberlin (London). Connor, however, refers to '3 lions' faces' and not 'three leopards' faces'.

[119] Anne Downes of Yalding, Kent, dau: of Robert Downes was the wife of Robert Chamberlain, son of Richard Chamberlain and therefore Elizabeth Stewkley's brother. These arms were granted in 1588 as a quarterly coat to Robert Chamberlain by Robert Cooke, Clarencieux.

[120] She was buried near her husband Hugh Stewkley who directed in January 1587 that he should be buried in

the Priory Church of Dunster 'over against his own seat or pew'.

121 The eldest son of George and Joan Luttrell

122 Brown's Somerset Wills, i, 79. Quoted by Connor, MBS 8

123 Connor MBS 8 (Presumably Ursula, stated to be 'unmarried' in the inscriptions on her mother's brass married after 1598 when Elizabeth died.)

124 Lyte H.D. Part II, 42 (Notes 2 and 3)

125 See Burke G.A. 984

126 Ibid. Part I 325 (Note2)

127 Lyte H.D. PartII, 332

128 Ibid. 120

129 Ibid. 332

130 Lyte H.D Part II, 332/3

CHAPTER 9

1 Ibid. 18 (quoting S.P Eliz., v, xcvi, p. 354)

2 Ibid. 18/19 (quoting S.P Eliz., v, cxvii, p. 45)

3 Ibid. 19. (quoting S.P Eliz., v cxxxviii, p. 20)

4 Ibid. (quoting S.P Eliz.., v, cxxxix, p. 49)

5 Ibid. (quoting S.P Eliz., v cxxxviii, p. 20)

6 Ibid. 25

7 Green S.A. 26 (quoting S.P Eliz., v. cxliii, p24)

8 Ibid.

9 Green S.A 34/35

10 Edward Popham was Commander against piracy for Somerset. J.P. and Recorder of Bridgwater He was the brother of Sir John Popham, Lord Chief Justice of England, grandfather of Jane Popham who married Thomas Luttrell in 1621.

11 Green S.A. 47/48 (quoting under Parks* S.P. Eliz., v. clxii. p.44)

12 Green S.A 49

13 Ibid.

14 Ibid.

15 Ibid. 49/50

16 Ibid. 86

17 Ibid. 87

18 Ibid. 106 (quoting British Museum 807, f.2.)

19 Lyte H.D. Part I, 88/9

20 Ibid. 132

21 Ibid. 140

22 Ibid.169

CHAPTER 10

1 Lyte H.D. Part I, 179

2 Ibid.

3 Lyte H.D. Part I, 177 (Note 2)

4 These arms are also displayed over the monument erected in the reign of James I in Dunster church.

5 Lyte H.D. Part II, 347/8 (Note 1 348)

6 George Luttrell the father of Thomas Luttrell was returned to parliament as one of the members for Minehead in 1584

7 Wedgwood K.P. 1637-41, 130

8 Lyte H. D. Part I, 179

9 Ibid. 180

10 Wedgwood K.P. 1637-1641, 128/9

11 Lyte H. D. Part I, 309/10 (Note 1 310)

12 Ibid. 305 (Note 3)

13 Lyte H.D. Part I, 305 (Note 2)

14 Ibid. 305/6 (Note 1 306)

15 Ibid. 241

16 John Poyntz of Iron Acton (Glos) was 'lawfull Fermor and Chieff officer…of the Forrest of Exmore in the Countyes of Somersett and devon for the tearme of his lieff' (see MacDermot H.F.E. 235).

17 MacDermot H.F.E 235/6 (see 236 for full text)

18 MacDermot H.F.E 237 (see 237/8 for full text)

19 Lyte H.D. Part I, 183. Registers quoted by Hancock, D.C.P., 102, give date as 7. Feb. 1643. This must be incorrect since his will is dated 25 May 1643 and contains the instructions that "My boddie I will to be buried decently in the parish church of Dunstarr in my isle (aisle) which is there." Lyte H.D. Part II, 427 (Note 1)

20 Davies, E.S. 1603 - 1660, 98

21 Lyte H.D. Part I, 182 (Note 2)

CHAPTER 11

1 Lyte H.D. Part I, 180

2i Exodus 20 verse 10

3 Wedgwood K.P., 96

4 Hancock D.C.P 107

5 Lyte H.D. Part II, 413

6 In the eighteenth century vicars of Dunster lived at Ellicombe.

7 Lyte H.D. Part II, 416

8 Wedgwood K.P. 1637-1641 99. Here we read 'The churching of women after child-birth was enforced although it was a ceremony repugnant to the extreme Protestant.'

9 Lyte H.D. Part II, 416

10 Wedgwood K.P. 1637-1641, 93

11 Ibid. 92

12 Lyte H.D. Part II, 428

13 Ibid. 403

14 Hancock D.C.P 180

15 Ibid. 184

16 Hancock D.C.P. 183

17 Ibid. 185

18 Ibid.

19 Eeles C of St G 12

20 Hancock D.C.P 181

21 Ibid. 179

22 Wedgwood K's P 1637/1641, 98

23 Davies E.S 1603-1660, 297 (Note 1)

24 Black R of E 1558-1603, 266

25 Ibid. 265

26 See Black R.E. 1558-1603. 264/5/6 for greater details re. vagabonds and beggars

27 Black R of E 1558-1603, 255 (Note I)

28 Hancock D.C.P. 132

29 Hancock D.C.P.132.

30 Ibid.

[31] Ibid. 143

[32] Davies E.S. 1603-1660, 297/298

[33] Hancock D.C.P. 137

[34] Ibid.

[35] Ibid.

[36] Hancock D.C.P 142

[37] Ibid.

[38] Ibid. 151

[39] Ibid.

[40] Ibid. 131/133

[41] George Luttrell heir of Thomas Luttrell

[42] Hancock D.C.P 131

[43] Hancock D.C.P

[44] See H.F.E references to Thomas Siderfin 350/2/370/3

[45] Hancock D.C.P 132

[46] Ibid. 142

[47] Ibid.147

[48] Ibid. 152

[49] Lyte H.D Part II 340/1

[50] Hancock D.C.P. 143

[51] Ibid. 147

[52] Ibid. 150

[53] My interpretation is open to argument.

[54] Hancock D.C.P 143

[55] Ibid.

[56] Hancock D.C.P 163

[57] Thomas Thorne does not appear as churchwarden in Hancock's list of churchwardens which for 1667, John Leigh and Thomas Dennis.

[58] Edmond Burington does not appear in Hancock's Dunster Overseers, but Edmond Brimpton is listed. See Hancock D.C.P 195, 203.

[59] Presumably occupier

[60] Hancock D.C.P 133/137

[61] Ibid. 132/148

[62] Hancock D.C.P 132/ 133/ 137-9/ 140/3 /141-5/ 147-9/ 150-2 These pages contain all quotes previously given from reference to Margaret Gardener onwards.

[63] Hancock D.C.P 140

[64] Ibid.

[65] Ibid. Curiously Hancock refers to "an act of parliament passed in the eighteenth year of Charles II. This must be incorrect since Charles II ascended the throne in 1660 and the eighteenth year would have been 1678. He gives the date of enactment as 2 Feb. 1665

[66] Hancock D.C.P 140

[67] Ibid. 143

[68] Ibid. 140

[69] Ibid. 142

[70] Ibid. 143

[71] Thomas Dennisford paid the rate for The Ship Inn now the Luttrell Arms.

[72] Hancock D.C.P 149

[73] Ibid. 141

[74] Ibid. 142

[75] Ibid. 144

[76] Hancock D.C.P 144/5

[77] Ibid. 141

[78] Ibid.

[79] Ibid. 138

[80] Ibid.

[81] Ibid.

[82] Ibid. 140

[83] Hancock D.C.P.148

[84] Ibid. 171

[85] Ibid. 148

[86] Ibid.

[87] Ibid.

CHAPTER 12

[1] His dukedom was achieved by the reversal of the attainder of his ancestor, Edmund Seymour the Lord Protector during the minority of Edward VI. His first wife was Lady Arabella Stuart (d 1615) cousin of James I.

[2] Wedgwood K.W., 113 (Note 2)

[3] Lyte H.D. Part I, 180 (Notes 4/5/6)

[4] Green S. and S.D.C 386

[5] Ibid. (Note 4)

[6] Sir John Stowell/Stawell of Cothelston Manor, a very large landowner.

[7] Green S. and S.D.C. 387

[8] Green S. and S.D.C. 387/8

[9] Lyte H.D. Part I 181

[10] One daughter, Katherine married John Frauncis of Coombe Florey, the grandson of George Luttrell (d1629) (see Green. S.and S.D.C 60). George Luttrell's daughter Susan married John Francis (Senr) of Coombe Florey in 1612 (see Lyte H.D. Part I 177).

[11] MacDermot H.F.E. 296. Chapter IX is devoted to The Tithe War. 277/298

[12] Popham W.C.F.P 59

[13] Ibid.

[14] Francis Popham had 'accompanied the Earl of Essex on his expedition against the Spaniards and was present at the sacking of Cadiz, where Essex knighted him for his services'. (see Popham .W.C.F.P 58)

[15] Popham H.W.C.F.P 58

[16] Lyte H.D. Part I, 181

[17] From this point Greene's account gives information additional to that given by Lyte (see Lyte H.D Part I) 182

[18] Greene S and S.D.C 388/9

[19] Lyte H.D. Part I, 177 (Note 1)

[20] Ibid. 183 *History of the Rebellion* (ed. 1826) vol. iv p.110

[21] Lyte H.D. Part I, 183

[22] Ibid. 184

[23] Ibid. (Note 1)

[24] Lyte H.D. Part 1, 184

[25] Hancock D.C.P 102

[26] Lyte H.D Part I, 185

[27] Ibid.

[28] Ibid. Part II, 427 (Note 1)

[29] Ibid. 427

[30] As Silvestra Capps she became the second wife of George Luttrell.

[31] Lyte H.D. Part I, 170
[32] Lyte H.D. Part I, 186
[33] Lyte H.D. Part I, 186
[34] Ibid.
[35] Hancock D.C.P 100
[36] Lyte H.D. Part I, 187 (Note 2)
[37] Hancock D.C.P 103
[38] Lyte H.D. Part I, 187
[39] Ibid.
[40] Ibid.
[41] MacDermot H.F.E. 12/13
[42] Davies E.S. 1603-1660, 141 (Note 1)
[43] Lyte H.D. Part I, 188/194
[44] 'With the arrival of the parliamentary levies the vicar, Robert Snellling, no doubt, had to fly. Until the end of the year 1649 the entries in the Dunster registers are made by the 'clarke', John Brimscombe.' See Hancock D.C.P 100.
[45] Green S. and S.D.C. 389 *Perfect Passages* No 56 (Parliamentary Newspapers).
[46] Green S. and S.D.C. 389 *Perfect Diurnal* No 125 (Parliamentary Newspapers)
[47] Ibid. *Moderate Intelligencer* No 38
[48] Ibid. (Blake's principal battery was, it is believed, behind *The Ship* . In the nineteenth or beginning of the twentieth century a few cannon balls were found on the Tor.)
[49] Ibid. 390 *Perfect Ocurrences*
[50] Ibid. *Moderate Intelligencer* No 44
[51] Thomas Wentworth 1st Earl of Strafford was executed in 1641. This must be a reference to his successor
[52] Green S. and S.D.C. 391 *Mercurius Academicus* No 3
[53] See Lyte H.D. Part I, 190 (Note 2)
[54] Green S. and S.D.C. 391 *Mercurius Civicus* No 136
[55] Ibid. *Mercurius Britannicus,* No 114
[56] Ibid. *Perfect Passages* No 6
[57] Ibid. *Mod Intell* No 44
[58] Ibid. *Weekly Account* No 2
[59] Ibid. 392 *Perfect Passages* No 65
[60] Green S. and S.D.C. 392 *Carte. T.*
[61] Ibid. *Perfect Passages* No 68
[62] Ibid. *Mod Intell.* No 50
[63] Ibid. *Moderate Intell* No 59
[64] Ibid. 393 *The Taking of Michael's Mount,* etc
[65] Green S. and S.D.C. 393/4 *Mercurius Civicus* No 152
[66] Ibid. 394 *Four Strong Castles Taken etc.* Lyte adds Colonel Blake's comment that 'the place was strong and of importance, for the passage into Ireland (see H.D. Part I, 194 (Note 2)
[67] Green S. and S. D. C. 394 *Perfect Diurnal* No 144
[68] Ibid. 389/394

CHAPTER 13

[1] Lyte H.D. Part I, 195 (Note 2)
[2] Lyte H.D. Part I, 195 (Note 4)
[3] Ibid. 195
[4] Ibid. 195/6 (Note 1, 196)
[5] Ibid. 196.
[6] In 1659 Desborough, now a Major-General, together with Colonel Fleetwood overthrew Richard Cromwell as Lord Protector.
[7] Lyte H.D. Part I, 196 (Note 2).
[8] Ibid. (Note 3)
[9] Lyte H.D. Part I, 196. (Note 4)
[10] Ibid. (Note 5)
[11] Ibid. (Note 6)
[12] Ibid. 197 (Note 1)
[13] Lyte H.D. Part II, 367
[14] See Ridley The R's, 153
[15] See Ridley The R's. 154
[16] Lyte H.D. Part I, 198 (Note 1)
[17] Ibid. (Notes 2, 3) Lyte himself was Deputy Keeper of the Records at the Tower of London.
[18] Lyte refers to this letter as having been written 'six months later', i.e. later than the 20th August 1650 that is Feb 1651. see Lyte H.D. Part I, 196/7.
[19] Ibid. 197 (Note 2)
[20] These are illustrated in Chapter I (Vol 2)
[21] Lyte H.D. Part I, 160/1 (Note 1 on 161)
[22] Sotheby Wilkinson and Hodge's *Catalogie of the Phillipps Collector,* Lot 545
[23] Lyte Preface Vol 1, vii.viii.
[24] Lyte H.D. Part I, 198/9 (Note 1 on 199)
[25] Ibid. 199 (Note 1)
[26] Ibid. 199/200 (Note 2 on 200)
[27] Hancock D.C.P. 100
[28] Ibid. 103
[29] Thorn, Lockyer and Smith H.E. 342
[30] For full details see Davies E.S. 1603-1660, 233
[31] Hancock D.C.P 103
[32] Ibid. 98
[33] Lyte H.D. Part I, 200 (Note 3)
[34] Ibid. 201
[35] Hancock D.C.P. 96/107. For details of the registers from 1598 to 1751 see Hancock D.C.P. 96/113
[36] Hancock D.C.P 108
[37] Davies E.S. 1603-1660 202/3 (Notes 1 and 2)
[38] Ibid. 203/4
[39] Ibid. 204
[40] Cross O.D.C.C. 1167
[41] Hancock D.C.P. 109
[42] Ibid.
[43] Davies E.S. 1603-1660 203.
[44] Ibid.
[45] The memorial brass to Richard Blackford lies on the north side of the nave of the parish church.
[46] Hancock D.C.P. 109/10

PEDIGREE OF MOHUNS OF DUNSTER

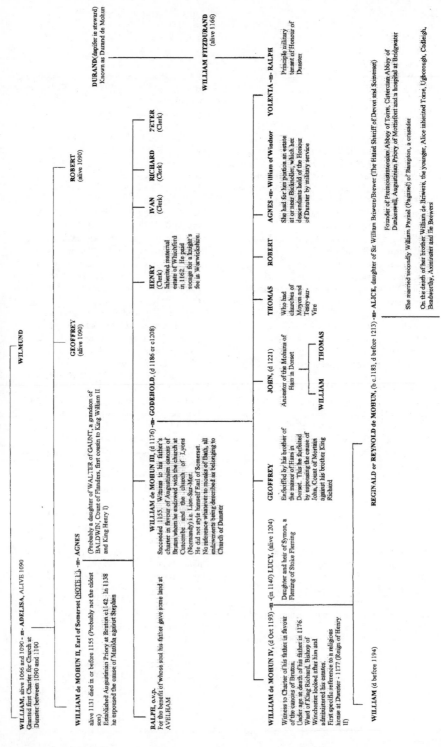

WILLIAM, alive 1066 and 1090 - m - **ADELISA**, ALIVE 1090
Granted first Charter for Church at
Dunster between 1090 and 1100

WILMUND

WILLIAM de MOHUN II, Earl of Somerset (NOTE 1) - m - **AGNES**
(Probably a daughter of WALTER of GAUNT, a grandson of
BALDWIN, Count of Flanders, first cousin to King William II
and King Henry I)

alive 1131 died in or before 1155 (Probably not the eldest
son)
Established Augustinian Priory at Bruton c.1142. In 1138
he espoused the cause of Matilda against Stephen

GEOFFREY
(alive 1090)

ROBERT
(alive 1090)

DURAND (dapifer ie steward)
Known as Durand de Mohun

RALPH, o.v.p.
For the benefit of whose soul his father gave some land at
AVELLHAM

WILLIAM de MOHUN III, (d 1176) - m - **GODEHOLD**, (d 1186 or c.1208)

Succeeded 1155. Witness to his father's
charter in favour of Augustinian canons of
Bruton whom he endowed with the church at
Cutcombe and the church of Lyons
(Normandy) i.e. Lion-Sur-Mer.
He did not style himself Earl of Somerset.
No reference whatever to monks of Bath, all
endowments being described as belonging to
Church of Dunster

HENRY
(Clerk)
inherited maternal
estate of Whichford
in 1162. He paid
scutage for a Knight's
fee in Warwickshire.

IVAN
(Clerk)

RICHARD
(Clerk)

PETER
(Clerk)

WILLIAM FITZDURAND
(alive 1166)
Principle military
tenant of Honour of
Dunster

WILLIAM de MOHUN IV, (d Oct 1193) - m (n 1140) **LUCY**, (alive 1204)
Daughter and heir of Symon, a
Fleming of Stoke Fleming

Witness to Charter to his father in favour
of the canons of Bruton.
Under age at death of his father in 1176.
Ward of King Richard, Bishop of
Winchester looked after him and
administered his estates.
First specific reference to a religious
house at Dunster - 1177 (Reign of Henry
II)

GEOFFREY
Enfeoffed by his brother of
the manor of Ham in
Dorset. This he forfeited
by espousing the cause of
John, Count of Mortain
against his brother King
Richard

JOHN, (d 1221)
Ancestor of the Mohuns of
Ham in Dorset

WILLIAM   **THOMAS**

THOMAS
Who had
churches of
Moyon and
Tessy-sur-
Vire

ROBERT

AGNES - m - **William of Windsor**
She had for her portion an estate
at or near Bicknoller, which her
descendants held of the Honour
of Dunster by military service

YOLENTA - m - **RALPH**

WILLIAM, (d before 1194)

REGINALD or REYNOLD de MOHUN, (b c.1183, d before 1213) - m - **ALICE**, daughter of Sir William Briwere/Brewer (The Hated Sheriff of Devon and Somerset)

Founder of Premonstratensian Abbey of Torre, Cistercian Abbey of
Dunkeswell, Augustinian Priory of Mottisfont and a hospital at Bridgwater

She married secondly William Paynel (Paganel) of Bampton, a crusader

On the death of her brother William de Briwere, the younger, Alice inherited Torre, Ugborough, Cadleigh,
Bradworthy, Axminster and Ile Brewers

Continued

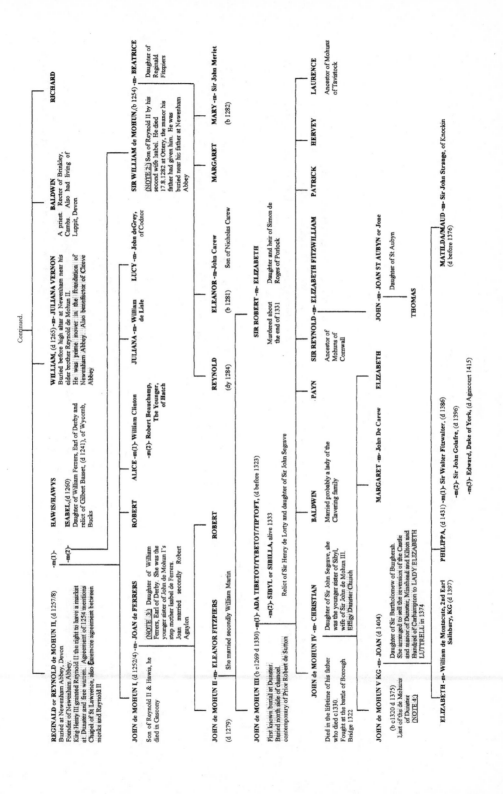

The Luttrell Genealogy: Table 1

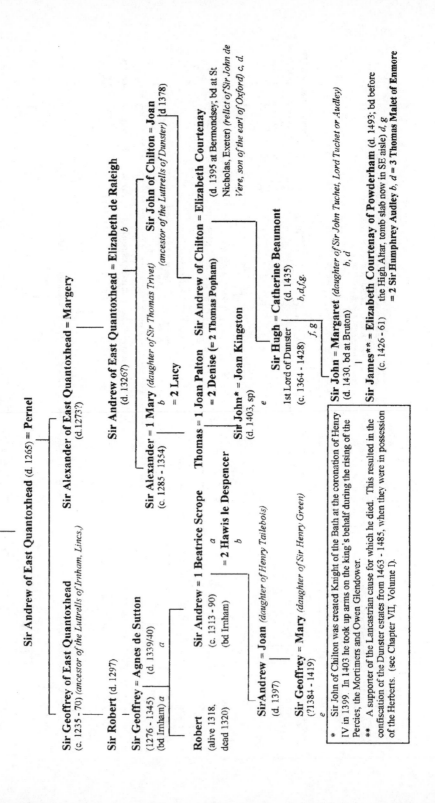

* Sir John of Chilton was created Knight of the Bath at the coronation of Henry IV in 1399. In 1403 he took up arms on the king's behalf during the rising of the Percies, the Mortimers and Owen Glendower.

** A supporter of the Lancastrian cause for which he died. This resulted in the confiscation of the Dunster estates from 1463 - 1485, when they were in possession of the Herberts. (see Chapter VII, Volume I).

The Luttrell Genealogy: Table 2

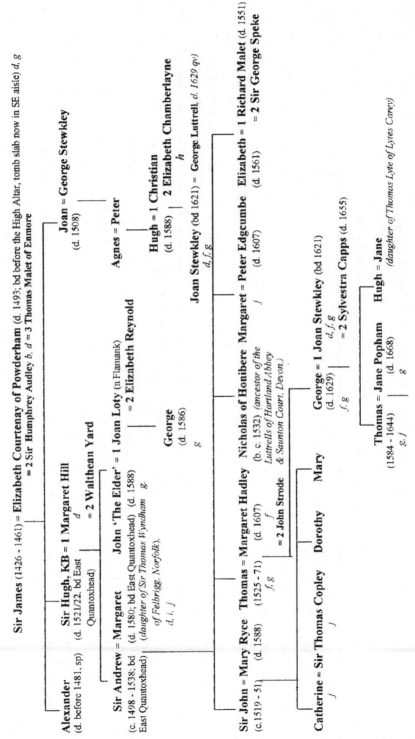

Common Ancestors of Thomas Luttrell and Margaret Hadley

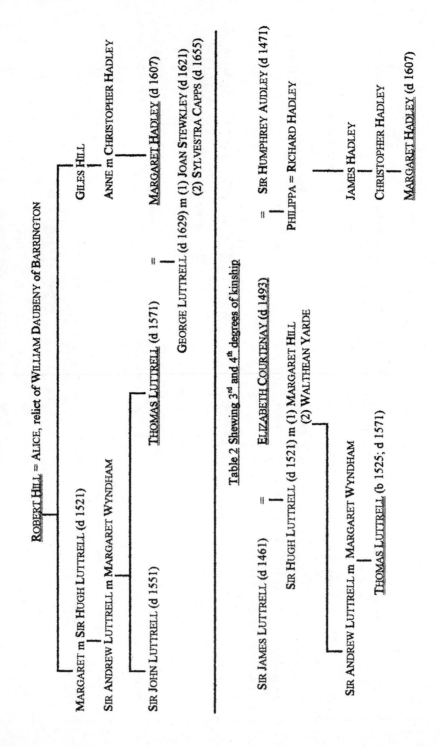

ROBERT HILL = ALICE, relict of WILLIAM DAUBENY of BARRINGTON

MARGARET m SIR HUGH LUTTRELL (d 1521)

SIR ANDREW LUTTRELL m MARGARET WYNDHAM

SIR JOHN LUTTRELL (d 1551)

GILES HILL

ANNE m CHRISTOPHER HADLEY

THOMAS LUTTRELL (d 1571) =

MARGARET HADLEY (d 1607)

GEORGE LUTTRELL (d 1629) m (1) JOAN STEWKLEY (d 1621)
(2) SYLVESTRA CAPPS (d 1655)

Table 2 Shewing 3rd and 4th degrees of kinship

SIR JAMES LUTTRELL (d 1461) =

SIR HUGH LUTTRELL (d 1521) m (1) MARGARET HILL
(2) WALTHEAN YARDE

SIR ANDREW LUTTRELL m MARGARET WYNDHAM

THOMAS LUTTRELL (b 1525; d 1571)

ELIZABETH COURTENAY (d 1493)

= SIR HUMPHREY AUDLEY (d 1471)

PHILIPPA = RICHARD HADLEY

JAMES HADLEY

CHRISTOPHER HADLEY

MARGARET HADLEY (d 1607)

POYNTZ

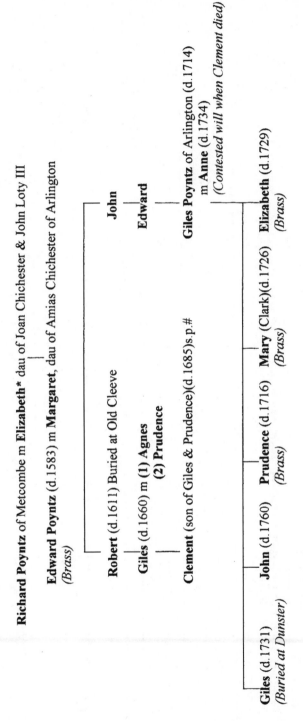

Richard Poyntz of Metcombe m **Elizabeth*** dau of Joan Chichester & John Loty III

Edward Poyntz (d.1583) m **Margaret**, dau of Amias Chichester of Arlington
(Brass)

John

Edward

Robert (d.1611) Buried at Old Cleeve

Giles (d.1660) m (1) Agnes
(2) Prudence

Clement (son of Giles & Prudence)(d.1685)s.p.#

Giles Poyntz of Arlington (d.1714)
m **Anne** (d.1734)
(Contested will when Clement died)

John (d.1760)

Prudence (d.1716)
(Brass)

Mary (Clark)(d.1726)
(Brass)

Elizabeth (d.1729)
(Brass)

Giles (d.1731)
(Buried at Dunster)

***Elizabeth** or **Joan** (See text). Both sisters-in-law of Joan Flamank who married their brother Robert (d.1510)

#s.p. 'sans prole', i.e. without issue.

PEDIGREE OF STEWKLEY

FROM A HISTORY OF DUNSTER PART II, p417 by SIR H.C. MAXWELL LYTE

MONUMENTAL BRASSES IN SOMERSET pp. 8/9 by A.B. CONNOR

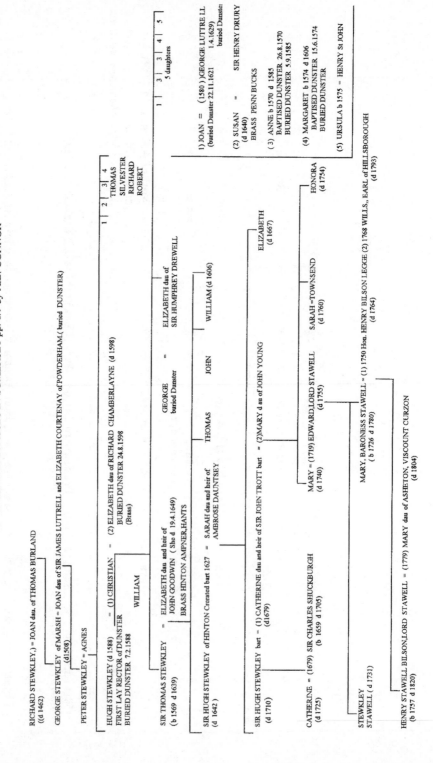

GLOSSARY

agistment
L.M.E.
(O). Fr
agistement]

The action or process of agisting livestock. L.M.E.
 A rate levied upon the owner or occupier of pasture land. Esp. in agistment tithe. E 16.
 The rate levied or profit made by agisting another's livestock. L.16.The herbage of a forest, or the right to it. L 16.

ambergris
L.M.E.
(O). Fr.
ambre gris
ambrejaune

Grey amber, as distinct from the later *ambre jaune* yellow ambre (the resin). An odiferous pale grey wax-like substance, which originates as a secretion in the intestines of the sperm whale and is found floating in tropical seas.
 Used in perfumery.

angel`

In full *angel-noble*. A gold coin having as its device the archangel Michael piercing the dragon (c.f. *Angelot* [(O).Fr, dim. of O.Fr. *angele* angel. Weight 80gr currency value 6s 8d. Fineness 23ct., 3½gr. (1509-26)
 "   "   "   " 7s 6d "   "   "   (1526-44).
 "   "   "   "   8s "   "   "   (1544-7)
 The Wolsey coinage of 1526-44 included the angel (7s 6d) and a half-angel (3s 4d). In the last years of Henry VIII, the angel was valued at 8s and there were half-angels and quarter-angels.Their fineness was reduced to 22 and finally 20 carats. In the reigns of Mary Tudor and Elizabeth the angel and the half-angel were of 23 carats, 3½gr.

angelot
(O) Fr., *angele*
angel.

A French gold coin. Same device as angel.

apparitor

A servant or attendant of an ecclesiastical or civil court. M.E. a herald, an usher. M 16.

armiger

An esquire: orig., a person who attended a knight to bear his shield; now a person! entitled to heraldic arms. M.18

base

A pleated skirt appended to a doublet, reaching from the waist to the knees; an imitation of this in mailed armour for man or horse. Also the skirt of a woman's outer petticoat or robe.

billman/ byllman

A soldier, watchman, etc, armed with a bill L 15. Various bladed or pointed hand weapons, such as broadswords mentioned in Old English poetry, a weapon like a halberd with a hook instead of a blade; a similar long-handled weapon was carried by constables of the watch.

bixgay/bisgay

A tool for rooting, consisting of a combination of a heavy mattock and a small axe,called also a Visgy, two-tailed.

bisgy/bisgee

Somersetshire name for a double-axe, having two faces, opposite and transverse to each other. Variant of besague. 15c.

caliver
M.E.

[Var.] of Calibre prob. first in Fr *arquebuse, pièce de calibre*]
 a light kind of harquebus fired without a rest.

camysaddo

Camisado, an attack on one's shirt, i.e. a night-attack.

carsie/kersey
A.L.*pannus*
cersegus
carsea

A kind of coarse cloth woven from a short-stapled wool. L.M.E.
 Prob. of Kersey in Suffolk
 A make or variety of kersey (usually in pl. kerseys/sies.
 Formerly also, a piece of kersey of a definite size. L.M.E.

caylys
  cayles/cailes
  kayles
	A variety of nine-pins or skittles; the set of wood or bone pins in this.

close
  M.E
  (O). Fr. *clos*
 	
  L *clausum*.
	Closed place, enclosure.
	An enclosure about or beside a building, M.E.
	The precinct of a cathedral, also the precinct of any sacred place, a cloister L.M.E.
	A farmyard. Now *dialect* L.M.E.
	A field, an enclosed piece of land. Now *dial* L.M.E. and Law.
	An entry, a passage, an alleyway. chiefly *Scottish*, an entry form a street to a common stairway or court, at the back of a building, also a common stairway or court with such an entry. L.M.E.

closh	An obsolete game with a ball or bowl, prohibited in many successive statutes in the 15c-16c. It was obsolete before the time of Cromwell (1554-1611), who supposed it to be equivalent to nine-pins or skittles. (Cowell. Choshe in an unlawful game forbidden by the statute which is casting of bowle at ninepinnes of wood). (*Lambarde Eiren* 1588). Every Justice of the Peace may... enter into any common house or place where any playing at the Bowles. Coites, Closh, Cailes...or any other game prohibited...schal he suspected to be used. From the 16c Dutch lexicographers and Dutch descriptions, it appears that the bowl used in the game had to be driven from a spade – or chisel-shaped implement, the *klos-beytel,* through a hoop or ring, as in croquet.
conventicles L.M.E	Place of assembly, formally dim. of *conventus* meeting. A regular assembly or meeting L.M.E. – M 17c. A meeting or assembly of a private, clandestine, irregular or illegal nature. L.M.E. A clandestine or unlawful religious meeting esp. of Noncomformists or Dissenters in England, or of Covenanters in Scotland. E.16. A place of (irregular etc.) meeting esp. a Noncomformist or Dissenting meeting-house. L.M.E. Asmall convent. M 16-E. 17.
corregidor/	The chief magistrate of a Spanish town or in former Spanish territory.
corslets	A soldier wearing a corslet in 16c-E. 18c. A corslet was a piece of armour covering the body, originally from the head to the thighs, later just the upper trunk.

coyting/
  quoiting
  also **curling**
	Coyte/Coite etc. In origin and widest sense (now only with ref. to the Greek and Roman discus), a flat disc of stone or metal, thrown as an exercise of strength or skill, spec. in mod. use, a heavy flattish ring of iron, slightly convex on the upper side and concave on the under, so as to give it an edge capable of cutting into the ground when it falls, if skilfully thrown. Also, the ring of rope, rubber, etc. used in *deck-quoits* and similar games. (see also under Closh).

cresset	A blazing cresset; the light of a crescent; a beacon light [(O). Fr. *cresset, craisset*]
crown	Any of various coins, orig. bearing the figure of a crown, *esp* an English or British coin of the value of 5s. L.M.E. Of 22 carats

fineness (1526-44). 20 carats (1544-47)
Also half-crown also of 22 carats fineness.

demi-lance A light horseman armed with a 'half-lance', i.e. a lance with a short-shaft, chiefly used in 15c and 16c.

diurnal Daily.

dowlas A coarse kind of linen. M.E. Now a strong calico made in imitation of it. (from *Daoulas* – a village in Brittany).

empryse Enterprise.

escheat Provision of feudal law whereby a fief reverted to the lord when the tenant died without leaving a successor qualified to inherit underthe original grant; the lapsing of land to the Crown, or to the lord of the manor, on the death of the owner intestate without heirs.

faldstool A seat, frequently folding used by a bishop or other priest when not occupying the throne and when officiating in any church other than his own. (L.OE).

Also a movable folding stool or desk at which worshippers kneel; especially one used by a monarch at his/her coronation. (L.OE.).

Also a small desk at which the Litany is said or sung. (E 17c).

feudal aids Taxes on knights' fees. The king had a legal right to levy such aids of his vassals for his ransom, if he were made prisoner, and the knighting of his eldest son and when his daughter was married.

full To full, to clean or thicken cloth by treading or beating. Now clean, shrink and felt (woollencloth) by heat, pressure or moisture.L.M.E.

frank-pledge An old English form of security by which each group of ten freemen stood mutually pledged for the good behaviour of each individual.

galloon/galoon A piece of ornamental fabric, *esp.* close-woven silk braid.

hackbutter Soldier armed with a hackbut. Fr.*Haguebot* Gun, firearm *(c.f. blunderbuss)*.

halberd A weapon, in use *esp.* during the 15c and 16c., consisting of a long handle ending in a combined spearhead and battle-axe.

half-bowl A game played with a hemisphere of wood and fifteen small pins of a conical form. Called in Hertfordshire, rolly-polly.

helvys Handles.

hoye/hoy A small sailing vessel, usually rigged as a sloop for carrying passengers and goods *esp.* for short coastal journeys.

impropriate Annex (an ecclesiastical benefice) to a corporation or person as corporate or private property *esp.* place. (tithes or ecclesiastical property) in lay hands.

jessimy/ jessamy Jessimy gloves, perfumed gloves; scented with jasmine. Fashionable in 16c. and 17c. Often imported from the Continent, very expensive.

jointure Originally the joint holding of property by a husband and wife for life, or intail as a provision for the latter in the event of her widowhood. M.E. Now an estate settled on a wife for the period in which she survives her husband. A dowry. L.M.E.

justiciar/steward Senior administrative post.

lance	A mounted soldier armed with a lance; a lancer.
	A spear with a long wooden shaft and an iron or steel head held by a charging horseman.
lay-rector	In the Church of England, a layman receiving the rectorial tithes of a benefice. By custom he enjoys the right to the chief seat in the chancel of the parish church for himself and his family and the freehold of the whole church, but this gives him no right of possession or of entering it when not open for divine service. He also has the duty of repairing the chancel, for the neglect of which duty he may be sued by the county court. He may compound for the liability, however, with the Board of Finance, subject to the approval of the Diocesan Dilapidations Board.
logat/logating	A game played in which thick sticks were thrown as close as possible to a mark. Usually called 'loggatts'; a missile used in this game.
matriculate	Enter a name in the register of a university, college or polytechnic, admit as a member of a university, college or polytechnic
matriculation	The act or an act of matriculating; esp. formal admission into a university, college or polytechnic. Also, an examination to qualify for this, a crtificate of matriculation
messuage	The portion of land intended to be or actually occupied as a site for a dwelling-house and its appurtenances. Now (Law) a dwelling house with its outbuildings and the adjacent land assigned to its use.
moiety	Half.
monytyone	Munition.
morion/murrion	A kind of helmet, without beaver or visor, worn by soldiers in the 16c and 17c.
mortmain	The statute of Mortmain was passed in 1279. It prohibited all grants of land to ecclesiastical corporations, thus preventing persons making over their property to the Church and then receiving it back as tenants, with a view to escaping their feudal obligations to the King. The statute was made more stringent in 1391 and extended to corporations other than ecclesiastical. So called from the fact that the Church is a *dead hand* (FR. *morte main*) in that property cannot be shifted away from it.
noble	The 'Wolsley' coinage of 1526-44 included the gold coin, the George noble (6s 8d) and a half-George noble (3s 4d) so called because they bore on their reverse side the figures of St George and the Dragon.
petronel	A carbine or large pistol used in the 16c. and 17c., *esp.* by cavalry in 16c. A soldier armed with a petronel.
pikeman/pykner/ pykyner	Soldier armed with a pike, an infantry weapon consisting of a long wooden shaft and a pointed iron, or steel head. E.16c
pincernaria regis	The King's cup-bearer.
plevins	Pledges, assurances, a warrant (chiefly Law).
pluralist	A person who holds two or more offices or positions, *esp.* ecclesiastical offices or benefices.
praemunire	Forewarn, admonish. So called from the words *praemonere facias*

	(that you warn).
predial tithes	Tithes accruing from, or produced from land or farms.
procurations	Management, superintendence; attention, care stewardship. The action of appointing a person with legal authority to act on one's behalf; the authority to delegate, the function or action of one's agent. (L.M.E.)
receiver- general	Chief financial officer
rother	An ox; generally horned animal, also Rother beast.
sallet	A light round helmet without a crest and with a lower part curving outwards behind, wore as part of medieval armour.
sawte	Assault.
shallop	A large heavy boat fitted with one or more masts and carrying fore-and-aft or lug sails and sometimes furnished with guns. Also a boat for use in shallow waters, a dingy L 16c.
sovereign	'Wolsey' coinage of 1526-44 included the sovereign (22s 6d), 22 carats 3½ gr fineness. In the last years of Henry VIII (1544-47) the sovereign and half-sovereign had their weight severely cut down and their fineness reduced from 23 to 22 and finally 20 carats. Mary Tudor's sovereign was 23 carats 3½gr and was worth 30s. Same for Elizabeth I.
somners	Summoners or apparitors were officers of court of law. The allusion in Lyte, *History of Dunster* Part 1, 143 is here to pieces of artillery.
synodal	Of, pertaining to, or connected with a synod or an episcopal visitation. A payment made by inferior clergy to a bishop, originally the occasion for a synod, later at an episcopal or archidiaconal visitation. M. 16c.
tenter	A framework on which milled or printed cloth stretched so that it can dry without shrinking or loosing shape. (M.E). To stretch (cloth) on a tenter or tenters (17c L.M.E.). hence tenter-hooks, to hurt, as by stretching, rack, torture (the feelings etc) *Note.* In the gardens of The Courts, Holt, Wiltshire. N.T. may be seen eight stone pillars, which until their removal during World War II had chains hung between them for drying of cloth produced at the mill there.
tuck	To dress or finish (woven cloth), stretch (woven cloth), on tenters. M.E.
twill/ twille	A woven fabric with a surface of diagonal parallel ridges produced by passing the weft threads over one and under two, or more threads of the warp instead of over and under in regular succession. M.E.
valletus	Yeoman.
villein	One of the class of serfs in the feudal system; peasant occupier or cultivator entirely subject to a lord or attached to a manor.
villein	Variable measure of land (30 acres on average).
vivario	Pond stocked with live fish.
volucrum	Bird.

BIBLIOGRAPHY

H.A.C.M.	BANNISTER FLETCHER, SIR, *A HISTORY OF ARCHITECTURE ON THE COMPARATIVE METHOD*.
I.C.P.S.	BATES, E.H., *INVENTORY OF CHURCH PLATE IN SOMERSET*.
(Proc	Proceedings of the Somerset Archaeological and Natural History
S.A.N.H.S)	Society, Vol. XLVI (1900) Part 2, 149-187.
F.A.	BAZIN, JEAN FRANCOIS, *FONTENAY ABBEY, MOYON*.(See THOMPSON)
M.M.N.O.G.	BELTZ, GEORGE, FREDERICK, K.H., LANCASTER HERALD, *MEMORIALS OF THE MOST NOBLE ORDER OF THE GARTER*. LONDON. WILLIAM PICKERING. 1841.
C & C.	BETTEY, J.H., *CHURCH and COMMUNITY*, ALPHA BOOKS. 1979
F.M.A.	BOASE, T.S.R., *MORTALITY, JUDGEMENT and REMEMBRANCE* in *THE*
(M.J.R.)	*FLOWERING OF THE MIDDLE AGES*. EDITED BY JOAN EVANS. THAMES and HUDSON. 1985.
R E.	BLACK, J.B., *THE REIGN of ELIZABETH*. OXFORD. Second Edition, 1959
B.H	BOUTELL, R.H., *BOUTELL'S HERALDRY*, revised by J.P. Brooke-Little. Richmond Herald of Arms. FREDERICK WARNE and CO. LTD. LONDON and NEW YORK. 1973.
	BRUSHFIELD, T.N., *RALEGHANA*. Report and Transactions of the Devonshire Association, Vol. 32. 1900.
B.G.A.	BURKE, BERNARD SIR, Ulster King of Arms, *GENERAL ARMORY*. HERALDRY TO-DAY. (RAMSBURY. WILTS) Fourth Impression 1989.
S.S.	BUSH, R.J., .*SOMERSET STORIES*. DOVECOTE PRESS LTD. DORSET. 1990.
N.C.`	BUSH, R.J., and CORBETT, G.U.S., *NETTLECOMBE COURT*. (Guide)
W.S.W.	CHATWIN, PHILIP, *WHICHFORD, SOUTH WARWICKSHIRE*. (B.A.S. TRANS), BIRMINGHAM ARCHAEOLOGICAL SOCIETY TRANSACTIONS. VOL 63. 1939/40.
	CHEETHAM, A., *THE HOUSE of YORK*. see K.Q.E. (under FRASER).
17c	CLARK, G.N., *THE SEVENTEENTH CENTURY*. OXFORD. Second Edition, 1947.
H.C.S.	COLLINSON, JOHN (REV.), F.A.S., *A HISTORY OF THE COUNTY OF SOMERSET*. 1791.
C.P.	*COMPLETE PEERAGE* (VARIOUS VOLUMES). SUTTON PUBLISHING LTD.
M.B.S.	CONNOR, B., *MONUMENTAL BRASSES IN SOMERSET*. KINGSMEAD REPRINTS. BATH. 1970.
O.D.C.C.	CROSS, F.L., *THE OXFORD DICTIONARY of the CHRISTIAN CHURCH*. Edited by F.L. Cross. OXFORD UNIVERSITY PRESS, NEW YORK, TORONTO. 1958.
E.S.	DAVIES, G., *THE EARLY STUARTS*, OXFORD. Second Edition. 1989
D.C.	DODD, D., *DUNSTER CASTLE*. National Trust. 1990. (Guide)
D.S.N.Q.	DORSET AND SOMERSET NOTES AND QUERIES.
C of St G.	EELES, F.C., *THE CHURCH of St GEORGE DUNSTER*. PRESS and PUBLICATIONS BOARD of the CHURCH ASSEMBLY. WESTMINSTER.
D.J.E.	EVELYN, J., *THE DIARY of JOHN EVELYN*. DENT. 1951,1952,1973.
P.D.A.	FLEMING, HONOUR AND PEVSNER, *PENGUIN DICTIONARY OF ARCHITECTURE*.
K.Q.E.	FRASER, ANTONIA (ED), *THE KINGS and QUEENS of ENGLAND* (see ASHLEY, CHEETHAM, EARLE, GILLINGHAM, WILLIAMS). WEIDENFELD and NICOLSON. LONDON. 1975
D.P.C.	FREEMAN, E. A., M.A., *DUNSTER PRIORY CHURCH*. Proceedings of the
(PROC. S.A.N.H.S.)	Somerset Archaeological and Natural History Society, Vol VI. (1885), Part 2, 1-16.

E.T.D.	FREEMAN, E. A., M.A., *ENGLISH TOWNS AND DISTRICTS*. MACMILLAN. 1883.
N.D.H.	FRIAR, STEPHEN (ED), *A NEW DICTIONARY OF HERALDRY*.
M.E.S.	FRYER, A.C., *MONUMENTAL EFFIGIES IN SOMERSET*. Proceedings of the Somerset
(PROC. S.A.N.H.S.)	Archaeological and Natural History Society, Part 3, Vol LXII (1917), Part 2, 1-20; Part 8, Vol LXVIII (1922), Part 2, 27-63; Part 10, Vol LXX(1924), Part 2, 45-85.
V.E.S.G.	GALICKI. M., *VICTORIAN and EDWARDIAN STAINED GLASS*. ENGLISH HERITAGE PUBLICATIONS
C. of A.[N.P.]	GODDARD, RICHARD, *NOSTRO PELICANO*. The Coat of Arms Magazine of the Heraldry Society. N.S. Vol VI. Nos 13 5/6.
S.A.	GREEN, E., 'THE PREPARATIONS IN SOMERSET AGAINST THE SPANISH ARMADA. 1558-1588*. HARRISON and SONS. LONDON 1888.
S & S.D.C.	GREEN, E., *THE SIEGE and SURRENDER of DUNSTER CASTLE. 1645/6*. ARCHAEOLOGICAL JOURNAL. VOL 37. 1880.
D.B.S.	GUNNIS, R., *DICTIONARY of BRITISH SCULPTORS 1660- 1851*. ABBEY LIBRARY. LONDON. 1953.
G.M (H.A.D.).	HAMPER, W., *HISTORY and ANTIQUITIES of DUNSTER. GENTLEMAN'S MAGAZINE*. Vol LXXVIII, part 2 1808.
D.C.P.	HANCOCK, F., *DUNSTER CHURCH and PRIORY*. BARNICOTTT and PEARCE. TAUNTON. 1905.
W.C. (H.P.W.)	HANCOCK, F., *A HISTORY of WIVELISCOMBE. WIFELA'S COOMBE*. BARNICOTTT and PEARCE. 1911.
C & R.	HIBBERT, C, *CAVALIERS and ROUNDHEADS. THE ENGLISH WAR 1642-1649*. HARPER- COLLINS. 1993.
H.A.D.	HUTCHINS, J., M.A., *THE HISTORY AND ANTIQUITIES OF DORSET*. VOLS 1,3,4.
Y.B. and E.C.P.	IRWIN, M., *YOUNG BESS and ELIZABETH, CAPTIVE PRINCESS*. 1953.
E.G.	JACKSON, Sir C., *ENGLISH GOLDSMITHS and THEIR MARKS*. (1921). Edited by I. PICKFORD. ANTIQUE COLLECTORS' CLUB. 1989
15c	JACOB, E.F., *THE FIFTEENTH CENTURY. 1399-1485*. OXFORD. 1961.
E.C.M.	KEMP, B., *ENGLISH CHURCH MONUMENTS*. B.T. BATSFORD. LTD
C.B.	LARKWORTHY, P., *CLAYTON and BELL, STAINED GLASS ARTISTS and DECORATORS*. ECCLESIOLOGICAL SOCIETY. 1984.
M.M.	LAWRENCE, C.H., *MEDIEVAL MONASTICISM*. LONGMAN. 1984/8
E.W.D.	LITTEN, J., *THE ENGLISH WAY of DEATH — THE COMMON FUNERAL SINCE 1450*. HALE. 1991.
D.L.	LYTE, H.C., *DUNSTER and ITS LORDS*. 1882.
H.D. (PART I and II)	LYTE, H.C, *A HISTORY of DUNSTER*. St CATHERINE PRESS LTD. LONDON. 1909.
H.F.E.	MacDERMOT,. E., *THE HISTORY of the FOREST of EXMOOR*. BARNICOTT and PEARCE. TAUNTON. 1911.
E.T.	MACKIE, J. D., *THE EARLY TUDORS. 1485-1558*. OXFORD. 1952.
M.B.	MACKLIN, H., D.D., *MONUMENTAL BRASSES*. CHARLES OMAN. 1953.
R.S.B.	McCANN, JULIAN, O.S.B., (TRANS), *THE RULE OF ST BENEDICT*. BURN OATES.
14c.	McKISACK, MAY, *THE FOURTEENTH CENTURY (1307-1399)*. OXFORD. 1959
L.H.D.	MERCHANT. H.F., *THE LUTTRELL HATCHMENTS at DUNSTER*. THE COAT of ARMS MAGAZINE of the HERALDRY SOCIETY. (N.S. VOL VI, nos 135/6). 1985/6. de MONSTRELET, ENGUERRAND, see THOMPSON.
T.A.	MONTGOMERY, F., *TEXTILES IN AMERICA, 1650-1870*. McLEOD. TORONTO
D.A.A.	MURRA, P. and L., *DICTIONARY of ART and ARTISTS*. PENGUIN BOOKS. 1957.
D.O.A.	PAPWORTH, J.W., *AN ALPHABECTICAL DICTIONARY of COATS of ARMS*. T. RICHARDS. 1874.
S.W.S	PEVSNER, N., *SOUTH and WEST SOMERSET*. (B. of ENGLAND). PENGUIN.1958.
D.C.	POLE, Sir W., *COLLECTIONS TOWARDS a DESCRIPTION of the COUNTY of*

                     DEVON. (1791)

D.M.C.   POOLE, A.L., '*DOMESDAY to MAGNA CARTA. 1087-1216.* OXFORD. 2nd Ed. 1954.

W.C.F.P.   POPHAM, F.W., *A WEST COUNTRY FAMILY: THE POPHAMS from 1150.* THE
                    AUTHOR, KEMSING. SEVENOAKS. KENT

13c   POWICKE, M., *THE THIRTEENTH CENTURY. 1216-1307.* OXFORD.
                    Second Edition 1962

P.C.T.S.   POYNTZ WRIGHT, P., *THE PARISH CHURCH TOWERS OF SOMERSET (1350-
                    1550).* AVEBURY PRESS, 1981.

L.H.E.   RICHARDSON, JOHN, *THE LOCAL HISTORIANS' ENCYCLOPEDIA.* HIST. ASS.

R's   RIDLEY, J., *THE ROUNDHEADS.* CONSTABLE. LONDON. 1976.

B.E.   SALZMAN, L.F., *BUILDING IN ENGLAND DOWN TO 1540.* OXFORD

H.H.C.   SAVAGE, JAMES, *HISTORY OF THE HUNDRED OF CARHAMPTON IN THE
                    COUNTY OF SOMERSET.* 1830

H.E.8   SCARISBRICK, J.J., *HENRY VIII.* EYRE AND SPOTTISWODE. 1968.

H.S.P.   SMOUT, T. C., *A HISTORY of the SCOTTISH PEOPLE. 1560- 1830.* COLLINS.
                    FONTANA. 1972.

H.T.   STEINBERG, S.H., *HISTORICAL TABLES.* MACMILLAN and CO LTD. N.Y.
                    Seventh Edition. 1964.

                    TAYLOR, G., *SILVER.* PENGUIN ORIGINAL.

H.Y.W.   THOMPSON, PETER, *CONTEMPORARY CHRONICLES OF THE HUNDRED
                    YEARS WAR* (including JEAN le BEL, JEAN FROISSART, ENGUERRAND de
                    MONSTRELET). FOLIO SOCIETY. 1966.

H.E.   THORNE, J., LOCKYER. R., SMITH D., *A HISTORY of ENGLAND.* ERNEST BENN.

R by R.   USHERWOOD, S., *REIGN by REIGN.* MICHAEL JOSEPH.

V.C.H.   VICTORIA HISTORY of the COUNTIES of ENGLAND, *SOMERSET.* Edited by R.W.
                    DUNNING (esp Vol 5 WILLITON and FREEMANORS HUNDRED).

V.C.D.   VIVIAN, J.L., *THE VISITATIONS of the COUNTY of DEVON.* PRIVATELY
                    PUBLISHED. PRINTED by S. ELAND. EXETER.

V.C.S.   WEAVER, F.W., *VISITATIONS of the COUNTY OF SOMERSET.* W. POLLARD.
                    EXETER.

K.J.   WARREN, W.L., *KING JOHN.* METHUEN.

A.B.M.A.   WEBB, G., *ARCHITECTURE IN BRITAIN. THE MIDDLE AGES.* PELICAN. 1956.

K.P.   WEDGWOOD, C.V., *THE KING'S PEACE 1637-1641.* COLLINS FONTANA. 1958.

K.W.   WEDGWOOD, C.V., *THE KING'S WAR. 1641-1647.* ditto.

C.S.   WICKHAM, K., *CHURCHES IN SOMERSET.* DAVID and CHARLES. NEWTON
                    ABBOT. MACDONALD 1965

                    WILLIAMS, N., *THE TUDORS.* see K.Q.E. (under FRASER)

S.G.S   WOODFORDE, C., *STAINED GLASS IN SOMERSET. 1250-1830.* OXFORD
                    UNIVERSITY PRESS. 1946.

F.H   WYNDHAM, H.A., *THE FAMILY HISTORY, 1410-1688: the WYNDHAMS of
                    NORFOLK and SOMERSET.* GENEALOGY. I. 1939.

D.E.E.   Various volumes and compilers of the *ENCYCLOPÆDIA.* DAILY EXPRESS
                    PUBLICATIONS. 1934.

R.A.   ZARNECKI, GEORGE, *ROMANESQUE ART.* WEIDENFELD AND NICOLSON. 1971.

INDEX